DISABILITY LAW AND POLICY
AN ANALYSIS OF THE UN CONVENTION

DISABILITY LAW AND POLICY

AN ANALYSIS OF THE UN CONVENTION

Edited by

Charles O'Mahony
BA, LL.B., LL.M., LL.M., PhD

and

Gerard Quinn
BA, LL.B., LL.M., S.J.D.

CLARUS
PRESS

Published by
Clarus Press Ltd,
Griffith Campus,
South Circular Road,
Dublin 8.
www.claruspress.ie

Typeset by
Gough Typesetting Services, Dublin

Printed by
CPI Group (UK) Ltd,
Croydon, CR0 4YY

ISBN
978-1-905536-90-0

ABOUT THE CONTRIBUTORS

Aisling de Paor is a lecturer in the School of Law and Government at Dublin City University. She is a former Irish Research Council Scholar and former PhD candidate at the Centre for Disability Law and Policy at NUI Galway. In 2013 Aisling defended her PhD entitled `Advancing Science and Controlling the Misuse of Genetic Information in Employment and Insurance? Towards an Effective European Union Regulatory Framework.?

Andrea Broderick is assistant professor at the Department of International and European Law at Maastricht University, having previously been a Marie Curie Research Fellow and a lecturer (docent) at Maastricht University. Andrea holds a Ph.D. in international and comparative disability equality law from Maastricht University.

Andrew Power is currently Lecturer in Human Geography. He joined Geography and Environment at the University of Southampton in April 2011. He received his PhD from the Geography Department at National University of Ireland Maynooth. He was an ESRC Post-Doctoral Fellow at the University of Lancaster. He subsequently worked as a Research Associate at the Centre for Disability Law and Policy (School of Law) at the National University of Ireland.

Anna Arstein-Kerslake is a lecturer in the Melbourne Law School at the University of Melbourne and the Academic Co-ordinator of the Disability Research Initiative (DRI). She has developed and co-ordinates the Disability Human Rights Clinic (DHRC) at Melbourne Law School. She holds a PhD in Law from the National University of Ireland, Galway (NUIG), a JD from the City University of New York (CUNY) School of Law and a BA in Sociology from San Diego State University (SDSU).

Anna Lawson is a Professor of Law and Director of the Centre for Disability Studies at the University of Leeds. She works in the Law School, where she is co-ordinator of the Disability Law Hub (whose home is in the Centre for Law and Social Justice). Anna has played lead roles in a range of interdisciplinary national and multinational research projects, for NHS England, the EU Agency for Fundamental Rights and the European commission. She has delivered papers in over 30 countries and regularly advises national and international organisations on disability issues.

Barbara Phillips is a researcher at the Empowerment, Participation and Social Integration Unit, Swiss Paraplegic Research, Nottwil, Switzerland. Nicole Emmenegger is a research fellow at the Swiss Paraplegic Foundation.

Bernadette McSherry is a Professor at the University of Melbourne where she is the Foundation Director of the Melbourne Social Equity Institute. She is an internationally recognised legal academic in the fields of criminal law and mental health law and became an Australian Research Council Federation Fellow in December 2007. After working as a solicitor at Coltmans and as an Associate for the then Justice James Gobbo at the Supreme Court of Victoria, Professor McSherry commenced her academic career in the Monash Law School in 1991. She was appointed in 2005 to the position of Louis Waller Chair of Law and Associate Dean (Research). She became the Director of the Centre for the Advancement of Law and Mental Health in June 2011 and in that year she was elected a Fellow of the Academy of Social Sciences in Australia and a Fellow of the Australian Academy of Law.

Bronagh Byrne is a lecturer in the School of Sociology, Social Policy and Social Work at Queens University Belfast. Her research interests lie in two main areas; disability rights and children's rights. She has a keen interest in disability policy and the relationship between international human rights law and policy development and implementation with respect to disability issues.

Bruno Trezzini holds a PhD in sociology. He taught economic and development sociology at the University of Zurich as well as organizational behavior and research methods at the business school of the Nanyang Technological University in Singapore. In 2009 he joined Swiss Paraplegic Research where he is currently a group leader in the Empowerment, Participation and Social Integration unit. At the University of Lucerne, he is involved in teaching qualitative research methods at the graduate level.

Charles O'Mahony is a lecturer at the School of Law, NUI Galway. He completed a Ph.D at the Centre for Disability Law and Policy, NUI Galway in 2013 entitled "Diversion: A Comparative Study of Law and Policy Relating to Defendants and Offenders with Mental Health Problems and Intellectual Disability". Charles previously worked as Amnesty International Ireland's Legal Officer on its mental health campaign.

Charlotte May-Simera is a PhD student (Irish Research Council Scholar) exploring the future of sheltered workshops at the Centre for Disability Law and Policy at NUI Galway. Charlotte worked as a research assistant at the Centre for Disability Law and Policywhere she primarily worked on the European Yearbook of Disability Law, while also preparing country reports for ANED (Academic Network of European Disability experts).

Ciara Hackett is a lecturer in the School of Law at Queens University Belfast. Ciara began her law degree in 2002 graduating in 2005 with an LLB (Hons) from Queen's University Belfast. In 2006 she graduated with an LLM in Corporate Governance and Public Policy (QUB). Arising from her LLM thesis, Ciara was accepted into the PhD programme at QUB, funded by a DEL scholarship. Ciara successfully defended her thesis in 2009 entitled "Dependent States, Global Capital and the Capacity to Regulate: Why can't small open countries like Ireland have robust Corporate Social Responsibility?"

Claire Bruton is a practising barrister specialising in employment and equality law.

She appears regularly in employment law for and civil courts for employees and employers dealing with statutory claims, breach of contract, injunctions, judicial review, personal injuries, etc. She is a published author and regular speaker on employment law issues at conferences and seminars.

David Hosking completed a PhD entitled "A Critical Study of European Union Law and Policy Related to Disability" at the University of Leicester. His research examined the extent to which European Union law and policy reflect an approach to disability consistent with critical disability theory.

Eilionóir Flynn is Deputy Director of the Centre for Disability Law and Policy and Senior Lecturer with the School of Law, NUI Galway. Her interest in disability law stemmed from a broader interest in social justice and a recognition of the invisibility of people with disabilities at the time in broader human rights discourse. Her current passions in this field include assisted and supported decision-making, rights-enforcement mechanisms and access to justice.

Elizabeth Kamundia is a doctoral candidate at the University of Pretoria, writing her thesis on Article 12 of the CRPD. She holds an LLM in International and Comparative Disability Law and Policy from the Centre for Disability Law and Policy, National University of Ireland Galway. Elizabeth has worked with the Centre for Disability Law and Policy as a Legal Researcher and the Centre for Human Rights, University of Pretoria (Disability Rights and Law Schools Project Coordinator).

Fiona Morrissey completed a Ph.D. in mental health law at NUI Galway in 2014. She is specifically interested in legal tools, which promote recovery and human rights in mental health care and is actively involved in current law reform in this area. Fiona has published in the *Medico-Legal Journal of Ireland,* the *European Journal of Health Law* and the Journal of *Ethics, Medicine and Public Health* and has prepared legislative submissions to the Department of Health on behalf of the Mental Health Commission and other bodies.

Francisco J Bariffi is coordinator of the Ibero-American Network of Experts on the International Convention on the Rights of Persons with Disabilities and Co-Director of the Center for Research and Human Rights Education, Law Faculty, National University of Mar del Plata. He is Professor at the Law Faculty of the National University of Mar del Plata, and at the Carlos III University of Madrid, Spain. He is also Director of the Latin American Disability Rights Research and Teaching Project, funded by the Open Society Foundations.

Gerard Quinn is a leading authority on international and comparative disability law and policy and is a professor of law at NUI Galway. He directs the Director of the Centre for Disability Law and Policy at the School of Law, which was established by a grant from Atlantic Philanthropies in 2008. The Centre is a founding member of the Lifecourse Policy Research Institute at the University. He was called to the Irish Bar in 1983, and holds a masters (LL.M) and doctorate in law (SJD) from Harvard Law School as well as a BA (Political Science) and LL.B from NUI Galway.

Ignacio Campoy Cervera is a Professor at the Carlos III University of Madrid.

He holds a degree in Law from the Autonomous University of Madrid and Doctor of Law from the Carlos III University of Madrid.

János Fiala-Butora is Research Fellow at the Institute for Legal Studies, Centre for Social Sciences, Hungarian Academy of Sciences and Director of the Central Europe Program at the Harvard Law School Project on Disability.

Joyce Mortimer is a PhD candidate at the Centre for Dissability Law and Policy at NUI Galway. Her research focuses on the right to education for children with disabilities. Joyce worked previously as a law lectuer at Galway and Mayo Institute of Technology and as the Human Rights Executive to the Incorporated Law Society of Ireland.

Jukka Kumpuvuori is a PhD candidate at the Institute for Human Rights, Åbo Akademi University in Finland. His PhD research project is entitled "Impact of the Process Towards A United Nations Disability Rights Convention and Existing International Human Rights Treaties to the Making of Ugandan Disability Legislation: Interplay of International Human Rights Law and Ugandan Legislation on Human Rights of Disabled People".

Lana Kerzner is a lawyer in Toronto, Canada who specializes in disability law and policy work. She works, often in collaboration with disability organizations, to advance the rights of people with disabilities through law reform and education. She has written and published on several disability law topics. Lana speaks at conferences, both nationally and internationally, and teaches Disability and the Law at the Law Society of Upper Canada and Ryerson University. Her work currently focuses on capacity, decision-making and the international law implications of the United Nations Convention on the Rights of Persons with Disabilities.

Liz Brosnan is a researcher at the Centre for Disability, Law and Policy at National University of Ireland Galway. She completed a doctorate in sociology on mental health service-user involvement, examining the inherent tensions for service-users, service-providers and movement actors in involvement practices and policies at the University of Limerick. She has been active in social movement politics for over a decade and represented a service-user perspective to national statutory and NGOs' advisory committees.

Mary Keogh has worked for over 10 years at an international level on disability rights and international development. Completing her doctorate in 2014, her research focus was a comparative analysis of how the US, Finland and Australia mainstream disability in their development aid programmes. Mary currently works with CBM Australia as an adviser on disability inclusive development. Prior to this, she worked with CBM Ireland, CBM International and the International Disability Rights monitor holding research, advocacy and policy positions.

Mary Keys is a leading authority on mental health law and policy. She is a lecturer in the School of Law, NUI Galway. She was awarded a Ph.D. by the Cardiff University Law School, University of Wales, in 2006 on the topic of human rights and mental health law. Her main research focus is in mental health law and policy. Mary is currently serving a second term as a member of the Mental Health Commission, having being reappointed as the representative of the public interest, in 2012.

Meredith Raley is a researcher at the Centre for Disability, Law and Policy at National University of Ireland Galway. Meredith completed a PhD at the Centre, which explored Article 33 of the Convention on the Rights of Persons with Disabilities. Article 33 focuses on the domestic implementation of the rights enshrined in the Convention, and is an innovation not only in the field of disability law, but in human rights law in general.

Noelin Fox is Course Director of Social Care degree courses at the Open Training College. She worked in disability services in Ireland for many years both in service development and in service management. Noelin is a graduate of University College Dublin and the University of Limerick. She completed her PhD with the Centre for Disability Law and Policy in the National University of Ireland, Galway in 2013. Her PhD thesis explored implementing Article 19 of the UN Convention on the Rights of Disabled Persons in Ireland.

Olivia Smith lectures law at the School of Law and Government, Dublin City University and is a member of DCU's Socio-Legal Research Centre. Her work is mainly in the area of equality and discrimination law. Recent work includes the tensions in law and public policy relating to carers, and a book, Disability Discrimination Law. Her current work includes a project on gender and judging in Ireland and the invisibility of older women's experiences under discrimination law.

Omolara Funmilola Akinpelu is a Research Project Coordinator in the Burton Blatt Institute (BBI). She earned her Bachelor's and Master's degrees in Special Education from the University of Ibadan, Nigeria. She received her PhD in Guidance and Counseling with an emphasis on multicultural perspectives of hearing impairment at the University of Ilorin, Nigeria. She is a Senior Lecturer at the University of Ilorin where she teaches and supervises research projects at both undergraduate and graduate levels.

Paula Campos Pinto holds a PhD in sociology from York University, Toronto, Canada. She is an Assistant Professor at the School for Social and Political Sciences at the University of Lisbon. She is the co-coordinator of the Observatory on Disability & Human Rights, a platform that brings together academics, disability organisations and decision-makers to support disability research in Portugal.

Riku Virtanen is a Ph.D candidate in the Institute for Human Rights Åbo Akademi University in Finland. Riku's thesis is entitled "Persons with Disabilities and Their Inclusion in Development Cooperation in the Light of the United Nations Convention on Rights of Persons with Disabilities (UN CRPD)".

Sándor Gurbai is a Senior Legal Advisor, OPCAT NPM Department, Hungary. He previously worked as a project manager for the Mental Disability Advocacy Centre (MDAC). MDAC is an international human rights organisation that uses the law to secure equality, inclusion and justice for people with mental disabilities worldwide, operate at the global level as well as regional and domestic levels in Europe and Africa.

Shivaun Quinlivan is a graduate of Trinity College Dublin, NUI, Galway, King's College London and The Honourable Society of King's Inns. Shivaun has recently completed a PhD in Trinity College Dublin; her research addressed the efficacy of public interest litigation in the context of the right to education for children with disabilities. Shivaun has been a lecturer at the School of Law, NUI Galway since September 2000 where she teaches primarily in the area of Constitutional Law and Disability Law and Policy on a variety of programmes.

Sinead O'Donnell is a graduate of the School of Law, NUI Galway where she was awarded BA and LLB degrees. Sinead is currently undertaking a PhD at the Centre for Disability Law & Policy on the Right to community living in Ireland under Article 19 of the UN Convention on the Rights of Persons with Disabilities.

Suzanne Doyle graduated from Nottingham Trent University with a LL.B. (Honours) in Irish Law in 2004. In 2005 she graduated with an LL.M. from Trinity College Dublin. She is also a qualified barrister, having graduated with Merit from the King's Inns and called to the Irish Bar in 2006. She is currently completing her PhD thesis with the Faculty of Law at University College Cork. It is entitled "The Involuntary Detention of Persons with Mental Disabilities and the UN Convention on the Rights of Persons with Disabilities" and is being supervised by Dr. Darius Whelan and Dr. Mary Donnelly.

Tabitha Collingbourne has been teaching at University Centre Doncaster since 2007. Her past work experience includes front-line independent legal advice provision in both private and voluntary sectors, followed by work at national level as Assistant Director of a national disability advice network. Her research interests include international human rights and their implementation in the UK, social welfare and equality law, the administrative justice system, and (disabled) people's experience of the above.

Tina Minkowitz represented the World Network of Users and Survivors of Psychiatry in the drafting and negotiation of the Convention on the Rights of Persons witih Disabilities. She served on the steering committee of the International Disability Caucus and was a member of the 40-person drafting group that created the official text of the treaty for negotiation. She is credited with much of the paradigm-shifting character of the CRPD in the areas of legal capacity, liberty and respect for integrity of the person. Ms. Minkowitz is an attorney admitted in the state of New York. She is a survivor of psychiatry and believes in the development of authentic user/survivor perspectives in human rights.

Tsitsi Chataika is a senior lecturer in the department of Educational Foundations in the Faculty of Education at the University of Zimbabwe. She is a disability mainstreaming advocate and researcher with international reputation and she serves in various international editorial boards. Dr Chataika conducted work in several African countries, Malaysia and the United Kingdom. She recently developed a gender and disability-mainstreaming manual and she is also contributing to the Southern African Development Community Inclusive Education Strategy.

TABLE OF CONTENTS

PART 6: EMPLOYMENT AND PERSONS WITH DISABILITIES

INTRODUCTION

Gerard Quinn and Charles O'Mahony (Eds)

This book is an edited volume that undertakes a multidisciplinary examination of the United Nations Convention on the Rights of Persons with Disabilities (CRPD). The book evolved from an event entitled 'Global PhD and Researchers Colloquium on Disability Law & Policy' organised by the Centre for Disability Law and Policy in NUI Galway in April 2010. The Colloquium was organised in conjunction with the Burton Blatt Institute of Syracuse University, New York, and the University of Haifa, Israel. The Colloquium brought together an emerging community of scholars whose research in the field of disability examines the significance of the CRPD and the barriers to its operationalisation and implementation.

The rights-based perspective on disability is a relatively new lens through which disability law and policy is considered. This is despite the fact that persons with disabilities are often described by the United Nations as the world's largest minority. There are approximately 1 billion persons with disabilities in the world (15 per cent of the world's population), the vast majority of whom live in developing countries. Notwithstanding the obvious human rights issues that affect persons with disabilities, the default setting for considering disability has not generally been human rights. It has been a mixture of charity, paternalism and social policy. It was clear from many of the papers presented at the Colloquium that the general social policy response was to maintain people with disabilities rather than to forge pathways for them into the mainstream.

The papers contained in this edited collection comprise the bulk of presentations made at the Colloquium. A number of cross-cutting themes emerged from the papers presented. As such this edited collection has been organised into parts, in a such a way as to reflect these themes. Part 1 focuses on disability and intersectionality; Part 2 addresses the ongoing debate about the meaning of Article 12 of the CRPD and the right to equal recognition before the law. The chapters contained in Part 3 address the emerging discourse on the right to liberty as contained in Article 14 of the CRPD and the barriers facing persons with mental health problems in realising the full spectrum of human rights contained in the CRPD. Part 4 examines the right to live independently and to be included in the community. The right to inclusive education and employment for persons with disabilities are explored in Parts 5 and 6. The final part of the book, Part 7, examines how the CRPD is being implemented regionally and in a number of jurisdictions.

It is evident from the different chapters contained in this collection that migrating the issue of disability to the core of the human rights agenda has been a slow journey. It appears that this slow progress has something to do with the way that disability has traditionally been perceived. It emerges from the thematic examination of issues in this collection that the accumulated baggage from the past is now firmly on the defensive as the move to the human rights framework of reference takes root and the CRPD is being used to drive reform.

It is suggested throughout this collection that the movement to a new framework of reference, as provided for by the CRPD, is significant. It enables issues such as segregated education, denial of legal capacity and segregation in institutional settings to be seen as pressing human rights issues, whereas before these practices were simply accepted without question. It is suggested that the CRPD provides a mechanism that advances a whole new agenda based on ensuring equal respect for human rights regardless of the presence of disability. That this revolution has taken so long to happen in the field of disability is curious since one of the fundamental tenets of human rights is its supposedly universal equality. In its essence, therefore, the human rights revolution in the context of disability has to do with making the human being behind the disability visible, and extending the benefits of the rule of law to all and not just to some or, indeed, to most. A theme running throughout the different parts of this book, importantly, it that the human rights' perspective requires the treatment of persons with disabilities as subjects with full legal personhood, as distinct from objects to be managed and cared for.

Another theme running through the chapters of this edited collection centres on the significance of the CRPD, which many authors regard as the single-most exciting development to take place in the disability field for many decades. For the authors in this collection the CRPD represents an opportunity to push forward a positive worldwide process of law reform in the field of disability. A hope of the commentators is that the CRPD will clarify its underlying values and help to accelerate reform trends internationally.

It was widely expected that the CRPD would become one of the most widely ratified human rights treaties in the UN system. Indeed, the Convention received sufficient ratifications in a relatively short period of time, meaning that it came into force on 3 May 2008. As of April 2016, there are 163 ratifications of the CRPD and 160 signatories. The CRPD is the first human rights treaty of the twenty-first century, and its clever combination of civil, political, economic, social and cultural rights under an overarching theory of non-discrimination are explored in the different thematic areas in this collection. It is of note that the CRPD has an Optional Protocol, which, if ratified, enables the relevant treaty monitoring body (the CRPD Committee) to receive individual and group petitions. As of April 2016, there were eighty-eight ratifications of the Optional Protocol and ninety-two signatories.

The chapters in this edited collection examine the application of the human rights contained in the CRPD across the thematic areas, and identify that this application is greatly instructive for several reasons. The CRPD forces us to think through the concept of human difference on the ground of disability and to reflect on when or whether the difference requires separate or special treatment. The difference of disability forces us to expand our concept of non-discrimination to require the would-be discriminator to take positive account of the disability and to 'reasonably accommodate' it. The notion of 'reasonable accommodation' is a signature feature of the non-discrimination tool in most comparative disability discrimination law, and a key feature of the CRPD; it is examined in a number of chapters in this collection. The case of disability tends to provide tangible proof of the much vaunted – but little understood – thesis concerning the interdependence and indivisibility of both sets of human rights (civil and political, as well as economic, social and cultural). As will be seen in this collection, disability brings out the truth in the nexus between both sets of rights. This is so because breaking down barriers that are in the way of persons with disabilities through, for example, non-discrimination law, is not sufficient. Some positive acts of social solidarity are also often required to underpin freedom. This is in fact true for all persons, and only more obviously true in the case of persons with disabilities. So the disability field vividly demonstrates how economic, social and cultural rights underpin, and do not undermine, freedom.

It is evident from the chapters in this collection that the CRPD is hastening the trend throughout the world toward respecting and advancing the rights of persons with disabilities. The CRPD reinforces reform efforts in many countries. A number of authors have pointed out that the work of the Committee on the Rights of Persons with Disabilities is crucial in guiding law reform and disability policy development. A key challenge for the Committee is to address ambiguities as to the scope and meaning of the rights contained in the CRPD. A central message running through the chapters in this collection is that disability has moved to the core of the UN human rights agenda, and that there is unprecedented opportunity for persons with disabilities to influence law and policy locally, nationally and globally.

PART 1: DISABILITY & INTERSECTIONALITY

CHAPTER 1

GENDER, DISABILITY AND ACCESS TO JUSTICE: AN INTERSECTIONAL EXPLORATION OF ARTICLE 13 OF THE CRPD

*Eilionóir Flynn**

1. INTRODUCTION

The right to access justice has attracted significant attention in international human rights law discourse in recent years. It has been highlighted as crucial to securing universal human rights from a wide variety of rights-based perspectives, and social movements throughout history have sought to articulate how this right should apply to them to ensure that they can assert and enforce all other human rights.[1] This chapter will explore the development of a right to access justice in international human rights law, focusing primarily on perspectives from feminist theory and how these concepts translate to disability in order to contextualise the current framing of the right to access justice in Article 13 of the UN Convention on the Rights of Persons with Disabilities (CRPD). This intersectional approach should add value to the debate on the scope and potential of a right to access justice, and is appropriate given the mandate of the drafters of the CRPD whose role was not to create 'new rights' but to reformulate existing rights as they apply to persons with disabilities.

In the first section I consider how the concept of a 'right to access justice' has evolved at a theoretical level – using Bahdi's feminist conceptualisation of access to justice as a guiding framework – and how this might apply in the context of persons with disabilities. Throughout the second section, I explore the trajectory of a right to access justice in international human rights law prior to the entry into force of the CRPD, and examine the development of Article 13 during the negotiation of the Convention. Thirdly, I discuss some insights into the interpretation of this article to date, keeping in mind the intersectional approach to accessing justice. In the

* This chapter is partly based on an article co-authored with Anna Lawson, 'Disability and Access to Justice in the European Union: Implications of the UN Convention on the Rights of Persons with Disabilities' (2012) 4 European Yearbook of Disability Law (forthcoming). I am particularly indebted to Anna for her many valuable insights on this topic, and to the students of my LLM course on Advocacy and Access to Justice for inspiring me to think about this issue in a different light.

1 See e.g. Y Ghai and J Cottrell (eds), *Marginalised Communities and Access to Justice* (Routledge 2010); I Van de Meene and B Van Rooij, *Access to Justice and Legal Empowerment: Making the Poor Central in Legal Development Co-operation* (Leiden University Press 2008); F Francioni (ed), *Access to Justice as a Human Right*, (OUP 2007); H Genn, *Judging Civil Justice* (CUP 2010); J M Jacobs, *Civil Justice in the Age of Human Rights* (Ashgate 2007); D Rhode, *Access to Justice* (OUP 2005).

conclusion I will address how the scope of Article 13 might impact on other access to justice protections in existing human rights law – and enhance the potential for women, persons with disabilities, and other marginalised groups to assert and enforce their human rights.

2. Access to Justice as a Human Right? Perspectives from Feminist Scholarship

The term 'access to justice' is generally used to describe access to the legal system and the availability of appropriate remedies for breach of rights; as such, it is a relatively new concept in international law. However, a consensus has emerged, particularly from feminist scholarship, that 'access to justice' has a much broader meaning than simply the right to engage with the legal system and to obtain an effective remedy.[2] The key intersection between feminist and disability scholars in terms of access to justice is a sense that this is a more multi-faceted issue than formal access to the courts, or to legal representation. This broader approach views access to justice as encompassing procedural safeguards, substantive equality, representation and participation in decision-making, and symbolic concerns about citizenship, belonging and empowerment.[3]

Therefore, for the purpose of this chapter, 'access to justice' is broadly construed to include rights associated with participatory democracy, due process, and even social contract theories of justice, which unpack how societal and political institutions should operate. Cappelletti and Garth are proponents of this broader approach, and define access to justice as follows:

> The words 'access to justice' are admittedly not easily defined, but they serve to focus on two basic purposes of the legal system–the system by which people may vindicate their rights and/or resolve their disputes under the general auspices of the state. First, the system must be equally accessible to all; second, it must lead to results that are individually and socially just.[4]

---

2 See for example R Bahdi, *Background Paper on Women's Access to Justice in the MENA Region* (International Development Research Centre (IDRC), Women's Rights and Citizenship (WRC) Programme, and the Middle East Regional Office (MERO) Middle East and North African (MENA) Regional Consultation 9–11 December 2007 Cairo, Egypt); D Rhode, *Justice and Gender* (Harvard University Press 1989) and 'Missing Questions: Feminist Perspectives on Legal Education' (1992-1993) 45 Stanford Law Review 1547; M J Mossman, 'Gender Equality, Family Law and Access to Justice' (1994) 8 International Journal of Law and the Family 357; R Hunter, 'Border Protection in Law's Empire: Feminist Explorations of Access to Justice' (2002) 11 Griffith Law Review 263.

3 See for example L Clements and J Read 'The Dog that Didn't Bark: The Issue of Access to Rights under the ECHR by Disabled People' in A Lawson and Caroline Gooding (eds), *Disability Rights in Europe: From Theory to Practice* (Hart 2005); Bahdi (n 2); and D Rhode, 'Missing Questions: Feminist Perspectives on Legal Education' (1992–1993) 45 Stanford Law Review 1547. For more on the intersection between disability and gender in the CRPD, see Barbara Phillips et al 'Raising awareness about awareness: insights from the feminist movement on interpreting Article 8 CRPD' in this volume.

4 M Cappelletti and B Garth, 'Access to Justice: the Newest Wave in the Worldwide Movement to Make Rights Effective' (1978) 27(2) Buffalo Law Review 181.

In the context of her analysis of women's access to justice in the Middle East and North Africa, Bahdi identifies three distinct but interlinking components of access to justice – substantive, procedural and symbolic.[5] This conceptualisation provides a useful starting-point for the analysis of access to justice within an intersectional context and will be used to frame the remainder of this section.

According to Bahdi, the substantive element of access to justice 'concerns itself with an assessment of the rights claims that are available to those who seek a remedy'.[6] It thus concerns itself with the substance or content of the legal rules and principles, which shape the decisions made in favour or against those who seek a remedy. The process of ensuring substantive justice extends beyond court rulings on the rights of people with disabilities to require inclusive law reform processes (including Constitutional reform), and ensure that parliaments take individuals' claims to an equal share of public resources into account in determining how public services are provided.

Bahdi contends that the substantive element of access to justice requires the development of laws and policies which promote substantive equality, and stresses that this cannot be effectively achieved without the involvement of the disadvantaged group in question and an in-depth understanding of social context. In the context of gender inequality, she states that 'such an approach proves respectful of the right to self-determination. It also results in an understanding of the real barriers to equality and the kinds of solutions which must be fashioned to produce such results'.[7]

Other feminist scholars support this participatory approach to substantive equality and access to justice. Rhode contends that in order to achieve substantive equality

> [e]ffective strategies for gender equality [are required which involve] a re-assessment of ends as well as means. The paradigmatic liberal prescription–equal opportunity–is a necessary but never sufficient social objective. The ultimate goal is not simply to ensure women's full participation in organizations that wield social, economic, and political power; it is rather to change the nature of those organizations and the way power is distributed and exercised.[8]

This statement about the fundamental importance of participation in achieving substantive justice is closely linked to the concept of 'Nothing About Us Without Us' which emanated from the self-advocacy movement,[9] and which became the rallying cry of persons with disabilities during the drafting of the CRPD.[10]

---

5 Bahdi (n 2).

6 ibid 3.

7 Bahdi (n 2) 28.

8 Deborah Rhode, *Justice and Gender* (Harvard University Press 1989) 320.

9 D Goodley, *Self Advocacy in the Lives of People with Learning Disabilities* (Open University Press 2000).

10 This slogan was adopted by the International Disability Caucus during the negotiations. See R Dyson, 'Statement for Formal Ceremony at the Signing of the Convention on the Rights of Persons with Disabilities' (UN DESA, 13 March 2007) <www.un.org/esa/socdev/enable/documents/Stat_Conv/nzam.doc> last accessed 31 March 2016.

This idea of structural reform to achieve substantive access to justice leads to a consideration of procedural justice, the second component of access to justice in Bahdi's categorisation. She claims that procedural justice

> should be broadly understood to mean the types of institutions where one might bring a claim, the rules that govern the complaint and conduct of the parties once the complaint is brought within a particular institution, the particular mandate of a given institution and the factors – outside of the substantive law itself — which influence the nature and quality of the encounter for women within a particular legal institution.[11]

Bahdi's notion of the extra-legal factors which influence the nature and quality of encounters with the justice system can also be read to include participation in all levels of the justice system – an issue which is equally relevant to persons with disabilities as it is to women, although arguably women have had more success in achieving this form of participation[12] than persons with disabilities to date (in terms of representation of women in the legal profession, the judiciary, jury members etc).

Hunter demonstrates the inter-linked nature of substantive and procedural as she examines how laws are framed, and interpreted, with respect to women's rights:

> Apart from the difficulties of framing legal rules that adequately respond to women's concerns, there is also the matter of how and by whom legal rules are implemented. In most cases, it was simply assumed that the traditional court system and its personnel would provide a friendly home for feminist-inspired doctrinal revisions and new causes of action. Yet two border protection mechanisms stand in the way here: the rules of evidence, and the rules and practices of procedure.[13]

Similar concerns have pre-occupied persons with disabilities, as rules of evidence and procedure can pose particular barriers to access to justice. These include physical accessibility of courts and other buildings used in the administration of justice, the availability of sign-language interpreters for deaf jurors, defendants, or witnesses,[14] the failure to adapt court procedures such as cross-examination to ensure that these are accessible to persons with intellectual or communication disabilities,[15] and the difficulties for those who are thought to lack capacity to instruct a lawyer in securing appropriate legal representation.[16] Of course, if access to justice is read broadly to include access to mechanisms outside the formal legal system, ensuring procedural justice will entail securing both access to the legal system (access to legal representation, accessibility of court and tribunal processes) and access to

---

11 Bahdi (n 2) 28.

12 Deborah Rhode, 'Missing Questions: Feminist Perspectives on Legal Education' (1992–1993) 45 Stanford Law Review 1547.

13 R Hunter, 'Border Protection in Law's Empire: Feminist Explorations of Access to Justice' (2002) 11 Griffith Law Review 263, 266.

14 M Schwartz, 'Serving Hearing Impaired Clients' (1991–1992) 18 Barrister 45.

15 Neta Ziv, 'Witnesses with Mental Disabilities: Accommodations and the Search for Truth – The Israeli Case' (2007) 27(4) Disability Studies Quarterly 51.

16 M Bach and L Kerzner, 'A New Paradigm for Protecting Autonomy and the Right to Legal Capacity' (Toronto: Law Commission of Ontario, 2010).

the political system (transparency and accountability of executive decisions and determinations of public bodies). Again, this broader access to political and social justice is an issue which concerns both women and persons with disabilities.

The third component of Bahdi's definition of access to justice is 'symbolic justice.' To achieve symbolic justice, Bahdi claims we must '[step] outside of doctrinal law and [ask] to what extent a particular legal regime promotes citizens' belonging and empowerment.'[17] Thus, for Bahdi, the symbolic component of access to justice involves a social structure in which women are fully included and empowered to participate as equal citizens. There may well be a relationship between the enactment of progressive laws and policies and the increase in belonging and empowerment – however, Bahdi notes the difficulties associated with proving the impact on wider social structures and relations of specific statutes, judicial decisions or the justice system as a whole. Recognition of the importance of the symbolic element of access to justice suggests that monitoring of the levels of inclusion and participation of the relevant group is a necessary process – a process which, like the identification of the ingredients of substantive equality, cannot be effectively conducted without the involvement of the group concerned, whether women, persons with disabilities or others.

Therefore, in the context of disability, the concept of symbolic justice reaffirms Bahdi's claim that achieving access to justice involves some consideration of what 'justice' for the particular marginalised group entails. For persons with disabilities, as for women, this will involve a broader examination of 'justice' outside the narrow confines of the legal system – incorporating political, social and cultural activities which further the participation of persons with disabilities and their recognition as equal citizens. As Lawson and I have argued elsewhere,[18] it is worth adding a fourth category to Bahdi's conceptualisation – one of participatory justice. This, while echoed in substantive, procedural and symbolic justice, deserves its own space to ensure that citizenship, belonging and empowerment become realities for persons with disabilities. As will be addressed in the following section, the participatory process used to draft Article 13, and indeed the CRPD as a whole, sheds new light on the concept of participatory justice and may prove useful when read in conjunction with other international human rights instruments, in furthering access to justice for women and other marginalised groups.

3. The Development of a Right to Access Justice in International Human Rights Law – from Universal Declaration to CRPD

In general, the right to access justice is regarded as having evolved from two pre-existing rights – the right to an effective remedy and the right to a fair hearing.[19] Both these rights are contained in the founding instrument of international human

17 Bahdi (n 2) 3.

18 E Flynn and A Lawson, 'Disability and Access to Justice in the European Union: Implications of the UN Convention on the Rights of Persons with Disabilities' (2013) 4 European Yearbook of Disability Law 7–44.

19 See Fundamental Rights Agency, *Access to Justice in Europe: An Overview of Challenges and Opportunities* (FRA 2011).

rights law – the Universal Declaration of Human Rights,[20] and in the International Covenant on Civil and Political Rights (ICCPR).[21] As mentioned in the introduction, a specifically enumerated right to access justice did not exist in international human rights law until the adoption of the CRPD – however, previous Conventions echoed the existing rights to an effective remedy and to a fair hearing in civil and criminal contexts.[22]

The right to an effective remedy is seen as reinforcing the notion of State-sanctioned consequences where a violation of rights has occurred;[23] whereas the right to a fair hearing is traditionally associated with due process rights in the context of criminal trials in particular.[24] Both rights are closely linked to a narrow conception of the justice system as the formal legal system – and focus almost exclusively on judicial or administrative remedies for breach of rights, and procedural rights in terms of how a judicial or administrative hearing is conducted. Some elements of these rights do, however, connect with a broader understanding of access to justice echoed in feminist jurisprudence and disability scholarship[25] – in particular relating to legal representation and assistance, the availability of interpreters in a fair and public hearing, the existence of an independent and impartial forum for hearing legal disputes, equality of arms in pursuing a legal right, and equal access to courts and tribunals without discrimination.[26]

Before turning to the development of the specific right to access justice in the CRPD, it is worth considering to what extent the rights of women in international human rights law contributed to framing a concept of access to justice. There is no specific articulation of a right of access to justice in the Convention on the Elimination of All Forms of Discrimination Against Women (CEDAW), although Thater contends that Articles 1, 2(c), 3 and 15 read together infer a right to access justice, closely

---

20 art 8 UDHR protects the right to an effective remedy and art 10 protects the right to a fair hearing.

21 art 2(3) ICCPR protects the right to an effective remedy and art 14 protects the right to a fair and public hearing. See also General Comments 13 and 32 of the Human Rights Committee on the Right to a Fair Hearing, Human Rights Committee, General Comment 13 – Equality before the courts and the right to a fair and public hearing by an independent court established by law 04/13/1984 and General Comment No. 32–Article 14: Right to equality before courts and tribunals and to a fair trial 23/08/2007, CCPR/C/GC/32.

22 See for example Committee on Economic, Social and Cultural Rights, General Comment 9 – The domestic application of the Covenant 03/12/98, E/C.12/1998/24. In this comment, the Committee provided guidance as to what constitutes an effective remedy for breach of economic, social and cultural rights, specifying that it may take the form of a non-judicial, administrative remedy. This General Comment also stresses that effective remedies should be accessible, affordable, timely and effective.

23 See R Provost, *International Human Rights and Humanitarian Law* (CUP 2002) 44.

24 See Human Rights Committee, General Comment No. 32–Article 14: Right to equality before courts and tribunals and to a fair trial 23/08/2007, CCPR/C/GC/32.

25 See R Hunter, 'Border Protection in Law's Empire: Feminist Explorations of Access to Justice' (2002) 11 Griffith Law Review 263 and Neta Ziv, 'Witnesses with Mental Disabilities: Accommodations and the Search for Truth – The Israeli Case' (2007) 27(4) Disability Studies Quarterly 51.

26 These components of the right to a fair hearing were identified as connecting to a broader right to access justice by Human Rights Law Resource Centre, 'The Right to a Fair Hearing and Access to Justice: Australia's Obligations' (Melbourne 2009) www.hrlrc.org.au/files/hrlrc-submission-access-to-justice-inquiry.pdf last accessed 31 March 2016.

linked to the right to equal recognition before the law.[27] Article 2(c) is of particular relevance, as it requires States Parties to 'establish legal protection of the rights of women on an equal basis with men and to ensure through competent national tribunals and other public institutions the effective protection of women against any act of discrimination.'[28]

In the CEDAW Committee's General Recommendation on this Article, States Parties are requested 'to facilitate access to and provide for the full realization of women's rights'[29] which includes ensuring that women 'have access to information about their rights under the Convention and are able to effectively promote and claim those rights.'[30]

The Committee's recommendation also addresses the participatory element of access to justice, by requiring States Parties to ensure that women are able to participate actively in the development, implementation and monitoring of policies designed to prohibit discrimination, and states that 'to this end, resources must be devoted to ensuring that human rights and women's non-governmental organizations are well-informed, adequately consulted and generally able to play an active role in the initial and subsequent development of the policy.'[31]

Aside from this general comment, the CEDAW Committee has made little reference to the barriers to accessing justice for women generally, but has highlighted additional problems which specific groups of women such as women migrant workers may face in accessing justice,[32] and has asked States Parties to take steps to address this in reports to the Committee. CEDAW has also acted as a tool for national and regional activists to monitor women's access to justice at grassroots level.[33]

However, since the comparatively narrow scope of CEDAW focuses on preventing discrimination and does not address broader issues of participation and representation in the justice system, it is arguably of limited assistance in understanding how the notion of access to justice might be expanded beyond a right to access the courts in order to seek a remedy for a violation of rights. For this deeper understanding of access to justice, and the intersection between feminist and disability theory on this issue, I now turn to examine Article 13 of the CRPD, to consider how it addresses

---

27 See G Thater, 'Equality Before the Law and Access to Justice' (paper presented at Joint Seminar of CEDAW Committee and UNHCR Examining the particular relevance of the Convention on the Elimination of All Forms of Discrimination Against Women to the protection of women of concern to UNHCR, New York, 16–17 July 2009).

28 art 2(c), Convention on the Elimination of All Forms of Discrimination Against Women (1979).

29 Committee on the Elimination of All Forms of Discrimination Against Women, General recommendation No. 28 on the core obligations of States Parties under Article 2 of the Convention on the Elimination of All Forms of Discrimination against Women, 16/12/2010, CEDAW/C/GC/28 para 20.

30 ibid para 27.

31 ibid.

32 Committee on the Elimination of All Forms of Discrimination Against Women, General recommendation No. 26 on Women Migrant Workers, 05/12/2008, CEDAW/C/2009/WP.1/R para 21.

33 See for example KARAT, 'Regional Coalition on CEDAW and Access to Justice (2010-2012)' www.karat.org/programmes/womens-human-rights/regional-coaltion-on-cedaw-access-to-justice-2010-2012/ last accessed 31 March 2016..

these broader issues of access to justice, while building on existing rights to a fair hearing and an effective remedy.

As mentioned in the Introduction, the mandate of the Ad Hoc Committee which drafted the CRPD was not to create any new rights for persons with disabilities, but simply to enumerate how existing human rights norms applied in the context of disability. In the first draft of a set of articles produced in January 2004 by the Working Group of the Ad Hoc Committee,[34] there was no article on access to justice. However, in a footnote to the Working Group's report on Article 4 (which concerned General Obligations), it was noted that other (rejected) versions of that Article had included specific provisions on remedies.[35] These had not been incorporated into the Working Group's text since the group noted that the right to an effective remedy appeared in the ICCPR but not in the International Covenant on Economic, Social and Cultural Rights, and that there was insufficient consensus in international human rights law on the issue to justify including a specific article on remedies or access to justice.[36]

In response to the draft articles developed by the Working Group, the Asia-Pacific Forum of National Human Rights Institutions suggested an addition to draft Article 4 regarding the right to an effective remedy, which was already well-established in international human rights law.[37] Although the suggested addition appeared at first glance to follow the wording of the right to an effective remedy in the UDHR and ICCPR,[38] closer scrutiny reveals the presence of some elements which appear to go beyond the pre-existing right. These new elements included the recognition of the need for legal aid in order to access justice, the need for flexibility in existing laws of procedure and evidence to accommodate witnesses and defendants with disabilities, and the reaffirmation of a positive obligation on the competent authorities of the State to enforce such remedies.[39]

In June 2004, in the third session of the Ad Hoc Committee,[40] Chile added to this debate by suggesting that there should be a separate article on access to justice.[41] Chile proposed that, in order to guarantee this right, courts would have to train judges and court personnel to ensure effective access to justice for persons with disabilities.

---

34 See United Nations Enable, Ad Hoc Committee, Working Group to draft a Comprehensive and Integral International Convention on the Protection and Promotion of the Rights and Dignity of Persons with Disabilities, 'Report to the Ad Hoc Committee, Annex I' (UN DESA, 16 January 2004) www.un.org/esa/socdev/enable/rights/ahcwgreporta4.htm last accessed 31 March 2016.

35 See United Nations Enable, Ad Hoc Committee, Working Group to draft a Comprehensive and Integral International Convention on the Protection and Promotion of the Rights and Dignity of Persons with Disabilities, 'Report to the Ad Hoc Committee, Annex I Draft Article 4' (UN DESA, 16 January 2004) www.un.org/esa/socdev/enable/rights/ahcwgreporta4.htm last accessed 31 March 2016.

36 ibid n 18.

37 See United Nations Enable, 'NGO Comments on the draft text – Draft Article 4, Proposal by Asia Pacific Forum of National Human Rights Institutions' (UN DESA, 25 May 2004) <www.un.org/esa/socdev/enable/rights/ahc3ngoa4.htm> last accessed 31 March 2016.

38 ibid.

39 ibid.

40 Landmine Survivors Network, *Daily summary of discussion at third session of UN Convention on the Rights of Persons with Disabilities Ad Hoc Committee 3 June 2004*, (Landmine Survivors Network 2004), Volume 4 (8).

41 ibid.

By the end of the fourth session of the Ad Hoc Committee in August 2004,[42] despite the proposals of Chile and the Asia-Pacific Forum, there had been no movement to draft a separate article on access to justice. Instead, access to justice issues were deemed to be addressed within what was then a draft Article 9 on recognition as a person before the law, which at that time, required States Parties to:

> [E]nsure that persons with disabilities who experience difficulty in asserting their rights, in understanding information, and in communicating, have access to assistance to understand information presented to them and to express their decisions, choices and preferences, as well as to enter into binding agreements or contracts, to sign documents, and act as witnesses.[43]

During the discussion of the draft Article 9 in the fifth session of the Ad Hoc Committee, the question of whether a separate article was needed in order to guarantee equal access to justice for disabled people arose once again. Many delegations supported this proposition, including Costa Rica, Mexico, Chile, the EU, Norway and Japan. Several delegations then met informally to draft Article 9 bis, which read as follows:

> States Parties shall ensure effective access to justice for persons with disabilities on an equal basis with others, facilitating their effective role as direct and indirect participants in all legal proceedings, including the investigative and other preliminary stages.[44]

Ultimately, that text was removed from its parent article, which was the recognition as a person before the law provision (which became Article 12), and took its final place as Article 13 of the CRPD. Article 13 now reads as follows:

> 1. States Parties shall ensure effective access to justice for persons with disabilities on an equal basis with others, including through the provision of procedural and age-appropriate accommodations, in order to facilitate their effective role as direct and indirect participants, including as witnesses, in all legal proceedings, including at investigative and other preliminary stages.
>
> 2. In order to help to ensure effective access to justice for persons with disabilities, States Parties shall promote appropriate training for those working in the field of administration of justice, including police and prison staff.

The final text of Article 13 incorporates some elements of earlier drafts, as well as some innovative additions, including the 'provision of procedural and age-

---

42 Landmine Survivors Network, *Daily summary of discussions on Article 9 at fourth session of UN Convention on the Rights of Persons with Disabilities Ad Hoc Committee 26 August 2004,* (Landmine Survivors Network 2004), Volume 5 (4).

43 See United Nations Enable, Ad Hoc Committee, Working Group to draft a Comprehensive and Integral International Convention on the Protection and Promotion of the Rights and Dignity of Persons with Disabilities, 'Report to the Ad Hoc Committee, Annex I Draft Article 9' (UN DESA, 16 January 2004) <www.un.org/esa/socdev/enable/rights/ahcwgreporta9.htm> last accessed 31 March 2016.

44 United Nations Enable, 'Article 13, Status of Discussions, Fifth Session, Ad Hoc Committee, Report of the Coordinator' (UN DESA, 4 February 2005) <www.un.org/esa/socdev/enable/rights/ahcstata13fisrepcoord.htm> last accessed 31 March 2016.

appropriate accommodations' – an element with connections to Article 7 on children with disabilities and which draws on the Asia Pacific Forum of National Human Rights Institutions' proposal regarding flexible application of evidence and procedural law to accommodate people with disabilities. Its scope and potential interaction with existing international law – including women's human rights (and the rights of women with disabilities in particular) – will be addressed in the following section.

4. Interpretation and Scope of Article 13 of the CRPD

As Article 13 represents the first statement of a stand-alone right to access justice in international law, it is worth considering further the scope of this new right and whether it does in fact go beyond the substance of earlier law. The first point to note is the novelty of the broad scope of Article 13 as compared, for example, with articulations of the right to an effective remedy or to a fair hearing, or, indeed, the right to legal protection from discrimination in Article 2(c) of CEDAW. For example, in order to assert the right to an effective remedy, the person must first demonstrate the violation of some other fundamental right. Article 13 departs from this as it treats access to justice as a stand-alone right.

Kayess and French praise the approach taken in Article 13, which they view as an extension of the traditional right to equality before the law,[45] and rightly so, as the article was initially contained within what became Article 12 on equal recognition before the law. Throughout the entire drafting process of the CRPD, many delegations referred to these core concepts as being intertwined – as being enabling rights which reinforce each other. Without the recognition of legal personality, there can be no recourse to justice, and without access to justice the right to be recognised as an equal before the law is meaningless, since it cannot be asserted, applied to specific contexts or enforced.

The interlinked nature of access to justice and equal recognition before the law highlights the symmetry between the various interpretations of access to justice: substantive, procedural, symbolic, and participatory, as discussed in the previous section. In particular, reading access to justice for people with disabilities as an expansion of the right to an effective remedy which emanates from the right to equal recognition before the law, reinforces the notion that this is a right which is central to equal citizenship, and supports the full participation of people with disabilities in all aspects of the justice system – the political, the legal and the social.

Since this chapter is focused on the intersection between gender and disability, it is worth considering the relationship between Article 6 of the CRPD on women with disabilities and Article 13 on access to justice. It should be noted in terms of the evolution of Article 6 that the initial draft articles for the CRPD did not include an interpretative article on women with disabilities, as it was felt that gender mainstreaming throughout the text of the CRPD would be sufficient to protect

---

45 R Kayess and P French, 'Out of Darkness Into Light? Introducing the Convention on the Rights of Persons with Disabilities' (2008) 8(1) Human Rights Law Review 1, 29.

women's rights.[46] However, following significant lobbying from women's groups and the testimonies of women with disabilities regarding the discriminatory and unjust treatment they experienced, the Ad Hoc Committee agreed to its inclusion.[47]

Article 6 recognises the multiple discrimination experienced by women and girls with disabilities, and reaffirms the obligation on States Parties to 'ensure the full development, advancement and empowerment of women, for the purpose of guaranteeing them the exercise and enjoyment of the human rights and fundamental freedoms set out in the present Convention.'[48] Since the CRPD is a relatively new Convention, the Committee on the Rights of Persons with Disabilities has yet to consider access to justice issues impacting on women with disabilities in either its concluding observations on State Reports, or via the individual complaints mechanism. Beyond acknowledgements of the barriers to accessing justice caused by multiple discrimination, and the impact this has on women with disabilities, little exploration of how a gendered understanding of 'justice' might impact on Article 13 has occurred to date.

However, Article 13 remains an innovative expression of the right to access justice which does push boundaries and raise questions. These may, in time, be addressed by the Committee on the Rights of Persons with Disabilities. However, an examination of its initial reports and concluding observations reveals that the Committee has not to date engaged extensively in defining the scope of Article 13. Instead, it has focused on other substantive articles which are connected to, and can be read in conjunction with, Article 13 (especially Article 5 on Equality and Non-Discrimination, Article 6 on Women with Disabilities, Article 9 on Accessibility and Article 12 on Equal Recognition Before the Law).

Nevertheless, some emerging trends can be seen in the Concluding Observations of the Committee on access to justice issues. These include concerns about legal information, advice and representation for persons with disabilities – especially in the context of free legal aid.[49] The links with other CRPD rights to legal capacity and liberty are also made clear – especially in the context of criminal procedures[50] and for people with psycho-social disabilities.[51]

The intersections between gender and disability have also been recognised, including the additional barriers which may face women and girls in seeking access to justice.

---

46 See Report of the Ad Hoc Committee on a Comprehensive and Integral International Convention on the Protection and Promotion of the Rights and Dignity of Persons with Disabilities, 5th Session, 23 February 2005, A/AC.265/2005/2 para 46.

47 See Report of the Ad Hoc Committee on a Comprehensive and Integral International Convention on the Protection and Promotion of the Rights and Dignity of Persons with Disabilities, 6th Session, 17 August 2005, A/60/266 paras 23–26.

48 art 6(2), CRPD (2006).

49 See for example, United Nations Committee on the Rights of Persons with Disabilities, Concluding Observations: El Salvador, (2013), CRPD/C/SLV/CO/1, para 30(b); United Nations Committee on the Rights of Persons with Disabilities, Concluding Observations: China, (2012), CRPD/C/CHN/CO/1, para 23.

50 See for example, United Nations Committee on the Rights of Persons with Disabilities, Concluding Observations: Paraguay, (2013), CRPD/C/PRY/CO/1, para 32.

51 United Nations Committee on the Rights of Persons with Disabilities, Concluding Observations: Australia, (2013), CRPD/C/AUS/CO/1, para 29.

This was explicitly addressed by the Committee in its Concluding Observations on El Salvador, where the Committee noted that women and girls with disabilities were at higher risk of becoming 'victims of abuse or neglect owing to the low credibility ascribed to their witness statements'[52] and requested the States Parties to '[a]dopt measures to secure access to justice for women and girls with disabilities, with due consideration paid to their role as witnesses and victims during the trial phase.'[53]

Finally, the need for training of those involved in the administration of justice is clarified in the Committee's observations to date – and this obligation on States Parties has been extended beyond the narrow confines of the justice system to health and social care workers[54] as well as judges, lawyers, police and prison staff.

However, because the Committee has at the time of writing published its concluding observations in relation to only ten countries (Spain, Tunisia, Peru, Argentina, Hungary, China, Paraguay, Australia, Austria and El Salvador) it may well address substantive issues relating to the scope of Article 13 in the forthcoming dialogues with other States Parties. In the absence of a specific General Comment from the Committee on Article 13, its concluding observations to date provide a useful starting point to guide States Parties, and these are further complemented by references to accessing justice in the Committee's General Comments on Articles 9 and 12 which make specific reference to access to justice issues. In General Comment 1 on Article 12, the links between Articles 12 and 13 are again made explicit, beginning with the recognition of a person with disabilities as a person before the law, which recognition is required to assert and enforce rights in the justice system. The historical and ongoing exclusion of persons with disabilities from key roles in the justice system (from acting as witnesses, lawyers or judges, for example) was also highlighted. This general comment also requires States Parties to implement provisions for recognising and accommodating testimony of persons with disabilities, and support for the exercise of legal capacity (including recognition of diverse communication methods) in the legal system.[55] Similarly, General Comment 2 on Article 9 highlighted the need for accessibility of physical locations in which justice is administered, as well as accessibility of services connected to the justice system (e.g. legal services, interpretation services etc.)[56]

Of course, the scope of Article 13 is not solely left to the Committee to determine, but will also be shaped by States Parties in the ways in which they report on the achievement of access to justice for persons with disabilities, including women with disabilities at domestic level. Therefore, it is important for States Parties to acknowledge the broad scope of Article 13, as being concerned with procedural and participatory access to justice which play a powerful role in facilitating substantive and symbolic access to justice.

---

52 United Nations Committee on the Rights of Persons with Disabilities, Concluding Observations: El Salvador, (2013), CRPD/C/SLV/CO/1, para 30.

53 ibid, paras 30(a) and (d).

54 See for example, United Nations Committee on the Rights of Persons with Disabilities, Concluding Observations: El Salvador, (2013), CRPD/C/SLV/CO/1, para 30(c).

55 Committee on the Rights of Persons with Disabilities, *General Comment on Article 12* (CRPD/C/GC/1), paras 34–35.

56 Committee on the Rights of Persons with Disabilities, *General Comment on Article 9* (CRPD/C/GC/2) para 33.

5. Conclusion

Since Article 13 represents a unique and broad-ranging right to access justice it is worth considering its potential for impact on other access to justice protections in existing human rights law. The focus of this chapter has been on the relationship between meaningful access to justice for women and how this understanding of access to justice has shaped and inspired the development of a specific right to access justice for persons with disabilities. As Lawson and I have argued elsewhere,[57] Article 13's primary contribution to international human rights discourse is to clearly articulate an element of 'participatory justice' into the framework of this right – adding to Bahdi's conceptualisation of access to justice as substantive, procedural and symbolic. This could have a knock-on impact not only on the rights to an effective remedy and to a fair hearing from which access to justice developed, but on statements of the broader right to access justice in other core human rights conventions, including CEDAW. It will be interesting to track the use of Article 13 in future general comments and recommendations issued by the relevant UN treaty-monitoring bodies on the issue of 'participatory' access to justice, which could enhance the potential for women, persons with disabilities, and other marginalised groups to assert and enforce their human rights.

---

57 E Flynn and A Lawson, 'Disability and Access to Justice in the European Union: Implications of the UN Convention on the Rights of Persons with Disabilities' (2013) 4 European Yearbook of Disability Law 7–44.

Chapter 2

IDEAS FOR THE CONSTRUCTION OF A HUMAN RIGHTS MODEL FOR CHILDREN, WITH OR WITHOUT DISABILITIES[1]

Ignacio Campoy Cervera

1. Introduction

In our society today the two prevailing models which determine, respectively, the recognition and protection systems for children's rights, and the rights of people with disabilities are the 'renewed' protectionism model and the social model of disability.[2] However, the solutions offered by both models continue to be unsatisfactory in terms of what should be a suitable system of recognition and protection for children's rights in general and disabled children's rights in particular: a system which fits within the framework of the human rights model.[3]

Both models are unsatisfactory because when resolving the conflict between protecting the best interests of children and desiring to grant greater legal relevance to the children's will through the protection of their right to participate in the decision-making process regarding all the questions affecting them, the ideas inherent in the protectionism model still prevail ie that children, due to their inherent incapacities, cannot freely exercise their rights. This idea is cognisant of all the important exceptions established in current legal texts, in which children only gradually, as they

---

1 This work forms a part of the following Projects: the Consolider-Ingenio 2010 Project 'El tiempo de los derechos,' CSD2008-00007, and the Research Project 'Los derechos de los niños con discapacidades,' within the Programme 'Estancias de movilidad de profesores e investigadores sénior en centros extranjeros de enseñanza superior e investigación, excepcionalmente españoles, incluido el programa "Salvador de Madariaga," 2010-2011,' funded by the Spanish Ministry of Science and Innovation, reference no. PR2010-0112, thanks to which I was able to carry out research at the Centre for Disability Law and Policy – National University of Ireland, Galway, and profit from the knowledge and teaching of the Director of the Centre, Professor Gerard Quinn.

2 An in-depth analysis of the protectionism model, which includes what I refer to as 'renewed' protectionism, as well as the previous model, which I call 'traditional' protectionism, can be found in my book: I Campoy Cervera, *La fundamentación de los derechos de los niños. Modelos de reconocimiento y protección* (Dykinson 2006). And with respect to the models for the rights of people with disabilities, see the excellent book A Palacios, *El modelo social de discapacidad: orígenes, caracterización y plasmación en la Convención Internacional sobre los Derechos de las Personas con Discapacidad* (CERMI 2008).

3 The considerations I explain with regard to this in this chapter are more fully developed – justified by the evolution observed in both models of rights recognition and protection – in the article by I Campoy Cervera, 'The construction of a human rights model for children, with or without disabilities' (forthcoming).

grow up and mature, acquire the legal capacity to exercise their own rights. Therefore, the idea is that children's will – although worthy of suitable consideration according to the child's age and maturity – cannot be legally binding, as it is assumed that if children could exercise their rights without control they would constitute a danger to others as well as to themselves. This implies an inadequate solution to the need to reconcile, first, consideration of the child, with or without disability, as a person endowed with equal dignity, and whose possibilities of drawing up life plans and acting so as to accomplish them must therefore be respected on an equal basis with everyone else; and secondly, the adoption of justified paternalistic measures, which mean denying – where necessary – the legally binding force of the will manifested by the child to take a certain course of action. Since, in accordance with protectionist principles, despite the great importance which can be recognised and attributed (which is still far from being the case) to the child's participation in the decision-making process for all the questions affecting them – and also in determining what their real interests are and how to fulfil them – in general the wills of others, usually the parents, are still allowed to dominate the corresponding decisions concerning children's lives; so that paternalistic measures which unjustifiably limit the freedom of children, with or without disabilities, continue to be imposed and thus also, ultimately, limit the free development of their personalities. This result will be inevitable so long as mechanisms are not developed to allow children to exercise their rights freely, according to their own desires and opinions, and according to what could be considered to be their 'real' will, despite recognising children as holders of all rights.

In order to solve this current problem, I will first explain that I am starting out from an ethico-juridical assumption that the ultimate aim of a society which respects the human rights model is that the greatest possible number of people should fulfil, to the greatest possible extent, the life plan which each has independently chosen, and thus attain the free development of their own personality. Afterwards, I will analyse cases in which the paternalistic measures applied to children, with or without disabilities, can be considered to be justified; and finally, I will examine the implications which have arisen from the previous considerations for shaping a system of recognition and protection for the rights of children, with or without disabilities, in accordance with the human rights model.

2. The Human Rights Model: Autonomy, Dignity and Rights

For Professor Peces-Barba, the central role of liberty is derived from its direct connection with human dignity. In his book *La dignidad de la persona desde la Filosofía del Derecho*[4] Peces-Barba presents a series of characteristics which are proper to human nature and which shape the idea of human dignity: free choice

---

4 G Peces-Barba Martínez, *La dignidad de la persona desde la Filosofía del Derecho* (Dykinson 2002). In what I explain later on in the main body of the text, in order to construct my own arguments, I will be referring to some of the principal ideas from Professor Peces-Barba's theory of human dignity and its relationship to the foundation of fundamental rights, which he develops in several different books; although perhaps his most comprehensive work in this respect is G Peces-Barba Martínez with the collaboration of Rafael Asís, Carlos Fernández Liesa and Àngel Llamas, *Curso de derechos fundamentales. Teoría General* (Boletín Oficial del Estado-Universidad Carlos III 1995).

(that is to say, free will), the capacity to build general concepts and to reason, the capacity to communicate by means of a complex language, the capacity to create art, sociability and moral freedom (that is to say, humankind's utopian objective of happiness through self-fulfilment as a moral being). However, as I understand it, of all these characteristics only the first and the last are fully significant when it comes to determining the core of justice which law must contain.

Freedom of choice is the capacity human beings have which allows them to take different courses of action. This capacity is denied from the viewpoint of determinism, but is a principle we have to accept if we wish to give any moral sense to human beings' actions; if we wish to recognise any trait of dignity in mankind. As I understand it, moral freedom ultimately coincides with the free development of one's own personality, achieved through drawing up our life plans, and taking appropriate action in order to effectively fulfil them.

As we can see, these freedoms are essentially linked. First, the free development of one's own personality can only be achieved through the suitable exercise of one's freedom of choice. If we consider that our objective is to attain the development of the individual's own personality, then his or her life plans and choice of how to realise them cannot be imposed from outside; the creation, selection and acceptance of those life plans must be the product of a decision taken freely by the individual in accordance with his or her will, desires and preferences. And, secondly, it is the continuous exercise of freedom of choice in designing and redesigning life plans and taking action in an attempt to put them into practice which, finally, allows a person to attain the maximum possible development of his or her own personality.

It follows that the attainment of this common objective must be what we are attempting to achieve with the rule of law models through the recognition and protection of fundamental rights which, in this way, will be constituted in the most suitable politico-juridical instruments for allowing the greatest possible number of people to design their life plans and act towards their effective fulfilment, thus achieving the maximum possible development of their own personalities.[5]

In this way, it must be understood that this free development of personality to the greatest possible extent, through the free design of a life plan and the actions freely realised in order to fulfil it, represents the ultimate common objective for society and, consequently, an opportunity to achieve it must be guaranteed to everyone on an equal basis; to children as well as adults, to people with disabilities as well as those without; to females as well as males; and to children with disabilities as well as those without. So that any restriction which society may impose on people's free action in terms of designing and attaining their own life plans, in the free exercise of their rights, can only be justified if it is considered necessary for the attainment of this fundamental common aim and is implemented in accordance with objective, regulated criteria which are the same for everyone.

Above, I stated that the solutions offered by 'renewed' protectionism and the social

---

5 See the justification for this idea in I Campoy Cervera, 'Una revisión de la idea de dignidad humana y de los valores de libertad, igualdad y solidaridad en relación con la fundamentación de los derechos' (2004) 23 Anuario de Filosofía del Derecho 143.

model of disability were unsatisfactory with regard to the human rights model. I will now attempt to find an interpretation of both principles more in harmony with a recognition and protection system for the rights of children with or without disabilities, in keeping with the human rights model, taking into account, essentially, the two basic principles on which the current system of children's rights recognition and protection is based: protection of the child's best interests – in accordance with Article 3.1 of the Convention on the Rights of the Child (CRC) and as stated in Article 7.2 of the Convention on the Rights of Persons with Disabilities (CRPD) – and the child's right to participate in the questions which affect him or her – in accordance with Article 12.1 of the CRC and as stated in Article 7.3 of the CRPD.[6]

If we wish to give an objective meaning to the term 'the best interests of the child' – with or without disability – within human rights discourse, I think we should seek none other than the meaning which can be attributed to the 'best interests' of any other person: to attain the free development of one's own personality, the possibility of drawing up one's own life plans and taking action so as to effectively fulfil them.[7] Therefore, attending to the need to protect the child's best interests means supposing that there are certain measures which must be taken in order to succeed in protecting the free development of one's own personality.[8] Thus, it can be understood that 'the best interests of the child' which must be protected in law

6 The Committee on the Rights of the Child itself has identified arts 2, 3.1, 6 and 12 of the Convention as those which set out its general principles, which adds other articles as general principles. However, while arts 2, 6 and 12.2 of the Convention are clearly of a principal nature, they do not have the essential nature of arts 3.1 and 12.1 in terms of understanding the theoretical and legitimising basis of the new system. Articles 2 and 6 recognise, respectively, the right to non-discrimination and the right to life, development and survival. Thus, art 2 stipulates the States Parties' obligation to respect the rights mentioned in the Convention and to ensure their application to every child subject to their jurisdiction without any distinction whatsoever. Article 6 recognises the intrinsic right every child has to life, and the fact that the States Parties have to guarantee their survival and development as far as possible. In this way, what the two articles constitute is the fundamental basis for ensuring that all children can enjoy the rights recognised in the Convention. Article 12.2 itself simply specifies more precisely the necessary application of the principle established in art 12.1, on the respect owed to the child's opinion in the corresponding judicial and administrative proceedings.

7 A concept which therefore exists within the framework of what I take to be the culture of human rights. From the point of view of other cultures, it is clear that the concept of the child's best interests can be viewed in very different ways. With regard to this, Philip Alston alerted us some time ago to the different interpretation which the principle of the child's best interests could have in different cultures, in P Alston, 'The best interests principle: towards a reconciliation of culture and human rights' in P Alston (ed), *The Best Interests of the Child. Reconciling Culture and Human Rights* (Oxford University Press 1994) 5.

8 With regard to this, the contribution made by the Inter-American Court of Human Rights (IACHR) in its Advisory Opinion OC-17/02, of 28 August 2002, Series A No. 17, *Juridical status and human rights of the child*, is interesting in that it states in para 56 that 'This regulating principle regarding children's rights is based on the very dignity of the human being, on the characteristics of children themselves, and on the need to foster their development, making full use of their potential, as well as on the nature and scope of the Convention on the Rights of the Child.' And Elizabeth Salmón takes this opinion of the Court into consideration as expressed in the resolution of the cases *Bulacio v Argentina* and *Hermanos Gómez Paquiyauri v Perú*, to infer, precisely, that 'as we can appreciate from the definitions offered, the principle of the child's best interests safeguards the free development of the personality of the male and female child.' In any case, in accordance with that stated by the Court in the subsequent paras 60, 101 and 102, it appears that its opinion finally continues to adhere to the principles of 'renewed' protectionism. E. Salmón, *Los derechos de los niños y las niñas en la Jurisprudencia de la Corte Interamericana de Derechos Humanos: estándares en torno a su protección y promoción*

under 'renewed' protectionism, includes recognising and protecting certain basic aspects of the child's life, such as full and effective enjoyment of his or her rights and the full development of his or her own personality.[9]

Furthermore, the participation of the child in the decision-making process for all those questions which affect him or her is fundamental because it is based on the idea that the free development of each individual's personality can only be achieved if he or she is free to draw up his or her own life plans and to take action for their effective fulfilment. Each individual is, therefore, the only person who can decide how to effect the free development of their personality. And it is precisely for this purpose that people are protected in the free exercise of their rights, according to their will. So, taking into consideration the need to protect children's involvement also means understanding that there are certain measures which must be taken in order to be able to guarantee that it is the children themselves who act in order to attain the free development of their own personalities. And for this reason we must guarantee that children are protected in the free exercise of their rights, according to their will.

In this way, the possible conflict between the two principles would arise if a child, with or without disability, in the free exercise – according to their will – of their rights, were to act against attainment of the free development of their own personality. This is an apparent logical inconsistency, which involves observing that although the only way to attain the free development of our own personality is to act according to our will, on occasion it is precisely an action taken according to our will which would run counter to the free development of our own personality – an apparent incoherence which places us right in the arena of paternalism, justified or unjustified.

3. Some Considerations Regarding Paternalism, Justified and Unjustified

As I have just observed in the preceding section, individuals may on occasion make decisions in the exercise of their freedom of choice which, were they to be carried out, would end up significantly hindering attainment of the free development of their own personalities. The idea is that on these occasions it would be justified for a third party, for example the authorities, to intervene so as to prevent the individual from taking

(Cooperación Alemana al Desarrollo 2010) (Translations of the texts quoted originally in Spanish are always my own).

9 In the time that has passed between when this work was submitted for publication and its effective publication, the Committee on the Rights of the Child has adopted General Comment No. 14, On the right of the child to have his or her best interests taken as a primary consideration (art 3, para 1), CRC/C/GC/14 (2013). In any case, the line marked by the Committee can be understood according to what is said in the main text, so that the content of this General Comment does not alter the ideas that I develop in this work. In this respect, the Committee on the Rights of the Child explicitly noted: 'The concept of the child's best interests is aimed at ensuring both the full and effective enjoyment of all the rights recognized in the Convention and the holistic development of the child'; clarifying the Committee itself, as already noted in para 12 of its General Comment No. 5, that the term 'development' is to be interpreted 'as a "holistic concept, embracing the child's physical, mental, spiritual, moral, psychological and social development"' (General Comment No. 14, On the right of the child to have his or her best interests taken as a primary consideration (art 3, para 1), CRC/C/GC/14 (2013), para 4).

this course of action; but it must be quite clear that the purpose of such intervention on the part of the authorities or third parties is, precisely, to allow the individual to attain his or her own moral freedom, the free development of his or her own personality. However, by directly affecting the dynamism of freedom – in fact, by preventing the exercise of free choice – it is necessary to analyse carefully the different situations. On one hand, there are cases in which an individual is prevented from taking a course of action because a third party considers that the individual would thereby be moving away from what that third party considers to be the attainment of the individual's moral freedom (and subsequent imposition of the third party's own moral choices, alien to the individual concerned, with a consequent preventing or hindering the attainment of the free development of the individual's own personality – an unjustified paternalism). On the other hand, there are cases in which one respects the attainment of the free development of the individual's personality – a justified paternalism. In the latter cases – those of justified paternalism – it would be necessary to determine how it is possible to affect someone's freedom of choice and yet continue to believe that even then it is possible to attain the fulfilment of the individual's moral freedom, of the free development of their own personality. In other words, one would have to identify the criteria that make it possible to justify the application of suitable paternalistic measures.

The subject of paternalism is extremely broad and complex; below I will merely attempt to explain, very briefly, the main criteria which one would have to consider in order to determine the existence of a kind of paternalism which could be justified in accordance with the aim of respecting the free development of individuals' personalities – including, evidently, children, with or without disabilities – and, consequently, in order to construct a recognition and protection system for the rights of children, with or without disabilities, in conformity with the human rights model.[10]

From what we have discussed so far, it should be understood that justified paternalistic measures refer to situations where it would be justified to act in opposition to a person's express wishes in the free exercise of their will, because it is thought that if the person was permitted to perform such an action, one would be allowing considerable harm to be done to the free development of his or her own personality.[11] The apparent contradiction which seems to arise between acting

10 An elaboration of the main ideas explained here regarding children's education can be found in I Campoy Cervera, 'La educación de los niños en el discurso de los derechos humanos' in I Campoy Cervera (ed), *Los derechos de los niños: perspectivas sociales, políticas, jurídicas y filosóficas* (Dykinson 2007); and, concerning the effective exercise of the rights of disabled people, in I Campoy Cervera, 'La discapacidad y su tratamiento conforme a la Constitución española de 1978' in I Campoy Cervera and A Palacios (eds), *Igualdad, no discriminación y discapacidad. Una visión integradora de las realidades española y argentina* (Dykinson 2007).

11 In fact, justification of paternalistic measures is often considered to be found in the attainment of the person's autonomy, although then there are differences with respect to what exactly this means and how it can be achieved. Thus, for example, Garzón indicates, as the 'ethical normative' component necessary to consider a paternalistic measure justified: that which is taken to overcome the deficit caused by a basic incompetence 'justly, for the sake of autonomy and equality;' and similarly, Victoria Camps proposes the justification of paternalistic measures in terms of the final objective of this same attainment of a person's autonomy. Regarding this, see E Garzón Valdés, '¿Es éticamente justificable el paternalismo jurídico?' (1989) 5 Doxa. Cuadernos de Filosofía del Derecho 155 and V Camps, 'Paternalismo y bien común' (1989) 5 Doxa. Cuadernos de Filosofía del Derecho 195.

Freeman's ideas on children's rights are also interesting. In the opinion of this English Professor, when recognising children's rights, one must pay attention to both children's needs,

against the will expressed by the person, and respect for the life plans which they have freely made in the exercise of their free will, is resolved by considering that this respect means giving priority to what constitutes the person's 'real' will, as opposed to their manifest will. That is to say, one must accept that on occasion the will expressly declared by a person may not correspond to what must be considered to constitute their 'real' will, the exercise of which would permit the free development of the individual's personality.

This kind of paternalism can be justified, therefore, because the aim pursued by the persons or institutions acting paternalistically consists in all cases of respecting and fulfilling the 'real' will of the person to whom the paternalistic measure is applied. For this reason, I consider that this way of conceiving paternalism could properly be called 'paternalism of the will.' And so it will be necessary to explain in more depth how we can identify this 'real' will of the individual.

In this regard it is necessary to bear in mind that the significant lack of one of the following three factors could distort a person's will, thus modifying their 'real' will: the possibility of using the faculties of reason; sufficient information about the circumstances relevant to the decision to be taken; and the experience to be able to evaluate this information properly. This makes it possible to understand that the fulfilment, on such occasions, of the will expressly indicated by the individual could produce significant harm to the proper development of their own life plans, and that this could justify a paternalistic measure being adopted, acting in opposition to that which the person has expressly declared. Or, in other words, we could understand that these are the three factors which allow a person to exercise their 'real' will, to take judicious decisions, to be aware of the consequences of the act which they are going to perform or omit, and accept them. In any case, one would always have to be aware that the stricter the conditions believed necessary in order to consider that a person possesses this capacity to take judicious decisions, the closer one gets to moral perfectionism, and that, therefore, these conditions should not be interpreted too rigorously.

On this point, regarding children's rights, it is extremely important to observe that these factors, which make up the capacity to take judicious decisions, could be understood also to constitute what both the CRC and the CRPD refer to as the 'maturity' of the child. In fact, the CRC itself clarifies that '[m]aturity refers to the ability to understand and assess the implications of a particular matter, and must therefore be considered when determining the individual capacity of a child.

---

which, due to their particular incapacity and vulnerability they cannot satisfy themselves, and to the respect owed to their autonomy, present or future, which they share as a human characteristic with everyone else (and which he recognises as existing, frequently at age 7 and in the majority of cases by age 10); indicating precisely, as a limit to this respect for the child's autonomy, those acts which could seriously endanger their own autonomy, either in the present or the future. Thus, acts which could undermine future life plans or irreparably harm their interests should be expressly considered as irrational acts. In these cases, and only to the extent strictly necessary to prevent serious and irreparable harm, intervention by means of paternalistic action would be justified; as it must be considered that nobody, not even a child, would want to prevent themselves from becoming a rational, autonomous being capable of deciding upon their own aims. An exposition of these ideas of Freeman's can be found in M D A Freeman, 'Taking Children's Rights more Seriously', in P Alston, S Parker and J Seymour (eds), *Children, Rights and the Law* (Oxford University Press 1995).

Maturity is difficult to define; in the context of Article 12, it is the capacity of a child to express her or his views on issues in a reasonable and independent manner.'[12]

In any case, taking seriously the fact that the 'real' will of the person – the child, with or without disability – must always be respected means that when we act contrary to the will expressed by the person, we must be able to justify very clearly that the will expressed does not correspond to his or her 'real' will, and that the consequences of the proposed action would significantly harm the attainment of his or her own life plans. This in turn means, first, that the harm which would supposedly arise from the course of action taken in accordance with the will expressed by the person must clearly run contrary to what we could presuppose would be acceptable to that person, had he or she the possibility of using the faculties of reason, adequate information and experience (ie sufficient 'maturity');[13] and secondly, that such harm must be probable and considerable.[14] Thus, the less the consequences of the manifestly wished-for action would affect the present and future development of the person's potential life plans, the less paternalistic action contrary to this expressly indicated will would be justified.[15]

---

[12] General Comment No. 12 – The right of the child to be heard CRC/C/GC/12 (2009), para 30.

[13] The approach I support regarding justified paternalistic measures implies, therefore, that justification for a paternalistic action can never lie in the consent which the person concerned may subsequently give – which we might call paternalism 'a posteriori.' First, because the paternalistic measure is not being justified by a hypothetical future will, but by a hypothetical present will, which the person, the child, cannot express, exclusively because they lack the possibility of using the faculties of reason, or adequate information or experience – which could also be understood as sufficient 'maturity.' And, secondly, because the future will of the subject could be modified precisely by the implementation of the paternalistic measure itself, and so, by changing the subject's will, we would be acting without justification from two points of view. First, because precisely the harm which we were trying to avoid by applying the paternalistic measure would occur: damage would be done to the development of the life plans which the person had freely chosen, as, by modifying their will we would necessarily modify the life plans the person would have made if the paternalistic measure had not been applied. And, secondly, because one cannot consider that an action (the paternalistic measure) is justified by its acceptance by a will transformed precisely by the carrying out of that action as, clearly, the will which gives its acceptance may have assumed the values of those who applied the paternalistic measure, and that it why its consent is given; but perhaps this would not be given if the person had been able to develop their own personality freely. If we were to find this criterion valid, we would find ourselves in the undesirable situation where the more effective the forming of the personality of the person to whom the paternalistic measure is applied in accordance with the values of those applying it, the more the paternalistic measure adopted could be justified.

This 'a posteriori' paternalism is also criticized from the 'renewed' protectionism viewpoint, as can be seen, together with other critical considerations, in T D Campbell, 'The rights of the minor: as person, as child, as juvenile, as future adult' in P Alston, S Parker and J Seymour (eds), *Children, rights and the law* (Oxford University Press 1995); and also in C Lowy, 'Autonomy and the appropriate projects of children: a comment on Freeman,' in P Alston, S Parker and J Seymour (eds), *Children, rights and the law* (Oxford University Press 1995).

[14] Regarding this, Gerald Dworkin's observation is interesting when he writes that for justified paternalism in the 'hypothetical consent' it turns out to be just as necessary to verify some deficiency in the competence of the person, 'irrational propensities, deficiencies in cognition and emotional capacities, and avoidable and unavoidable ignorance,' as that the decision is 'far-reaching, potentially dangerous and irreversible' (see G Dworkin, *The Theory and Practice of Autonomy* (Cambridge University Press 1988).

[15] Once again the opinion of the CRC is important here, when it states: 'The impact of the matter on the child must also be taken into consideration. The greater the impact of the outcome on the life of the child, the more relevant the appropriate assessment of the maturity of that child. General Comment No. 12 – The right of the child to be heard CRC/C/GC/12 (2009) para 30.

However, when judging in real cases whether a certain paternalistic measure is justified or not, the answer may not be so simple. In each case one would have to clarify how these two elements could be combined: the probability that harm to the person's life plans would really be done, and the extent of such harm. Thus, and in accordance with the above, to facilitate deciding on the justification or non-justification of the paternalistic measure to be taken, I consider that three closely linked considerations would have to be taken into account.

The first would be to comprehend that the paternalistic measure would only be justified if it could be established that there is a high probability of producing serious harm to the life plans which can legitimately be presupposed to be according to the will which the person, the child, with or without disability, would express at the time if he or he had sufficient use of the faculties of reason, information and experience, ie sufficient 'maturity.' The more probable and serious the harm which could be caused by allowing the subject to act according to the will he or she has expressed, the less demanding we should be when collecting data which allows us to determine whether the will expressed coincides with his or her 'real' will, with regard to putting the paternalistic measure into practice, as one would then be more likely to be acting to the detriment of the life plans of the person by not adopting the paternalistic measure.[16] And, conversely, the less probable and serious the harm of carrying out the action expressed by the person, the more stringent we should be when collecting data to allow us to determine that it does not coincide with their 'real' will, with regard to implementing the paternalistic measure, because it is less likely that one would be acting to the detriment of the person's life plans by not adopting the paternalistic measure.

The second consideration one would have to bear in mind is that probability and seriousness function here in inverse proportion to each other: the more serious the harm produced by not implementing the paternalistic measure, the less necessary is the requirement of the probability of the harmful consequence, and the more probable it is that harm will be done to the person's life plans, the less necessary it is to insist on the seriousness of the harm (though we should never consider harm to be insignificant or trivial, as we would be failing to fulfil that established by the first consideration).

And the third consideration is that in this calculation of probabilities and harm which must be carried out in order to weigh up the justification or lack of justification of the implementation of the paternalistic measure, we must consider not only how performing or not performing the action to be taken in accordance with the individual's expressly stated will would harm the development of his or her personality, but also how the consequences of implementing the paternalistic measure itself could harm this development.

---

16 Although supposing it could be reliably proved that the person was fully aware of the consequences of their action or omission and accepted them after due deliberation – ie this corresponded with their 'real' will, if one were then to prevent them from carrying out this course of action, this would not be a justified paternalistic measure, even though the consequences arising for the person's life might seem to others to be extremely serious and probable.

4. Implications for the Construction of a Recognition and Protection System for the Rights of Children, with or without Disabilities, which would be in Harmony with the Human Rights Model

From all the considerations examined in the two preceding sections we may draw five important conclusions which directly affect the recognition and protection system for the rights of children, with or without disabilities, which must be developed in accordance with the human rights model.

The first is that one way of clearing up the underlying conflict which may exist between the two basic principles of the protection of the child's best interests and the protection of the child's right to take part in all the questions which affect him or her is by understanding that, with both, what one really has to do is protect what must be considered as constituting the 'real' will of the child.

The second conclusion is that the possible conflict which may arise in the practical application of the two principles can be resolved by applying the same justification criteria for any paternalistic measures which it may be considered necessary to adopt with respect to any person's decision – regardless of their personal condition.

The third is that we must always respect the will expressly indicated by the child, with or without disability, when taking a decision in the exercise of his or her rights (as must be done towards any person, regardless of personal condition), except when there are good reasons to justifiably presuppose that the child, due to not having the possibility of using the faculties of reason, or due to not having enough information or experience to be able to process that information properly, that is to say, due to lack of 'maturity,' is not really aware of the consequences which may arise from the course of action which he or she expressly declares he or she wishes to carry out, or not carry out, in this exercise of his or her rights, and, in addition, there exists a considerable probability that as a result of these unforeseen consequences the attainment of his or her plans, or the free development of his or her own personality will be prevented or hindered (or, obviously, third parties may be unlawfully harmed in a similar way).

The fourth conclusion is that should the corresponding paternalistic measure be taken, if one is acting towards the attainment of the free development of the child's personality (even if this is done while claiming that one is acting to protect the best interests of the child) in spite of what the child declares (participation to express the child's opinions on the subject is always necessary), one must make the decision which one could presuppose the child, with or without disability, would make, for that specific case and at that precise time in their life, if they had sufficient 'maturity.' That is to say, one would have to take the child's particular personal situation into account and act in a way which was coherent with what, until then, had been the design and development of the child's life plans, and the development of his or her own personality. In other words, one would have to act in accordance with what one understood to be, at that time and for that specific decision, the 'real' will of the child.[17] In this way, it is important to observe that these considerations apply to any child, with or without a disability, whatever their personal condition or age.[18]

The fifth conclusion is that the criteria of age and disability cannot be general criteria for limiting the capacity to act. Although it is possible to use these criteria for isolated limitations to the capacity to act, their use must be kept to a minimum and must be clearly justified. In this regard, it is understood that age and disability can occasionally be sufficient criteria to presuppose that the child suffers from lack of sufficient 'maturity' to freely exercise some of his or her rights. However, it would be necessary to provide solid reasons for this, regarding the specific right in question (as the legislator would have to carry out an individualised study of these criteria for each right), which would make it possible to justifiably presuppose that the child under the proposed age threshold or with a certain disability lacked sufficient 'maturity' to be able to freely exercise this right, as there existed a considerable probability that as a result of the consequences of the free exercise of this right the attainment of his or her life plans or the free development of his or her personality would be prevented or significantly hindered (or similar harm would unlawfully

[17] On this point the ideas of Eekelaar are of interest; after also identifying, in 'The Importance of Thinking that Children have Rights,' the need to pay attention to what the children themselves think and to encourage them to express themselves as much as possible, he finally underlines that in any case it can never be considered sufficient simply to claim that an action is performed to ensure a child's welfare; instead, one should be thinking of carrying out the action which we believe would very probably be what the child itself wanted. At any rate, later on, in 'The interests of the child and the child's wishes: the role of dynamic self-determinism,' he explains the meaning of his interesting concept of 'dynamic self-determinism,' which serves to reconstruct the meaning of the principle of the child's best interests, by considering that although on occasion it is necessary to have recourse to the method of 'objectivation' – ie a supposedly objective interpretation made by competent people – of what should be understood by these best interests, he expressly states the danger using this method involves of imposing the ideologies and interests of others, and not those of the child; and so it is necessary to accept the relevance of the method of 'dynamic self-determinism,' which acts in parallel to that of 'objectivation' and which requires one to pay attention to the desires and points of view of the child itself when determining what his or her interests are, so that the child reaches adulthood with the maximum number of opportunities to form and pursue their life plans, and these will reflect an autonomous choice as faithfully as possible. But, as he makes quite clear, this does not mean simply delegating to children the taking of all the decisions which affect them, nor seeking the decisions to be taken from them, although it does mean that they have to take an active part in accordance with their own evolution. Adults must try to provide the right conditions for the child to develop this dynamic self-determinism which will foster the development of their personality; for this purpose one must pay attention to the child's desires, as well as their stability and the coherence of these desires with the child's process of self-fulfilment (see these ideas in J Eekelaar, 'The Importance of Thinking that Children have Rights' in P Alston, S Parker and J Seymour (eds) *Children, rights and the law* (Oxford University Press 1995); and in J Eekelaar, 'The interests of the child and the child's wishes: the role of dynamic self-determinism' in P Alston (ed), *The best interests of the child. Reconciling Culture and Human Rights* (Oxford University Press 1994).

[18] With regard to this, the opinion of the Committee on the Rights of the Child is interesting, in General Comment No. 7 – Implementing child rights in early childhood CRC/C/GC/7/Rev.1 (2005) para 14: 'The Committee wishes to emphasize that Article 12 applies both to younger and to older children. As holders of rights, even the youngest children are entitled to express their views, which should be 'given due weight in accordance with the age and maturity of the child' (art 12.1). Young children are acutely sensitive to their surroundings and very rapidly acquire understanding of the people, places and routines in their lives, along with awareness of their own unique identity. They make choices and communicate their feelings, ideas and wishes in numerous ways, long before they are able to communicate through the conventions of spoken or written language.'

be done to third parties).[19] In any case, the reduction of those criteria of age and disability to a minimum also means that the necessary discretion which the setting of any limit involves must be suitably attenuated by structuring the recognition and protection system for children's rights, in line with the human rights model, in an open way. That is to say, in such a way that if it is proved that a child, with or without disability, regardless of age or disability, has the 'maturity' required for the free exercise of the right concerned, then he or she may have the means necessary to have the legal capacity for the free exercise of this right recognised in a simple way – in the same way that, if it was proved that a person lacked sufficient 'maturity' for the free exercise of the right in question, there would have to be a simple way of accessing the support measures necessary to suitably exercise this right in accordance with what could be considered to constitute 'real' will.[20]

The application of these conclusions to the construction of a suitable recognition and protection system for the rights of children, with or without disabilities, would mean passing beyond the limits which we have seen 'renewed' protectionism and the social model of disability confine them to, and setting up a system in line with the human rights model. The most important consideration here is the child's freedom,

---

19 Regarding this point, the proposals of Foster and Freed, on the need to surpass the establishment of a general criterion for the age of majority in terms of rights recognition (as this is arbitrary and characterised by exceptions which highlight the lack of rational criteria for such recognition) and on the need to maintain different age thresholds for recognition of the capacity to exercise different rights, prove interesting. The way in which these age thresholds would be established would be by taking into consideration the maturity and behaviour of young people with regard to the activity which would be permitted in the exercise of the right concerned, and it would be according to these criteria that the functioning and efficacy of the right would be determined; and thus the age threshold set for that right would be periodically reviewed. And, in line with this idea, they explicitly propose that we should recognise children's individual freedom according to their maturity and development; and anyone who sought to limit this freedom would have to prove that such a limitation was necessary, and really applied in the child's best interests (see H Foster, Jr. and D J Freed, 'A Bill of Rights for Children' (1974) 6 Family Law Quarterly 343). Also of interest is Rodham's analysis, following the ideas of Foster and Freed, as this also points to the possibility of abolishing a general minority age and considers that if age can be a valid criterion for the distribution of legal benefits and burdens, a rationality test should be carried out before the criterion is applied (see her exposition of this in H Rodham, 'Children Under Law' (1974) 9 Harvard Educational Review 1).

20 Here too the opinion of the CRC is relevant, on stating that 'By requiring that due weight be given in accordance with age and maturity, Art. 12 makes it clear that age alone cannot determine the significance of a child's views. Children's levels of understanding are not uniformly linked to their biological age. Research has shown that information, experience, environment, social and cultural expectations, and levels of support all contribute to the development of a child's capacities to form a view. For this reason, the views of the child have to be assessed on a case-by-case examination.' General Comment No. 12 – The right of the child to be heard CRC/C/GC/12 (2009) para 29.

In fact, in Spain, for example, notaries, as officials responsible for guaranteeing legal certainty, have to look into each individual case to determine the capacity of the child or disabled person in certain circumstances. As García Pons recalls, 'The capacity to act of minors or people with disabilities will be assessed by the notary by means of a direct, personal examination, and then, on their responsibility, the corresponding judgement of capacity will be issued, which will state if this is sufficient or not, not only regarding the intellective faculties or natural capacity to understand and want which the subject may have, but also regarding the nature of the act or contract they intend to execute'; A García Pons, 'Algunas consideraciones a propósito del vigésimo aniversario de la Convención Internacional de los Derechos del Niño, y su relación con la Convención Internacional sobre los Derechos de las Personas con Discapacidad. Consecuencias en la actuación notarial' (2009) 72 Revista Jurídica del Notariado 195.

like that of any other person, and, consequently, the legally binding force of their will in the exercise of their rights.[21] The introduction of this system does not only mean that children, with or without disabilities, must take part in the decision-making process regarding questions which affect them, but also that children, with or without disabilities, are also citizens of society like any other, with the possibility of exercising their rights according to the same criteria as any other person. This also means understanding that it is not that children, with or without disability, are holders of all rights and that their legal capacity to exercise some rights is recognised, and, in all cases, their participation in the decision-making process regarding questions which concern them should be required, although always under the supervision of the parents or a third party qualified to do so (as used to happen under 'renewed' protectionism and the social model of disability); but, rather, that they are holders of all rights and their legal capacity to exercise them on an equal basis with everyone else in society is recognised and protected.

Therefore, a support model for decision-making, for the exercise of rights, must be established, through which the rights, the will and the preferences of the person – and also, logically, the child – whose right is to be exercised must be respected, and, consequently, the will substitution model must be withdrawn. Such a support model has already been established under Article 12 of the CRPD for persons with disabilities,[22] and it is this which must be extended to include children, with or without disabilities. It is in this way that the end of Article 7.3 of the CRPD should be interpreted, which, let us recall, establishes that the States Parties must guarantee the right of disabled children on an equal basis with everyone else to express their opinion freely on all the questions affecting them 'and to be provided with disability and age-appropriate assistance to realise that right.' Appropriate assistance is particularly important for the exercise of the right to participation, due to the transcendence which we have already seen that this right (and principle) has in the recognition and protection system for children's rights; but it is obvious that such suitable assistance should not be limited to this right to participation, but in fact should be provided for the child whenever they need it, in the exercise of any right.[23]

---

[21] Since, as the Office of the United Nations High Commissioner for Human Rights correctly observed in the document 'Children's rights: Creating a Culture of Human Rights,' 'children are people: as members of the human family they have the same consideration as adults. They are not the property of their parents, nor products of the State, nor people in training. Governments have the moral responsibility of recognizing the human rights of children as citizens in their own right on all levels of society.' Office of the High Commissioner for Human Rights, *Children's Rights: Creating a Culture of Human Rights* (1998) 12 (Translation is my own).

[22] In this regard the reflections of De Asís, Barranco, Cuenca and Palacios are very clear when they state that 'Article 12 of the Convention establishes a fundamental change in the way of approaching the question of legal capacity in situations where a disabled person may need help from a third party. This change could be called passing from the 'substitution in decision-making' model to the 'support or assistance in decision-making' model. It is, doubtless, the greatest challenge which the Convention faces. Article 12 includes, within the concept of legal capacity, the capacity to act, ie the faculty of creating, modifying or extinguishing legal relationships; and restricts, or we could even say prohibits, the incapacitation instrument (in the case that this should be interpreted as a mechanism for revoking the capacity to act and, therefore, now legal capacity too)' (R de Asís Roig, M C Barranco Avilés, P Cuenca Gómez and A Palacios Rizzo, "Algunas reflexiones generales sobre el impacto de la Convención Internacional de los Derechos de las Personas con Discapacidad en el Derecho Español' in P Cuenca Gómez (ed), *Estudios sobre el impacto de la Convención Internacional sobre los Derechos de las Personas con Discapacidad en el Ordenamiento jurídico español* (Dykinson 2010)

[23] Regarding this, see, for example, arts 16, 20 and 24 of the CRPD itself, which concern,

This support model entails recognition of the legally binding force of the 'real' will of the child, with or without disability, ie their manifest will where it is considered that they have sufficient 'maturity' to exercise the right concerned, or the will which it is considered would be theirs if they possessed at that time the 'maturity' required; and the model thus excludes the imposition of the will of anyone who might exercise the right for them (even though they could try to justify this by arguing that they are acting in order to protect the child's best interests). The contrary would mean assuming that Article 12 of the CRPD establishes the support model instead of the will-substitution model for all people with disabilities, regardless of type or extent, but excludes (without justification) children from this concept of a person, permitting the will-substitution model to continue in force only for the child. This model previously ran counter to a suitable recognition and protection system for children's rights,[24] but now runs counter to international human rights law, as it openly contradicts the spirit of a regulation/treaty as important as the CRPD.[25]

In this regard, it must be understood that the CRPD goes further than the social model of disability (and also 'renewed' protectionism), aiming towards the construction of a human rights model,[26] which must also be valid for children. For this reason, we cannot continue to think that the will-substitution model, which is not valid for disabled people, could be valid for children. To continue with a system of recognition and protection of children's rights based on the interpretation and application inherited from 'renewed' protectionism, and its principles of the child's best interests and participation, really constitutes another unjustified exclusion of children from the human rights model. On the contrary, integrating children into the human rights model means recognising that their legal capacity is also guaranteed on an equal basis with other people in all aspects of life, and that consequently a system which takes into consideration their 'real' will, for the proper exercise of their rights, must be found for them too.

---

respectively: protection against exploitation, violence and abuse, participation in cultural life, recreational activities, leisure and sport, and education.

24 As I have explained in several different works; though for the first time in the 'Epílogo' of I Campoy Cervera, *La fundamentación de los derechos de los niños. Modelos de reconocimiento y protección* (Dykinson 2006).

25 In this regard it could be said that they were also approaching the ideas of García Pons, who initially observes (he is referring to the Spanish legal code, but his reflections can be generalised) that '[i]t is to be hoped that the systems of substitution and complement of a person's capacity to act, currently constituted by the legal representation institutions (parental authority, guardianship) and tutorship, most of which involve legal incapacitation, will also be subject to review. The legislative tendency is towards the implementation of a system of assistance or support for the capacity to act which does not involve said incapacitation of the person and avoids, as far as possible, the substitution system;' later on he points out that, from the CRPD onwards, 'the question of minors with disabilities should also be contemplated from the perspective of non-discrimination, equal opportunities and universal accessibility, as the basic principles established by the above mentioned 2006 Convention,', and finally goes on to link these safeguards from art 12 of the CRPD precisely with the principle of the child's best interests, remarking that this is 'perfectly subsumable within what art 12 of the Convention of 13 December 2006 calls 'suitable and effective safeguards for preventing abuses in accordance with international human rights law' (García Pons (n 19)).

26 As indicated, for example, in the 'Study of Disability in EC Development Cooperation,' which describes our progress through four different paradigms: charitable, medical, social, and human rights, observing that 'The CRPD is based on the human rights approach which has also been adopted by the EU.' P Coleridge, C Simonnot and D Steverlynck (experts), *Study of Disability in EC Development Cooperation*, (Final Report Draft 2010) 30.

Thus, in accordance with the human rights model, it will be necessary to adhere to the following two general considerations in order to guarantee this suitable system of protection for the exercise of rights by children, with or without disability. The first is that it would be based on the fact that the child, with or without disability, can exercise his or her rights freely (ie according to his or her manifest will), and that any limitation to the exercise of their rights would have to be previously justified.

The second is that when it is considered that a child does not possess the sufficient 'maturity' required to freely exercise a right – which could be connected to an age threshold or some kind of disability – one must always try to ensure that the exercise of the right corresponds as far as possible to whatever the child's 'real' will would be. This means that the child, with or without disability, must be guaranteed participation in the exercise of the right to the greatest possible extent and must be given all the support needed for the proper exercise of the right at all times, and that his or her 'real' will should never be replaced by that of whoever takes the final decision regarding the exercise of the right (not even with the traditional justification of acting to protect his or her best interests).

This second consideration affects two possible situations. One would occur when it is considered that the child, with or without disability, cannot freely exercise the right in question, but that they could do so after receiving the necessary support. In this case the child must be able to access all these support measures and then be able to freely exercise his or her right. The other possible situation would occur when it is considered that the child, with or without disability, cannot freely exercise the right concerned even if he or she receives the necessary support. In this case the right in question will be exercised by a third party qualified to do so, after due participation by the child and after he or she has received the necessary support; and one must always try to ensure that such exercise corresponds with what it would be reasonable to think would in this case be the 'real' will of the child, with or without disability, who holds the right.

Chapter 3

RAISING AWARENESS ABOUT AWARENESS: INSIGHTS FROM THE FEMINIST MOVEMENT ON INTERPRETING ARTICLE 8 OF THE CRPD[1]

Barbara Phillips, Nicole Emmenegger, Bruno Trezzini and Mary Keogh

1. Introduction

This chapter discusses the concepts of awareness-raising and consciousness-raising as they pertain to Article 8 ('Awareness-raising') of the Convention on the Rights of Persons with Disabilities (CRPD). 'Awareness' and 'consciousness' are two words often used interchangeably, with only a slight difference in meaning but, as we argue in this chapter, with far-reaching consequences. Compared to other articles of the CRPD,[2] Article 8 addresses rather uncontroversial objectives, and the suggested measures to meet these objectives seem straightforward.[3] However, by examining Article 8 more closely, by drawing parallels between the disability and feminist movements, and by comparing the CRPD to previous legal disability tools, it becomes obvious that the article only comprises the notion of awareness-raising; consciousness-raising does not feature. We see this as a fundamental omission, and propose an interpretation of Article 8 of the CRPD that clearly distinguishes between awareness- and consciousness-raising, so as to enhance the successful implementation of Article 8 of the CRPD and, as a result, to effectively empower persons with disabilities.

In Section 2 we start off by considering the history of the disability movement and the paradigm shift from the medical to the social model of disability, highlighting parallels with and differences to the feminist movement. We then clarify what we mean by awareness-raising and consciousness-raising. Furthermore, we show that while persons with disabilities could of course be simply subsumed under 'society'

---

1 We would like to thank Jerome Bickenbach for his helpful comments at various stages of this chapter.

2 In particular, art 12 ('Equal recognition before the law') with its reference to legal capacity comes to mind. During the deliberation process an interpretational tug-of-war ensued revolving around the notions of supported and substituted decision-making (see A Dhanda, 'Legal Capacity in the disability rights convention: Stranglehold of the past or lodestar for the future' (2006–2007) 34 *Syracuse Journal of International Law and Commerce* 429).

3 United Nations Conventions on the Rights of Persons with Disabilities (CRPD), art 8 [2006], A/RES/61/106.

they are in effect not the addressees of Article 8. This is followed by a discussion of the implications of the fact that women and persons with disabilities are both heterogeneous groups. To gain a better understanding of the origins of Article 8 and the neglect of consciousness-raising, we perform in Section 3 an in-depth analysis of the previous disability tools on which the CRPD was based. We also revisit the deliberations and negotiations of Article 8 of the CRPD. Finally, with regard to how Article 8 has been implemented to date, we briefly examine in Section 4 a number of reports by States Parties submitted to the Committee on the Rights of Persons with Disabilities.

2. Parallels in the Development of the Feminist and Disability Movements: Biological Determinism v Social Construction

Before the disability movement gained momentum and political clout, the medical, or individual, model of disability was dominant.[4] The medical model has been criticised by many disability activists for treating disability as a personal problem and for assuming that it is the individual who has to adjust or be 'fixed', thus neglecting the role of society in accommodating people with disabilities.

In the wake of the emerging disability movement, the social model of disability has shifted attention away from individuals and their physical or mental deficiencies and focuses instead on the ways in which society includes or excludes them.[5] According to the social model, disability is primarily a product of social arrangements, and can thus be reduced or possibly eliminated.[6] The disablement is socially created and the experience of disability is another form of social oppression.[7] Supporters of the social model argue that the physical or mental state of health is of secondary importance compared to the oppression persons with impairments experience in society.

Similarly, feminists questioned biological determinism, ie the purportedly inexorable influence of the biological fact of being female.[8] They also argued that being female is of secondary importance to the oppression women experience in society. Furthermore, feminist scholars found it imperative to make a distinction between biological sex (impairment) and socially constructed gender (disability). This distinction enabled them to argue that many differences between women and men were socially produced and, therefore, changeable.[9]

The bio-psycho-social model of disability, first introduced in the International Classification of Functioning, Disability and Health (ICF) by the World Health Organization (WHO),[10] combines elements of the two contending perspectives by

---

4 M Oliver, *Social Work with Disabled People* (Macmillan 1983).

5 M Oliver, *The Politics of Disablement* (Macmillan 1990).

6 T Shakespeare, *Disability Rights and Wrongs* (Routledge 2006).

7 M Lloyd, 'Does she boil eggs? Towards a feminist model of disability' (1992) 7 Disability, Handicap & Society 207.

8 S de Beauvoir, *The Second Sex* (Vintage 1989).

9 R J Stoller, *Sex and Gender: On The Development of Masculinity and Femininity* (Science House 1968).

10 World Health Organisation, *International Classification of Functioning, Disability and Health (ICF)* (2001).

defining disability as the outcome of the interaction between a health condition, or impairment, and societal barriers. Based on the Preamble, section (e),[11] and Article 1, it would appear that the CRPD is drawing on the bio-psycho-social model of disability.[12] However, although the limitations a person experiences through his or her actual impairment are especially important in the legal realm, this is not the case in the CRPD.[13] Rather, the CRPD is based heavily on the social model of disability, which emphasises that limitations result from disability and not impairment.[14] The somewhat simplistic idea that 'people are disabled by society'[15] is also reflected in the wording of Article 8 of the CRPD. Thus, the social model's focus on the role of society in removing barriers may also account for the absence of consciousness-raising in Article 8.

3. Distinction between Awareness-Raising and Consciousness-Raising

'Awareness-raising' refers to activities that raise public awareness of social issues, such as disability rights and the need for their enforcement. It is directed at people who are not themselves part of the social group whose problems are the focus of the awareness-raising efforts.

'Consciousness-raising,' by contrast, involves similar awareness-raising activities, but is directed inwards, targeting the affected group itself.[16] Consciousness-raising is awareness-raising, but for and by the oppressed group itself. Activities to that effect encompass anything from gathering information to meeting in small groups to discuss personal issues and recognise personal oppression.[17] Table 1 provides an overview of four ideal-typical forms of awareness- raising and consciousness-raising.

---

11 art 1(e), CRPD, 'Recognizing that disability is an evolving concept and that disability results from the interaction between persons with impairments and attitudinal and environmental barriers that hinder their full and effective participation in society on an equal basis with others' United Nations, *From Exclusion to Equality: Realizing the Rights of Persons with Disabilities* (United Nations 2007).

12 ibid '(…) Persons with disabilities include those who have long-term physical, mental, intellectual or sensory impairments which in interaction with various barriers may hinder their full and effective participation in society on an equal basis with others.'

13 This, for example, is the case in anti-discrimination laws which require proof of discrimination based on difference and in welfare laws which require proof of impairment as the basis for eligibility for benefits.

14 R Lang, 'The United Nations Convention on the right and dignities for persons with disability: A panacea for ending disability discrimination?' (2009) 3 ALTER, European Journal of Disability Research 266.

15 R Kayess and P French, 'Out of darkness into light? Introducing the Convention of Persons with Disabilities' (2008) 8 Human Rights Law Review 1.

16 K Sarachild, 'Consciousness-Raising: A Radical Weapon' (1978) <http://library.duke.edu/rubenstein/scriptorium/wlm/fem/sarachild.html> last accessed 31 March 2016.

17 R Rosen, *The World Split Open: How the Modern Women's Movement changed America* (Viking 2000); K Sarachild, 'A Program for Feminist "consciousness-raising,"' pp 78–80 in S Firestone and A Koedt (eds), *Notes From The Second Year: Women's Liberation* (Redstockings 1970).

Table 1: Types of consciousness-raising and awareness-raising

		Target of action / measure	
		In-group (affected people)	Out-group (general public)
Source of action / measure	In-group (affected people)	Bottom-up consciousness-raising (eg self-help group meetings)	Bottom-up awareness-raising (eg public rallies by advocacy groups)
	Out-group (government)	Top-down consciousness-raising (eg information on legal regulations by equal opportunities office)	Top-down awareness-raising (eg sensitivity training; media campaigns)

However, consciousness-raising goes further than just being aware of a certain problem or situation; it has to do with people recognising their common experiences as oppressed people. Marx, for instance, gave the examples of peasants and factory workers not effectively questioning the rule of the aristocracy or the owners of the means of production as long as they were not fully conscious of their common social position and oppression.[18] More recently, Nussbaum[19] and Sen[20] have pointed out that societal barriers exist to acquiring full justice because of 'adaptive preferences,' preferences that have adjusted to the persons' second-class status.

Many social movements have loosely followed Marx's thinking on consciousness, but it was very prominently re-introduced by one faction of the feminist movement in the 1960s and 1970s.[21] More specifically, in the women's movement this was called 'raised consciousness' and involved 'raising something from the unconscious to the conscious mind; to heightened consciousness of oneself or of a state of affairs; to an altered consciousness.'[22] Cassell referred to it as, 'having your head in a different place.'[23]

4. The Individual is Political

Consciousness-raising creates the necessary 'lens through which ideas, individuals, and relationships are newly viewed.'[24] This 'lens' identifies the problem as societal

18 K Marx, *The German Ideology* (1845) <www.marxists.org/archive/marx/works/1845/german-ideology/ch01a.htm> last accessed 31 March 2016.

19 M Nussbaum, 'Capabilities as fundamental entitlements: Sen and social justice' (2003) 9 *Feminist Economics* 33.

20 A Sen (ed), *Gender Inequality and Theories of Justice* (Clarendon Press 1995).

21 J Freeman, *The Politics of Women's Liberation* (David McKay Company 1975).

22 J Cassell, *A Group Called Women: Sisterhood and Symbolism in the Feminist Movement* (David McKay Company 1977) as quoted on p 13 in S N Barnartt, 'Disability Culture or Disability Consciousness?' (1996) 7 Journal of Disability Policy Studies 1.

23 ibid.

24 M F Katzenstein, 'Comparing the women's movements of the United States and Western

rather than an individual problem. It also invokes the necessity for collective action,[25] and impels its adherents to take that action.[26] As Lambert points out:

> A home birth, the purchase of fair trade coffee, and a woman's provisions of unpaid caring labour in the home all have profound public policy implications. At their heart each of these acts rejects elements of the dominant culture and envisions that a different world is possible. As long as these acts are considered non-political then their potential for improving women's internal efficacy and political interest remains small. Once the acts are named political, then women can perceive their private choices as having broader political consequences and can see the intersections of politics and their lives.[27]

This issue was prominently discussed in Carol Hanisch's famous essay: 'The Personal Is Political.'[28] Early second-wave feminists argued that women were isolated from each other, and as a result many problems in women's lives were misunderstood as 'personal,' or as the results of conflicts between the personalities of individual men and women, rather than systematic forms of oppression. One way to raise consciousness is to get together and talk about personal problems, to realise that many problems are not personal at all. Hanisch states that it is important to learn to draw conclusions and make connections from experiences and feelings that get discussed in a consciousness-raising group.[29] The people in the group are then empowered to do the necessary awareness-raising in a successful manner that could lead to a change of the system and the potential removal of the problem identified by the consciousness-raising group and the oppression that accompanies it.

This brings us back to the social model of disability, which also identifies the barriers for persons with disabilities as a societal rather than a personal issue. Even after several decades of progress in feminist and disability issues, consciousness-raising is still required to advance key concerns. We accept the feminist precept that consciousness-raising has to be done by the group itself. However, the impulse for consciousness-raising can also come from the outside, for example, as information given to the affected group or as a legal tool like the CRPD. Such external impulses may be necessary because contemporary societies still condone the inequality of women[30] and the disadvantages faced by people with disabilities.[31] More importantly, people with disabilities potentially internalise such beliefs and attitudes as well. As mentioned above, people tend to accept inequalities when they are embedded in

---

Europe: An Overview,' pp 3-22 in M F Katzenstein and C McClurg Mueller (eds), *The Women's Movements of the United States and Western Europe* (Temple University Press 1987).

25 E Klein (ed), *The Diffusion of Consciousness in the United States and Western Europe: An Overview* (Temple University Press 1987).

26 S N Barnartt (n 22).

27 L Lambert, 'Women's Motivations for Political Participation' (Annual Meeting of the Canadian Political Science Association 2008).

28 C Hanisch, 'The Personal Is Political' (1969) <www.carolhanisch.org/CHwritings/PIP.html> last accessed 31 March 2016.

29 ibid.

30 United Nations, *The World's Women 2010 Trends and Statistics* (2010).

31 Disability Rights Promotion International, 'Monitoring the Human Rights of People with Disabilities in Canada Toronto Monitoring Site Fact-Sheet on Social Participation' (2010) <www.disabilityalliancebc.org/docs/100210_torontofactsheet10.pdf> last accessed 31 March 2016.

legitimising ideologies. They accept their status and their subordination and will not recognise oppression.

For the CRPD to play such a galvanising role it has to explicitly address its beneficiaries. It could well be argued that '[t]o raise awareness throughout society…,' as stated in Article 8, includes everyone and, therefore, persons with disabilities are indeed included in the wording. However, grammar alone draws a seemingly slight, but definite line as the sentence continues with: '(…) regarding persons with disabilities,' suggesting that the CRPD's beneficiaries are not the addressees of its Article 8. This is further supported by examining the measures suggested in Article 8(2) of the CRPD. All the measures listed in paragraph 2 of Article 8 are targeted at the general public and encourage the 'acceptance' of persons with disabilities as valuable members of society. By implication, they therefore do not provide any explicit reference or measures towards awareness-raising for people with disabilities.

Even if one were to consider the differences between awareness-raising and consciousness-raising as pure semantics, one would have to acknowledge that the general public and the disabled community are two target groups with very different backgrounds and needs, who therefore have to be addressed appropriately.

5. Target Groups

The main target group of the CRPD are persons with disabilities whose rights are being secured through such a Convention. People with disabilities have the personal experience of living with impairment and disability; they have first-hand experience of oppression, which differentiates them from the able-bodied members of society. Abstract commitment to human rights and equal opportunity remains vague because it is missing the personal experience and might therefore lead only to short-lived action. In contrast, support based on personal experience is more likely to lead to empowerment, continued action and fundamental changes. Shakespeare, drawing on arguments put forward by Klein,[32] emphasises that there is a clear distinction between the 'feminist sympathy of men' on the one hand and the 'feminist consciousness of women' on the other.[33]

We do not wish to deny that, in the context of Article 8 of the CRPD and in accordance with the social model of disability, the general public is an important target group as well, because they are disabling persons with disabilities by putting up barriers, or not removing barriers, and by not eliminating prejudices and stereotypes. However, Article 8, by addressing the general public and speaking about persons with disabilities only by using the term 'regarding,' excludes the very people whom the Convention is supposed to empower. Unless the alleged 'objects' of the Article – for this is the way people with disabilities are depicted – are turned into subjects and become agents of their own situation, the prejudices and stereotypes that Article 8 is trying to erase, will prevail.

[32] E Klein, *Gender Politics* (Harvard University Press 1984).

[33] T Shakespeare, 'Disabled people's self-organisation: a new social movement?' (1993) 8 Disability, Handicap and Society 249.

6. Heterogeneity of the Main Target

An important issue in the present context is that neither the disability nor the feminist community are homogeneous groups.[34] Just as the feminist movement, for instance, had to acknowledge that there are black women, white women, women with disabilities, rich women, poor women etc or some combination of the different dimensions, it must be acknowledged that people with disabilities are not a homogeneous group either, which of course complicates addressing their needs and makes raising consciousness difficult. Even though people with disabilities all encounter exclusion, discrimination and oppression,[35] there are different impairment groups that may not share the same agenda, nor are they subjected to the same discrimination and oppression. The experience of discrimination may vary greatly and so could the social response to different impairments.[36] One example is the need of wheelchair users for access. The introduction of curb-cuts has made wheelchair use considerably easier. At the same time, curbs-cuts are a useful tool for blind people to orientate themselves and find their way around. We can see from this example that the needs of people with disabilities are diverse, which makes collective action and consciousness-raising within this group all the more difficult. This, as Lang reiterates, impacts on the CRPD as well.[37] To be effective and to encompass all impairments with all levels of severity at the same time, the national bodies mandated with monitoring the CRPD need to consult with the broadest range of impairments possible to avoid continued discrimination of disabled persons.

7. Legal Tools and Instruments referencing Disability Rights Prior to the Convention

Previous legal tools implicitly mentioned consciousness-raising. This raises the question as to why Article 8 of the CRPD no longer does so. Since earlier disability-specific human rights tools formed the historical background of the CRPD, we shall first look more closely at each of the major human rights documents in chronological order. We shall then turn to the deliberations and negotiations of the Ad Hoc Committee and the Working Group for the CRPD.[38]

The World Programme of Action Concerning Disabled Persons (WPA 1982)[39] proclaimed by the United Nations was one of the major outcomes of the International

---

34 J Morris, 'Impairment and disability: Constructing an ethics of care that promotes human rights' (2001) 16 Hypatia 1.

35 C Barnes, *Disabled People in Britain and Discrimination* (Hurst & Co 1991); M Oliver (n 5).

36 T Shakespeare (n 6); J E Bickenbach, S Chatterji, E Badley and B Ustun, 'Models of disablement, universalism and the international classification of impairments, disabilities and handicaps' (1999) 48 Social Science and Medicine 1173.

37 R Lang (n 14).

38 In order to track the discussions that led up to the drafting process of art 8 of the CRPD and to get an understanding of the deliberation process of the Ad Hoc Committee, we took into account all the official documents filed under the homepage of the United Nations. United Nations Enable, 'United Nations Negotiation Archives' (2010) <www.un.org/disabilities/default.asp?id=1423> last accessed 31 March 2016; United Nations Enable, 'Background Documents' (2014) <www.un.org/esa/socdev/enable/rights/ahcstata8bkgrnd.htm> last accessed 31 March 2016.

39 United Nations General Assembly 'World Programme of Action Concerning Disabled Persons', A/RES/37/52, 3 December 1982.

Year for Disabled Persons (1981).[40] The WPA as a global strategy, but not a legally binding instrument, declared as its primary goal the full participation of persons with disabilities on the basis of equality in all aspects of social and economic life as well as national development. It also declared the need to approach disability issues from a human rights perspective instead of a social welfare point of view. Under the heading 'Information and public education'[41] Member States are recommended to establish a comprehensive public information programme about the rights, contributions and unmet needs of disabled persons that would reach all concerned, 'including the general public.' Furthermore, it is stated that public authorities are responsible for adapting their information so that it reaches everybody, 'including disabled persons.'[42] Measures in the WPA are therefore clearly directed at two different target groups. Thus, the WPA does indeed talk about consciousness-raising without explicitly using this expression.

The WPA was followed by the Standard Rules on the Equalization of Opportunities for Persons with Disabilities, which came into effect in 1993.[43] The Standard Rules consist of twenty-two rules summarising the WPA. Although not a legally binding instrument either, the Standard Rules create a strong moral and political duty on States to take action to attain equalisation of opportunities for persons with disabilities and also serve as an instrument for policy-making.[44] The term 'equalisation of opportunities' means the process through which the various systems of society, such as services, activities, information and documentation, are made available to everyone, but in particular to persons with disabilities.[45]

The Standard Rules[46] use the terminology of awareness-raising. Under preconditions for equal participation, the UN Standard Rules state the following: 'States should initiate and promote programmes aimed at raising the level of awareness of persons with disabilities concerning their rights and potential. Increased self-reliance and empowerment will assist persons with disabilities to take advantage of the opportunities available to them.'[47] Even though the term consciousness-raising is not referenced explicitly, persons with disabilities are also mentioned as a group that needs to be addressed. Furthermore, programmes aimed at raising the level of awareness of persons with disabilities, ie consciousness-raising programmes according to our definition, are mentioned in a separate paragraph, thus emphasising the importance of specifically addressing people with disabilities.

---

40 United Nations, International Year of Disabled Persons, A/RES/36/77, 8 December 1981.

41 United Nations Enable, 'World Programme of Action Concerning Disabled Persons – Part 2' (2014) <www.un.org/disabilities/default.asp?id=24> last accessed 31 March 2016.

42 United Nations Enable, 'World Programme of Action Concerning Disabled Persons' (2014) <www.un.org/disabilities/default.asp?id=23> last accessed 31 March 2016.

43 United Nations General Assembly Standard Rules on the Equalization of Opportunities for Persons with Disabilities, A/Res/48/93, 20 December 1993.

44 United Nations Enable, 'The Standard Rules on the Equalization of Opportunities for Persons with Disabilities' (2007) <www.un.org/esa/socdev/enable/dissre00.htm> last accessed 31 March 2016.

45 United Nations Enable, 'The Standard Rules on the Equalization of Opportunities for Persons with Disabilities' <www.un.org/disabilities/default.asp?id=75> last accessed 31 March 2016.

46 United Nations Enable, 'The Standard Rules on the Equalization of Opportunities for Persons with Disabilities' (2007) <www.un.org/esa/socdev/enable/dissre00.htm> last accessed 31 March 2016. United Nations Enable (n 44).

47 United Nations Enable, 'Preconditions for Equal Participation' (2006)<www.un.org/esa/socdev/enable/dissre03.htm#1> last accessed 31 March 2016.

8. CRPD Deliberations and Negotiations

The CRPD was negotiated during eight sessions held by the Ad Hoc Committee of the UN General Assembly from 2002 to 2006, making it the fastest-negotiated human rights treaty in UN history.[48] The wording of Article 8 of the CRPD was the result of the Ad Hoc Committee and the Working Group surveying and discussing the language of the first draft of the CRPD, which had been delivered by the Working Group.[49] The Working Group was assigned to take into account all the earlier disability-specific instruments and all previous contributions submitted to the Ad Hoc Committee.

As already highlighted, the element of consciousness-raising is not found in the wording of Article 8 nor the Ad Hoc Committee's deliberations. Since the element of consciousness-raising is indeed implicitly mentioned in both pre-existing disability specific instruments, but the deliberations of the Ad Hoc Committee unfortunately do not give many clues as to why this aspect is missing, we can only speculate why the wording of Article 8 does not include consciousness-raising. The main focus of the Ad Hoc Committee during the deliberations seems to have been to come up with positive and appropriate wording.[50] Much of the discussion focused on the appropriate phrasing of the Article so as not to be offensive to people with disabilities. This raises the question whether Article 8 could have fallen victim to 'political correctness', discussing language issues instead of content.

Another explanation could be that the Ad Hoc Committee worked under the assumption that the affected group is already conscious and therefore consciousness-raising is not needed. This could be due to the fact that the members of the Ad Hoc Committee and the Working Group were not only country representatives but also members of major disability groups who, of course, are conscious of the issues, having tackled exactly these for many years prior to the establishment of a legal tool. But, as we have previously seen with regard to the feminist movement, not all women are conscious of their oppressed state just because they happen to be women, and neither are all people with disabilities conscious of their situation regarding disadvantages and oppression just because they have a disability. It

---

48 T Degener, 'Disabled Women: How they will benefit from the Convention on the Rights of Persons with Disabilities' (presentation made on the occasion of the Special Event at Human Rights Council 2008) <www.un.org/disabilities/default.asp?navid=14&pid=150> last accessed 31 March 2016.

49 All official documents relevant to the deliberation and negotiation process of the CRPD can be accessed under the Negotiation Archives at UN enable <www.un.org/disabilities/default.asp?id=1423> last accessed 31 March 2016.

50 See for example the contribution from Thailand in the Afternoon Session of the Working Group on 14 January 2004, in which Thailand draws attention to the reference to promoting an image of persons with disabilities as 'full and capable members of society.' Its delegate suggested substituting 'productive' in place of 'full.' In addition, he added that the word 'capable' should probably come first so that it reads 'capable and productive members of society.' Thailand also pointed to the language 'to foster an attitude of respect for the rights of PWD' and proposed that the word 'positive' be inserted before 'attitude.' Furthermore, there was a contribution from the Landmine Survivors Network. They made the point that in some instances, 'positive' portrayals of people with disabilities may not be accurate, and may inadvertently contribute to societal stereotypes. Consequently, they suggested an alternative title like 'Stereotyping of Groups' or 'Awareness-Raising Measures.' www.un.org/esa/socdev/enable/rights/wgsuma5.htm last accessed 31 March 2016.

also again raises the question of how the addressees of the CRPD, ie people with disabilities, will avail themselves of the legal tool now at their disposal if they do not know of its existence.

A third possibility could be that the social model of disability influenced the drafters. If the drafters followed the thought process that disability is created by society one could assume that consciousness-raising is not needed, as disability will disappear if society's attitudes and barriers are eliminated. But people with disabilities cannot be left out. The CRPD is a legal instrument to be used by people with disabilities, therefore, requiring them to know of its existence as a legally binding tool that can be used in a court setting.

9. Examination of States Parties Reports to Date

We now take a look at the reports by States Parties that have been submitted to the Committee on the Rights of Persons with Disabilities under Article 35 to check if there is any reference to consciousness-raising of people with disabilities under Article 8. According to Article 35 of the CRPD, States Parties have to submit periodically a comprehensive report on measures taken to give effect to its obligations under the CRPD. The role of the Committee on the Rights of Persons with Disabilities is to consider the reports submitted by States Parties (see Article 36 of the CRPD) and make suggestions and general recommendations on these reports. The first report submitted to the Committee was from Tunisia on 1 July 2010. It only mentions the measure of awareness-raising to satisfy Article 8, and it does not mention people with disabilities mentioned as a target group.[51] This is an early example of how States Parties interpreted Article 8 of the CRPD and clearly adhere to the wording and the measures suggested therein without interpreting it further.

To date twenty-seven initial reports have been submitted.[52] These reports mostly show that the main activities and measures taken under Article 8 are targeting the general public. However, a survey of the reports submitted[53] also found a number of activities related to people with disabilities. For example, countries like Austria, the UK and the Cook Islands that run peer counselling (Austria) and training programmes that specifically target people with disabilities. Croatia, as another example, has implemented a programme to prevent domestic violence against women, and specifically domestic violence against women with disabilities. They also run other programmes under the slogan 'Nothing About Us Without Us.' Germany has published a guide for people with a disability and various countries publish the CRPD in Braille and plain language for people with cognitive disabilities.

Also important to note is the fact that the Committee on the Rights of Persons with Disabilities did not mention explicitly the need to target people with disabilities in its first concluding observations about the Tunisia report, but stated it would do

---

51 Office of the High Commissioner for Human Rights, 'Committee on the Rights of Persons with Disabilities – Sessions for CRPD' (2014) <http://tbinternet.ohchr.org/_layouts/treatybodyexternal/SessionDetails1.aspx?SessionID=362&Lang=en> last accessed 31 March 2016.

52 Office of the High Commissioner for Human Rights, 'Committee on the Rights of Persons with Disabilities – Deadlines for the submission of documentation' (2014) <http://tbinternet.ohchr.org/_layouts/TreatyBodyExternal/MasterCalendar.aspx> last accessed 31 March 2016.

53 For the purposes of this chapter, we reviewed 16 of the 27 State Reports (April 2012).

so in the two following concluding observations about Spain and China.[54] This, it could be argued, further supports our thesis that the Committee also realises that consciousness-raising should be an integral part of Article 8 of the CRPD.

10. Conclusion

In this chapter, we have aimed to clarify the crucial difference between consciousness-raising and awareness-raising as it pertains to Article 8 of the CRPD. We have done so by drawing on the striking parallels existing between the feminist and the disability movements and by showing that consciousness-raising forms an important aspect of awareness-raising. The challenges stemming from the fact that in our view Article 8 of the CRPD needs to address two fundamentally different target groups have been explained, and the complicating issue that people with disabilities are not a homogeneous group has been highlighted as well. Furthermore, we have argued that the CRPD has great potential as a legal tool, but that without the knowledge that such an instrument exists, the CRPD cannot be effectively implemented to promote human rights.

Our main conclusion, then, is that for a consistent and comprehensive implementation of the CRPD and in order to realise its great potential as a legal tool securing human rights for persons with disabilities, Article 8 needs to be interpreted in such a way that it includes awareness-raising and consciousness-raising. Without becoming critically conscious of their own situation, real improvements will be elusive for people with disabilities.

But maybe the situation is not quite this bleak. In the Communication on the EU's Disability Strategy by the European Commission[55] it is stated that 'the Commission will work to ensure that people with disabilities are aware of their rights, paying special attention to accessibility of materials and information channels.'[56] Furthermore, the concluding observations of the Committee on the Rights of Persons with Disabilities are now pointing out the importance of targeting people with disabilities. We are also seeing increasing numbers of countries include consciousness-raising in their agendas. As long as awareness-raising and consciousness-raising are both actively included in States Parties' activities, there is a good chance that the CRPD will indeed 'empower the world's largest minority to claim their rights'[57] and thus introduce social change.[58]

---

54 Office of the High Commissioner for Human Rights, 'Committee on the Rights of Persons with Disabilities – Session 5, 6 & 8 for CRPD' (2014) <http://tbinternet.ohchr.org/_layouts/TreatyBodyExternal/SessionsList.aspx?Treaty=CRPD> last accessed 31 March 2016.

55 European Commission, 'Communication From the Commission to the European Parliament, The Council, The European Economic and Social Committee Of The Regions European Disability Strategy 2010-2020: A renewed Commitment to a Barrier-Free Europe' (European Disability Strategy), COM(2010) 636 final <http://eur-lex.europa.eu/legal-content/EN/ALL/;ELX_SESSIONID=LHmNT1fPQYhJr8qp93F154KhPQtRCnWmQV1sQvBwfmxG6Cx8BTDt!2061451643?uri=CELEX:52010DC0636> last accessed 31 March 2016.

56 ibid at 2.2.

57 R Kayess and P French (n 15).

58 V Illagan and C Zubiaga, 'UN Convention on the Rights of Persons with Disabilities, shared by Carmen Zubiaga, speech of Ms Illagan on the brief overview of CRPD delivered during the Philippine Celebration of entry into force May 12, 2008' (2008) http://pwag.org/issues-and-news-items-about-disability/un-convention-on-the-rights-of-persons-with-disabilities-overview-shared-by-ms-carmen-zubiaga/ last accessed 31 March 2016.

CHAPTER 4

DISABILITY, GENDER AND DEVELOPMENT

Mary Keogh

1. INTRODUCTION

This chapter explores the potential of using an intersectional approach for analysing the discrimination and exclusion experienced by women with disabilities in a development context. Intersectionality is a relatively new research paradigm and while some suggest that it has yet to gain traction at an operational level,[1] its potential to broaden our analysis and understanding of the causes of exclusion and discrimination faced by women with disabilities is worth considering. The main focus of the discussion in this chapter centres around the role intersectionality can play in facilitating policy-makers to move beyond a single-lens approach to one which applies a more nuanced contextual understanding of how people with impairments interact with their environment in low-income countries, and in particular the intersection of disability and gender.

The first section introduces the specific issues affecting women with disabilities. It considers the relationship between disability and gender in development and illustrates how responses through a single-lens/category approach, ie disability or gender, may not capture the full experience of discrimination faced by women with disabilities and, indeed, may inadvertently render the specific needs of women with disabilities invisible to policy solutions which tackle gender and disability discrimination. The second section gives a brief overview of the Convention (CRPD) and discusses its progress from previous international laws and policies in recognising the multiple identities of persons with disability. It then introduces intersectionality and considers its contribution to a more nuanced understanding of the particular issues specific to women with disabilities that are not captured by viewing women with disabilities through the unitary categories of either disability or gender. The final section provides a summary by highlighting how intersectionality can enhance the emphasis on multiple discrimination faced by women with disabilities, which is recognised by the CRPD, and how applying this to Article 32 can move women with disabilities beyond being viewed through a single lens.

2. WOMEN WITH DISABILITIES IN DEVELOPMENT

The World Report on Disability estimates that the population of people with disabilities worldwide is one billion, the majority of whom who live in developing

---

1 See O Hankivsky and R Cormier, 'Intersectionality and Public Policy: Some lessons from existing model' (2010) 64 (1) Political Research Quarterly 217.

countries.[2] The United Nations and other agencies have highlighted that persons with disabilities, especially women with disabilities, have been largely absent from development processes.[3] All of these factors, it could be said, lead to the logical conclusion that people with disabilities, including women with disabilities, are among the most vulnerable to poverty, have less access to basic services and in many cases have less chance of survival. Linked to this vulnerability to poverty is the fact that people with disabilities face discrimination in a number of areas. Women with disabilities in particular are widely recognised as being subject to discrimination on a number of grounds in that they not only face discrimination and exclusion from the perspective of being disabled, but also from being women, therefore posing additional challenges to developing an effective policy that responds adequately to the discrimination and exclusion that they face.

3. Disability and Gender

From the outset it is important to recognise that disability and gender in the developing world are inextricably linked. Studies show that gender can be considered a risk for acquiring a disability. The World Health Organisation estimates that more than 30 women every minute are seriously injured or disabled during labour, thus rendering vast numbers of women in the developing world physically and socially disabled. For every woman who dies from complications of pregnancy, between thirty and 100 more live with painful and debilitating consequences.[4] Equally, women with disabilities are excluded from the majority of development interventions due to the fact that they are disabled and also female, rendering them vulnerable to poverty. As the UN reports, 'the combination of male preference in many cultures and the universal devaluation of disability can be deadly for disabled females.'[5] Furthermore, research from the UN Special Rapporteur on the right of everyone to the enjoyment of physical and mental health concurs with this and highlights the double disadvantage facing women with disabilities, finding that they are more likely to suffer from discrimination than able-bodied women and men due to the stigma attached to both gender and disability.[6] The list of issues facing women with disabilities in the poorest of the poor countries is lengthy. The limited statistics that are available seem to give credence to this. For example, the UNDP reports the literacy rate for women with disabilities may be as low as one percent; USAID reports that women with disabilities are at increased risk of being sicker, poorer and more socially isolated that men with disabilities or able-bodied women; in terms of access to rehabilitation services, UNICEF reports that women and children with

2 See Economic and Social Council, 'Mainstreaming Disability in the Development Agenda report' E/CN.5/2008/6, which reports that '(a)n estimated 80 per cent of these persons live in developing countries, many in conditions of poverty.'

3 See Disability Rights, Gender and Development, 'An Inclusive Approach to Disability Rights, Gender and Development' (2008) Module 3, 17.

4 See World Health Organisation, 'Female Genital Mutilation' (2012) www.who.int/mediacentre/factsheets/fs241/en/ last accessed 31 March 2016.

5 See United Nations Enable, 'Rights of Special Groups with Disabilities, International Norms and Standards relating to disability' (2003) www.un.org/esa/socdev/enable/comp001.htm last accessed 31 March 2016.

6 See P Hunt, 'Report of the Special Rapporteur on the right of everyone to the enjoyment of the highest attainable standard of physical and mental health', submitted in accordance with Commission Resolution 2002/31, E/CN.4/2003/58, para 67.

disabilities receive twenty percent less rehabilitation services, and finally, studies on women with disabilities in rural areas of many countries have found that more than eighty percent of women with disabilities have no independent means of livelihood and are totally dependent on others for their very existence.[7] The exclusion of women with disabilities from access to services is a challenge facing policy-makers to figure out how best to respond to ensure inclusive development. The European Disability Forum (EDF) contends that the issues facing women with disabilities – and in particular their experience of discrimination and resulting exclusion – cannot simply by summarised by adding together their needs as disabled persons and women; rather a different and special status arises that must be understood and recognised, one which requires a specific innovative and long-term approach. The EDF, it could be argued, hints at a much more holistic approach for understanding the needs of women with disabilities.

4. Invisible Women

While there is limited data on women with disabilities, what we do know to date is that women with disabilities, along with facing discrimination on a number of grounds, also face the problem of a double invisibility as women and as disabled people. This double invisibility, it could be argued, leads to inadequate policy responses from both a disability and a gender perspective where women with disabilities are further marginalised.

Groce claims that policies within a development context focus on either 'disability' or on 'women' rather than on the common problems shared by both, and that because of this women with disabilities have been disenfranchised.[8] The disenfranchisement Groce speaks of could be attributable to a number of factors, but for the purposes of this chapter the suggestion is that one of the factors is the dominance of an identity-based lens or category approach to policy-making eg viewing the issues faced by women with disabilities through a unitary lens (either disability or gender, neither of which adequately respond to the myriad of issues faced by women with disabilities in developing countries). The following examples illustrate how an emphasis from the viewpoint of disability and gender has not adequately considered the issues of women with disabilities.

Taking disability first, if the dominant lens is from a disability perspective, some academics suggest that the diversity which exists within disability can be overlooked. Two particular examples highlight this. First, the dominance of the social model in disability discourse, some academics felt, has resulted in an over-emphasis on social barriers and does not leave much room for discussing the experience of persons impairment.[9] In addition to this, other academics, such as Priestly, have suggested

---

7 For facts about people with disabilities see USAID, 'Fact Sheet on Women with Disabilities' www.usaid.gov/our_work/cross-cutting_programs/wid/disability/wwd_statistics.html last accessed 31 March 2016; United Nations Special Rapporteur on Disability, 'International Women's Day' (2005) www.un.org/esa/socdev/enable/womenday05.htm last accessed 31 March 2016.

8 N Groce, 'Women with Disabilities in the Developing World, Arenas for Policy Revision and Programmatic Change' (1997) 8 Journal of Disability Policy 177.

9 See T Shakespeare, *Disability Rights and Wrongs* (Routledge 2006).

that the social model and its focus on enhanced civil rights and barrier-removal tends to stress commonality at the expense of difference.[10] So, in terms of theory and conceptual understanding in disability, one could plausibly argue that finding a space for recognition of difference or in the case of women with disabilities, a gendered approach to disability, is limited. From a practical perspective, the second example illustrates this. Groce and Driedger in their research illustrate this difficulty with regard to women with disabilities accessing rehabilitative services in post-conflict countries. They state that even with disability-specific services, the needs of disabled women were not considered and that there was lack of gender-awareness when the focus is solely on disability, as it would be from a rehabilitative purpose. They cite examples of health and rehabilitation services that were developed post-conflict catering more for male veterans than to the needs of disabled women; the rehabilitation centres were located in urban locations, meaning that disabled women needed to travel long distances to reach them, and leave behind their family and support networks.[11]

Similarly, from a gender lens, women with disabilities have been traditionally marginalised from the mainstream women's movement. Some disability academics have suggested that what inclusion there was mostly took place under the guise of research carried out by feminists, which led to a failure to take on board the subjective reality of disabled women, objectifying women with disabilities instead, so that any research is alienated from experience.[12] Additionally, other academics suggest that feminists have been shown to incorporate discriminatory attitudes towards disabled women in an attempt to contest the normative viewpoint of dependency that both people with disabilities and women face.[13] Again, if we look from a practical level, we can see this marginalisation of women with disabilities from mainstream women's issues evidenced through a number of initiatives, for example, the Millennium Development Goals (MDGs). The MDGs represent a universally accepted approach to poverty reduction, which include eight goals. The MDG's have been widely criticised for not having a disability focus;[14] however, they do have a focus on gender (MDG 3) and issues that are specific to children (MDG 4) and women (MDG 5).[15] Desk research to find where disability has been cited in reports

---

10 See M Priestly, 'Constructions and Creations; Idealism, materialism and disability theory' (1998) 13 Disability and Society 1.

11 Research by D Driedger and N Groce (1991) in 'Women with Disabilities in the Developing World, Arenas for Policy Revision and programmatic change' (1997) 8 Journal of Disability Policy 177.

12 For further reading on feminism and disability see J Morris, 'Pride and Prejudice: Transforming attitudes to disability' (1991) 10 The Women's Press; J Morris, 'Feminism and Disability' (1993) 43 Feminist Review.

13 See R Galvin, 'Identity Politics: The Paradox of Disability Culture, the need to combine versus the imperative to let go' (2003) 8 Disability and Society (5) 675.

14 See United Nations General Assembly – Realizing the Millennium Development Goals for Persons with Disabilities through the implementation of the World Programme of Action concerning Disabled Persons and the Convention on the Rights of Persons with Disabilities A/64/180; United Nations General Assembly –Keeping the promise: realising the Millennium Development Goals for persons with disabilities towards 2015 and beyond A/65/173; United Nations Enable, 'Disability and the Millennium Development Goals; a review of the MDG Process and Strategies for Inclusion of Disability in Millennium Development Goals Efforts' (2011) www.un.org/disabilities/default.asp?id=1470 last accessed 31 March 2016.

15 See United Nations Millennium Development Goals, 'MDG 3 – Promote Gender Equality and Empower Women; MDG 4 – Reduce Child Mortality' and MDG 5 – Maternal Health' (2012) www.un.org/millenniumgoals/aids.shtml last accessed 31 March 2016.

detailing MDG implementation found that under MDG 3 references to disability were made for the most part on the impact of disability on gender e.g. women acquiring an impairment through poor maternity services, poverty etc. For example, one country report highlighted the issue of women as caregivers of persons with disabilities.[16] Another report stressed the need to understand how gender equality was affected by different factors, such as disability. The only initiative mentioned specific to women with disabilities cited under the report was a one-time financial assistance for women with disabilities. Finally, under MDG 4 and MDG 5, the report also highlighted how the lack of obstetric, prenatal and postnatal care was a cause of disability. So it could be suggested that the focus of these reports primarily is through a gender lens and the consideration of disability is concerned primarily with the impact of disability on gender, for example, the burden of caring for disabled people falling to women or women acquiring a disability themselves through inadequate health care and situations of poverty. While there is no disputing that developing appropriate neo- and postnatal care is a vital component to any health care programming in developing countries for women to mitigate against preventable disabilities, what is demonstrably missing from these reports is the consideration of what would be an appropriate response to women with disabilities who are also exposed to the same risks in maternal health.

These examples were intended to illustrate how using a single-lens approach can create gaps for women with disabilities and can lead to the potential for policy responses to be blinkered or siloed[17] towards the predominant category, eg gender or disability, therefore rendering the specific needs of women with disabilities invisible. In practice, however, assigning people to categories is how law and policy has traditionally worked. For example, most national anti-discrimination laws require that membership of a group or category be proven in order to seek protection. Additionally, while international laws such as the Universal Declaration of Human Rights, the International Covenant on Civil and Political Rights and the International Covenant on Economic, Social and Cultural Rights all promote universal rights, there are also a number of thematic conventions which serve to clarify rights from the prospective of particular groups eg the Convention on the Elimination of Discrimination against women, the Convention on the Rights of the Child and most recently, the Convention on the Rights of Persons with Disabilities.[18] Along with law, the need for categorisation is also found at policy-making level where policies are generally designed to respond to a particular set of needs faced by a group of individuals. While assigning categories or giving special emphasis from a policy perspective has its merits in terms of creating visibility of a particular group's needs or issues, there can be a tendency for the group to be viewed as homogenous without any recognition of specific needs and also the potential for further stigmatisation, all of which impact of women with disabilities.[19]

---

16 See United Nations General Assembly – Realizing the Millennium Development Goals for Persons with Disabilities through the implementation of the World Programme of Action concerning Disabled Persons and the Convention on the Rights of Persons with DisabilitiesA/64/180.

17 See United National General Assembly – Report of the Special Rapporteur on violence against women, its causes and consequences (2011) A/HRC/17/26.

18 For example, under the Americans with Disabilities Act (1990) and the Irish Equal Status Act (2000), to claim protection, you must be able to prove membership of the disability community.

19 See M Minnow, *Making all the Difference: Inclusion Exclusion and American Law* (Cornell

5. The Convention and its Recognition of Difference

The CRPD has made progress on moving away from a homogenous view of disability to one where multiple identities are recognised. Degener describes it as 'the only Convention [...] which explicitly refers to multiple discrimination in the binding text.'[20] From the perspective of human rights, the CRPD provides us with a normative framework calling for States Parties 'prohibit all discrimination on the basis of disability and guarantee to persons with disabilities equal and effective legal protection against discrimination on all grounds.'[21] The Convention does not define disability, but it does recognise more so than previous law and policy the different identities that a person with a disability may have and the resulting propensity for discrimination. For example, previous measures, such as the World Programme of Action on Disability, made minimal references to diversity within disability, recognising women and children with disability within the category of special groups rather than integrated throughout its actions.[22] The UN Standard Rules reference women and children with disabilities at different junctures; however, the CRPD explicitly references them throughout the text and also in specific articles explained below, which in turn raise visibility for their specific issues. For example, its preamble recognises the diversity of people with disabilities (see preamble (i)), and (p)–(s) recognise that people with disabilities experience multiple or aggravated forms of discrimination, and that women and children with disabilities face distinct forms of discrimination, in particular violence and abuse. The Convention text has specific articles recognising the needs of specific groups such as women (Article 6) and children (Article 7). In addition to the specific articles, the Convention was authored from a gender-sensitive viewpoint; Articles 6 and 7 are cross-cutting, and are therefore applicable to all of the Conventions articles, including Article 32 on inclusive development. At first glance the Convention could be said to have made much progress on recognising diversity within the disability community, and in particular the specific needs of women with disabilities which heretofore have been relatively invisible. In practical terms, though, as the Convention and its provisions, in particular Article 32, are implemented, it will be interesting to track the Committee's jurisprudence over the coming years on how discrimination based on multiple identities is captured in the reporting process and dealt with within the commentary. The Convention has been described as having an intersectional approach;[23] however, what is not clear is whether this is from a multiple approach

University 1990); M Fineman, *The Vulnerability Theory;* A Satz, 'Disability, vulnerability, and the limits of anti-discrimination' (2008) 83 Washington Law Review, 153.

20 The CRPD, being the youngest of the treaties, has had the benefit of building on recent years' commentary coming from UN treaty bodies on multiple discrimination, for example the Committee on the Elimination of Discrimination Against women, 'General Comment 18' (1991). <www.un.org/womenwatch/daw/cedaw/recommendations/index.html> last accessed 31 March 2016; D Shiek and A Lawson (eds), *European Union Non-Discrimination Law and Intersectionality – Investigating the Triangle of Racial, Gender and Disability Discrimination* (Ashgate 2011).

21 Article 5(2) CRPD.

22 For example, see World Programme of Action on Disability, which categorises women and children with disabilities within a special group status; United Nations Enable, 'World Programme of Action concerning Disabled Persons' (2012) www.un.org/disabilities/default.asp?id=23#current last accessed 31 March 2016.

23 De Silva is currently progressing work in this area and suggests that the Convention has the potential to enable the different human rights treaties affecting women and children with disabilities 'to be implemented together within an interlocking web of the human rights

with disability remaining the main lens and identities, such as being a woman or a child being added on, or whether this is from an intersectional perspective.[24] Degener, it could be argued, supports this view by suggesting that the measures the Convention does take to combat multiple discrimination are limited only to gender. It could be argued that this limits the potential of the Convention to have an intersectional approach that spans the life cycle of persons with disabilities.[25]

6. Intersectionality: Moving Beyond the Single Lens

The earlier sections of this chapter discussed the difficulties faced by women with disabilities in a development context. Some of them are attributable to discrimination based on gender, some to disability, while others are not so clear-cut or easy to define. Along with the multiple forms of discrimination faced by women with disabilities, I also outlined the invisibility faced by women with disabilities within the categories of both gender and disability when a unitary-lens approach is taken to analyse and develop appropriate responses to their needs. Creating challenges for developing policy responses that avoid these 'blind spots,' while also recognising the experience of women with disabilities when faced with discrimination on an intersectional basis could have the potential to respond in a more holistic way. This final section will discuss the potential that intersectionality has to achieve this. It will also highlight where, as a theory, it resonates with different aspects of disability theory.

As a concept, intersectionality is relatively new. Crenshaw, one of its original theorists, developed the thinking in response to black women's experience in employment. She claimed that the single-axis framework that is dominant in anti-discrimination erases black women in the conceptualisation, identification and mediation of race and sex discrimination. From the outset, it is important in terms of understanding intersectionality to briefly describe where it fits with regard to other types of discrimination, such as multiple and compound discrimination. Makkonen differentiates between three categories of discrimination. The first is multiple discrimination, which he describes as a situation where a person can experience discrimination on one ground in one situation and on another ground in another situation. The next is compound discrimination, which occurs on the basis of being two of more grounds at the same time and where one ground compounds or adds to discrimination on another ground eg gender and disability. Lastly, he describes intersectional discrimination occurring where several grounds operate and interact with each other at the same time in such a way that they are inseparable. Therefore, singling out grounds as in the other two models is not applied.[26]

---

framework,' and that this 'will provide the necessary safeguards against multiple and cross cutting forms of discrimination against women and children with disabilities.' See also Rangita de Silva de Alwis, 'Mining the Intersections: Advancing the Rights of Women and Children with Disabilities within an interrelated web of Human Rights' (2009) 18 Pacific Rim Law and Policy Journal Association 1.

24 For further discussion on the difference between additive or multiple identity and intersectionality see A Hancock, 'When multiplication doesn't equal quick addition: Examining Intersectionality as a Research Paradigm (2007) 5 Perspectives on Politics (1) 63.

25 See T Degener, 'Intersections between Disability, Race, and Gender in Discrimination Law' in D Shiek and A Lawson (eds), *European Union Non-Discrimination Law and Intersectionality – Investigating the Triangle of Racial, Gender and Disability Discrimination* (Ashgate 2011).

26 See T Makkonen, 'Multiple, Compound and Intersectional Discrimination: Bringing the

Intersectionality's potential to move beyond a one-axis understanding of discrimination is not only exclusive to law. Within the social science field, it has also become prominent in a number of different ways: first, in how it considers the interaction of such categories as organising structures of society (eg disability and gender), recognising that these key components influence political access, equality and potential for any form of justice[27] as a way to analyse the intertwining of social and cultural categories;[28]secondly, as a mechanism for moving beyond a single-category perspective to a more complex understanding of difference and power which understands that one voice does not represent all, and that the voices of those who are marginalised must be recognised;[29] and finally, as recognising that the context in which we situate ourselves is vital, in particular taking into account the historical, social and political context and the experience of the individual.[30] Some of these points, it could be argued, have resonance with existing disability theory, particularly the recognition that the social model has gained in situating the marginalisation of people with disabilities as an inadequate response by society, and the need for the voice of people with disabilities to be included in all aspects of life.

In discussing how intersectionality could be advantageous in shaping effective policy-response for women with disabilities, I would like to put forward three main areas for consideration:

(a) its potential to widen the lens of policy analysis, moving away from an identity-based or category-based approach which is traditionally used in law and policy. In moving beyond the single lens, the intersectional approach has two advantages. First, it departs from what is called additive/compounds lens and provides us with the opportunity to investigate disabled women's experience of discrimination and exclusion through a contextualised approach rather than focusing on individual characteristics or a single identity. Moser describes how having a number of identities can cause an 'unmasking of each other' and that in particular contexts this unmasking can bring forward one identity over another. If that one identity becomes the dominant one through which problem-solving occurs, this has the capacity to cause other experiences to be overlooked. This is particularly relevant in the earlier illustrated examples of disabled women's access to vital services in areas such as rehabilitation and maternal health care in developing countries. Secondly, it could be helpful

---

experiences of the most marginalized to the fore' (Institute for Human Rights, Åbo Akademi University, 2002).

27 A Hancock, 'When multiplication doesn't equal quick addition: Examining Intersectionality as a Research Paragidm' (2007) 5 Perspectives on Politics (1) 63.

28 S Knudsen, 'Intersectionality – A Theoretical Inspiration in the Analysis of Minority Cultures and Identities in Textbooks' (2006) www.caen.iufm.fr/colloque_iartem/pdf/knudsen.pdf. last accessed 31 March 2016. Knudsen describes it is where the relationship between gender, race, ethnicity and disability are examined.

29 T Grillo, 'Anti-essentialism and intersectionality: Tools to dismantle the master's house' in R Dhamoon, 'Considerations on Mainstreaming Intersectionality' (2011) 62 Political Research Quarterly 230 describes an important element of intersectionality is the move away from a uni-dimensional viewpoint such as gender or race to a more complex understanding of difference and power. This move to a more complex understanding, it could be argued, resonates with the social model of disability.

30 See Human Rights Commission, 'An Intersectional Approach to Discrimination Addressing Multiple Grounds in Human Rights Claims' (Ontario Human Rights Commission 2001).

in bridging the gap that exists from focusing solely on an individual strand of identity eg disability and gender, which in turn makes women with disabilities invisible in the development of policy and programmes to one which focuses on the historical, social and political contexts of women with disabilities. This wider focus is particularly relevant in a development context as there are a number of issues at play. For example, an intersectional approach would consider the cultural practices that are harmful to women, the stigma faced by both people with disabilities and women and the subsequent vulnerabilities as a result of these issues. In taking into consideration this wider set of factors, it creates a more holistic understanding of discrimination faced by women with disabilities and how to develop appropriate responses.

(b) The second reason for its consideration is its emergence into international law.[31] As human rights have evolved, the focus is now increasingly on a contextualised approach to discrimination which places less emphasis on an individual's characteristics and more on society's response to a person.[32] This point, it could be argued, resonates strongly with the principles of the social model of disability, which influenced the foundations of the CRPD's approach to disability. Grillo, referenced earlier, described intersectionality as shining a light into 'the positioning that constitutes everyday life and the power relations that are central to it.' Interestingly, it could be argued that the disability movement since the 1970s has held a similar viewpoint. Academics, such as Oliver, advocated for shifting the view of disability as an individual deficit to one that places responsibility on society and its inadequate responses to including persons with disabilities.

(c) The final point worth considering is where intersectionality gives a voice to the marginalised particularly in terms of policy development. Some academics have suggested that intersectionality has the potential to involve the lived experience of those facing discrimination and exclusion. As Grillo puts it 'one of the aspects of an intersectional approach is recognising that helping marginalised women speak ... does not mean speaking for them but instead acknowledging their voices by placing a microphone in front of them.'[33] Similarly, Hancock suggests that intersectionality goes beyond designing policies that create small improvements for a defined percentage of a group and looks at how policies can ensure that all members of any marginalised group are enabled to empower themselves.[34] Both of these points have particular resonance for persons with disabilities and, in particular, women with disabilities, who traditionally were omitted from decision-making. It could be argued that the emergence and subsequent adoption of the mantra 'Nothing About Us Without Us', which was the mantra of the international disability community during the Ad Hoc Committee negotiation for the

---

31 Intersectionality made its first appearance in an international legal context at the UN World Conference Against Racism, Racial Discrimination, Xenophobia and Related Intolerance held in Durban 2011.

32 See Human Rights Commission (n 29).

33 See T Grillo 'Anti-essentialism and intersectionality: Tools to dismantle the Masters House' (1995) 10 Berkeley Journal of Gender, Law and Justice 16.

34 See A Hancock (n 23).

Convention, referenced in policy documents, shares the sentiments of ensuring that marginalised groups are empowered. Additionally, the text of the Convention itself references the need for consultation and representation throughout the Convention. For example, the Convention's preamble, recognises that persons with disabilities should have the opportunity to be actively involved in decision-making processes about policies and programmes. Article 4(3) states that 'in the development of legislation and policies to implement the present Convention, and in other decision-making processes concerning issues relating to persons with disabilities, State Parties shall closely consult with, and actively involve persons with disabilities.'[35]

7. Conclusion

The CRPD has made progress with increasing awareness of the multiple forms of discrimination faced by people with disabilities and particularly women with disabilities. A number of articles throughout the Convention impact on development and people with disabilities living in low-income countries. Article 32 in particular focuses on international cooperation and development programmes, requiring States Parties to take measurable actions to ensure that their international cooperation is accessible to and inclusive of persons with disabilities. Reading Article 6 on women with disabilities coupled with the aspects of the Convention which promote a gender-mainstreaming approach, it is hoped, will improve States Parties' measures (through their bilateral donor agencies) for the inclusion of women with disabilities in development. However, whether this is through the simple addition of gender to disability issues, or comes from a true understanding of the unique circumstances faced by women with disabilities, taking into account their contextual surroundings, is something we will have to monitor closely in future Committee comments on multiple discrimination.

[35] art 4(3), United Nations Convention on the Rights of Persons with Disabilities (CRPD) (2006).

CHAPTER 5

ARE WE RIGHT OR ARE WE RIGHT?: 'RIGHT APPROACH' IN THE ADVOCACY WORK OF ORGANISATION OF PERSONS WITH DISABILITIES[1]

Jukka Kumpuvuori and Riku Virtanen

1. INTRODUCTION

The aim of this chapter is to look at the possibilities of organisations of persons with disabilities (DPOs) in promoting human rights of persons with disabilities through a human-rights based approach, which we call the 'Right Approach.'[2]

Persons with disabilities and DPOs have been excluded not only from the processes of mainstream decision-making locally, nationally, regionally and globally, but also from the specific processes concerning this specific group of people. The authors also share the view of Banks that persons with disabilities themselves cannot be excluded, when looking for reasons of exclusion of persons with disabilities and DPOs in decision-making.[3] In the context of human-rights protection, there is a trend of, and need for preventive human rights strategies and mechanisms. This is because weaknesses in the international mechanisms put in place are predominantly restorative and international by nature. It is evident that stronger protection of human rights calls for mechanisms and strategies that are preventive and closer to the right-holders, the individuals whose rights are in focus.[4] Ramcharan points out that preventive human-rights strategies are the way forward in all levels of human rights protection.[5]

After presenting a hypothetical case to illustrate the role of DPOs, this chapter

---

1 The authors would like to express their gratitude to Ambrose Murangira, Pirkko Mahlamäki and Stefan Trömel for their precious and insightful comments, which made this chapter better.

2 We see 'DPO' as an organisation that is established and run by persons with disabilities themselves but we also recognise the variation in the definition and usage of the concept in various contexts.

3 Banks argues that the disability advocacy movement reflects an ongoing silencing of people with disabilities by disempowering them, often from within. See R Banks, 'More Than Law: Advocacy for Disability Rights' in M Jones and L Basser Marks (eds), *Disability, Divers-ability and Legal Change* (Kluwer Law International 1999) 343.

4 *See* O Chinedu Okafor, *The African Human Rights System. Activist Forces and International Institutions* (Cambridge University Press 2007) 300, where Okafor concludes his book by emphasising the significance of grassroots civil society organisations in human rights work.

5 B G Ramcharan, *Preventive Human Rights Strategies* (Routledge 2010) 1.

establishes the basis for participation of DPOs in various decision-making processes. Following this, the chapter then looks at the various levels and methods of participation in which DPOs aim to promote the human rights of persons with disabilities. Finally, the chapter concludes by developing the Right Approach and illustrating this approach within the context of the case presented next.

2. Case of 'Our Life'

'Our Life' (OLDPO) is a hypothetical DPO in Kampala, Uganda. It is a cross-disability DPO with most of its governing bodies run by persons with disabilities. It works in the Kampala region and focuses on the realisation of human rights of persons with disabilities in general and educational rights in particular. A deaf student of the Makerere University in Kampala, Ms Vagabond, has faced discrimination in the form of the university denying her rights to education by refusing to provide for any sign language interpretation. Ms Vagabond turns to OLDPO as their member and asks them to help her in her fight for human rights. OLDPO takes the matter seriously and starts to plan how to proceed to make the educational human rights of Ms Vagabond a reality.

3. Basis for the Participation of DPOs

3.1. Nothing About Us Without Us

The development of the slogan 'Nothing About Us Without Us' has gone hand-in-hand with the global disability rights movement. The slogan emanates from the point of view that persons with disabilities themselves need to be involved in the processes involving them in order to avoid dependence, control and paternalism of the surrounding society.[6] The slogan sets out a mandate to include persons with disabilities in everything that concerns them. The slogan can be seen as starting from the presumption that the needs and rights of persons with disabilities can only be met if they are included in all processes of decision-making that concern them. If we think more closely about the legitimacy of the demand of including persons with disabilities in everything that concerns them, we can say that it is mostly based on pursuing change in societal circumstances in itself instead of trying to rationally explain why persons with disabilities need to be included. Even though, or because of this, the slogan contains a strong impetus to include persons with disabilities in everything and anything that concerns them. The slogan was also introduced repeatedly during the negotiations within the United Nations, which eventually led to the adoption of the CRPD.[7]

---

6 J Charlton, *Nothing About Us Without Us – Disability Oppression and Empowerment* (University of California Press 2000) 3.

7 Trömel describes the meaning of the slogan within the negotiations in S Trömel, 'A personal perspective on the drafting history of the United Nations Convention on the Rights of Persons with Disabilities', in G Quinn and L Waddington (eds), *European Yearbook of Disability Law. Volume 1* (Intersentia 2009). '"Nothing About Us Without Us" was soon to become the slogan of the IDC [International Disability Caucus], signaling to the world that the times had definitely passed when legislation and policies affecting persons with disabilities were prepared without their active involvement.'

3.2. Interest Group or Expert Group?

In debates relating to enabling persons with disabilities to participate in the processes that concern them, one usually enters into discussions on whether persons with disabilities will be partial in those processes. The consequence of claimed partiality ultimately often leads to demands to exclude persons with disabilities from those processes. The authors want to differentiate between grounds for demands of participation of DPOs, namely into arguments of interest-group presentation and expert-group presentation. By interest-group presentation we mean including some groups in the processes concerning them with the role of presenting the interests of that particular group. By expert-group presentation we mean the inclusion of experts on a particular topic in to processes concerning those particular topics.

Considering that DPOs represent interest groups, it could be claimed that these representatives are impartial. However, it would be far-fetched to claim that including DPOs in processes concerning persons with disabilities as such would lead to illegitimacy of the processes. It would also be incorrect to claim that persons with disabilities cannot be experts on disability. This kind of thinking can be identified within the process of negotiating the parts of the CRPD that concern the Committee set up to monitor the CRPD. While the International Disability Caucus[8] was of the opinion that all or at least the majority of the Committee members should be persons with disabilities themselves, some states suggested that the text should refer to 'experts and persons with disabilities' which would, according to Trömel, give the impression that persons with disabilities could not be experts. The final wording refers to 'experts with disabilities.'[9]

The authors claim that DPOs need to be considered not only as interest groups or expert groups but as both. It is evident that DPOs carry both strong legitimacy in representing a particular group of people (interest group) and they possess a strong expertise on lives of persons with disabilities (expert group). Thus, both interest group and expert group arguments make a strong point of including persons with disabilities and DPOs in every process that concerns them.

3.3. Normative Obligation to Include DPOs

As the newcomer in the field of human rights and disability, the CRPD gives a new meaning to the inclusion of DPOs. It is no exaggeration to say that the level of involvement of DPOs in the preparation process of the CRPD was historical within the United Nations system and gave impetus to the inclusion of DPOs in

---

8 Reina describes the International Disability Caucus in Maria Reina, 'How the International Disability Caucus Worked During Negotiations for a UN Human Rights Convention on Disability' (2008), <www.globalaging.org/agingwatch/events/CSD/2008/maria.htm> last accessed 31 March 2016, as follows: 'The IDC was the representative voice of persons with disabilities in the process of the Ad Hoc Committee, made up of government delegates. The IDC was composed of more than 70 world-wide, regional and national Disabled People's Organisations (and allied NGOs) who had decided to work together and coordinate their efforts.'

9 Trömel (n 6) 134. See also art 34(4), CRPD A/RES/61/106 (2006), which regulates: 'The members of the Committee shall be elected by States Parties, consideration being given to equitable geographical distribution, representation of the different forms of civilization and other principal legal systems, balanced gender representation and participation of experts with disabilities.'

the national sphere as well. This phenomenon was bound to be seen as an inherent part of the CRPD itself.

Several articles of the CRPD address the topic, starting from the General Principles in Article 3, which sets out full and effective participation and inclusion in society as one of the principles of the CRPD (Article 3(c)) and ending up in the duty to include DPOs in some of the specific areas of the CRPD, such as international cooperation (Article 32) and national implementation and monitoring (Article 33). There is some difference in the references to organisations of persons with disabilities in the Articles of the CRPD,[10] but the authors are of the opinion that they all refer to the same complex concept of 'DPO' defined above.

All in all, this means that States Parties that have committed to the CRPD can no longer exclude DPOs in processes that concerns them. One could argue that everything has to do with persons with disabilities, and therefore DPOs would need to be included in everything. The above anecdote could well serve as a starting point to illustrate the need and demand for inclusion of DPOs. The authors are of the opinion that the normative demand of inclusion of DPOs in processes concerning persons with disabilities is very broad, practical and strong. Thus it needs to be addressed in relation to corresponding efforts of various stakeholders.

4. Contemporary Strategies of DPOs to Promote Human Rights of Persons with Disabilities

4.1. Levels of Participation

In this chapter we identify various levels of participation of DPOs by looking closer at non-participation, illusionary participation and full participation. As 'non-participation,' we consider situations in which DPOs are not at all included in processes concerning persons with disabilities and their situation in society. Generally, participation of DPOs has been very minimal historically, in all parts of the world. If DPOs do not actively take part and thus are not included in decision-making processes, the needs of this particular group are easily ignored.

Participation of DPOs is 'illusionary' if it is only formal without any actual opportunity to take part in decision-making. In other words, DPOs can be involved in decision-making processes formally without effective possibilities to provide their expertise. This can occur in situations wherein the knowledge and skills of DPOs is not enough or the participation of DPOs only occurs during the late phase of the process.[11] Further, consultancy and involvement of DPOs is illusionary when

[10] art 4(3) refers to 'their [persons with disabilities] representative organisations'. The same goes with art 33(3). Article 32(1) refers to 'organisations of persons with disabilities.' All the references carry the notion of organisations of persons with disabilities and through this exclude the possibility to make an interpretation that the references would include also organisations for persons with disabilities, which has been and still is an important but vague distinction. Also, there is an issue of what means 'representative.' In order to carry its weight, the term would need to address both diversity of persons with disabilities and not leaving any group out, but it would also need to look at the coverage of the organisation in geographical terms, among others.

[11] For example, this was the case with the Committee that considered the reform of the Equality

authorities give an opportunity to present opinions but these opinions are not taken into account. We understand 'full participation' to mean DPOs taking part in decision-making processes effectively, and in an effective manner, from the beginning to the end of the process. It is a strategic choice of DPOs to take part in all relevant activities at all appropriate levels locally, regionally, nationally and globally.

4.2. Strategic and Practical Methods of DPO Participation

In this chapter, we identify some strategic and practical approaches to DPO advocacy. When discussing 'strategic' methods of DPO participation we differentiate between political and legal advocacy. With 'political advocacy,' we mean that both the arguments and methods used are basically political.[12] There is a long history[13] of political advocacy on rights of persons with disabilities. Indeed, the birth of the disability movement was a result of severe violations against the rights of persons with disabilities, and the political response thereto. Various forms of political advocacy include public demonstrations, collecting signatures and utilising personal contacts with politicians. In 'legal advocacy,' both the arguments and methods used are basically legal.[14] DPOs take part in preparation of legislation, implementation and monitoring mechanisms, but also use legal arguments in advocacy in general and are not limited to the 'traditional' legal processes. However, political and legal approaches to DPO advocacy closely intertwine and complement each other.[15]

By 'practical' methods of DPO participation we refer to shadow reports, political participation, awareness-raising and scholarship activism. In recent years, DPOs have taken an active role in 'shadow reporting.' DPOs are often only actors who are able to collect information about the human rights situation of persons with disabilities and to prepare 'shadow reports' for national monitoring mechanisms and international treaty bodies. Through shadow reporting, DPOs act as watch dogs and make available their view of the situation. This can happen at local, regional, national or global level.

'Political participation' can be divided into two types. First, persons with disabilities themselves can act as politicians. Another method is to involve representatives of DPOs or persons with disabilities in decision-making processes. Politicians, including MPs, with disabilities can be found in almost all societies, both in

---

Act of Finland (21/2004). A representative of DPOs was included in the Committee only at very final stages of the work of the Committee in 2009.

12 See J Kumpuvuori and H Katsui, 'Achieving human security through political advocacy: Linking Ugandan and Finnish DPO advocacy work to Article 14 of the UN CRPD' in J Kumpuvuori and M Scheinin (eds), *United Nations Convention on the Rights of Persons with Disabilities. Multidisciplinary Perspectives* (The Center for Human Rights of Persons with Disabilities VIKE 2009) 214, where the authors describe political advocacy: 'In political advocacy, both the arguments and methods used are primarily political. This mean using arguments such as 'you politicians should change the law, otherwise your political support from our group will decrease rapidly.'

13 D F Stroman, *The Disability Rights Movement. From Deinstitutionalization to Self-Determination* (University Press of America 2003).

14 See Kumpuvuori and Katsui (n 11) 213, where the authors describe legal advocacy: 'In legal advocacy, both the arguments and methods used are primarily legal. This means using arguments such as '[w]e PWDs have the constitutional right to X' and employing legal methods such as filing complaints to legal bodies.'

15 See Kumpuvuori and Katsui (n 11) 214.

developed and developing countries. Often their background is in the disability movement. In the Ugandan Parliament there is a quota system where five members of the Parliament who represent persons with disabilities have to be from a DPO structure.

According to Article 8 of the CRPD, States Parties are obliged to facilitate and promote 'awareness-raising' activities regarding persons with disabilities. DPOs utilise various types of awareness-raising; actually almost all the activities of DPOs can be seen as a manifestation of awareness-raising. Raising awareness among societies is crucial since awareness is key to enabling changes in the perceptions of various stakeholders in society and, through that, changes in society and the situation of persons with disabilities.[16] One element of awareness-raising is to promote positive perceptions and greater social awareness towards persons with disabilities in public. It is important that the media is sensitive toward issues of persons with disabilities. According to Article 8(2)(c), States Parties are expected to encourage all organs of the media to portray persons with disabilities in a manner consistent with the purpose of the CRPD.

Academic research is an essential part of participation. Many DPOs in different parts of the world do research of their own or provide expert support to academic institutions working in close cooperation with them. All this can be called 'scholarship activism.'[17] As scholars ourselves, we are convinced of the role of this increasing practical method as one of the most promising ways to promote human rights of persons with disabilities.

5. 'Right Approach'

We will now proceed to introduce some elements of an approach which we call 'Right Approach' (RA). The elements introduced herein are not in any way final, and the authors wish to initiate a process leading to more thorough formulation of

---

16 G Quinn and T Degener see human rights as a 'visibility project' in the context of disability. They write: 'The disability rights movement has sunk deep roots in many countries around the world, especially over the past decade. It is in many ways a "visibility project". Its prime message is to remind us of something that we should not need reminding about, namely that persons with disabilities are human beings and therefore share the same human rights as everybody else and the right to enjoy them to the same degree.' G Quinn and T Degener, 'The moral authority for change: human rights values and the worldwide process of disability reform' in G Quinn and T Degener, *The current use and future potential of United Nations human rights instruments in the context of disability* (United Nations 2002) 26.

17 Kumpuvuori and Scheinin describe scholarship activism as, '[a]cademia and disability rights often come hand-in-hand. The writing of academic articles, chapters and books has become a part of global disability rights activism. This could be called scholarship activism. By this we mean that because much of the lack of realisation of human rights for persons with disabilities can be explained by a lack of awareness amongst relevant stakeholders, producing and receiving information will raise the level of awareness, and ultimately have a real chance of changing the mindset of the reader.' J Kumpuvuori and M Scheinin (n 11) 9. See also R Traustadóttir, 'Disability studies, the Social Model and legal developments', in O M Arnadóttir and G Quinn (eds), *The UN Convention on the Rights of Persons with Disabilities. European and Scandinavian Perspectives* (Martinus Nijhoff Publishers 2009) 15, where the author highlights the role of disability studies: 'Disability studies has influenced legal developments in various ways, most importantly by re-defining the "problem" by directing the focus away from the individual bio-medical understanding towards a social-contextual view of disability.'

the RA. We stress the importance of enabling various types of advocacy approaches to develop.[18]

We call the approach developed here the Right Approach, since we want the name to highlight two basic ideas behind the approach. First, the approach is based on human rights, and is thus in the realm of human-rights based approaches to disability.[19] Secondly, the approach is based on the strategic point of view of being right. By this we mean that the utilisation of the approach does not mean looking for actual, confirmed (through adjudication), content of a human rights norm, but rather making our own interpretation of those norms, with the goal of reaching the desired result in advocacy.

Pertaining to the dichotomy of preventive and restorative human rights strategies, the RA falls in the middle, leaning a bit more to the side of preventive. The utilisation of the RA can typically begin at a very early stage when it is not even clear that human rights violations are likely to occur in the near future. In the very early stage of the process this means, inter alia, conceptualising the issue into 'human rights talk' and starting advocacy work by establishing networks with relevant stakeholders. We argue that, typically, the RA is more effective as a preventive strategy for human rights than a restorative one. This is mainly because the RA is based predominantly on subjective interpretations of the person or organisation employing the RA. If the process develops and the RA is employed after the distinguishable human rights violation, the subjective interpretations are subjected to the scrutiny of authoritative organs, such as courts. This does not mean that the RA cannot be used as a restorative human rights strategy but for maximum effect the preventive strategy is preferable.

The RA is based on four main elements, namely those of normative obligation to include DPOs, full participation of DPOs, prioritising legal advocacy and recognising the emotional consequences and benefits that are an inherent consequence of the utilisation of the RA. Within the RA, the participation of DPOs in processes concerning persons with disabilities and the legitimacy of participation is not grounded merely on good-will or morals but on normative demand.[20] The normative

---

18 Banks and Kayess argue that 'Advocacy must adopt a diversity of models to remain appropriate for all people with impairments. It is clear that no two people experience their impairments in entirely same way. Similarly, the social barriers which create disability operate in variety of ways and take a multitude of forms, some obvious and some oblique,' see R Banks and R Kayess, 'Disability advocacy: Too much talk and not enough action', in M Hauritz, C Sampford and S Belncowe (eds), *Justice for People with Disabilities. Legal and Institutional Issues* (The Federation Press 1998) 163. We can argue that the variety of approaches is relevant both at the levels of individual and DPOs.

19 See for example Quinn and Degener et al (n 16), which employs comprehensively a human-rights based approach to disability. Stein and Stein take a step forward to develop a theory based on a human-rights based approach to disability, which they call 'The Disability Human Rights Paradigm' in M A Stein and P Stein, 'Beyond Civil Rights' (2007) 58 Hastings Law Journal 1203. See also discussion on human-rights based approach to development, which both acts as an example of developing rights-based approaches to disability, but also carries a significant importance in the context of disability in P Uvin, *Human Rights and Development* (Kumarian Press 2004).

20 G Quinn, 'Civil society: current use of the United Nations human rights system and future choices', in G Quinn and T Degener (n 16) 243, where he lists grounds for including DPOs in the making of that report to include the moral imperative to listen to the voices of those most directly affected and the impact the involvement of DPOs would have in the credibility of the

ground of participation of DPOs can be found particularly in Article 4(3) of the CRPD, which regulates as a general obligation that States Parties should '(...) closely consult with and actively involve persons with disabilities, including children with disabilities, through their representative organisations.'[21] The RA promotes full participation of DPOs, stressing that no other level of participation is enough to realise human rights of persons with disabilities to the fullest possible standard. As long as DPOs remain at the periphery of the decision-making processes, their voices will be too silent and their potential not benefited from.

Even though we consider that within the RA other forms of advocacy can be used in a way that results in legal dialogue, like raising awareness of human rights issues for persons with disabilities in the media, legal advocacy is the primary advocacy according to the RA. Within the RA, legal advocacy is considered to include, primarily, actions that have the result of directly imposing legal responsibility on someone, like taking court action. Everyone has the right to interpret human rights in the way that they wish to and everybody is entitled to take part in that discussion, whether addressing human rights specifically or discussing these issues without making an explicit reference to human rights. There are some practical limitations to an interpretation process based on the strategic choice of being right, such as requiring the rule of law and basic tenets of logic. The strategic choice of being right is more legitimate when it is a layman or DPO staff utilising this principle. If used by lawyers or other organisations that professionally deal with legal issues, the requirement to formally make the correct interpretation, ie play by the rule of law, are stricter. However, interpretation of law is, *per definitionem*, very prone to differing interpretations and thus 'playing by the rules' does not prevent even these actors from adopting anything other than a status quo interpretation of the law.

The authors want to make a link to the legal system and its formation.[22] The utilisation of human rights could and should be more flagrant in order to change society. If a DPO adopts and publicises only when the leaders of that DPO think that this 'is the confirmed and universal interpretation', no change in society will happen. This we term as 'going out' which means speaking out for human rights, both at the individual level and DPO level.[23] Although it is good to be systematic in advocacy and know the basics of how society works, we think it is important to keep the threshold of entering into advocacy as low as possible. There is a risk of impotency to take any action, if DPOs are afraid of 'being wrong.'[24]

---

study itself and the recommendations it is making. We see Quinn's elaboration on the topic in wide spectrum and see that the same grounds could very well be listed as criteria of including DPOs in various types of processes other than research, such as policy or law making.

21 art 4(3) CRPD (2006) UN Doc A/Res/ 61/106.

22 Offord points out this idea: '(...) human rights are translated through the lens of being human and in everyday life more than we think. They do not simply lie in the legal or political theatres of our lives' in Baden Offord, 'Activating Human Rights through questions of value and activism', in E Porter and B Offord (eds), *Activating Human Rights* (Peter Lang AG, International Academic Publishers 2006) 25.

23 Banks and Kayess (n 18) 166.

24 There can be some tendencies in the literature and societal discussions on this phenomenon of considering the advocacy activities towards the society and policies as very difficult and professional processes. See for example Raymond Lang and Ambrose Murangira, 'Barriers to the inclusion of disabled people in disability policy-making in seven African countries', in Kumpuvuori and Scheinin (n 9) 174, where the authors write: '(...) DPOs do not understand the complexity of policy-making.' See also Banks and Kayess (n 18) 166, where the authors

The RA recognises the emotional consequences of utilising this approach. Utilising the RA can lead to strong opposition, since the demands set within the RA are inherently an exaggeration, and are bound to confront the attitudes of the surrounding society, which, it can be argued, may be hostile. When someone gets blamed for discriminating against persons with disabilities, the defence very easily turns to blaming the victim, turning the discussion upside down.

The emotional consequences of facing such a resistance could be harsh also for DPOs. The authors want to stress the fact that DPOs consist of individuals, who are susceptible to emotional stress as are all individuals. Dependant on the strength of the DPO and individuals acting within, the stress related to the utilisation of the RA could lead to withdrawal. However, if the DPO and individuals acting within are strong and have good coping strategies, the RA can be utilised very effectively, converting the opposition experienced into added value by using it against the other party.[25]

6. The Case of Ms Vagabond – An Illustration of the Right Approach

Assuming that OLDPO utilises the RA within its advocacy approach, we can now consider how the scenario would develop. OLDPO takes the message of Ms Vagabond very seriously from the beginning, and want to champion her human rights and win the case. OLDPO takes immediate action in multiple arenas. They make it very clear to everyone they approach that they have the mandate to represent Ms Vagabond not only because they have a letter of attorney from her but also because it concerns her human rights and thus there is a possibility for external intervention. They stress that it is their normative right and obligation to proceed with this particular case.

OLDPO files a complaint to the Office of the Rector of the Makerere University claiming the rights of Ms Vagabond. They also contact the police and ask them to take action. They also contact several reporters and make the issue visible in the media. Further, they file a law suit in the Constitutional Court of Uganda claiming that the treatment of Ms Vagabond is unconstitutional. In addition to the Constitution of Uganda, they refer to the CRPD and the Persons with Disabilities Act of Uganda.

They argue that these international human rights norms and national laws oblige the university to provide the accommodation that Ms Vagabond requires. They cite some parts of those legal instruments which provide for this. Further, they do not enclose some elements relating to those instruments that are not in favour of their

explain: 'Systemic advocacy requires a high level of skill in political analysis and policy development.'

25 Even though, the negative emotional consequences of utilising the RA are definitely a challenge for the approach, which is worthy of attention for future empirical research. H Katsui, 'Downside of the Human Rights-Based Approach to Disability in Development' (2008) Working Paper 2/2008, The Institute of Development Studies, Helsinki University. Hisayo Katsui points out that '(…) there is an acute need of more critical (self-) reflection of the HRBA to understand its both positive and negative sides in a particular context so that the HRBA is a helpful tool on the ground rather than in theory.'

argument, such as the fact that the CRPD is not yet domesticated in Uganda and therefore is not in itself legally binding upon the Ugandan legal system.

OLDPO faces strong resistance. Many people, including some prominent characters of Ugandan society, contact them and tell them that they are demanding too much and exaggerating. They think that Ms Vagabond should settle for attending fewer lectures and getting the notes from other students. The Constitutional Court responds and informs them that they could consider the case; however, they run the risk of the Court dismissing the case based on demands that constitute 'unreasonable accommodation,' and thus the university's actions would not be a breach of the Constitution.

Now, it is all up to the fighting spirit of OLDPO and its management. If they surrender in this situation it will all be over for them and Ms Vagabond. However, the management of OLDPO is strong in spirit and keeps on advocating. Eventually, they receive a call from the Makerere University telling them that they have managed to secure funding for the accommodation of Ms Vagabond needs. They are disgruntled by OLDPO and the whole issue, since they do not favour the public debate. OLDPO and Ms Vagabond celebrate the victory and Ms Vagabond is able to concentrate on her studies.

7. Conclusion

In this chapter, we have demonstrated the basis of DPO-advocacy and their strategies. We have also developed an approach we call the Rights Approach and applied its usage to a hypothetical case. Having discussed the topic, we want to make the following conclusions:

1. Legal advocacy can be much more than the mere utilisation of traditional legal mechanism, like law suits. Legal advocacy can also involve a wide-range of actions such as utilising the media and private correspondence [26] to name a few, through which one can reach the goals much more speedily and effectively than through the 'traditional' types of legal advocacy.
2. It is worth considering the element of the RA of 'being right'. Thinking about human rights advocacy as a novel attempt to change somebody's life situation, the authors are of the view that every possible move needs to be taken. Here, it is important to bear in mind that one respects also the human rights of other individuals. For example, one has to restrict the methods used to the ones that do not infringe the personal security of others.
3. We feel that even though the elements we think to be the basis for the RA are valid and sound, they are somewhat anecdotal. Thus, some empirical research would need to be done in order to show how the RA would work in real-life advocacy processes. In spite of this, though, we feel that the basis laid down in this piece of work for the preliminary development of

[26] Madison presents nicely the utilisation of performance as a tool in the fight for human rights and social justice in S D Madison, *Acts of Activism Human Rights as Radical Performance* (Cambridge University Press 2010).

the RA is strong enough, and we are convinced that the elements described in this article will remain focal points for future development of the RA and other approaches relating to the advocacy processes of DPOs.

PART 2: LEGAL CAPACITY

CHAPTER 6

LEGAL CAPACITY AND SUPPORTED DECISION-MAKING: RESPECTING RIGHTS AND EMPOWERING PEOPLE

Anna Arstein-Kerslake

1. INTRODUCTION

Sándor Harmati is an advocate, an activist, a man with Down syndrome, and an individual living under a plenary guardianship that denies his right to\ legal capacity.[1] Mr Harmati is a Hungarian man who has worked with disability advocacy groups in Hungary to lobby for the reform of Hungary's restrictive guardianship laws which have resulted in Mr Harmati suffering violations of many of his human rights, such as being prohibited from voting,[2] working and marrying.[3] Unfortunately, the realities of life without legal capacity, and the human rights violations that one suffers when placed under guardianship, are not unique to Hungary. Instead, they are endemic across the globe.

The Convention on the Rights of People with Disabilities (CRPD) is the first international treaty to recognize that all people, including those with disabilities, should enjoy legal capacity on an equal basis in all areas of life. It was the fastest-negotiated human rights treaty in the history of the United Nations.[4] Eighty-two countries signed on the opening day, the highest number of any UN Convention on its opening day.[5] Disability rights is an area that people from a broad range

---

1 Information gained from the Legal Capacity Conference at Harvard Law School on 20 February 2009 in which Sándor Harmati was the Keynote Speaker.

2 The Hungarian Constitution, art 70(2). For most of Mr Harmati's life he has been prevented from exercising his right to vote because we was placed under a plenary guardianship; however, it is important to note that on 20 May 20 2010, the European Court of Human Rights ruled that an automatic exclusion from voting for people under guardianship violates the European Convention on Human Rights, Protocol 1, art 3, the Right to Free Elections. *Alajos Kiss v Hungary* (application no. 38832/06). See also *European Court of Human Rights upholds the right to vote of persons with disabilities*, Mental Disability Advocacy Center (20 May 2010). The ruling of the European Court of Human Rights has a binding effect on Hungary, as a member of the European Union (EU), because it is a prerequisite of membership in the EU that a country ratify the Council of Europe's European Convention of Human Rights and accept the jurisdiction of the European Court of Human Rights: *The Human Rights System: European Union* Human Rights Education Associates (2007).

3 See *Human Rights and Guardianships in Hungary*, Mental Disability Advocacy Center (2007) 45.

4 A Geisinger and M A Stein, 'Rational Choice, Reputation and Human Rights Treaties' (2008) 106(6) Michigan Law Review 1129, 1142.

5 Information on signatories to the Convention on the Rights of People with Disabilities (CRPD)

of political affiliations are willing to support. However, the resistance to Article 12 of the Convention is palpable. It has been one of the most contentious areas in the Convention.[6] Article 12 seems to touch a nerve – it asks us to strip away the paternalistic instinct to protect people with disabilities; not only that, it asks us to deconstruct centuries-old systems of substituted decision-making, such as guardianship, conservatorship, deputyship, wardship etc. This resistance to Article 12 may reveal the truth behind the willingness of governments to ratify the Convention: an ever-pervasive stigma related to perceived 'difference' in people labelled as disabled, which is perpetuated via pity and a willingness to provide merely paternalistic protection and charity, rather than real opportunities for individuals to be respected and recognised as full citizens.

2. Defining 'Legal Capacity' and the Obligations in the CRPD

The recognition of a right to legal capacity in the CRPD signifies that all people have an equal right to make decisions on their own behalf.[7] Without the right to make fundamental decisions, such as where to reside and what kind of medical care to receive, a person is relegated to the status of an object rather than an independent human being with thoughts, emotions and opinions.[8] The recognition of legal capacity is the tool that allows an individual access to make these decisions. It is the freedom to be a holder of rights and obligations as well as the freedom to exercise those rights and undertake those duties by way of one's own conduct and without representation by a third party.[9]

There is a strong argument to be made that Article 12 dictates that there is an irrebuttable presumption in favour of legal capacity.[10] This amounts to universal legal capacity,[11] which requires that States Parties refrain from denying legal capacity – obviating the need for capacity assessments – and simultaneously obligating States Parties to provide support for the exercise of capacity, where desired by the individual. Essential to a system of supported decision-making is the provision

as well as general information on the CRPD can be found on the UN Enable website at www.un.org/disabilities.

6 This is evidenced by the high number of reservations, understandings and declarations that have been lodged on art 12. A list of them can be found on the UN Enable website at www.un.org/disabilities.

7 General Comment No 1, art 12: Equal Recognition Before the Law, Paragraph 8, UN Committee on the Rights of Persons with Disabilities, UN Doc. No. CRPD/C/GC/1 (April 2014); M Bach and L Kerzner, 'A New Paradigm for Protecting Autonomy and the Right to Legal Capacity' prepared for the Law Commission of Ontario (October 2010).

8 See G Quinn and T Degener, et al, Human Rights and Disability: The current use and future potential of United Nations human rights instruments in the context of disability, 14-16, United Nations Doc. No. HR/PUB/02/1 (2002).

9 Office of the United Nations High Commissioner of Human Rights, *Legal Capacity* (Background Conference Document 2005) 1 and 13

10 G Quinn, Statement to the Oireachtas Joint Committee on Justice, Defence and Equality, Re: Hearing on the Mental Capacity Bill (29 February 2012).

11 General Comment No 1, art 12: Equal Recognition Before the Law, Paragraph 25, UN Committee on the Rights of Persons with Disabilities, UN Doc. No. CRPD/C/GC/1 (April 2014).

of tools for augmenting capacity[12] – with an assumption that every individual has decision-making abilities, although may need assistance developing those skills and expressing their wills and preferences. Article 12 requires that the individual is the decision-maker. The support persons or people are merely there to explain details, when necessary, and interpret the signs and desires of the individual when it is needed.[13]

Recognising that differing abilities call for differing amounts of outside aid in making decisions, Article 12 of the Convention demands that supported decision-making systems replace all forms of substituted decision-making systems, such as guardianship.[14] It requires States Parties to support individuals who are in need of it and to safeguard against abuse within that support system.[15] This calls for a system of supported decision-making that could take many different forms including one trusted support person or a network of support people providing assistance on a one-time basis or consistently throughout an individual's life.

3. The Support Paradigm

3.1. Respect for an Individual's Autonomy and the Support Paradigm

The denial of decision-making power to individuals with disabilities is a pervasive and harmful form of discrimination.[16] Article 12 of the CRPD recognizes that every person has a will, desires, and needs – and that every person is capable of making choices accordingly. Not every person is able to express choices through conventionally accepted methods of communication. Some people communicate through words, others through signs, others through writing and others simply through smiles. When a person communicates with the world in unconventional ways, others may not recognize that he or she is communicating and expressing his

---

12 G Quinn, 'Rethinking Personhood: New Directions in Legal Capacity Law & Policy' paper presented at University of British Columbia, Vancouver (29 April 2011).

13 General Comment No 1, art 12: Equal Recognition Before the Law, para 29, UN Committee on the Rights of Persons with Disabilities, UN Doc. No. CRPD/C/GC/1 (April 2014); The Department of Economic and Social Affairs (UN-DESA), the Office of the United Nations High Commissioner for Human Rights (OHCHR); Inter-Parliamentary Union (IPU) *From Exclusion to Equality: Realizing the Rights of Persons with Disabilities* (2007).

14 As is stated in the UN Committee on the Rights of Persons with Disabilities General Comment and its Concluding Observations in response to the reports from Spain, Peru and Tunisia. General Comment No 1, art 12: Equal Recognition Before the Law, para 26, UN Committee on the Rights of Persons with Disabilities, UN Doc. No. CRPD/C/GC/1 (April 2014). *Consideration of reports submitted by States parties under article 35 of the Convention: Concluding observations, Tunisia,* Committee on the Rights of Persons with Disabilities, 5th Session at 4, UN Doc. CRPD/C/TUN/CO/1 (11–15 April 2011); *Consideration of reports submitted by States Parties under article 35 of the Convention: Concluding observations, Spain,* Committee on the Rights of Persons with Disabilities 6th Session UN Doc. CRPD/C/ESP/CO/1 (19–23 September 2011); *Consideration of reports submitted by States Parties under article 35 of the Convention: concluding observations,* Peru, Committee on the Rights of Persons with Disabilities, 7th Session, 25, UN Doc CRPD/C/PER/CO/1 (16–20 April 2012).

15 This is clear upon a reading of art 12 of the CRPD, which protects the right to legal capacity on an equal basis, in conjunction with art 16, securing the right to freedom of exploitation, violence and abuse. CRPD arts 12 and16 (13 December 2006) A/RES/61/106.

16 See generally B J Winick, 'On Autonomy: Legal and Psychological Perspectives' (1992) 37 Villanova Law Review 1705, 1755–1768.

or her likes and dislikes, needs and desires. Whichever way an individual is able to communicate, conventional or not, Article 12 requires that his or her desires not be ignored. The support paradigm is a system in which people work together to understand an individual's desires and choices and then provide the means for that person to exercise legal capacity and live life in the way he or she chooses as opposed to a way imposed by someone else's decision made on his or her behalf.

3.2. Positive Effects of the Support Paradigm

When the law recognizes that an individual is competent to make his or her own decisions it has broad effects. It fosters equality across many areas of life such as employment and personal relationships. It also affirms the power of choice, thereby enabling individual development.[17] When the law permits support for individuals when making decisions, there are also significant effects. The support paradigm fosters social solidarity without sacrificing the recognition of equal legal capacity. By offering the choice of assistance, the supported decision-making paradigm removes the illusion that legal capacity can only be exercised through self-sufficiency. This opens the door for a societal dialogue about the interdependence of all individuals.[18]

The support paradigm's humanistic approach – adapting to the needs of all individuals and not allowing the law to sanction one person taking control of the decisions of another person – has the potential to provide a much lower risk of exploitation than guardianship and other substituted decision-making systems. Studies have shown that where autonomy is fostered and where individuals are given meaningful choices, intrinsic motivation is increased and the overall well-being of the individual is enhanced.[19] Therefore, it can be argued that legal capacity systems, which recognize every individual as a decision-maker, serve to foster autonomy and create stronger individuals who are better able to protect themselves from abuse and exploitation. Of course, meaningful safeguards are still necessary to ensure an effective system of support that is free from abuse – as required by Article 12(4).[20]

The paradigm of support adapts to a sliding scale of abilities[21] rather than being a binary model of capacity or incapacity as are many substituted decision-making models.[22] It does not create a separate category of people who are 'legally

---

17 See B Winick, 'The Side Effects of Incompetency Labeling and the Implications for Mental Health Law' (March 1995) 1(1) Psychology, Public Policy and Law 6; R M Ryan and E L Deci, 'Self-Determination Theory and the Facilitation of Intrinsic Motivation, Social Development, and Well-being' (Jan 2000) 55 American Psychologist 68; E L Deci and R M Ryan, 'The "What" and "Why" of Goal Pursuits: Human Needs and the Self-Determination of Behavior' (2000) 11 Psychological Inquiry 227.

18 'Rethinking Personhood: New Directions in Legal Capacity Law & Policy' (n 12); G Quinn with A Arstein-Kerslake, 'Restoring the 'Human' in 'Human Rights' – Personhood and Doctrinal Innovation in the UN Disability Convention' (Forthcoming 2012).

19 Self-determination theory supports this statement. For a discussion of self-determination theory, see Ryan and Deci, 'Self-Determination Theory and the Facilitation of Intrinsic Motivation, Social Development, and Well-being' (n 16); 'The "What" and "Why" of Goal Pursuits: Human Needs and the Self-Determination of Behavior' (n 16).

20 General Comment No 1, art 12: Equal Recognition Before the Law, paras 20–22, UN Committee on the Rights of Persons with Disabilities, UN Doc. No. CRPD/C/GC/1 (April 2014).

21 See eg M Bach and L Kerzner, *A New Paradigm for Protecting Autonomy and the Right to Legal Capacity* prepared for the Law Commission of Ontario (October 2010).

22 See S S Herr, 'Self-Determination, Autonomy, and Alternatives for Guardianship, in S S Herr, L

incapacitated,' which, it has been argued, amounts to institutionalized discrimination and subordination.[23] This categorization of individuals, whereby there is one category of persons whose decisions are recognized and another category of persons whose are not, is fraught with pitfalls[24] and can be profoundly disempowering for the group of people labelled 'incapacitated.'[25] The support paradigm asks that a system begin with the assumption that all individuals have decision-making ability and then asks what support each individual needs in augmenting her decision-making ability and expressing her preferences.[26] In this system, no labels are needed; instead, it is merely a question of determining what type of support any given individual might need.

3.3. The Nuts and Bolts of a Supported Decision-Making System

Substituted decision-making systems include guardianship models, conservatorships, wardships and other models where the guardian, conservator or other representative is authorized by the court to make decisions on behalf of or in the place of an individual who is deemed to be legally incapable.[27] These regimes usually follow a paternalistic 'best interests' model in which the substitute makes decisions based on what he or she believes to be the 'best interests' of the individual[28] – as opposed to what might be decisions based on the actual preferences of the individual.

In contrast, the support paradigm reflects the social model of disability.[29] The social model perceives disability as a creation of a society that is unwilling to make the slightest bend to address the needs of those that may be outside of the 'norm.' It says that if a person with a 'disability' is unable to function, it is because society is unwilling to interact with the person in a way that allows the person to function.[30] The support paradigm demands that society adjust to individuals' differing needs and act in a way that eliminates the barriers to legal capacity by providing adequate assistance for the exercise of that legal capacity.

O Gostin, H H Koh (eds) *The Human Rights of Persons with Intellectual Disabilities: Different But Equal* (Oxford University Press 2003) 440; A Dhanda, 'Legal Capacity in the Disability Rights Convention: Stranglehold of the Past or Lodestar for the Future?' (2006–2007) 34 Syracuse Journal of International Law and Commerce 429.

23 T Minkowitz, "The United Nations Convention on the Rights of Persons with Disabilities and the Right to Be Free from Nonconsensual Psychiatric Interventions" (2006–2007) 34 Syracuse Journal of International Law and Commerce 405.

24 See generally G S Owen, F Freyenhagen, G Richardson, and M Hotopf, 'Mental Capacity and Decisional Autonomy: An Interdisciplinary Challenge' (February 2009) 52 Inquiry 79.

25 Winick (n 16); S Stefan,'Silencing the Different Voice: Competence, Feminist Theory, and Law' (1993) 47 University of Miami Law Review 763.

26 G Quinn, 'Personhood & Legal Capacity: Perspectives on the Paradigm Shift of Article 12 CRPD' (Harvard: Harvard Project on Disability, 20 February 2010).

27 General Comment No 1, art 12: Equal Recognition Before the Law, para 27, UN Committee on the Rights of Persons with Disabilities, UN Doc. No. CRPD/C/GC/1 (April 2014) eg New York State Mental Hygiene Law, NY CLS Men Hyg § 81.02(c)(4)(ii–iii) (2007); Mental Capacity Act 2005 c 9 (England and Wales); the Lunacy Regulation Act 1871 c 22 (Ireland).

28 eg Mental Capacity Act 2005 c 9, pt 1(4) (England and Wales).

29 M Jesperson, 'PO-Skåne–Personal Ombudspersons in Skåne' presentation available at <www.peoplewho.org/documents/jesperson.decisionmaking.doc>.

30 For a description of the social model of disability see R Kayess and P French, 'Out of Darkness into Light – Introducing the Convention on the Rights of Persons with Disabilities' (2008) *8* Human Rights Law Review 1, 5–8; C Barnes and G Mercer (eds), *The Social Model of Disability: Europe and the Majority World* (The Disability Press, Leeds 2005).

The support paradigm of Article 12 acknowledges that the answer is not forced intervention or substituted decision-making when an individual is faced with challenges when attempting to exercise his or her legal capacity in the conventional manner. Instead, in a supported decision-making system, outside assistance for decision-making should generally be minimal and should be based on the needs of the individual. The individual is the centre of the decision-making process and the support person is not permitted to utilize his or her judgment in place of the individual's judgment. The support person is merely an interpreter of the will and preferences of the individual.[31]

There are some people who require almost complete outside support for decision-making, such as people who have disabilities which affect their communication with the outside world. For people in this situation, the support person should still enable, to the fullest extent possible, the individual to exercise his or her legal capacity.[32] This may mean a variety of things, including spending time learning the communication methods that the individuals does have (such as movements of the eyelids, hand-squeezing, smiling etc.), researching past communications (if available), or other means to ascertain the individual's desires and decisions. The support person should try to ascertain, by any means available, the wishes of the individual. If it is not possible to discover the wishes of the individual, the support person should make a decision, *not* based on what the support person believes are the best interests of the individual, but instead based on what the support person believes are the true wishes of the individual.[33]

There are many different possible forms of supported decision-making systems.[34] Because substituted decision-making systems nearly completely dominate in modern legal systems, there are very few clear, functioning examples of what a supported decision-making system should look like.[35] This leaves room for states to establish supported decision-making systems that conform to their particular cultural and political landscapes.

3.4. Concluding Remarks on Supported Decision-Making

Self-determination may be daunting for many people. Families of individuals with disabilities may fear that their family member with a disability will not be able to make the best decisions for him or herself. People with disabilities may themselves be fearful of a new responsibility to make important decisions about their own lives

---

[31] The Department of Economic and Social Affairs (UN-DESA), the Office of the United Nations High Commissioner for Human Rights (OHCHR), and the Inter-Parliamentary Union (IPU), *From Exclusion to Equality: Realizing the Rights of Persons with Disabilities* (2007); and General Comment No 1, art 12: Equal Recognition Before the Law, para 29, UN Committee on the Rights of Persons with Disabilities, UN Doc. No. CRPD/C/GC/1 (April 2014).

[32] The Department of Economic and Social Affairs (UN-DESA), the Office of the United Nations High Commissioner for Human Rights (OHCHR), and the Inter-Parliamentary Union (IPU), *From Exclusion to Equality: Realizing the Rights of Persons with Disabilities* (2007).

[33] *Submission on Legal Capacity: the Oireachtas Committee on Justice, Defence & Equality* (Centre for Disability Law and Policy (CDLP) at NUI Galway 2011) 21.

[34] General Comment No 1, art 12: Equal Recognition Before the Law, para 29, UN Committee on the Rights of Persons with Disabilities, UN Doc. No. CRPD/C/GC/1 (April 2014).

[35] ibid.

that they may have never been faced with before. However, no person is an island.[36] People with disabilities and people without disabilities are faced with decisions every day and are assisted in varying ways in making those decisions. The paradigm of supported decision-making is not proposing a radical change in how an individual makes decisions. It is merely requiring that the freedom to make decisions is not removed from an individual. It recognizes that many people need more assistance than others in making decisions and that this assistance should be provided to the fullest extent desired by the individual.

Currently, people without disabilities are generally free to make decisions on a much wider scale than people with disabilities. People without disabilities are free to make decisions that serve their interests or their loved ones' interests or, in the alternative, do not serve their interests. Article 12 is merely requiring that a person with a disability should be equally free to exercise his or her legal capacity and make his or her own decisions whether or not the outside world views them as 'good'.[37]

Autonomy and interdependence can and should coexist in supported decision-making systems. An individual with a disability should be free to make his or her own decisions and concurrently he or she should be offered the support needed to fully understand that decision and to make his or her desires and choices known to the world. The supported decision-making model enables self-determination while encouraging communal involvement and support.[38]

4. Legal Capacity Systems in Need of Reform

One of the reasons that Article 12 of the CRPD has been so contentious is that it requires real changes to existing legal systems and challenges people's notion of people with disabilities as lacking decision-making skills. This notion has fostered the paternalistic legal capacity systems that dominate the world today, violate Article 12 of the CRPD and are in need of reform.

Although there is debate about exactly what Article 12 requires of States Parties, there is general consensus on a few key issues, including, but not limited to:[39] the recognition of legal capacity on an equal basis for all;[40] the primacy of the will

---

36 J Donne, 'Devotions Upon Emergent Occasions, Meditation XVII' (1624) <www.luminarium.org/sevenlit/donne/meditation17.php> from H Alford (ed) 'The Works of John Donne vol III.' (John W. Parker 1839) 574–5.

37 'Personhood & Legal Capacity: Perspectives on the Paradigm Shift of Article 12 CRPD' (n 26).

38 'Rethinking Personhood: New Directions in Legal Capacity Law & Policy' (n 12).

39 See *Essential Principles: Irish Legal Capacity Law*, Amnesty Ireland, The Centre for Disability Law and Policy (CDLP) at NUI Galway, et al (April 2012)

40 'Legal capacity on an equal basis' has had multiple interpretations – and, at the time of writing, the CRPD committee has yet to publish a general comment on the subject. For the argument that a functional test of capacity fulfills this requirement, see Tribunal Supremo, Sala de la Civil, sentencia no. 282/2009 (30 March 2009) (Spain), a decision of the Spanish Supreme Court that found that the tudor/curador complies with Article art 12. For the argument that, reading Article art 12 as a whole, only *universal* legal capacity respects legal capacity on an equal basis for all, see Minkowitz (Footnote n 2123); CRPD, Article art 12(2) (Dec 13, 2006) A/RES/61/106.

and preference of the individual;[41] the construction of adequate safeguards;[42] and the replacement of substituted decision-making systems with supported decision-making systems.[43] Currently, there are very few jurisdictions that fulfill these requirements. For example, as in many jurisdictions,[44] in New York State, a diagnosis of developmental disability can be used as evidence to deny an individual his or her legal capacity. The individual also has no statutory right to be at the hearing that determines whether to remove legal capacity from that individual.[45] There is also no further reporting process required in New York after the individual is placed under a guardian.[46] In Wisconsin, an individual can be denied legal capacity and, once under a guardianship, loses the right to vote, to marry, or to consent to sterilizations without a court specifically finding otherwise.[47] In California, by statute, the court can grant a conservator the power to consent to the sterilization of the conservatee[48] and to specify that a consertavor has control over the social and sexual contacts of a conservatee.[49] These concerning examples are all within the United States, which is thought of as having some of the most progressive protections for the rights of

---

41 'Submission on Legal Capacity: the Oireachtas Committee on Justice, Defence & Equality' (Centre for Disability Law and Policy (CDLP) at NUI Galway, Page 6 (2011) 6; M. Bach and L. Kerzner, *'A New Paradigm for Protecting Autonomy and the Right to Legal Capacity'* (prepared for the Law Commission of Ontario, Page 61 (October 2010) 61; CRPD, Article art 12(4).

42 Although the Wingspan Guardianship Conference in the United States is not based on the principles of the CRPD or the right to legal capacity on an equal basis, it does provide an example of modern trends in safeguarding legal capacity regimes. See National Guardianship Network, *Third National Guardianship Summit Releases Standards and Recommendations*, Recommendation Number 2: Guardian's Relationship to the Court 6 (October 2011). CRPD, Article art 12(4).

43 General Comment No 1, art 12: Equal Recognition Before the Law, UN Committee on the Rights of Persons with Disabilities, UN Doc. No. CRPD/C/GC/1 (April 2014); *Consideration of reports submitted by States parties under article 35 of the Convention: Concluding observations, Tunisia,* Committee on the Rights of Persons with Disabilities (CRPD), 5th Session at 4, UN Doc. CRPD/C/TUN/CO/1 (11–15 April 2011); *Consideration of reports submitted by States parties under article 35 of the Convention: Concluding observations, Spain,* Committee on the Rights of Persons with Disabilities , 6th Session at 5, UN Doc. CRPD/C/ESP/CO/1 (19–23 September 2011); *Consideration of reports submitted by States parties under article 35 of the Convention: concluding observations,* Peru, Committee on the Rights of Persons with Disabilities, 7th Session, at 25, UN Doc CRPD/C/PER/CO/1 (16–20 April 2012).

44 eg The England and Wales Mental Capacity Act 2005 states that 'a person lacks capacity in relation to a matter if at the material time he is unable to make a decision for himself in relation to the matter because of an impairment of, or a disturbance in the functioning of, the mind or brain.' The Law Commission concluded that a diagnostic threshold of metal disability has more protective value than potential for prejudice. Gordon Ashton (ed), *Court of Protection Practice 2012* (Jordan Publishing 2012) 113; The Mental Capacity Act (2005), ch 9, UK Public General Acts (England and Wales).

45 Matter of Chaim A K, 8/26/2009 NYLJ 41 (col 1) (Sur Ct, New York County); New York Surrogate's Court Procedure Act (art 17-A) § 1750.

46 Matter of Mark C H, 5/10/2010 NYLJ 243 (Sur Ct, New York County).

47 "Guardianship of Adults: A Decision-Making Guide," Sections 1 through 3, Wisconsin Department of Health Services (24 October 2008).

48 California Probate Code § 1950-69.

49 California Probate Code § 2351.5(b)(6).

the people with disabilities;[50] some countries with less developed protections have even more oppressive legal capacity laws.[51]

England and Wales, like the United States, have been lauded for having a robust system of rights protections for people with disabilities.[52] However, although their legal capacity system was reformed relatively recently,[53] when compared with the standards established in Article 12, it falls short in several aspects. Although there is not space in this article to do a thorough analysis of the 2005 Mental Capacity Act (MCA),[54] a few key flaws can be highlighted.[55] Most significantly, it can be argued that the MCA's mere categorization of individuals as 'incapacitated' is a violation of Article 12 simply because it denies those individuals their right to legal capacity. This raises the issue of the MCA's conflation of the concepts of 'legal capacity' and 'mental capacity.' It is important to distinguish between decision-making ability (mental capacity) and legal capacity. All individuals have varying levels of decision-making ability. However, Article 12 suggests that decision-making ability is not something that should have any impact on an individual's right to legal capacity.[56] Irrespective of decision-making ability, according to Article 12, every person has an inherent right to legal capacity and equal recognition before the law.[57] The MCA provides a functional assessment of mental capacity – denying legal capacity to those who do not pass the test. Article 12, instead, requires that a system never deny legal capacity and instead provide appropriate assessments limited to what

---

50 During the recent hearings regarding the United States ratification of the CRPD, Dick Thornburgh stated: 'We are indeed at this time the most progressive country in the world when it comes to the domestic protection of disability rights.' D Thornburgh, Former Attorney General of the United States and Under-Secretary-General of the United Nations, 'Respecting the Convention on the Rights of Persons with Disabilities', testimony before the Foreign Relations Committee of the United States Senate (12 July 2012) 8.

51 For examples of jurisdictions with legal capacity laws that do not sufficiently protect the rights of people with disabilities, see the reports produced by the Mental Disability Advocacy Centre (MDAC) eg *Guardianship and Human Rights in Serbia*, Mental Disability Advocacy Center (2006) and *Guardianship and Human Rights in Hungary*, Mental Disability Advocacy Center (2007).

52 The United Kingdom has been listed as one of the countries with the most comprehensive definitions of disability discrimination. T Degener and G Quinn, *A Survey of International, Comparative and Regional Disability Law Reform*, Disability Rights Law and Policy International and National Perspectives, M L Breslin and S Yee (eds), Disability Rights Education and Defence Fund (2002).

53 The England and Wales Mental Capacity Act was created in 2005 in response to a finding by the Law Society's Mental Health Sub-Committee that legislation was lacking in this area. G R Ashton, 'Preface to the First Edition' in G Ashton (ed) *Court of Protection Practice 2012* (Jordan Publishing 2012) 9.

54 The Mental Capacity Act 2005, ch 9, UK Public General Acts (England and Wales).

55 For a more thorough analysis, see L Series, A Arstein-Kerslake, P Gooding, and E Flynn, *The Mental Capacity Act 2005, the Adults with Incapacity (Scotland) Act 2000 and the Convention on the Rights of Persons with Disabilities: The Basics*, Mental Capacity Law Discussion Paper, Thirty Nine Essex Street Mental Capacity Law Newsletter; and L Series, *The Mental Capacity Act 2005 And The Institutional Domination Of People With Learning Disabilities*, Doctoral Thesis in Law, University of Exeter (January 2013)

56 CRPD, art 12(3); and General Comment No 1, art 12: Equal Recognition Before the Law, paras 13–15, UN Committee on the Rights of Persons with Disabilities, UN Doc. No. CRPD/C/GC/1 (April 2014)

57 See T Minkowitz, "The United Nations Convention on the Rights of Persons with Disabilities and the Right to Be Free from Nonconsensual Psychiatric Interventions," 34 Syracuse Journal of International Law and Commerce 405, 408 (2006–2007)

type of supports a particular individual needs in order to be able to exercise his or her legal capacity.

The Act requires a two-stage test of capacity, which begins with determining whether the person has an impairment of the mind or brain.[58] This automatically places individuals with intellectual disabilities or mental illnesses on unequal standing with all others being assessed for legal capacity, violating Article 12(2) of the Convention which states that persons with disabilities shall enjoy legal capacity on the same basis as others and in all aspects of life.[59] The second step of the capacity test in the MCA is to ask whether the person is able to make the specific decision in question at the time it needs to be made.[60] However, in order to recognize legal capacity for all, there should not be an assessment of *whether* a person is able to make a decision, but simply an assumption that they can and an effort to determine their wishes. Furthermore, the MCA places the power to assess capacity in the hands of almost any third party who needs a decision to be made – without significant procedural protections.[61] Article 12(4) requires that any assistance provided in decision-making must be accompanied by appropriate procedural safeguards,[62] which are lacking when doctors, lawyers and others are permitted to make ad hoc determinations of whether an individual has sufficient decision-making skills. Finally, while the MCA does mention the importance of giving weight to the wishes of the individual,[63] it still maintains the best interest standard as the primary means for decision-making. Article 12 makes no mention of best interests, and instead requires States Parties to 'respect the rights, will and preferences' of the individual.[64]

The MCA was a step in the right direction and is a distinct improvement upon the prior guardianship system in England and Wales.[65] However, with the UK's signature of the Convention and its ratification, England and Wales must modify their system further to come into compliance with the Convention and to uphold the human rights of individuals with disabilities. As is evident from these examples, there is an immediate need for legal capacity reform around the globe.

5. Conclusion

Without the recognition of the human right to legal capacity, individuals are treated as mere objects of the state and may not be given the opportunity to develop to their desired potential. It is highly beneficial for individuals, as well as for society,

---

58 *Mental Capacity Act 2005 Code of Practice*, issued by Lord Falconer, Secretary of State for Constitutional Affairs and Lord Chancellor, Department for Constitutional Affairs, 41 (23 April 2007); *The Mental Capacity Jurisdiction*, G Ashton (ed), *Court of Protection Practice 2012*, Section 2.58 (Jordan Publishing 2012) 113.

59 CRPD art 12(2.).

60 *Mental Capacity Act 2005 Code of Practice* (n 54) 41; The Mental Capacity Act (2005), ch 9, UK Public General Acts, pt 1 (2)(1) and pt 1 (3)(1) (England and Wales).

61 Ashton (n 58) at Section 2.100, 126.

62 CRPD art 12(4).

63 Mental Capacity Act (2005), ch 9, UK Public General Acts, pt 1 (3)(6)(a) (England and Wales).

64 CRPD art 12(4).

65 G R Ashton, *Mental Capacity: The New Law*, 5 P.C.B. 299–302 (2006). Gordon R Ashton describes how the previous guardianship system was more restrictive, provided the individual with very little control, and did not provide an assumption of capacity.

that everyone is given the opportunity to fully explore their capabilities in order for each individual to realize the expanse of their abilities and share the benefits of them with society.[66] Substituted decision-making systems are paternalistic and highly restrictive and do not allow individuals to exercise their right to legal capacity and do not foster development or self-determination. The support paradigm offers a system that meets the goals of the CRPD, protects the right to legal capacity and allows for individuals to be empowered to develop their own capabilities as full members of society – in this way, respecting a right to legal capacity is not only a human rights imperative, it is also simply smart policy.

[66] Amaryta Sen's work supports this assertion, in that it merges individual capability expansion with economic development and concludes that one cannot exist without the other. See A Sen, "Development as Capability Expansion," in K Griffin, J Knight (eds), *Human Development and International Development Strategy for the 1990s* (Macmillan 1990) 41–58; and A Sen, "Development and Thinking at the Beginning of the 21st Century," Suntory and Toyota International Centers for Economics and Related Disciplines, Research Paper No. DEDPS 02 (1997).

Chapter 7

ARTICLE 12 OF THE UN CONVENTION ON THE RIGHTS OF PERSONS WITH DISABILITIES AND THE EUROPEAN CONVENTION ON HUMAN RIGHTS

Mary Keys

1. Introduction

The UN Convention on the Rights of Persons with Disabilities (CRPD) is widely regarded as a major breakthrough for human rights of persons with disabilities. Quinn comments that '…the human rights revolution in the context of disability has to do with making the human being behind the disability visible and extending the benefits of "the rule of law" to all and not just to some, or indeed to most.'[1] The core purpose of the CRPD is to promote equality and to ensure the full and equal enjoyment of all human rights and fundamental freedoms by all persons with disabilities. The CRPD exposes the essential interdependence of civil and political rights and economic, social and cultural rights, previously viewed as separate. It emphasises the need to break down barriers to the achievement of these rights for persons with disabilities. Disability rights have become a global challenge and in the European region, the European Union (EU) has ratified the CRPD to the extent of its area of competence. Article 26 of the Charter of Fundamental Rights of the EU refers to persons with disabilities and 'supports measures designed to ensure their independence, social and occupational integration and participation in the life of the community.'[2] In a growing number of legal actions the European Court of Human Rights (ECtHR) has referred to the CRPD as an important interpretative source.[3] Both the EU and the Council of Europe have disability action plans.[4] It is clear that the focus on disability has become much more concentrated at a variety of levels.

---

1 G Quinn, 'A Short Guide to the United Nations Convention on the Rights of Persons with Disabilities, in G Quinn and L Waddington (eds), *European Yearbook of Disability Law* (Vol 1, Intersentia, 2009) 90.

2 available at <http://www.europarl.europa.eu/charter/pdf/text_en.pdf> last accessed October 10, 2016.

3 *Kiss v Hungary* (App No 38832/06) 20 May 2010; *Kiyutin v Russia* App No 2700/10 (ECtHR, 10 March 2011; *Stanev v Bulgaria* App No 36760/06 (ECtHR, 17 Jan 2012); *DD v Lithuania* App No 13469/06; *MH v United Kingdom* (App No 11577/06) 22nd October 2013.

4 The Disability Action Plan for the EU is set out in COM/2003/650. The Council of Europe plan is found in the Committee of Ministers of the Council of Europe, Recommendation Rec (2006)5 '*on the Council of Europe Action Plan to promote the rights and full participation of people with disabilities in society: improving the quality of life of people with disabilities in Europe 2006–2015*', 5 April 2006.

At the core of the CRPD, in Article 12, is the key right to the recognition of legal capacity. Legal capacity is essential to opening up all other rights to persons with disabilities and to safeguarding decision-making and destiny. The importance of legal capacity is recognised by Quinn who said that 'the legal tool of capacity ... helps to secure notions of personhood ... allows for an expression of the will ... opens up zones of personal freedom ... facilitates uncoerced interactions.'[5] The denial of legal capacity affects a disproportionate number of people who are prevented from making decisions and who are often in a continuous cycle of disempowerment and invisibility.[6] This impacts on many fundamental rights including the right to liberty, to consent to treatment, and to control and manage one's own money and property. Each of these deprivations lead to a further cascade of intrusions on autonomy, so the space of self-determination can be extremely narrow. The ECtHR equates the right to legal capacity as 'at least equally important' as the right to liberty.[7] Reform of capacity law, the protection of autonomy and the right to make one's own decisions are among the challenges currently facing policy makers and legislators who must 'envisage an alternative to the cognitive approach to legal capacity, particularly since it remains central to guardianship regimes.'[8]

The principle of equality and the mandate to mainstream the human rights of persons with disabilities underpins the CRPD. Article 1 provides an illustrative description, rather than a definition, that persons with disabilities are 'those who have long-term physical, mental, intellectual or sensory impairments which in interaction with various barriers may hinder their full and effective participation in society on an equal basis with others.' The focus is on equality and the 'interaction with various barriers' requiring society to remove the barriers to 'full and effective participation,' highlighting the social construct of disability. This shift from a reliance on a narrower medical model, focusing solely on fixing the person to fit society, towards a social and human rights model which focuses on removing barriers to inclusion and opening up society, is fundamental in order to achieve equality. The challenges regarding the detention and forced medical treatment of persons with psychosocial disability are particular evident in this regard.

The ECtHR has begun to refer to the CRPD as an authoritative interpretative aid in a number of cases, although this is unpredictable and the extent of influence is not yet clear.[9] First acknowledged by the ECtHR in 2009, the CRPD was referred to

---

5 G Quinn, 'Personhood & Legal Capacity Perspectives on the Paradigm Shift of Article 12 CRPD' (HPOD Conference, Harvard Law School, 20 February 2010). <www.nuigalway.ie/cdlp/staff/gerard_quinn.html > last accessed 31 March 2016.

6 Mansell et al suggests a figure of 1.2 million in institutions in the EU and Turkey, excluding Germany and Greece. J Mansell and others, *Deinstitutionalisation and Community Living – Outcomes and Costs: Report of a European Study Volume 2: Main Report* (University of Kent 2007) 25. In addition, EHRLR 1 estimates that 80 million Europeans live with a disability. T Hammarberg, *Disability rights: from charity to equality* (2011). O Lewis estimates upwards of 2.5 million people live in residential institutions for disabled people. O Lewis, 'Stanev v Bulgaria: On the Pathway to Freedom' (2012) 19(2) Human Rights Brief 7.

7 *Shtukaturov v Russia* App No 44009/05 (ECtHR, 27 March 2008) para 71.

8 M Bach and L Kerzner, 'A New Paradigm for Protecting Autonomy and the Right to Legal Capacity' (Law Commission of Ontario 2010) 1, 9. B McSherry, 'Legal Capacity under the Convention on the Rights of Persons with Disabilities' (2012) 20 Journal of Medical Law 22, 25.

9 *Kiss v Hungary* App No 38832/06 (ECtHR, 20 May 2010); *Kiyutin v Russia* (App No 2700/10) 10 March 2011; *Stanev v Bulgaria* App No 36760/06 (ECtHR, 17 Jan 2012) in which the

'as the basis for the existence of a European and universal consensus on the need to protect persons with disabilities from discriminatory treatment.'[10] Since then, the denial of legal capacity has led to more challenges being taken under the ECHR, highlighting the widespread restrictive practices and profound negative impact of the automatic removal of legal capacity.[11] A significant number of States Parties to the ECHR are also parties to the CRPD, supporting a growing consensus among these countries that disability rights must be promoted, protected and fulfilled.[12] At domestic level in both English and Irish case law there is evidence of some awareness and acknowledgement of the CRPD.[13]

In recognition of the needs of millions of people whose lives are blighted by wholly negative substitute decision-making systems, like plenary guardianship or wardship, both law and policy reform are required. This chapter considers the requirements of Article 12 of the CRPD and identifies areas of commonality with the ECHR as well as areas of incompatibility that must be addressed.

2. Article 12 and Legal Capacity

Legal capacity was first mentioned in the Convention on the Elimination of Discrimination Against Women 1979, although the right to equal recognition before the law was provided for in the UN Declaration of Human Rights and the International Covenant on Civil and Political Rights.[14] Now Article 12 of the CRPD presents an unprecedented shift in the traditional understanding of legal capacity and personhood.[15] Dhanda comments that disability and the 'reality of difference can be accommodated in this new paradigm of universal legal capacity.'[16]

Essential to an understanding of law and policy reform is the realisation that legal

majority failed to examine the core legal capacity issue; *DD v Lithuania* App No 13469/06 (ECtHR, 14 February 2012). *Campeanu v Romania* (2014) ECHR 789; *Ivinovic v Croatia* (Application No 13006/13) 18 September 2014. See also E Flynn, 'Cases on Denial of Legal Capacity to Persons with Disabilities' Human Rights in Ireland, 1 May 2012) http://humanrights.ie/mental-health-law-and-disability-law/echr-cases-on-denial-of-legal-capacity-to-persons-with-disabilities last accessed 31 March 2016.

10 *Glor v Switzerland* App NO 13444/04 (ECtHR, 30 April 2009), para 25; Part 11 *Annual Review of European Law and Policy* 'The Council of Europe' 253. The recognition of disability as included in 'other status' in art 14 was significant, indicating an expansion of the law on reasonable accommodation. Despite Switzerland not having signed the CRPD it was referenced for the first time indicating the emerging consensus.

11 *Shtukaturov* (n 7); *Stanev* (n 3); *DD* (n 3).

12 J Clifford, 'The UN Disability Convention and its Impact on European Equality Law' (2011) 6 Equal Rights Review 21.

13 *MX (APUM) v HSE* [2012] IEHC 491, *AH v West London Mental Health Trust & Secretary of State for Justice* [2011] UKUT 74(AAC).

14 art 15, www.un.org/cedaw 9 October 2014.

15 A Dhanda, 'Legal Capacity in the Disability Rights Convention: Stranglehold of the Past or Lodestar for the Future?' (2007) 34 Syracuse Journal of International Law and Commerce 429–462; A Kämpf, 'Involuntary Treatment Decisions: Using Negotiated Silence to Facilitate Change?' in B McSherry and P Weller (eds), *Rethinking Rights-Based Mental Health Laws* (Oxford 2010).

16 A Dhanda, 'Universal Legal Capacity as a Universal Human Right' in M Dudley, D Silove and F Gale (eds), *Mental Health and Human Rights, vision: praxis, and courage* (Oxford 2012) 179.

capacity and mental capacity are distinct concepts, although they have been conflated in legislation in many jurisdictions, so where a person is believed to have impaired capacity this results in a denial of legal capacity. The CRPD presumes legal capacity with the emphasis on support for the person with decision-making difficulties. The concept of legal capacity in Article 12 is two-fold: it means the ability to hold rights and duties along with the freedom to exercise these rights and duties. Mental capacity focuses on the decision-making and communication skills of a person, which, universally, vary from one person to another. The General Comment on Article 12 states that 'perceived or actual deficits in mental capacity must not be used as justification for denying legal capacity.' [17]

The guiding principles of the CRPD focus on inherent dignity, autonomy, and freedom to make one's own choices and participate fully in society without discrimination due to disability. Direct and indirect discrimination are prohibited and reasonable accommodation is unequivocally incorporated into the non-discrimination requirement of the CRPD. These are essential elements in the effort to ensure that human rights are enjoyed by disabled people 'on an equal basis with others.'[18] Reasonable accommodation is defined as 'necessary and appropriate modification and adjustments not imposing a disproportionate or undue burden' to ensure equality.[19] Lawson refers to the duty to accommodate 'the specific circumstances of a particular disabled person by adjusting physical and organisational structures and practices.'[20] Normally this is a duty to take positive steps to remove barriers placing the person at a disadvantage compared to a non-disabled person. States are required to 'take all appropriate measures, including legislation, to modify or abolish existing laws, regulations, customs, and practices that constitute discrimination against persons with disabilities.'[21] In its Report on Austria the Committee on the CRPD recommended that supported decision-making structures must

> 'respect the person's autonomy, will and preferences, and be in full conformity with article 12 of the Convention, including with respect to the individual's right, in his or her own capacity, to give and withdraw informed consent for medical treatment, to access justice, to vote, to marry, to work and to choose his or her place of residence.'[22]

Lewis and others highlight the interdependent nature of all our lives stating that the 'CRPD is a declaration of interdependence; grounded in liberal individualism and it recognises that all our lives are pursued in conjunction with others.'[23] Dhanda comments that Article 12(2) 'reconstituted the person in the person with disabilities and underpinned the person as interdependent ...'[24] Against this background of principle and obligation, Article 12 starts with a presumption of legal capacity for all

---

17 General Comment No. 1 (2014) CRPD/C/GC/1, para 13.

18 A Lawson, 'Disability equality, reasonable accommodation and the avoidance of ill-treatment in places of detention: the role of supranational monitoring and inspection bodies,' (2012) 16 International Journal of Human Rights 6, 845.

19 art 2.

20 A Lawson (n 18).

21 art 4(1)(b) and (e).

22 UN Committee on the Rights of Persons with Disabilities (2014) *Concluding Observations of the Committee on the Rights of Persons with Disabilities Austria* CRPD /c/aut/co/1, para 28

23 O Lewis, 'Advancing legal capacity jurisprudence' (2011) 6 EHRLR 707.

24 A Dhanda, (n 16) 180.

persons with disabilities and the right to enjoy legal capacity on an equal basis with others in all aspects of life.[25] Article 12(3) requires States Parties to take appropriate measures to provide access by persons with disabilities to the support they may require in exercising their legal capacity. Measures relating to the exercise of legal capacity must respect the rights, will and preferences of the person and the state must provide safeguards to prevent abuse in accordance with human rights law.[26] The terms 'will and preference' are used to focus on the person in keeping with supported decision-making and the avoidance of what might resemble substitute decision-making in a 'best interests' approach.[27] Substitute decision-making systems, like guardianship, often the only response to a finding of incapacity, result in the automatic loss of a host of rights, effectively rendering the person legally invisible. There is considerable debate on whether substitute decision-making is ever acceptable under the CRPD.[28]

The recognition in Article 12 of an individual as a person who holds and exercises rights on an equal basis with everyone else is essential to living as one chooses and being part of the community. Article 19, for example, underpins this right to inclusive and independent living so that denial of legal capacity and choice is contrary to its provisions. Included in this article is the opportunity to make decisions that have a significant impact as well as decisions that are more basic but are core to quality-of-life decisions that are taken for granted by most people These are highly valued decisions about where and with whom to live, how to spend one's money and what health care decisions to make. It should be remembered, though, that physical change to the community is not sufficient to ensure inclusion; essential is choice equal to others to full inclusion and participation. The impact of a denial of legal capacity has a major impact on lives and means that basic choices concerning quality of life cannot be made by the person with the disability.

A not untypical scenario occurs when adults with intellectual disability are pressured to move into residential care as a perceived 'necessary protective measure' following the illness or death of an older parent. The reassurance of other family members or of well-meaning professionals trumps potential supports to remain in the familiar community to which the person belongs. In these circumstances the dominant position of service providers often assumes authority in decision-making and in the efficient management of the lives of people they support.[29]

Once an adult has been placed under guardianship, that person's guardian can, under current provisions in many jurisdictions, send the person against their will to a social care institution.[30] Some are in remote places, have poor conditions, allow no choice about any aspect of life and are often not subject to scrutiny.[31] An institution is defined by the European Coalition for Community Living as

---

25 arts 12(1) and (2).

26 art 12(4).

27 Ireland has adopted the 'will and preference' wording and omitted 'best interests' in its current proposals on legal capacity law reform in the Assisted Decision-Making (Capacity) Bill 2013.

28 A Kampf (n 15), A Dhanda (n 15), M Bach and L Kerzner (n 8), General Comment No 1 (n 17).

29 M Bach and L Kerzner (n 8).

30 Lithuania, Bulgaria and Ireland are examples.

31 Adults with an intellectual disability living in residential centres in Ireland have not yet benefited from an independent inspection and monitoring system although it is promised. This is despite

> '... any place in which people who have been labeled as having a disability are isolated, segregated and/or compelled to live together. An institution is also any place in which people do not have, or are not allowed to exercise control over their lives and their day to day decisions. An institution is not defined merely by its size.'[32]

Institutionalisation and guardianship are closely linked in some jurisdictions resulting in total social exclusion.[33] Detention in an institution can take place solely at the request of the guardian and without any independent control or judicial review, as well as under mental health laws. Review or restoration of legal capacity is controlled by the guardian or the institution. Closure of institutions is, therefore, an important policy priority to aid reform of legal capacity laws provided the alternatives are compliant with human rights standards.

One of the basic tools of freedom and participation in society is to access one's money and to decide how it is spent. Yet this is a frequently denied right, often informally, on the basis of perceived incapacity to make the 'right' decisions and in the interest of efficient management. The freedom to own, manage or inherit property or deal with financial matters is contained in Article 12(5). A key associated right is accessing justice but, without a high level of support from an NGO or a particularly insightful lawyer, this is often unavailable. Participation in the political life of the community as one of the markers of citizenship is expressed by most in the right to vote, and is supported in the CRPD.[34] This fundamental right is often denied to a person with a disability, or restricted based on nothing more than a presumption of incapacity to understand the issues involved due to a disability.[35] Often there are no criteria for this judgement and no formal recourse to challenge the decision. Rarely is that denial associated with a notion that support may be required to affect this fundamental right.

3. Mental Health Law

Recognition of legal capacity is important in mental health law where the right to liberty and bodily integrity are often denied on the basis of a range of justifications. Dhanda suggests a need to 'examine the prejudicial underpinnings of these justifications.'[36] She questions whether the impact of denial of capacity along with the availability of force and compulsion 'have impeded the capability development of the mental health profession, who due to the easy presence of force, have not felt the need to develop skills of dialogue, persuasion and understanding.' The detention and treatment of persons in mental health care is regarded as a form of

---

many reports pointing to the high levels of abuse of people with intellectual disabilities. See also Health Services Executive, *Report of the Working Group on Congregated Settings: Time to Move on from Congregated Settings: A Strategy for Community Inclusion* (Dublin, 2011).

32 European Coalition for Community Living< www.community-livinginfo/ > last accessed 31 March 2016.

33 *Shtukaturov* (n 7); *Stanev* (n 3); *DD* (n 3).

34 CRPD art 29.

35 *Kiss* (n 3).

36 A Dhanda (n 16) 187.

clinical guardianship where control rests, usually, with the consultant psychiatrist.[37] This denial of legal capacity for persons with psychosocial disabilities also leads to exclusion from the general safeguards against arbitrary detention under mental health law in many jurisdictions.[38] Persons admitted for mental health care as so-called voluntary or informal patients are frequently informally deprived of their legal capacity to consent to admission or treatment.[39] This is also true of people admitted to all manner of care facilities in the community.

Mental health laws that tend to rely on substitute decision-making, based on criteria permitting broad interpretation and long detention periods with limited or no review, have been the subject of criticism.[40] Some commentators have proposed that mental health laws violate the CRPD, particularly Articles 12 and 14, and that these laws should be abolished and replaced by consensual practices, with services 'based on a social model with room for medical support …'[41] Clearly this element will need to be given greater consideration due to the possible incompatibilities with Article 5(1)(e) of the ECHR. Phil Fennell suggests that what is required under the CRPD is dismantling the medical model of mental disorder and replacing it with a model based on psychosocial disability.[42] Arbitrary deprivation of liberty under Article 5 has been established in many cases, including persons who have been informally detained.[43] Such detention has frequently been a direct result of being in guardianship.

Article 5(1)(e), which permits the deprivation of liberty based on 'unsound mind,' appears to conflict with Article 14 of the CRPD. Article 14 provides for the liberty and security of the person in a somewhat similar way to Article 5(1)(e) of the ECHR, but then there is a clear difference stating '…that the existence of a disability shall in no case justify a deprivation of liberty.' The last sentence is key in terms of the incompatibility with the ECHR which permits detention on the grounds of 'unsoundness of mind.' The interpretation of Article 14 has further raised concerns particularly for states that are party to both the ECHR and the CRPD. A further challenge arises in the requirement for states to have ratified the ECHR in order to be members of the EU. The response of the CRPD Disability Rights Committee to these states will be important in understanding how conflicting obligations might be addressed.

Article 14 has been interpreted as requiring a disability-neutral approach to detention for mental health care and treatment. The interpretation by the Office of the UN High Commissioner for Human Rights in 2009 is forthright in stating that the Convention forbids 'deprivation of liberty based on the existence of any disability, including

37 Victoria Law Reform Commission, *Consultation Paper: Guardianship* CP 10, 2011.

38 Ireland, for example, has wardship legislation in Lunacy Regulations Act 1871 (Ireland). Wards are excluded from safeguards under the Mental Health Act 2001. Law reform is proposed.

39 The Irish Mental Health Act 2001 has a broad definition of 'voluntary' patient with no safeguards or support for persons with that status who have difficulty with making decisions.

40 A Kamphf (n 15), 145.

41 T Minkowitz 'Abolishing Mental Health Laws to Comply with the Convention on the Rights of Persons with Disabilities' in B McSherry and P Weller (eds) *Rethinking Rights Based Mental Health Laws* (Hart 2010) 151.

42 P Fennell, *Mental Health: Law and Practice* (Jordan 2011), para 2.86; P Fennel and U Khalik, 'Conflicting or complementary obligations? The UN Disability Rights Convention, the European Convention on Human Rights and English Law' (2011) 6 EHRLR 662.

43 *HL v United Kingdom* (2004) 40 EHRR 761 *Stanev* (n 3).

mental or intellectual, as discriminatory.'[44] The Council of Europe Commissioner for Human Rights commented on the continuing recognition of the exception to the right to liberty in Article 5(1)(e) of the ECHR permitting the detention of 'persons of unsound mind', justifying the limitation of legal capacity. This, he said, was evidence that 'the ECHR system has not fully incorporated the paradigm shift in Article 12 and the granting of a primary right to support in decision-making.'[45] This is a key challenge; Article 5 permits what the Victoria Law Reform Commission referred to as 'clinical guardianship' arguably like other forms of guardianship.[46] It is one of the starkest examples of a conflict with the intention of Article 14. In its report on Austria, and other jurisdictions, the Committee on the CRPD urged all necessary legislative, administrative and judicial measures to ensure that no one is detained against their will in any kind of mental health facility, and to develop de-institutionalization strategies based on the human rights model of disability. It stated that all mental health services should be based on free and informed consent with emphasis on community-based outpatient services.[47] It also recommended that states 'allocate more financial resources to persons with intellectual and psychosocial disabilities who require a high level of support, in order to ensure that there are sufficient community-based outpatient services to support persons with disabilities.'[48]

The approach to legal capacity in the CRPD is echoed in *Shtukaturov v Russia* and, like *Winterwerp v Netherlands*, untangled legal capacity from mental disorder, stating that '...the existence of a mental disorder, even a serious one cannot be the sole reason to justify full incapacitation.'[49] The ECtHR recognised the deprivation of legal capacity as a 'serious intrusion on the right to respect for private and family life' protected by Article 8, and necessitating a tailor-made response. The response of the Council of Europe Commissioner for Human Rights indicates that the interpretation of the ECtHR in *Shtukaturov* is in line with the CRPD.[50]

The automatic link between a loss of legal capacity and institutionalisation or deprivation of liberty in a social care home for people with psychosocial disabilities was established in the important case of *Stanev v Bulgaria*.[51] Despite the case arising as a result of deprivation of legal capacity the approach of the ECtHR in avoiding the Article 8 issues was surprising. The applicant, Mr Stanev was placed in partial guardianship without notice or participation, was deemed incapable of expressing

44 United Nations High Commissioner for Human Rights and Reports of the Office of the High Commissioner and the Secretary General, *Thematic Study by the Office of the United Nations High Commissioner for Human Rights on enhancing awareness and understanding of the Convention on the Rights of Persons with Disabilities* (A/HRC/10/48, 26 January 2009).

45 ibid 17, referring to Parliamentary Assembly Resolution 1642 in 2009 points explicitly in the direction of this shift.

46 Victoria Law Reform Commission (n 37)

47 UN Committee on the Rights of Persons with Disabilities (2014) *Concluding Observations of the Committee on the Rights of Persons with Disabilities Austria* CRPD /c/aut/co/1, paras 30, 31. Also Denmark CRPD/C/DN/CO/1, 30 October 2014 and Spain CRPD/C/ESP/CO/1, 19 October 2011.

48 UN Committee on the Rights of Persons with Disabilities (2014) *Concluding Observations of the Committee on the Rights of Persons with Disabilities Sweden* CRPD/c/SWE/CO/1 12 May 2014.

49 *Shtukaturov* (n 7) 94; *Winterwerp v Netherlands* (1979) 2 EHRR 387.

50 T Hammarberg, 'Persons with mental disabilities should be assisted but not deprived of their individual human rights' (Council of Europe, Viewpoint, 21/09 2009)

51 *Stanev* (n 3).

his wishes, and never met his first guardian who was later replaced by the director of the care home. Forced to live 'voluntarily' in the institution for eight years, he alleged he was arbitrarily deprived of liberty under Article 5(1)(e) with no means of leaving due to extreme isolation, lack of money and retention of his identity papers.[52]

Objectively, he made no decisions, and was subject to constant supervision and a strict daily routine, leading to a health deterioration, onset of institutionalisation and potential loss of ability to reintegrate in his community. Subjectively, he had not wanted to leave his home, had not been consulted, nor had he consented to the placement.[53] A psychiatric assessment in 2006 stated that he did not have schizophrenia and identified damage to his health by remaining in the home, stating that he was capable of re-integration in the community.

Affirming earlier statements in *Shtukaturov,* the ECtHR did not question the basis for his deprivation of legal capacity.[54] Mr Stanev's placement was based on out-of-date medical assessments, and there had been no assessment of his mental health and no review of his ongoing detention.[55] The Court believed he 'was well aware of his situation and ... at least from 2004 he had explicitly expressed his desire to leave the social care home ... to have his legal capacity restored and to be released from guardianship.'[56] The Court recognised the impact of the lack of support in that he was unable to challenge his status, and had no alternative measures, along with the failure to strike a fair balance between his social needs and his right to liberty. The Court reiterated its important statement on the right to liberty as

> '... too important in a democratic society for a person to lose the benefit of Convention protection for the single reason that he may have given himself up to be taken into detention especially when it is not disputed that the person is legally incapable of consenting to or disagreeing with the proposed action.'[57]

His detention was found to be a breach of Article 5(1) with no appropriate remedy available, and to be a breach of Article 5(4) involving the right to regular review of detention. Significantly, the finding of a breach of Article 3, which prohibits inhuman and degrading treatment, based on the eight years of appalling living conditions, followed a number of earlier negative independent reports,[58] one commenting that, 'in most cases, placement of people with mental disabilities in a specialised institution led to a *de facto* deprivation of liberty.'[59] The breach of Article 3 was the first to apply to a social care home and potentially broadens the scope to other community

---

52 *Stork v Germany* 43 EHRR 6.

53 His guardian signed the placement contract within six days of being appointed.

54 *Shtukaturov* (n 7) para 108.

55 *Stanev* (n 3) para 135.

56 ibid para 130.

57 *Stanev* (n 3); *HL v UK* (n 43) para 90.

58 Council of Europe Committee for the Prevention of Torture, *Report to the Bulgarian Government on the visit to Bulgaria carried out by the European Committee for the prevention of torture and inhuman and Degrading Treatment or Punishment* (CPT) CPT/Inf (2004); Amnesty International, Bulgaria, *Far from the Eyes of Society: Systematic Discrimination against people with mental disabilities* (2002) EUR 15/005/2002.

59 CPT Report 2004, (n 58), para 11.7 cited in *Stanev* (n 3), para 83; *Stanev* (n 3), para 85. A CPT report in 2006 identified the need for assistance with the contracts which should specify legal rights of residents and complaints systems.

residential centres.[60] Many efforts at deinstitutionalisation have resulted in extending the institutional mindset to the community; *Stanev* highlights obligations on the state to examine life in community facilities.[61] The subtleties of control and lack of personal choice are potentially more difficult to identify in community situations, requiring a rigorous approach to the recognition of legal capacity and ensuring a truly supportive environment.

The disconnect between the stance taken by the ECtHR on legal capacity and the refusal of the majority to examine the alleged violation of his Article 8 rights was striking and difficult to comprehend as the case was fundamentally about legal capacity.[62] The ECtHR stated 'it seems clear to the Court that if the applicant had not been deprived of legal capacity on account of his mental disorder, he would not have been deprived of his liberty', a statement regarded by Oliver Lewis as the most important statement in the decision. [63] A minority of judges dissented on the refusal to examine the Article 8 element and were strongly of the view that Article 8 was breached by failing to ensure that Mr Stanev's wishes and preferences, which he was capable of expressing, were respected. Judge Kalaydjieva recognised legal capacity as 'the primary issue' in the case. She stated:

> 'No justification was offered for the fact that Mr Stanev was stripped of the ability to act in accordance with his preferences to the extent determined by the courts and the law and that instead of the due assistance from his officially appointed guardian, the pursuit of his best interests was made completely dependent on the goodwill or neglect shown by the guardian. In this regard the lack of respect for the applicant's recognised personal autonomy violated Mr Stanev's right to personal life and dignity as guaranteed by Article 8 and failed to meet contemporary standards for ensuring the necessary respect for the wishes and preferences he was capable of expressing.'[64]

The judge was outspoken about access to justice as a result of being dependent on the guardian, referring to

> '... the failure to subject to separate scrutiny the absence of safeguards for the exercise of these rights in the face of a potential or even evident conflict of interests, a factor which appears to be of central importance for the requisite protection of vulnerable individuals against possible abuse and is equally pertinent to the applicant's complaints under Article 8 and Article 6.'[65]

---

60 It is also the first time that the ECtHR examined detention in non-prison or psychiatric facility – this could have a much broader impact than at first thought.

61 D Doherty and ors, *Happy Living Here, An Evaluation of community residential mental health services* (2007) Mental Health Commission and Health Research Board < http://www.mhcirl.ie/File/happylivinghere.pdf > last accessed October 10, 2016.

62 L Nelson, 'DD v Lithuania, Mental Health and Mental Capacity Law' <www.mentalhealthandcapacitylaw.worldpress.com/2012/03/22>, last accessed 31 March 2016. L Nelson was one of the lawyers representing Mr Stanev and was the Litigation Director of the MDAC; O Lewis, 'Stanev v Bulgaria: On the Pathway to Freedom' (2012) 19 Human Rights Brief, Issue 2–7 referring to *Stanev* (n 3) Para 154.

63 O Lewis (n 62) 2–7.

64 *Stanev* (n 3) partly dissenting opinion of Judge Kalaydjieva, 41.

65 ibid.

The apparent distancing of the majority from addressing the legal capacity concerns directly would appear to be at odds with Article 12 of the CRPD and the requirement of safeguards against exploitation. However, the decision is regarded as significant

> '... for the rights of thousands of persons with psychosocial disabilities and intellectual disabilities throughout Europe and whether the Court is willing to broaden its approach in acknowledging the CRPD in terms of the international standards and engage with the paradigm shift of the CRPD.'[66]

The reluctance of the Court was evident when it resisted commenting on whether, 'any placement of a legally incapacitated person in a social care institution constitutes a "deprivation of liberty" within Article 5.1' and limited its decision to the facts of the case.[67] Nelson comments that the Court's

> '... explicit limitation seems to deny the systemic nature of involuntary placement of persons with psycho-social and intellectual disabilities in institutions and of the inter-relationship between guardianship and institutionalisation even though the facts before it clearly arose from systemic practices... [and] avoided the larger question of States' obligations to ensure that persons with psycho-social disabilities and intellectual disabilities have choices equal to others in all aspects of life.'[68]

The commentary from this decision exposes the real tensions arising from the failure to address the deprivation of legal capacity. The Council of Europe Commissioner for Human Rights made a strong recommendation to end 'voluntary' placements of persons in closed wards and social care homes against their will but with the consent of a guardian and that such placements 'should always be considered a deprivation of liberty...'[69]

4. Access to Justice

The lack of any right of appeal and review of guardianship, based on the total control of the guardian or the lack of an effective appeal system, breaches Article 6 of the ECHR and the right to a fair trial. Opposition to the restoration of legal capacity can pose difficulties even where expert support is available.[70] The ECtHR reiterated that the right to ask a court to review a declaration of incapacity is one of the most important rights for the person concerned and any restrictions on access to court must be justified. Access to court to challenge a finding of legal incapacity 'is one of the fundamental procedural rights for the protection of those who have been partially deprived of legal capacity.'[71] The Court has strongly supported the

---

66 L Nelson, (n 62).

67 *Stanev* (n 3).

68 L Nelson (n 62). Similar issues arose in *DD v Lithuania* (n 3).

69 Commissioner for Human Rights, *Who Gets to Decide? Right to legal capacity for persons with intellectual or psychosocial disabilities* (Council of Europe 2012).

70 *Shtukaturov* (n 8); *Stanev* (n 3); *Zehentner v Austria* App no 20082/02 (ECtHR, 16 July 2009) concerning the loss of applicant's home due to partial guardianship; *Dudarev v Latvia* App No 28621/10 (ECtHR, 14 June 2011) para 19.

71 *Stanev* (n 3), para 241.

'right of effective access to a mechanism' enabling a person lacking capacity to challenge the lawfulness of a deprivation of liberty.[72] Access to justice is strongly supported in Article 13 of the CRPD.

5. Impact of Loss of Legal Capacity

A profound loss of control and loss of self-esteem is experienced following deprivation of legal capacity. Being deemed incapable followed by the removal of control over one's own life is increasingly seen as a 'social and legal harm'[73] to that person involving 'harmful side effects.'[74] It also removes the opportunity to learn the very decision-making skills that may have been necessary to avoid being deprived of legal capacity in the first place. To offset such consequences Donnelly advocates a view of autonomy as achievement which she regards as more in keeping with the view of autonomy in the CRPD and proposes

> '... a legal framework for autonomy... concerned with issues such as the adequacy of choice and with the development of autonomy-building measures aimed at enhancing individual agency and affecting a shift in decision-making power to the individual.'[75]

A wide range of research, ongoing for many years, indicates that feelings of control are crucial to our outlook in life, a fact that has been consistently ignored by the law. Fox, a neuroscientist, suggests that 'if we have a real sense that we control our destiny, this not only helps us bounce back from setbacks but also maximises our enjoyment of life.'[76] Fox refers to the deceptively simple Arden House study in the 1970s, worth recounting here as a reminder of how choice and control impact in the long-term.[77] The purpose of the study was to examine whether the inability of nursing home residents to make decisions was caused by the lack of control over their environment. Two separate groups of residents were each given the same tasks of minding a plant and watching a weekly film. One group was allowed to choose their own plant, decide when to water it and choose the time of the film; in the second group staff chose and watered the plants and decided on the film night. Returning after 18 months, the researchers found the people given the choices were happier and healthier than the second group, in which twice as many people had died. In the context of the highly controlled environments of institutions and some community settings these and other findings are useful.[78]

---

72 *MH v United Kingdom* (n 3).

73 M Bach and L Kerzner (n 8) 7.

74 A Dhanda (n 16) 180.

75 M Donnelly, *Healthcare Decision-Making and the Law: Autonomy, Capacity and the Limits of Liberalism* (Cambridge 2010).

76 E Fox, *Rainy Brain Sunny Brain* (London 2012) 190.

77 J Rodin and E Langer, 'The Effects of Choice and Enhanced Personal Behaviourality for the Aged: A Field Experiment in an Institutional Setting' Journal of Personality and Social Psychology (1976) 191.

78 European Union Agency for Fundamental Rights, *Choice and control: the right to independent living-Experiences of persons with intellectual disabilities and persons with mental health problems in nine EU Member States 2012* available at Luxembourg Publications Office of the European Union.

6. Supported Decision-Making

Article 12 represents the most significant change of approach to decision-making, from substitute decision-making to supported decision-making. Support to make decisions is a central element in Article 12(3), but is no more than a reflection of the norm and does not compromise a person's legal capacity. Dinerstein defines supported decision-making as 'a series of relationships, practices, arrangements, and agreements, of more or less formality and intensity, designed to assist an individual with a disability to make and communicate to others decisions that the person chooses to make.'[79] Bach and Kerzner refer to supports to exercise legal capacity including: life planning, independent advocacy, communicational, interpretive, representational and relationship-building.[80] Some commentators hold that substitute decision-making may be seen as a last resort as long as all practicable steps are taken to support decision-making using advocacy, advance decisions or lasting powers of attorney.[81] Opposing views believe supported decision-making measures only should apply.[82]

Assessment of a person's capacity for decision-making may be contrary to the universality principle of the presumption of legal capacity and the shift to the supported decision-making approach. A number of assessment approaches have been traditionally used in the attribution of legal incapacity. The status or stereotyping approach presumes that a person with a particular type of disability lacks legal capacity; the outcome approach is based on the actual decision which is regarded as 'irrational' based on the expectation or disagreement of the assessor; and the functional test is based on a person's cognitive ability to meet a particular standard in 'understanding and appreciating' the nature of the decision having been given appropriate information.

Ordinarily, in arriving at a significant decision people discuss the issues with family and friends, seek clarification to assist in understanding and appreciating consequences in so far as one can, before making the decision. The functional approach is regarded as more acceptable by providing for a tailor-made approach to determining capacity, reflected in recent reforms of capacity law.[83] This may conflict with the intention of Article 12 and universal legal capacity on the basis of equality with others. Without recognition of the need for support, the functional approach may ensure continued exclusion and denial of legal capacity. The test of rationality does not take account of factors in decision-making like emotion, environment and intention. The Council of Europe Commissioner for Human Rights commented on the functional approach as having 'given too little attention to the importance of support. [It] may yet have a future not as a yardstick by which to withdraw capacity

---

79 R Dinerstein, 'Implementing Legal Capacity Under Article 12 of the UN Convention on the Rights of Persons with Disabilities: The Difficult Road From Guardianship to Supported Decision-Making' (2012) 19 Human Rights Brief, Issue 2, 10.

80 M Bach and L Kerzner, (n 8), 74.

81 A Kamphf, (n 15), 140; P Fennell and U Khaliq, (n 42), 672.

82 A Dhanda (n 15); T Minkowitz 'Legal Capacity: Fundamental to the Rights of Persons with Disabilities' (2007) 56 International Rehabilitation Review 1, 25, General Comment No 1 (n 17). See also P Gooding 'Supported Decision-Making: A Rights Based Disability Concept and its Implications for Mental Health Law.' Psychiatry, Psychology and Law, 22 August 2012, DOI: 10.1080/13218719.

83 *Shtukaturov* (n 7); Mental Capacity Act 2005 England and Wales; proposed Assisted Decision-Making (Capacity) Bill 2013 in Ireland.

[...] but rather as a measure to help determine what type of supports should be made available.'[84] Dhanda refers to the 'objective evaluation of the competence of a person with disabilities and the rejection of the subjective in doing so' and asks 'how can we reconcile self determination with a determination by someone else ... the only justification for having any determination is for the "practical needs of social functioning."'[85]

Bach and Kerzner propose reformulating the functional test or the 'understand and appreciate' test, describing instead three distinct decision-making statuses.[86] The first is a legally independent status, where the person understands information and appreciates the consequences of the decision, and is able to communicate that understanding and intention to a third party understandably and free of coercion. Support in making the decision would not affect their legally independent status.

The next level involves being in a supported decision-making status where a recognised representative knows the person's will and intention and represents this in decisions. Minkowitz makes the point that '[m]aking support available without the loss of autonomy can make it easier for people to acknowledge a need for support and accept such support if desired.' She comments that '[s]upport can only merit the name when it is truly voluntary and when those providing support understand their role as facilitative rather than directive, that is as an adjunct to the person's own decision-making process rather than as a central participant in that process.'[87] Ensuring people have opportunities to have trusting relationships with others is a key element to the success of this status.[88]

The third level is for a facilitated decision-making status at the level where a person is unable to communicate and there is little to indicate their 'will and intention.' There may be evidence of a person's wishes in an advance directive or a lasting power of attorney. Otherwise a facilitator would construct a view of what the person would have wished based on the narrative of her or his life. Where no information is available for the person a principle of 'best interests' would apply, which should be clearly defined to focus on the person's quality of life.[89]

The use of the best interests principle is contentious due to its entrenched negative association with paternalism. Shifting from the perceived certainty of guardianship or control towards the perceived lack of certainty in relying on a construction of the person's intention is one of the most challenging elements for legislators and policy makers. The key difference in a facilitated decision-making approach is that the person retains legal capacity, unlike current guardianship/wardship. Different levels of oversight would necessarily form part of the system.

---

84 Commissioner for Human Rights (n 69) 10.

85 A Dhanda (n 16) 181.

86 M Bach and L Kerzner (n 8) 83.

87 T Minkowitz (n 41) 158.

88 E Flynn and A Arstein-Kerslake, 'Legislating Personhood: Realizing the Right to Support in Exercising Legal Capacity' (2014) 10 International Journal of Law in Context 1, 81–104.

89 M Bach and L Kerzner (n 8) 98. See C O'Mahony, 'Legal capacity and detention: implications of the UN disability convention for the inspection standards of human rights monitoring bodies' (2012) 16 International Journal of Human Rights 6, 883.

7. Safeguards

The risk of abuse of vulnerable adults even when guardianship systems are in place is well-documented.[90] Article 12(4) of the CRPD requires 'appropriate and effective safeguards to prevent abuse … respect the rights, will and preferences of the person…' The real cause of risk is the absence of appropriate community services and supports. Often the focus is on abuse in institutions with less attention paid to the paucity of community supports.[91] Positive obligations under the ECHR require prevention of abuse and exploitation.

Respect for human rights safeguards apply independently of legal capacity status. Violations of many of these rights have been raised in relation to persons with disabilities, including access to essential economic and social activities, an appropriate range of recreational and cultural activities, and the prohibition on discrimination. Specific obligations arise in relation to: the prohibition on torture, inhuman and degrading treatment in Article 3; freedom from arbitrary removal of liberty in Article 5, including the right to information in Article 5(2); the right to a fair trial in decisions concerning civil rights in Article 6; and, importantly, the right to respect for private life in Article 8, including rights to consent to treatment and to uphold dignity.[92] Access to the ECtHR to complain depends on access to legal representation often from an NGO, such as MDAC, rather than supported by the state through legal aid.[93] In an analysis of the success in affirming the rights of persons with a mental health disability, the ECHR was found to be better in protecting against unwarranted interferences with liberty and treatment rather than ensuring equal access to treatment and care.[94]

The right to respect for private life in Article 8 has as its core the recognition of legal capacity. The preservation of mental stability is, in that context, an indispensable precondition to effective enjoyment of the right to respect for private life.[95] Included is the right to dignity, identity and personal development, and the right to communicate and develop relationships with the outside world. These are some of the essential elements of an ordinary life as compared with life in the controlled and isolated environment of an institution.[96] The ECtHR has affirmed the equal importance of the deprivation of legal capacity with the right to liberty.[97] Legal

---

90 C. Cooper, A Selwood and G Livingston, 'The Prevalence of Elder Abuse and Neglect: A Systematic Review' (2008) 37 Age and Ageing 151; C. Naughton and others, *Abuse and Neglect of Older People in Ireland: Report on the National Study of Elder Abuse and Neglect* (Dublin 2011).

91 L Clements, 'Disability, dignity and the cri de coeur' (2011) 6 *EHRLR* 675–785.

92 *Price v United Kingdom* (2002) 34 EHRR 1; Stanev (n 3); *Winterwerp* (n 49); *Pretty v United Kingdom* (2002) 35 EHRR 1; *HL* (n 44) *Storck* (n 53); *Bensaid v United Kingdom* (2001) 33 EHRR 205; *Botta v Italy* (1998) 26 EHRR 241.

93 G Niveau and J Materi, 'Psychiatric Commitment: Over 50 years of case law from the European Court of Human Rights' (2007) 22 European Psychiatry 59. Of 118,000 decisions 108 concerned psychiatric commitment. The study concluded that access to the ECtHR depends on the level of democracy and legal assistance from NGOs. Mental Disability Advocacy Centre www.mdac.info. Since the introduction of the CRPD challenges to the removal of legal capacity have increased.

94 T Kallert, 'Coercive Treatment in Psychiatry' 342 in M Dudley, D Silove, F Gale (eds) (n 9).

95 *Bensaid (*n 92)

96 *Stanev* (n 3)

97 *Shtukaturov* (n 7).

capacity restrictions must be proportionate to comply with the ECHR, and full incapacity, as in plenary guardianship or wardship, does not meet this requirement.[98]

Denial of legal capacity can lead, for example, to an absolute ban on the right to vote in some jurisdictions. The applicant in *Kiss v Hungary,* who was in partial guardianship due to mental illness, alleged a violation of his right to vote based on Article 3 of Protocol 1 of the ECHR.[99] The Court held the ban 'constituted an unjustified deprivation of his right to vote, which was not susceptible to any remedy…'[100] Referring to the absolute bar from voting by anyone under guardianship, the important statement by the Court has broader application

> … if a restriction on fundamental rights applies to a particularly vulnerable group in society, who have suffered considerable discrimination in the past, such as the mentally disabled, then the State's margin of appreciation is substantially narrower and it must have very weighty reasons for the restrictions in question…The reason for this approach, which questions certain classifications *per se*, is that such groups were historically subject to prejudice with lasting consequences, resulting in their social exclusion. Such prejudice may entail legislative stereotyping which prohibits the individualised evaluation of their capacities and needs.[101]

A higher bar is applied to people with disabilities based on the status approach and the presumption of incapacity arising from a disability.[102] National authorities accept the historical position on voting that only those capable 'of conscious and judicious decisions' and resisting undue influence are permitted to vote.[103] The influence of emotion on voter behaviour, well established in research, challenges the adoption of these restrictions widely held in domestic law.[104] Being readily identified as having a disability has disadvantages and clearly places persons with disabilities in a wholly unequal position contrary to the intent of the CRPD.

---

98 *Drobnjak v Serbia* App no36500/05 (ECtHR, 13 October 2009); Shtukaturov (n 7).

99 *Kiss v Hungary* (n 3).

100 *Hirst v United Kingdom* App No 74025/01 (ECtHR, 6 October 2005) and *Kiss* (n 3) para 18. The court did not rule out the possibility of deprivation of this right in certain circumstances.

101 *Kiss* (n 3) para 42; The European Union Agency for Fundamental Rights (FRA) *The right to political participation of persons with mental health problems and persons with intellectual disabilities* (2010) < www.fra.europa.eu/ fraWebsite/attachments/Report-vote-disability_EN>. The report established that 17 Member States exclude persons with intellectual disabilities and mental health problems from political participation.

102 T Hammarberg, (n 70) in which the Council of Europe Commissioner for Human Rights stated, '… persons with mental health and intellectual disabilities should have the right to vote in elections and stand for election. Though this is stated clearly in the CRPD, individuals in a number of European countries are excluded. Being deprived or restricted of their legal capacity they have been denied these rights as well. This has further exacerbated their political invisibility.'

103 Kiss (n 3) para 38.

104 T Brader, 'Striking a Responsive Chord: How Political Ads Motivate and Persuade Voters by Appealing to Emotions' (2005) 49 (2) American Journal of Political Science 388–405. Brader demonstrates that political ads can change the way citizens get involved and make choices by using images and music to evoke emotion. T Grisso and ors, 'The McArthur Treatment Competence Study II: Measures of Abilities Related to Competence to Consent to Treatment' (1995) 19 Law and Human Behaviour 127. Research carried out on the capacity of people in general hospital care indicates many lacked capacity but their decision-making abilities are generally not questioned.

8. Challenges: Consultation and Communication

Communication and sharing information are crucial in ensuring satisfactory decision-making and choice. A positive obligation to inform arises in Article 5(2) of the ECHR which safeguards the right to information in the specific area of the right to liberty, while Article 8 safeguards the right to informed consent. Different levels of communicational support are required ranging from basic explanations to having a representative fully informed to act on the person's will and preferences. Accessible communication, as required in Article 21 of the CRPD, is referred to as 'the first step' in making sure that persons with disabilities are enabled to exercise legal capacity, and is core to the support obligation in Article 12(3).[105] Accessible information is a support that can be tailored to a particular context and 'not restricted but used in practice by lawyers, health professionals, bankers, judges and court personnel in situations where legal capacity is being exercised, and training should be provided for this purpose.'[106]

The CRPD provides at Article 4(3) that the views of people with disabilities, including children, must be consulted in order to achieve equality. It should be clear that, without involvement,

> 'persons with disabilities will inevitably be burdened with laws and procedures that do not account for their individual experiences and that reproduce the paternalistic approach that has sustained historic disadvantage.'[107]

The UN Special Rapporteur on the Right to the Highest Standard of Physical and Mental Health highlighted that 'the right of persons with mental disabilities to participate in decision-making processes that affect their health and development, as well as in every aspect of service delivery, is an integral part of the right to health.'[108] He emphasised the importance of the involvement of persons with mental disabilities 'at all stages of the development, implementation and monitoring of legislation, policies and programmes and services relating to mental health and social support, as well as broader policies and programmes.'[109] He includes family members as having an important contribution to make in these areas also.

An example of positive consultation is found in the Fundamental Rights Agency (FRA) report on *Choice and Control: the right to independent living,* which used interview-based research in nine EU Member States with persons with intellectual

---

[105] Minkowitz (n 41). Article 21 includes a reference to the right to information on an equal basis with the general public in an accessible formal and appropriate for different disabilities.

[106] See, for example, *Making Your Decisions,* a partnership project involving people with intellectual disabilities, students and academic staff at the Centre for Disability Law and Policy, School of Law, NUI Galway, as an example of easier-to-read information that will be useful not only to people who use services but to the frontline staff who support them <www.nuigalway.ie/cdlp/>. Contact makingyourdecisions@gmail.com.

[107] J. Clifford (n 12).

[108] P Hunt, 'Annual Report to the Human Rights Commission by the UN Special Rapporteur on the right of everyone to the enjoyment of the highest attainable standard of physical and mental health' (2005) in O Lewis and N Munro 'The Right to Participation of People with Mental Disabilities in Legal and Policy Reforms' 589 in M Dudley, D Silove, F Gale (eds) (n 16).

[109] ibid.

and mental health disabilities.[110] The findings provide 'a platform to those individuals whose voices are seldom heard' and provides invaluable information on how the 'lives of individuals are affected by laws and policies, or by the lack of them.'[111] This direct-consultation method is an important measure in influencing policy makers and legislators.

At a different level, the ECtHR has a growing practice of accepting 'third party interventions' or *amicus curiae* briefs.[112] As a result, civil society organisations have had a new opportunity to intervene in the 'interests of justice.'[113] Coomber comments on this 'growing window of exceptional importance to European level disability NGOs interested in advancing the engagement of the Court in this field.'[114] This approach adds value to the requirement of consultation in Article 4(3) of the CRPD.

9. Conclusion

Legal capacity recognition is relatively new territory, although recent decisions of the ECtHR indicate a growing awareness of the importance of the CRPD as an interpretative source. The emerging principles around legal capacity, the decisions of the ECtHR, and developments at EU level, indicate a growing recognition of CRPD obligations, while significant concerns remain. One of these is the use of disability criteria for detaining persons with mental health problems and the prohibition on such practice in the CRPD. This poses a significant challenge for legislators and policy makers to upend such long-held practices. Recognition of the substitute decision-making practices involved are at the core of such concerns. Such practices and associated attitudes have remained unchallenged in any formal sense, so the demand for reform is fragmented at an early stage and necessitates guidance.

Positive indicators come from the ratification of the CRPD by the EU along with the growing number of countries in the Council of Europe region addressing law reform. The Council of Europe recommends supported decision-making alternatives to guardianship.[115] The European Union Agency for Fundamental Rights has examined aspects of the CRPD and provided comparative analysis of the legal frameworks of EU Member States against current international and European legal standards, making recommendations for change.[116] Dhanda insightfully maintains that '[t]he paradigm of the CRPD is up against the barrier of the mind' requiring significant

110 European Union Agency for Fundamental Rights, *Choice and control: the right to independent living – Experiences of persons with intellectual disabilities and persons with mental health problems in nine EU Member States 2012*, available at Luxembourg Publications Office of the European Union.

111 ibid.

112 Rule 44 of Rules of the ECtHR.

113 Examples are in *DD v Lithuania* (n 3) para 12 by the European Group of National Human Rights Institutions and the Harvard law School Representatives; *Kiss v Hungary*, (n 3) para 34; *Stanev* (n 3).

114 A Coomber, Part 11 Annual Review of European Law and Policy, 'The Council of Europe' (Intersentia 2010) para 2.2.

115 Council of Europe Commissioner for Human Rights (n 69).

116 European Union Agency for Fundamental Rights, *The Right to Political Participation of Persons with Mental Health Problems and Persons with Intellectual Disabilities* (n 101).

changes in attitude and practice.[117] Action must be taken to ensure awareness of disability rights at all levels, to enable and empower people with disabilities to be centrally involved in driving change in order to avoid the fragmentation and inappropriate laws and policies that have beset past reforms.

---

[117] Dhanda (n 16) 185.

CHAPTER 8

LEGAL CAPACITY: ALTERNATIVES TO FUNCTIONAL CAPACITY

Tina Minkowitz

People with disabilities, along with children, remain the last vestige of those who may be consigned to the status of dependent wards. Modernising reforms in legal capacity have created a presumption of capacity that applies to all adults,[1] so that the mere fact of disability does not entail being treated as 'naturally and legally incapable,' an automatic equation of disability with incapacity still in force in some jurisdictions.[2] However, the criteria for determining that someone lacks capacity almost always include disability as a decisive factor. Older persons with age-related disabilities are a large and growing population at risk of being deprived of their legal capacity.[3]

Disability can be a threshold criterion (e.g. note the titles of relevant laws in UK and Scottish: 'Mental Capacity Acts')[4]. Disability can be the underlying substantive meaning of incapacity itself, for example in definitions of functional or transactional capacity as the 'ability' to understand and appreciate the nature and consequences of a legal act[5] – an adult who failed to demonstrate this ability to the satisfaction of a person who questions it (and who is recognised as having the authority to make such a determination) would be treated as a person with an intellectual, psychosocial or cognitive disability.

Even if a law is facially neutral, disability is generally understood to be the underlying issue – it is hard to imagine that legal incapacity on grounds of poor education or lack of familiarity with local customs would be acceptable under the International Covenant on Civil and Political Rights, for example. Laws permitting restriction of legal capacity on grounds of dissipation may be an exception to this.[6] Provisions allowing nullification of legal acts on a showing that one party exploited the other's need, recklessness or experience to obtain an unjustified financial benefit,[7] on the

---

1 NY MHL art 81; cf NY SCP art 17A.

2 Ibero-American Network of Experts on the United Nations Convention on the Rights of Persons with Disabilities, 'First Report on the Existing Legal Situation Regarding the Legal Capacity of Persons with Disabilities in the Member States of the Network' (Mar de Plata, Argentina, 21 March 2011).

3 Report of the United Nations High Commissioner for Human Rights, E/2012/51 (20 April 2012) IV.B.

4 Mental Capacity Act 2005 (UK MCA) 2; Adults with Incapacity Act 2000 1(6) (Scotland).

5 UK MCA 3; see also Health Care (Consent) and Care Facility (Admission) Act [RSBC 1996] Ch 181 (BC, Canada).

6 P Varul, A Avi and T Kivisild, 'Restrictions on Active Legal Capacity' (2004) Juridica International IX 99.

7 Cod. Civ. Art. 954 (Arg 1871).

other hand, do not appear to be incapacity laws and can be admitted in a framework of support.

Even before the Convention on the Rights of Persons with Disabilities (hereafter CRPD), a number of jurisdictions had adopted measures for supported decision-making and other means of legally expressing autonomy, intentionality and individuality in situations where there are challenges to creating or ascertaining contract-like decisions. Recognition of support relationships and direct provision of support services mean greater freedom and autonomy, particularly for persons with intellectual disabilities who may have gone directly into guardianship upon reaching adulthood.[8] Designating a relationship as one of support places a duty on the supporter to inquire into the person's own choices and facilitate carrying them out. Advance directives and powers of attorney allow a person to document choices to be followed if it becomes difficult to communicate effectively, to share responsibility for financial tasks, to rely on a chosen advocate in health care settings, and to prepare for the future by considering and planning for anticipated needs.[9]

Practices of support developed by people with psychosocial disabilities have not focused on legal mechanisms. The emphasis has been on avoiding the adverse legal actions of coercive mental health treatment and civil commitment through a combination of support and advocacy that respects the person's worldview and makes a space to 'sit with discomfort' while moving toward the state of affairs the person desires.[10] Advance directives and powers of attorney are used defensively within an incapacity-based system, but generally cannot prevent involuntary admissions. The German Living Will is an exception that allows a person to refuse medical assessment as well as treatment, and is promoted by a group of lawyers and NGOs as effective in preventing involuntary hospitalisation and other restrictions of freedom as well.[11]

In the context of a legal system where capacity is a rebuttable presumption, ie one that allows 'incapacity' to be proven and assigned as a status, advance directives and powers of attorney, while beneficial, can be unduly restrictive. Once a determination of incapacity is made, the person's choices expressed in the present cease to be treated as meaningful. Only the autonomy, intentionality and individuality of the person's past is legally relevant, although a caring and trustworthy supporter acting as agent can fulfil the person's wishes expressed in the present if given that scope in the instrument. Similarly, support services and relationships that exist alongside substituted decision-making arrangements, as is the case with all the innovations described by Herr, are constrained by the potential for restriction of autonomy that still exists in the system. Legal capacity remains a privilege rather than a right as applied to persons with disabilities, and the loyalty of supporters is

8 S S Herr, 'Self-Determination, Autonomy, and Alternatives for Guardianship' in S S Herr, L O Gostin, and H H Koh (eds) *The Human Rights of Persons with Intellectual Disabilities* (Oxford University Press 2003).

9 L Ziegler, 'Upholding Psychiatric Advance Directives' in P Stastny and P Lehmann (eds), *Alternatives Beyond Psychiatry* (2007) [ABS].

10 S Mead, 'Intentional Peer Support: An Alternative Approach' (2005/2007/2008); M Jesperson, 'Personal Ombudsman in Skåne,' in ABS (n 9).

11 Civil Code ss 1896 and 1901 (FRG); 'Advance Medical Directive (pursuant to § 1901 a German Civil Code),' < www.patverfue.de/cms-96TK/media/patverfue-en_neu.pdf> last accessed 31 March 2016.

necessarily compromised if they are empowered to declare that support has failed and substitution is needed.

The Committee on the Rights of Persons with Disabilities has established a simple standard with regard to Article 12 in early jurisprudence: the obligation is to replace substituted decision-making regimes with supported decision-making, which respects the person's autonomy, will and preferences.[12] This standard nicely encapsulates the expectations of the disability community from Article 12[13] and as such enjoys both popular legitimacy and authoritative legitimacy from the body designated to interpret the CRPD in its practical applications. In order to explore what such a standard might mean in practice, this chapter will examine one law reform proposal in detail and contrast it with two others.

A recent law reform proposal prepared by the Centre for Disability Studies at NALSAR University of Law in Hyderabad, India, takes Article 12 as its starting point and substantially complies with that standard.

The NALSAR proposal has appeared in three guises: as amendments to the National Trust Act, a law providing for support and guardianship for people with developmental disabilities (hereafter "NTAA");[14] as part of the draft Rights of Persons with Disabilities Act (hereafter "RPDA1");[15] and in a revised version of the draft RPDA (hereafter "RPDA2").[16] As of this writing, it had not yet been introduced in the legislature.

The approach taken is to adapt the CRPD provisions to function in domestic law. Rather than attempting to review and repeal every inconsistent law, it is established that persons with disabilities have legal capacity on an equal basis with others notwithstanding any other provision of law.[17] In addition, the version in RPDA1 declares as void 'any legislation, rule, notification, order, by-law, regulation, custom or practice that deprives any person with disability of their legal capacity' and RPDA2 furthermore voids 'any act, order or proceeding that has the effect of depriving a person with a disability of legal capacity or which questions the legal capacity of a person with disability on the grounds of disability'; both versions

---

12 Concluding Observations of the Committee on the Rights of Persons with Disabilities: Spain, CRPD/C/ESP/1 (2011) para 34; Concluding Observations of the Committee on the Rights of Persons with Disabilities: Peru, CRPD/C/PER/1 (20 April 2012) para 25.

13 International Disability Alliance CRPD Forum, 'Principles for Implementation of CRPD Article 12' (2007) < http://social.un.org/ageing-working-group/documents/egm/Article12.pdf > last accessed 31 March 2016.

14 'A proposal to amend the National Trust for Persons with Autism, Cerebral Palsy, Mental Retardation and Multiple Disabilities Act of 1999 and to rename it the Legal Capacity and Support Act 2010 (Draft for Discussion)' https://d3gqux9sl0z33u.cloudfront.net/AA/AG/chrusp-biz/downloads/113281/Final_draft_NT_Amdment-02-03-2010.doc. last accessed 31 March 2016.

15 'Working Draft of the Rights of Persons with Disabilities Act, 2010' (Center for Disability Studies, NALSAR University of Law, Hyderabad, India) [RPDA1].

16 'The Rights of Persons with Disabilities Bill, 2011' (Center for Disability Studies, NALSAR University of Law, Hyderabad, India 30 June 2011) [RPDA2].

17 NTAA (n 14), s 12A (1); RPDA1 (n 15), s 7A (1); RPDA2 (n 16), s 18(1).

provide for a complaint remedy.[18] RPDA2 adds a specific guarantee of the financial rights of persons with disabilities as specified in Article 12 (5).[19]

RPDA2 provides for limited guardianship, defined as 'a limited system of joint decision-making which operates on mutual understanding and trust between the guardian and the person with disability.'[20] All plenary guardianships would be replaced by limited guardianships, and 'limited guardians shall act in close consultation with the person with disability to arrive at legally binding decisions.'[21] Read together with the provision that voids any acts or proceedings that have the effect of depriving an individual of legal capacity, it appears that the person would have a remedy against such guardianship being ordered or undertaken against his or her will.

All versions address the provision of support, the establishment of safeguards and the rights of third parties by setting out broad principles and creating mechanisms for further elaboration and functioning of the system. Individuals have a right to access required support in accordance with their own will and preferences, and governments have duties to both mobilise community support arrangements and to take particular measures to put in place support for persons living in institutions or who need to have high levels of support, as well as to assist those exiting from plenary guardianship to set up support arrangements other than limited guardianship, and assisting those currently in a limited guardianship to set up suitable support.[22] NTAA and RPDA1 give examples of support arrangements, providing for 'registration of advance directives, recognition of support networks, registration of enduring powers of attorney, terms of appointment of a personal assistant or any other suitable mechanism of customary law or community practice by which support can be effectively provided to a person with disability.'[23]

Safeguards are addressed in NTAA and RPDA1 by creating mechanisms to solicit feedback from support recipients on its suitability and usefulness, and whether they desire any modification or addition to it, and to conduct awareness-training and sensitisation programs.[24] RPDA2 omits a general feedback mechanism and provides for review only of how the system of deemed limited guardianship is working for persons with disabilities.[25]

Further safeguards against the abuse of support are provided by the following: prohibiting the denial or questioning of legal capacity due to the person's accessing support; prohibiting the exercise of undue influence by supporters and requiring them to respect the person's autonomy, dignity and privacy; and requiring supporters to abstain from providing support in a particular transaction in respect of which a conflict of interest exists (conflict cannot be presumed from the existence of a

18 RPDA1 (n 15), s 7A(2) and (11); RPDA2 ss 18(2) and 21.
19 RPDA2 (n 16), s 18(3).
20 RPDA2 (n 16), s 19.
21 ibid.
22 NTAA (n 14), ss 12A (4), 12B and 12C (1); RPDA1 (n 15), ss 7A (5) and (6), 7B, 7C and 7D (1); RPDA2 (n 16), ss 18(4) and 20.
23 NTAA (n 14), s 12A(8); RPDA1 (n 15), s 7A(12).
24 NTAA (n 14), s 12C(2) and (3); RPDA1 (n 15), s 7D(2) and (3).
25 RPDA2 (n 16), s 20(c).

relationship of blood, affinity or adoption).[26] A person receiving support can change or dismantle a support relationship and replace it with another.[27] RPDA1 emphasises that no person with a disability shall be obliged to seek support.[28]

The system protects the rights of third parties by ensuring that alteration of support arrangements is prospective and does not nullify third-party transactions entered into with such support.[29]

With respect to health care decisions, legal proceedings and other areas of life in which legal capacity is exercised the NALSAR proposal is silent, except as the RPDA drafts may provide for these rights separately under other rights. Both versions of RPDA recognise a right to freedom from civil commitment while not yet abolishing it entirely,[30] in this area falling short of the standard in CRPD Article 14. RPDA1 states that 'no person shall be deprived of personal liberty only on the ground of disability' this is corrected in RDPA2 which also calls for phasing out of civil commitment through review of all cases and re-organisation of the care and treatment of persons with disabilities, as well as development of programmes for community-based non-violent conflict resolution and promotion of respect for diversity.[31]

While phasing out civil commitment is a progressive step, and goes farther than any country has to date, the continuation of coercive measures for any period of time is unwarranted and constitutes a human rights violation. In contrast to the situation with limited guardianship, the proposal to phase out civil commitment does not have any clear remedy for an individual who does not wish to be subjected to these measures.

It is possible that the remedy against measures that have the effect of depriving any person of legal capacity could be used to exit civil commitment. However, this may depend on how civil commitment is understood in domestic law, for example whether it is treated as a matter of health or as a security measure, and on the degree to which informed consent in health care is protected as a legal right. Both RPDA drafts treat informed consent as an ethical obligation rather than a legal one,[32] and neither includes protection against forced mental health interventions under respect for physical and mental integrity. RPDA1 mentions as a form of violence placing a person in an institution or subjecting the person to an intervention or invasive treatment with electric current, chemicals or other techniques;[33] however, the provision requires intent to cause harm, so that the application of electroshock or psychotropic drugging against the person's will that is seen by the perpetrator as a therapeutic treatment would be in doubt. In this respect, the NALSAR proposal falls short of both the CRPD and standards promulgated by the Special Rapporteur on Torture.

---

26 NTAA (n 14), s 12A (3), (5) and (6); RPDA1 (n 15), s 7A (7), (8) and (9); RPDA2 (n 16), s 18 (5), (6) and (7).

27 NTAA (n 14), s 12A (7); RPDA1 (n 15), s 7A (10); RPDA2 (n 16), s 18(8).

28 RPDA1 (n 15), s 7A (2).

29 NTAA (n 14), s 12A (7); RPDA1 (n 15), s 7A (10); RPDA2 (n 16), s 18(8).

30 RPDA1 (n 15), s 10 (5)(b); RPDA2 (n 16), s 23 (5)(b).

31 RPDA1 (n 15), s 10(3); RPDA2 (n 16), s 23(3) and (6).

32 RPDA1 (n 15), s 21B; RPDA2 (n 16), s 67.

33 RPDA1 (n 15), s 13 ((1)(a)(iii).

The NALSAR proposal can be seen as creating a national framework for implementation of Article 12, and, with the reservations just mentioned (which could be corrected in subsequent initiatives), it is a worthy one. It does not attempt to resolve all issues that may arise, but sets out the parameters within which resolution must take place. It leaves such resolution to the complaint mechanism and to the mechanisms for promoting and providing access to support and reviewing such support. Support is treated as a practical matter of creating appropriate relationships for this purpose, and substituted decision-making arrangements would be ended or phased out of existence. The system is designed to be user-friendly and accessible, bringing legal capacity closer to ordinary life and eliminating barriers while maintaining the essential nature of law and legal acts as binding and certain.

While it may be argued that the devil is in the details and that NALSAR only postpones grappling with difficult questions, it may be wisest to proceed in this way, from the broad principles of the CRPD to the creation of a framework and mechanisms in national law, to the operation of those mechanisms in a context of new values. By creating a new system and providing for it to replace the old one, social and legal institutions as well as customs and practices are compelled to change. Forms of thought can follow as people begin to cooperate in the exercise of legal capacity and mutual safeguarding of autonomy, beginning with persons with disabilities and taking on wider relevance.

The NALSAR proposal can be usefully compared with a framework for legislation proposed by the Canadian Association for Independent Living ("CAIL") in 1992.[34] The CACL framework intended to make a complete paradigm shift and create an alternative system through enabling legislation, and pioneered an understanding of interdependent decision-making that respects the legal capacity of all individuals – for example, insisting that 'no individual should be assessed to determine his or her competency.'[35] However, it takes pains to assure us that the conventional understanding of what is required to give legitimacy to legal acts is not being disturbed.

For example, CACL notes that 'a model must be developed that respects informality while providing enough formality and certainty to give it legitimacy from the point of view of third parties (for example, doctors, bankers, service providers, etc.)' and in that vein sets out a procedure for steps to be followed in order that legal validation attach to specific decisions.[36] The approach of making room for people with disabilities within a discriminatory legal framework is captured in this paragraph on contractual decision-making:

> 'The law is a barrier to participation. Nevertheless, we recognise that legal tests requiring the need to understand the terms of a contract meet a legitimate economic and social goal of making people accountable for the contracts they enter into. We recognise that contract law cannot be completely re-written.

---

34 'Report of the CACL Task Force on Alternatives to Guardianship' (August 1992) [CACL].

35 CACL (n 36) pt III (ix)

36 CACL (n 36), pt V 'Procedural Framework for Supported Decision-Making'

> Yet the law must accommodate people with disabilities so they can participate in this aspect of social and economic life.'[37]

Much of the CACL framework remains valuable as a way of envisioning how support might function. But in catering to third parties who doubt the legitimacy of decision-making by persons with disabilities, CACL maintains a deferential stance towards the existing system and may limit innovation. The perspective shifts from that of the person with disability seeking inclusion, to that of the doubter questioning whether inclusion is possible.

The CACL framework has not been faithfully enacted into law, while British Columbia has enacted a Representation Agreement Act 1996 that recognises supported decision-making, while retaining substituted decision-making as a parallel system.[38] The innovation is to allow for a lower threshold of competency to enter into a support arrangement than that which is required for other legal acts, and then to provide that decisions made under such an arrangement can be recognised as legally valid.[39] Contrary to the CACL framework, capacity tests are a central feature. Other objectionable elements include the potential to give a durable permission for restraint and other coercive acts,[40] and the exclusion of any authorisation to refuse consent to mental health services and admission made compulsory under the Mental Health Act 1996.[41]

Later initiatives based loosely on this framework have abandoned the premise of respect for individual will and preferences, and opted for a graduated incapacity system aimed at assigning individuals to 'appropriate' decision-making statuses: independent, supported and facilitated.[42] Whereas in the original CACL proposal the Public Facilitator was an office designated to provide interim support (imperfect, because it could not be said to be based on a relationship of trust) until the individual could develop true support relationships, 'facilitation' is now used as a virtual euphemism for substituted decision-making.[43]

A proposal introduced by deputies of the Costa Rican Legislative Assembly, the Proyecto de Ley Autonomía de las Personas con Discapacidad ("PLA"), is an alternative approach based on treating support for legal capacity as a service, such as personal assistance. The PLA creates a large-scale government programme to provide various forms of support for the exercise of autonomy.[44] It repeals the laws of interdiction and guardianship,[45] while maintaining the government's obligation to resolve questions concerning the capacity to act[46] and retaining the mechanism

---

37 CACL (n 36), pt VI 'Supported Contractual Decision-Making.'

38 Representation Agreement Act (RSBC 1996) ch 405.

39 RAA (n 40), ss 3, 4, 8, 13, 15, 19.

40 RAA (n 40), ss 9(1) and 9.1(a).

41 RAA (n 40), s 11.

42 M Bach and L Kerzner, 'A New Paradigm for Protecting Autonomy and the Right to Legal Capacity: Prepared for the Law Commission of Ontario' (October 2010) [New Paradigm] pt III.

43 Bach and Kerzner, New Paradigm (n 44), pt VI.D.3 and VI.E (in particular).

44 Proyecto de Ley Autonomía de las Personas con Discapacidad (2009) [PLA] chs III, IV, V, VII, VIII.

45 PLA (n 46), ch IX ss II Art 86 and VIII Art 94.

46 PLA (n 46), ch I art 4 (h).

to nullify legal acts if found to have been performed by a person who lacked the volitional or cognitive capacity to consent in relation to the specific act.[47] It has been pointed out that there are many grounds for alleging that one's capacity was compromised, including force, fear, threat, ignorance and deceit, so that lack of capacity does not exclusively refer to disability.[48]

The PLA lacks a comprehensive legal framework to ensure recognition of the legal capacity of persons with disabilities without discrimination of any kind. Such a guarantee could be inserted into Article 4 on state obligations, for example; the purpose of the law (to promote, protect and ensure the autonomy of persons with disabilities)[49] is broad enough to encompass anti-discrimination as well as obligations related to the creation and functioning of support.

A distinction between private and public responsibilities,[50] and definition (negotiation) of the boundaries between them, may be appropriate to clarify the author's preference for the NALSAR approach overall. In the course of the CRPD negotiations and subsequently at conferences, proponents of a robust public responsibility have often urged explicit recognition and regulation of substituted decision-making, saying that it will happen anyway, in the name of support or informally, and that it is better to provide safeguards both on the transition from support to substitution, and on the conduct of substitute decision-makers. The International Disability Caucus ("IDC"), on the other hand, advocated both complete equality and recognition of interdependence, recognising that it is impossible to police the transition from support to substitution without negating the person's autonomy, since this requires a complete outsider acting as representative of a supervening authority to decide not only when as a matter of fact the transition has occurred but also when it must occur.[51] Members of the IDC found it helpful to illustrate with a concrete example: 'If I am in a coma and then come out of it, I don't need to go to court to get my legal capacity back.'

As we now know even in the physical sciences, there is no such thing as neutral observation that has no effect on the system on being observed: the determination of incapacity creates a new situation independent of the person's expression of will and choices in any given moment. Besides being faulty epistemologically, a public responsibility that fails to recognise its limitations can negate the private space that inheres in each person and that gives rise to subjectivity, which is the value that gives rise to an institution in which individuals can create and modify legal relationships.

The public responsibility is to recognise the legal validity of the exercise of autonomy by all individuals irrespective of disability, and to ensure the availability of support, as well as reasonable accommodation and accessible information and communication, to make the exercise of legal capacity most effective and meaningful. This dual responsibility reflects the principle of formal equality plus substantive

47 PLA (n 46), ch IX ss VII art 91 and VIII art 93.

48 Personal communication by Rodrigo Jiménez to the author, 'Comentarios de Tina' (2008).

49 PLA (n 46) ch I art 1.

50 A similar distinction in relation to prevention of suicide was suggested in a personal communication by Piers Gooding to OzMad email group (18 June 2012).

51 World Network of Users and Survivors of Psychiatry, 'Advocacy Note on Legal Capacity' (2005).

equality.[52] Neither one alone is sufficient; without formal equality, substantive equality is not equality but paternalism. Without substantive equality, formal equality is a mockery that does not take account of diversity.

The private responsibility of supporters is to develop relationships based on trust and to work with the person to meet their particular needs in relation to exercising legal capacity; whether it be to explain legalese or medicalese, to fill in forms, to advocate with service providers, even to make certain decisions while checking in to ascertain that it is what the person wants. The development of trust is key, and may well be the most difficult part of supported decision-making in many situations.[53] It is also difficult to police and regulate beyond the basic standards of avoiding conflict of interest and refraining from undue influence.

Regulating the boundary between private and public responsibilities is the role of safeguards under Article 12 paragraph 4. As a boundary, there should be some negotiation or mutuality between the public and private, rather than having safeguards function purely as public responsibility.

The NALSAR approach functions very much along these lines, which can be understood also as incorporating a new paradigm of legal capacity into the method and mechanisms for dealing with legal capacity, and even into the implementation process. The paradigm is democratic in that it requires continual consultation, feedback and participation by persons with disabilities and by all members of the community acting in solidarity.

With a view to prospective law reform initiatives elsewhere, the following might be considered as a starting point based on lessons drawn in this chapter. The legislation adheres to a perspective of solidarity between persons with disabilities and their communities. Concepts, language, mechanisms and the process of development of the legislation itself should be subject to continual reflection in this regard. The fundamental premise that persons with disabilities have the right to having legal capacity on an equal basis with others is stated explicitly in legislation. The legislation provides that any laws, customs, practices, orders and proceedings that have the effect of depriving any person of legal capacity on the basis of disability or of questioning a person's legal capacity on the basis of disability; and it creates a complaint remedy for such deprivation.

The legislation establishes a programmatic framework for promoting the creation of support networks, promoting the establishment of services for cultivation of personal autonomy and expression, and providing particular attention to individuals who have need of high support and those needing to leave institutions; also creating a mechanism for individuals to provide feedback as to how support is working for them and whether they desire any change or addition to the support.

The legislation prohibits discrimination based on a person's use of support to exercise legal capacity. Supporters are obligated to respect the will and preferences, autonomy,

---

52 T Minkowitz, 'Legal Capacity and Psychosocial Disability' (Proyecto Dignidad International Seminar, Buenos Aires 10–11 May 2012).

53 A12 Principles (n 13), para 4.

dignity and privacy of the person they are supporting; exercise of undue influence by supporters is prohibited and supporters are obligated to refrain from providing support in any transaction in respect to which they have a conflict of interest with the person whom they are supporting.

All collateral areas involving an exercise of legal capacity, including health care decisions and personal liberty, are fully guaranteed in accordance with Article 12 and standards found elsewhere in CRPD. The legislation creates processes and mechanisms for implementation and feedback, with active engagement by persons with disabilities and their communities to consider periodically how the system is working and whether any further legislation, regulation or other activities may be needed.

CHAPTER 9

SUPPORTED DECISION-MAKING INNOVATIONS: THE CANADIAN EXPERIENCE

Lana Kerzner

1. INTRODUCTION

Canada's decision-making laws have attracted much international notoriety, especially during the negotiation, coming into force and international implementation efforts in relation to the Convention on the Rights of Persons with Disabilities (CRPD). Indeed, British Columbia's Representation Agreement Act 1996 ("RAA") was selected as an outstanding example of good policy in an international study on the implementation of the CRPD.[1] The United Nations Handbook for Parliamentarians on the CRPD, too, states that British Columbia is 'one of the leading jurisdictions in incorporating supported decision-making into law, policy and practice.'[2] British Columbia is but one of a number of Canadian jurisdictions whose laws recognise supports for decision-making. This chapter explores the unique features of Canada's supported decision-making laws. The purpose of which is to answer the following questions: what features of Canada's laws are a guiding light? What can other jurisdictions learn from Canada's supported decision-making innovations?

Recognition of the role played by supports in decision-making is progressively permeating Canada's legal landscape. Over the past 15 years legislative models of supported decision-making have gradually been erupting in Canada. This trend has been buttressed by decisions of the Supreme Court of Canada recognizing the interplay between and significance of the rights to autonomy and legal capacity. In *Starson v Swayze,*[3] the Supreme Court of Canada stated that '[u]nwarranted findings of incapacity severely infringe upon a person's right to self-determination.'[4] With specific reference to supports, the Ontario Court (General Division) stated that '[i]t is to be remembered that mental capacity exists if the appellant is able to carry out her decisions with the help of others.'[5]

1 *Zero Report* 9 and 160–161, online: http://www.bclaws.ca/civix/document/id/complete/statreg/96405_01

2 *Handbook for Parliamentarians on the Convention on the Rights of Persons with Disabilities*, online: http://www.un.org/disabilities/default.asp?id=212

3 *Starson v Swayze*, 2003 SCC 32, [2003] 1 S.C.R. 722. The Supreme Court also advanced the value to be placed in autonomous decision-making in *Nova Scotia (Minister of Health) v J.J.*, 2005 SCC 12, [2005] 1 SCR 177

4 *Starson v Swayze* (2005) SCC 12, [2003] 1 SCR 722 at 759.

5 *Koch (Re)* (1997) 33 OR (3d) 485 (Gen. Div.) 521. Also see the following decisions, which recognize the role of supports: *Clark v Clark*, (1983) 40 OR (2d) 383; *Kacan v Ontario Public Service Employees Union* (2010) HRTO 795, File No. 2008-00381-I at para. 22, and *Gray v Ontario* [2006] OJ No. 266 at para 47.

Nonetheless, this trend is far from complete in Canada if Article 12 of the CRPD is taken as the benchmark. This chapter describes tools that Canadian legislation employs which recognize supports for decision-making and makes some observations about existing gaps, with recommendations aimed to guide law and policy reform in jurisdictions in the process of implementing Article 12.

2. Canada's Capacity Laws: Supported Decision-Making in Context

Laws in Canada that have implications for whether, and to what extent, an individual has the right to exercise his or her legal capacity form a complex web of both legislation and common law. Legislation includes laws specific to decision-making, adult protection and mental health Acts.[6] Consistent with Canada's Constitution, each Canadian province and territory is responsible for its own laws relating to capacity, decision-making and mental health.[7] There is no uniform law across Canada. This means that a review of Canadian laws in these areas requires examining each jurisdiction's individual laws.

Additionally, there are some spheres of activity that have their own, unique capacity requirements which are separate from broader decision-making laws. Some legislation addresses capacity as a necessary but ancillary component of their scheme eg legislation which requires a level of capacity to act as a director of a corporation[8] or give evidence in court.[9] A common law articulation of what it means to be capable in certain circumstances also governs some aspects of people's lives. For example, Canadian courts have articulated tests specifically relating to capacity to enter into a contract,[10] make a will[11] and get married. However, the legislative articulation of capacity tends to be clearer than the common law, as it is not always possible to discern from jurisprudence a clear common law approach to capacity.

In addition to transaction-specific laws, each Canadian jurisdiction has legislation that covers decision-making broadly. Rather than focussing on specific types of transactions, it regulates generally the ways in which people exercise their legal capacity. Commonly, guardianship, planning documents, such as powers of attorney and consent to health care, are covered. These laws specify what it means to be

---

6 Both adult protection and mental health Acts in Canada have implications for whether, and to what extent, an individual has the right to exercise his or her right to make decisions. These types of legislation, in general, can both be said to be inconsistent with art 12.

7 Legislation in Canada is governed by the Constitution, which includes both the distribution of legislative authority between the federal and provincial/territorial parliaments and the Canadian Charter of Rights and Freedoms. In general, the power to legislate with respect to legal capacity issues falls within provincial and territorial jurisdiction as a result of the division of powers established under the Constitution Act 1967, s 92(13). Canadian Charter of Rights and Freedoms, Pt 1 of the Constitution Act 1982, being Sch B of the Canada Act (1982) (UK) 1982, c 11. Explanatory Memorandum on the United Nations Convention on the Rights of Persons with Disabilities, Tabled before the House of Commons, Parliament of Canada, December 2009, online: http://www.chrc-ccdp.ca/pdf/memorandum_ratification_note.pdf. Mental health Acts are also the responsibility of provincial and territorial governments.

8 Business Corporations Act R.S.O. 1990, c B.16, s 118(1).

9 Evidence Act R.S.O. 1990, c E 23, s 18.

10 G H L Fridman, *The Law of Contract* (5th edn, Carswell 2006) 158; *The Canadian Encyclopedic Digest* (4th edn, vol 12, Carswell 2010) 727, para 175.

11 *Brydon* v *Malamas* [2008] BCJ No. 1179, (2008) BCSC 749 paras 47–50.

'capable' and have the legal right to make one's own decisions, describe how people can choose, in advance of incapacity, substitute decision-makers for themselves, and the process and rules relating to the appointment of a substitute decision-maker by a court or other legal authority (often referred to as 'guardianship'). Many statutes in Canada define capacity in relation to a person's cognitive functioning ie having the status of being considered capable is determined based on a person's own ability to understand information and appreciate the consequences of making a decision.

Legislation in some Canadian jurisdictions also provide for supported decision-making. The manner in which this is achieved is also unique to each jurisdiction, although commonalities exist. That said, substitute decision-making continues to predominate and there is not a single Canadian jurisdiction that has abandoned it. Further, many provinces/territories do not provide for any recognition of supports or do so only minimally, such as New Brunswick, Ontario and Prince Edward Island. This mosaic of decision-making options is here to stay, although likely with a shift towards greater emphasis on supported decision-making over time, consistent with Article 12 and Canada's reservation and declaration in relation to the CRPD.

3. Canada and Article 12 of the CRPD

Canada signed the CRPD on 31 March 2007 and ratified it on 11 March 2010. Canada's ratification of the CRPD included a declaration and reservation, which is of particular relevance to Article 12. Canada's declaration and reservation makes it clear that there is an intention to maintain both substitute and supported decision-making in its legal framework. Canada interprets Article 12 as securing supported decision-making as a right while ensuring that availing oneself of supports does not undermine his or her full legal capacity. It has taken the position that, while not prohibiting substitute decision-making regimes,[12] Article 12 places particular emphasis on the importance of supported decision-making.[13]

There has been much discourse about the recognition of supported decision-making found in the CRPD, but the wording of Article 12 does not give specific and clear direction to States Parties as to how to operationalise the right to exercise legal capacity on an equal basis, and as to the State's duty to provide access to supports to exercise legal capacity. Adopting legislation as a means of implementation is a specific requirement of the CRPD.[14] Given the challenge of advancing supported decision-making from a conceptual idea to the clarity required for implementation, each State Party, in its implementation efforts, should inform itself of all laws internationally that recognize supports for decision-making.

In what ways do Canadian laws incorporate supported decision-making? Has Canada fully implemented Article 12? While Canada provides plenty of examples from which to learn, this chapter illustrates that there is no single piece of Canadian legislation, on its own, that meets all of the criteria in Article 12. However, if the

---

12 A Dhanda, 'Legal Capacity in the Disability Rights CRPD: Stranglehold of the Past or Lodestar for the Future?' (2007) 34:2 *Syracuse Journal of International Law & Commerce* 429, 460–461.

13 ibid 455–456.

14 CRPD, art 4(1)(a) and (b).

aspects of supported decision-making found in the various pieces of legislation were combined, one could create legislation that might come closer to meeting the requirements of Article 12. The following sections describe the methods by which supports for decision-making are legally recognized in Canada.

4. Recognition of Supports and Supported Decision-Making in Canadian Legislation

Supports and supported decision-making are recognized in Canadian laws by three broad methods:

1. Supporters are recognized to assist with decision-making by way of:
   a.) legislation which allows an individual to create a planning document appointing support people to assist him or her with decision-making;
   b.) legislation which allows a court to appoint support people to assist an individual with decision-making; and
   c.) the legislated role of third parties to facilitate and encourage the use of supports in decision-making.
2. Legislation which creates a role for the government in providing or arranging for the provision of supports
3. Legislative requirements not to appoint a guardian or co-decision-maker if less-restrictive alternatives exist, including supports.

5. Notable Features of Supported Decision-Making in Canadian Legislation

5.1 Supporters are Recognized to Assist with Decision-Making

5.1.1 Supported Decision-Making Planning Documents

Yukon, British Columbia and Alberta each have legislation that provide for the creation of supported decision-making planning documents. These allow an individual to create a document in which he or she grants legal authority to others to help him or her make decisions. Yukon's Adult Protection and Decision-making Act 2003 describes their purpose as follows:

> (a) to enable trusted friends and relatives to help adults who do not need guardianship and are substantially able to manage their affairs, but whose ability to make or communicate decisions with respect to some or all of those affairs is impaired; and
> (b) to give persons providing support to adults under paragraph (a) legal status to be with the adult and participate in discussions with others when the adult is making decisions or attempting to obtain information.[15]

British Columbia's Representation Agreement Act is perhaps the best-known model for these types of documents. This is partly because it was the first piece of

[15] Adult Protection and Decision-Making Act 2003, s 4.

Canadian legislation to recognize them.[16] Additionally, the RAA is well known for the extent to which disability organizations and seniors' groups played a role in its development.[17] People's knowledge and use of provisions is enhanced by Nidus Personal Planning Resource Centre & Registry (Nidus)[18] which continues to play a pivotal role in supporting and educating people about representation agreements as a tool for supported decision-making.

British Columbia's Representation Agreement Act is also unique for the manner in which capacity is addressed. The test to determine whether an adult is incapable of making a Representation Agreement involves consideration of four factors, including a desire to have the representative help make decisions and consideration of whether there is a trusting relationship between the adult and representative.[19] This test recognizes the shades of grey inherent in capacity and is a more flexible approach than the most commonly used statutory test in Canada, which requires an assessment of an individual's ability to understand information and appreciate the consequences of a decision.

Yukon, as well as Alberta, also have legislative provisions which allow people to create supported decision-making planning documents. A significant distinguishing feature between the planning documents in British Columbia, Yukon and Alberta is the type of decisions that they can cover. Supported decision-making planning documents in Yukon have a broad coverage. An adult can authorize a support person to help make decisions with respect to his or her 'affairs', which includes activities of daily living and other personal matters, health care, legal matters and financial affairs.[20] British Columbia's form of planning document, known as Representation Agreements, can only cover routine management of financial affairs, personal and some health care decisions. Alberta's supported decision-making authorizations cover personal matters only.[21]

5.1.2 Court Appointment of Support People

When someone is able to make decisions with supports, in addition to supported decision-making planning documents, supporters can be imposed on them by a court appointment. This contrasts with planning documents where an individual himself or herself chooses his or her own supports. The provinces of Alberta, Quebec and Saskatchewan each have legislation which recognizes court appointment of decision-making support, assistance or advice. The term 'co-decision-making' is used in both Alberta and Saskatchewan, but without a consistent meaning. In Quebec, a court

---

16 The Representation Agreement Act was first enacted in 1993 and came into force in February, 2000.

17 Representation Agreement Resource Centre and Nidus eRegistry, 'BC's Representation Act for Assisted Decision-making: Is It Meeting A Need?', Handout produced for workshop at Canadian Conference on Elder Law (October, 2005).

18 The Nidus Personal Planning Resource Centre is a non-profit, charitable organisation. Nidus provides information to British Columbians about personal planning. It also operates a centralised Registry for personal planning documents. http://www.nidus.ca/

19 Representation Act s 8(2)

20 Adult Protection and Decision-Making 2003 Act ss 1 and 4.

21 Adult Guardianship and Trusteeship Act S.A. 2008, c A4.2, Pt 2, Div 1.

may appoint an 'advisor', whose role it is to assist a person with those transactions specified by the court.[22]

In general, this mechanism refers to a legally recognized decision-making support relationship where a court orders that an adult make decisions with support, assistance or advice. It is not the same as supported decision-making in its purest form in that the adult himself or herself does not choose his or her own supports, nor is there assurance that the relationship is a long-standing and trusting one. That said, a factor to be considered in whether the court will appoint a co-decision-maker is the relationship between the proposed co-decision-maker and the adult.[23] Additionally, although not the same as choosing one's own supports, Alberta's Adult Guardianship and Trusteeship Act 2008 requires that the adult consent to the appointment of the co-decision-maker.[24] However, Saskatchewan's Adult Guardianship and Co-Decision-Making Act and Quebec's Civil Code each allow a court to appoint a co-decision-maker without any requirement that the adult consent. Further, Saskatchewan and Alberta's laws are somewhat patronising in that the court's appointment is partly based on its own assessment of whether co-decision-making is in the best interests of the adult.[25] While Saskatchewan's form of co-decision-making can apply to both personal and property decisions, Alberta and Quebec's forms are more limited. Alberta's applies to personal decisions only, while Quebec's applies to property decisions only. In each case, there is a required assessment of capacity, based on the principle that co-decision-making is appropriate when the adult's capacity is impaired to the extent that he or she requires assistance in making decisions[26]

5.1.3 Legislated Role of Third Parties to Facilitate and Encourage the use of Supports in Decision-Making

Do laws ever provide a role for health care professionals or other third parties to take active steps to involve supports in the decision-making process? For example, if a doctor suggests to her patient that he should have heart surgery, is there a law that speaks to the doctor's role in relation to the patient's decision-making supports? This type of duty is different than the vast majority of Canada's supported decision-making laws which focus either on an adult's right to have his or her supports legally recognised or on the State's role in support provision.

Examples exist in both Newfoundland and Labrador, and Yukon. Newfoundland and Labrador's Adult Protection Act provides that in the delivery of programs and services to an adult who lacks capacity and is in need of protective intervention, the adult should be '...encouraged to obtain support, assistance and advice from family and friends ...' to help the adult make and communicate decisions.[27] Although in a

---

22 The legal existence of advisorship is threatened by Bill 45, which, if passed, would repeal the provisions relating to advisers to persons of full age in Quebec's *Civil Code*.

23 Adult Guardianship and Co-Decision-Making Act s 13(1)(e)(viii) and s 39 (1)(f)(viii); Adult Guardianship and Trusteeship Act s 14(1)(b)(ii).

24 Adult Guardianship and Trusteeship Act s 4(c).

25 Adult Guardianship and Trusteeship Act s 4(a)(iv) and Adult Guardianship and Co-Decision-Making Act s 14(1)(a) and 40(1)(a).

26 Adult Guardianship and Co-Decision-Making Act s 14(1)(a)(i) and 40(1)(a)(i) and Adult Guardianship and Trusteeship Act s 13(4)(a).

27 Adult Protection Act s 8(g).

different context (ie consent to care), Yukon's *Care Consent Act* specifies that a care provider, when seeking a person's consent to care or deciding whether a person is incapable, may allow the person's spouse, relatives or friends who accompany the person to help them understand the proposed care.[28]

5.2 Government's Role in Provision of Supports

None of the mechanisms described thus far provides for a State role relating to accessing supports for decision-making. However, the CRPD requires governments to take positive action to provide supports in the decision-making process. More specifically, Article 12(3) obliges States Parties to take 'appropriate measures to provide access by persons with disabilities to the support they may require in exercising their legal capacity.' Manitoba's supported decision-making legislation, the Vulnerable Persons Living with a Mental Disability Act 1993 (VPA),[29] is the only Canadian legislative scheme that, at least partly, responds to the requirement of Article 12(3).

Pursuant to the VPA, applications may be made to a Commissioner for the appointment of substitute decision-makers. In this way, it is similar to guardianship applications. However, there is an important emphasis on supports in relation to Article 12(3). If an application is made for the appointment of a substitute decision-maker, but the person does not have a support network, the Commissioner may make a request that steps be taken by a government program to involve a support network.[30] The government assistance, legislatively created to involve a support network, may avoid the outcome whereby a person who lacks capacity without a support network would automatically be placed under substitute decision-making. What is interesting about Manitoba's scheme is that while it contains mechanisms to promote access to and respect for the role of supports, support networks, in and of themselves, are not legally recognized. That is, if a person avoids substitute decision-making because of the role of their support network, this does not guarantee that third parties will honour the role of the supporters. There is, in fact, no legal requirement for them to do so. This is a significant limitation of the VPA. It illustrates the necessity of legislatively recognized supports, such as through supported decision-making planning documents, in combination with a legislative requirement for government to play a role in the creation of support relationships.

5.3 Consideration of Supports in Co-Decision-Making and Guardianship Appointments

Manitoba's VPA is also noteworthy for its recognition of the existence and role of a support network in considerations of whether to grant substitute decision-making orders. A substitute decision-maker shall be appointed only if, among other things, the person is incapable by himself or herself or with the involvement of a support network.[31] This provision ensures that substitute decision-making is ordered only

---

28 Yukon Care Consent Act s 7(b).

29 The Vulnerable Persons Living with a Mental Disability Act 2003 C.C.S.M. c. V90. VPA only applies to people with intellectual disabilities.

30 ibid s 50(2) and 85(2).

31 The Vulnerable Persons Living with a Mental Disability Act 2003 C.C.S.M. c. V90, s 53(1) and 88(1).

if the person is incapable despite the involvement of a support network. There are several additional Canadian examples of this type of mechanism.[32] For example, Saskatchewan's Adult Guardianship and Co-Decision-Making Act 2000 states that a court cannot appoint a co-decision-maker or guardian unless alternative ways to assist the adult in making decisions, including less intrusive forms of support or assistance, have been tried or carefully considered.[33]

This type of requirement concretely acknowledges the important role that supports play in decision-making, but is deficient in that it does not specifically give any legal recognition to supported decision-making per se, as do the legislative tools described above. Nonetheless, and most importantly, by requiring that supports be considered, the development of decision-making support arrangements will be encouraged, perhaps to avoid more draconian guardianship or co-decision-making orders.

6. How do Canadian Legislative Approaches Measure Up to Article 12?

Some people have natural support networks in their lives. The hurdle they encounter occurs when those with whom they interact refuse to accept their supporters in the decision-making process. Being able to create a supported decision-making planning document would solve their problem. However, currently in Canada they can only do so in some jurisdictions and not for all types of decisions. For example, in Alberta, a supported decision-making authorization only applies to personal matters. What happens in Alberta when a person wants to open a bank account with the assistance of members of their support circle? Others may live in a remote rural area and have no supports in their lives. To make supported decision-making a reality for them would require assistance in creating and facilitating relationships of support. It would also require that the supported relationships that are created are recognized as a legal status. However, Manitoba is the only jurisdiction in which legislation provides some opportunity for this type of assistance, but falls short in that it provides no legal recognition to supporters. While co-decision-making, recognized in some Canadian jurisdictions, is a less restrictive court-appointed alternative to guardianship, it is not supported decision-making; the adult's choice of supports and control over the support relationship is absent.

Thus, comparing Canada's supported decision-making models leads to the conclusion that while incorporation of supports has taken hold in some jurisdictions, a fulsome recognition of supported decision-making as articulated in Article 12 has not come to fruition. There is no piece of Canadian legislation in which supported decision-making covers all situations. A more complete supported decision-making scheme could be created by merging the various tools available across Canada into one piece of legislation. It would recognize:

- supported decision-making planning tools
- state assistance in the development of support networks and

[32] eg Substitute Decisions Act ss 22(3) and 55(2); Yukon Adult Protection and Decision-making Act s 32(1)(c)

[33] Adult Guardianship and Co-Decision-Making Act 2000 s 14(2)(a) and 40(2)(a).

- co-decision-making and substitute decision-making as last resorts, where clear and convincing evidence establishes that true supported decision-making is impossible.

There is still hope that Canada will, one day, create a comprehensive legislative scheme which recognizes supported decision-making, fully implementing Article 12. Another attempt at a CRPD-compliant decision-making legislative model may soon be seen in Newfoundland and Labrador. In June 2011, leaders representing persons with disabilities, seniors, community agencies, the government of Newfoundland and Labrador and international experts gathered at a symposium to chart a new direction in securing the right to legal capacity in light of Article 12. Since then, the government of Newfoundland and Labrador has publicly stated its commitment to following the principles in the CRPD, including respect for autonomy and an adult's right to make his or her own decisions with supports if he or she chooses.[34] Key members of community groups are engaging in dialogue with government in an effort to make these commitments a reality.

7. Complexity of Decision-Making Laws: Do they Promote or Hinder Autonomy?

Even though they are conceptually and practically interrelated, the models described in this chapter are sometimes standalone pieces of legislation while others come closer to a complete decision-making code. For example, in Yukon, the Decision-Making, Support and Protection to Adults Act 2003 provides a comprehensive, unified approach. It covers all of supported and substitute decision-making arrangements, guardianship, adult protection and consent to care.[35] In contrast, Newfoundland and Labrador addresses adult protection, mental health, enduring powers of attorney, health care decisions, including advance health care directives, each in separate Acts. The absence of unity in this type of legislative approach leads to inconsistencies, which is exemplified in Newfoundland and Labrador where terminology and tests of capacity differ.

One commonality between models is their sheer complexity. The more decision-making options available, the more complex the law is. The complexity is, of course, exacerbated in jurisdictions whose decision-making laws are fragmented. However, the primary reason for the complexity is that there may be several legal tools, each of which covers different types of decisions and have different rules applicable with respect to their formalities and content.

Alberta's laws can be used as an illustration. Alberta allows for three types of planning tools. Personal directives for substitute decision-making for personal matters; enduring powers of attorney for substitute decision-making for financial/

[34] *Access. Inclusion. Equality: Provincial Strategy for Inclusion of Persons with Disabilities in Newfoundland and Labrador*, April, 2012, 29, online: http://www.aes.gov.nl.ca/disabilities/dpo_access_inclusion_equality.pdf; *New Energy,* 2011 Policy Blue Book, PC Party of Newfoundland and Labrador, 68, online: http://newenergynl.ca/the-blueprint/2011-policy-blue-book/.

[35] However, it does omit mental health provisions and enduring powers of attorney, which are addressed in separate legislation.

property decisions; and supported decision-making authorizations for supported decision-making for personal matters. Additionally, there are three different types of court appointments: Co-decision-making orders for personal matters; guardianship orders for substitute personal decisions; and trusteeship orders for substitute financial decisions. Additional provisions relate to health care substitute decision-making.

Complexity in this context is not necessarily something to be avoided. Indeed, it is a necessary aspect of protecting people's right to legal capacity and autonomous decision-making, by providing a range of decision-making options geared to a wide variety of individual circumstances. With respect to Manitoba's supported decision-making legislation, it has been observed that simplifying the legal process may come with unacceptable results, by making it simpler to invoke substitute decision-making: the exact opposite of the intention behind these laws.[36]

Rather than attempting to simplify decision-making models, efforts must be made to lessen the burden of their complexity so that they are comprehensible and usable. It is thus essential to educate the public, professionals (e.g. legal, health care and financial), and government in the various decision-making legal mechanisms and rules related to them. Some jurisdictions in Canada have produced valuable information tools which promote public awareness. For example, both British Columbia's Public Guardian and Trustee and Yukon's government Department of Health and Social Services have made publicly available written material as well as charts outlining, in an easily accessible format, the various legal tools, their features and their governing statutes.[37] Nidus, too, is well known as a resource centre for planning tools in British Columbia.

8. Supported Decision-Making in Practice

While there is a diversity of legislative approaches in Canada which recognize supports, legislation, in and of itself, can be a misleading barometer of the virtues and flaws of the schemes and tools it creates. It does not tell us how much its tools, mechanisms and safeguards are being used, and whether they, in fact, achieve the purposes for which they were designed. When considering how successful a law is, or how consistent it is with the CRPD, it is essential to look at three things: first, the specific legislative language; secondly, gaps in the legislative language; thirdly, what the experience is in practice ie do the laws achieve what they were intended to? Do people understand them? Do people use the planning tools that the law creates? What do stakeholders, such as people with disabilities, older adults, lawyers, health professionals and financial institutions consider to be positive features of the laws? What aspects do they find to be impractical and unworkable? The answers to these questions have equal importance to the legislative language and schemes themselves. It is futile to craft what appears to be skilfully worded legislation that only the drafters, and perhaps lawyers, understand. There are also no utility creating planning tools that are of practical benefit to people with disabilities and older adults.

---

36 Lutfiyya et al *Report on the Examination of the Implementation and Impact of The Vulnerable Persons Living with a Mental Disability Act (VPA)* (September 2007) 103.

37 See http://www.hss.gov.yk.ca/pr_seniors.php; http://www.trustee.bc.ca/pdfs/STA/It's_Your_Choice-Personal_Planning_Tools%20Mar%202012.pdf

In relation to supported decision-making planning documents, there is no mandatory registry in Yukon, Alberta or British Columbia, so there is no mechanism for tracking use of these documents. Objective evidence of the extent of their use and people's satisfaction with them is lacking. However, some anecdotal evidence does exist. For example, interviews conducted by Michelle Browning of stakeholders in Yukon revealed that supported decision-making and representation agreements in that jurisdiction have been used only to a limited extent.[38] With respect to Alberta, there is no clear evidence of the extent to which supported decision-making authorizations are being used or the impact they are having.[39] Somewhat conflicting perspectives exist with respect to the experience with British Columbia's representation agreements. Nidus promotes representation agreements as having a very positive impact on the lives of people with disabilities and older adults. However, there has been some resistance in the legal community to their use.[40] Given the absence of more definitive research,[41] Nidus recommended that '[t]here is a need for qualitative research to gain insight into the motivations and experiences of adults and their personal supporters with respect to the making and using of Representation Agreements with standard powers.'[42]

Quebec's form of co-decision-making, referred to as advisorship, is at risk of being eliminated altogether by a Bill that, at the time of writing, had not been passed, and was awaiting debate in a parliamentary committee. The explanatory notes to the Bill do not explain the rationale for its elimination, but one wonders whether the conclusion to be drawn is that it is being eliminated because of lack of use or inherent flaws. Further exploration of the Bill's background might help devise future laws which take account of Quebec's experience, and any currently existing shortcomings.

Manitoba is the one province that has conducted a detailed and extensive review of the implementation and impact of the VPA.[43] Participants interviewed for the review noted that, as a result of the VPA, there seemed to be more support networks and adults are more involved in choosing who will be members of their support network.[44] The general consensus was that the VPA had a positive impact on the lives of people with intellectual disabilities, to whom the VPA applies.[45] This is so notwithstanding the observation that even though the VPA calls for an active role for the Vulnerable Persons' Commissioner regarding the identification, establishment and support of support networks before moving to the appointment of a substitute decision-maker, the Commissioner has ignored and/or avoided this provision.[46]

---

[38] M Browning, *To investigate new models of guardianship and the emerging practice of supported decision-making* (Report by Michelle Browning 2010 Churchill Fellow) 29.

[39] ibid. Michelle Browning's report states that people are not using supported decision-making authorizations to a large degree (23–24). But the Victorian Law Reform Commission states that supported decision-making authorizations have been very popular (128).

[40] M Hamilton, *Planning for Personal and Health Care Decisions*, paper prepared for the Continuing Legal Education Society of British Columbia, June, 2011, 3.1.2; M Browning (n 38) 31.

[41] M Browning (n 38) 35.

[42] *A study of Personal Planning in British Columbia* (Vancouver: Nidus) 4. Available at: http://www.nidus.ca/PDFs/Nidus_Research_RA7_InAction.pdf.

[43] Lutfiyya et al.

[44] ibid 52.

[45] ibid 89.

[46] ibid 141.

This is unfortunate given that this provision, highlighted earlier in the chapter, is Canada's sole legislative tool that most responds to the demands of Article 12(3).

9. Transforming Legislation into Lived Experience

How can we enhance the impact that supported decision-making laws have on people's lives? How can we ensure that they function consistent with their original intent and are free from abuse? If ensuring that they are free from abuse increases their utilization because of greater confidence in them, how can this be achieved? Some underrated and less widely known features of Canada's models have great potential for responding to these concerns. Preamble/principle/purpose provisions, being easily identifiable with people's lived experience, can influence people's behaviour, including their use of and respect for supports. At the same time, legislated safeguards, both standard and innovative ones, can protect the integrity and viability of support relationships over time.

Each jurisdiction in Canada that explicitly recognizes supported decision-making as a legal status, also contains legislative language setting out principles meant to guide interpretation and administration of the Act.[47] Of all the dense statutory provisions and mechanisms described above, surprisingly, the preamble, principle and purpose provisions may have the greatest direct impact on people's behaviour and actions. They have the potential to guide the manner in which people plan for their own decision-making, and the way in which others, such as family members, health care providers and financial institutions interact with people who have issues with their capacity.

While the exact text of these types of provisions differs, there are important similarities. Some common principles include:

- adults are presumed to have capacity to make decisions unless the contrary is demonstrated[48];
- an adult's autonomy must be preserved and independence must be enhanced[49];
- the least restrictive and intrusive form of assistance, support or protection must be ensured[50]; and
- adults are entitled to be informed about and, to the best of their ability, participate in decisions affecting them.[51]

Many people can easily identify with these statements and associate them with some aspect of their own lives or the lives of those with whom they interact. Thus, they can be a beacon of light that is not found in the complex legislative language that

---

47 Sask principles clause s 3; Alberta principles clause s 2; Yukon guiding principles clause s 2; Manitoba preamble; BC purpose s 2.

48 Sask 3(b); mb preamble; Alberta 2(a); separate section in BC (ie not preamble/purpose/principle) s 3.

49 Mb preamble; Alberta 2(c).

50 Yukon 2(c); Sask 3(d); MB preamble; Alberta 2(c).

51 Sask 3(f); Yukon 2(b).

follows them. However, they do not have specific application to situations where the support relationship is breaking down. Safeguards are required for this purpose.

Article 12(4) requires that States Parties ensure that all measures that relate to the exercise of legal capacity provide for appropriate and effective safeguards to prevent abuse. Having the right to have matters relating to substitute or supported decision-making arrangements reviewed by a court or other legal authority is a fundamental safeguard. However, such rights are not, in and of themselves, sufficient to safeguard the integrity of substitute and supported decision-making. The time, expense and complexity often associated with pursuing this route can be a barrier for many people, especially people with disabilities and older adults. Thus, there is a need for additional safeguards, which would work in concert with review and appeal rights, to ensure that supporters and substitutes are not abusing their power. Examples of safeguards exist in Canada, which, in addition to reviewing and appealing rights, enhance the integrity of decision-making arrangements and prevent abuse. They are currently being used to a very limited degree, but their potential makes them noteworthy. Two such safeguards are monitors and registration systems. They have the advantages of being more informal and less expensive, and they can serve as prevention and/or early resolutions to abuse.

Monitors can be appointed under British Columbia's Representation Agreement Act as a safeguard against abuse by the representative/supporter. The purpose of the role of a monitor is to ensure that the representative/supporter is complying with his or her duties.[52] British Columbia's Representation Agreement Act provides that a person can appoint a monitor in his or her representation agreement.[53] If the monitor believes that the representative/supporter is not complying with his or her duties and the matter cannot be resolved, the monitor is required to report to the Public Guardian and Trustee. This gives the monitor the power to intervene and take steps in response to inappropriate action of representatives/supporters. In some situations appointment of a monitor is voluntary, while others require the appointment. A study conducted by Nidus Personal Planning Resource Centre and Registry received positive feedback about the use of monitors in British Columbia. Even though monitors are only mandatory in some circumstances, Nidus found that they are being used often, and are being used voluntarily as well as when required under the Act.[54]

A registry can be housed in an office whose purpose is to hold copies of all planning documents and decision-making appointments in the jurisdiction, and make details of these available to members of the public in appropriate circumstances. Registration ensures that people who interact with a supporter or substitute know that the supporter or substitute has legitimate authority to act in the manner in which he or she is proposing. Members of the public can thus satisfy themselves that people who hold themselves out as acting as supporters or substitutes, prima facie, have legitimate authority to do so. Without a registry, people will, inadvertently or intentionally,

---

52 Duties and powers of monitors are set out in s 20 of RAA. Under British Columbia's RAA, if the monitor believes that the representative is not complying with his/her duties, and the matter cannot be resolved, the monitor must inform the Public Guardian and Trustee

53 Representation Agreement Act s 12.

54 *A Study of Personal Planning in British Columbia* (Vancouver: Nidus) 4. Available at: http://www.nidus.ca/PDFs/Nidus_Research_RA7_InAction.pdf.

represent themselves as either substitutes or supporters when they have no legal authority to do so. An additional benefit of a registry is the assurance that people's wishes and directions, as expressed in their planning documents, are known.

The following observation, made in a report of the implementation and impact of Manitoba's Vulnerable Persons Living with a Mental Disability Act highlights the need for a registry as a safeguard:[55]

> We found when speaking with family members and vulnerable people that there was considerable uncertainty about whether or not the vulnerable person has a substitute decision maker and, if he or she did, whether or not the family member, the Public Trustee, or a third party was, in fact, the substitute decision maker. Some family members had indicated that they were the substitute decision maker but upon hearing other participants describe the application process, realized that they were not the substitute decision maker.[56]

Of the Canadian jurisdictions that allow for supported decision-making planning documents, only British Columbia has a personal planning registry, which is operated by Nidus.[57] Documents that can be registered include representation agreements, powers of attorney and advance care plans. However, Nidus is a non-profit, charitable organization and the registry is not legislatively created nor government funded. Ideally, from the standpoint of safeguarding a decision-making system, the registry should be mandatory and apply to all decision-making arrangements, whether planning tools or appointments. Consulting a voluntary registry does not provide any assurance that other legally valid supported or substitute decision-making arrangements do not exist.

Even with measures designed to enhance people's understanding of and confidence in supported decision-making tools, we are left searching for explanations for their underutilization, which, in the absence of evidence, can only be based on conjecture. One possible explanation is that some adults do not have close trusting relationships with people who could act as their supporters.[58] This may more likely be the case for people who live in remote rural areas, or people whose disabilities result in social isolation and exclusion. Another possible explanation is exactly the opposite. Some people have a long-standing practice of making decisions with supports informally. This has worked for them practically and they have had no difficulties conducting their lives in this manner, including doing their banking, managing their finances and making health decisions. For them, there would be no benefit to taking steps to formalize their support relationship. However, the ability to conduct their affairs informally can change over time. For example, in the future, financial institutions may insist on more formal evidence of the support relationship or health care providers may begin to routinely exclude supporters. Evolution of laws and practice may necessitate legal recognition of supports which does not currently exist for this group of people. Lastly, a lack of familiarity with supported decision-making tools may have an impact on the extent of their use. This may be exacerbated by an initial

---

55 This observation is likely common to many jurisdictions. There is no reason to believe it to be uniquely a Manitoba phenomenon.

56 Lutfiyya et al 81.

57 See www.nidus.ca.

58 M Browning (n 38) 29.

resistance to charting these new waters given that substitute decision-making tools have an entrenched existence in our legal system. Given the relative newness of supported decision-making tools, their use must be preceded by knowledge of their features and an associated comfort level with the practicalities of creating and using them. Developing knowledge takes time and is reliant on the availability of publicly available resources. While some Canadian provincial/territorial governments have produced educational materials, Nidus, in British Columbia, is currently the only community-based resource in Canada devoted to personal planning.[59]

10. Conclusion

Canada's supported decision-making models have become well-known internationally, especially in light of the CRPD. Although no Canadian supported decision-making model entirely meets the dictates of Article 12, the Canadian experience provides plenty of guidance to governments internationally in their implementation efforts. The best known tools in Canada are planning documents which allow an individual to appoint his or her legally recognized supporters. Additional mechanisms include court appointment of supporters, and a legislated role for government to assist with establishing and facilitating support networks. However, little discussed but critical components to the success of these types of models include effective safeguards and strongly worded preamble/principle/purpose provisions.

The existence of supported decision-making models, in and of themselves, are not necessarily indicative of the extent to which people are able to use supports in practice when conducting their day-to-day affairs. Canada is a case in point, where despite the promise of many supported decision-making models, they appear to be underutilized. Thus, the laws themselves give an incomplete picture of people's life experiences. Good law must be coupled with research and evaluation mechanisms intended to assess whether they have been successful and where there is need for reform. Unfortunately, these activities are insufficient in Canada.

Given the significance of implementing Article 12, jurisdictions in the process of doing so should place equal emphasis on legislative drafting as well as those efforts required to ensure that the legislation achieves its goals. The Canadian experience provides greater guidance with respect to the former than the latter. Building on Canada's examples, supported decision-making laws must be coupled with legislatively mandated reviews to ensure that appropriate reforms will respond to lived experience and political and social change. Equally important is a commitment to public education and community resources to increase awareness and facilitate the creation of support relationships.

---

[59] See http://www.nidus.ca/?page_id=2329.

Chapter 10

THE CRPD AND LEGAL CAPACITY REFORM IN HUNGARY: COMPROMISE OF WHAT?

János Fiala-Butora

1. Introduction

Hungary was the first country in the world to reform its guardianship system after the ratification of the CRPD. The Civil Code, adopted in 2009, was drafted with the intention of implementing the new international standard. The result is somewhat perplexing, a mix of progressive and regressive elements, which does not seem to be fully in line with the CRPD. This chapter will look into the CRPD's impact on the Hungarian law reform process, and strategies to reach its full potential.

2. The 2009 Civil Code in Light of the CRPD

Sándor Gurbai, in his chapter 'Unfulfilled Dream about Moving from Civil Death to Visible Citizens: Legal Capacity Law Reform in Hungary' explains in detail the content of the 2009 Civil Code and the process leading to its adoption. For the purposes of this chapter, I only recall that it did not fully implement a supported decision-making model. It abolished plenary guardianship, but retained partial guardianship, although in a more limited form. It also introduced two new legal institutions, 'supported decision-making' and 'advance directives.' The new regulation was thus a mix of two paradigms, one based on substituted, the other on supported decision-making. The Civil Code enabled both regimes to coexist, with supported decision-making having an advantage in application.[1]

Allowing guardianship to remain part of the law seems to be problematic. Article 12(2) of the CRPD requires that 'persons with disabilities enjoy legal capacity on an equal basis with others in all areas of life'.[2] If persons with disabilities can be subject to restrictions of their legal capacity, and others cannot, they are arguably not treated equally in this respect. Guardianship, in whatever limited form, constitutes such a restriction, and therefore seems to be contrary to the CRPD. This is not the only position on the interpretation of Article 12,[3] but as it was the one adopted by

---

1 According to 2.23§ (4) of the Civil Code, guardianship should only be applied if less restrictive alternatives are insufficient to safeguard the person's interest.

2 art 12(2), United Nations Convention on the Rights of Persons with Disabilities (2006) (CRPD).

3 M Keys, 'Legal Capacity Law Reform in Europe: An Urgent Challenge' in G Quinn and L Waddington (eds), *European Yearbook of Disability Law* (Intersentia 2009) 65; A Dhanda, 'Legal capacity in the Disability Rights Convention: Strangehold of the past or lodestar for the future?' (2007) 34 Syracuse Journal of International Law and Commerce 429, 460.

the Hungarian disability rights organisations during the reform process, I will take it as a starting point.[4] The purpose of this chapter is not to decide whether they were right, but to highlight the complexities of the CRPD's implementation going beyond mere textual analysis.

If the CRPD prohibits guardianship, at least in the opinion of Hungarian disability advocates, the new Civil Code is in violation of it. This can be explained by the fact that the law was a result of political compromise. It was obviously not drafted and adopted by civil society, but by other actors. That is certainly true, but not fully satisfactory. In the following I will look into the question of what it compromised, and the reasons for this compromise.

3. The Nature and Sources of the Domestic Opposition

International law theories of compliance typically analyse factors which lead states to respect their international obligations.[5] In the following, I would like to take the opposite approach, and look at the forces which pushed the guardianship reform in a different direction than the interpretation of the CRPD offered by disability advocates.

3.1. The CRPD and Domestic Political Process

The Hungarian guardianship reform was pressed for by persons with disabilities, their family members and the organisations representing them.[6] The opponents of the reform came from mainly three camps: judges deciding guardianship cases, represented by justices of the Supreme Court's Family Law Division; legal scholars of civil law; and representatives of guardianship authorities. Their positions were based on different motivations, but shared the core argument: getting rid of guardianship is impossible, because there exist no alternatives for persons with severe disabilities who would be left without legal protection and who would become vulnerable to abuse.[7]

This opposition was not based on a textual interpretation of Article 12. The CRPD was relied upon by members of civil society to strengthen their position. To the

---

4 Guardianship reform coalition of 15 Hungarian organisations, *A gondnoksági rendszer módosításának javasolt alapelvei' [Proposed principles for the guardianship system's reform]* (Hungarian coalition for guardianship reform 2007).

5 See, for example, A Chayes and A H Chayes, *New Sovereignty: Compliance with international Regulatory Agreements* (Harvard University Press 1995); J Goldsmith and E Posner, *The Limits of International Law* (Oxford University Press 2005); R Goodman and D Jinks, 'How to influence states: Socialization and international human rights law' (2004) 54 Duke Law Journal 621; H Koh, 'Transnational legal process' (1996) 75 Nebraska Law Review 181.

6 In June 2007, 15 organisations formed a Coalition for Guardianship Reform to communicate a common position towards the government. Among them were DPOs representing persons under guardianship and NGOs working on guardianship issues, and also DPOs and NGOs not directly affected by guardianship issues who wanted to support the process by expressing their solidarity.

7 I took part in the legislative process as a representative of the guardianship reform coalition of 15 organisations. Unless otherwise noted, the references to other parties' arguments come from my own reflection on the process.

extent it was countered, it was mostly by denying its importance for domestic private law, and its apparent conflict with other higher sources of law, such as the Hungarian Constitution. No opponent seriously argued that the interpretation offered by civil society is incorrect, and that the CRPD allows for some limited form of guardianship.[8] This came as a surprise, since disability advocates expected that this point would be contested, and prepared a detailed argument supporting their position.[9] But neither the Hungarian Ministry of Foreign Affairs, nor international law academics, who could have elaborated on a contrary opinion, joined the debate.

Therefore, the first experience of the Hungarian reform is that perhaps too much emphasis has been put by advocates on the question of the CRPD's interpretation, when in fact this was not decisive. The domestic implementation is not simply a technical legal process, where the wording of the highest norm in the hierarchy is 'translated' to ordinary laws. Rather, it is a political process not too different from any other. The international norm is taken as a starting point, and various alternatives achieving various levels of compliance are considered.[10] The political cost of these alternatives is measured against the political cost of non-compliance at the international level.

This is not say that the international norm does not matter. It matters, but how much it matters depends on several factors. If the norm is clear-cut and easy to implement, the norm in itself can prevent the adoption of various alternatives violating it. If it, however, provides for differing interpretations, the difficulty of implementing some of them might play an important role in giving advantage to others.

3.2. The Opponents' Motivations

In the case of the Hungarian legal reform, it is useful to understand the political motivations of the different stakeholders. Judges, who were the most vocal opponents of the reform, were interested in simple, easy to administer guardianship rules, which will not overburden the already stressed judicial system.[11] Law professors expressed scepticism over whether new legal institutions imported from common law countries could organically fit the natural development of Hungarian private law.[12] Guardianship authorities also expressed preference for a simple system, where the person under guardianship can be 'helped' by their well-intentioned guardians, who have sufficient tools at their disposal, including plenary guardianship, in those rare cases when they might need it.

These groups shared each other's position to some extent, and they also shared a pessimistic view about the abilities of persons with disabilities, and the seriousness

---

8 G Gadó, 'Eltérő és egyező álláspontok az új Ptk. előkészítése során' [Opposing and concurring views on the preparation of the new Civil Code] (2008) 6 Magyar Jog 386.

9 Mental Disability Advocacy Center, *A fogyatékos-jogi egyezmény 12. cikkének értelmezése* [Interpretation of Article 12 of the CRPD] (MDAC 2007).

10 See A Chayes and A H Chayes (n 5) 17, on the more general point that the goal of international law is not perfect, but is an acceptable level of compliance.

11 L Vékás, 'Bírálat és jobbító észrevételek a kormány Ptk. Javaslatához' [Critique and constructive comments on the government's Civil Code proposal] (2008) 9 Magyar Jog 577.

12 G Jobbágyi, 'A kormány Ptk. Tervezetéről' [On the government's Civil Code proposal] (2009) 2 Magyar Jog 98.

of the condition of those in the system. They were also generally sceptical about the allegations related to massive human rights abuses generated by the Hungarian guardianship system.[13] This was not surprising, given that persons under guardianship had not been represented in debates at this level before, and their problems are generally hardly known to others.

However, it would be wrong to characterise the opposition as overly conservative. Many of them accepted that there are problems with the current guardianship system, which needs to be changed. The advocacy efforts of non-governmental organisations, and the fact that persons with disabilities themselves were involved in the reform,[14] helped to convince many about the gravity of the issues. Open denial was therefore not a problem, and a more or less general consensus was reached that reform indeed must take place.[15] The question was, what kind of reform and how far it should go?

3.3. The Obstacles to Full Implementation

All domestic stakeholders accepted partial improvements of the system. However, the CRPD requires a completely new paradigm, one without guardianship. What the CRPD did not answer was how the paradigm might work. Would it not produce more problems than it solves? Would it not be too difficult to operate? Would it provide enough protection for everybody? Perhaps it is better for some people, but worse for others. These were valid concerns, not to be dismissed lightly. In the Hungarian context, they resulted in questioning the reasonableness of the rule expressed by Article 12 of the CRPD, respectively its interpretation offered by disability advocates.

If the rule expressed in the CRPD rejects all forms of guardianship, then states have to provide legal protection to every person through alternative means. This can be mandated by law; technically it is easy to draft a Civil Code abolishing all forms of guardianship. It is not that clear, however, what the facilitation of decisions taken by a severely disabled person would look like. This is a heavily under-examined question in the academic literature as well. Arguing from the authoritative position of the CRPD does not solve this problem. Neither does emphasising the need of protecting the autonomy of persons with disabilities 'to the maximum extent possible' – everybody can agree with the principle in its abstract form, but that does not bring us closer to solving the mystery of what the 'maximum extent' actually is and how is it 'possible' to support a person in a near-vegetative state to manage his finances.

The aim of legal reform is not about answering these questions in the abstract, but prescribing duties for agents of the state (in Hungary, mostly courts and guardianship authorities) about how they should react to various situations in practice. This

13 Reports documenting violations, such as the Mental Disability Advocacy Centre's (MDAC) guardianship reports, were not contested, and the potential for abuse was acknowledged, but in the absence of statistics it was difficult to agree on how widespread the problems are.

14 Some persons with disabilities were involved in the governmental-level negotiations, and they also spoke on the conferences and round-tables organised by NGOs and attended by representatives of the government and the judiciary

15 A Kőrös, '"Jót s jól" – helyes célok, alkalmatlan megoldások a cselekvőképesség tervezett szabályozásában" ['"Good and well!" – right aims, inappropriate solutions in the proposed regulation of legal capacity'], (2009) 2 Magyar Jog 104.

involves advance assessment of risk by potential sources of abuse, about which we have very little information until the system comes into operation.

An example may help to clarify this problem: in Hungary, guardians are notorious for failing to establish the wishes of the persons they represent. Article 15/A(1) of the Civil Code, which requires guardians to communicate with persons under guardianship 'if possible' is insufficient to solve this problem, because if they do not have daily contact, guardians make very little effort to talk to the person. We know that this is a problem, because we have ample anecdotal and some empirical evidence from observing it in practice.[16] The erroneous application, however, could not be deduced from the text of the provision itself. A similar provision in another country might be interpreted in a very different way, for various reasons. Also, a similarly worded provision of the Hungarian Civil Procedure Code concerning the attendance of persons in court hearings on their own legal capacity, is applied without major difficulties in Hungary[17] – contrary to some other countries in the region,[18] Hungarians with disabilities are typically present when judges deprive them of legal capacity. In hindsight, we might understand that the large number of persons under guardianship locked up in social institutions far away from their guardians, the large number of persons under guardianship per guardian, and the impossibility for the person under guardianship to challenge his/her guardian's decision before courts, were responsible for developing a very lax understanding of the 'if possible' requirement in Hungary, which had contagious effects. That, however, would have been hard to predict and react to before it materialised in practice.

Enacting a new Civil Code based on Article 12 must therefore not simply end all guardianship and replace it with supported decision-making. It should also equip it with the necessary safeguards and procedures able to prevent practical problems and abuses. This should be achieved to an extent at which stakeholders opposing it can be convinced that they will be able to practise their mandate efficiently in the new system. This is needed to reduce or eliminate the political cost of their resistance, and make the CRPD a viable alternative. And this, at least in Hungary, manifests itself as a very practical problem.

3.4. The Heavy Baggage of Institutional Culture

Hungary is a country with a developed guardianship infrastructure. Restrictions of legal capacity have been used since medieval times, and guardianship in its modern form exists since the nineteenth century.[19] Currently, there are around 70,000 persons under guardianship in the country, for a population of ten million.[20] Many of them live in long-term social care institutions, and most of them have 'professional'

---

16 Mental Disability Advocacy Center, *Guardianship and Human Rights in Hungary* (MDAC 2007).

17 ibid.

18 ibid.

19 K Györök, 'A gondnokság alá helyezési eljárás fejlődése Magyarországon 1945-től 2001-ig' [The development of guardianship procedure in Hungary from 1945 to 2001], (2008) 2 Iustum Aequum Salutare IV, 135.

20 The number was 66,955 on 1 January 2009 and is constantly growing; Office of the National Judiciary Council 'Letter No. 10586/2011/2. OIT Hiv.' (Letter from the Office of the National Judiciary Council (OITH) to author on the number of persons under guardianship) (18 March 2009).

(public) guardians appointed by the state. Public guardians are employed, and all guardians are supervised by the guardianship authorities, which have local offices in municipalities all over the country. There is no data about how many people are involved in administering the system, but they number several thousand in public administration alone, not counting judges and other court personnel involved in legal capacity cases and employees of social protection services.

This massive system has its own interests, and maximising the autonomy of persons with disabilities has not been high on their agenda. Quite the contrary, placement under guardianship is typically initiated by the guardianship authority, and is often motivated by the system's needs. There is ample anecdotal evidence about how the provision of social assistance by the state is informally conditioned on the appointment of a guardian, and the statistical analysis of Verdes and Tóth showed that on a regional level, increasing the supply of institutional social care services correlates with increase in the number of placements under guardianship.[21] Persons under guardianship are the perfect clients: they never make trouble, they cannot refuse the service or payment, they cannot complain, since their guardian, another public employee, makes all decisions on their behalf. Guardianship has therefore become an arm of the social welfare state, with post-communist reflexes aimed at isolating persons with disabilities rather than empowering them.

Of course not all public guardians have ill intentions. Quite the contrary, the poorly compensated positions attract people who have true desire to help vulnerable persons with disabilities, and many I met do this passionately. However, the system was structured in a way that resulted in an institutional culture firmly set in the old paradigm of substituted decision-making. Persons under guardianship are not thought of as autonomous beings able to decide for themselves, but as objects of care.

This institutional culture, and the similar wider societal culture in which it is embedded, is probably the main obstacle for implementing the CRPD in Hungary. Laws can be changed fast. Even resources can be reallocated to new types of services, although not without a political fight. However, if the state is to play a role in ensuring that persons with disabilities have access to the support they require,[22] and safeguards preventing abuse are available to them,[23] it will most likely do it utilising the same personnel currently running the guardianship system. For reasons of experience, job preservation, and financial efficiency, the new framework will inherit the infrastructure and people of the old one, with the uncomfortable baggage of existing institutional attitudes towards the abilities and independence of persons with disabilities.

4. The Disability Advocates' Position

Supported decision-making is a new legal institution, with which different segments of society have no experience. It must be developed in practice, by which I mean

---

[21] T Verdes and M Tóth, *A gondnoksági rendszer társadalmi funkcióiról* [On the societal functions of guardianship], (TASZ 2008).

[22] art 12(3), CRPD.

[23] art 12(4), CRPD.

that it has to be accepted and operationalised by retailers, banks, doctors, landlords, employers, the public administration and many other bodies with whom persons with disabilities interact. This will not take place without tensions. What supported decision-making will turn into very much depends on how these problems will be resolved.

The novelty of supported decision-making thus leads to its fragility: there is no experience with problems and abuses to build on, therefore it is hard to predict what kind of safeguards will most suit the system, and how it should be organised. The more rigid the rules, the bigger the mistakes that are bound to happen. However, flexibility should be exercised with care: placed in the wrong hands, it can bring supported decision-making very close to guardianship.

These were the reasons which led disability advocates in Hungary to reject the possibility that the state should be the main actor in charge of developing supported decision-making and running its infrastructure. A conscious decision was made that guardianship authorities should not appoint and supervise supporters, should not handle complaint procedures, and should not play any other role in managing the supported decision-making system.

This, however, meant that in the initial stages, the task of developing supported decision-making falls on NGOs. They certainly do not have capacity to run the system for every person in need, but for those for whom they do, the outcome will be much better. Once supported decision-making becomes established in practice, and its safeguards develop, the state can step in to ensure that it becomes available for everybody else.

This strategy means that for a temporary period, supported decision-making will be available only to a narrow circle of persons with disabilities, while others will remain under guardianship. It can be argued that this is not in line with what the CRPD requires. Indeed, Hungary is certainly not reaching its full potential in maximising the autonomy of person with disabilities, regardless of how one defines it. However, the alternative was even worse: abolishing guardianship and replacing it with supported decision-making overnight would mean that the latter would be developed by those very people currently running the former system. Regardless of its name and what the law says, the new system would be bound to become a new version of guardianship.

The ideal alternative – developing a system based on no restriction on legal capacity – was simply not available. Legislative reform can change legal rules, what it cannot change is mind-sets and attitudes. At least not overnight.

5. Lessons for the International Community

The Hungarian situation is certainly not unique, but I also do not claim that it is universal. Other countries, already running more autonomy-enhancing versions of guardianship, might find it easier to adapt their infrastructure to the requirements of Article 12. Others, who have no public guardianship system in place, and will be faced with the requirement to invest resources in developing a support system, will also have no reason to experiment with limitations of legal capacity. However, countries with a restrictive form of guardianship, with a lot of vested interest and a repressive culture, are likely to face the same obstacles as Hungary.

5.1. How we should Approach the CRPD's Interpretation

It is not clear what the Hungarian experience means for the interpretation of the CRPD. The reform revealed a weakness of the CRPD's principled interpretation: if it requires creating a system based on no restrictions of legal capacity overnight, it likely requires the impossible. Very few, if any, governments will be able to meet this standard, and some compromise with practicality must be made. However, there are also good reasons against relaxing the standard. The CRPD negotiations did not explicitly accept the existence of guardianship, which is a success that should not be given up easily.

A possible solution is to accept that no guardianship is the goal established by Article 12, which, however, cannot be achieved immediately. I can understand why many disability advocates are sceptical about 'progressive realisation' schemes, which are often neither progressive nor lead to the realisation of the right. The interpretation of Article 12 proposed here is different. In countries like Hungary, it is not the allocation of resources which constitutes the main obstacle, but the changing of societal culture and institutional attitudes relating to the autonomy of persons with disabilities. Therefore, the state should be under an obligation to immediately adopt laws and allocate resources aimed at changing this culture and attitudes, and more specifically, to start developing a system based on supported decision-making. If it does that effectively, it should be commended for it, while at the same time it should be emphasised that it is not yet reaching the standard. This could be done openly, by admitting that some of the changes will take effect only over time, or covertly, by not making clear what the standard is, only emphasising that the country is still in violation of it. The latter seems to be more in line with the practice of the Committee on the Rights of Persons with Disabilities, which criticised Tunisia,[24] Spain[25] and Peru[26] for their guardianship practices, without mentioning what would be in line with Article 12.

5.2. The CRPD as *Ultima Ratio*

The CRPD's other weakness in light of the Hungarian experience lies in its relative lack of persuasive power. Its text and its interpretation do not authoritatively end all debates. In the domestic legal process, it is worth only as much as the sense

---

[24] Committee on the Rights of Persons with Disabilities – Concluding observations of the Committee on the Rights of Persons with Disabilities – Tunisia (2011) <www2.ohchr.org//SPdocs/CRPD/5thsession/CRPD-C-TUN-CO-1_en.doc> last accessed 31 March 2016, paras 22-23.

[25] Committee on the Rights of Persons with Disabilities – Concluding observations of the Committee on the Rights of Persons with Disabilities – Spain (2011) <www.ohchr.org/Documents/HRBodies/CRPD/6thsession/CRPD.C.ESP.CO.1_en.doc> last accessed 31 March 2016, paras 33-34.

[26] Committee on the Rights of Persons with Disabilities – Concluding observations of the Committee on the Rights of Persons with Disabilities – Peru (2012) <www.ohchr.org/Documents/HRBodies/CRPD/7thsession/CRPD.C.PER.CO.1-ENG.doc> last accessed 31 March 2016, paras 24–25.

governments can make of it in convincing opponents that the alternative presented by the CRPD is not only a legal obligation, but is also one which is practically possible and leads to better results on the ground. As an international legal obligation it is certainly an important consideration, but does not trump all other ones. The government has to take into account the position and arguments of other stakeholders as well, to make sure that by adhering to the international principle it does not cause more trouble on the ground than it solves.

This weakness is quite understandable, given that the CRPD introduced a completely new paradigm, going against hundreds of years of worldwide practise, with not much practical experience to build on. This, indeed, stresses that it is a ground-breaking instrument, which was worth fighting for. That, however, does not make it less of a weakness.

5.3. Ways to Strengthen the CRPD

How can this weakness be overcome? The text is, of course, set, and will not be changed anytime soon. However, academic literature can help a lot in clarifying it. And since the question is not what the CRPD means but how that meaning can be achieved in practice, this academic literature should not be restricted to legal literature only. Psychologists, sociologists, social workers, doctors and others should all explore the implications of supported decision-making for their practice area. In Hungary, a psychological-sociological academic research project about decision-making by persons with intellectual disabilities started simultaneously with the legislative reform.[27] Its results will be a valuable contribution to any legal reform in the future.

The practice of other countries also proved to be very persuasive in the Hungarian context. Of course, there are not many international examples related to supported decision-making to rely on, but even less-restrictive guardianship regimes were an important reassurance for the government that it is not alone in moving away from substituted decision-making. The situation is likely to improve over time as more countries experiment with implementing the CRPD, and it is important that their experience is widely shared and studied. The Hungarian reform was already used as an argument in influencing similar reforms in the Czech Republic,[28] Slovakia,[29] and other countries of the region, and as more countries change their laws to implement the CRPD, the confidence of the resisting ones should be somewhat weakened.

Support from other international bodies could also strengthen the CRPD. Hungary ratified a number of international treaties, and is bound to comply with all of them; it is therefore important to consider their comments on legal capacity. The European

27 K György PhD, DSc, *Pszichoszociális fogyatékossággal élő személyek jog-, illetőleg cselekvőképessége, valamint a támogatott döntéshozatal az evidencián alapuló gyakorlat és irányelvek fényében [Legal capacity of persons with psychosocial disability in light of evidence-based practice and principles]* (Interdisciplinary research report, Budapest, 2008).

28 Czech coalition for guardianship reform, *Připomínky k návrhu občanského zákoníku [Comments on the Civil Code proposal] (*Czech coalition for guardianship reform 2009).

29 Slovak coalition for guardianship reform, *Osnova návrhu reformy opatrovníctva v Slovenskej republike [Outline of the proposal of the Slovak Republic's guardianship system]* (Slovak coalition for guardianship reform 2012).

Court of Human Rights, with its elaborate reasoning and monetary sanctions, is particularly important. The decision of *Shtukaturov v Russia* provided important arguments for disability advocates to argue why plenary guardianship should not be part of any progressive system.[30]

Last but not least, the Committee on the Rights of Persons with Disabilities can play a decisive role. Over time individual complaints, concluding observations and general comments will add more clarity and substance to our understanding of Article 12. It is unsurprising that the Committee is cautious with exercising its powers, and is not jumping to any unwarranted detailed elaborations on what the standard should look like. However, the strength of its opinions would be greatly enhanced if it added more reasoning about why it adopts a certain position. Governments can perhaps be satisfied with knowing what the norm is, but if they are to convince other domestic stakeholders about implementing it, it is important for them to understand why the specific norm was adopted, and why the alternatives are not satisfactory.

The Hungarian legal reform did not benefit from much of the above. The only support it could rely on was the enthusiasm and hard work of disability advocates. The end result was certainly not in full compliance with the CRPD, far from it in fact, but it has perhaps set the country on the right track. That, at least, can be stated in light of the very gloomy starting point, and gives hope for future stages of the reform. If other states will be able to make some use of the Hungarian experience, the advocates' work was not in vain.

[30] *Shtukaturov v Russia* App no 44009/05 (ECtHR 27 March 2008).

CHAPTER 11

UNFULFILLED DREAM ABOUT MOVING FROM CIVIL DEATH TO VISIBLE CITIZENS: LEGAL CAPACITY LAW REFORM IN HUNGARY

Sándor Gurbai

1. INTRODUCTION

Individuals are more than just passive holders of rights and obligations; we are active subjects who have the capacity to exercise these rights and to enter into legal relationships with others. Legal capacity is a term used to define both of these aspects. Individuals having full legal capacity can make independent decisions. On the other hand, individuals deprived of their legal capacity are denied the ability to make decisions about their lives. Around the world, including in Hungary, people with intellectual disabilities and/or psycho-social disabilities (mental health problems) are widely divested of their legal capacity and placed under the guardianship of another person. These adult guardianship systems are based mainly on substituted decision-making.

Hungary was the first state in Europe and second in the world to ratify the UN Convention on the Rights of Persons with Disabilities (CRPD); the CRPD entered into force on 3 May 2008. Despite ratifying the CRPD, current Hungarian legislation still allows courts to deprive and restrict the legal capacity of persons with intellectual disabilities and psycho-social disabilities; there are alternatives to guardianship, but these are not in compliance with the CRPD.[1] According to statistics, in August 2013 there were 61,259 people under guardianship from which 34,174 persons were placed under plenary guardianship, with 24,442 persons under partial guardianship. There is no information about the remaining 2643 people.[2]

Legal capacity law reform in Hungary targeted to make '[r]espect for inherent dignity, individual autonomy including the freedom to make one's own choices, and

---

1 See eg Mental Disability Advocacy Center & Hungarian Civil Liberties Union, *Written submission on the Follow-up to the Concluding Observations on Hungary CRPD/C/HUN/CO/1* (2013) http://tbinternet.ohchr.org/Treaties/CRPD/Shared%20Documents/HUN/INT_CRPD_NGS_HUN_16889_E.doc last accessed 31 March 2016.

2 Hungarian Government, *Information provided under the follow-up procedure to the concluding observations of the Committee [on the Rights of Persons with Disabilities]* (2013) 13. <http://tbinternet.ohchr.org/Treaties/CRPD/Shared%20Documents/HUN/INT_CRPD_AFR_HUN_16078_S.doc>.

independence of persons'[3] a reality for all adults with intellectual disabilities and psycho-social disabilities. In other words, the goal of self-advocates and disability rights advocates in Hungary was to bring people under guardianship out of the shadows and enable them to become visible citizens.

The CRPD compliance of the Hungarian legal capacity law reform, and the adoption of the Act CXX of 2009 on the Civil Code (Civil Code) is excellently analysed in János Fiala-Butora's chapter elsewhere in this volume. The aim of this chapter is to focus on the law reform process and to give an overview on the legal-capacity related provisions of the Civil Code and the current legal-capacity legislation.

2. Legal Capacity Law Reform

In 1998, the Hungarian Government decided to modernise the civil law which was rooted in the Act IV of 1959 on the Civil Code and to prepare a new civil code. It was highlighted that 'the direct aim of the revision is the creation of a modern civil code, which measures up to international practice and expectations.'[4] In 2002, the concept of a new Civil Code was issued by the Codification Chief Committee consisting mainly of law professors, and the drafting process started. Although in 2001 a new type of partial guardianship was introduced that was based on limitation of legal capacity,[5] civil society organisations active in the field of disability rights were unsatisfied with this reform and continued advocating for further actions. However, the drafting committee was closed off to engaging with disability rights advocates in the drafting process. At the end of August 2007, an important change happened in the process; the Ministry of Justice and Law Enforcement took over the draft for further work. This resulted in a completely new type of cooperation with civil society organisations; the consultation process was built on the obligation under Article 4(3) of the CRPD, according to which '[i]n the development and implementation of legislation and policies to implement the present Convention, (…) States Parties shall closely consult with and actively involve persons with disabilities, including children with disabilities, through their representative organizations.'[6]

This change could happen because the CRPD was adopted by the United Nations General Assembly in 2006 and Hungary signed the Convention on 30 March 2007. A coalition of disabled persons organisations and non-governmental organisations (NGO) developed a CRPD-inspired proposal on the principles for the guardianship reform. Our document highlighted that the new Hungarian Civil Code should be built on the support model without any restriction on legal capacity. At the same time, the text took into consideration the circumstances in Hungary, and acknowledged that for a transitional period the subsistence of guardianship based on the restriction

[3] Art 3(a), United Nations Convention on the Rights of Persons with Disabilities (2006) (CRPD).

[4] Hungarian Government (2014) Government Resolution No 1050/1998 (IV. 24).

[5] Until the 2001 reform, the 1959 Civil Code contained two types of guardianship measure: 'total deprivation of legal capacity' and 'general limitation of legal capacity.' For more information on the 2001 reform see: I Hoffman and G Könczei, 'Legal Regulations Relating to the Passive and Active Legal Capacity of Persons with Intellectual and Psychological Disabilities in Light of the Convention on the Rights with Disabilities and the Impending Reform of Hungarian Civil Code' in Loyola of Los Angeles International and Comparative Law Review 33: (1) 165–167.

[6] art 4(3) CRPD.

of legal capacity in a modified form could be acceptable. The proposal highlighted the importance of introducing legal instruments which might empower people with disabilities in their decision-making without restricting their legal capacity. In addition, a civil society coalition prepared a legislative proposal. The civil society proposal served as a basis for further work of the working group on legal capacity consisting of representatives from the NGO coalition, judges from the Supreme Court and the Budapest Metropolitan Court and employees of the Ministry.

Throughout the drafting process, opponents of the proposal firmly argued that some people with severe intellectual and psycho-social disabilities need to be protected by placing them under plenary guardianship. Despite these push-backs, the Bill which was presented to the Parliament did not contain plenary guardianship but had provisions on supported decision-making and advance directives. Despite Parliament adopting the Act on the Civil Code in June 2008, the President of the Republic of Hungary did not agree with the Act and the way it was adopted. As a result, he sent it back to the Parliament for further consideration. On 9 November 2009, the Parliament took the President's objections into account and voted for and adopted a new Civil Code.[7] This Civil Code did not contain any provisions regarding its entry into force; consequently, a different legal instrument dealing with this issue had to be adopted.

In December 2009, the Hungarian Parliament adopted the Act on the entry into force and implementation of the Civil Code. The President of Hungary disagreed with this Act as well, and few days before Christmas sent it back to the Parliament for further consideration. In his 'response' letter, the President highlighted that 'the Civil Code includes welcome innovations, such as the new foundations of the provisions on legal capacity.'[8] On 15 February 2010, the Hungarian Parliament passed the 'Act on the entry into force and implementation of the Civil Code,'[9] and it was published in the Official Journal of Hungary. According to this Act, the Civil Code would have entered into force in two steps: Book I and Book II of the Civil Code[10] on 1 May 2010, and the remaining sections of the Civil Code on 1 January 2011.

On the same day as the 'Act on the entry into force and implementation of the Civil Code' was published in the Official Journal, a Member of Parliament from the opposition party submitted a petition to the Constitutional Court. In his petition, the Member of Parliament drew the Constitutional Court's attention to the provisions which provided that different parts of the Civil Code were to come into force at different times. According to the petitioner, this kind of regulation makes the relevant basic provisions of civil law inapplicable. He also argued that the limited preparation time (a little more than five months)[11] for the changes were insufficient for stakeholders and for those who have to implement the Civil Code. The petitioner

7 Act CXX of the Civil Code (2009).

8 László Sólyom President of Hungary, Letter to Béla Katona President of the Parliament. No. II-1/04986-1/2009. Budapest, 22/12/2009, 2.

9 Act XV on the entry into force and implementation of the Civil Code (2010).

10 While Book I (Introductory Provisions) and Book II (Persons) of the Civil Code contain 105 articles, the whole Civil Code consists of more than 1200 articles. Legal capacity legislation can be found in Book II of the Civil Code (2009).

11 The Act CXX of the Civil Code (2009) was published in the Official Journal of Hungary on 20 November 2009, and the date of the entry into force of Book I and II were determined for 1 May 2010.

also mentioned that the date of the entry into force of the Civil Code was uncertain until the Act on the entry into force and implementation of the Civil Code was published in the Official Journal on 2 March 2010. According to the petitioner's arguments, these circumstances violate the constitutional principle of the Rule of Law and Legal Certainty. As a response to this submission, a coalition of civil society organisations submitted an *amicus curiae*-type petition to the Constitutional Court arguing for the rejection of the above-mentioned petition by proving that there was sufficient time provided to apply the Civil Code.

On 25 April 2010, the opposition party won the general election in Hungary and on 26 April 2010, the Constitutional Court delivered its decision on the unconstitutionality of those provisions of the 'Act on the entry into force and implementation of the Civil Code' that concerned the entering into force of the Civil Code. The Constitutional Court's *Decision 51/2010. (IV. 28.) AB* held that:

> The constitutionality of the preparation period granted for the application of a legal norm can be assessed on the basis of the case-by-case evaluation of the character and the quantity of the provisions contained in the statutory regulation concerned, as well as the other factors influencing the preparation for the enforcement of (or the voluntary compliance with) the statutory regulation. The preparation period is not deemed to be opened due to the mere fact of the text of the statutory regulation being known, if the date of its taking effect is unknown or uncertain. The preparation period can only be started when the sure date of the introduced changes taking effect becomes known.[12]

Here, the Hungarian Constitutional Court did not say that the new legal capacity legislation, or generally the whole Act on the Civil Code was unconstitutional. Rather, it stated that the short preparation period which was regulated in the Act had an unconstitutional effect. Shortly after the elections, the new Hungarian Parliament adopted the 'Act on the not entering into force of the Act CXX of 2009 on the Civil Code,'[13] which made it clear that the '[a]ct CXX of 2009 on the Civil Code does not enter into force.'[14]

Even though the new Hungarian legal capacity legislation did not enter into force, it is not only useful but also important to learn about and analyse legal capacity related measures of the Civil Code, since it was the first attempt to implement Article 12 of the CRPD after the entry into force of the Convention.

3. Legal Capacity Related Measures of the Act CXX of 2009 on the Civil Code

The Civil Code abolished plenary guardianship, contained guardianship restricting legal capacity in groups of matters, and introduced two brand new measures in the Hungarian legal system ie advance directives and supported decision-making.

---

12 *AB* [2010] Constitutional Court Decision 51/2010 (IV. 28.).

13 The Act LXXIII of 2010 was published in the Official Journal of Hungary on 12 July 2010.

14 art 1, Act LXXIII on the not entering into force of the Act CXX of 2009 on the Civil Code (2010).

The common feature of the latter measure is that legal capacity of the adult person remains intact.

3.1. Advance Directives

According to the Civil Code, every adult having full legal capacity may make decisions on his or her financial and personal matters for the future.[15] Wishes expressed in advance directives shall enter into force when a court rules on a case restricting the legal capacity of an adult person with respect to one or several groups of affairs.[16] The court shall rule on the advance directives or a specific part thereof coming into force instead of restricting the legal capacity of the adult person if the provisions of the advance directives ensure the necessary protection of the person concerned.

Even though the provisions regarding advance directives in the Civil Code are steps forward for Hungary, they are still not in compliance with the CRPD. When advance directives are prepared for the time when the person's legal capacity is restricted or denied, Article 12(2) of the CRPD is not respected. Equal enjoyment of legal capacity in all aspects of life without any limitation on the basis of disability should be the basis for any kind of advance directives.

3.2. Supported Decision-Making

Under the Civil Code, supported decision-making is based on relationships of trust and written agreements between the person with a disability and his or her supporter(s). Besides this, the appointment of the supporter(s) shall be made by the court, either in a procedure initiated especially for this purpose or in a guardianship procedure. In the latter case, the court shall consider whether the adult person can deal with his or her affairs with support and whether it is necessary to limit his or her legal capacity and to appoint a guardian for him or her. According to the Civil Code, supporter(s) are entitled to be present when the supported person is making a legal statement, and to provide the supported person with necessary advice and information.

Provisions of the Civil Code on supported decision-making took into account the general principles of the CRPD, in particular Article 12, and aimed to respect the autonomy, will and preferences of the person concerned.

---

[15] People may dispose of the following issues in particular by means of an advance directive:

a) specify one or more person(s) who may give them support for making their decisions, legal statements under the rules of supported decision-making, moreover whom they propose to have appointed as their guardian or substitute guardian;
b) exclude certain individuals from the scope of support persons and guardians
c) apply for or prohibit their placement in residential social institutions;
d) name a guardian for their children under the legal age or may exclude specific person(s) from those who may be appointed as guardians;
e) grant a power of attorney for the management of their financial transactions; and
f) dispose of the manner in which their movable assets or real estate, as well as income, is managed.

[16] Regarding restriction of legal capacity, see Section 3.4 of this chapter.

3.3. Professional Supporter

Under the Civil Code, a court is responsible for appointing a professional supporter who can assist in the framing of supported decision-making where it is impossible to appoint a supporter because of a lack of trust and where the person's placement under guardianship is not necessary. Professional supporters must not be appointed without the consent of the person concerned. The appointment of professional supporter(s) can be crucial when people with disabilities are in the process of leaving large institutions with the view to living independently and being included in the community.[17]

3.4. Guardianship Restricting Legal Capacity

The Civil Code abolished plenary guardianship and general partial guardianship. According to the new Civil Code, only partial limitation of legal capacity can be ordered by the court.

The Civil Code allows for the restriction of legal capacity only when an adult is unable to act independently, or with assistance, as a result of his or her intellectual or psycho-social impairments, addiction, or additional social barriers. The new Civil Code incorporated a highly important safeguard with respect to this provision; legal capacity can be restricted only when it is necessary to protect the adult from harm and less restrictive measures are insufficient for the protection of the person concerned. Limiting someone's legal capacity must be based on an expert's opinion which should include medical, rehabilitation, pedagogical and psychological examinations. Importantly, the new Civil Code pointed out that the manner of a person's communication shall not in itself be a ground for restricting their his or her capacity.

In summary, the Civil Code allows for the restriction of legal capacity. This is not in line with Article 12(2) of the CRPD according to which 'persons with disabilities enjoy legal capacity on an equal basis with others in all aspects of life.'[18] In 2009, the Mental Disability Advocacy Center and the Hungarian Association for Persons with Intellectual Disability submitted a paper on the right to equal recognition before the law based on the case of Hungary,[19] to the Committee on the Rights of Persons with Disabilities. Regarding guardianship restricting legal capacity, the submission highlighted:

> The remaining form of guardianship (in its itemised form) requires courts to assess a person's capacity in all matters, and allow restriction only in affairs where less restrictive (and more supportive) measures are insufficient to protect the person concerned. Even though in such cases a joint decision-making process is envisaged with the mutual agreement of the person with

---

17 The idea was to create a 'community connector' type of possibility in order to assist persons concerned in building support networks around them. Cf. <http://plan.ca/about-plan/what-we-do/networks/connectors> last accessed 31 March 2016.

18 art 12(2), CRPD.

19 Mental Disability Advocacy Center, 'Written submission on the right to equal recognition before the law: Based on the case of Hungary' (2009) <www2.ohchr.org/SPdocs/CRPD/DGD21102009/MDACHungary.doc> last accessed 31 March 2016.

disability and his guardian, we still affirm that such measure is a restriction of legal capacity and is in contradiction with the principle of equal recognition before the law.[20]

3.5. The 'Last Resort' Case of the Independent Conduct of the Guardian

A court may also allow a guardian to act independently with respect certain matters subject to restriction. The independent conduct of the guardian may be based on the joint request of the guardian and the person under guardianship, concerning the recurring affairs of the person under guardianship and/or those that demand making regular legal statements. On the other hand, the guardian may act as a substitute decision-maker

i. on the basis of the joint request of the guardian and the guardianship authority, if
ii. an opinion based on complex expert's examination has confirmed that in connection with the given affair or group of affairs, the guardian is not able to communicate with the person under guardianship even with the assistance of a specialist with expertise in the field of communication with people with disabilities, and
iii. the protection of the person under guardianship cannot be ensured in another way.[21]

This *ultima ratio* clause was introduced to address the concerns of those who were worried about people with severe intellectual and psycho-social disabilities and about individuals in a coma.

There are two main differences between plenary guardianship and the guardian's independent decision-making in the Civil Code. First, the court must not order the denial of legal capacity and must not appoint a guardian as a general substitute decision-maker for the adult in all areas of life. Second, the court, before authorising the guardian to act as a substitute decision-maker, shall examine whether there is any way to establish communication with the person under guardianship.

The Civil Code incorporated safeguards against abuse with regard to the independent conduct of the guardian:

> 'Upon making decisions that affect the person under guardianship, guardians shall be obliged to hear the person under guardianship – adapting to the mode of communication and intellectual capacity of the person under guardianship – and take the opinion of the person under guardianship into account to the greatest possible degree. If it is impossible to determine the opinion of the person under guardianship, the guardian shall proceed in accordance with the previously-expressed instructions of the person under guardianship. Where previously-expressed wishes are impossible to determine, the guardian shall

---

[20] ibid para 13.
[21] art 2:25, Civil Code (2009).

> be obliged to proceed on the basis of the set of values of the person under guardianship, in a manner that best serves his or her interests.'[22]

Here, the legal capacity of the person concerned is restricted which violates the persons' rights, will and preferences. However, the UN Committee on the Rights of Persons with Disabilities underlines that rights, will and preferences of the person with disabilities shall always be respected.[23] If the will and preference of the person cannot be ascertained then the 'best interpretation of will and preference' shall be applied instead of the 'best interest' model.[24]

The Civil Code did not enter into force due to the Constitutional Court decision and due to the 'Act on the not entering into force of the Act CXX of 2009 on the Civil Code.' On 11 February 2013, the Hungarian Parliament adopted a new Civil Code (2013 Civil Code) which has been in force since 15 March 2014.

4. Current Legal Capacity Legislation

The 2013 Civil Code allows for 'full restriction of legal capacity'[25] which is equivalent to 'total deprivation of legal capacity' under the 1959 Civil Code. Both of these categories result in placement under plenary type of guardianship which can be characterised as follows:

i. legal statements of persons concerned are null and void unless these are insignificant contracts (eg buying an ice-cream);
ii. people concerned cannot make independent decisions – their guardian makes decisions on their behalf;
iii. people concerned are automatically deprived of several rights including, among others, the right to marry, to bring up children, to adopt children, to decide where to live, to give and withdraw informed consent for medical treatment, to access to justice, to make a will, to work, to freedom of association.

According to the Hungarian Government, the novelty of 'full restriction of legal capacity' is that it can be used as a last resort and only in those situations when 'the person concerned is unable to make a legal statement even jointly with his or her guardian and if it is absolutely necessary that somebody acts on his or her behalf.'[26] However, in 2012 the UN Committee on the Rights of Persons with Disabilities was 'concerned about the possibility of maintaining a modified regime of substitute decision-making in the drafting of the new Civil Code.'[27] Moreover, in July 2013

---

22 ibid art 2:36(3).

23 Committee on the Rights of Persons with Disabilities – General Comment on Article 12 of the CRPD. CRPD/C/GC/1, para 20.

24 ibid para 21.

25 arts 2:21 – 22, Act V of the Civil Code (2013).

26 Hungarian Government, *Information provided under the follow-up procedure to the concluding observations of the Committee [on the Rights of Persons with Disabilities]* (2013) 4.

27 Committee on the Rights of Persons with Disabilities – Concluding observations of the Committee on the Rights of Persons with Disabilities on Hungary 22/10/2012, CRPD/C/HUN/CO/1, para 25.

the Hungarian Commissioner for Fundamental Rights submitted a petition to the Constitutional Court claiming that the measure of 'full restriction of legal capacity' is unconstitutional and violates Article 12 of the CRPD and Article 8 of the European Convention on Human Rights.[28] The motion of the ombudsperson was rejected by the Constitutional Court in April 2014.[29]

The 2013 Civil Code allows for 'partial limitation of legal capacity' which results in placement of the person concerned under partial guardianship. In this case, the adult has full legal capacity in all areas of life with the exception of certain matters, in which his/her legal capacity is limited. These groups of matters are not defined by the 2013 Civil Code but they can cover, for example, matters concerning inheritance, health/medical care, disposition on personal property or real estate etc. Individuals placed under this type of guardianship can act independently in those areas in which their legal capacity is not limited. They can also make decisions on the matters in which they are restricted, but in these situations they need the approval of their guardian without which the legal act of the person concerned is void.

The 2013 Civil Code introduces two alternatives to guardianship: supported decision-making[30] and advance directives.[31] Supported decision-making can be described as follows:

i. it does not affect the adult's legal capacity
ii. it is available only for people who 'due to a minor decrease in their mental capacity need help in dealing with some of their affairs and in making decisions'
iii. the support person is appointed by the guardianship authority either based on the request of the person concerned or on the basis of a court decision in a guardianship procedure
iv. a support person can only be appointed in agreement with the adult person.

Under the Act CLV of 2013 on Supported Decision-Making the guardianship authority can appoint a 'professional supporter' for the person concerned if there is nobody to be appointed as support person. Although a professional supporter can only be appointed in agreement with the person concerned, these supporters can be professional guardians and are entitled to 'support' up to 45 people at the same time.[32]

In its concluding observations on Hungary the UN Committee on the Rights of Persons with Disabilities was concerned that 'the process of drafting of the new Civil Code has not been used to provide for a detailed and viable framework for supported decision-making in the exercise of legal capacity in accordance with the provisions of article 12 of the Convention.'[33]

---

28 Commissioner for Fundamental Rights, *Petition Re. unconstitutionality of full restriction of legal capacity of the 2013 Civil Code.* No. AJB-2580/2013. Budapest, July 2013.

29 *AB* [2014] Constitutional Court Decision 11/2014 (IV. 4.).

30 art 2:38, Act V of the Civil Code (2013). Detailed provisions can be found in the Act CLV of Supported Decision-making (2013).

31 arts 2:39 – 2:41, Act V of the Civil Code (2013).

32 art 7, Act CLV of Supported Decision-Making (2013).

33 Committee on the Rights of Persons with Disabilities – Concluding Observations of the

Under the 2013 Civil Code, advance directives can be made by every adult having full legal capacity to be used in the event of their losing legal capacity either fully or partially. In advance directives, eligible people may

i. specify one or more persons whom they propose to have appointed as their guardian;
ii. exclude certain individuals from the scope of guardians;
iii. dispose of the manner in which their financial and personal matters are managed.

In summary, the 2013 Civil Code follows neither the CRPD nor the Basic Law of Hungary which states that regarding the *pacta sunt servanda* principle, 'Hungary shall ensure harmony between international law and Hungarian law in order to fulfill its obligations under international law.'[34]

5. Conclusions

The United Nations Convention on the Rights of Persons with Disabilities decisively shifts the predominant paradigm of substituted decision-making towards systems of supported decision-making. Even so, the question remains: what is the best way to implement Article 12? This chapter presented the Hungarian experiences in the special context of Central Europe. Although the reform was well-intentioned, the results are incompatible with the CRPD.

There are an increasing number of legal capacity law reform initiatives across the globe, and different cultures play a role when States Parties to the CRPD want to implement Article 12. However, Article 12 holds a strong message according to which 'persons with disabilities enjoy legal capacity on an equal basis with others in all aspects of life.'[35] This is not dependent on cultures and continents; it means that people with disabilities have universal legal capacity which should never be limited or excluded on the basis of disability. Article 12 places an obligation on States Parties regarding implementation of the right to legal capacity; they 'shall take appropriate measures to provide access by persons with disabilities to the support they may require in exercising their legal capacity.'[36] However, it is not enough to modify and abolish existing laws and prepare new ones; discriminatory practices, negative attitudes, stigma and abuse should be also addressed in an effective way.

Information-sharing on legal capacity law reform is important in order to avoid traps and to gain knowledge on bad, best and promising practices. The aim of this chapter was to contribute to this information-sharing. I am convinced that a real shift from guardianship systems to the support paradigm can be achieved only by overcoming numerous barriers including social, legal, financial, attitudinal and political. We all have responsibilities to build societies in which people with

---

Committee on the Rights of Persons with Disabilities on Hungary 22/10/2012, CRPD/C/HUN/CO/1, para 25.

34 art Q(2) of the Basic Law of Hungary (2011).

35 art 12(2) CRPD.

36 ibid art 12(3).

intellectual disabilities and people with psycho-social disabilities are visible citizens with equal rights with others.

PART 3: MENTAL HEALTH LAW AND DISABILITY

Chapter 12

ARTICLE 14 OF THE CRPD IN LIGHT OF ARTICLE 5 OF THE ECHR: THE CHALLENGE FOR COUNCIL OF EUROPE MEMBER STATES REGARDING THE INVOLUNTARY DETENTION OF PERSONS WITH MENTAL DISABILITIES

Suzanne Doyle

1. Introduction

In this chapter the case law of the European Court of Human Rights (ECtHR) regarding the right to liberty of person with mental disabilities under the European Convention on Human Rights (ECHR) will be examined in light of the requirements of Article 14 of the United Nations Convention on the Rights of Persons with Disabilities (CRPD). As will be shown below, post-ratification of the CRPD, the Members of the Council of Europe who have ratified the CRPD will therefore be bound by two different legal standards when analysing the validity of the involuntary detention of persons with mental disabilities.

In respect of the United Nations instruments, although a gradual move away from a strictly paternalistic, medical model of the right can be traced, pre-CRPD Declarations and Principles had, for the most part, simply reflected the legal position that existed in many States.[1] In addition, one of the UN's strongest statements on the issue of involuntary detention, the MI Principles,[2] is generally agreed to provide a very low level of protection in respect of the right to liberty[3] and have been rejected by the majority of the disability community (albeit still referred to by States themselves) as having been antiquated at their inception.

---

1 See eg United Nations, 'The Declaration on the Rights of Mentally Retarded Persons,' Proclaimed by General Assembly Resolution 2856 (XXVI) of the 20 December 1971; United Nations, 'The Declaration on the Rights of Disabled Persons,' Proclaimed by General Assembly resolution 3447 (XXX) of 9 December 1975.

2 United Nations General Assembly–Principles for the Protection of Persons with Mental illness and the Improvement of Mental Health Care (1991) G. A. Res 46/119.

3 M Jones, 'Can international law improve mental health?' (2005) 28 International Journal of Law and Psychiatry 183, 202.

Council of Europe instruments have taken a similar approach to their United Nations counterparts. However, the Council of Europe 'soft law' instruments have produced stronger standards regarding the review of detention, reflecting their connection to the ECHR.[4] In addition, a noticeable social model influence became more obvious in the instruments drafted during the twenty-first century.[5]

However, none of these instruments made any attempt to address the more fundamental issue of the infringement of the right to liberty of persons with mental disabilities by way of involuntary detention. Its validity was taken as a presumption which did not require re-examination. As will be demonstrated in this chapter, as a result of Article 14 of the CRPD this can no longer be presumed.

2. Article 5 of the European Convention on Human Rights – Case Law from the European Court of Human Rights

The validity of the principle of involuntarily detaining persons with mental disabilities has been relatively unproblematic for the European Court of Human Rights (the Court) to date. This has been due to the fact that Article 5(1) of the ECHR provides that, '[e]veryone has the right to liberty and security of person. No one shall be deprived of his liberty save in the following cases and in accordance with a procedure prescribed by law, (…), (e) the lawful detention of persons for the prevention of the spreading of infectious diseases, of persons of unsound mind, alcoholics or drug addicts or vagrants, (...)'.[6]

Article 5(1) also contains a number of other grounds for the detention of particular classes of person. In addition to this general provision concerning the detention of persons with mental disabilities, Article 5 contains a number of procedural requirements. Article 5(2) states that '[e]veryone who is arrested shall be informed promptly, in a language which he understands, of the reasons for his arrest and of any charge against him.'[7] Further, Article 5(4) states that '[e]veryone who is deprived of his liberty by arrest or detention shall be entitled to take proceedings by which the lawfulness of his detention shall be decided speedily by a court and his release ordered if the detention is not lawful.'[8]

Both the procedural and substantive principles which the European Court of Human Rights has established with respect to the deprivation of the liberty of persons with mental disabilities will be examined. This is necessary in order to compare and

---

4 See e.g. Council of Europe – Recommendation (83) 2 of the Committee of Ministers to Member States concerning the legal protection of persons suffering from mental disorder placed as involuntary patients (Adopted by the Committee of Ministers on 22 February 1983 at the 356 meeting of the Minister's Deputies).

5 See Council of Europe – Recommendation (2004) 10 of the Committee of Ministers to Member States concerning the protection of the human rights and dignity of persons with mental disorder (Adopted by the Committee of Ministers on 22 September 2004 at the 896th meeting of the Ministers' Deputies).

6 Council of Europe, Convention for the Protection of Human Rights and Fundamental Freedoms (European Convention on Human Rights, as Amended) (ECHR) 1950, art 5(1)(e).

7 Council of Europe, Convention for the Protection of Human Rights and Fundamental Freedoms (European Convention on Human Rights, as Amended) (ECHR) 1950, art 5(2).

8 ibid art 5(4).

contrast the jurisprudence of the Court in these two areas with the interpretation which has thus far been given to Article 14 by the UN Committee on the Rights of Persons with Disabilities.

2.1 The Right to Liberty of Persons with Mental Disabilities – The Definition of Deprivation of Liberty

In *Guzzardi v Italy*[9] the ECtHR sought to define the meaning of 'deprivation of liberty' in the context of Article 5 and stated that '(…) the starting point must be (the individual's) concrete situation and account must be taken of a whole range of criteria such as the type, duration, effects and manner of implementation of the measure in question.'[10]

In *Ashingdane v The United Kingdom*[11] the Court clarified that '[t]he distinction between deprivation of and restriction upon liberty is merely one of degree, and not one of nature or substance.'[12]

2.2 The Right to Liberty of Persons with Mental Disabilities – Substantive

In the context of the Court and the substantive right to liberty of persons with mental disabilities, its decisions in *Johnson v The United Kingdom*[13] and *H.L. v The United Kingdom*[14] provide contrasting examples of the levels of protection which it will attract under Article 5.

In *Johnson v The United Kingdom*,[15] the Court held that the applicant's continued detention after a tribunal found that he was free of the mental illness which had initially formed the basis of his detention, but that he was not fit for absolute discharge without first going through a period of rehabilitation in a hostel, constituted a breach of Article 5(1). The Court held that a finding by an expert authority that a person was no longer suffering from the mental illness which led to his confinement did not inevitably lead to his immediate and unconditional discharge into the community. The expert authority enjoyed discretion to assess what was the most appropriate course to take in the circumstances, balancing the interests of the individual and those of the community. However, the Court emphasised that it was of paramount importance that discharge be not unreasonably delayed and that safeguards existed to prevent this.

The Court also based its finding of a violation of Article 5 on the fact that while it might be justified in principle to defer the applicant's discharge until a hostel best suited to his needs was arranged, the tribunal lacked the powers to ensure that a placement was secured within a reasonable time. In addition, the applicant could not petition the tribunal in between the annual reviews to have the terms of the hostel condition varied or reconsidered. There was therefore a lack of adequate safeguards,

---

9 *Guzzardi v Italy* App no 7367/76 (ECtHR 6 November 1980).
10 ibid para 92.
11 *Ashingdane v The United Kingdom* App no 8225/78 (ECtHR 28 May 1985).
12 ibid para 41.
13 *Johnson v The United Kingdom* (1997) 27 European Human Rights Reports 296.
14 *H.L. v The United Kingdom* (2004) 1 Mental Health Law Reports 236.
15 *Johnson v The United Kingdom* (n 14).

including provision for judicial review, to ensure that the applicant's release from detention would not be unreasonably delayed.

Despite these findings, however, the Court held that the applicant did not automatically acquire an immediate right to an unconditional release and that:

> Such a rigid approach to the interpretation of that condition would place an unacceptable degree of constraint on the responsible authority's exercise of judgment to determine in particular cases and on the basis of all the relevant circumstances whether the interests of the patient and the community into which he is to be released would in fact be best served by this course of action. It must also be observed that, in the field of mental illness, the assessment as to whether the disappearance of the symptoms of the illness is confirmation of complete recovery is not an exact science.[16]

Johnson is perhaps the best example of the practice of the Strasbourg Court of taking a hard line on procedural guarantees but being a great deal weaker on the substantive core of the right to liberty in respect of persons with mental disabilities. This can, for the most part, be attributed to the terms of Article 5 itself. However, the decision of the court in *Johnson* took a particularly broad interpretation of Article 5, which arguably stretched its validating powers in respect of involuntary detention too far. Bartlett and Sandland submit that the Court's reasoning seems to amount to 'an extraordinarily conservative reading of the phrase "person of unsound mind" in Article 5.1(e).'[17]

In contrast to the conservative approach taken towards the right to liberty of persons with mental disabilities in *Johnson*, the high-water mark in the Courts' jurisprudence on deprivation of liberty in respect of persons with mental disabilities is generally agreed to be its decision in *H.L. v United Kingdom*[18] which concerned an applicant who lacked capacity and had been 'informally' admitted to a psychiatric hospital and therefore was not entitled to the statutory reviews of detention provided for under the UK's Mental Health Act 1983. The Court concluded that the applicant had been deprived of his liberty based on the following facts:

- The health care professionals treating and managing the applicant exercised complete and effective control over his care and movements.[19]
- His responsible medical officer was clear that, had the applicant resisted admission or tried to leave thereafter, she would have prevented him from doing so and would have considered his involuntarily committal.[20]
- The applicant's contact with his carers (who wished to have the applicant released to their care immediately) was directed and controlled by the hospital.[21]

---

16 ibid para 61.
17 P Bartlett and R Sandland, *Mental Health Law: Policy and Practice* (Oxford University Press 2007) p 29.
18 *H.L. v The United Kingdom* (n 15).
19 ibid para 91.
20 ibid.
21 ibid.

The Court stated that it was not determinative of a deprivation of liberty whether the ward was 'locked' or 'lockable.'[22] The Court further held that the right to liberty was too important in a democratic society for a person to lose the benefit of ECHR protection 'for the single reason that he may have given himself up to be taken into detention, especially when it is not disputed that that person is legally incapable of consenting to, or disagreeing with, the proposed action.'[23] It was therefore held that the applicant had been deprived of his liberty and that although he did suffer from a mental disorder, the common law which governed his 'informal' admission was insufficiently precise and predictable to satisfy the requirements of Article 5(4).[24]

Gledhill notes that central to the reasoning of the Court in *H.L.* was that the formal process of detention brought with it safeguards that were necessary in the circumstances to guard against 'arbitrariness.' Therefore, he notes that in the context of Article 5(1) of the ECHR, the existence of a disability leading to a vulnerability has to be taken into account in assessing the adequacy of the regime that governs detention.[25] *H.L.* might therefore represent the beginnings of a subtle infusion of social model theory by the European Court in respect of its substantive interpretation of the right to liberty of persons with mental disabilities.

Johnson and *H.L.* represent opposing ends of the spectrum in terms of the Court's analysis of the substantive right to liberty of persons with mental disabilities. Yet they do not comprise the totality of that Court's jurisprudence on this point. There have been a number of other judgments which have been instructive regarding the Court's position on this topic. For example, in *Reid v UK*,[26] it was held that there was no requirement imposed by Article 5(1)(e) that detention in a mental hospital be conditional on the illness or condition being of a nature or degree amenable to medical treatment. The applicant in that case had anti-social personality or psychopathic disorder. Most of the psychiatric reports stated that his condition was not treatable, but the Court stated that treatability was not required for detention.

Most recently, the Grand Chamber of the ECtHR examined the right to liberty of persons with mental disabilities in *Stanev v Bulgaria.*[27] In 1975 the applicant was diagnosed as suffering from schizophrenia. By Court orders, and at the request of certain members of his family, the applicant was partially deprived of his legal capacity and placed under trusteeship. Since 2002, he had been placed in a social care home for adults with mental disorders, based on a request made by his guardian, a social worker. The director of the social care home then became his guardian. On

---

22 ibid para 92.

23 ibid at para 90.

24 For a sample of the voluminous analysis of the decision in *H.L.*, see P. Bartlett, O. Lewis and O. Thorold, *Mental Disability and the European Convention on Human Rights* (Martinus Nijhoff 2007) 36–37, P. Fennell, 'The Mental Capacity Act 2005, the Mental Health Act 1983, and the common law' (2005) 163 Journal of Mental Health Law 165; K. Keywood, 'Detaining mentally disordered patients lacking capacity: The arbitrariness of informal detention and the common law doctrine of necessity' (2005) 13(1) Medical Law Review 108; D. Hewitt, 'Effective, unqualified control' (2004) 154 New Law Journal 1553.

25 K. Gledhill, 'Disability law and mental health' in Lawrence Gostin, P. Bartlett, P. Fennell, J. McHale and R. Mackay (eds), *Principles of Mental Health Law and Policy* (Oxford University Press, 2010) p 917.

26 *Reid v UK* (2003) 37 European Human Rights Reports 9.

27 *Stanev v Bulgaria* App no 36760/06 (ECtHR 17 January 2012).

numerous occasions the applicant had requested that he be removed from trusteeship but was barred from bringing proceedings without the consent of his guardian. The applicant alleged a violation of Articles 5(1), (4) and (5) on account of his placement in care homes against his will, the fact that it was not possible under Bulgarian law to have the lawfulness of his detention reviewed, and the absence of a judicial procedure to seek compensation. The applicant also alleged that there were violations of Article 3 (on account of the poor living conditions at the care home), of Article 6 (due to his lack of access to court to request the restoration of his legal capacity) as well as Articles 8 and 13 of the ECHR.

In its judgment, the ECtHR found a violation of Article 5(1) in that it observed that the applicant's placement in the home was not ordered 'in accordance with a procedure prescribed by law,' and that his deprivation of liberty was not justified by sub-paragraph (e) of Article 5(1).[28] The Court noted that Bulgarian law envisaged placement in a social care institution as a protective measure taken at the request of the person concerned and not a coercive one ordered on one of the grounds of detention listed in Article 5(1) of the ECHR. However, in the applicant's case, the measure in question entailed significant restrictions on personal freedom giving rise to a deprivation of liberty with no regard for the applicant's will or wishes.[29]

Regarding whether a procedure prescribed by law was followed, the Court noted that under domestic law, the guardian of a person partially lacking legal capacity was not empowered to take legal steps on that person's behalf. Any contracts drawn up in such cases are valid only when signed together by the guardian and the person under guardianship. The Court therefore concluded that the decision by the applicant's guardian to place him in a social care home for people with mental disorders without having obtained his prior consent was, prima facie, invalid under Bulgarian law. This conclusion was therefore, in itself, sufficient for the Court to establish that the applicant's deprivation of liberty was contrary to Article 5.[30] However, in any event, the Court considered that that measure was not lawful within the meaning of Article 5(1) of the ECHR since it was not justified on the basis of any of the grounds of detention listed in that provision.[31] Further, as the applicant was legally unable to challenge or seek compensation for his detention, Articles 5(4) and 5(5) of the ECHR had been violated.

The Court also held unanimously that the applicant had been subjected to degrading treatment in violation of Article 3 of the ECHR by being forced to live in unsanitary and unliveable conditions, and that domestic law did not provide him with any mechanism to seek redress for such violations.

H.L. and *Stanev* represent the European Court of Human Rights' most extensive examination of the right to liberty of persons with mental disabilities to date, and are certainly welcome steps forward in terms of safeguarding the right to liberty of persons with mental disabilities who may be incapable of consenting to voluntary admission to a psychiatric facility. Yet, ultimately, the Court is bound by the content

28 ibid para 159.
29 ibid para 149.
30 ibid para 150.
31 ibid para 151.

of Article 5(1)(e) which expressly permits the involuntary detention of persons with mental disabilities. Inevitably, therefore, its case law will only ever be able to address the regulation of that practice, not the lawfulness or justifications for the practice itself.

2.3 The Right to Liberty of Persons with Mental Disabilities – Procedural Guarantees

The Court took its first major foray into such regulation in its decision in *Winterwerp v The Netherlands*.[32] In this case the court set down certain procedural safeguards which Member States had to apply in relation to involuntary detention. The Court held that in order for such detention to be lawful, the following three conditions had to be met:

1. Except in emergency situations, the person must be reliably shown to have a mental disorder by way of objective medical expertise.
2. The mental disorder must be 'of a kind or degree warranting compulsory confinement.'[33]
3. The continuation of the detention will only be valid for so long as that mental disorder persists.

The Court also held that the relevant domestic law must be reasonably clear. The detained person should also have prompt and regular access to a Court or tribunal to challenge the validity of their detention and, during these proceedings, should have the right to be heard and to be legally represented.[34] The Court held that the procedure followed by the domestic courts fell short of the system envisaged by Article 5(4) of the ECHR, in that the applicant was neither notified of the proceedings and their outcome, nor given an opportunity to argue his case. Further, the public prosecutor's rejection of the applicant's requests for discharge complied with domestic law but did not qualify as the decision of a Court within the meaning of Article 5(4). Moreover, the ECHR did not impose a requirement on the applicant to appoint himself a legal representative and the respondent State could not rely on his failure to do so to excuse their handling of the proceedings. The rights of the applicant under Article 5(4) of the ECHR had accordingly been breached.

In the decision of *Aerts v Belgium* the ECtHR held that the institution in which the applicant had been detained was not an appropriate environment for a person such as the applicant and that the detention of an individual as a mental health patient was lawful for the purposes of Article 5(1)(e) of the ECHR if it was effected in a hospital, clinic or appropriate institution. The relationship between the aim of the detention and the conditions of the detention was found to be deficient in this case, and it followed that there had been a breach of Article 5(1) of the ECHR.

32 *Winterwerp v The Netherlands* (1979–1980) 2 European Human Rights Reports 387.

33 ibid para 39.

34 However, it is worthy of note that on this issue of the substantive right to liberty that the court in *Winterwerp* ultimately held that the behaviour of the applicant had warranted the use of emergency confinement and that his detention was carried out in accordance with domestic measures which conformed to the requirements of the Convention. There had, therefore, been no breach of art 5(1) of the Convention.

In terms of the scope of the review of detention under Article 5(4), the Court held in *X v The United Kingdom*[35] that, '[t]he review should, (...) be wide enough to bear on those conditions which, according to the Convention, are essential for the 'lawful' detention of a person on the ground of unsoundness of mind, especially as the reasons capable of initially justifying such a detention may cease to exist.'[36] On that basis, the Court held that a review of detention by way of habeas corpus was not capable of satisfying the requirements of Article 5.

In *Shtukaturov v Russia*[37] the applicant, who had been declared legally incapable at a hearing which had lasted ten minutes and of which he had not been notified, complained that, inter alia, his detention was in breach of Article 5. Specifically in relation to his right to liberty, the Court held that Article 5(4) requires that a person of unsound mind compulsorily confined in a psychiatric institution for an indefinite or lengthy period be entitled, at any rate where there is no automatic periodic review of a judicial character, to take proceedings at reasonable intervals before a court to put in issue the lawfulness of his detention. The Court noted that it was not clear whether the inquiry carried out by the prosecution authorities concerned the lawfulness of detention and, in any event, found that it had not been a judicial review satisfying Article 5(4). The applicant's detention was not voluntary and the last court assessment of his capacity was ten months before his admission to the hospital in proceedings that were seriously flawed and did not consider the necessity of his placement in a closed institution. No court assessed this when it occurred. In the circumstances, the Court held that the applicant's inability to obtain judicial review of his detention breached Article 5(4).[38]

The right of a person deprived of their liberty based on the existence of a mental disability to challenge their detention was recently endorsed again by the ECtHR in *D.D. v Lithuania*[39] where the Court also referred to the CRPD in its considerations.[40]

The preceding case law shows that the ECtHR has been increasingly stringent regarding the requirements for the valid detention of persons with mental disabilities based on the existence of that disability. As will be demonstrated below, however, such measures, in and of themselves, are not sufficient to bring ECHR jurisprudence in line with the substantive requirements of Article 14 of the CRPD.

3. Article 14 of the UN Convention on the Rights of Persons with Disabilities

Article 14 of the CRPD states:

> 1. States Parties shall ensure that persons with disabilities, on an equal basis with others
>   (a) Enjoy the right to liberty and security of person;

---

35 *X v The United Kingdom* (1981) 4 European Human Rights Reports 188.

36 ibid para 58.

37 *Shtukaturov v Russia* (2008) Mental Health Law Reports 238.

38 ibid at 240.

39 *D.D. v Lithuania* App no 13469/06 (ECtHR 14 February 2012).

40 ibid para 84.

(b) Are not deprived of their liberty unlawfully or arbitrarily, and that any deprivation of liberty is in conformity with the law, and that the existence of a disability shall in no case justify a deprivation of liberty.

2. States Parties shall ensure that if persons with disabilities are deprived of their liberty through any process, they are, on an equal basis with others, entitled to guarantees in accordance with international human rights law and shall be treated in compliance with the objectives and principles of the present Convention, including by provision of reasonable accommodation.[41]

3.1 The Interpretation of Article 14 by the United Nations Committee on the Rights of Persons with Disabilities

The Committee on the Rights of Persons with Disabilities addressed this issue in April 2011 when it adopted its first Concluding Observation[42]– a response to the Country Report submitted to it by Tunisia.[43] Here it stated that: '[w]ith reference to Article 14 of the Convention, the Committee is concerned that having a disability, including an intellectual or psychosocial disability, can constitute a basis for the deprivation of liberty under current legislation.'[44]

The Committee went on to recommend that Tunisia:

> '(…)[R]epeal legislative provisions which allow for the deprivation of liberty on the basis of disability, including a psychosocial or intellectual disability. The Committee further recommends that until new legislation is in place, all cases of persons with disabilities who are deprived of their liberty in hospitals and specialized institutions be reviewed, and that the review include the possibility of appeal.'[45]

This interpretation of Article 14(1)(b) by the Committee has continued in the two subsequent Concluding Observations which it has adopted. In response to Spain's periodic report, the Committee has stated:

> 'The Committee takes note of the legal regime allowing the institutionalization of persons with disabilities, including persons with intellectual and

---

[41] art 14, CRPD (2006).

[42] Consideration of reports submitted by states parties under art 35 of the CRPD. Committee on the Rights of Persons with Disabilities – Concluding observations of the Committee on the Rights of Persons with Disabilities – Tunisia (2011) <www2.ohchr.org//SPdocs/CRPD/5thsession/CRPD-C-TUN-CO-1_en.doc> last accessed 31 March 2016.

[43] The attitude of the Committee towards art 14(1)(b) was somewhat predictable given the initial List of Issues which it published at the foot of Tunisia's report at their Fourth Session which was held from the 4–8 of October 2010. At para 15 of this document they ask Tunisia to 'indicate whether having disabilities, including intellectual, mental and psychosocial disabilities, constitute a basis for the deprivation of liberty under current legislation, either alone or in combination with other grounds. If so, please explain: Whether steps are taken to repeal or amend this legislation, (...)' Both Tunisia's Periodic Report and the Committee's response by way of its List of Issues are available at: <www.ohchr.org/EN/HRBodies/CRPD/Pages/Session4.aspx> last accessed 31 March 2016.

[44] CRPD (n 43) para 24.

[45] ibid para 25.

> psychosocial disabilities ("mental illness"). It is concerned at the reported trend of resorting to urgent measures of institutionalization which contain only ex post facto safeguards for the affected individuals. It is equally concerned at the reported abuse of persons with disabilities who are institutionalized in residential centres or psychiatric hospitals.
>
> The Committee recommends that the State party: review its laws that allow for the deprivation of liberty on the basis of disability, including mental, psychosocial or intellectual disabilities; repeal provisions that authorize involuntary internment linked to an apparent or diagnosed disability; and adopt measures to ensure that health-care services, including all mental-health-care services, are based on the informed consent of the person concerned.'[46]

Similar statements have been contained in many subsequent Concluding Observations including those in respect of Peru,[47] China,[48] Hungary[49] and Paraguay.[50]

The matter has now been put beyond all doubt by the adoption by the Committee on the Rights of Persons with Disabilities of its first General Comment which set out its interpretation of Article 12 of the CRPD ('Equal Recognition before the Law')[51]. Within its analysis of that provision, the Committee noted that:

> 'Recognition of legal capacity is inextricably linked to the enjoyment of many other human rights provided for in the Convention on the Rights of Persons with Disabilities, including, but not limited to, the right to access justice (art. 13); *the right to be free from involuntary detention in a mental health facility*

---

46 Consideration of reports submitted by states parties under art 35 of the CRPD. Committee on the Rights of Persons with Disabilities – Concluding observations of the Committee on the Rights of Persons with Disabilities – Spain (2011) <www.ohchr.org/Documents/HRBodies/CRPD/6thsession/CRPD.C.ESP.CO.1_en.doc> last accessed 31 March 2016, paras 35–36.

47 Consideration of reports submitted by states parties under art 35 of the CRPD. Committee on the Rights of Persons with Disabilities – Concluding observations of the Committee on the Rights of Persons with Disabilities – Peru (2012) <www.ohchr.org/Documents/HRBodies/CRPD/7thsession/CRPD.C.PER.CO.1-ENG.doc> last accessed 31 March 2016, para 28.

48 Consideration of reports submitted by states parties under art 35 of the CRPD. Committee on the Rights of Persons with Disabilities – Concluding observations of the Committee on the Rights of Persons with Disabilities – China (2012) <http://docstore.ohchr.org/SelfServices/FilesHandler.ashx ?enc=6QkG1d%2fPPRiCAqhKb7yhsrBkvDLHrFFq8wSOe2z9g3jLWXscOK3cW%2bh6NEqWxDjRLAKgX49CP9xOmOS0nj0fJI6mx6njq3Tv58P4WDFvkFwfkKJ4vgykAxFZLMUDgW7S> last accessed 31 March 2016, para 26.

49 Consideration of reports submitted by states parties under art 35 of the CRPD. Committee on the Rights of Persons with Disabilities – Concluding observations of the Committee on the Rights of Persons with Disabilities – Hungary (2012) <http://docstore.ohchr.org/SelfServices/FilesHandler.ashx?enc=6QkG1d%2fPPRiCAqhKb7yhsmg8z0DXeL2x2%2fDmZ9jKJskZ6Y9eRc8 3PT5FhFy95TQZkyGQot9vWZBNEf0eAwM4AH0py5P0KQ9jmr6ZHdZ17dnUAKIzS4Qpi81YhvnXxVrA> last accessed 31 March 2016, paras. 27-28.

50 Consideration of reports submitted by states parties under Art. 35 of the CRPD. Committee on the Rights of Persons with Disabilities – Concluding observations of the Committee on the Rights of Persons with Disabilities – Paraguay 2013 <http://docstore.ohchr.org/SelfServices/FilesHandler.ashx?enc=6QkG1d%2fPPRiCAqhKb7yhsgS19RWfPJldrCFmmb%2b7m2ungB6Pi9l9xVGXNTsk%2fsLPwJa73BTPaIjO%2bm7iKKquuDLwB3ZOqV4uVBs6N951vV01thhR8Q%2bWcPiMHUSrGf79> last accessed 31 March 2016, paras 33–36.

51 Committee on the Rights of Persons with Disabilities, General Comment No. 1–Article 12: Equal recognition before the law (2014) <http://daccess-dds-ny.un.org/doc/UNDOC/GEN/G14/031 /20/PDF/G1403120.pdf?OpenElement> last accessed 31 March 2016.

> *and not to be forced to undergo mental health treatment (art. 14)*; the right to respect for one's physical and mental integrity (art. 17); the right to liberty of movement and nationality (art. 18); the right to choose where and with whom to live (art. 19); the right to freedom of expression (art. 21); the right to marry and found a family (art. 23); the right to consent to medical treatment (art. 25); and the right to vote and stand for election (art. 29). Without recognition of the person as a person before the law, the ability to assert, exercise and enforce those rights, and many other rights provided for in the Convention, is significantly compromised.'[52]

The Committee further elaborated its position on Article 14 in the context of Article 12 when it stated:

> 'Respecting the right to legal capacity of persons with disabilities on an equal basis with others includes respecting the right of persons with disabilities to liberty and security of the person. The denial of the legal capacity of persons with disabilities and their detention in institutions against their will, either without their consent or with the consent of a substitute decision-maker, is an ongoing problem. This practice constitutes arbitrary deprivation of liberty and violates articles 12 and 14 of the Convention. States Parties must refrain from such practices and establish a mechanism to review cases whereby persons with disabilities have been placed in a residential setting without their specific consent.'[53]

The Committee has therefore clearly affirmed that the involuntary detention of persons on the basis of their mental disability, whether intellectual or psychosocial, is contrary to the requirements of Article 14, and that the imposition of safeguards such as mandatory periodic review (as have been crafted by the ECtHR) will not be sufficient to cure that basic violation of the individual's right to liberty. It has instead clarified, quite predictably, that the right of persons with disabilities to not be involuntarily detained based on the existence of their psychosocial disability is inextricably linked to, and in fact an extension of, the right of all individuals to recognition of their legal capacity (regardless of the requirement an individual might have for support in making or communicating that decision).

Little doubt therefore remains regarding the requirements placed on States Parties to the CRPD with respect to their involuntary detention laws based on Article 14.

3.2 External Commentary on Article 14 of the CRPD

It is worth noting that even prior to the Committee on the Rights of Persons with Disabilities' authoritative interpretation of Article 14, the United Nations High Commissioner for Human Rights had already interpreted Article 14(1)(b) as prohibiting the removal of a person's liberty on the basis of the existence of a mental disability (ie including their involuntary detention under mental health legislation). It noted that proposals made during the drafting of the CRPD to limit the prohibition of detention to cases 'solely' determined by disability were rejected.

---

52 ibid para 31.

53 ibid para 40.

Therefore 'unlawful detention' under the CRPD even encompasses situations where the deprivation of liberty is grounded in the combination of factors such as a mental or intellectual disability and other elements such as dangerousness, or care and treatment. Since such measures are partly justified by the person's disability, they are to be considered discriminatory and in violation of the prohibition of deprivation of liberty on the grounds of disability contained in Article 14.[54] This interpretation of the implications of Article 14 of the CRPD has also been endorsed by the UN's Special Rapporteur on Torture and Other Cruel, Inhuman or Degrading Treatment or Punishment.[55]

The UNHCHR clarified that Article 14 of the CRPD should not be interpreted to mean that persons with disabilities cannot be lawfully subject to detention for care and treatment or to preventive detention, but that the legal grounds upon which restriction of liberty is determined must be de-linked from the disability and neutrally defined so as to apply to all persons on an equal basis.[56]

4. Conclusion

The difference in legal standards which is currently applied by the European Court of Human Rights to the involuntary detention of persons with disabilities under Article 5(1)(e) of the ECHR on the one hand, and the interpretation which has been given by Committee on the Rights of Persons with Disabilities to Article 14 of the CRPD on the other hand, presents a substantive issue for Member States of the Council of Europe who have ratified or will ratify the CRPD.

The Court has not been slow to reference the CRPD in the context of disability. Their decision in *Glor v Switzerland*[57] saw the Court expressly endorse the CRPD concept of 'reasonable accommodation' and found that on the basis of the CRPD there was 'a European and universal consensus on the necessity to protect persons suffering from a disability from discriminatory treatment.'[58] This general approval of the CRPD has continued in subsequent decision touching on the rights of persons with disabilities such as *Kiss v Hungary*,[59] *Jasinskis v Latvia*,[60] *Seal v The United Kingdom*[61] and *Kiyutin v Russia*.[62] However, none of these decisions touched on the right to liberty or the compatibility of Article 5 of the ECHR with Article 14 of the CRPD. Ultimately, despite these laudable endorsements of the CRPD, the Court is faced with the reality that Article 5(1)(e) of the ECHR specifically provides for

54 United Nations High Commissioner for Human Rights and the Secretary General, 'Thematic Study by the Office of the United Nations High Commissioner for Human Rights on Enhancing awareness and Understanding of the Convention on the Rights of Persons with Disabilities' (2009) A/HRC/10/48, para 48.

55 United Nations General Assembly, M Nowak, 'Interim report of the Special Rapporteur on Torture and other cruel, Inhuman or Degrading Treatment or Punishment' (2008) A/63/175 para 64.

56 Committee on the Rights of Persons with Disabilities (n 43) para 49.

57 *Glor v Switzerland* App no 13444/04 (ECtHR 30 April 2009).

58 ibid 9.

59 *Kiss v Hungary* App no 38832/06 (EctHR 20 May 2010).

60 *Jasinskis v Latvia* App no 45744/08 (ECtHR 21 December 2010).

61 *Seal v The United Kingdom* App no 50330/07 (ECtHR 7 December 2010).

62 *Kiyutin v Russia* App no 2700/10 (ECtHR 10 March 2011).

action by States Parties and their agents which is contrary to Article 14 the CRPD. Indeed, the *Winterwerp* criteria, the touchstone of ECHR jurisprudence in this area, are themselves incompatible with Article 14 of the CRPD in that they base the lawfulness of detention on the existence of a 'mental disorder.'

As a result, while it would appear that its procedural guarantees on this issue are, at the very least, not inconsistent with those contained in Article 14 of the CRPD, there is a clear disparity between its substantive protection of the right to liberty of persons with mental disabilities and the corresponding right contained in Article 14. The implications of these two levels of protection are all the more apparent for EU Member States in light of the 'confirmation' (ratification) by the EU of the CRPD on 23 December 2010,[63] and its implications for Member States of the EU.

A possible means by which Member States of the Council of Europe who have ratified the CRPD could reconcile these divergent standards regarding the substantive right to liberty of persons with mental disabilities would be to accede to the international shift in legal opinion on this issue and to alter its legislation and future jurisprudence accordingly. Nothing in Article 5(1) of the ECHR prohibits Member States from applying disability-neutral criteria to legislation which involves the detention of individuals. It simply provides a lawful justification for such detention if it is part of the domestic legal framework. There is therefore no legal impediment within the ECHR to a Member State choosing to apply, at a legislative level, such a disability-neutral standard, and this could not be a basis upon which the ECtHR could find a violation of Article 5 of the ECHR. In other words, the formulation of legislation compatible with Article 14 would also ensure ECHR compliance, whereas the reverse would not be true.

Realistically, however, this may prove to be a bridge too far at present for countries that have ratified both international instruments and which have had a historical practice of justifying the involuntary detention of persons with mental disabilities based on the existence of that disability. The UN Committee on the Rights of Persons with Disabilities' statements on this point, both by way of its Concluding Observations, its General Comment on Legal Capacity and its responses to individual petitions under the CRPD's Optional Protocol (where that has been ratified by a State Party), will undoubtedly play a crucial role in affecting such shifts in the legal landscape of disability rights for those in Council of Europe countries.

---

[63] Council Decision of 26 November 2009 concerning the conclusion, by the European Community, of the United Nations Convention on the Rights of Persons with Disabilities – 2010/48/EC [2010] OJ L 23/35.

Chapter 13

MENTAL HEALTH LAW: A PARADIGM FOR ITS DISSOLUTION

Tina Minkowitz

1. Introduction

The unstated premise of mental health law is the need for a body of law to maintain control over the lives and bodies of people with psychosocial disabilities. While mental health legislation also encompasses laws for accreditation and quality control of mental health services, the issues that interest mental health lawyers are issues such as civil commitment, compulsory treatment, guardianship and the insanity defence. While these practices exist, there is certainly a need for lawyers to defend people against them to the best of the lawyer's ability. However, the new paradigm of human rights law as applied to people with psychosocial disabilities requires that coercive measures based on the existence of a psychosocial disability be abolished. Mental health lawyers need to participate in the move towards abolition, and join in the creation of a new field of human rights law from a psychosocial-disability perspective.

This chapter will review the relevant provisions of the Convention on the Rights of Persons with Disabilities (CRPD)[1] and their application by the Committee on the Rights of Persons with Disabilities and other relevant UN bodies, with regard to the issues of concern to mental health lawyers. As guardianship is addressed in another chapter by this author in the same volume, this chapter will cover civil commitment, compulsory treatment and the insanity defence, along with related issues in the policing and prison systems. The rights of children and young people in the mental health system are not addressed here, but it is noted that such exploration is needed.

2. Civil Commitment and the CRPD

Civil commitment is prohibited by Article 14 paragraph 1(b), which requires States to ensure that deprivation of liberty shall in no case be justified by the existence of a disability. During the negotiations, States Parties rejected proposals to add the term 'solely' to this phrase, and the chair of negotiations summed up discussion by saying that it was a non-discrimination provision, and that a person with a disability who posed a danger to others should be dealt with as anyone else in that situation.[2]

---

1 UN Convention on the Rights of Persons with Disabilities (CRPD) (2006) A/Res/ 61/106.

2 Daily Summaries, 26 January 2005 <www.un.org/esa/socdev/enable/rights/ahc5sum26jan.htm >; 18 January 2006 <www.un.org/esa/socdev/enable/rights/ahc7sum18jan.htm>; and 19

The Ad Hoc Committee struck a balance so as to ensure that persons with disabilities were not exempt, on the ground of disability, from the operation of otherwise lawful processes for the deprivation of liberty such as criminal arrest, while also prohibiting any measure that drew its justification from the existence of the disability itself. By rejecting the term 'solely', negotiating parties avoided creating a loophole for civil commitment based on the existence of a disability in combination with other factors, such as likelihood of harm to the person or to others, or need for care and treatment, which are typical criteria found in mental health legislation.[3]

The Office of the High Commissioner for Human Rights ('OHCHR') provided some early guidance on legislative measures necessary for implementation of the CRPD. OHCHR said:

> 'Legislation authorizing the institutionalization of persons with disabilities on the grounds of their disability without their free and informed consent must be abolished. This must include the repeal of provisions authorizing institutionalization of persons with disabilities for their care and treatment without their free and informed consent, as well as provisions authorizing the preventive detention of persons with disabilities on grounds such as the likelihood of them posing a danger to themselves or others, in all cases in which such grounds of care, treatment and public security are linked in legislation to an apparent or diagnosed mental illness. This should not be interpreted to say that persons with disabilities cannot be lawfully subject to detention for care and treatment or to preventive detention, but that the legal grounds upon which restriction of liberty is determined must be de-linked from the disability and neutrally defined so as to apply to all persons on an equal basis.'[4]

The last sentence in this paragraph risks being misunderstood. It allows for the possibility that States might maintain a system of preventive detention, or a system of detention for care and treatment without violating Article 14 if such measures apply equally to all people, and do not target persons with disabilities. Although such systems may be objectionable for other reasons, the grounds for challenging them cannot be found in Article 14 of the CRPD, which is a non-discrimination provision.

'De-linking' and 'neutral definition' need to be understood in light of the definition of discrimination based on disability in Article 2, that is:

> 'any distinction, exclusion or restriction on the basis of disability which has the purpose or effect of impairing or nullifying the recognition, enjoyment or exercise, on an equal basis with others, of all human rights and fundamental freedoms in the political, economic, social, cultural, civil or any other

---

January 2006, <www.un.org/esa/socdev/enable/rights/ahc7sum19jan.htm> last accessed 31 March 2016.

3 Interim Report of the Special Rapporteur on Torture and other cruel, inhuman or degrading treatment or punishment, A/63/175 (28 July 2008) [SRT] para 64; Thematic Study by the United Nations Office of the High Commissioner for Human Rights on enhancing awareness and understanding of the Convention on the Rights of Persons with Disabilities, A/HRC/10/48 (26 January 2009) [OHCHR Study] paras 48–49.

4 OHCHR Study (n 3) para 49.

field. It includes all forms of discrimination, including denial of reasonable accommodation.'

If a law were passed that only superficially de-linked the grounds for detention from disability, while targeting persons with disabilities indirectly or through differential application in practice, it would continue to violate Article 14. Detention 'for care and treatment' in particular would need to be scrutinized because of the overlap between health conditions and disability; it is likely that responding to any health condition with compulsory treatment would be evidence of a social barrier such that persons having that condition would be covered under the CRPD as persons with disabilities.

The Committee on the Rights of Persons with Disabilities in its early jurisprudence has confirmed that Article 14 requires States Parties to repeal legal provisions authorizing the deprivation of liberty of persons with psychosocial and intellectual disabilities.[5] The Committee has also elaborated that this refers to 'provisions which authorize involuntary internments linked to an apparent or diagnosed disability' (adopting the language of OHCHR), and further called on the States Parties to 'ensure that all health care services including all mental health care services are based on informed consent of the person concerned.'[6]

The Committee's decision to address informed consent under Article 14 underscores the shift that needs to be made in inpatient as well as outpatient services, so that all hospital admissions as well as the treatment offered are enabled to function for the sole purpose of meeting the needs of clients as clients themselves wish those needs to be met.

It should be noted that access to justice, as required by Article 13 of the CRPD, is insufficient on its own to address civil commitment, as the standard to be applied by a court in ruling on the lawfulness of detention is found in Article 14, under which no instance of civil commitment would be lawful. Article 19 similarly is insufficient to address civil commitment, which entails confinement to a particular place as well as a deprivation of the right to not be compelled to live in a particular living arrangement.

Finally, the Special Rapporteur on Torture points out the harm that is done by civil commitment, such that in some cases the pain and suffering inflicted may rise to the level of torture and ill-treatment.[7] The length of institutionalization, conditions of detention and the treatment inflicted must be taken into account in making this assessment.[8]

---

5 Concluding observations of the Committee on the Rights of Persons with Disabilities: Tunisia, C/CRPD/TUN/CO/1 (29 April 2011) [CO-Tunisia] paras 24 and 25; Concluding observations of the Committee on the Rights of Persons with Disabilities: Spain, C/CRPD/ESP/CO/1 (2011) [CO-Spain] paras 35 and 36; Concluding observations of the Committee on the Rights of Persons with Disabilities: Peru, C/CRPD/PER/CO/1 (20 April 2012) [CO-Peru] paras 28 and 29.

6 CO-Spain (n 5), para 36.

7 SRT (n 3), para 65.

8 ibid; see also T Minkowitz, 'Forced interventions and institutionalization as torture/CIDT from the perspective of persons with disabilities,' Annex III to Final Report of OHCHR Expert Seminar on Torture and Ill Treatment and Persons with Disabilities (11 December 2007) [Forced

3. Compulsory Treatment and the CRPD

Compulsory mental health treatment is prohibited by the CRPD under several articles read separately and together. We have already seen that Article 14 is interpreted to require mental health services based on informed consent of the person concerned, and particularly prohibits detention or involuntary confinement in a psychiatric hospital or institution.

Article 12 requires States to recognize that persons with disabilities enjoy legal capacity with others in all aspects of life, and to provide access to support that may be needed by persons with disabilities to exercise their legal capacity, while also establishing safeguards to prevent abuse of any such measures. This includes exercise of legal capacity to make decisions about health care and treatment.[9]

The Committee on the Rights of Persons with Disabilities has interpreted the core requirement of Article 12 to be replacement of substituted decision-making regimes by supported decision-making, which respects the person's autonomy, will and preferences.[10] To the extent that coercive mental health services function systemically as a regime of substituted decision-making, Article 12 requires that this system be replaced by one of supported decision-making, in which all actions are governed by respect for the person's autonomy, will and preferences. A number of practices developed as alternatives to the medical model of mental health are designed to function in this way.[11] Peer advocates can be helpful to assist people with finding out the information they need to make a decision about mental health services and alternatives, and with getting the services that they want.[12]

4. Article 19 CRPD

Article 19 on living independently in the community mandates a shift not only from institutions to community services, but also from services where care providers are the primary protagonists, to services and supports that are designed to be auxiliary to the person's own life, agency and needs as experienced by that person. Mental health services, and peer-run alternatives to such services, need to provide space for people to experience healing and recovery and connections with others while not becoming in themselves a source of isolation and segregation from the community.

4.1 Articles 15, 16, 17 and 25 of the CRPD

Articles 15, 16, 17 and 25 directly address the issue of compulsory treatment. Article 25 paragraph (d) obligates States to require health professionals to provide health care to persons with disabilities which is of the same quality as that which

interventions] <www.ohchr.org/EN/Issues/Disability/Pages/UNStudiesAndReports.aspx> last accessed 31 March 2016.

9 SRT (n 3), para 44.

10 CO-Spain (n 5), para 34; CO-Peru (n 5), para 25.

11 T Minkowitz, 'Abolishing Mental Health Laws to Comply with the CRPD,' in B McSherry and P Weller (eds), *Rethinking Rights-Based Mental Health Laws* (Hart 2010) 162–166.

12 World Network of Users and Survivors of Psychiatry, 'Implementation Manual for the United Nations Convention on the Rights of Persons with Disabilities' (February 2008) 37–38.

is available to others, including on the basis of free and informed consent. The principle of free and informed consent needs to be understood as a right of the person designed to protect his or her autonomy and personal integrity – not as a formality required to satisfy legal principles or defend health care providers against unjustified lawsuits. This approach dovetails with the shift in legal capacity from a concern with criteria for validity of a legal act, to the promotion of autonomy and mutuality in and through legal relations.[13]

The practical implication of the provision requiring free and informed consent, read together with Article 12 on legal capacity, is to require that mental health services are based on free and informed consent of the person concerned. A logical corollary of the right to free and informed consent is the right to refuse treatment,[14] which must be incorporated into legislation so that individuals can have a remedy. Any legal permissions or immunities for compulsory mental health treatment need to be voided or abolished.

4.2 Articles 15, 16 and 17 of the CRPD

Articles 15, 16 and 17 all deal with issues of the integrity of the person. Article 15 incorporates the universal right to freedom from torture and ill-treatment, including freedom from non-consensual medical and scientific experimentation, and requires States to take all effective measures to prevent persons with disabilities from being subjected to torture or other ill-treatment. Article 16 requires States to take measures to protect persons with disabilities from all forms of exploitation, violence and abuse; to prevent abuse by means such as educating persons with disabilities and their families and caregivers on how to avoid abuse; to ensure independent monitoring of services and facilities designed to serve persons with disabilities; to promote recovery and social reintegration of persons with disabilities who are victimized by exploitation, violence and abuse, in an environment that fosters health, welfare, self-respect, dignity and autonomy of the person; and to ensure that instances of exploitation, violence and abuse against persons with disabilities are identified, investigated and, where appropriate, prosecuted. Article 17 states that every person with disabilities has a right to respect for his or her physical and mental integrity on an equal basis with others.

The three articles are both overlapping and complementary with each other. Article 15 brings a disability dimension to the obligations of States under the torture-prevention framework in international and domestic law and mechanisms. The obligation is to take effective prevention measures irrespective of whether particular violations are characterized as torture or ill-treatment.[15] This author has argued that forced psychiatric interventions meet the definition of torture set out in Article 1 of the Convention Against Torture,[16] and has also set out an alternative framework

---

13 See article by this author in the chapter on legal capacity.

14 Committee on Economic, Social and Cultural Rights, General Comment No. 14, E/C.12/2000/4 (2000) paras 8 and 34 (note that in para 34, the exceptional permission for coercive treatment for mental illness relies on outdated standards and cannot be maintained in light of the CRPD); Situation of detainees at Guantánamo Bay: Report, E/CN.4/2006/120 (2006) para 82.

15 See also Committee Against Torture, General Comment No. 2, CAT/C/GC/2/CRP.1/Rev.4 (2007) para 3.

16 T Minkowitz, The United Nations Convention on the Rights of Persons with Disabilities and

of factors that support the characterization of these practices as forms of torture and ill-treatment.[17] The Special Rapporteur on Torture has accepted this premise and set out detailed guidelines for assessing such claims, which this chapter will address in further detail below.

The Committee on the Rights of Persons with Disabilities has expressed concern under Article 15 about 'continuous forcible medication' with neuroleptics in psychiatric institutions.[18] The Committee also urged the State Party to investigate allegations of ill-treatment, review the legality of individuals' placement in institutions, and create community-based mental health services to facilitate inclusion in communities and people's ability to leave institutions.

4.3 Article 16 and 17 of the CRPD

Article 16 takes a practical and holistic approach to violence-prevention and remedies, which is relevant to healing and recovery from psychiatric abuse, and to educating mental health workers and monitoring services so as to ensure a true transformation of the mental health system, from a culture of compliance to one of respect and mutual learning. Individuals may need help to go off psychiatric drugs, and to rebuild their lives after losing homes, jobs and relationships to long- or short-term compulsory hospitalisation or institutionalisation. The post-traumatic stress that people experience as a result of psychiatric abuse has consequences that need to be acknowledged politically, socially and legally, as well as being a matter for individuals' own healing.[19]

Article 17 recognizes the right to respect for integrity, which people with disabilities enjoy on an equal basis with others. Integrity includes autonomy and dignity, as well as respect for diversity. Persons with disabilities have the right to experience themselves as being different from others without having that difference condemned and violently attacked, even when that violence is done under the mistaken belief that it is therapeutic or curative. Under Article 17, the Committee on the Rights of Persons with Disabilities has urged States Parties to incorporate into law the abolition of compulsory medical treatment.[20]

5. Special Rapporteur on Torture

The Special Rapporteur on Torture in 2008 devoted a section of his report to the General Assembly to the subject of 'Protecting persons with disabilities from torture.'[21] A substantial part of the report focused on abuse in the medical context, and it went into considerable detail on forced psychiatric interventions.

---

the Right to be Free from Nonconsensual Psychiatric Interventions, 34 Syracuse J of Intl L and Commerce (2007) [Freedom from Nonconsensual Interventions] 405.

17 T Minkowitz, Forced interventions (n 8).

18 CO-Peru (n 5), paras 30–31.

19 Basic Principles and Guidelines on the Right to a Remedy and Reparation for Victims of Gross Violations of International Human Rights Law and Serious Violations of International Humanitarian Law, A/RES/60/147 (21 March 2006) (Reparation Guidelines).

20 CO-Tunisia (n 5), paras 28–29; CO-Spain (n 5) para 38.

21 SRT (n 3).

Practices of concern to the Rapporteur included segregation in institutions, deprivation of liberty against the person's will or without the person's free and informed consent, severe forms of restraint and seclusion, medical experimentation and 'intrusive and irreversible medical treatments without their consent (eg sterilization, abortion and interventions aiming to correct or alleviate a disability, such as electroshock and mind-altering drugs including neuroleptics).'[22] 'Such practices,' the report stated, 'when perpetrated against persons with disabilities, remain invisible or are being justified, and are not recognized as torture or other cruel, inhuman or degrading treatment or punishment.'[23]

The broad principle recognizing that compulsory medical treatments may amount to torture is devised in relation to an assessment of the level of pain and suffering, which is one of the four elements of the definition of torture in Article 1 of the Convention Against Torture (the others are intent, purpose and state involvement).

Whereas a fully justified medical treatment may lead to severe pain or suffering, medical treatments of an intrusive and irreversible nature, when they lack a therapeutic purpose or aim at correcting or alleviating a disability, may constitute torture and ill-treatment if enforced or administered without the free and informed consent of the person concerned.[24]

As noted above, the category of intrusive and irreversible treatments aimed at correcting or alleviating a disability includes 'electroshock and mind-altering drugs including neuroleptics.' The principle combines respect for personal autonomy, respect for integrity, and respect for diversity. Non-discrimination, in the form of the right to be different, is invoked in the acknowledgement that correcting or alleviating a disability, when forced or coerced, can be an infliction of severe pain and suffering.[25]

The Rapporteur recalls that the definition of torture expressly proscribes the infliction of pain and suffering for reasons based on discrimination of any kind (under the element of purpose),[26] and says that the intent required for torture can also be satisfied when a person has been discriminated against on the basis of disability. Medical professionals in particular cannot be excused when 'good intentions' mask severe violations and discrimination, while 'purely negligent treatment' not constituting an act of discrimination could nevertheless amount to ill-treatment.[27]

State responsibility, the final element of the torture definition, attaches to the obligation to enforce the prohibition of torture in all institutions, and to exercise due diligence to investigate, prosecute and punish violations in private as well as public institutions.[28]

Applying these elements to compulsory treatment with mind-altering drugs or

---

22 ibid para 40.
23 ibid para 41.
24 ibid para 47.
25 T Minkowitz, Freedom from Nonconsensual Interventions (n 16).
26 SRT (n 3), para 48.
27 ibid para 49.
28 ibid para 51.

electroshock qualifies such treatment as torture. Discrimination is always present since the intervention is aimed at correcting or alleviating a disability, and States incur responsibility when they allow private and public institutions to enforce or administer treatment without the free and informed consent of the person concerned.

The Rapporteur takes a case-by-case approach to the question of whether forced psychiatric interventions constitute torture or ill-treatment, saying that this depends on the circumstances of the case, the suffering inflicted and the effects on the person's health.[29] If this standard is used in evaluating individual claims regarding compulsory treatment, the right to a remedy and reparations should be kept in mind, adopting a standpoint in solidarity with the person who has been victimized.[30] In particular, credence should be given to the person's experience of suffering and of ill-effects on health. It would be a further infliction of abuse to allow mental health professionals to offer justification for compulsory treatment on the ground that the person's mental health was deemed to have improved.

6. Insanity Defence and Issues in Policing and Prison Systems

CRPD requires a re-thinking of international standards on the treatment of persons with psychosocial disabilities by police, prisons and other detention settings, and penal law and procedure. The Standard Minimum Rules on the Treatment of Prisoners, a non-binding instrument adopted in 1955, is currently under review by the United Nations Commission on Crime Prevention and Criminal Justice, and this presents an opportunity to conform the Rules to the requirements of the CRPD as well as other human rights treaties and updated standards.[31]

Article 12 provides that persons with disabilities have legal capacity on an equal basis with others in all aspects of life. Legal capacity entails responsibilities as well as rights, and there is no reason why criminal responsibility should be excluded from the standard of equal legal capacity of persons with disabilities, unlike the comparable rule in the Convention on the Elimination of all Forms of Discrimination against Women, which is limited to civil matters.[32] While it may seem counter-intuitive to have a right to responsibility, it is a matter of social inclusion and participation. As stated in Article 29 of the Universal Declaration of Human Rights, '[e]veryone has duties to the community in which alone the free and full development of his [or her] personality is possible.'

The Office of the High Commissioner for Human Rights adopted this position, saying:

---

29 ibid para 63.

30 Reparation Guidelines (n 19), Preamble and 10.

31 Commission on Crime Prevention and Criminal Justice, Report on the twenty-first session (13 December 2011 and 23–27 April 2012) E/2012/30, E/CN.15/2012/24 ch I.A.I; T Minkowitz for World Network of Users and Survivors of Psychiatry, 'Persons with Psychosocial Disabilities and the Standard Minimum Rules on the Treatment of Prisoners' (Inter-governmental Expert Meeting on the Standard Minimum Rules on the Treatment of Prisoners) <www.chrusp/org/media/AA/AG/chrusp-biz/downloads/198693/SMR_and_PWPD.docx> last accessed 31 March 2016.

32 UNTS vol 1249 p 13, adopted 18 December 1979, entered into force 3 September 1981, art 15.

> 'In the area of criminal law, recognition of the legal capacity of persons with disabilities requires abolishing a defence based on the negation of criminal responsibility because of the existence of a mental or intellectual disability. Instead disability-neutral doctrines on the subjective element of the crime should be applied, which take into consideration the situation of the individual defendant. Procedural accommodations both during the pre-trial and trial phase of the proceedings might be required in accordance with article 13 of the Convention, and implementing norms must be adopted.'[33]

Article 13 requires States to ensure effective access to justice for persons with disabilities on an equal basis with others, including procedural accommodations, and to promote appropriate training for police and prison staff. Article 13 focuses on practical implementation, and establishes the principle that justice must be equally effective for persons with disabilities as it is for other persons. Beyond procedural accommodations in conventional legal proceedings, effective access to justice can also be served by alternative approaches to both civil and criminal responsibility from a restorative justice paradigm, that aim to do substantive justice for all persons concerned rather than focusing narrowly on blame and punishment.[34] In exploring restorative justice approaches, it is essential that as all persons concerned agree to use such practices, and that outcomes are consistent with the CRPD. 'Diversion' from the criminal justice system into the mental health system is not consistent with the CRPD if the person is not free to refuse treatment at any time without penalty, or if mental health services are the only option being offered to people with psychosocial disabilities who may not see their needs as being defined by mental health issues.

Article 14 paragraph 2 provides that persons with disabilities who are deprived of their liberty are entitled on an equal basis with others to guarantees in accordance with international law. This provision applies to guarantees in the context of arrest, legal proceedings related to the deprivation of liberty, and conditions of detention, including those contained in the International Covenant on Civil and Political Rights, Articles 9, 10, 11, 14 and 15.[35] For example, persons with disabilities are entitled to the presumption of innocence and to have a fair trial to adjudicate guilt on an equal basis as other persons. Diversion to disability-based security measures in lieu of a conventional trial violates this principle.

Also under Article 14 paragraph 2, persons with disabilities are entitled to be treated in compliance with objectives and principles of the CRPD, including by provision of reasonable accommodation. In places of detention, persons with disabilities have the right to be considered eligible for all programs, housing and services on an equal basis with others.[36] Traumatising and demeaning practices like strip-searches should be replaced by measures in keeping with human dignity, lessening the need to modify such practices as an accommodation for prisoners with psychosocial

---

33 OHCHR Study (n 3), para 47.

34 W D McCaslin (ed), *Justice as Healing: Indigenous Ways* (Living Justice Press 2005); K Pranis, 'Restorative values,' in G Johnstone and D W Van Ness (eds), *Handbook of Restorative Justice* (Willan Publishing 2007).

35 UN *International Covenant on Civil and Political Rights* (1966) A/Res/2200.

36 See World Network of Users and Survivors of Psychiatry, 'Discussion Paper on Mental Health and Prison Systems' <www.chrusp.org//media/AA/AG/chrusp-biz/downloads/200273/WNUSPDiscussionPaperPrisonsMH.doc> last accessed 31 March 2016.

disabilities and any others with a history of past trauma. Placement in a mental health unit or under medical supervision should not be done routinely based on a person's history of receiving mental health services, or without the person's free and informed consent; a person should also be entitled to receive desired mental health services and supports in the general population, without having to enter a special unit. Compulsory mental health treatment is unjustified in any setting.

7. Conclusion

Mental health law, as it has been known up to this time, is changed beyond recognition by the CRPD. If the CRPD is fully implemented, the subjects dealt with by mental health law will become obsolete. Furthermore, following the model of the CRPD, it should be a branch of non-discrimination law and a critical disability/madness perspective that deals with the rights of persons with psychosocial disabilities, and not a branch of health law that reduces people to the status of 'mental patients.'[37]

[37] World Network of Users and Survivors of Psychiatry, 'Position Paper on the Principles for the Protection of Persons with Mental Illness' <http://wnusp.rafus.dk/position-paper-on-principles-for-the-protection-of-persons-with-mental-illness.html> last accessed 31 March 2016.

CHAPTER 14

'NEW' RIGHTS FOR MENTAL HEALTH LAWS? THE RIGHT TO THE ENJOYMENT OF THE HIGHEST ATTAINABLE STANDARD OF HEALTH AND THE RIGHTS OF CARERS

Bernadette McSherry

1. INTRODUCTION

In 2005, Murray Allen, then President of the Western Australian Mental Health Review Board, posed the question:

> We don't have (or presumably need) a Cancer Act or a Dementia Act, so what is the purpose of the various Mental Health Acts and other similar legislation?[1]

The existence of specific mental health legislation has traditionally been justified on the basis of what Genevra Richardson terms 'three broad goals: the provision of access to health care, the protection of the patient and the protection of others'.[2]

Much of the debate about mental health laws has focused on the latter two goals rather than the first one of the provision of access to health care. Other chapters in this volume explore the implications of the right to legal capacity and the right to liberty set out in the Convention on the Rights of Persons with Disabilities 2006 (CRPD) in relation to those with mental and intellectual impairments.[3] The focus in these chapters is on the 'proper' scope of state authority in encroaching upon the rights of the individual.

The right to liberty and legal capacity are generally referred to as 'negative' rights in the sense that they encompass freedom from state interference. The CRPD, however, goes further than other conventions in including economic, social and cultural rights,

---

1 M Allen, 'Why Specific Legislation for the Mentally Ill?' (2005) 30(3) Alternative Law Journal 103, 103.

2 G Richardson, 'Balancing Autonomy and Risk: A Failure of Nerve in England and Wales?' (2007) 30 International Journal of Law and Psychiatry 71, 71.

3 The term 'mental impairments' is used throughout this chapter as this is the term used in art 1 of the Convention on the Rights of Persons with Disabilities (CRPD). That Article states: 'Persons with disabilities include those who have long-term physical, *mental*, intellectual or sensory *impairments* which in interaction with various barriers may hinder their full and effective participation in society on an equal basis with others' [emphasis added].

which are often referred to as 'positive' rights in placing obligations on States Parties to ensure certain rights are upheld. While these two sets of rights have been described as 'indivisible and interrelated',[4] in practice, civil and political rights 'have dominated the international agenda.'[5] The CRPD is significant in outlining a number of obligations to ensure non-discrimination in the areas of employment, education, health, housing, transport and access to justice.[6]

This chapter is concerned with two sets of rights that are not often discussed in relation to mental health laws. The first is the 'positive' right set out in Article 25 of the CRPD, which refers to 'the right to the enjoyment of the highest attainable standard of health without discrimination on the basis of disability'. As explained below, this encompasses a right to the enjoyment of those services that are necessary for the realisation of the highest attainable standard of health.

The second set of rights deals with carers' rights and how these may be included in mental health laws. There is no reference to carers in the CRPD. There is, however, a reference to the family in the Preamble with paragraph (x) stating that:

> '...the family is the natural and fundamental group unit of society and is entitled to protection by society and the State, and...persons with disabilities and their family members should receive the necessary protection and assistance to enable families to contribute towards the full and equal enjoyment of the rights of persons with disabilities... .'

These two sets of rights necessitate a rethinking of the aims of mental health laws, assuming that they remain in place for some time to come.[7] As part of an Australian Research Council Federation Fellowship project,[8] sixty-five semi-structured interviews were conducted in Australia, New Zealand, Canada and the United Kingdom with mental health professionals, consumer and carer representatives, lawyers, academics and judges/decision-makers who had current or past involvement in their relevant mental health systems. While the methodology used and some analyses of these interviews have been published elsewhere,[9] it is worth noting here that two common themes that emerged unprompted from the interviews were

---

4 United Nations, 'The Vienna Declaration and Programme of Action: Report of the World Conference on Human Rights, UN Doc A/CONF. 157/24 (13 October 1993) 5.

5 P Alston, 'Putting Economic, Social and Cultural Rights Back on the Agenda of the United States' in W F Schulz (ed), *The Future of Human Rights: U.S. Policy for a New Era* (University of Philadelphia Press 2008) 120.

6 See in general, A Lawson, 'People with Psychosocial Impairments or Conditions, Reasonable Accommodation and the Convention on the Rights of Persons with Disabilities' in B McSherry (ed), *International Trends in Mental Health Laws* (Federation Press 2008) 62.

7 There is of course a strong argument that mental health laws should be abolished: T Minkowitz, 'Abolishing Mental Health Laws to Comply with the Convention on the Rights of Persons with 'Disabilities' in B McSherry and P Weller, *Rethinking Rights-Based Mental Health Laws* (Oxford: Hart Publishing, 2010) 151.

8 The five-year Australian Research Council Federation Fellowship commenced in 2007: Project No: FF0776072. The main aim of the Federation Fellowship project entitled *Rethinking Mental Health Laws* is to explore the role the law has and should have in improving access to optimal mental health care and promoting and maintaining good mental health.

9 B McSherry and K Wilson, 'Detention and Treatment Down Under: Human Rights and Mental Health Laws in Australia and New Zealand' (2011) 19(4) Medical Law Review 548; K Wilson, 'Law Reform or Systemic Reform? Stakeholder's Perceptions of Resource Constraints in

(a) resource constraints preventing access to good quality mental health care and (b) the lack of information given to carers and families about the civil commitment and tribunal processes and treatment issues.

The next section focuses on Article 25 and what it may mean for mental health laws while the ensuing section turns to carers' rights and the ways in which these are beginning to be incorporated into legislation.

1.1 The Right to the Enjoyment of the Highest Attainable Standard of Health

The first broad goal of mental health legislation referred to by Genevra Richardson – the provision of access to health care – has generally been taken to mean the necessity for a legislative scheme to enable treatment via a 'substitute' decision-making process. That is, the decision to provide treatment to an individual with mental impairment is generally made by a psychiatrist who substitutes his or her decision for that of the individual concerned.

Although many mental health acts now contain provisions referring to involuntary detention and treatment as permissible only where there are no less-restrictive means of providing treatment available, the very existence of mental health legislation enabling involuntary treatment generally means that the mental health system becomes an emergency-driven one with a lack of resources available for access to voluntary treatment. The Victorian Government Department of Human Services has stated that 'services are too focused on the most severely mentally ill'.[10] The same may be said of mental health laws.

While some mental health laws contain separate provisions for those who are being treated on a voluntary basis,[11] most laws focus on involuntary detention and treatment. This skews the system such that those who want treatment may be refused access because they are not 'ill enough', while those who do not want treatment are detained and/or treated without their consent. In the interviews conducted as part of the Australian Research Council Federation Fellowship, half of the interviewees (thirty-seven out of sixty-five) were concerned about resource constraints preventing people with mental impairments obtaining access to treatment, at times with tragic consequences. Kay Wilson points out in this regard:

> 'There was a general concern about the lack of services for voluntary patients. The problem was perceived to be that people seeking treatment for themselves or their children are turned away because they are not sick enough. This means that they are left to deteriorate in the community without treatment until they

Mental Health in Australia, New Zealand and Canada' (2013) 20(4) Psychiatry, Psychology and Law 553.

[10] Victorian Government Department of Human Services, Because Mental Health Matters: A New Focus for Mental Health and Wellbeing in Victoria: Consultation Paper (Department of Human Services, 2008) 13.

[11] For an overview of Australian laws in this regard, see B McSherry, 'The Right of Access to Mental Health Care: Voluntary Treatment and the Role of the Law' in B McSherry and P Weller, *Rethinking Rights-Based Mental Health Laws* (Hart Publishing, 2010) 379.

either commit a crime (and enter the forensic system) or satisfy the criteria for involuntary treatment (and are civilly committed).'[12]

Article 25 of the CRPD can be viewed as shifting the focus away from involuntary treatment towards voluntary access to services. Paragraph (b) of Article 25 requires States Parties to:

> provide those health services needed by persons with disabilities specifically because of their disabilities, including early identification and intervention as appropriate, and services designed to minimize and prevent further disabilities.

Article 25 can be viewed as helping to develop the interpretation of the right to the highest attainable standard of health set out in General Comment No. 14 of the United Nations Committee on Economic, Social and Cultural Rights.[13] Paragraph 9 of the General Comment states that

> the right to health must be understood as a right to the enjoyment of a variety of facilities, goods, services and conditions necessary for the realization of the highest attainable standard of health.

This right to the enjoyment of services marks a significant challenge for mental health laws, given that it is difficult for tribunals and courts to 'force' governments to resource mental health services. Nancy K Rhoden has pointed out in relation to mental health care in the United States that:

> since judicial decrees can grant rights against government infringement of liberty far more easily than they can establish positive entitlements to care and services, the result was that mental patients obtained their liberty, but at the expense of the community care they so desperately needed.[14]

Some laws in fact make it clear that there is no obligation on clinicians to admit those with mental impairments into hospital. For example, section 6(1) of New Brunswick's Mental Health Act 1973[15] states that 'admission to a psychiatric facility may be refused by the authorities at the facility if the immediate needs in the case of the proposed patient are such that hospitalization is not urgent or necessary.'

One existing example that reflects the right to the enjoyment of services relates to powers to review a decision by a clinician not to admit an individual to a mental health facility. Section 25(9) of the Mental Health and Related Services Act (Northern Territory) states:

---

12 K Wilson, 'Law Reform or Systemic Reform? Stakeholder's Perceptions of Resource Constraints in Mental Health in Australia, New Zealand and Canada' (2013) 20(4) Psychiatry, Psychology and Law 553, 567.

13 United Nations Committee on Economic, Social and Cultural Rights, The Right to the Highest Attainable Standard of Health (Art 12 of the International Covenant on Economic, Social and Cultural Rights, General Comment No 14 (22nd Sess), UN Doc E/C12/2000/4, 11 August 2000.

14 N K Rhoden, 'Law and Psychiatry Part II: The Limits of Liberty: Deinstitutionalization, Homelessness, and Libertarian Theory' (1982) 31 Emory Law Journal 375.

15 Mental Health Act, RSNB 1973, c M-10.

> On refusing to admit a person or to confirm the admission of a person under this section, the medical practitioner or authorised psychiatric practitioner:
> (a) must inform the person of the grounds of the decision and that the person has a right to apply to the Tribunal for a review of the decision; and
> (b) must explain the review procedure to the person.

The Mental Health Review Tribunal under section 127(5) has the following powers in relation to reviewing a decision to refuse admission:

> Following a review in relation to an application made under subsection (1), the Tribunal may:
> (a) affirm, vary or set aside the decision or order
> (b) make any decision or order that the medical practitioner or authorised psychiatric practitioner may have made
> (c) refer the matter back to the medical practitioner or authorised psychiatric practitioner for further consideration, or
> (d) make any other order it thinks fit.

This means that the Mental Health Review Tribunal may order that the person concerned be admitted to the facility.

In New South Wales, an individual can apply to the 'medical superintendent' (the psychiatrist in charge of the mental health facility) for a review of a decision not to be admitted to the facility.[16] The New South Wales Minister for Mental Health, Kevin Humphries, has signalled that this may be reformed to enable a right of appeal to the Mental Health Review Tribunal for 'those who are refused access to ensure that mental health services remain open and accessible to consumers.'[17]

There has as yet been no study carried out as to how often the Northern Territory and New South Wales provisions are used. Applying to another psychiatrist for a review of a decision not to admit may not be a popular option for those with mental impairments because of the reviewer's connection to the mental health facility. Review by a Tribunal has the benefit of being seen to be independent from the mental health facility.

The main drawback, however, is that some clinicians would not want to be ordered by a Tribunal to admit a person to a mental health facility. In a recent report on the New South Wales Mental Health Review Tribunal's powers to review involuntary commitment decisions, it was noted that:

> '...the Tribunal is now reviewing whether the care of the person is appropriate. Some clinicians had the view that the Tribunal was entering into the domain of clinical practice, which at times has created friction between lawyers and clinicians.'[18]

---

16 Mental Health Act 2007 (NSW), s 11.

17 K Humphries, 'NSW Government Response to the Release of the Report into the Evaluation of the Efficacy and Cost of the Mental Health Inquiry System', NSW' Media Release 15 March 2012 <www.health.nsw.gov.au/news/2012/20120315_00.html>.

18 Communio, 'Evaluation of Efficacy and Cost of the Mental Health Inquiry System, Final Report'

Provisions for the review of a refusal to admit an individual to mental health services may thus be viewed as interfering with clinical decision-making rather than putting the onus on the government to provide more services. These provisions also only deal with individuals who have been refused admission as inpatients – they do not translate to a refusal to treat in community-based services.

Despite these drawbacks, such provisions at the very least indicate that there is a role for the law in providing access to hospital services on a voluntary basis. This is in line with the obligations placed on States Parties under Article 25. The time is right to explore other options that may address current concerns with resource constraints in the mental health arena.

2. The Rights of Carers

The move away from institutions towards community-based models of health care without adequate resources has led to families bearing the brunt of caring for those with mental impairments. Carers are a vital source of information and expertise, but legislation has failed to reflect this.[19] Reviews of mental health laws have identified as a matter for concern a lack of participation and respect for carers.[20]

Carers have reported feeling disenfranchised and excluded by health providers.[21] Specifically, carers have identified as a significant concern a lack of consultation with them as to the appropriateness of commencing or discontinuing treatment.[22] This is despite research suggesting that early family and carer engagement with mental health services, and the inclusion of carers in decision-making processes, are important in obtaining the best outcomes for individuals with mental impairments.[23]

There have been some legislative reforms that have attempted to meet these concerns. One way of incorporating carers' rights into legislation is to set them out as guiding principles. For example, the Carers Recognition Act 2005 (SA) has seven principles including 'recognising the role carers can play' and that 'views of … carers must be taken into account along with the views, needs and best interests of people receiving care, when decisions impact on carers.' In Scotland, section

(Sydney: Mental Health and Drug and Alcohol Office, NSW Ministry of Health: 2012) p 7. <www.health.nsw.gov.au/resources/whatsnew/pdf/communio_report.pdf>.

19 Victorian Mental Health Carers Network, *Response to the Review of the Mental Health Act (Vic), Submission No 105* <www.health.vic.gov.au/mentalhealth/mhactreview/submissions/sub105.pdf> last accessed 31 March 2016.

20 The Millan Committee, *Report on the Review of the Mental Health (Scotland) Act 1984* (January 2001) Ch 16 <https://www.mhtscotland.gov.uk/mhts/files/Millan_Report_New_Directions.pdf> (Millan Committee Report) last accessed 31 March 2016; I Bidmeade, *Paving the Way: Review of Mental Health Legislation in South Australia, Report* (Review Committee on Mental Health Legislation, Department of Health, South Australia, April 2005) 8.

21 ibid Bidmeade 19.

22 Millan Committee Report, Ch 16 48.

23 M Chambers, A A Ryan and S L Connor, 'Exploring the Emotional Support Needs and Coping Strategies of Family Carers' (2001) 8 Journal of Psychiatric and Mental Health Nursing 99; J Reid, C Lloyd and L de Groot, 'The Psychoeducation Needs of Parents Who Have an Adult Son or Daughter with a Mental Illness' (2005) 4(2) Australian e-Journal for the Advancement of Mental Health 65; E Walker and B Jane Dewar, 'How Do We Facilitate Carers' Involvement in Decision-making?' (2001) 34(3) Journal of Advanced Nursing 329.

1(3)(b) of the Mental Health (Care and Treatment) (Scotland) Act 2003 requires that the views of carers to be taken into account when discharging functions under the Act, unless it is unreasonable and impractical to do so.

Another way to take carers' rights into account is to set them out in detail in the legislation. The Mental Health (Care and Treatment) (Scotland) Act 2003 provides a good example of this. Under the Scottish scheme, carers have specific rights to be consulted before an involuntary treatment order is made and when determining a care plan.[24] They also have a right to attend tribunal hearings and present information.[25] However, such a right may remain unused as some carers may be reluctant to air views that disagree with those under their care, in order to maintain their relationship. Carers may wish to provide information in confidence, but this must be balanced against natural justice considerations. Scotland has attempted to balance these competing interests by empowering tribunal members to accept information by carers in confidence if the tribunal believes it is in the interests of the individual concerned.[26]

The tension between the rights of carers and individuals with mental impairments is perhaps the most acute in relation to the disclosure of patient information. A cornerstone of medical ethics is doctor–patient confidentiality, and its importance is inculcated in health professionals throughout their training.[27] It assists therapeutic outcomes by encouraging disclosure and facilitating the health professional to provide appropriate care.[28] However, carers, for the similar objective of providing optimal care, desire access to information that health professionals may have obtained in the course of providing treatment.

There are three approaches that can be discerned in legislation that attempt to improve carers' access to information. It may be done via:

- highlighting the carer's right to access information as a guiding principle of the legislation
- allowing disclosure and
- mandating disclosure in certain circumstances.

3. Disclosure as a Guiding Principle

The legislation in Scotland and South Australia provides examples of guiding principles concerning the provision of information to carers. Section 1(5) of

---

[24] Mental Health (Care and Treatment) Act 2003 (Scotland) ss 61, 62.

[25] ibid s 64.

[26] On this point see eg Mental Health Tribunal for Scotland (Practice and Procedure) (No 2) Amendment Rules 2008; and Limited Review of the Mental Health (Treatment and Care) (Scotland) Act 2003: Report (Scottish Government, March 2009) 6 < www.scotland.gov.uk/Resource/Doc/281409/0084966.pdf>.

[27] See, in general, A Kämpf, B McSherry, J Ogloff and A Rothschild, *Confidentiality: Ethics and Law for Mental Health Professionals* (Australian Academic Press 2009).

[28] G Szmukler, 'Family Involvement in the Care of People with Psychosis. An Ethical Argument' (1997) 171(11) British Journal of Psychiatry 401.

the Mental Health (Care and Treatment) (Scotland) Act 2003 states that persons discharging duties under the Act 'shall have regard' to:

> (a) the needs and circumstances of any carer of the patient which are relevant to the discharge of the function and of which the person is aware; and
> (b) the importance of providing such information to any carer of the patient as might assist the carer to care for the patient.

Similarly, section 7(i) of the Mental Health Act 2009 (SA) states:

> 'patients (together with their family or other carers or supporters) should be provided with comprehensive information about their illnesses, any orders that apply to them, their legal rights, the treatments and other services that are to be provided or offered to them and what alternatives are available.'

Such provisions provide a framework for the right of carers to access adequate information.

3.1 Allowing Disclosure

More specific provisions can allow for the disclosure of certain information to carers. For example, section 106(2)(c) of the South Australian Mental Health Act 2009 states that mental health professionals are not prevented from:

> 'disclosing information to a relative, carer or friend of the person to whom the information relates if—
> (i) the disclosure is reasonably required for the treatment, care or rehabilitation of the person; and
> (ii) there is no reason to believe that the disclosure would be contrary to the person's best interests.'

The South Australian legislation contains a proviso that the disclosure of personal information is not authorised 'in contravention of a direction given by the person to whom the information relates.'[29] Similarly, section 346(2)(g) of the Victorian Mental Health Act 2014 states that disclosure of health information is permitted if:

> 'the disclosure is made in general terms to a friend, family member or carer of the person to whom the health information relates and the disclosure is not contrary to the views and preferences expressed by the person that the health information must not be disclosed to that friend, family member or carer.'

Section 346(2)(h) of the Victorian Mental Health Act 2014 further permits disclosure if:

> the person to whom the health information relates is a patient and—
> (i) the disclosure is reasonably required by a carer of the patient to determine the nature and scope of the care to be provided to the

---

29 Mental Health Act 2009 (SA) s 106(3).

patient and to make the necessary arrangements in preparation for that role or to provide care to the patient; and

(ii) regard has been had to the patient's views and preferences, including those expressed in any advance statement that the patient may have prepared

3.2 Mandating Disclosure

In Scotland, the Mental Health Tribunal and health professionals are required to notify the 'named person' (a person nominated to support the individual concerned through the process of involuntary detention and treatment) and, less routinely, the 'primary carer' when certain events occur, such as the making of an involuntary treatment order, changes to treatment and tribunal hearings.[30] The named person may be nominated by the individual concerned, or if there is no such nomination, the default setting is for the primary carer or nearest relative to be given this role. There is an obligation placed on Mental Health Officers to establish if there is a named person and, where there is no nomination, to determine who will become the default named person.

Interestingly, the Scottish approach of mandating disclosure has caused some concerns among carers. Some carers have reported being upset when they unexpectedly (as they were unaware that they were the named person) received detailed papers causing them to discover things they had previously not known or had known but were forced to relive.[31]

Overall then, there have been varying attempts in mental health laws to include the rights of carers to be involved in decisions to detain and treat involuntarily those under their care. Access to information is perhaps the most difficult area for the law to find an appropriate balance between the rights of individuals with mental impairments and the rights of carers. Any law reform endeavours should ensure that information provided to carers is limited to that necessary for their role and avoids the unnecessary harm that excessive disclosure causes to both the individuals concerned and their carers.

4. Conclusion

To date, a focus on the involuntary commitment of those with severe mental impairments has meant that much of the analysis concerning the 'proper' scope for mental health laws has centred on the rights to liberty and autonomy.[32] Most

---

30 A Dawson, I Ferguson, K Mackay and M Maxwell, *Assessment of the Operation of the Named Person Role and Its Interaction with Other Forms of Patient Representation* (Scottish Government Social Research, 2009) 14 <www.scotland.gov.uk/Resource/Doc/263258/0078745.pdf>.

31 'Limited Review of the Mental Health (Treatment and Care) Act 2003 (Scotland): Report' (Scottish Government, March 2009) 16 <www.scotland.gov.uk/Resource/Doc/281409/0084966.pdf>.

32 See further on this point M Donnelly, 'From Autonomy to Dignity: Treatment for Mental Disorders and the Focus for Patient Rights' in B McSherry (ed) *International Trends in Mental Health Laws* (Federation Press 2008) 37.

debates are still framed in terms of balancing the rights of individuals with mental impairments with the need for treatment to prevent deterioration in mental state or to prevent harm to self or others.

Article 25 of the CRPD can be viewed as shifting the focus to the right to service delivery for those who want treatment, but who are unable to obtain it. This is an area that is ripe for further investigation. Having a legislative right to appeal a decision to refuse to admit an individual to a mental health facility goes some way towards ensuring that those who want treatment can access it. However, there are still barriers that need to be overcome in relation to legal decision-makers ordering clinicians to ensure admission and to provide treatment in the absence of adequate government funding.

There have been more inroads made in relation to incorporating carers' rights into mental health laws than in relation to the right to the enjoyment of the highest attainable standard of health. John Dawson has made the point that the state 'has strong interests…in fostering the support of families and carers for the mentally ill' and that any human rights analysis in relation to mental health laws should take into account the interests of third parties in the relationship between the individual and the state.[33] Introducing carers' rights into mental health laws, no matter what form this takes, can be seen as a way of addressing the needs of families and carers in this regard.

Because of the focus in mental health laws on negative rights and on individual rights versus those of the state, until recently debates about the scope of such laws have largely ignored the right to the enjoyment of health services and the rights of carers. Article 25 of the CRPD and the developing inclusion of carers' rights in legislation serve to broaden these debates considerably.

[33] J Dawson, 'Compulsory Outpatient Treatment and the Calculus of Human Rights' in B McSherry and P Weller (eds) *Rethinking Rights-Based Mental Health Laws* (Hart Publishing 2010) 327, 338.

Chapter 15

ADVANCE DIRECTIVES: SUPPORTING LEGAL CAPACITY IN MENTAL HEALTH CARE

Fiona Morrissey

1. Introduction

The UN Convention on the Rights of Persons with Disabilities (CRPD)[1] requires us to engage in new approaches to decision-making in mental health care, and to develop a range of support strategies. Mental health law has traditionally authorised conduct which would otherwise be unlawful, including the loss of liberty and forced treatment.[2] Many individuals with disabilities still have little influence over their destiny and are excluded from meaningful participation in decisions relating to treatment and care. The CRPD marks a new era for persons with psychosocial disabilities[3] through the social model of disability and the adoption of support strategies.[4] The emphasis on dignity and autonomy, including freedom to make choices, is infused in the Preamble and runs throughout the CRPD. Article 12 requires the adoption of a new generation of measures which can support legal capacity in the mental health context.[5] Advance directives are considered to be appropriate vehicles for supporting legal capacity by allowing individuals to identify their treatment preferences and other life choices prior to a mental health crisis. This measure is increasingly recognised as an important decision-making tool which enables the explicit wishes of the person to be respected during periods when decision-making autonomy may be reduced.[6] A major goal of advance directives in mental health care is to support the exercise of decision-making capacity by providing a communication forum where the values and preferences of the individual can be articulated. This serves to restore the 'voice' of the person and provides an alternative to coercive measures. Advance directives provide the opportunity to realise the social model of disability and embed values such as equality, participation, autonomy and inclusion in mental health care.

---

1 United Nations Convention on the Rights of Persons with Disabilities (CRPD) opened for signature on 13 December 2006, GA Res 61/106. UN Doc A/Res/61/106 (entered into force on 3 May 2008).

2 N Rees, 'The fusion proposal: A next step?' in B McSherry and P Weller (eds), *Rethinking Rights-Based Mental Health Law* (Hart Publishing 2010) 76.

3 Persons with psychosocial disabilities are those who experience mental health issues, and/or who identify as 'mental health consumers' or 'psychiatric survivors.'

4 A Lawson, 'The United Nations Convention on the Rights or Persons with Disabilities: New era or false dawn?' (2007) 34 (2) Syracuse Journal of International Law 563.

5 art 12(3), United Nations Convention on the Rights of Persons with Disabilities (2006).

6 ibid art 12(4).

2. Legal Capacity

Legal capacity is an important component of modern mental health law. It enables the individual to make choices and to have those decisions respected. In the absence of legal capacity, everyday decisions, including those relating to mental health treatment, have no legal force. The Commissioner for Human Rights in the Council of Europe described this approach as 'civil death.'[7] This is a reality for many thousands of people in modern society. The CRPD Committee distinguishes between mental and legal capacity.[8] Legal capacity is the ability to hold rights and to exercise those rights. Mental capacity, in comparison, refers to the decision-making skills of the individual, which naturally vary.[9] Article 12 does not permit perceived or actual deficits in mental capacity to be used as a justification for denying legal capacity.[10] State Parties must instead provide access to supports, such as advance directives, to enable individuals to exercise legal capacity.

Persons with psychosocial disabilities are often treated as individuals who need to be controlled, protected and limited in the scope of their decision-making for the protection of themselves or others.[11] The decision to forgo treatment is often viewed as an irrational decision rather than an informed choice.[12] Concerns and requests are frequently dismissed, causing a sense of worthlessness and diminished sense of self.[13] The adverse consequences of the incapacity label are detrimental for persons with mental health difficulties. The sense of helplessness can have a critical impact on psychological well-being[14] and further accentuate feelings of stigmatisation, lack of control and demotivation.[15] Participation has a number of therapeutic benefits which can contribute to dignity and well-being. It enables the person to actively engage in life activities and builds decision-making capacity.[16]

The CRPD requires respect for legal capacity without discriminating on the basis of disability.[17] The 'will and preferences' of the person are the key determining factors in decisions. Persons with psychosocial disabilities are considered to have

---

7 T Hammarberg, 'Rights-based Approach needed in New Law on Legal Capacity' *The Irish Times* (1 March 2012).

8 Committee on the Rights of Persons with Disabilities, 'General comment No. 1, Article 12: Equal recognition before the law' para 13, Adopted by the Committee at the eleventh session on 31 March–11 April 2014.

9 ibid.

10 ibid.

11 P Longmore, 'Medical decision-making and people with disabilities: A clash of cultures' (1995) 23 (1) Journal of Law, Medicine and Ethics 82.

12 P Corrigan, B Angell, L Davidson, S Marcus, M Salzer, P Kottsieper, J Larson, C Mahoney, M O'Connell and V Stanhope, 'From adherence to self-determination: Evolution of a treatment paradigm of people with serious mental illnesses' (2012) 63 (2) Psychiatric Services 169.

13 J Bromley and S Cunningham, 'You don't bring me flowers any more': An investigation into the experience of stigma by psychiatric inpatients' (2004) 25 Psychiatric Bulletin 371.

14 L Salzman, 'Rethinking guardianship (again): Substituted decision-making as a violation of the integration mandate of Title II of the American with Disabilities Act' (2010) 81 University of Colorado Law Review 157.

15 M Donnelly, 'From autonomy to dignity: Treatment for mental disorders and the focus of patient rights' (2008) 26 (2) Law in Context 49.

16 L Salzman, 'Guardianship for persons with mental illness – A legal and appropriate alternative?' (2011) 4 Saint Louis University Journal of Health Law & Policy 279.

17 art 5, United Nations Convention on the Rights of Persons with Disabilities (2006).

legal capacity on an equal basis with others.[18] Mental health treatment decisions should, therefore, be made independently or with support. The challenge is to break the assumption that a person has less decision-making capability due to a mental health disability. The MacArthur Treatment Competence Study[19] demonstrated that although decision-making abilities were compromised in some individuals with mental health difficulties, more than half had capacity levels similar to their counterparts in physical health care. The research suggests that individuals with mental health conditions are capable of developing advance directives, but some may require support for completion.[20] Decision-making ability can be enhanced by providing information in the appropriate context/format and allowing time for discussion with trusted persons.[21] The side effects of treatment and the episodic nature of a condition should also be considered.[22] A study by Gunn showed a marked improvement in the level of understanding achieved by persons with mental health conditions when information was made more accessible.[23] The CRPD requires an exploration of ways of providing information adapted to the needs of the individual.[24]

3. Advance Directives in Mental Health Care

Advance directives are considered to be appropriate measures for supporting legal capacity by recognising the 'will and preferences' of the person. Comparative jurisdictions have a range of legal frameworks, with some adopting provisions under mental health legislation and others providing for advance directives under general health care decision-making legislation. The CRPD implies that the principles and objectives underpinning advance directives must be considered in the broader legislative context.[25] The principles of equality and non-discrimination require the elimination of differential standards and exceptions to enforceability. The integration of mental health decisions with general health care decisions legislation minimises discrimination and limits the extent to which advance directives can be overridden by existing mental health laws. The CRPD requires respect for the legal capacity of all persons, including those detained under mental health legislation.[26] The right

---

18 ibid art 12(2).

19 P Appelbaum and T Grisso, 'The MacArthur treatment competence study I: Mental illness and competence to consent to treatment'(1995) 19 Law and Human Behaviour 105; T Grisso, P Appelbaum, E Mulvey and K Fletcher, 'The MacArthur treatment competence study II: Measure of abilities related to competence to consent to treatment' (1995) 19 Law and Behaviour 127; P Appelbaum and T Grisso, 'The MacArthur treatment competence study III: Abilities of patients to consent to psychiatric and medical treatments' (1995) 19 Law and Human Behaviour 149.

20 T Peto, D Srebnik, E Zick and J Russo, 'Support needed to create psychiatric advance directives' (2004) 31 (5) Administration and Policy in Mental Health 409.

21 P Weller, 'The Convention on the Rights of Persons with Disabilities and the social model of health: New perspectives' (2011) (Spring) Journal of Mental Health Law 74.

22 ibid.

23 M Gunn, I Clare, A Holland and J G Wong, 'Decision-Making Capacity' (1999) 7 Medical Law Review 269.

24 Amnesty International, 'Essential Principles: Irish Legal Capacity Law' (April 2012) 4 (a) <http://www.amnesty.ie/reports/essential-principles-irish-legal-capacity-law> last accessed 31 March 2016.

25 A Dhanda, 'Legal capacity in the disability rights Convention: Stranglehold of the past or lodestar for the future' (2006–2007) 34 Syracuse Journal of International Law 429.

26 art 12 provides for equal recognition before the law, art 14 provides for the right to liberty, and art 17 provides a right to physical and mental integrity.

to physical and mental integrity requires respect for the treatment choices of all persons, and decisions involving these rights should only be taken with the free and informed consent of the person.[27]

The CRPD Committee recently stated that mental health laws that permit forced treatment should be abolished to ensure that the legal capacity of persons with disabilities are respected on an equal basis with others.[28] Legislative provisions for advance directives should, therefore, apply equally to all health care decisions, including those relating to mental health treatment. Advance directives can facilitate collaboration, promote respect and reduce discrimination in mental health care.[29]

3.1. Development

Advance directives originated in the United States. Thomas Szasz first suggested the notion of a 'psychiatric will' in the early 1980s.[30] This involved taking an express refusal or consent to future mental health treatment into account. The first reported court decision occurred in 1991, when a New York court denied the authorisation of electroshock therapy in the case of *Rosa M.*[31] Mental health advance directives have since received extensive legislative support internationally. They can be distinguished from end-of-life directives in two ways. First, persons executing end-of-life directives are usually making decisions regarding treatments they may have never experienced. Persons with psychosocial disabilities, in contrast, are often dealing with a condition which is episodic in nature and they are more likely to have experience of treatment and managing crises. The goal of general advance directives is usually to increase dignity and autonomy at the end of life, whereas the objective of an advance directive in mental health is often to maximise recovery while minimising unwanted intervention and treatment.[32] Legal requirements vary between jurisdictions resulting in a lack of single definition.[33] Phrases used to describe legally binding and non-legally binding advance planning measures include psychiatric advance directives (PADs), Ulysses directives, advance statements, advance decisions, advance agreements and joint crisis plans. The CRPD implies that the title of advance directives should be non-discriminatory and should not distinguish between mental health and other health care decisions.

3.2. Benefits

The potential benefits of advance directives in mental health care are described extensively in the literature. The discussions can be divided between the benefit of creating a directive and the benefit of invoking a directive.

---

27 Committee on the Rights of Persons with Disabilities (n 8), para 42.

28 ibid para 7.

29 P Weller, *New Law and Ethics in Mental Health Advance Directives: The Convention on the Rights of Persons with Disabilities and the Right to Choose* (Routledge 2013).

30 T Szasz, 'The psychiatric will: A new mechanism for protecting people against psychosis and psychiatry' (1982) 37 American Psychologist 762.

31 *Matter of Rosa M*, 155 Misc. 2d 103 NY Sup. Ct. (1991).

32 Harvard Medical School, 'Making the most of psychiatric advance directives' (2007) 24 (6) Harvard Mental Health Letter 1.

33 J Atkinson, 'Advance directives' in P Barker (ed), *Mental Health Ethics: The Human Context* (Routledge 2011) 306.

The benefits of creating an advance directive are particularly apt under the supported decision-making model. The creation of an advance directive yields capacity building and recovery benefits beyond the legislative aspects. The development process provides an opportunity for dialogue and reflection and ongoing engagement with the person's will and preferences, even if the directive is never legally invoked. The increased sense of choice, of being listened to and respected, and ownership can improve self-efficacy and hope for recovery.[34] The creation of a directive can also assist the identification of relapse triggers and recovery strategies, thereby reducing the need for hospital admission or coercion.[35] One of the most significant benefits is that directives provide users with a sense of control over future treatment.[36]

Invoking a directive can give the individual the opportunity to have his or her choices respected and eliminate the need for involuntary admission or treatment.[37] Advance directives can also impact on the conceptualisation of persons with psychosocial disabilities and their ability to make decisions.[38] The CRPD obligates States Parties to take appropriate steps to raise awareness of the capabilities of persons with disabilities and to counter unfounded prejudices and stereotypes in society.[39] Advance directives represent a broader attitudinal shift in the law in relation to individuals with mental health conditions, as subjects of rights rather than objects of treatment and protection.

3.3. Involuntary Detention and Treatment

Advance directives are at the forefront of contemporary measures to reduce the need for involuntary detention and treatment.[40] Concern over the expansion of coercion led to a broadened view of directives as alternatives to involuntary treatment and as vehicles for 'self-directed care.'[41] The psychological effect of the loss of autonomous control and non-consensual invasion of the body is significant.[42] Coercive treatment can be anti-therapeutic, negatively impact on self-esteem and

---

34 C Wilder, E Elbogen, L Moser, J Swanson and M Swartz, 'Medication preferences and adherence among individuals with severe mental illness and psychiatric advance directives' (2010) 61 (4) Psychiatric Services 380; R Miller, 'Advance directives for psychiatric treatment: A view from the trenches' (1998) 4 (3) Psychology, Public Policy and Law 728; B Winick, 'Advance directives for those with mental illness' (1996) 51 University of Miami Law Review 57.

35 ibid.

36 A Scheyett, 'University students' views on the utility of psychiatric advance directives' (2012) 60 (1) Journal of American College Health 90.

37 P Backlar, 'The longing for order: Oregon's medical advance directive for mental health treatment' (1995) 31 (2) Community Mental Health Journal 103.

38 J Swanson, M Tepper, P Backlar and M Swartz, 'Psychiatric advance directives: An alternative to coercive treatment' (2000) 63 (2) Psychiatry 160.

39 A Lawson, 'People with psychosocial impairments or conditions, reasonable accommodation in the UN Convention on the Rights of Persons with Disabilities' (2008) 26 (2) Law in Context 62.

40 T Bogdanoski, 'Psychiatric advance directives: The new frontier in mental health law reform in Australia?' (2009) 16 Journal of Law and Medicine 891.

41 D Srebnik and J La Fond, 'Advance directives for mental health treatment' (1999) 50 (7) Psychiatric Services 919; D Srebnik, J Russo, J Sage, T Peto and E Zick, 'Interest in psychiatric advance directives among high users of crisis services and hospitalisations' (2003) 54 (7) Psychiatric Services 981.

42 D Srebnik, L Rutherford, T Peto, J Russo, E Zick, C Jaffe and P Holtzheimer, 'The content and utility of psychiatric advance directives' (2005) 56 Psychiatric Services 592.

induce feelings of apathy, distrust, submissiveness, dehumanisation and frustration.[43] Consistent findings suggest that individuals are more likely to engage in treatment and to experience better outcomes when given a choice.[44] The MacArthur Research Network studies found that individuals who believed they had a 'voice' experienced less coercion during the hospital admission process.[45] Coercive interventions were reduced by half for individuals who completed facilitated advance directives in a previous study.[46] Henderson also found decreased use of mental health legislation and reduced readmission rates for a group who used 'joint crises plans' (a form of directive) in the UK.[47] Individuals who believe their choices are respected are more likely to engage and benefit from treatment than those who feel coerced and disrespected.[48]

Advance directives can still be overridden by mental health laws in many jurisdictions. However, the CRPD requires respect for the legal capacity of all persons, including those detained under mental health legislation.[49] A decision of the Constitutional Court of Germany based on CRPD principles found advance directives to be legally binding and to indicate the natural 'will' of the person in the context of involuntary treatment.[50] The court referred to the right to be treated equally before the law and to exercise legal capacity with support. The need to facilitate genuine engagement and flexibility regardless of capacity was recognised. The risk of harm to others was not considered to be a justifiable ground for overriding a valid directive when detention can be used for this purpose. Clinicians fear this will lead to individuals being left untreated, but the international evidence suggests that advance directives are rarely used to refuse all treatment.[51] The measure is generally used to express a preference for particular treatments and to inform providers of concerns.[52] Current mental health laws should, therefore, be amended to ensure

---

43 E Gallagher, 'Advance directives for psychiatric care: A theoretical and practical overview for legal professionals' (1998) 4 (3) Psychology Public Policy and Law 746.

44 L Davidson, D Roe, E Stern, *Y Zisman-Ilani, M O'Connell* and P Corrigan, 'If I Choose it: Am I more Likely to Use it?' (2012) 2 (3) The International Journal of Person-Centred Medicine 577.

45 J Monahan, H Steadman, E Silver, P Appelbaum, P Clark Robins, E Mulvey, L Roth, T Grisso and S Banks, *Rethinking Risk Assessment: The MacArthur Study of Mental Disorder and Violence* (Oxford University Press, 2001).

46 J Swanson, M Swartz, E Elbogen, R Van Dorn, H R Wagner, L Moser, C Wilder, and A Gilbert, 'Psychiatric advance directives and reduction of coercive crisis interventions' (2008) 17 Journal of Mental Health 255.

47 C Henderson, C Flood, M Leese, G Thornicroft, K Sutherby,and G Szmukler, 'Effect of joint crises plans on use of compulsory treatment in psychiatry: single blind randomised controlled trial' (2004) 329 British Medical Journal 136.

48 D Wexler and B Winick, *Essays in Therapeutic Jurisprudence* (Carolina Academic Press, 1991).

49 art 12 provides for equal recognition before the law; art 14 provides for the right to liberty, and art 17 provides a right to physical and mental integrity.

50 Leitsätzezum Beschluss des Zweiten Senats vom März 23, 2011, BVerfGE–2 BvR 882/09, <http://www.bverfg.de/entscheidungen/rs20110323_2bvr088209.html> last accessed 31 March 2016.

51 D Srebnik; J Reilly and J Atkinson, 'The content of mental health advance directives: Advance statements in Scotland' (2010) 33 International Journal of Law and Psychiatry 116; P Backlar, B MacFarland, J Swanson, and J Mahler, 'Consumer, provider and informal caregiver opinions on psychiatric advance directives' (2001) 28 (6) Administration and Policy in Mental Health 427.

52 P Appelbaum, 'Law and Psychiatry: Psychiatric advance directives and the treatment of committed patients' (2004) 55 (7) Psychiatric Services 751.

advance directives are equally available to all persons to minimise the need for coercion and to ensure that the preferences of the person are respected during any future periods of hospitalisation. The use of advance planning under the CRPD can transform traditional responses to mental health crises by providing treatment in accordance with the person's wishes and change the legal model of care from one of 'coercion to contract'.[53]

3.4. Comparative Provisions

Many jurisdictions have provided for advance directives for mental health through extended common law or legislative provisions. Some directives are legally binding while others are accorded due respect and consideration. Provisions can usually be found in capacity legislation, continuing powers of attorney, health and mental health legislation. The various approaches are based on diverse models of care and the development of human rights. Approaches range from a minimalist approach in New Zealand to an embedded human rights model in Scotland. In the United States, two-thirds of states have statutes explicitly authorising 'psychiatric advance directives' (PADs) or proxy decision-making, and other states permit them through health care directives or power of attorney statutes.[54]

Advance directives for mental health care are recognised in a number of European jurisdictions. However, the legal status of advance directives is disparate and validity remains unclear in many countries.[55] Only half of the twenty-eight EU Member States currently have legislative provisions.[56] The Czech Republic introduced CRPD-based capacity law reform, which included written advance directives.[57] In *Jehovah's Witnesses of Moscow v Russia,*[58] the European Court of Human Rights stated that advance directives should be legally binding as far as possible. The Court also stated that a proxy decision-maker[59] should be obliged to make health care decisions in conformity with the instructions of the individual not in his/her 'best interests.' Advance directives are recognised as the principal means of self-determination in the Council of Europe Recommendations and Resolutions[60] and the Biomedicine Convention.[61] The most recent Council of Europe Resolution provides more specific

---

53 R Bonnie, 'Advance Directives: A tool for reducing coercion' (2012) 63 (5) Psychiatric Services 411.

54 Services Effectiveness Research Program, Department of Psychiatry and Behavioural Sciences, 'Duke University Program in Psychiatric Advance Directives' (2012) <http://pad.duhs.duke.edu/statutes.html> last accessed 31 March 2016.

55 R Andorno, Nikola Biller-Andorno, S Brauer, 'Advance health care directives: Towards a coordinated European policy?' (2009) 16 European Journal of Health Law 207.

56 Laws addressing advance directives have not yet been approved in Bulgaria, the Czech Republic, Greece, Ireland, Italy, Latvia, Lithuania, Poland, Portugal, Slovakia and Sweden.

57 Mental Disability Advocacy Center, Budapest, 'Czech Republic Enacts Legal Capacity Law Reform' (Mental Disability Advocacy Center 2012) <www.mdac.info/en/news/czech-republic-enacts-legal-capacity-law-reform> last accessed 31 March 2016.

58 *Jehovah's Witnesses of Moscow v Russia* App No 302/02 (ECtHR, 10 June 2010).

59 The proxy decision stems from knowledge of the person's will and preferences when they are unable to communicate them. The hybrid directive combines the appointment of a proxy with the person's instructions.

60 Council of Europe, European Committee on Legal Co-operation, CM/Rec (2009) 11, 1073; Council of Europe, Parliamentary Assembly Resolution 1859 (Council of Europe 2012).

61 art 9, Convention for the Protection of Human Rights and Dignity of the Human Being with regard to the Application of Biology and Medicine (Oviedo 1997).

guidance and states an urgent need for Member States to enact and fully implement legislation in this area to ensure the human rights and dignity of all citizens.[62]

3.5. Types of Advance Directives

Advance directives can take varying forms, enabling different decisions to be made.[63] Although there is general consensus on the appropriateness of advance directives, significant differences exist as to how they are implemented.[64] Preferences can be expressed through instructional directives which provide directions regarding treatment or, proxy directives, where the authority to communicate choices is given to a trusted person, or hybrid directives, which include a combination of both features.[65] A directive can be either positive or negative in that it is not only used to refuse treatment, but to proceed to certain agreed treatments. An advance refusal is generally agreed to be legally binding whereas a treatment request is non-legally binding. While advance directives usually include personal treatment preferences, they can also include information regarding other life choices eg childcare, household finances. Personal directives are considered to be particularly beneficial for the enhancement of autonomy.[66] The basic information in all directives covers treatment preferences, information on crisis and relapse symptoms, persons to be notified and, if relevant, a proxy decision-maker.[67]

The provision of third-party support for completion is a key component of advance directives[68] under the CRPD. Originally, advance directives were designed to be completed independently without support. Due to low usage rates, several features were introduced to promote development including the provision of facilitated support,[69] information and training sessions,[70] and computer-assisted directives.[71] Structured facilitation is a process that emphasises the use of reflective listening and non-directive discussion to help the individual clarify and articulate values and

---

62 Council of Europe, Parliamentary Assembly Resolution 1859 (Council of Europe 2012) paras 3, 4, 6.

63 J Atkinson, *Advance Directives in Mental Health: Theory, Practice and Ethics* (Jessica Kingsley 2007).

64 R Andorno, N B Andorno and S Brauer, 'Advance health care directives: Towards a coordinated European policy?' (2009) 16 European Journal of Health Law 207.

65 J La Fond and D Srebnik, 'The impact of mental health advance directives on patient perceptions of coercion in civil commitment and treatment decisions' (2002) 25 (6) International Journal of Law and Psychiatry 537.

66 In one study, up to 20% of the plans contained non-treatment choices.

67 P Nicaise, V Lorant and V Dubois, 'Psychiatric advance directives as a complex and multistage intervention: A realist systematic review' (2012) 21(1) Health and Social Care in the Community 1.

68 ibid.

69 J Swanson, M Swartz, E Elbogen, R Van Dorn, J Ferron, R Wagner, B McCauley, and M Kim, 'Facilitated psychiatric advance directives: A randomised trial of an intervention to foster advance treatment planning among people with severe mental illness' (2006) 163 American Journal of Psychiatry 1943; E Elbogen, J Swanson, P Appelbaum, M Swartz, J Ferron, R Van Dorn and H R Wagner, 'Competence to complete psychiatric advance directives: Effects of facilitated decision-making' (2007) 31 Law and Human Behaviour 275.

70 D Srebnik and L Brodoff, 'Implementing psychiatric advance directives: Service provider issues and answers' (2003) 30 Journal of Behavioural Health Services and Research 253.

71 P Sherman, 'Computer-assisted creation of psychiatric advance directives: Service provider issues and answers' (1998) 34 Community Mental Health Journal 351.

choices.[72] The facilitated directive allows the statement of treatment preferences without the involvement of a clinician, thereby maintaining autonomy.[73] Other forms of directives such as 'joint crisis plans' involve a negotiated completion process between the individual, clinician and other third parties, such as family or friends.[74] The goal of this directive is to form a therapeutic alliance between clinicians and mental health service users.[75] Most studies report a feeling of self-determination and empowerment when completing any form of advance directive.[76] However, individuals using unsupported directives report a lack of information and the need for assistance.[77] The CRPD requires States Parties to provide access to appropriate support to exercise legal capacity, including assistance to complete an advance directive.[78]

4. Advance Directives under the CRPD

The CRPD implies that mental health treatment decisions should be guided by the same criteria as general health decisions.[79] The Bazelon Centre for Mental Health Law urges that advance directives for mental health should operate in the same way as other directives, subject to legitimate emergency situations where there is an immediate threat to the life of the person.[80] Discrimination continues to exist between the provision of advance directives in general and mental health care. Most statutes permit preferences to be overridden where a person is detained under mental health legislation. This is often justified on the premise that involuntary detention without treatment will result in lengthy periods of hospitalisation or excessive restraint.[81] However, the international research suggests that the refusal of all treatment is rare.[82] In Ontario, detained persons have been able to use advance decisions to refuse treatment since the 1980s.[83] In England and Wales, the Mental

72 J Oliver, 'Promoting the use of advance directives by people with serious mental illness under Virginia's Health Care Decisions Act: Implementation study update' (2012) 31(6) Developments in Mental Health Law 1.

73 P Nicaise, V Lorant and V Dubois (n 67).

74 C Henderson, C Flood, M Leese, G Thornicroft, K Sutherby and G Szmukler, 'Views of service users and providers on joint crisis plans' (2009) 44 Social Psychiatry and Psychiatric Epidemiology 369.

75 C Henderson, J W Swanson, G Szmukler, G Thornicroft and M Zinkler, 'A typology of advance statements in mental health care' (2008) 59 (1) Psychiatric Services 63.

76 P Nicaise, V Lorant and V Dubois (n 67).

77 P Backlar, B MacFarland, J Swanson, and J Mahler (n 51); M Swartz, J W Swanson, R A. Van Dorn, E B. Elbogen and M Shumway, 'Patient preferences for psychiatric advance directives' (2006) 5 International Journal of Forensic Mental Health 67.

78 art 12 (3), United Nations Convention on the Rights of Persons with Disabillities (2006).

79 A Kampf, 'Involuntary treatment decisions' in B McSherry and P Weller (eds), *Rethinking Rights-Based Mental Health Law* (Hart Publishing 2010) 143.

80 Bazelon Centre for Mental Health Law, 'Power in Planning Self Determination through Psychiatric Advance Directives' <http://www.bazelon.org/LinkClick.aspx?fileticket=kdy5IA1a7To=&tabid=104> last accessed 31 March 2016.

81 R O'Reilly, 'The capacity to execute an advance directive for psychiatric treatment' (2008) 31 International Journal of Law and Psychiatry 66.

82 D Srebnik, L Rutherford, T Peto, J Russo, E Zick, C Jaffe and P Holtzheimer (n 47); J Reilly and J Atkinson, 'The content of mental health advance directives: advance statements in Scotland' (2010) 33 International Journal of Law and Psychiatry 116; J Swanson, M Swartz, E Elbogen, R Van Dorn, J Ferron, H R Wagner, B McCauley, and M Kim (n 83).

83 Health Care Consent Act SO 1996 c.2, SCH A.

Capacity Act 2005 recognises advance refusals of treatment, but excludes those subject to mental health legislation despite the fact that the National Institute for Clinical Excellence (NICE) includes advance directives as a standard of care for persons with schizophrenia.[84] Discriminatory standards re-reinforce stigma and diminished citizenship. After filing a legal challenge for differential treatment in *Hargrave v Vermont*,[85] Nancy Hargrave asserted:

> 'it seems fundamentally unfair that I choose or refuse chemotherapy which is saving my life, but I don't have the same right to choose or refuse psychiatric medication.'[86]

4.1. Supporting Legal Capacity

The supported decision-making model marks a paradigm shift from one where a person is divested of the right to make decisions to one that respects legal capacity and provides appropriate support if needed.[87] Support measures can be extremely beneficial for persons with psychosocial disabilities.[88] Individuals who have been institutionalised or suffer exclusion may find it difficult to make decisions. The support model maximises interaction with others providing an opportunity to develop capacity in an integrated manner.[89] Advance directives are multistage interventions that develop decision-making capacity by encouraging dialogue and reflection on mental health experiences. The incorporation of a 'values history' in the directive can assist clarification and reduce the risk of ambiguity.[90] Directives also provide for regular communication and discussion whether a mental health crisis has taken place or not. If a crisis has occurred, it is crucial that the experience is discussed and appropriate revisions are made.[91] The directive may then become a vehicle for learning and enhance the dignity of the individual in future mental health experiences.[92]

4.2. Supported Advance Directives

A major theme in developing directives is whether they are made independently or with support. The complexity of the decision-making process often requires the involvement of a trusted support person to facilitate completion. The evidence suggests that supported directives achieve significantly higher completion rates, are more responsive to user needs and contain more valuable information.[93] Studies in

---

84 National Institute for Clinical Excellence, *Schizophrenia Core Interventions in the Treatment of and Management of Schizophrenia in Adults in Primary and Secondary Care* (NICE 2009).

85 *Hargrave v State of Vermont,* No. 2: 99-CV 128 (2001); *Hargrave v State of Vermont,* 340 F 3d 27 (2nd Cir 2003).

86 ibid.

87 L Salzman (n 14).

88 ibid.

89 ibid.

90 D Doukas and D Gorenflo, 'The values history: The evaluation of the patient's values and advance directives' (1993) 4 Journal of Clinical Ethics 41.

91 R Berghmans and M Van Der Zanden, 'Choosing to limit: Self-binding directives in Dutch mental health care' (2012) 35 International Journal of Law and Psychiatry 11.

92 R Kogstad, 'Protecting mental health clients: Dignity-The importance of legal control' (2009) 57 International Journal of Law and Psychiatry 383.

93 J Swanson (n 83); E Elbogen (n 83).

the United States and Ireland have shown that the majority of mental health service users' prefer support to complete advance directives.[94] In the US study, participants with severe mental health conditions needed help articulating preferences or getting information on treatment options.[95] A study of crisis cards in the UK showed that all of the participants chose to make a joint card over an independent card.[96] The research also indicated that mental health service users were interested in designating a proxy decision-maker.[97] In a trial of joint crisis plans, a trusted person was frequently nominated.[98] The research is consistent with suggestions that family, friends or other trusted individuals[99] should assist with completion.[100] However, a significant proportion of mental health service users lacked a trusted person to act on their behalf suggesting a need to build support networks and to provide independent facilitators.[101] In times of crisis, persons with psychosocial disabilities often receive less support from family and friends due to stigma.[102] While clinicians may not be appropriate support persons due to the power imbalance in the therapeutic relationship, the content of the directive should be communicated to them to ensure it is respected and implemented. 'A one size fits all' approach is unlikely to work in the mental health context as some individuals may prefer a directive which is agreed jointly while others may want to make one independently. The research suggests a need for a choice of directives to accommodate various needs and preferences under the CRPD.

Self-determination infers that the person decides the direction and nature of treatment with providers only acting in a consultative and supportive role.[103] Decisions by others should only be accepted if the person has nominated a representative to communicate his or her wishes, or if he or she has given legal authority to a proxy decision-maker.[104] The CRPD principles developed for Irish capacity law state that the 'will and preferences' of the individual should be clearly represented in any

---

94 T Peto, D Srebnik, E Zick and J Russo, 'Support needed to create psychiatric advance directives' (2004) 31 (5) Administration and Policy in Mental Health 409; F Morrissey, 'The introduction of a legal framework for advance directives in Irish mental health care', The views of service users and consultant psychiatrists, PhD thesis, Unpublished (National University of Ireland Galway 2014).

95 ibid T Peto.

96 K Sutherby, G Szmukler, A Halpern, M Alexander, G Thornicraft, C Johnson and S Wright, 'A study of crisis cards in a community psychiatric service' (1999) 100 (1) Acta Psychiatrica Scandinavica 56.

97 M Amering, P Stastny and K Hopper, 'Psychiatric advance directives: Qualitative study of informed deliberations by mental health service users' (2005) 186 British Journal of Psychiatry 247; J Swanson (n 83); F Morrissey (n 116).

98 C Henderson (n 90).

99 J Rogers and J Centifanti, 'Beyond "self-paternalism": Response to Rosenson and Kasten' (1991) 17 (1) Schizophrenia Bulletin 9.

100 E Howe, 'Lessons from advance directives for PADs' (2000) 63 Psychiatry 173; J Swanson (n 43).

101 P Backlar, B MacFarland, J Swanson, and J Mahler (n 59); D Ambrosini, D Bemme, A Crocker and E Latimer, 'Narratives of individuals concerning psychiatric advance directives: A qualitative study' (2012) 6 Journal of Ethics in Mental Health 1; F Morrissey (n 116).

102 J Bromley (n 13).

103 P Corrigan (n 12).

104 L Kerzner and M Bach, *A New Paradigm for Protecting Autonomy and the Right to Legal Capacity* (October 2010) 140 <www.lco-cdo.org/disabilities/bach-kerzner.pdf> last accessed 31 March 2016.

support, including the appointment of a representative.[105] The General Comment on Article 12 also states that the person has the right to end or change the support relationship at any time he or she chooses.[106] Concerns have been expressed that proxy decision-makers are more likely to use a 'best interest' standard than decide according to the person's preferences.[107] Proxy decisions have been shown to poorly correlate with the individual's preferences, even where the representative is familiar with the person.[108] The legislation should, therefore, clearly distinguish between proxy decision-making and 'best interests' to safeguard against substitute decision-making. A legal duty should also be placed on proxy decision-makers to make decisions in accordance with the person's values and preferences, and training should be provided for representatives. A UK study found mental health service users experienced more discrimination from people with whom they had regular contact suggesting that carers and mental health professionals need to be educated on the supported decision-making role.[109] The research suggests a need for measures to safeguard against discrimination and substitute decision-making by proxies and other supported decision-makers.

4.3. Peer Support

Peer support plays a critical role in supporting the development of advance directives and increasing completion rates. The research suggests peers may provide appropriate support because of their independence from the treatment relationship, unique knowledge and shared experience.[110] Peer support refers to the process whereby a person of equal standing advocates on behalf of another person who shares the experience.[111] Previous research found service users were more comfortable with facilitators from outside the mental health system with no stake in their treatment preferences.[112] Peers are now being used to support the development of advance directives in a number of US states.[113] A peer facilitator may also act as a mediator and advocate for the person ensuring their choices are respected if a directive is facilitated by a provider, family member or other support person. The CRPD Committee refers to peer support as a potential measure under Article 12, making it an appropriate support measure for the completion of advance directives.[114]

---

105 Amnesty International (n 24).

106 Committee on the Rights of Persons with Disabilities, para 29 (g) (n 8).

107 D Srebnik and John La Fond (n 41).

108 A Seckler and ors, 'Substituted Judgment: How accurate are Proxy Predictions?' (1991) 115 (2) Annals of Internal Medicine 92.

109 C Henderson, E Corker, E Lewis-Holmes, S Hamilton, C Flach, D Rose, P Williams, V Pinfold and G Thornicraft, 'England's time to change antistigma campaign: One year outcomes of service user-rated experiences of discrimination' (2012) 63 (5) Psychiatric Services 451.

110 S Mead and C MacNeil, 'Peer Support: What makes it unique?' (2006) 10 (2) International Journal of Psychosocial Rehabilitation 29.

111 World Network of Users and Survivors of Psychiatry, *Implementation Manual for the United Nations Convention on the Rights of Persons with Disabilities* (February 2008), 29 <http://wnusp.rafus.dk/documents/WNUSP_CRPD_Manual.pdf> last accessed 31 March 2016.

112 C Henderson and others, 'How should we implement psychiatric advance directives? Views of consumers, caregivers and mental health providers and researchers' (2010) 37 (6) Administration and Policy in Mental Health and Mental Health Services Research 447.

113 Georgia, Washington, New York and Virginia. M Salzer, E Schwenk and E Brusilovskiy, 'Certified peer specialist roles and activities: Results from a national survey' (2010) 61 (5) Psychiatric Services 520; T Peto, D Srebnik, E Zick and J Russo (n 20); M Amering, P Stastny and K Hopper (n 118).

114 Committee on the Rights of Persons with Disabilities, para 17 (n 8).

5. Capacity Requirements under the CRPD

The CRPD requires a re-evaluation of capacity determinations for the activation and deactivation of advance directives. Mental capacity has traditionally been used as a threshold for executing, invoking and revoking advance directives. The validity of the directive often depends on whether the person was considered capable at the time it was executed and becomes operational when the person is deemed incapable. Many individuals are excluded from using directives because of the high level of capacity required for execution. The challenge is to separate advance directives from legal frameworks that use capacity as a threshold for activation and deactivation. The emphasis should move from capacity determinations and deficits to the identification of appropriate supports to execute a directive.[115] The presumption of capacity in the CRPD necessitates the development of directives which are designed to communicate wishes during mental health crises, while maintaining legal capacity.[116] This form of directive does not categorise a person as 'legally incapable' or represent a judgment on cognitive abilities.

Capacity judgments are fraught with ethical, legal and pragmatic complexities.[117] Determinations are often based on the perceived rationality of a decision-making persons with psychosocial disabilities particularly vulnerable to findings of incapacity.[118] The law does not attribute lack of capacity to individuals with physical health conditions, so the capacity to execute or revoke an advance directive is generally not questioned.[119] The German Constitutional Court considered advance directives to be legally binding even if doubt arises in relation to capacity at the time of execution.[120]

5.1. Invoking an Advance Directive

The requirement for an individual to be declared legally incapable for an advance directive to be invoked severely limits their use and fails to comply with the presumption of capacity under Article 12. The CRPD requires the use of more widely defined directives, which allow the person to set out the circumstances in which he or she wishes the statement to be activated or deactivated and when trusted proxy decision-makers should be consulted eg when the person goes into crisis or is hospitalised. The directive then acts as a communication tool, which ensures the person's preferences are respected without any impact on legal capacity. Bach suggests individuals should identify the triggering event in the directive and specify guidelines so the parameters are clearly established within the terms of

115 art 12 (3), United Nations Convention on the Rights of Persons with Disabilities (2006).

116 World Network of Users and Survivors of Psychiatry, *Implementation Manual for the United Nations CRPD on the Rights of Persons with Disabilities* (WNUSP 2008).

117 F Callard, N Sartorius, J Arboleda-Flores, P Bartlett, H Helmchen, H Stuart, J Taborda and G Thornicraft, *Mental Illness: Discrimination and the Law* (Wiley 2012) 47.

118 M Perlin, *The Hidden Prejudice: Mental Disability on Trial* (American Psychological Association, 2000) 155, 156; M Donnelly, 'From autonomy to dignity: Treatment for mental disorders and the focus of patient rights' (2008) 26 (2) Law in Context 49.

119 A Dhanda, 'Universal legal capacity as a universal human right' in M Dudley, D Silove and F Gale (eds) *Mental and Human Rights: Vision, Praxis and Courage* (Oxford University Press 2012) 184.

120 Leitsätze zum Beschluss des Zweiten Senats (n 58).

the directive. [121] In some jurisdictions, being subject to capacity or mental health legislation automatically invokes an advance directive.[122] In British Columbia, an adult can enter into a representation agreement with a trusted person or support network without compromising legal capacity.[123] The Representation Agreement Act creates a presumption that the person has capacity unless specific criteria finds otherwise.[124] The agreement provides broad legally binding powers to act according to the terms and the individuals known wishes or preferences. A flexible and non-judgmental approach to capacity and a relationship of trust is apt for advance directives under the CRPD.

5.2. Revoking an Advance Directive

The circumstances in which an advance directive can be revoked must also be considered. Some jurisdictions specify that the person must have decision-making capacity to revoke the directive, while others allow the advance directive to be revoked at any time. Other jurisdictions allow the person to choose whether the document is revocable during crisis periods.[125] The research suggests that a significant proportion of service users prefer advance directives to be revocable at any time, but few are actually revoked in practice.[126] The Irish study suggested that over half of service users were interested in an advance directive which allowed them to change their mind when unwell.[127] Some individuals fear they may change their mind about aspects of the instructions or experience a limitation in treatment not intended in their previously expressed will. The presumption of legal capacity in the CRPD implies that an advance directive can be revoked at any time. In Germany, an advance directive can be revoked informally even with limited decision-making capacity.[128] While this clearly confers autonomy, issues arise in mental health where a person expresses preferences in the knowledge that he or she will change the instructions when unwell and wishes to override his/her own future objections. Many individuals self-bind to avoid deterioration and the need for involuntary commitment, or to avoid behaviour they exhibit during mental health crises. The revocability issue can be resolved by allowing the advance directive to be changed at any time, unless a Ulysses clause has been executed by the person. The Ulysses clause allows the person to clearly specify if he or she wishes the directive instructions to stand over objection during crisis periods.[129] The clause may include safeguards to ensure it

---

[121] M Bach, 'Supported decision-making under Article 12 of the UN Convention on the Rights of Persons with Disabilities: Questions and Challenges' (Conference on Legal Capacity and Supported Decision-Making Parents' Committee of Inclusion Ireland, Athlone November 2007).

[122] Mental Health (Care and Treatment) (Scotland) Act 2003.

[123] Representation Agreement Act, RSBC, ch 405, pt 3, 26 (1996), s 6 (36).

[124] ibid ch 405, pt 3, 26 (1996), s 1 (3), 2 (8).

[125] Arizona, Washington.

[126] In one US study, 106 clients with advance directives and 487 crisis events, a directive has never been revoked as a whole, although in 105 (22%) of the crises, clients changed their minds about some specific instruction. D Srebnik and S Kim, 'Competency for creation use and revocation of psychiatric advance directives' (2006) 34 (4) Journal of the American Academy of Psychiatry and the Law 501.

[127] F Morrissey (n 116).

[128] U Wiesing, R Jox, H J Hebler and G Borasio, 'A new law on advance directives in Germany' (2010) 36 Journal of Medical Ethics 779.

[129] Self-binding directives are available in a number of US States, Canadian provinces and the Netherlands.

reflects the 'will and preferences' of the person at execution. Concerns have been expressed that this form of directive may result in undue coercion and negate the wishes of the unwell self in favour of the well self.[130] However, the optional clause has proven popular with service users in some jurisdictions.[131] The CRPD requires that the 'will and preferences' of the person are respected in all supports for legal capacity and should never amount to substitute decision-making.[132] The self-binding directive should, therefore, be subject to safeguards and review to ensure that it reflects the 'will and preferences' of the person and apply for a limited period.

5.3. Other Implementation Issues

A range of legal and practical issues accompany the implementation of advance directives under the CRPD. The varying forms of advance directives across comparative jurisdictions make their overall purpose unclear.[133] From an international perspective, a more substantial agreement beyond a minimal consensus on their scope needs to be formulated. The appropriate legal framework for supporting legal capacity requires consensus among States Parties to the CRPD. The structure of the legislation can perpetuate stigma and limit the use of advance directives in mental health care.[134]

Once advance directives are enshrined in legislation, considerable attention must be given to implementation. While advance directives have received extensive legislative support, little is known about how they can be effectively implemented into practice. The implementation of the legislation requires a systematic and coordinated approach to build trust, reduce barriers and promote a cultural shift towards respect for individual preferences. Further studies are needed to document the impact of advance directives on developing decision-making capacity, empowerment, recovery, engagement and service satisfaction. The effective implementation of the measure in different legal and system contexts also needs to be addressed.

Education plays a key role in the successful implementation of advance directives. The perceived barriers increased for groups who were not educated on their use in the Virginia stakeholder survey.[135] Each of the stakeholder groups (service users, clinicians, administrators, families and advocates) had specific educational needs or areas where additional training was needed. The barriers also increased for service users who were unfamiliar with the measure in the Irish survey.[136] Provider education is viewed as critical for the effective implementation of advance directives. The Gundersen Lutheran programme in Wisconsin achieved over 90% participation and

---

[130] R Dresser, 'Ulysses and the psychiatrists: A legal and policy analysis of the voluntary commitment contract' (1982) 16 (3) Harvard Civil Rights–Civil Liberties Law Review 777.

[131] Approximately 50% of service users in the state of Virginia in the United States are executing a Ulysses clause.

[132] Committee on the Rights of Persons with Disabilities, para 17 (n 8).

[133] P Nicaise, V Lorant and V Dubois (n 67).

[134] P Corrigan, A Watson, M Heyrman, A Warpinski, G Gracia, N Slopen and L Hall, 'Structural stigma in state legislation' (2005) 56 (5) Psychiatric Services 557.

[135] C Wilder, J Swanson, R Bonnie, T Wanchek, L McLaughlin and J Richardson, 'A survey of stakeholder knowledge, experience, and opinions of advance directives for mental health in Virginia' (2013) 40 (3) Administration and Policy in Mental Health 232

[136] F Morrissey (n 116).

compliance through training with providers on planning for end-of-life care.[137] In Scotland, a number of steps were recommended to increase usage including greater publicity and assigning responsibility for development.[138] Other proposals included involving independent advocates, encouraging staff in the recovery process to discuss them and requiring medical professionals to review any treatment in conflict with the 'will and preferences' of the person. The implementation of advance directives should be a continuous process facilitated by a central co-ordinating body and ongoing research.[139]

6. Comparative Models

6.1. Virginia, USA

An innovative health care law in Virginia allows individuals to plan for mental health crises using an integrated advance directive.[140] A major objective of the directive is to allow persons with psychosocial disabilities more control over their care and reduce the need for coercion.[141] Prior to the amendments to the Health Care Decisions Act, the law in Virginia only provided for advance directives for end-of-life care. The law is novel in that it provides for an integrated directive when the capacity to make health care decisions becomes impacted by mental health, dementia or other disability.[142] The Virginia directive provides for all types of health care decisions, including mental health treatment decisions, thus eliminating the need for separate directives. The Commission decided that a stand-alone statute perpetuated the practice of singling out mental health for differential treatment.[143] A health care proxy can be appointed to communicate treatment decisions or the individual can make an instructional directive or a combination of both features. The revisions to the Health Care Decisions Act (HCDA) were preceded by a three-year period of consensus-building with a range of stakeholders. The attempt to implement the law are still ongoing, with the goal of optimising benefits for persons with psychosocial disabilities, enhancing quality of care, reducing coercion and promoting mental wellbeing in the community.[144]

The Virginia legislation provides a model for other jurisdictions seeking more ethical and person-centred approaches to mental health decision-making. The legislation promotes the CRPD principles of equality and non-discrimination and provides a presumption of capacity by providing legally binding directives that are easily executable and revocable by all persons. The framework provides for flexibility and choice in relation to the revocability of the directive and the appointment of a

---

137 B Hammes, B Rooney and J Gundrum, 'A comparative, retrospective, observational study of the prevalence, availability and specificity of advance care plans in a county that implemented an advance care planning microsystem' (2010) 58 (7) Journal of the American Geriatrics Society 1249.

138 Scottish Government, 'Limited review of the Mental Health (Care and Treatment) (Scotland) Act 2003: Report' (March 2009).

139 R Bonnie, J Reinhard, P Hamilton and E McGarvey, 'Tragedy and mental health system transformation in Virginia' (2009) 28 Health Affairs 793.

140 Virginia Code Annotated (2010), s 54.1-2981.

141 C Wilder (n 135).

142 R Bonnie (n 139).

143 ibid.

144 C Wilder (n 135).

proxy decision-maker. The grounds on which advance directives can be overridden by mental health law are confined to defined emergencies, providing respect for preferences during involuntary detention and minimizing the need for coercion. The implementation points to the importance of accompanying the introduction of advance directives with resources, stakeholder education and support. The provision of peer support for completion is a critical feature of the model, which complies with the supported decision-making model in the CRPD. The reform shows the value of adopting a consensus-building approach and for system and law reform to proceed in tandem with each other. The Virginia experience suggests that a planned consensus-building process with substantial participation by service users can break down barriers, facilitate understanding and help develop a shared vision of reform.[145]

6.2. Germany

Germany introduced a new law on advance directives in 2009.[146] The law provides legal certainty, emphasises autonomy and flexible legal regulations.[147] The legislation is liberal in the international context, due to the lack of formal legal requirements.[148] The directive does not require certification or specific review and can be revoked informally.[149] Advance directives must be respected in any decision concerning medical treatment regardless of the stage of the condition and are legally binding during involuntary detention.[150] Individuals have the option to communicate their 'will and preferences' directly or through a proxy decision-maker. If any doubt exists as to applicability, the physician, proxy decision-maker and other trusted persons determine the persons 'will.' Where there is no written directive, treatment preferences or the person's presumed 'will' is determined on concrete evidence such as previous verbal statements.[151] The directive can be revoked even with limited decision-making capacity.[152] The legislation complies with many of the CRPD principles by providing for advance directives that are easily executable and revocable by all persons and are legally binding during involuntary detention. The CRPD recognises the right to be free from involuntary detention and forced treatment in a mental health facility.[153] States Parties must provide supports to exercise legal capacity and measures such as advance directives to eliminate the need for involuntary detention and forced treatment.

---

145 R Bonnie (n 139).

146 Bunderministerium der Justiz, Drittes Gesetz zur Änderung des Betreuungsrechts, *Bundesgestezblatt* Teil 1 Nr 48 (2009) <www.bmj.bund.de/files/-/3906/Drittes_Gesetz_Aenderung_Betreuungsrecht_Bundesgesetzblatt.pdf> last accessed 31 March 2016.

147 U Wiesing, R Jox, H J Hebler and G Borasio.

148 Advance directives are considered legally binding if they are in writing and can be registered centrally.

149 U Wiesing, R Jox, H J Hebler and G Borasio.

150 German Civil Code, s 1901a. Bunderministerium der Justiz, Drittes Gesetz zur Änderung des Betreuungsrechts, *Bundesgestezblatt* Teil 1 Nr 48, 31 July 2009.

151 A verbal statement has some legal value although it is not recognised as an advance directive. R Jox, H J Hebler and G Borasio (n 162).

152 ibid.

153 Committee on the Rights of Persons with Disabilities, para 31 (n 8).

7. Conclusion

The CRPD era provides an opportunity to clarify and extend the purpose of advance directives and to reduce barriers to implementation. Advance directives are more than legal documents that are completed at a single point in time, but involve engagement with the 'will and preferences' of the person over a prolonged period.[154] The expanded vision of advance directives views them as vehicles for supporting the exercise of legal capacity, which allow the person to articulate his or her values and preferences and to identify effective recovery strategies, thereby avoiding the need for coercion.

Advance directives are a key driver in the cultural shift towards respect for the 'will and preferences' of the person. A spectrum of legal measures will be required to implement the supported decision-making model in the CRPD.[155] Advance directives are amongst a host of measures which can be embedded into the legal framework to support legal capacity, autonomy, equality and non-discrimination. In conjunction with other support measures such as advocacy, life-planning and peer support, advance directives can act as powerful tool for supporting legal capacity. The threat of coercion in mental health care suggests an increased need for legally binding non-discriminatory directives with accountability mechanisms to ensure respect for the preference of the person. The implementation of advance directives can strengthen the framework for participation and assist the paradigm shift towards respect for all persons. The adoption of a legal model for advance directives, whereby the preferences of individuals with mental health conditions are respected on an equal basis with others, can reduce stigma and discrimination. The establishment of a strong philosophical ethos of respect may be the most important aspect of the measure in mental health care. Ultimately, the implementation of CRPD-compliant advance directives requires respect for the 'voice' of all persons. The potential implications demand their introduction by State Parties.

154 C Peters and P Chiverton, 'Use of a values history in approaching medical advance directives with psychiatric patients' (2003) 41 Journal of Psychosocial Nursing Mental Health 28.

155 J Brayley, 'Decisions about supported accommodation: Advocacy and supported decision-making vs substituted decision-making. Rights, responsibilities and rhetoric: unpacking policy and practice issues' (National Mental Health Law, Guardianship and Trusteeship Conference, Adelaide, 7 October 2009).

CHAPTER 16

THE CRPD AND HUMAN-RIGHTS BASED APPROACHES: A MAGIC WAND FOR INCLUSION?

Liz Brosnan

1. INTRODUCTION

Marginalised and oppressed groups – mental health service-users[1] in particular – have much to gain from engaging with and becoming familiar with the discourses around human rights. Since the Universal Declaration of Human Rights was adapted by the UN assembly in 1948,[2] much has been debated and indeed tested in the courts, about what human rights mean for marginalised and oppressed groups. Human rights laws have evolved into instruments that can provide remedies for failures of government to either positively or negatively provide for people's rights. Perhaps more importantly human rights discourses provide opportunities to help people improve their lives because of the moral persuasion that can be used to effect change. The most recent Convention on the Rights of Persons with Disabilities[3] (CRPD) in many ways illustrates the extent to which the right to participate in policy and service delivery has become accepted as the norm.[4] This chapter primarily aims to explain to peer-advocates[5] and other activists how human-rights based approaches can offer a different way for mental health service-users/survivors to engage with the psychiatric system and influence improvements in how care is delivered.[6] Before

---

1 The terms used to refer to individuals who have first-hand experience of use and/or survival of the psychiatric system are varied and contested. Service-user and survivor are the most commonly used terms in Ireland and the UK so both are used in this chapter; for further discussion, see P Beresford, *A Straight Talking Introduction to Being a Mental Health Service User* (PCCS Books Ltd 2010). I personally identify with, and use both terms, and many other intersecting identities, depending on the context in which I find myself.

2 United Nations, Universal Declaration of Human Rights 1949, GA Res. 217 (III), UN Doc. A/810 (1948) 71.

3 United Nations Convention on the Rights of Persons with Disabilities (CRPD) (2006) A/Res/61/106 (CRPD).

4 A Dhanda and T Narayan, 'Mental health and human rights' (2007) 370 The Lancet 1197; P Bartlett, 'The United Nations Convention on the Rights of Persons with Disabilities and the future of mental health law' (2009) 8 Psychiatry 496.

5 Peer advocates are those who have personal experience of psychosocial difficulties and offer, usually non-legal, advocacy support to other service-users. For further discussion, see A Plumb, 'The challenge of self-advocacy' (1993) 3 Feminism & Psychology 169; D Brandon, 'Peer support and advocacy–International comparisons and developments' in R Jack (ed), *Empowerment in Community Care* (Chapman & Hall 1995); www.irishadvocacynetwork.com. last accessed 31 March 2016.

6 There is a wide body of opinion within the service-user/survivor community about whether to engage in participation opportunities with services in an effort to influence change by 'winning hearts and minds' or to resist what many consider to be an oppressive, abusive system, which denies human rights to people under their control. For those who do engage, unequal power

considering what benefits there may be for advocates of change in adopting human rights-based approaches I will examine briefly some of the concepts and debates around what is meant by human rights and how they have been understood by legal theorists, reviewing some of the tensions and paradoxes inherent in discourses and practices of human rights.

2. Human Rights Theory

Donnelly discusses the general principles of human rights in terms of their impact on individuals and society.[7] Rights holders can be said to be entitled to X, eg participate in decisions which affect them, while duty bearers have an obligation to provide, or move towards providing X. Rights are held by individuals and the individual can claim his or her rights from the duty bearers and seek legal remedies if they are not forthcoming. Rights empower, not just benefit, those who hold them because the very act of claiming them causes a reaction, according to Donnelly. In their absence, claiming a right is a powerful action, even if just at a moral or symbolic level. When States do not respect rights, rights holders may need to take action to demand or 'assertively exercise' such rights. This is where the power of human rights law is most potent, in demanding that the State actively respect a duty they have towards fulfilment of a right.

Under the Universal Declaration of Human Rights there are some core features of human rights, which are understood as given in the discussions of them and the ways they might be used.[8] Human rights are considered to be equal; everyone has them by virtue of being human; they are inalienable, they cannot be taken away; and they are universal – every human being has the same rights. As well as being 'moral rights of the highest order', which 'imply a manifesto for political change,' human rights rest on a priori moral (and international legal) entitlements.[9] They can be used through moral arguments to secure legal entitlements. Donnelly also emphasised that human rights form part of an independent and indivisible whole, not a menu, prohibiting States from deciding which rights they will recognise or which they would ignore. Therefore, social and economic rights, he argues, are on an equal basis with civil and political rights.

Another feature of rights discussed by Donnelly is the distinction between the positive and negative duties of States associated with every right. Traditionally, conservative legal theorists argued that because negative rights were cost neutral ie the State simply desists from action (prohibiting torture or police brutality) they were more likely to be realisable than more costly positive rights which imply duties of provision on States, eg to provide adequate health care.[10] However, negative rights do imply action on the part of the State – to train the police forces

---

dynamics are a common obstacle. See L Brosnan, 'Power and participation: An examination of the dynamics of mental health service-user involvement in Ireland' (2012) 6 Studies in Social Justice.

7 J Donnelly, *Universal Human Rights in Theory and Practice* (2nd edn, Cornell University Press 2003) ch 1.

8 ibid ch 2.

9 ibid 12.

10 M Cranston (1964) and H Bedau (1979) cited in J Donnelly (n 7) 28–30.

in anti-discrimination policies, in non-conflict resolution etc – and thus do have cost implications. And under the UN system, resource arguments are not acceptable justifications for inaction: States are obliged to demonstrate that they are making reasonable movement towards progressive realization of human rights.[11]

Claiming rights domestically, and the complex question of what rights are justiciable or amenable to legal adjudication, is a complicated matter because it involves the interaction of the courts and other branches of the State to resolve questions about conflicts between different interpretations of constitutional text and judicial precedent.[12] International human rights law in many jurisdictions is not used as common practice by Irish judges in arriving at their decisions, in part because international human rights law may not be incorporated into domestic law. Exercising rights through legal action may require an interpretation by individual judges; therefore one would need to have an expectation of a positive outcome, which is unlikely given the conservative nature of the current Supreme Court in Ireland.[13] It is questionable if it is worth getting a result that sets back the social progress of a movement towards realising rights, especially for marginalised and oppressed groups.[14]

Before leaving this brief discussion of human rights theory, it is worth noting two other themes of critique in the scholarship around human rights. First, a significant critique analyses the discourses within which rights are framed. Mullally examined the separation of the ethic of care from that of justice and rights. She argued for a widening of legal discourse to include a politics of recognition of diversity and discrimination of women bound by networks of reciprocal obligations.[15] Ziv also highlighted the individualist-liberal conceptualisation of rights corresponding to the fulfilment of responsibilities, with the individual assumed to be autonomous and independent, achieving choice and participation through maximising available opportunities.[16] This approach fails to recognise the concept of capabilities, people's abilities to pursue freedom, the constraints in particular on persons with disabilities and others in need of protection from harm or material deprivation. Ziv outlined Sen's (1992) concept of justice which critiques this liberal notion, and called for

---

11 ibid. Technically this point is outlined in the International Convention Economic Social and Civil Rights but it is accepted as applying to States generally.

12 Mégret argues that the CRPD removes the emphasis on litigation, which fails to address structural inequalities, instead emphasising rights action within policy frameworks. See Frédéric Mégret, 'The Disabilities Convention: Towards a holistic concept of rights' (2008) 12 The International Journal of Human Rights 273.

13 For example, by conservative I mean that the Irish Supreme Court understands its role in narrow terms, failing to move beyond a restricted, traditional, liberal interpretation of the Constitution, indeed often arguing to protect the State against citizens' rights. For further discussion, see G Whyte, 'The Role of the Supreme Court in our democracy: A response to Mr Justice Hardiman' (2006) 28 Dublin University Law Journal 1; S Mullally, 'Feminist jurisprudence' in T Murphy (ed), *Western Jurisprudence* (Thomson Round Hall 2004).

14 While many successes have been achieved in different jurisdictions in human rights advocacy, for example in the US in relation to racism, by the 1980s Critical Race scholars were writing about the rolling back of gains made earlier. For further discussion, see R Delgado and J Stefancic, 'Critical Race Theory: Past, present and future' (1998) 51 Current Legal Problems 467.

15 Mullally (n 13).

16 N Ziv, 'The Social Rights of People with Disabilities' in D Barak-Erez and A M Gross (eds), *Exploring Social Rights: Between Theory and Practice* (Hart 2007) 370.

recognition of the actual ability of the person to do certain things that can improve their situation or overall wellbeing. Ziv developed Sen's concept of justice as it operates in relation to the rights of people with disabilities, highlighting an ethics of care which regards people as interdependent, with everybody likely to require and be reliant on others for care and support at different stages in their lives. While individuals are rights holders, the practice of human rights and in particular human rights-based approaches are realised and exercised in webs of social relationships.[17]

Another theme within critical legal scholarship was illustrated by Pieterse.[18] He argued 'the transformative potential of rights is significantly thwarted by the fact that they are typically formulated, interpreted, and enforced by institutions that are embedded in the political, social, and economic status quo'[19] – mental health legislation allowing detention and forced treatment being a pertinent example. Critical legal scholars have demonstrated how liberal rights discourse has been used to 'silence challenges by vulnerable sectors of society to existing social power structures and, second, to thwart state efforts at social redistribution.'[20] He illustrated how the South African Constitutional Court, in many ways a shining example of judgments positively influencing socioeconomic policies, interpreted human rights obligations in terms of the State's abstract procedural duties to progressively realise rights rather than immediately enforce concrete entitlements. In other words, by showing it was developing policies to improve access to health rights, the State could argue it was meeting its duties to respect human rights. In the meantime, the applicants could die, or remain homeless.[21]

Yet although critical legal scholarship has questioned the advances made and the real danger of appropriation by liberal discourses or dominant interest groups, Patricia Williams offered a powerful, eloquent and moving defence of human rights and their role in the emancipation and empowerment of dispossessed groups such as African Americans.[22] Her argument remains compelling:

> 'Rights' feels so new in the mouths of most black people. It is still so deliciously empowering to say. It is a sign for and a gift of selfhood that is very hard to contemplate reconstructing (deconstruction is too awful to think about!) at this point in history. It is the magic wand of visibility and invisibility, of inclusion and exclusion, of power and no-power. The concept of rights, (…) is the marker of our citizenship, our participatoriness, our relation to others.[23]

17 J Nedelsky, 'Reconceiving rights as relationship' (1993) 1 Review of Constitutional Studies/ Revue d'études constitutionnelles 1; M Minow 'Interpreting rights: An essay for Robert Cover' (1987) Yale Law Journal 1860; M Minow and M L Shanley, 'Relational rights and responsibilities: Revisioning the family in liberal political theory and law' (1996) 11 Hypatia 4.

18 M Pieterse, 'Eating socioeconomic rights: The usefulness of rights talk in alleviating social hardship revisited' (2007) 29 Human Rights Quarterly 796.

19 ibid 797.

20 ibid 800.

21 Mégret (n 12) 265. Mégret argues that the CRPD had overcome this distinction between positive and negative rights, which is an advance for the potential power of human rights in the lives of all marginalised people.

22 P J Williams, 'Alchemical notes: Reconstructing ideals from deconstructed rights' (1987) Harvard Civil Rights-Civil Liberties Law Review 401.

23 ibid 431.

I would argue that this is how most persons with disabilities feel about the newly won recognition for their human rights with the CRPD.

3. Social Model of Disability and Human Rights

The social model asserts that disability is a product of disabling environments, rather than an inherent attribute of a person.[24] The social model was a major development of the Disability Movement, which challenges the paternalistic and reductionist conception of people enshrined in the medical model of disability, providing an intense sense of liberation from individualised deficit attention for disabled people. Space does not permit adequate discussion of the immense importance of this development here; much has been written about its enormous impact in changing the paradigms and discourses around disability. Its influence is obvious within the CRPD, which introduces the social model of disability into international human rights law. There is, however, an inherent tension between asserting the importance of environmental restrictions on individuals and recognising the costs for disabled people of asserting and exercising their rights. For instance, Baily has described how it fails to recognise the effort the disabled person must make with and through their bodies, and she theorised about recognition of 'doing impairment,' or 'doing energy management,' actual daily practices by people which allow them participate in daily activities taken for granted by able-bodied people.[25] This recognition of the reality of 'doing the body,' or indeed the broader concept of the ethics of care are sharp critiques of the dominant language and discourses around disability and human rights.[26] The applicability of the social model of disability to explain psychosocial distress has been the subject of interesting research within the service-user/survivor community, but space prohibits discussion here.[27]

There is a substantial body of work which focuses on the right of people to participate, and the central importance of the concept of citizenship in contemporary theories of disability and disability rights.[28] Claiming citizenship, and the dignity and equality this entails, is fundamental to overcoming dehumanisation and exclusion. For persons with disability, the effective denial of citizenship through failure to accommodate effects of impairment results in a denial of the opportunity to participate in everyday activities but also in public policy formulation and decision-making, which affects

24 M Oliver, *The Politics of Disablement* (Macmillan 1990); M Oliver and C Barnes, *Disabled People and Social Policy: From Exclusion to Inclusion* (Longman 1998). R Garland-Thomson, '*Feminist Disability Studies*' (2005) 30 Signs: Journal of Women in Culture and Society 1557.

25 R Bailey, 'Doing Impairment: Towards a Non-Normative, Socially Shaped Understanding of Impairment' (Paper presented at BSA Annual Conference: 'Inequalities & Social Justice,' 7–9 April 2010, Glasgow Caledonian University).

26 Mégret (n 12) 274. Megret argues that the reality of the lives of persons with disabilities which underpins the text and spirit of the CRPD has displaced the presumptive assumptions of the able-bodied subject and individual autonomy which underpins earlier understandings of human rights and thus transformed human rights into a more plural, relational understanding for all.

27 P Beresford, M Nettle and R Perring, *Towards a Social Model of Madness and Distress? Exploring What Service Users Say* (Joseph Rowentree Foundation 2010).

28 M A Stein and J Lord, 'JC' (2007) 13 Texas Journal on Civil Liberties and Civil Rights; J Hammel, S Magasi, A Heinemann, G Whiteneck, J Bogner and E Rodriguez, 'What does participation mean? An insider perspective from people with disabilities' (2008) 30 Disability & Rehabilitation 1445; R Kayess and P French, 'Out of darkness into light? Introducing the convention on the rights of persons with disabilities' (2008) 8 Human Rights Law Review 1.

their lives.[29,30] Widespread exclusion of people with disabilities from public policy formulation and decision-making processes is a profound distributive injustice, denying them the opportunity to argue for their needs and rights in the contest for social resources, and for the reform of oppressive laws.[31] This 'wrong' is intensified by the exercise of overt executive power over the lives of many persons with disability by means of compulsory assistance (or coercive treatment),[32] or more covertly, through effective control over the social resources that sustain people with disability. This history of disempowerment and paternalism has resulted in a demand for radical participation, encapsulated in the ethic 'Nothing About Us Without Us', a fundamental principle of social justice.[33]

4. Human Rights and Psychosocial Disability

Early recognition of disabled people in human rights law was paternalistic, and legitimised segregation through specialised services and institutions. While the 1991 adoption by the UN of the Mental Illness Principles[34] was the first time mental health conditions were included in human rights discourses, they were controversial as they enshrined the paternalistic medical model. The Principles established mental health care standards and procedural guarantees for the protection of people with mental illness against human rights abuses in mental health facilities.[35] However, the continued focus on treatment and protection has meant that the Principles have been critiqued by many legal theorists,[36] and rejected by survivor activists for their perpetuation of a paternalistic medical model of disability which authorised forced treatment on a best-interests principle.[37] Harding critiqued the Principles in several ways: they lacked formal international treaty status; there was no requirement on

---

29 art 3(c), art 4, art 8, art 29 and art 33 CRPD (n 3). For instance, art 3(c) enshrines 'full and effective participation and inclusion in society' of persons with disabilities; art 4 outlines the obligations on States Parties to ensure such participation; art 8 details the obligations on States Parties to raise awareness, including to combat disabling stereotypes and foster respect for people's capabilities; art 29 treats inclusion in public and political life; and art 33 requires that persons be included in national implementation and monitoring of the CRPD.

30 This social justice argument of exclusion and invisibility helped leverage the involvement of disabled peoples' organisations in the drafting of the CRPD and underpins the provisions of the CRPD that require the participation of persons with disabilities across all levels of society.

31 E Flynn, 'A socio-legal analysis of advocacy for people with disabilities – Competing concepts of 'best interests' and empowerment in legislation and policy on statutory advocacy services' (2010) 32 Journal of Social Welfare and Family Law 23.

32 T Minkowitz, 'The United Nations Convention of the Rights of Persons with Disabilities and the right to be free from non-consensual psychiatric interventions' (2007) 34 Syracuse Journal of International Law and Commerce 405.

33 Kayess and French (n 28).

34 United Nations General Assembly – Principles for the Protection of Persons with Mental Illness and for the Improvement of Mental Health Care (1991) G A Res. 46/119.

35 Kayess and French (n 28). These protections were against excessive or prolonged use of physical restraint or involuntary seclusion, sterilisation on the grounds of mental illness, psychosurgery and irreversible treatment.

36 E Rosenthal and LS Rubinstein, 'International human rights advocacy under the "Principles for the protection of persons with mental illness"' (1993) 16 International Journal of Law and Psychiatry 257; C Gendreau, 'The rights of psychiatric patients in the light of the principles announced by the United Nations' (1997) 20 International Journal of Law and Psychiatry 259; T Harding, 'Human rights law in the field of mental health: A critical review' (2000) 101 Acta Psychiatrica Scandinavica 24.

37 The World Network of Users and Survivors of Psychiatry (WNUSP) called for their abolition

States to adopt them as minimum standards; in relation to consent to treatment they removed rights rather than protected them; and finally, they failed to provide for a redress or any form of monitoring inspection and supervision by an independent international body.[38]

The CRPD covers mental health conditions, which is a core strategy of the disability movement, ie the inclusion of all people with disabilities in policies and frameworks rather than developing impairment specific frameworks or principles. It enshrines the same basic human rights for persons with disabilities as apply to others, affirming the universality, indivisibility, interdependence, and inter-relatedness of all human rights.[39] It was drafted with the active participation of people with disabilities themselves, who united and worked together through the International Disability Caucus, on which mental health service-users/survivors played a significant role. Survivor groups such as the World Network of Users and Survivors of Psychiatry (WNUSP), Mind Freedom/Support Coalition International (MF/SCI) and other user/survivor organizations from fifteen countries[40] participated in the negotiations on the text of the CRPD.[41]

From a service-user/survivor perspective the CRPD is a paradigm changer. It makes three basic contributions to the advancement of the rights of people with psychosocial disabilities; it enshrines a human-rights approach to all people, including those treated by the psychiatric system; it establishes the principle of non-discrimination based on grounds of a disability; and it provides for the autonomy and freedom to make one's own decisions about treatment, based on the principle of equal legal capacity, a freedom denied by mental health legislation.[42] It affirms the right to political participation of persons with disabilities,[43] including decision-making processes about mental health policies and programmes[44] and on the committees established to monitor the implementation of the Convention.[45] In the area of informed consent and legal capacity it represents a paradigm shift, moving to the

---

in 2001; see WNUSP, 'Position paper on Principles for the Protection of Persons with Mental Illness' (2001) <www.wnusp.net/> last accessed 31 March 2016.

38 T Harding (n 36).

39 United Nations Vienna Declaration and Programme of Action, 63-65, U.N. Doc A/CONF. 157/23 (World Conference on Human Rights, Vienna, June 1993).

40 Canada, Denmark, Ghana, Guinea, Hungary, Ireland, India, Japan, New Zealand, Nicaragua, Peru, Sweden, Uganda, the United Kingdom and the United States of America.

41 For an account of the process of participation of users/survivors see World Network of Users And Survivors of Psychiatry, 'Implementation Manual for the United Nations Convention On The Rights Of Persons With Disabilities' (WNUSP 2008) <www.wnusp.net/> last accessed 31 March 2016, 4–5.

42 M Kovary, 'The United Nations Convention on the Rights of Persons with Disabilities (CRPD) from the perspective of users and survivors of psychiatry' (2008) <www.wnusp.net> last accessed 31 March 2016.

43 art 29 CRPD (n 3).

44 art 4(3) CRPD (n 3). Article 4(3) ensures that '[i]n the development and implementation of legislation and policies to implement the (…) Convention, and in other decision-making processes concerning issues relating to persons with disabilities, States Parties shall closely consult with and actively involve persons with disabilities, including children with disabilities, through their representative organizations.'

45 ibid art 33(3). Article 33(3) ensures the participation of people with disabilities in domestic independent CRPD monitoring bodies.

concept of supported decision-making.[46, 47] This is discussed in greater detail in other chapters, while the focus of this chapter remains on the right to participate, a principle enshrined throughout the CRPD.[48]

It is evident from the overview presented above that much has been gained by the leverage of human rights in international and national legal and policy domains of society. There are also significant criticisms of the limitations of human rights discourse, including suggestions that the more powerful can appropriate rights talk to defend their privileges or to assimilate and subsume social movements.[49] Stammers argues for the need to examine the role and potential for social movements to challenge and redefine how human rights can contest some of the power plays of dominant interest groups.[50] Substantial gains have been made by adapting a social movement/community development approach to the use of human rights, and the CRPD offers new potential to advance the position of mental health service-users/survivors.[51] One such model is the human-rights based approach (hereafter HRBA), a social movement which seeks to engage local people on the ground with the ideas of human rights activism. The remainder of the chapter examines HRBA and the potential it offers for change, illustrated by the Participation and Practice of Rights (PPR) Project in Belfast and recent HRBA activity in the Republic of Ireland by survivors.

5. Human-Rights Based Approaches (HRBA) and Participatory Processes

HRBA seek to ensure that human rights are a central plank underpinning policy-

46 Ireland's utterly out-of-date capacity legislation is a significant obstacle to ratification of the CRPD. See E Flynn, 'Justice Committee Hearing on Capacity Legislation' (Human Rights in Ireland, 22 February 2012) <www.humanrights.ie/index.php/2012/02/22/justice-committee-hearings-on-capacity-legislation/> last accessed 31 March 2016; M Bach and L Kerzner, (2010) 'A new paradigm for protecting autonomy and the right to legal capacity' *Law Commission of Ontario* < http://www.lco-cdo.org/disabilities/bach-kerzner.pdf> last accessed 31 March 2016.

47 The committee of experts tasked with overseeing the interpretation of the CRPD has issued general comments in relation to the right of persons with disabilities to be accorded the same legal capacity (as distinct from mental capacity) as all others. This asserts that people, including those with psychosocial disabilities, must give free and informed consent to medical treatment, including psychiatric. General Comment No. 1, para 42, states that 'forced treatment by psychiatric and other health and medical professionals is a violation of the right to equal recognition before the law and an infringement of the rights to personal integrity (art. 17); freedom from torture (art. 15); and freedom from violence, exploitation and abuse (art. 16). This practice denies the legal capacity of a person to choose medical treatment and is therefore a violation of Art. 12 of the Convention. … States Parties must abolish policies and legislative provisions that allow or perpetrate forced treatment, as it is an ongoing violation found in mental health laws across the globe, despite empirical evidence indicating its lack of effectiveness and the views of people using mental health systems who have experienced deep pain and trauma as a result of forced treatment.' See Committee on the Rights of Persons with Disabilities, General Comment No. 1 (2014) Article 12: Equal recognition before the law. <http://www.ohchr.org/en/hrbodies/crpd/pages/crpdindex.aspx> last accessed 31 March 2016.

48 Bartlett (n 4).

49 Pieterse (n 19).

50 N Stammers, 'Social movements and the social construction of human rights' 21 Human Rights Quarterly 980.

51 See, for instance, WNUSP Implementation Manual (n 41).

making and political choices by ensuring that people have the political, institutional and material resources to demand, exercise and monitor their human rights, and to actively participate in decision-making processes.[52] It requires the integration of minimum standards into all plans, policies, budgets, processes and institutions. By definition HRBA is as concerned with the process as the outcome. In the context of mental health services, for instance, HRBA requires that strategies and goals be explicitly based on the norms and values of international human rights law, but also that those strategies be identified, applied and reviewed with active and informed participation of the relevant communities, in particular those who use services. The use of human rights language and participatory processes empowers rights holders to both assert their human rights and hold accountable those legally responsible for their delivery.

Five inter-connected principles have been internationally recognised as forming the core of HRBA. These are: Express application of the international human rights framework; empowerment; participation; non-discrimination and prioritisation of vulnerable groups; and accountability.[53] I will examine just one of these principles in more detail as it specifically relates to the emergent policy of service-user involvement in mental health services.

The active and informed participation of individuals, communities and populations is an integral component of the right to the highest attainable standard of health enshrined in Article 12 of the International Covenant on Economic, Social and Cultural Rights ('ICESCR').[54] This right includes participation in identifying overall health strategy, agenda-setting, decision-making, prioritisation, implementation and accountability.[55] Potts clearly distinguished participation in health policy development from education, informing or consultation, as none of these practices guarantees that the 'voice' of individuals and groups will be heeded, or that there will be follow-through on any information gathered during the conduct of these activities.[56] Potts described the learning from several projects that used HRBAs to look at participation in health-policy development in different countries. She argued that institutional mechanisms must be put in place to ensure that participation is fair.[57] These must address three issues: agenda-setting; rule-making and facilitation; and discussion.[58] Rules must be established to overcome the difficulties all participants can have as a result of personal, interpersonal and institutional dynamics, setting out how discussions are managed and decisions reached. Appointing an independent facilitator can also help to ensure that everyone has a chance to have their voice heard. Transparent information on which to base decisions must be available.[59]

---

52 Amnesty International, *Our Rights, Our Future. Human Rights Based Approaches in Ireland: Principles, Policies and Practice* (2006) 48.

53 ibid.

54 P Hunt, Foreword to H Potts, *Participation and The Right to The Highest Attainable Standard of Health* (Human Rights Centre, University of Essex 2008) 2.

55 H Potts, *Participation and The Right to The Highest Attainable Standard of Health* (Human Rights Centre, University of Essex 2008).

56 ibid 18.

57 ibid 18.

58 ibid 22. Participation does not preclude a preliminary, predetermined agenda as a starting point which is necessary in policy formation, but fairness means allowing everyone the same chance to put their concerns on the agenda.

59 ibid 26. This means complex topics must be explained in an accessible manner, free of jargon,

Finally, through the development of context-dependent indicators and benchmarks, the government can show how the 'voices' of people and groups are listened to in the process and how the final decisions are made.[60]

Potts reported on the way the HRBA worked in several health-related projects including the Participation and Practice of Rights (PPR) project in Belfast, which works with disenfranchised and disadvantaged local communities, including a mental health users and carers project.[61] The background context to this mental health project, concerned with reducing deaths by suicide, included a complex and weighty set of policy documents and government exercises which made frequent references to user involvement, which, however, had not resulted in any changes for people on the ground. The local group, in collaboration with PPR, demonstrated how participatory processes, from the bottom-up, resulted in concrete, user-defined outcomes and indicators. These indicators were established using WHO-designed instruments and indicators to monitor governments' progress on international human rights commitments. Local people, supported by the PPR, used these official measures, based on action research carried out by the group themselves on the mental health needs of their communities, to place the spotlight back on the State. Their experiences and research helped them identify four core concerns around mental health services in Northern Ireland: follow-up appointments; complaints; information from General Practitioners; and service-user participation. They developed six indicators to hold the government to account for progressive realisation of these issues, which they saw as critical to realisation of their human rights.[62] They took three key decisions after consultation on their indicators with an international panel of mental health and human rights experts. First, by holding the Minister for Health directly politically accountable for delivery on their indicators, they used his political authority to overcome the resistance of the Trust to making progressive changes. As a result, he announced the introduction of the 'card before you leave' scheme a few short months after the media campaign set up by the group, and made mental health follow-up care one of his top twelve health priorities.[63] The second key decision the group took was to avoid the existing government structures for consultation[64] as they had previous experience of the failures of these existing mechanisms. The group's issues and concerns had been frequently raised through these forums in the past without result. Instead, the group sought a ministerial liaison, a top-level civil servant who had specific responsibility to deliver on their indicators. Finally, they decided not to rely solely on the Minister or the liaison official to deliver but also exerted outside political pressure through a successful media campaign and

and that community perspectives and understandings of the health issues are available to, and listened to by, health services officials.

60 ibid 26.

61 F McMillan, N Browne, S Green, and D Donnelly, 'A card before you leave: Participation and mental health in Northern Ireland human rights' (2009) 11 Health and Human Rights 61.

62 [62] ibid 61.

63 ibid. This was considered vital because the group's research highlighted that post-discharge suicides peaked within the first 1–2 weeks, and UK-wide policy guidelines for people at risk suggested they be followed up within one week.

64 ibid. McMillan and colleagues defined 'existing consultative structures' as 'those structures, bodies, and forums designed and led by the government, which include mental health service-users as members and which have the express purpose of increasing "user involvement" in policy processes.'

alliances with other community groups, including international advocacy groups, trade unions etc.

An interesting aspect of this project was the rejection of the existing consultative structures.[65] McMillan and colleagues described some of the barriers to participation experienced by members of the local group.[66] Top-down consultative processes have often been criticised as failing to provide genuine opportunities for participation, whereas the projects developed in partnership with PPR from the ground up, building capacity in local groups through HRBA, supporting them in developing their own user-led benchmarks and indicators, can be the beginnings of real participation for service-users. In addition, this project demonstrated real power-subversion by adapting the WHO measures and indicators and using them to hold the government to account. There is a pressing need for more meaningful participation by people affected by mental health issues in professionally-led projects which employ human rights discourse and indicators to leverage change towards improved mental health services.[67]

International networks of (ex)users/survivors have engaged in legal advocacy[68] and developed tools which can form the basis of such action by the user/survivor movement.[69] One such HRBA action was recently taken by a group of (ex)users and survivors of psychiatry in Ireland, Recovery Experts by Experience (REE),[70] who produced a shadow report on mental health services to the fourth UN periodic review of Ireland under the International Covenant On Civil And Political Rights (ICCPR).[71] This report highlighted failures of the Irish State to respect Article 7 (the right to freedom from torture, cruel, inhuman or degrading treatment or punishment), Article 9 (on the right to liberty and security of person) and Article 10

---

65 ibid.

66 ibid. These included having decisions made without them, being made to feel stupid at meetings, the chair always filled by someone on the government side, having to constantly repeat their stories, and no real information about obstacles being presented.

67 An example of this approach was the establishment of an Expert by Experience Advisory Group (EEAG) by Amnesty International Ireland during their mental health campaign, whose role was to guide and inform their advocacy on mental health. See L Brosnan, 'Empowerment and development of an Irish advocacy movement' in A Higgins, and S McDaid (eds), *Mental Health in Ireland: Policy, Practice & Law* (Gill and Macmillan 2014) 81–100.

68 Mental Health Europe and European Network of (ex-)Users and Survivors of Psychiatry, 'Rights of people with mental health problems must not be restricted: Joint declaration about the new Constitution of Hungary by Mental Health Europe (MHE) and European Network of (ex-)Users and Survivors of Psychiatry (ENUSP)' (2011) <wwwmhe-smeorg/assets/files/press/MHE-ENUSP%20statement%20on%20HU%20Constitution%20 2011_28Aprilpdf> last accessed 31 March 2016; European Disability Forum, European Network of (ex-)Users and Survivors of Psychiatry, International Disability Alliance, World Network of Users and Survivors of Psychiatry, 'Mihailovs submission to The European Court of Human Rights (App no 35939/10)' (2012) <wwwenusporg/documents/mihailovs%20submission13%20February%202012Finalpdf> last accessed 31 March 2016.

69 WNUSP Implementation Manual (n 41).

70 REE emerged from the advisory group established by Amnesty in 2008.

71 Recovery Experts by Experience 'Recovery Experts by Experience (REE) Submission to the Un Human Rights Committee on the Examination of Irelands Fourth Periodic Report under the International Covenant on Civil and Political Rights (ICCPR)'(2014) Office of the High Commissioner for Human Rights http://tbinternet.ohchr.org/_layouts/treatybodyexternal/Download.aspx?symbolno=INT%2fCCPR%2fCSS%2fIRL%2f17491&Lang=en last accessed 31 March 2016.

(on the right of those deprived of liberty to be treated with humanity and respect for the inherent dignity of the person). In addition to a catalogue of failures to respect human rights in mental health services, the submission also calls for meaningful participation of users and survivors in national developments in mental health, a current review of mental health legislation and a committee charged with drafting of assisted decision-making legislation. REE argues that meaningful participation of users is necessary to ensure more appropriate and respectful mental health care. REE also developed a submission arguing for the need for legally binding advance health care directives in mental health in response to concern at being excluded from the process of drafting the long awaited Assisted Decision-Making (Legal Capacity) Bill. The document used Article 12 of the CRPD (Equal recognition before the law), and the deliberations of a Citizens' Jury established and supported by Amnesty International Ireland (AI), while the group was constituted as EEAG to AI.[72].This submission was used to both lobby politicians and make representations to government departments and parliamentary committees.[73]

6. Conclusion

This chapter has examined some of the issues and paradoxes of human rights discourses and practices. Initial enthusiasm for the expectation that human rights law would lead to progressive realisation of improvements in people's actual circumstances has been tempered by the reality of limited liberal interpretations by courts, and indeed outright subversion of rights talk by dominant interest groups, including the State itself. Such discourse was also shown to be limited by its failure to include the standpoint of women and other marginalised groups such as black persons, disabled persons and children. Scholars with such perspectives highlight the need to include an ethic of care and a concrete elaboration of people's realities and needs into abstract human rights discourses. Inclusion of persons with disabilities in the drafting of the CRPD has demonstrated how the resultant text can be a paradigm changer.[74]

We have entered a period of renewed optimism about making meaningful gains on the human rights of people with psychosocial difficulties – indeed, as Mégret has argued, for all people. Many stumbling blocks remain, not least the Irish Government's failure to ratify the CRPD because of inadequate capacity legislation. In the meantime, promising developments lie in the use of HRBA by social movements, such as those occurring internationally on the CRPD.[75] Two examples were used to illustrate this potential in the empirical discussion of the PPR projects in Belfast and REE in the Republic of Ireland. In Belfast people on the ground showed the power of HRBA, bypassed the established participation mechanisms, and used official indicators to hold the government to account to leverage some of the changes they decided could meet their needs. The second example is the REE

---

72 Amnesty International Ireland, *A Citizens' Jury on Legal Capacity Law* (Amnesty International Ireland 2012).

73 *Response of Recovery Experts by Experience (REE) to the Draft General Scheme for Advance Healthcare Directives* (2014) available from miseliz@gmail.com.

74 Mégret (n 12).

75 See www.disabilityrightsfund.org/; http://www.freedom-center.org/freedom-center-and-usnusp-collaborate-quothuman-rights-allquot-tour.

group's use of human rights instruments, notably the ICESCR and the CRPD, to highlight failures to protect human rights in mental health services, and to leverage for greater participation in forums that are traditionally exclusionary. These examples of human rights in action from the ground up demonstrate the continued power of human rights to be the: '[M]agic wand of visibility and invisibility, of inclusion and exclusion, of power and no-power.'[76]

---

76 Williams (n 22).

CHAPTER 17

THE CRPD AND THE FUSION OF MENTAL HEALTH AND LEGAL CAPACITY LEGISLATION

Charles O'Mahony and Ciara Hackett

1. INTRODUCTION

This chapter considers the proposal of fusing mental health and mental capacity legislation. As will be seen fusion of both sets of laws has been advanced as a positive law reform that would better respect the rights of persons with mental health problems. However, this claim will be examined from the perspective of the UN Convention on the Rights of Persons with Disabilities. It is important to note that guardianship laws respond to persons who are considered to have problems making decisions or, perhaps more accurately, are considered to have impaired decision-making. Mental health laws, on the other hand, specifically respond to persons who are considered to have mental health problems and who are considered to pose a risk to themselves and/or others. A key difference between guardianship laws and mental health laws manifest in respect of the powers relating to emergency intervention. While mental health laws in many jurisdictions empower police officers and other public officials to enter the home of persons suspected of posing risk to themselves or others, and force them to attend a medical setting for assessment for detention and treatment, guardianship laws generally do not have corresponding coercive provisions.[1] A more informal process is engaged in respect of emergency situations arising for persons who lack capacity and are being dealt with under guardianship. The less coercive guardianship approach is explained in that a person lacking mental capacity is more likely to comply than resist intervention, as opposed to persons being subject to mental health legislation.

2. ARGUMENTS FOR AND AGAINST THE FUSION OF MENTAL HEALTH AND GUARDIANSHIP LAWS

Dawson and Szmukler argue for the fusion of mental health and guardianship laws as they consider that law should respond to a question of lack of capacity in the same manner, regardless of the reason for the perceived lack of capacity.[2] They also argue that the criterion of a lack of capacity should be met in order for intervention

1 Rees 'The Fusion Proposal: A Next Step' in McSherry and Weller (eds) *Rethinking Rights-Based Mental Health Laws* (Hart Publishing 2010) 86.

2 Dawson and Szmukler 'Why Distinguish "Mental" and "Physical" Illness in Involuntary Treatment?' in Freeman and Goodenough (eds), *Law, Mind and Brain* (Ashgate, 2009) 174–175.

to occur.[3] Another suggested benefit of a fused approach is that it would address the discriminatory approach of having a separate legislative substitute decision-making framework for persons with mental health problems. When a person is considered to have lost the capacity to make decisions under the fused approach, the substitute decision-making power would shift from a public official to a family member or a trusted person (provided that these natural supports are present) or to a guardian as a last resort.[4] It is suggested that this would be a positive development in promoting 'the dignity and autonomy of the person who loses capacity because of mental illness, as in many instances the substitute decision-maker would be a close and trusted person rather than an unfamiliar doctor at a psychiatric hospital'.[5]

Separate mental health laws and guardianship laws serve to institutionalise the notion that mental illness requires coercion and control. In that regard even though mental illness and social control are theoretically and practically different, the separate approach results in the intertwining of both concepts. Campbell does not argue against the use of preventative detention; rather he argues for an equal application of the rules.[6] Richardson has suggested that the discrimination experienced by persons with mental health problems could be avoided if 'mental health care could be provided according to the same principles, including respect for patient autonomy, as those which cover all other forms of health care'.[7] The presence of separate mental health laws and guardianship laws serves to single out persons with mental health problems, and basing the legislation on different sets of principles means that 'mental disorder will be regarded as the more threatening and its pariah-status will thus be reinforced'.[8]

One of the main arguments in support of separate laws is that mental health laws represent special measures that promote the best interests of persons with mental health problems. As such, mental health laws are not discriminatory and 'do not infringe the equal protection and non-discrimination provisions in domestic and international human rights charters.'[9] In that regard 'special measures' are necessary to respond to persons with mental health problems, as 'mental illness is different to most other forms of disability because it is sometimes accompanied by a lack of awareness of impaired functioning'.[10] Therefore, it is argued that this difference justifies separate mental health laws, which after all seek to help persons by acting in their 'best interests' in involuntarily detaining and treating them. Peay points out 'in the tussle between autonomy and coercion, a short period of coercion may be a precursor to a long period of autonomy'.[11] The other argument that has been identified opposing fused legal capacity and mental health legislation is that the safeguards that have been developed over many decades and generations of mental health law could be undermined if legal capacity laws – as opposed to mental health

---

3 ibid.
4 ibid.
5 Rees (n 1) 87.
6 Campbell 'Mental Health Law: Institutionalised Discrimination' (1994) 28 Australian and New Zealand Journal of Psychiatry 554, 556.
7 Richardson "'Autonomy, Guardianship and Mental Disorder: One Problem, Two Solutions"' (2002) 65(Modern Law Review: 2002, 65, 450).
8 ibid 459.
9 Rees (n 1) 90.
10 ibid.
11 Peay (ed) *Seminal Issues in Mental Health Law* (Ashgate 2005) 199.

laws – were used to involuntarily detain and impose treatment on persons with mental health problems.[12]

The fusion approach is very problematical in the guardianship paradigm as it may result in vesting what has been the power of the states to impose detention and coercive treatment to a single person (eg the guardian) who will normally either be a family member or trusted person, or, where such a person does not exist, a third party appointed under guardianship laws to exercise the functions of a guardian. Vesting power in a guardian raises fundamentally important issues with regards to 'liberty and bodily integrity,' and there is a need for independence and transparency in the decision-making processes around involuntary detention and forced treatment, which is the hallmark of modern robust mental health legislation.[13] The same level of safeguards is not provided for under guardianship legislation. It also suggested that guardianship laws lack the necessary process provisions to respond effectively to the circumstances in which some people with a mental illness come to the attention of police and ambulance services'.[14] Mental health laws generally have detailed provisions to deal with emergency situations where a person with a mental health problem is experiencing a crisis, while guardianship laws tend not to have corresponding provisions. Also identified as a problem with fusing mental health law and guardianship laws is that guardianship laws are generally triggered when someone is considered to lack capacity. This, it is suggested, 'may not be an effective means of providing assistance in some cases involving people with a mental illness'.[15] If there is a debate as to the capacity of the person to make decisions for themselves, as is often argued in respect of persons with mental health problems, the provisions under guardianship laws to resolve disputes as to the person's capacity 'may be too slow and awkward to permit timely clinical intervention in many cases'.[16]

The other main argument against a fused approach is that persons acting as a guardian are required under the legislative framework to act in the best interests of the person and also to consider the person's own views. It is foreseeable that this could be problematic, as the guardian may be pressurised by clinical mental health professionals to make decisions on the person's behalf that are at odds with the person's 'will and preferences' and the paradigm shift required by Article 12 of the CRPD.[17] The guardian, who is often a family member or family friend, will make decisions in the person's best interests based on clinical advice. It is suggested that this is 'a recipe for conflict' with the 'on-going relationship between a friend or relative who accepts appointment as a guardian and the represented person may be irrevocably damaged in these circumstances'.[18]

---

12 Rees (n 1) 91.

13 ibid.

14 ibid.

15 ibid.

16 *Ibid*ibid.

17 See Chapter 2: Literature Review, Part 2.

18 Rees "(n 1)The Fusion Proposal: A Next Step" in McSherry and Weller (eds) *Rethinking Rights-Based Mental Health Laws* (Oxford: Hart Publishing, 2010), at page 92.

3. Fusion and the CRPD

The main arguments put forward opposing the fusion of mental health laws and legal capacity laws are based on more practical concerns on how guardianship law can accommodate the needs of persons with mental health problems rather than on any substantive ideological opposition to the rationale for fusing the legislative frameworks. Those practical oppositions are less defensible, as the CRPD requires abolition of both guardianship laws and mental health laws. At a conceptual level the fusion debate is a dead one in light of the statements of the UN Committee on the Rights of Persons with Disabilities on the scope of Articles 12, 14 and 17 of the CRPD. However, given that State Parties to the CRPD have not begun the process of decommissioning mental health laws and guardianship laws (based on mental capacity and substitute decision-making), the notion of fusion may have some currency. That currency may have most value if the fused laws are based on supported decision-making that complies with Article 12 of the CRPD. The positive elements of non-coercive guardianship law, which may be more susceptible to supported decision-making, could filter less coercive and restrictive approaches into provisions relating to persons with mental health problems. The law reform required by Article 12 provides a unique opportunity to critically review mental health laws and guardianship laws. A guardianship system that embraces supported decision-making system (even incrementally) may ensure that the rights of persons with mental health problems could be bolstered in a fused legislative regime, notwithstanding that the legislation will fail to comply with the CRPD.

4. Conclusion

Despite the strong arguments in favour of fusing mental health and legal capacity laws there has been a failure to achieve the goal in jurisdictions where there was an opportunity to fuse legislative regimes.[19] It has been suggested that the failure to implement the fusion proposal in England and Wales indicates that it will only succeed "if consensus can be reached among a coalition of consumers, clinicians, carers and human rights lawyers who are able to persuade the broader community that the suggestion is fair and workable. That consensus may not be easily achieved given the struggles that invariably accompany attempts to rewrite mental health laws".[20] While it might be argued that the fusion of mental health laws and legal capacity laws might go some way towards addressing the requirements of Article 14 of the CRPD, provided that the paradigm shift in thinking and recognition of universal legal capacity is embedded and involuntary detention and forced treatment are not a part of the legislative framework. The suggestion that permitting 'the concurrent operation of mental health and guardianship laws, so that either statutory regime may be used to authorise involuntary detention and treatment (in hospital or in the community) of persons with a mental illness … unable to consent to their own treatment' will be insufficient to address the requirements of the CRPD.[21]

---

19 Daw 'Mental Health Act 2007: The Defeat of the Ideal' (2007) Journal of Mental Health Law 131.

20 Rees (n 1) 92.

21 ibid.

Chapter 18

THE IMPLICATIONS OF THE UNITED NATIONS CONVENTION ON THE RIGHTS OF PERSONS WITH DISABILITIES ON CRIMINAL RESPONSIBILITY

Charles O'Mahony

1. Introduction

When the drafting of the UN Convention on the Rights of Persons with Disabilities (CRPD) was concluded in 2006 few would have considered that the Convention would have implications for domestic law governing the criminal responsibility of persons with mental health problems. It was surprising, then, that in 2009 the UN Office of the High Commissioner for Human Rights (OHCHR) made a number of statements declaring that the CRPD required the repeal of the defences in criminal law, such as the insanity defence, and their replacement with 'disability neutral' laws. The statements of the OHCHR were also unexpected as the UN Standard Minimum Rules on the Treatment of Prisoners (which predated the CRPD) clearly mandated defences such as the insanity defence, and stated that persons found to be 'insane' should not be held in prison, but removed to a mental institution. This chapter critically considers the UN Disability Convention, the statements of the OHCHR, and the rationale underling its statements. It also assesses the extent to which State Parties to the Convention have sought to bring their criminal laws into conformity with these statements, and the type of law reforms that are needed in order for State Parties to comply with the their obligations under the CRPD.

1.1 The United Nations Convention on the Rights of Persons with Disabilities

The first indication from the OHCHR that the CRPD requires State Parties to reconsider how its domestic laws deal with the criminal responsibility of persons with disabilities came in 2007. The OHCHR stated:

> 'It must be noted here that the recognition of the legal capacity of persons with disabilities on an equal basis with others in all aspects of life has a bearing on the issue of criminal responsibility and the insanity defence clauses in many legal systems. It must be noted here that the recognition of the legal capacity of persons with disabilities on an equal basis with others in all aspects of life

has a bearing on the issue of criminal responsibility and the insanity defence clauses in many legal systems.'[1]

It was not clear from this statement what 'bearing' Article 12 of the CRPD would have on legal capacity. However, the Office of the High Commissioner for Human Rights in 2009 formed a more certain view on the action required by State Parties to the Convention in respect of domestic laws on criminal responsibility. The OHCHR submitted a Report to the Human Rights Council pursuant to Resolution 7/9 entitled 'Human rights of persons with disabilities'.[2] The first debate held by the Council focused on the 'key legal measures for ratification and effective implementation of the Convention, including with regard to equality and non-discrimination'. The Council requested the OHCHR '... to prepare a thematic study to enhance awareness and understanding of the Convention on the Rights of Persons with Disabilities, focusing on legal measures key for the ratification and effective implementation of the Convention, such as those relating to equality and non-discrimination, in consultation with States, civil society organizations, including organizations of persons with disabilities, and national human rights institutions ...' in order to support this debate. In preparing the thematic study, the OHCHR called for written submissions from the different stakeholders. These included State Parties, intergovernmental organisations, national human rights institutions, NGOs and representative disability groups. The OHCHR also organised 'a one-day open-ended consultation' on the thematic study and organised meetings with other relevant experts.[3] The recommendations and discussions that emerged from this process informed the content of the OHCHR's Report. The Office of the United Nations High Commissioner for Human Rights stated that:

> 'In the area of criminal law, recognition of the legal capacity of persons with disabilities requires abolishing a defence based on the negation of criminal responsibility because of the existence of a mental or intellectual disability. Instead disability-neutral doctrines on the subjective element of the crime should be applied, which take into consideration the situation of the individual defendant. Procedural accommodations both during the pretrial and trial phase of the proceedings might be required in accordance with article 13 of the Convention, and implementing norms must be adopted.'[4]

---

1 'Dignity and Justice for Detainees Week: Persons with Disabilities' (Office of the United Nations High Commissioner for Human Rights (OHCHR), Information Note No. 4, 2007) 3. Available at: http://www.ohchr.org/EN/UDHR/Documents/60UDHR/detention_infonote_4.pdf.

2 This Resolution followed a decision of the Human Rights Council to hold an annual interactive debate on the rights of persons with disabilities. See 'Annual Report of the United Nations High Commissioner for Human Rights and Reports of the Office of the High Commissioner and the Secretary-General: Thematic Study by the Office of the United Nations High Commissioner for Human Rights On Enhancing Awareness and Understanding of the Convention on the Rights of Persons with Disabilities' (A/HRC/10/48, 26 January 2009) 15. Available at: http://www2.ohchr.org/english/bodies/hrcouncil/docs/10session/A.HRC.10.48.pdf. last accessed 31 March 2016.

3 This was held in Geneva, Switzerland, on 24 October 2008.

4 'Annual Report of the United Nations High Commissioner for Human Rights and Reports of the Office of the High Commissioner and the Secretary-General: Thematic Study by the Office of the United Nations High Commissioner for Human Rights On Enhancing Awareness and Understanding of the Convention on the Rights of Persons with Disabilities' (A/HRC/10/48 26 January 2009) 15. Available at: http://www2.ohchr.org/english/bodies/

The position that has been adopted by the OHCHR reflects the position of disability rights groups who lobbied the United Nations on this point. For example, the International Disability Alliance (IDA) advocated for this positions.[5] The IDA in its 2008 position paper referred to the UN Standard Minimum Rules on the Treatment of Prisoners, which predated the CRPD. The UN Standard Minimum Rules provide that States that persons found to be 'insane' should not be held in prison, but removed to a mental institution. In that regard the IDA stated that Article 12 of the CRPD superseded the UN Standard Minimum Rules, which mandated the use of the insanity defence. The IDA, in adopting this position, emphasised that Article 12 requires the recognition of legal capacity in all aspects of life, and was not limited to civil matters. However, the IDA did concede that in abolishing the insanity defence there would need to engage in further law reform. In that regard, the IDA also stated that the 'provision on removing persons found to be 'insane' to a mental institution is also superseded by Articles 14 and 19, which do not permit compulsory institutionalization based on disability.'[6]

The World Network of Users and Survivors of Psychiatry (WNUSP) took a similar position to that of the IDA in relation to the implications of the Convention for the insanity defence.[7] The WNUSP in its manual refers to concepts mentioned in the Preamble which do not reappear in the 'binding articles' in the actual text of the Convention.[8] The WNUSP states that '[t]he application of these principles will radically alter the lives of persons with psychosocial disabilities' and that the consequences include 'the abolition of mental health commitment laws, guardianship, and the insanity defense'.[9] The WNUSP goes on to state that abolition of the insanity defence requires the replacement of 'disability-neutral standards for adjudicating criminal responsibility… actual criminal intent, taking account of the circumstances of the crime, motivation'.[10] In setting out its position in calling for abolition of the insanity defence, the WNUSP states that it is unconvinced by arguments that abolition would result in extremely ill offenders facing the death penalty.[11] It states

hrcouncil/docs/10session/A.HRC.10.48.pdf. The OHCHR in its Report made a number of other significant statements on action required by States Parties in order to comply with the Convention. In particular, under the heading 'right to liberty and security of the person' the OHCHR that art 14 of the Convention means that involuntary detention and or treatment based on mental disability or a mental disorder is not permitted. See in this volume the chapter by Suzanne Doyle and the chapter by Tina Minkowitz.

5 The IDA states that its goal is to promote the effective and full implementation of the UN Convention on the Rights of Persons with Disabilities (CRPD) worldwide. It also seeks to realise compliance with the Convention within the UN system, through the active and coordinated involvement of organisations that represent persons with disabilities at national, regional and international levels.

6 'Position Paper on the Convention on the Rights of Persons with Disabilities (CRPD) and other Instruments' (International Disability Alliance, 25 April 2008). Available at: http://www.internationaldisabilityalliance.org/wp-content/uploads/2009/08/IDA_CRPD_paper_final.doc.

7 The WNUSP '… is an international organization of users and survivors of psychiatry advocates for human rights of users and survivors speaks internationally for users and survivors promotes the user/survivor movement in every nation around the globe links user/survivor organizations and individuals throughout the world'. See http://wnusp.rafus.dk/.

8 ibid.

9 'Implementation Manual for the United Nations Convention on the Rights of Persons with Disabilities' (World Network of Users and Survivors of Psychiatry, February 2008) 10–11. Available at: www2.ohchr.org/SPdocs/CRPD/.../WNUSP_CRPD_Manual.doc.

10 ibid 16.

11 ibid 38.

that Article 14 of the Convention requires reasonable accommodation for persons with 'psychosocial disability'. It also acknowledges that 'we must seek the reform of the whole criminal justice system to fully realize reasonable accommodation for persons with psychosocial disabilities. Furthermore, we support alternatives to incarceration and the discretion to refrain from prosecution where appropriate, so long as these measures do not involve compulsory psychiatric treatment.'[12] The WNUSP, while stating that it 'cannot agree with the insanity defense in principle', did concede that 'as a practical option' the insanity defence needs to be left open as long as the death penalty and other harsh measures are being used in the penal system.[13] Therefore, the WNUSP states that they seek abolition of the insanity defence as part of a broader comprehensive penal reform agenda, while still criticising compulsory psychiatric detention and treatment of persons acquitted by reason of insanity.[14]

2. The Insanity Defence

In all common law jurisdictions there is provision for what we understand to be the insanity defence.[15] The insanity defence is probably the most controversial of all of the defences in criminal law. The defence, when raised successfully, results in a defendant being deemed not guilty of the criminal offences with which they are charged, and, as such, punishment is in theory not administered. It is also argued that the 'insanity defence is a mark of the maturity and humanity of the criminal law.'[16] The insanity defence covers the most serious of criminal offences, including homicide. The consequences of successfully using the insanity defence is that the defendant will be required to undergo psychiatric treatment and will in almost all cases will be detained in a psychiatric facility while that treatment is being provided. In practice, a person found not guilty by reason of insanity will usually be detained for a longer period than the sentence which they would have served for the crime had they being convicted.[17] There has been a lot of discourse around the insanity defence over the past number of decades. The proponents of the insanity defence

---

12 ibid 38–39.

13 ibid 39.

14 ibid.

15 An examination of the operation, reform and different formats of the insanity defence is outside the scope of this paper. For further reading on the insanity defence across different jurisdictions see Simon and Ahn-Redding *The Insanity Defence the World Over* (Lexington Books 2006). The ongoing controversy in the field of disability studies – the definition of disability – is also a controversy in the area of the insanity defence. There is no definition of mental defect or mental disease, and insanity legislation has tended not to provide a statutory definition of insanity. The US Federal Courts have held that '[t]he definition of mental disease or mental defect is essentially a factual, medical question, not a legal issue. The court should not encroach upon the jury's function of resolving possibly competing psychiatric views of this definition.' See *Government of the Virgin Islands v Fredricks* 578 F.2d 927, 932 (3rd Cir. 1978); *Wade v United States* 426 F.2d 64, 41 (9th Cir. 1970). While the final determination on insanity will be assigned to jurors, the lack of a definition of these terms has meant that it is open to mental health experts to provide their own definitions. Here in the United States definitions are based on the *Diagnostic and Statistical Manual of Mental Disorders (DSM)*. (The *DSM* is the standard classification of mental disorders. Mental health professionals in the United States and throughout the world use the DSM. It is used by a wide range of health and mental health professionals, including psychiatrists, physicians, psychologists, social workers, nurses, occupational and rehabilitation therapists, and counsellors.)

16 Editorial 'Reforming the Insanity Defence' (2003) (Mar) Criminal Law Review 139.

17 Ewing *Insanity: Murder, Madness and the Law* (Oxford University Press 2008), Parry *Criminal*

argue that it is fundamental to the criminal justice system as it bars the punishment of persons whose mental condition meant that they were not responsible for their acts.[18] It is on this basis that '… although the insanity defence has been the subject of much judicial and legislative tinkering for centuries, and especially in recent decades, to this day it remains an honored, if sometimes tarnished, fixture in Anglo-American law.'[19]

Opponents of the insanity defence, on the other hand, argue that while the underlying rationale is laudable, in reality the defence is open to abuse and does not deliver on its goals.[20] The verdict of not guilty by reason of insanity is unpredictable. Critics of the defence argue that the verdict will turn on factors such as the nature of the crime, the defendants' lawyer, the expert that testified for or against him or her, and not on the criminal responsibility or mental status of the defendant at the time of the commission of the crime.[21] The studies that have examined the public perception of the insanity defence have revealed that the public see the insanity defence as a legal loophole used by defendants to escape punishment for their crimes.[22] However, the insanity defence is only raised in a small number of criminal cases, and when the defence is raised it is seldom successful. Different studies across many jurisdictions that provide for the insanity defence have demonstrated that the defence is used in less than 1% of cases and when raised it has a success rate of less than 25%.[23] Other research has indicated that positive attitudes toward capital punishment in the United States and misperceptions about overuse of the insanity defence were directly related to negative attitudes toward the insanity defence.[24]

3. Legal Capacity and Criminal Responsibility

It is clear that the OHCHR's calls for reform of domestic law on criminal responsibility are based on Article 12 of the Convention, which provides for equal recognition of persons with disabilities before the law. While there is no definition of legal capacity in Article 12 of the Convention, legal capacity is understood to recognise that persons with disabilities not only have rights but are entitled to exercise those rights on an equal basis with everyone else. Article 12 of the CRPD is one of a number of Articles that were included in the Convention with a view to restoring power to people or empower them for the first time to make decisions about their lives.[25] The recognition of decision-making is very often taken for granted by most people, but

---

Mental Health and Disability Law, Evidence and Testimony (ABA Commission on Mental and Physical Disability Law: Criminal Justice Section 2009).

18 Ewing (n 17) xvii.

19 ibid.

20 ibid.

21 ibid.

22 See for example: Silver, Cirincione and Steadman 'Demythologizing Inaccurate Perceptions of the Insanity Defense' (1994) (18) Law and Human Behavior 1.

23 Ewing (n 17) xxii.

24 Bloechl, Vitacco, Neumann and Erickson 'An Empirical Investigation of Insanity Defense Attitudes: Exploring Factors Related to Bias' (2007) International Journal of Law and Psychiatry (30) 153–161.

25 See A Dhanda, 'Legal Capacity in the Disability Rights Convention: Stranglehold of the Past or Lodestar for the Future?' (2007) 24 (2) Syracuse Journal of International Law and Commerce, 429–462.

is something that has been denied to persons with disabilities. One of the compelling arguments for a specific UN Convention on disability was the lack of visibility of the person with disabilities. Persons with disabilities have being regarded as 'objects' to be managed as opposed to 'subjects' with their own will and preferences and the legal capacity to make decisions in accordance with that will and preferences. Article 12 of the CRPD was designed to challenge restrictive guardianship laws that allowed third parties to lawfully substitute their own choices for the decision-making of persons with disabilities. Article 12 requires what is frequently referred to as a 'paradigm shift' to the 'supported decision-making approach' to legal capacity. There is a growing discourse around the meaning of Article 12 as State Parties to the Convention seek to reform guardianship laws and implement supported decision-making models in their stead.[26]

The Council of Europe Commissioner for Human Rights recently published an Issue Paper on legal capacity entitled 'Who gets to decide? Right to legal capacity for persons with intellectual and psychosocial disabilities'.[27] In the Paper the Commissioner for Human Rights identified that the 'right of persons with disabilities to make choices about their lives and enjoy legal capacity on an equal basis with others is one of the most significant human rights issues in Europe today'. The Commissioner acknowledged that the 'bulk of European legal capacity systems are out-dated and in urgent need of law reform', and he made a number of recommendations to Council of Europe Member States, with a view to ensuring that persons with mental health problems and intellectual disabilities effectively enjoy the right to legal capacity. Interestingly there was no reference to the implications for Article 12 to the area of criminal responsibility.

To date the UN Committee on the Rights of Persons with Disabilities have only issued Concluding Observations in respect of Tunisia, Spain and Peru. However, despite the limited jurisprudence from the Committee, its initial statements in respect of Article 12 of the CRPD are quite important. The Committee have added to the weight of opinion stating that the CRPD requires a 'paradigm shift' in thinking about legal capacity.[28] The UN Committee, in its concluding observations on Tunisia's Report on its implementation of the CRPD, expressed concern '… that no measures have been undertaken to replace substitute decision-making by supported decision-making in the exercise of legal capacity'.[29] The Committee recommended that Tunisia review its laws allowing for guardianship and trusteeship, in addition to taking action to develop laws and policies to replace regimes of substitute decision-making by supported decision-making.[30] The Committee also recommended that training be

[26] See 'Who Gets to Decide? Right to Legal Capacity for Persons with Intellectual and Psychosocial Disabilities' [Strasbourg: Comm DH/Issue Paper (2012) 2, 20 February 2012], 'Submission on Legal Capacity the Oireachtas Committee on Justice, Defence and Equality' (Centre for Disability Law and Policy, NUI Galway, August 2011). Available at: http://www.nuigalway.ie/cdlp/documents/cdlp_submission_on_legal_capacity_the_oireachtas_committee_on_justice_defence_and_equality_.pdf and 'Essential Principles: Irish Legal Capacity Law' (Dublin: April 2012) available at: http://amnesty.ie/sites/default/files/report/2012/04/PRINCIPLES_WEB.pdf.

[27] 'Who gets to decide? Right to legal capacity for persons with intellectual and psychosocial disabilities' (Strasbourg, 20 February 2012, CommDH/IssuePaper(2012)2). Available at: https://wcd.coe.int/ViewDoc.jsp?id=1908555.

[28] The Committee on the Rights of Persons with Disabilities is the body of independent experts which monitors implementation of the CRPD by the States Parties.

[29] Available at: http://www.ohchr.org/EN/HRBodies/CRPD/Pages/Session5.aspx.

[30] ibid.

provided on this issue to all relevant public officials and other stakeholders, reflecting the need to change mind-sets that sees persons with disabilities in terms of deficits.[31] The Committee adopted a similar approach in its concluding comments on Spain's first Report to the Committee.[32] It recommended that Spain review its laws allowing for guardianship and trusteeship, and take action to develop laws and policies to replace regimes of substitute decision-making by supported decision-making. According to the Committee, this recommendation was necessary in order to respect 'the person's autonomy, will and preferences'.[33] In addition, the Committee again recommended the provision of training on this issue to all relevant public officials and other stakeholders. The Committee took a similar approach in its concluding observations to Peru.[34]

It is unfortunate that the OHCHR in its 2009 Report did not clearly articulate its reasoning by Article 12 of the CRPD regarding repeal and reform of defences such as the insanity defence. Perhaps it is that Article 12 of the CRPD talks about legal capacity, and assessments of mental capacity are no longer appropriate considerations in relation to the decision-making of persons with mental health problems. Article 12 of the CRPD is essentially about augmenting the autonomy of persons with mental health problems and restoring or supporting decision-making. It is difficult to reconcile the statements of the OHCHR with the rationale and the evolving discourse around Article 12.

An interpretation of Article 12 as requiring abolition of the insanity defence is problematic, as the rationale actually erodes the option to a person with a mental illness to raise the defence. If we view the insanity defence as a type of reasonable accommodation of the strict application of Article 12 as equal recognition before the criminal law, then it is difficult to reconcile as it arguably erodes the rights and options of offenders with mental health problems. The OHCHR's interpretation of the CRPD as requiring the stripping away of the insanity defence demonstrates a failure to appreciate the underlying rationale of the insanity defence. The underlying rationale is that it would be wrong to hold a person with a mental illness responsible in criminal law in circumstances where their illness meant that they could not control or appreciate the consequences of their actions at the time that they committed the criminal offence. The IDA, WNUSP and OHCHR, in their statements on Article 12 of the CRPD and criminal responsibility, have engaged with this rationale that the person lacked capacity at the time of the commission of the offence. Article 12 of the CRPD can rightfully be seen as taking a universal approach to the issue of

---

31 ibid.

32 'Consideration of reports submitted by States Parties under Art. 35 of the Convention: Concluding observations of the Committee on the Rights of Persons with Disabilities' [Committee on the Rights of Persons with Disabilities: Sixth Session, 19–23 September 2011] at p 6. Available at: http://www.ohchr.org/EN/HRBodies/CRPD/Pages/Session6.aspx accessed 31 March 2016.

33 ibid.

34 'Consideration of reports submitted by States parties under Art. 35 of the Convention: Concluding observations of the Committee on the Rights of Persons with Disabilities' [Committee on the Rights of Persons with Disabilities: Seventh Session 16–20 April 2012] 4–5. Available at: http://www.ohchr.org/EN/HRBodies/CRPD/Pages/Session7.aspx (last accessed 31 March 2016)

legal capacity.[35] However, Article 12(3) recognises that persons may need support in making decisions and Article 12(4) outlines a number of safeguards around restrictions being placed on legal capacity. The recognition that persons with disabilities may require support in exercising legal capacity and recognition that restrictions may be imposed in respect of legal capacity suggest that the proposition that Article 12 requires abolition of defences such as the insanity defence is not as obvious.

The way in which the OHCHR has presented the issue is also problematical as it fails to connect the abolition of the insanity defence with the overarching human rights concern with the insanity defence – the indefinite detention of persons in a psychiatric facility following acquittal by reason of insanity. The failure to make this connection is problematical for State Parties trying to understand their obligations under the Convention. There was a significant time delay between the opening of the CRPD for signature and the development of the OHCHR's conclusion that Article 12 requires abolition of the insanity defence and other similar defences. The submissions from the IDA and the WNUSP demonstrate some engagement and understanding of this overarching human rights concern with the insanity defence – indefinite detention in a psychiatric facility. However, there is a failure to engage in a discussion of the rationale underlying the insanity defence. The IDA and the WNUSP have adopted a social model of disability and are applying it to issues that affect offenders with mental health problems. It is important to note that these bodies are not necessarily representative of the views of offenders with mental health problems. This raises the issue of the visibility of offenders with mental health problems and raises the question of whether these groups are representative of the views of offenders with mental health problems.

The OHCHR and the representative disability rights groups mentioned above have failed to engage with the debate as to whether it is right to punish a person with a mental illness where the mental illness was a significant factor in the commission of the criminal act. To interpret the CRPD as requiring abolition of defences in criminal law that can be regarded as reasonable accommodations to offenders with specific disabilities arguably runs counter to the principles of the Convention. The concern of some of the disability rights groups is focused on the stigma of the insanity defence and the presumption of incapacity that goes hand-in-hand with the defence. Reform of the insanity defence, or even a discussion of reform and refinement of the insanity defence, would be a more sensible and helpful approach for the Office of the High Commissioner for Human Rights and for disability rights groups to take. Such an approach would address the human rights concerns in relation to the indefinite detention of defendants acquitted under the insanity defence. However, such an approach fails to advance the agendas of disability rights organisations whose preference is to see the abolition of the insanity defence and the invisibility of offenders with mental health problems. This approach is short sighted as it fails to engage with a discussion on the rationale and understanding of the insanity defence.

In Ireland, the law has been clarified in relation to the insanity defence by way of the Criminal Law (Insanity) Act 2006. During the course of the Dáil Debates on the

---

35 See A Dhanda 'Universal Legal Capacity as a Universal Human Right' in Dudley, Silove and Gale (eds) *Mental Health and Human Rights* (Oxford University Press, 2012).

legislation, one of the proposed amendments to the Bill was aimed at addressing the politically incorrect and stigmatising term 'insanity'. The proposed amendment suggested changing 'insanity' to 'mental disorder' in the Short Title. However, the Minister of the Justice, Equality and Law Reform at the time, Michael McDowell, stated that the:

> '... amendment cannot be accepted because corresponding changes would have to be made to the rest of the Bill's terminology. It would also be undesirable because the use of the less pejorative terminology, 'mental disorder' instead of 'insanity', may result in a widespread use of the plea on a mischievous basis. It might also give the misleading impression that any mental disorder, no matter how trivial, would justify returning a verdict of not guilty. The word 'insanity' signifies a threshold of disorder which cannot be regarded as trivial or minor. If one claims a person is insane in ordinary parlance, it does not just mean the person is a bit odd.'[36]

The rationale of the Minister was that the focus of the Bill was criminal law and the term 'insanity' was used in connection with the criminal law. He felt that an amendment of the nature suggested could introduce 'doubt or uncertainty into the area'.[37] The Minister stated 'I do not want to wake up some morning, even after a restless night, to discover a judge has interpreted it in a way which was not originally envisaged by the House. This is an attempt to give direction to the courts as to how they should deal with these matters. Throwing up untried and vague language will prejudice, rather than advance, the administration of justice.'[38] The reluctance of the Minister for Justice to even consider using a less offensive term than the insanity defence is indicative of the significant obstacles faced in replacing the insanity defence with a disability-neutral defence. Given the level of scepticism surrounding the insanity defence, the OHCHR's recommendation for a broader all-encompassing defence is an unrealistic proposition and one that is unlikely to appeal to legislators. The recommendation of a disability-neutral defence fails to engage with a consideration of the underlying rationale of the defence and its purpose.

There are no guarantees that the values and principles set out in the CRPD will be realised by State Parties to the Convention. An examination of the experiences in implementing the obligations contained in the pre-existing body of human rights instruments reveals the difficulties in translating human rights obligations into practice at domestic level. There will be resistance, particularly when the changes and reforms required by the Convention clash with established practices.[39] This will inevitably be the case with the proposed abolition of the insanity defence. As discussed, the insanity defence, while probably the most controversial of the defences in criminal law, is nonetheless seen as important and has been reviewed,

---

36 See M McDowell in Dáil Éireann 'Criminal Law (Insanity) Bill 2002 [Seanad]: Report and Final Stages' (Volume 616 – 23 March 2006) 17. Available at: http://historical-debates.oireachtas.ie (last accessed 31 March 2016)

37 ibid.

38 The rationale of the Minister was that the focus of the Bill was criminal law and the term 'insanity' was used in connection with criminal law.

39 Quinn 'Resisting the "Temptation of Elegance": Can the Convention on the Rights of Persons with Disabilities Socialise States to Right Behaviour?' in Aranardóittir and Quinn (eds) *The UN Convention on the Rights of Persons with Disabilities: European and Scandinavian Perspectives* (Martinus Nijohoff 2009) 216.

reformed and recalibrated as an important component of criminal justice systems across the world. As such, a half-committed, ambiguous paragraph from the Office of the United Nations High Commissioner for Human Rights on the need to abolish the defence is unlikely to be effective in convincing State Parties to the Convention to abolish the insanity defence.

The different Articles of the CRPD will not be sufficient in ensuring that the principles embodied in the Convention will be realised. In particular, it would be unlikely that a reading of the CRPD would lead a reader to conclude that it required removal of the insanity defence. It will be difficult for State Parties to see such a fundamental amendment to their criminal justice systems as necessary without a developed and comprehensive understanding of the consequences of the removal. The failure of the United Nations, and of the bodies advocating for this reform, to engage with the practicalities of the proposed reform means that even the consideration by State Parties of abolition of the insanity defence is unlikely. International human rights law has had limited success in challenging national sovereignty and State control over domestic policies which are inconsistent with human rights norms.[40] In that regard it is unlikely that the Convention will coerce State Parties to '… to do what they otherwise would not do… as international law rarely has that effect and usually only where there is a court to make authoritative and binding pronouncements. Even then, such a court would need time to build its institutional legitimacy.'[41] Other views of how international law works see international human rights law as having a persuasive effect and being adopted by State Parties.[42] It remains to be seen whether the CRPD will have a persuasive effect on Member States through ratification and signature of the Convention.[43] Given the way in which the reform of the insanity defence has been framed, it seems unlikely that the interpretation of the CRPD by the United Nations Office for the High Commissioner for Human Rights will be successful in persuading State Parties to remove the defence from their statute books.

The advent of the Convention on the Elimination of Discrimination Against Women (CEDAW) did not result in women's rights groups campaigning for the abolition of the defences of infanticide or 'battered wife syndrome'. Nor did any children's rights organisations suggest that the provisions provided for in the United Nations Convention on the Rights of the Child (CRC) mandated the repeal of the doctrine of *doli incapax* which limits the responsibility of children for their actions in criminal law. While this analogy is somewhat problematic, and while there are obvious differences with the above and the situation as it relates to the insanity defence, it is nevertheless worth noting that it would be difficult to imagine a women's or children's rights group advocating a reform that eroded or could be considered to erode the rights of the groups for whom they represent. The problem in relation to disability rights groups is that there is a disjointed approach to offenders with mental health problems. This is clearly evidenced from the discussion above on the social model of disability and its application to the mental health area.

---

40 See, for example, Krasner 'Sovereignty' (Foreign Policy: 2001, 122 January–February, 20–29).

41 Quinn (n 39) 218.

42 Goodman and Jinks 'How to Influence States: Socialization and International Human Rights Law' (2004) (54) Duke Law Review 621.

43 For a discussion on this see Quinn (n 39) 218.

4. European Convention on Human Rights and the Insanity Defence

There is a body of literature that has questioned whether the insanity defence is compliant with international human rights law on a different basis than that set out by the OHCHR.[44] Despite the public perception that the insanity defence is a legal loophole to avoid criminal culpability, the reality is that a defendant that successfully raises the defence will almost certainly not walk freely away from court. Inevitably, the person receiving a verdict of not guilty by reason of insanity will be subject to some form of detention, and the relevant procedures and processes vary from jurisdiction to jurisdiction.[45] This detention will normally be mandatory and for an indefinite period of time, with the defendant having no say in or control over the process and being detained until such time as he or she is not considered dangerous. There are legitimate human rights considerations with this process. After all, the underlying rationale of the insanity defence is not to punish a person who meets the requirements of the insanity defence. However, the result of successfully raising the insanity defence is indefinite detention, normally in a forensic psychiatry setting with a complete curtailment on freedom.

Article 5 of the European Convention of Human Rights provides for the right to liberty and security stating that '[e]veryone has the right to liberty and security of person'. A number of exception are set out in Article 5(1). The relevant restriction on persons with mental illness is contained in Article 5(1)(e) where it states 'the lawful detention of persons for the prevention of the spreading of infectious diseases, of persons of unsound mind, alcoholics or drug addicts or vagrants'.[46] In the seminal case in this area, *Winterwerp v The Netherlands*, the European Court of Human Rights held that the Dutch national in this case should not have been deprived of his liberty unless it was shown that he was of 'unsound mind'.[47] The Court went on to say in its judgment that a person detained must have a mental disorder and that the mental disorder needed to be established before the relevant national court or tribunal, and needed to be supported with objective medical evidence. The Court held that the evidence needed to be of the kind and degree that required compulsory confinement and that the detention could only be considered lawful in circumstances where the mental disorder persists.[48] In *Winterwerp* the ECtHR developed criteria to assist States in avoiding arbitrary and unlawful detention of persons considered to be of 'unsound mind'. The problem of definition was also evident in *Winterwerp*, and the European Court of Human Rights stated that a 'person of unsound mind' could not be given a definitive interpretation. According to Ashworth, the *Winterwerp* decision has implications for the insanity defence in that it requires a close relationship between expert opinion and the definition of the mental state required in satisfying the defence; the court's decision on the

---

44 See Ashworth *Principles of Criminal Law* (3rd edn, Clarendon Press 1999) and Hopper & McSherry 'The Insanity Defence and International Human Rights Obligations' (2001) 8 Psychiatry, Psychology and Law 2, 161–173.

45 See Ewing *Insanity: Murder, Madness and the Law* (Oxford University Press 2008) xxii-xxiii and Simon and Ahn-Redding *The Insanity Defence the World Over* (Lexington Books 2006).

46 For a discussion on the jurisprudence of the ECtHR on the involuntary detention of persons with mental health problems, see Suzanne Doyle's chapter in this volume.

47 (1979) 2 EHRR 387.

48 The European Court of Human Rights did not rule that treatment was a necessary requirement in order to make the detention lawful.

impairment must be based on objective medical evidence and the court must have discretion available to it in deciding whether the mental state is 'of a kind or degree warranting compulsory confinement'.[49]

The insanity defence in many jurisdictions is based on the M'Naghten Rules in whole or part.[50] One of the most well-known rules is the requirement that an accused person suffer from a 'defect or reason, from disease of the mind, as not to know the nature and quality of the act he was doing; or that he did not know he was doing what was wrong.'[51] Ashworth has argued that the concept of the 'disease of the mind' is not consistent with the criteria set down by the European Court of Human Rights in *Winterwerp*, as the courts have ruled that medical conditions such as hyperglycaemia, sleepwalking and epilepsy under certain circumstances constitute 'diseases of the mind'.[52] The problem here is that these conditions, unlike mental disorders, cannot be considered to require involuntary detention. In England and Wales (as, indeed, elsewhere) the human rights issues and criticisms of the insanity defence is not with the defence *per se* but rather the consequence of the defence – mandatory indefinite detention. It is also clear that indefinite detention of a person who successfully raises the insanity defence is not consistent with the decision of the European Court of Human Rights in *Winterwerp*, particularly in relation to the court, which must have discretion available to it in deciding whether the mental state is 'of a kind or degree warranting compulsory confinement'.[53]

The conception of detention as understood from the European Court of Human Rights jurisprudence is at odds with the message of the OHCHR. The OHCHR is advancing repeal of the insanity defence as it is based on a person having a mental illness and this is inconsistent with Article 12 of the CRPD. The European Court of Human Rights on the other hand requires that a mental disorder be present in order to be involuntarily detained, and that independent medical evidence is provided and that the evidence demonstrates that the compulsory confinement is justified. Given the profound implications of the position adopted by the OHCHR, it is unfortunate that it has not engaged in a more comprehensive explanation of its position, particularly as it conflicts with the current body of human rights law and case law that informs State Parties of their human rights obligations.

5. Legal Capacity, the Convention, Criminal Law and Law Reform

The jurisprudence of the Committee on the Rights of Persons with Disabilities is quite limited, having to date only issued concluding observations in respect of Tunisia, Spain and Peru.[54] However, it noteworthy that the while Article 12 of the

---

49 (1979) 2 EHRR 387.

50 *M'Naghten Rules* (1843) 8 ER 718. For a comprehensive discussion of the different forms of the Insanity defence see Simon and Ahn-Redding *The Insanity Defence the World Over* (Lexington Books 2006).

51 *M'Naghten Rules* (1843) 8 ER 718.

52 Ashworth *Principles of Criminal Law* (3rd edn, Clarendon Press 1999) 216. See also and Hopper and McSherry 'The Insanity Defence and International Human Rights Obligations' (2001) 8 Psychiatry, Psychology and Law 2, 161–173.

53 (1979) 2 EHRR 387.

54 'Consideration of reports submitted by States parties under Art. 35 of the Convention: Concluding observations of the Committee on the Rights of Persons with Disabilities' [Committee on the

CRPD has been discussed in all of the concluding observations issued, there was no reference to compliance of the State Parties' domestic criminal law. The New South Wales Law Reform Commission is currently undertaking a number of law reform projects on criminal responsibility, and published a series of Consultation Papers on people with cognitive and mental health impairments in the criminal justice system. These papers looked at criminal responsibility, diversion and forensic samples. In setting out its approach to its work the Commission made reference to the human rights obligations informing its work, including the United Nations Convention on the Rights of Persons with Disabilities:

> 'In 2007, Australia signed the *Convention on the Rights of Persons with Disabilities*. The *Convention* provides for equality before the law for all people. It also identifies obligations to protect people with disabilities (including intellectual and psychiatric disabilities) from cruel, inhuman or degrading treatment or punishment, and from exploitation, violence and abuse; and to provide appropriate training for police and prison staff to ensure effective access to justice.'[55]

What is interesting is that the Law Reform Commission's work, while referencing the United Nations Convention on the Rights of Persons with Disabilities, does not engage with the conclusion from the Office of the High Commissioner for Human Rights that the insanity defence requires abolition. In its Consultation Paper on the defence of mental illness the Law Reform Commission confined its discussion to reformulation of the current law on the insanity defence. The abolition of the defence does not feature in the discussions in the Consultation Paper. Their focus is on retaining the common law *M'Naghten* rules but expanding its scope and/or making a clarification in the legislation. The second reform option considered by the Commission was to replace the *M'Naghten* rules with a completely new approach. Similarly, the Law Commission for England and Wales is currently undertaking law reform projects on the area of criminal responsibility. The Commission published a Consultation Paper in 2010 that made a number of provisional recommendations to reform the law and procedure on unfitness to plead.[56] The Commission also published a scoping paper on the defences of insanity and automatism.[57] However, it is interesting to note that there was no discussion of the CRPD and its implications on the area of criminal responsibility.

The lack of discussion on the Convention necessitating the abolition of the insanity

---

Rights of Persons with Disabilities: Fifth Session, 11–15 April 2011]; 'Consideration of reports submitted by States parties under Art. 35 of the Convention: Concluding observations of the Committee on the Rights of Persons with Disabilities' [Committee on the Rights of Persons with Disabilities: Sixth Session, 19–23 September 2011] and 'Consideration of reports submitted by States parties under Art. 35 of the Convention: Concluding observations of the Committee on the Rights of Persons with Disabilities' [Committee on the Rights of Persons with Disabilities: Seventh Session 16–20 April 2012].

55 'People With Cognitive and Mental Health Impairments in the Criminal Justice System: An Overview' (New South Wales Law Reform Commission: CP 5, 2010) 17–18. Available at: http://www.lawlink.nsw.gov.au/lawlink/lrc/ll_lrc.nsf/vwFiles/CP05.pdf/$file/CP05.pdf.

56 'Unfitness to Plead' (London: Law Commission for England and Wales, Consultation Paper No. 197, 2010).

57 'Insanity and Automatism: A Scoping Paper' (Law Commission for England and Wales, 18 July 2012).

defence and other similar laws does not represent a particular failure on the part of the New South Wales Law Reform Commission or the Law Commission for New South Wales. The work of these institutional law reform bodies is hugely important in developing, updating and modernising the law in common law jurisdictions in a systematic and ongoing manner. Institutional law reform bodies such as law reform commissions have a hugely significant role to play in producing quality research that informs reform across many areas of private, public and, indeed, international law. However, there is a problem when bodies such as these do not pick up the message of the United Nations. It may be the case that the Commissions were not aware of the 2009 Report of the OHCHR. After all, nowhere in the text of the Convention does it state that the Convention requires the abolition of the insanity defence, and it took the OHCHR a number of years following the finalisation of the Convention text to reach the conclusion that Article 12 necessitated such abolition.

While the insanity defence is only raised in a small number of cases it is an important component of the criminal law. The failure of the OHCHR to engage with that is disappointing, particularly as the concept of the insanity defence 'is at the heart of debates about the effect of the accused's mental condition on criminal liability. The scope and limits of insanity are a major factor in shaping other defences founded on states of automatism, intoxication and diminished responsibility.'[58] This is an important point. While the law on diminished responsibility, the procedural rules on fitness to be tried and the law on the insanity defence have different rules (that vary from jurisdiction to jurisdiction) and are justified very often on different grounds, they have common threads running through them. The most obvious thread is the rationale for making concessions to offenders who commit criminal acts while experiencing some sort of impairment. As such, the implications of abolishing the insanity defence have far-reaching consequences that merit greater discussion and consideration than that provided by the OHCHR. In that regard, what seems clear is that the UN needs to make a more concerted and comprehensive effort in explaining the rationale for abolition of the insanity defence and how State Parties can achieve compliance. As part of that it is clear also that a broader dialogue is required on these complex issues. The requirement also fails to consider or even attempt to tease out conflicts with other human rights issues. For example, there is no engagement on the vexed issue of the death penalty. If State Parties who use the death penalty as a sanction in their criminal law abolish the insanity defence, then persons found guilty of murder could potentially face the death penalty regardless of their mental state at the time of the commission of the offence. In addition to the problems, complexities and difficulties, the abolition of the insanity defence will also have consequences for diversion programmes that seek to divert persons with mental health problems from the criminal justice system at different points.

6. Conclusion

Policy makers, lawyers and psychiatrists might quickly disregard the United Nations calls for the insanity defence to be abolished as 'absurd' and 'adopt a hurt and

[58] Editorial 'Reforming the Insanity Defence' (2003) (Mar) Criminal Law Review 139.

somewhat defensive posture'.[59] However, that approach would not be constructive. There is a legitimate human rights issue at the heart of the calls for the abolition of the insanity defence. Bartlett suggests that '[i]f there are reservations about the approach propounded for the CRPD, it is for users, practitioners and others in the field to come up with an equally clear and intellectually defensible alternative.'[60] The replacement of the insanity defence with a disability-neutral defence runs counter to the rationale of criminal law and is unlikely to garner support for law reform. The repeal and replacement of the insanity defence with a disability-neutral defence would open up the insanity defence in a way that would be repugnant to legislators and the public who often view the defence with much distrust and scepticism. A more workable suggestion would be to address the core human rights concern with the insanity defence, the indefinite detention of persons who successfully raise the defence. It seems clear that the OHCHR will need to engage with this issue in a more comprehensive way if it is to realise any reform of the insanity defence. Perhaps the UN Committee on the Rights of Persons with Disabilities will address the issue as part of a General Comment on Article 12, which is to be expected in the coming years. At any rate, greater consultation beyond the narrower dialogue that has currently been generated is key to ensuring a greater understanding of the complex issues involved, and in securing buy-in from State Parties, many of whom are currently engaged in domestic law reform programmes aimed at bringing national law into compliance with the Convention. The failure of the OHCHR to engage in a discussion about the implications of the abolition of the insanity defence is also evident in the lack of discussion around the defence of diminished responsibility.

The Convention on the Rights of Persons with Disabilities will undoubtedly be instrumental in advancing the rights of persons with disabilities and driving law reform agendas that seek to bring domestic law of State Parties across the world into conformity with the Convention. One of the main rationales for the development of a Convention on the Rights of Persons with Disabilities was to provide greater clarity on the human rights of persons with disabilities. The Convention on the whole was successful in embodying this in the text of the Convention. However, the calls for the abolition of the insanity defence result in profound confusion. It will come as a surprise for State Parties who negotiated the Convention that their compliance with the Convention now requires abolition of the insanity defence and other similar laws. The way that the United Nations has currently framed the need for State Parties to abolish the insanity defence is problematical. The OHCHR has provided a weak statement on why this reform is necessary, which is unlikely to convince State Parties to adopt the action recommended.

The submissions made by disability rights groups calling for abolition of the insanity defence are interesting. The submissions highlight a theoretical divergence in how the social model of disability relates to offenders with mental health problems. The guiding principles of the Convention embody a social model of disability that does not relate in the same way as the lived experience of persons with mental illness who come into contact with the criminal justice system. The social model has been very influential in impacting on policy and advancing equality, as evidenced by its

---

59 Bartlett 'The United Nations Convention on the Rights of Persons with Disabilities the Future of Mental Health Law' (2009) 8 (12) Psychiatry 498.

60 ibid.

impact on CRPD, and its potential in achieving greater equality for persons with disabilities has been described as 'incalculable'.[61] However, there is a lack of research exploring the tensions between the social model and the mental health field. In particular, there is a lack of research exploring the social model and its application to offenders with mental health problems. The views advanced by disability rights groups and user/survivor bodies may not represent the views of offenders with mental health problems, and there is a need to ensure that the voice of this category of persons is not misrepresented.

61 Crow 'Renewing the Social Model of Disability' (1996) (July) Coalition News 5–9.

PART 4: THE RIGHT TO INDEPENDENT LIVING

Chapter 19

INDEPENDENT LIVING: THE POTENTIAL OF THE EUROPEAN COURT OF HUMAN RIGHTS

Noelin Fox

1. Introduction

At the outset it should be stated that the European Convention on Human Rights (ECHR) does not include a right to independent living. The advent of the UN Convention on the Rights of Persons with Disabilities (CRPD) in 2006 is the first time the right to Independent Living has been enshrined in international law. Article 19 of the CRPD specifically states that people with disabilities have the right to choose where and with whom they live and to have the supports needed to achieve this. The CRPD does not contain any new human rights, rather it specifies how existing human rights can be made real in the context of the experience and history of disabled people. While Article 19 may appear to describe a new right to independent living and community inclusion, in fact it '(…) has not created a new right to community inclusion and participation. Rather, it is intended to provide a clarification of the obligations on States Parties to ensure disabled people's full and equal enjoyment of this 'existing' right.'[1] It is important, therefore, to identify the core aspects of this right to independent living and locate them within mainstream human rights instruments. In relation to the ECHR the most pertinent is the right to respect for private and family life, home and correspondence in Article 8. While the right to liberty and security of person speaks directly to the institutionalisation of disabled people, this is primarily dealt with in the corresponding Article 14 of the CRPD.

The independent living philosophy recognises that people with disabilities have the same human rights as non-disabled people, but that in order to realise these rights disabled people may have additional support requirements either temporarily or throughout their lives. The denial of the assistance needed results, in effect, in a denial of human rights.

Mansell, in his report 'Deinstitutionalisation and Community Living – outcomes and costs' established that that there are almost 1.2 million people with disabilities living in residential establishments accommodating thirty people or more in the twenty-eight countries surveyed.[2] Ireland did not return details on the size of institutions; however, the Health Service Executive report 'Time to Move on From

1 C. Parker and L. Clements, 'The UN Convention on the Rights of Persons with Disabilities: a New Right to Independent Living' (2008) 1 *European Human Rights Law Review* 509.

2 J Mansell, M Knapp, J Beadle-Brown and J Beecham, 'Deinstitutionalisation and community

Congregated Settings' indicates that in Ireland there are over 4,000 people with intellectual disabilities living in residential units for ten people or more.[3] Along with this, a further 3,000 people live in long-stay psychiatric wards and in 'community residences' which accommodate between six and eighteen people.[4] So although the problems of institutionalisation of disabled people may be more acute in Eastern Europe, many of the issues raised by the ECHR will be relevant in Ireland.

This chapter examines the potential of the European Court of Human Rights (the Court) to assist in the recognition and realisation of the right to independent living (IL) in Europe, exploring both the limitations and the potentials of the Court. It also considers the implications of the incorporation of the ECHR into Irish law for IL, and the growing international consensus on the existence of such a right.

2. Article 8: Right to Respect for Private and Family Life, Home and Correspondence

The Court has drawn broad definitional lines around the concept of a 'private life' and has defined its key elements as:

1. One has a right to have relationships with others[5]
2. One's 'private life' is not restricted solely to activities within the home or private sphere[6]
3. Private life encompasses not only respect for an individual's physical welfare but also for psychological welfare and for unhindered personal development.[7]

An additional important element of the Article 8 rights is the obligation on States Parties not only to refrain from interfering with people's rights but also to act positively to ensure respect for these rights, ie positive obligations. In *Storck v Germany*[8] the Court found that the State's positive obligations extended to protecting people from interference with their rights from private individuals or institutions – in this case, this included the obligation of ensuring that private psychiatric institutions were properly licensed and monitored in order to ensure that the rights of patients were protected.[9] In the context of Ireland, where residential services for people with intellectual disabilities are largely provided by independent voluntary agencies, the lack of monitoring of such services by the State must raise an issue under its Article 8 positive obligations.

---

living – outcomes and costs: Report of a European study' (Tizard Centre, University of Kent 2007) 25.

3 Health Service Executive, 'Time to Move on From Congregated Settings: A Strategy for Inclusion' (HSE 2011) 50.

4 See 'Irish Psychiatric Units and Hospitals Census' (2006) Table 2.1 p 25; Mental Health Commission, 'Annual Report' (2008) 79 <www.mhcirl.ie> last accessed 31 March 2016.

5 *Niemietz v Germany* App no 13710/88 (ECtHR 16 December 1992) para 29.

6 ibid.

7 *Botta v Italy* App no 153/1996/772/973 (ECtHR 24 February 1998) para 32.

8 *Storck v Germany* App no 61603/00 (ECtHR 16 June 2005).

9 ibid para 149.

In relation to mental capacity legislation the Court has found that legislation which adopts an either/or approach to legal capacity and denies people's rights to make the most fundamental choices about how to live their lives is in breach of Article 8. The Court decided in *Shtukaturov v Russia* that Russian legislation, which automatically deprives a person taken into guardianship of all legal capacity, was deficient under Article 8.[10]

The extent of a State's positive obligations as they relate to people with disabilities were defined in 1998 by the Court in the case of *Botta v Italy.*[11] Positive obligations are conditional in three ways:

1. The need to strike a fair balance between the interests of the community and the interests of the individual
2. The wide 'margin of appreciation' allowed to States in striking this balance
3. The existence of an immediate and direct link between the action sought by the individual and the person's private life.

Demonstrating that a direct link exists between the action sought and the person's private life has proven difficult. In both *Botta v Italy* and *Zehnalova v Czech Republic,*[12] where the applicants attempted to show a direct link between public facilities and their right to a private life, they failed to convince the Court. In *Botta v Italy* the judge commented as follows:

> (…) the right asserted by Mr Botta, namely the right to gain access to the beach and the sea at a place distant from his normal place of residence during his holidays, concerns interpersonal relations of such broad and indeterminate scope that there can be no conceivable direct link between the measures the State was urged to take, (…) and the applicant's private life.'[13] Even where a direct link can be proven the margin of appreciation allowable to States and the need to balance the needs of the individual with those of the community proved insurmountable obstacles in the disappointing Stenges[14] case.

Mr Stenges sought funding for an assistive device which would greatly increase his level of independence and enable him to develop relationships independent of his carers. While acknowledging the direct link between the measure sought and Mr Stenges' private life, the Court found that State's margin of appreciation is wide in the context of allocating limited national resources. The case was judged inadmissible.

In *DD v Lithuania* the applicant failed to convince the Court that institutionalisation is a breach of Article 8.[15] However, in the recent highly significant case of *Stanev v Bulgaria* the Court found that the State was in breach of Article 5 of the CRPD in institutionalising the applicant for several years without his consent and commented that '(…) the objective need for accommodation and social assistance must not

---

10 *Shtukaturov v Russia* App no 44009/05 (ECtHR 27 June 2008) para 79.

11 *Botta v Italy* (n 7).

12 *Zehnalova and Zehnal v Czech Republic* App no 38621/97 (ECtHR 14 May 2002).

13 *Botta v Italy* (Footnote 7) para 35.

14 *Sentges v The Netherlands* App no 27677/02 (ECtHR 8 July 2003) Admissibility Decision.

15 *D.D. v Lithuania* App no 13469/06 (ECtHR 14 February 2012).

automatically lead to the imposition of measures involving deprivation of liberty.'[16] This could have major implications for the widespread practice of placing people in large institutions isolated from the community, especially in Central and Eastern Europe, and increase pressure to provide community-based alternatives.

3. Limitations of the Court

On the face of it the lack of success experienced by disabled people in pursuing Article 8 cases could engender pessimism about the potential of the Convention and the Court in developing a right to IL in the Council of Europe (COE) States. In addition to a poor record of success in Strasbourg, people with disabilities face other barriers in pursuing cases.

3.1. Access to Justice

The process of litigating rights in the European Court is long and arduous, and potential applicants, especially those with intellectual disability or mental illness, must overcome many barriers. Applicants must first exhaust all domestic legal procedures before lodging a complaint with the Court – this, in itself, is a time-consuming process requiring a high level of commitment and resources. There must be an individual applicant who is willing and able to take a case. For people with intellectual disability or mental illness this is a significant deterrent, as most people in this situation do not have the support or resources to undertake proceedings and many lack the capacity to do so. Further, a lack of successful cases brought by disabled people means that other people are less likely to be willing to attempt to take new cases – the 'catch 22' situation.

3.2. Legal Capacity

Despite the rulings of the Court and broader COE policy, many Member States still retain legislation which does not allow for a functional approach to legal capacity and operates within a system which means that individuals may be deprived of their right to make any decisions which have many legal implications. This includes the option of taking independent legal action in pursuit of the ECHR rights, which represents a major barrier. Article 12 of the CRPD affirms the right of people with disabilities to equal recognition before the law, to equal enjoyment of legal capacity and to support in exercising their legal capacity.

The ability to make personal decisions is of paramount importance in realizing the right to IL. As Quinn states '[w]ithout legal capacity to make life choices (big and small), to have choices equal to others and respected by others, and indeed to make one's own mistakes, it is hard to see how the promise of living an independent life and being included in the community can be made good.'[17] There is a circular

---

[16] *Stanev v Bulgaria* App no 36760/06 (ECtHR 17 January 2012) para 153.

[17] G Quinn (Statement by Professor Gerard Quinn, Director, CDLP, to the Oireachtas Joint Committee on Justice, Defence and Equality), 'Hearing on the Mental Capacity Bill' (Centre for Disability Law and Policy, NUI Galway 2012) p 3. <www.nuigalway.ie/cdlp/documents/cdlp_statement_to_oireachtas_justice_committee_on_mental_capacity_bill_final.pdf> last accessed 31 March 2016.

relationship between IL and legal capacity, and in reality one is not possible without the other. People with disability, like everyone else, must learn the skills needed to live self-determining lives in the community, and to learn these skills they must be accorded the right to make their own decisions. Where people are segregated from the community their opportunities to learn how to live in the community are severely restricted and so they may never acquire these skills. Recognition of legal capacity, then, provides the route for people to acquire IL skills and develop their capacity.

3.3. Marginalisation of Disability

One shortcoming of the Court identified by O'Cinnide is what he terms the 'marginalisation of disability' within mainstream human rights instruments and the Convention. Nowhere in the Convention is disability mentioned other than the reference to people of unsound mind in Article 5. He suggests that mainstream rights instruments

> [...] conceptualise the individual in essentially liberal terms as an autonomous being capable of operating in isolation from the state: civil and political rights are designed to protect this individual from unjustified state interference, and the state is only placed under a positive obligation to assist this independent individual in certain very specific contexts.[18]

Supports, which are essential for people with disabilities in realising their rights, are generally viewed as the exception by general human rights instruments, and are therefore not generally applicable, or only available in very specific circumstances.

4. The Potentials

4.1. Emerging International Consensus on the Right to Independent Living

Although there is no clearly defined right to IL in the Convention, the question arises as to whether such a right could potentially be read into it. The core elements of the right to IL are choice and control, personal autonomy, equality of access, access to support and a right to participate. These are also fundamental values of the Convention. In fact, the impact of the CRPD on the Court is already becoming evident – in the recent *Glor v Switzerland*[19] case the Court demonstrated that it will take the CRPD into account in coming to decisions.

Legal and policy developments internationally over the past ten years have seen significant progress in the recognition of the rights of people with disabilities. Of particular importance on the international stage was the *Olmstead*[20] judgment in the United States, regarding institutional living for people with mental disabilities and a care regime skewed towards placing people in institutional settings rather than

---

18 C O'Cinneide, 'Extracting protection for the rights of persons with disabilities from human rights frameworks: Established limits and new possibilities' in O M Arnardottir and G Quinn (eds), *The UN Convention on the Rights of Persons with Disabilities: European and Scandinavian Perspectives* (Martinus Nijhoff Publishers 2009) 165.

19 *Glor v Switzerland* App no 13444/04 (ECtHR 30 April 2009).

20 *Olmstead v LC* 527 U.S. 581 (1999).

providing community-based alternatives. In the majority judgment in this case it was noted that such biased system arrangements were in breach of the Americans with Disabilities Act 1990 which prohibits discrimination in the provision of public services and identified unjustified institutional segregation as discrimination which cannot be justified on the basis of lack of funding.

The essence of a right to IL is acknowledged in the earlier UN human rights instruments, but the significance of the CRPD cannot be underestimated in the development of the recognition of a right to IL internationally. Likewise in the EU, a right to independent living is recognised in the EU Charter of Fundamental Rights and the EU Disability Action Plan. The building of a consensus in Europe around the need to develop more substantial rights realisation for disabled people has been enhanced by the fact that with the ratification of the Lisbon Treaty in 2009, the EU acceded to the European Convention of Human Rights, and further by the ratification by the EU of the CRPD in 2010.

Within the Council of Europe (COE) policy framework the right to IL is specifically detailed in Article 15 of the Revised European Social Charter. The overall thrust of the COE Disability policy, as expressed in its Disability Action Plan, is that of promoting the independence and participation of people with disabilities in society. Although it not possible to assert with any certainty that the Court will read a right to Independent Living/Community into the Convention, the interplay of UN human rights instruments – in particular the CRPD – EU law and policy and the Council of Europe's own policies relating to disabled people, represents an evolving international recognition of the existence of such a right. Over time this emerging consensus holds the potential to be a powerful influence of the Court.

4.2. Article 8

The case law to date in this area does not appear to provide much scope for optimism, however; the restrictive interpretation by the Court of the scope of Article 8 positive obligations may mask the potential of this article to encompass the core elements of a right to IL. For example, the potential exists to argue that institutionalisation represents a violation of the right to private life by way of over-crowding, levels of staff supervision, limitations on choice of activities, lack of privacy and all the other features common to institutionalised living. The Court has traditionally emphasised personal autonomy and the need to provide clear justification for interference with a person's chosen lifestyle. This opens the possibility of making a convincing argument along the lines of *Olmstead* that a regime which is skewed towards institutional living for people with disabilities represents a violation of the Article 8 right to private and family life. Although this has not proven successful to date, the possibility remains that the Court will move towards this position as more cases are presented.

De Schutter offers a useful analysis of the reasons behind the so-far restrictive view of the Court in relation to the Article 8 positive obligations.[21] He suggests that the

---

21 O De Schutter, 'Reasonable accommodations and positive obligations in the European Convention on Human Rights' in A Lawson and C Gooding (eds), *Disability Rights in Europe: From Theory to Practice* (Hart 2005).

barriers to a broader interpretation of States' positive obligations by the Court are institutional, rather than due to a lack of an understanding of how Article 8 relates to disabled people and their rights to private life. These constraints are:

1. The 'all or nothing' approach, which exemplifies the judicial function of the Court. A ruling of the existence of a positive obligation, especially in relation to physical access issues, opens respondent States to the possibility of having to spend large amounts of national resources to meet this obligation. It does not leave open the possibility of the progressive realisation of rights.
2. The need for the Court to ensure that in addressing the needs of one applicant the interests of other citizens are not damaged in the process. The Court must be mindful of the implications of its decisions for everyone where an individual applicant seeks to have his or her rights realised but the State does not have the resources to solve the same problem for everyone else in similar situations.
3. The open-ended nature of the concept of 'respect for private life' and the potential scope of the positive obligations it could impose on Member States.[22]

Each of the preceding points also touch on the democratic mandate of the Court – does it have a right to impose priorities on Member States in relation to the expenditure of national resources? Is this not properly the role of national governments elected by their citizens?

Possible strategies which could be adopted to assist the Court in overcoming these restrictions include:

1. Requiring States to comply with and enforce their own domestic law to protect individual autonomy.
2. Assessing the extent of Article 8 positive obligations in the context of other international human rights instruments to which Member States have signed up – it would be difficult for a State to argue that it cannot adopt a particular measure if the State has already undertaken to adopt that measure by agreeing to other international instruments.
3. Focusing on the need to ensure that States' decision-making processes take account of the impact of proposed actions or policies on vulnerable groups, ie taking account of the perspective of disabled people and other marginalized groups in all policy formulation.
4. An obvious difficulty faced by the Court is the extant of positive obligations which it is willing or able to impose on States. Finding a means of setting boundaries on such obligations should be helpful in enabling the Court to require States to comply. Where the direct link has been established and the expenditure by national governments is limited to specific cases and is concrete – unlike the widespread environmental changes required in *Botta* and *Zehnalova* and *Zehnal* – the chances of succeeding in the European Court should be enhanced. This is a challenge for litigators.

---

[22] ibid. See fn.21.

4.3. Article 8 with Article 14– the Anti-Discrimination Right

Article 14, which prohibits discrimination, cannot be invoked independently. Combining Article 8 rights with the Article 14 obligation not to discriminate – including a focus on indirect discrimination – may offer a potentially fruitful route for people with disabilities. In the case of *Thlimmenos v Greece*[23] the Court outlined the dimensions of 'discrimination' as encompassing:

1. Where people in analogous situations are treated differently without reasonable justification
2. A failure to treat differently people whose situation is significantly different without reasonable justification.

The latter of these is particularly significant for disabled people, many of whom will require different treatment because their situation is different in order to exercise their rights. In *Price v the UK*[24] the State's failure to treat the applicant, who was being held in custody, differently in order to take account of her disability-related needs amounted to inhuman and degrading treatment and constituted a violation of Article 3.

For disabled people living in institutions the Article 14 prohibition on indirect discrimination in conjunction with Article 8 may offer potential by demonstrating:

1. the disproportionate impact on the right to private and family life of policies biased towards institutional rather than community-based residential provision
2. the disproportionate number of people with disabilities living in state-funded residential care facilities compared with the general population resulting from health, housing, or social policy decisions.

The findings in *DH v Czech Republic*[25] could be used to support the contention that institutional provision represents indirect discrimination. In that case the Court found that the psychological testing of Roma children and the consequent disproportionate numbers of Roma children referred to special schools for children with intellectual disability amounted to indirect discrimination, while recognising that this was an unintended consequence of a government policy decision.

4.4. Incorporation into Irish Law

With the passage of the European Convention on Human Rights Act in 2003 ("Act") the ECHR was incorporated into Irish law. Three important aspects of the Act are:

1. A requirement on Irish Courts to interpret and apply Irish law in a manner compatible with the ECHR and to take judicial notice of the decisions of the Court
2. An obligation on 'organs of the state' to carry out their functions in a manner compatible with the ECHR

---

23 *Thlimmenos v Greece* App no 34369/97 (ECtHR 6 April 2000).
24 *Price v United Kingdom* App no 33394/96 (ECtHR 10 July 2001).
25 *DH and Others v The Czech Republic* App no 57325/00 (ECtHR 13 November 2007).

3. A facility for the High Court or the Supreme Court to declare rules of law or statutory provisions incompatible with the Convention.

Two Declarations of Incompatibility have been issued by the High Court in relation to Section 62 of the Housing Act 1966, which is the process available to local authorities to re-gain possession of their property from tenants. Section 62 does not include an independent forum for tenants' objections to evictions to be heard – it is this aspect of the law that was declared incompatible with Articles 6 and 8 of the Convention. Both cases were appealed to the Supreme Court, and in 2012 the incompatibility of Section 62 was affirmed. This Declaration of Incompatibility has now been referred to the Taoiseach who is obliged to lay it before the Dáil in order for the necessary legislative changes to be made.

It is perhaps too early to properly evaluate the impact of incorporation of the Convention into Irish law but it is possible to point to the following potential benefits:

1. The Act brings the jurisprudence of the European Court into the Irish courts offering a wider and deeper interpretation and application of Convention rights than would have previously been the case. It makes available the accumulated knowledge and wisdom of the Court to our judicial system.
2. Enabling Irish citizens to challenge the Convention-compatibility of laws, rules or policies in the national courts means that such cases should no longer have to be pursued as far as Strasbourg. It would seem unlikely that an Irish 'organ of the state' would allow a measure deemed to be incompatible with the Convention by the Irish courts to proceed as far as the European Court.
3. The incorporation of the Act should directly impact on the process of law reform. As it 'beds down,' the Convention should become a touch stone in the development of all new legislation so that all new law should consider the rights protected by the Convention from the outset.

5. Conclusion

What then is the likelihood of a right to IL being recognised by the European Court in the future? An examination of international and regional policies in relation to disabled people clearly indicate that there is broad agreement on the emergence of such a right, despite the fact that practices on the ground in many European countries are far from realising this right. And it is precisely this developing consensus that holds the greatest potential for people with disability to live lives of their choosing in places of their choosing and have the supports needed to do this. There is still a long way to go but the thrust of policy formation over the past ten to fifteen years supports the momentum in the direction of community-based provision. The passage of the CRPD is very significant in explicitly naming a right to IL for people with disabilities. It is difficult to see how the Court will be able to operate in a way which is contrary to the developing international and European consensus, and the CRPD in particular.

Advocacy groups of disabled people, their supporters and civil society groups will need to continue to highlight human rights violations, increase awareness of the human rights of disabled people, be prepared to bring relevant cases to the Court and support and safeguard potential applicants in the process.

The power of the Court lies in its authority to compel States to amend legislation, policies or practices, which violates people's human rights. Realising that litigation is a powerful way of achieving change within social service systems, support groups of disabled people and legal advocates must work to bring pertinent cases before the Court. The underdeveloped legal supports for disabled people in Ireland remains a challenge.

Chapter 20

INDEPENDENT LIVING FOR PERSONS WITH DISABILITIES IN KENYA: CHARTING THE WAY FORWARD

Elizabeth Kamundia

1. Introduction

Prior to the Convention on the Rights of Persons with Disabilities (CRPD), no other human rights instrument contained an explicit right for all persons with disabilities to live in the community as equal citizens.[1] This chapter explores the concept of independent living and living in the community from the perspective of a developing country – Kenya.

The chapter sets off by defining independent living, identifying its key elements, examining its historical and theoretical underpinnings and exploring the position taken by African countries on Article 19[2] during the negotiations of the CRPD. This section also examines the comments made to Spain and Tunisia on Article 19 by the Committee on the Rights of Persons with Disabilities (CRPD Committee) in a bid to gain a deeper understanding of independent living. Following this, the chapter provides a rationale for exploring the right to independent living from the perspective of a developing country. It notes that although a significant amount of literature exists on the meaning of independent living with regard to developed countries, not much has been written from the perspective of developing countries. Third, the chapter looks at measures taken by the government of Kenya towards providing support to

---

1 European Coalition for Community Living, 'Focus on Article 19 of the UN Convention on the rights of PWD' (Focus Report 2009).

2 art 19, United Nations Convention on the Rights of Persons with Disabilities (CRPD) (2006) 'Living independently and being included in the community' reads as follows:

> States Parties to the present Convention recognize the equal right of all persons with disabilities to live in the community, with choices equal to others, and shall take effective and appropriate measures to facilitate full enjoyment by persons with disabilities of this right and their full inclusion and participation in the community, including by ensuring that:
>
> (*a*) Persons with disabilities have the opportunity to choose their place of residence and where and with whom they live on an equal basis with others and are not obliged to live in a particular living arrangement;
>
> (*b*) Persons with disabilities have access to a range of in-home, residential and other community support services, including personal assistance necessary to support living and inclusion in the community, and to prevent isolation or segregation from the community;
>
> (*c*) Community services and facilities for the general population are available on an equal basis to persons with disabilities and are responsive to their needs.

persons with disabilities, noting that no single measure is taken specifically with the aim of enabling persons with disabilities to live independently. Fourth, it analyses Kenya's State Report to the CRPD Committee with regard to Article 19.

The paper argues that independent living is as relevant for developing countries as it is for developed countries. Indeed, it argues that the concept of independent living does exist in Africa, except that it has been expressed through different concepts. In Africa, emphasis has been placed on habilitation and rehabilitation aimed at enabling persons with disabilities to achieve independence. The effect of this in Kenya has been a narrow focus on persons with physical and sensory disabilities, leaving out those with intellectual, psychosocial and dual diagnosis disabilities, as well as those with other forms of multiple disabilities.[3]

2. Defining Independent Living and Identifying its Key Elements

Article 19 provides that persons with disabilities have the right to live independently in the community. Community living (also known as independent living),[4] refers to persons with disabilities being able to live in their local communities as equal citizens, with the support that they need to participate in everyday life.[5]

The core elements of independent living are self-determination, choice, autonomy, equal access, living in community, inclusion and participation. These elements are universal and not context-specific.[6] Indeed, independent living 'has been regarded as a concept rather than an issue requiring specific legal definition.'[7] Article 19 has been said to extend the traditional right of liberty. In the words of Kayess and French, Article 19 equates the right to liberty with the right of persons with disability to live in and be a part of the community.[8]

Article 35 of the CRPD requires that State Parties submit to the CRPD Committee

---

3 Board Member of the Kenya Association of the Mentally Handicapped, Fatma Wangare, states that 'there are many parents that hide their children with disabilities in their house due to the social stigma attached to disability. People in the community often associate developmental disabilities with mental illness or traditional beliefs such as curses and witchcraft.' Kenya Association of the Intellectually Handicapped, 'Social Stigmatization and Self Advocacy–Kiambu' (Young People with Intellectual Disabilities Learn to Speak Out 2009) <http://kaihid.org/index.php?option=com_content&view=article&id=12&Itemid=55> last accessed 31 March 2016. Separately, the Kenya Society for the Mentally Handicapped website features a story of a person with intellectual disabilities who was tied, chained, and locked up for 35 years. Due to this, he developed muscular atrophy, and lost the use of his legs to date. Kenya Society for the Mentally Handicapped, 'Rescues and Home-based Interventions' <www.ksmh.org/ksmh-at-work/interventions/rescues> last accessed 31 March 2016.

4 European Coalition for Community Living (n 1).

5 European Coalition for Community Living, 'Creating Successful Campaigns for Community Living: An Advocacy Manual for Disability organisations and service providers' (2008) <www.community-living.info/.../ECCL-Manual-final-WEB.pdf> last accessed 31 March 2016.

6 Interview with Dr M Seifu, Independent Disability Consultant (Galway, Ireland, 24 February 2012).

7 C Parker and L Clements, 'The UN Convention on the Rights of Persons with Disabilities: A New Right to Independent Living?' (2008) 4 European Human Rights Law Review 509.

8 R Kayess and P French, 'Out of darkness into light? Introducing the Convention on the Rights of Persons with Disabilities' (2008) 8 Human Rights Law Review 1.

a report on the CRPD's implementation.[9] The Committee has since considered the state reports of Spain and Tunisia, and issued concluding observations in this regard. These observations serve to clarify the various rights in the Convention. On Article 19 and with regard to Spain, the CRPD Committee expressed concern at the lack of resources and services to guarantee the right to live independently and to be included in the community, in particular in rural areas.[10] This emphasises the need for the state to come into play to ensure that certain elements of this right are fulfilled. While the Committee did not issue comments directly on Article 19 to Tunisia, it recommended that Tunisia 'take steps to replace institutional care for boys and girls with disabilities with community based care.'[11] These comments further inform what Article 19 should look like in practice.

Article 19 is a clear demonstration of how the CRPD blurs the line traditionally established in human rights between the traditional civil and political rights and economic, social and cultural rights.[12] Indeed, it is hard to distinguish the civil and political aspects from the social, economic and cultural aspects of the right to independent living.[13]

2.1. Historical and Theoretical Underpinnings of Article 19

Independent Living is a civil rights movement of people with disabilities which grew in America at the end of the 1960s as a protest to living conditions in clinical institutions.[14] Theoretically, the right to independent living is grounded in the social model of disability,[15] which distinguishes between the impairments that people have and the oppression which they experience. Most importantly, it defines 'disability'

---

9 This is required within two years after the entry into force of the Convention for the State Party. United Nations Human Rights, Office of the High Commissioner for Human Rights, 'Committee on the Rights of Persons with Disabilities' (2012) <www.ohchr.org/en/hrbodies/crpd/pages/crpdindex.aspx> last accessed 31 March 2016.

10 The Committee encouraged Spain to ensure that an adequate level of funding be made available to effectively enable persons with disabilities: to enjoy the freedom to choose their residence on an equal basis with others; to access a full range of in-home, residential and other community services for daily life, including personal assistance; and to so enjoy reasonable accommodation so as to better integrate into their communities. Committee on the Rights of Persons with Disabilities, Sixth Session (Geneva, 19–23 September 2011) CRPD/C/ESP/1 <www.ohchr.org/EN/HRBodies/CRPD/Pages/Session6.aspx> accessed 19 March 2012.

11 Committee on the Rights of Persons with Disabilities, Fifth Session (Geneva, 11–15 April 2011) CRPD/C/TUN/Q/1 <www.ohchr.org/EN/HRBodies/CRPD/Pages/Session5.aspx> last accessed 31 March 2016.

12 M A Stein and J E Lord, 'Ratify the UN Disability Treaty' (2009) <www.fpif.org/articles/ratify_the_un_disability_treaty> last accessed 31 March 2016.

13 G Quinn, 'Reflecting Strategically about the UN Convention on the Rights of Persons with Disabilities' (Conference Interights Guest Speaker Series, London, December 2011).

14 The Independent Living Movement sees disablement primarily as a social and political problem. It follows the example of the issues and strategies of the black civil rights movement and of the feminist movement. The main issues are the articulation of one's own needs, self-determination, assistance geared to the consumer and participation in politics and administration. Independent Living Institute, 'The Concept of Independent Living; A New Perspective in Rehabilitation' (1994) <http://www.independentliving.org/docs5/Osterwitz.html> last accessed 31 March 2016.

15 Parker and Clements (n 7).

as the social oppression, not the form of impairment.[16] This is the model adopted by the CRPD.[17]

2.2. Africa's Contribution to Article 19 During the Negotiations of the CRPD

Article 19 of the CRPD is one of the Articles that saw a clear divide between the negotiating standpoints of the developing and the developed countries.[18] The issue presents differently in the North and South of Africa. The critical issue in the North is institutionalisation. As Parker and Clements argue, '[i]n many parts of Europe the predominant provision for disabled people (children as well as adults) continues to be institutionalisation (often for life).'[19] The critical issue in the South is unavailability of the required support services to enable independence and facilitate participation in the society.[20] Further, in most countries of the south, mutual caring and support in the community is a norm, and it is often felt that there is no need for disabled persons to live physically and financially apart from their families. The emphasis is on one becoming a contributing member of the family rather than to manage her/his own household alone. Thus, the concept of independent living associated with the developed countries is not always relevant in the developing countries.[21] As a result, during the negotiations, the South placed great emphasis on support to families taking care of persons with disabilities.[22] Further, states from the South emphasised the 'promotion' of supportive assistance rather than an 'obligation to provide' such assistance.[23]

2.3. Inter-Linkages within the Convention

To get the full import of Article 19, one must be aware of the linkages that exist

---

16 M Oliver, *The Politics of Disablement* (Macmillan 1990) 22.

17 The CRPD recognises that 'disability is an evolving concept and that disability results from the interaction between persons with impairments and attitudinal and environmental barriers that hinders their full and effective participation in society on an equal basis with others' 'Preamble, Article (e), United Nations Convention on the Rights of Persons with Disabilities (2006).

18 United Nations Enable, 'Daily Summary of Discussions Related to Article 15 – Living Independently and Being Included in the Community' (2004) www.un.org/esa/socdev/enable/rights/ahc3sum15.htm last accessed 31 March 2016; United Nations Enable, 'Daily Summary of Discussions Related to Article 15 Living Independently and Being Included in the Community' (2004). <www.un.org/esa/socdev/enable/rights/ahc4sumart15.htm> last accessed 31 March 2016.

19 Parker and Clements (n 7).

20 I Komardjaja, 'Independent living and self determination of women with physical disabilities in Bandung, Indonesia' (2004) 24 Disability Studies Quarterly.

21 Y Oka, 'Self-reliance in Interdependent Communities: Independent Living of Disabled Persons in the Asia Pacific Region' (Conference on Social Rehabilitation, Hamamatsu, Japan, 10–11 September 1988) <www.independentliving.org/docs4/oka.html> last accessed 31 March 2016.

22 For Morocco's position, United Nations Enable, 'Report of the Third Session of the Ad Hoc Committee on a Comprehensive and Integral International Convention on the Protection and Promotion of the Rights and Dignity of Persons with Disabilities' (2004) <www.un.org/esa/socdev/enable/rights/ahc3reporte.htm> last accessed 31 March 2016; for Kenya's position, United Nations Enable, 'Daily Summary of Discussions Related to Article 15 – Living Independently and Being Included in the Community' (2004) <www.un.org/esa/socdev/enable/rights/ahc4sumart15.htm> last accessed 31 March 2016.

23 For Sierra Leone's position, United Nations Enable, 'Daily Summary of Discussions Related to Article 15 – Living Independently and Being Included in the Community' (2004) <www.un.org/esa/socdev/enable/rights/ahc3sum15.htm> last accessed 31 March 2016.

throughout the Convention.[24] Article 19 has been classified alongside other autonomy and dignity articles,[25] that is Articles 12, 18, 17 and 22.[26] It is also closely linked with participation rights, enshrined in Articles 9, 13, 27, 25, 24, 20, 26, 21 and 29.[27] Article 12, on legal capacity, is particularly key to independent living. As argued by Gerard Quinn and Michael Stein,

> This right (to legal capacity) acknowledges that people with disabilities have an innate capacity to decide their destinies for themselves – where to live, who to live with, what education or employment to pursue – and to have those choices respected. And if there is to be an intervention on the part of the State, the primary impulse should be to support a residuum of capacity, and to intervene to support people to make decisions for themselves, with appropriate safeguards.[28]

While independent living is closely linked with the above rights, it is more than the sum of these rights.[29]

3. Rationale for Examining Independent Living for People with Disabilities in Kenya

Although a significant amount of literature exists on the meaning of independent living with regard to developed countries, not much has been written from the perspective of developing countries.[30] This chapter argues that there is a need to explore independent living from the perspective of a developing country and offers four reasons for this position. The first reason is based on the argument that the core elements of independent living are universal and not context-specific. The second reason is pragmatic and based on the statistics of persons living with disabilities in Kenya. The third reason is based on an assessment of the factual situation/lived reality of people with disabilities on the ground in Kenya. The fourth and final reason is the fact that Kenya has an enabling legal framework. Having ratified the

---

24 United Nations Enable, 'Report of the United Nations High Commissioner for Human Rights on Progress in the Implementation of the Recommendations contained in the Study on the Human Rights of Persons with Disabilities' (Geneva 17 January) A/HRC/4/75 para 19 <www.un.org/disabilities/default.asp?id=135> last accessed 31 March 2016.

25 E Flynn, 'UN Convention on the Rights of Persons with Disabilities' (9th Irish Human Rights Commission and Law Society Conference, Dublin, October 2011).

26 These are legal capacity, liberty of movement and nationality, personal integrity and privacy, respectively.

27 These are accessibility, access to justice, employment, health, education, personal mobility, habilitation, participation in private and public life and freedom of expression, respectively.

28 G Quinn and M A Stein, 'Challenges in realizing the right to live in the community', in I Bulic and C Parker (eds), 'European Coalition for Community Living – Focus on Article 19 of the UN Convention on the rights of PWD' (Focus Report 2009) 28.

29 Council of Europe Commissioner for Human Rights, 'The Right of People with Disabilities to Live Independently and be Included in the Community' (2012) (COMM (2012) 3, 13) <https://wcd.coe.int/ViewDoc.jsp?id=1917847#P188_14524> last accessed 31 March 2016.

30 Developing countries particularly experience a problem with data. Equal Rights Trust and Kenya Human Rights Commission, 'In the Spirit of Harambee: Addressing Discrimination and Inequality in Kenya' (2012) 1 ERT Country Report Series <www.equalrightstrust.org/ertdocumentbank/In_the_Spirit_of_Harambee.pdf> last accessed 31 March 2016, notes that '[i]t is difficult to carry out accurate research on the situation of those living with mental and intellectual disabilities in Kenya due to the lack of official data and information.'

CRPD, Kenya is required to report on its progress in the implementation of all the rights contained therein to the Committee on the Rights of Persons with Disabilities.

3.1 The Universality of Independent Living[31]

Human rights are universal. They are the natural born rights for every human being.[32] Further, while the right to independent living, thus worded, is only contained in the CRPD, it is not a new right, but rather a creative interpretation of existing rights that has been specially tailored to apply to the context of persons with disabilities.[33]

According to the UK Office for disability issues, '[i]ndependent living' does not mean doing things for yourself, or living on your own. Instead, it means having choice and control over the assistance and/or equipment needed to go about your daily life and having equal access to housing, transport and mobility, health, employment and education and training opportunities.'[34]

Clearly, these issues are relevant to people with disabilities living both in developed and in developing countries.

3.2 Statistics

According to the 2009 Population and Housing Census Report,[35] Kenya has a total population of 37 million people.[36] The World Report on Disability, 2011, estimates that including children, over a billion people (or about 15% of the world's population) live with disability.[37] This would translate to about 5.5 million people in Kenya, most of whom live with their families but without the necessary support to ensure their participation and inclusion in the community. Consequently, this issue is important because it affects a significant sector of the society.

3.3 The Situation of Persons With Disabilities in Kenya

The legal position of persons with disabilities in Kenya has radically improved since the early 2000s. In 2003, Kenya enacted the Persons with Disabilities Act (PDA),[38] which provided, for the first time, a right to non-discrimination on grounds

---

[31] For a discussion of the elements of independent living, see Section 2 of this chapter.

[32] United Nations General Assembly, 'Universal Declaration of Human Rights' 10 December 1948, 217 A (III) <www.unhcr.org/refworld/docid/3ae6b3712c.html> last accessed 31 March 2016.

[33] United Nations Enable, 'Convention on the Rights of Persons with Disabilities' <www.un.org/disabilities/default.asp?navid=14&pid=150> last accessed 31 March 2016.

[34] Office for Disability Issues, 'Independent Living: A Cross-Government Strategy about Independent Living for Disabled People' (HM Government 2008).

[35] Kenya National Bureau of Statistics, 'Kenya Census 2009, Nipo! Natambulika! Counting our people for implementation of vision 2030' (2009) <www.knbs.or.ke/> last accessed 31 March 2016.

[36] 76.7% live in rural areas, whereas 32.3% live in urban areas.

[37] World Health Organisation and The World Bank, 'World Report on Disability' (WHO 2011) 29. According to Kenya's Census Report, the population of persons with disabilities is 1,330,312 (647,689 – male and 682, 623 – female). This seems to be a gross underestimation in the light of the World Report on Disability estimation at 15%.

[38] Kenya Law Reports, 'Laws of Kenya' (2003) Act No 14 <www.kenyalaw.org/klr/index.php> last accessed 31 March 2016.

of disability. In 2008, Kenya ratified the Convention on the Rights of Persons with Disabilities, which became part of Kenyan law with the promulgation of the Constitution of Kenya 2010.[39] However, despite these positive changes in the law, 'the lives of people with disabilities in Kenya are marked by experiences of discrimination, prejudice and inequality.'[40]

As with the rest of the world, the earliest efforts in addressing the issues of people with disabilities in Kenya were structured within the charity model.[41] While there has been a considerable move towards the social model of disability, it still remains difficult to incorporate in practice.[42] Hence, people with disabilities in Kenya continue to be viewed as tragic victims of impairment, and as the beneficiaries of charity, alms, and services – for which they should be grateful.[43] This is further complicated by the fact that people in the community often associate disability with traditional beliefs such as curses and witchcraft.[44]

The majority of persons with disabilities in Kenya live with their families, and the primary responsibility for providing the necessary support is situated within the family.[45] In a study of people with disabilities conducted in Kenya in 2007, Benedicte and Lisbet note that '[i]ndividual independence can be a solution when the family is non-supportive, but we have seen that those who manage almost as a rule have a supportive family to rely on.'[46]

---

39 Equal Rights Trust and Kenya Human Rights Commission (n 29).

40 African Union of the Blind, Kenya Union of the Blind and Centre for Disability Rights Education and Advocacy, 'State of Disabled Peoples Rights in Kenya' (2007) 43. In preparing this report, the authors interviewed 95 persons with various forms of disability in three different regions of Kenya with the aim of identifying the barriers they faced and understanding the human rights situation of disabled people. 86% of respondents stated that they had experienced unequal treatment, 80% reported experiencing isolation, segregation and lack of support for their needs, and 74% felt they had been denied the right to make decisions on their own lives. The report identified three types of barriers preventing people with disabilities from participating in life on an equal basis: abuse and violence, discriminatory attitudes and limited access. 56.8% of participants in the study reported that they had experienced abuse and violence in the community or society at large, while almost three quarters (74.7%) of interviewees had experienced discriminatory attitudes in society.

41 ibid.

42 The Chief Executive Officer of the Kenya Society for the Mentally Handicapped and a person with psychosocial disabilities herself, Edah Maina, has stated that 'the general attitude of the government and health professionals towards persons with disabilities – that they should be treated with charity and that their condition can only be addressed through medical intervention – has created an environment where their rights can be ignored.' Equal Rights Trust and Kenya Human Rights Commission, 'In the Spirit of Harambee: Addressing Discrimination and Inequality in Kenya' (ERT Country Report Series: 1 London, February 2012) 143.

43 E Kamundia, 'Employment of Persons with Disabilities: A Critical Analysis of the Persons with Disabilities Act, 2003' (LLM Thesis University of Nairobi 2010).

44 This is especially so in the case of intellectual disabilities and psychosocial disabilities. Kenya Association of the Intellectually Handicapped, 'Social Stigmatisation and Self Advocacy: Kiambu. Young People with Intellectual Disabilities Learn to Speak out' (2009) <http://kaihid.org/index.php?option=com_content&view=article&id=12&Itemid=55> last accessed 31 March 2016.

45 'Most [...people in need of support services in Kenya] are isolated at home without the support they need.' Open Society Foundation's Blog, 'The Other Side of Kenya's Terrible Secret' (2011) <www.soros.org/voices/other-side-kenya-s-terrible-secret> last accessed 31 March 2016.

46 B Ingstad and L Grut, 'See me but do not forget me; people with disabilities in Kenya' (2007) SINTEF Health Research <http://siteresources.worldbank.org/DISABILITY/Resources/Regions/Africa/LCKenya2.pdf> last accessed 31 March 2016.

In spite of the central role of families, a 2012 report carried out by Equal Rights Trust and Kenya Human Rights Commission states:

> ERT's interviews with persons with different forms of disability found that prejudice, stigma and discriminatory attitudes towards disability prevailed within families, and that the discriminatory treatment which persons with disabilities experienced in the home often had far-reaching consequences for their ability to participate equally in other areas of life.[47]

Investigations carried out for the Universal Periodic Review found that approximately 74% of people with disabilities interviewed reported that they were denied the right to make decisions on issues affecting their own lives. They also described how they had been forced into situations against their will because they had been judged incapable of deciding on their own due to their disability.[48]

The right to live independently in Kenya is further hampered by poor education (and the poor self-image and self-motivation that follow), which hinder market entry at a level genuinely commensurate with abilities.[49] Furthermore, a lack of equally effective and accessible transport facilities hinders not merely labour market mobility, but also ordinary social intercourse.[50] Lack of access to the assistive devices needed to enable active and equal participation in life presents a particular problem for many of those with physical and sensory disabilities, which, in combination with direct discrimination against them,[51] act as a barrier to independent living. Other problems affecting persons with intellectual and mental disabilities include under-provision of specialist facilities and services and a lack of facilitation for Augmentative and Alternative Communications (AAC). All these issues profoundly affect the right to live in the community.

Kenya does not have a welfare system to support sectors of the population who are less advantaged such as those who are unemployed, or who are unable to meet their basic needs for whatever reasons. It does however provide piecemeal support to a few specific groups of disadvantaged people. According to the United Nations Development Programme Human Development Report 2009, Kenya is rated as being of medium human development, ranking at number 147 out of 182 countries.[52] According to the Central Intelligence Agency WorldFact Book, 50%

---

47 Equal Rights Trust and Kenya Human Rights Commission (n 29).

48 Kenya UPR Stakeholders Coalition, 'An Assessment by Stakeholders of Government's Performance in Implementation of UPR Recommendations' (2011) <http://www.upr-info.org/IMG/pdf/follow-up_kenya_stakeholders_annual_progress_report_2011.pdf> last accessed 31 March 2016.

49 Committee on Economic Social and Cultural Rights – Concluding Observations on Kenya, UN Doc. E/C.12/KEN/CO/1, 2008 paras 16, 34. The CESCR in its concluding observations on the Government of Kenya's 2007 State Report drew attention to the fact that many persons with disabilities remained unemployed and had limited access to education.

50 G Quinn, 'The International Covenant on Civil and Political Rights and disability: A conceptual framework', in T Degener and Y Koster-Dreese (eds), *Human Rights and Disabled Persons' Essays and Relevant Human Rights Instruments* (Martinus Nijhoff Publishers 1995).

51 Equal Rights Trust and Kenya Human Rights Commission (n 29). The report further notes that '[i]n many parts of the country, access to assistive devices and specialist services for persons with physical and sensory disabilities is low, creating substantial problems across all areas of life.'

52 United Nations Development Programme, 'Summary Human Development Report 2009' (2009)

of the population of Kenya live below the poverty line.[53] People with disabilities in developing countries are over-represented among the poorest people. Poverty causes disabilities, and can furthermore lead to secondary disabilities for those individuals who are already disabled, as a result of the poor living conditions, health-endangering employment, malnutrition and poor access to health care and education. Together, poverty and disability create a vicious cycle.[54] This situation prevails in Kenya, and further hampers the realisation of independent living for people with disabilities.

3.4 Legal Basis

Kenya ratified the CRPD on 19 May 2008.[55] On 27 August 2010, the Constitution of Kenya 2010 was promulgated. Its Article 2(6) states: 'Any treaty or convention ratified by Kenya shall form part of the law of Kenya under this Constitution.'[56]

Hence, the CRPD is part of the law of Kenya and hence Kenya must report on the progress it is making on the implementation of the rights therein, including the right to independent living. It is therefore necessary to analyse this right in the context of the country, to ensure its implementation and to facilitate monitoring.

3.4.1 Measures taken by the Government of Kenya towards providing support to persons with disabilities[57]

The Government of Kenya has taken both legislative and programmatic measures towards addressing disability. Legislative measures were discussed above.[58] Programmatic measures constitute cash transfers and strategy papers. Under cash transfers is the National Development Fund for Persons with Disabilities,[59] the Economic Empowerment Project 2010,[60] and the Cash Transfer Programme for Persons with Severe Disabilities.[61] Persons with disabilities are also exempted

---

<http://hdr.undp.org/en/media/HDR_2009_EN_Summary.pdf> last accessed 31 March 2016.

53 Central Intelligence Agency, 'The World FactBook: Kenya' (2012) <www.cia.gov/library/publications/the-world-factbook/geos/ke.html> last accessed 31 March 2016. In terms of its population living under $1.25 and $2.00 a day, it ranks at 70.7% and 80.0% respectively. Wikipedia, 'List of Countries by Percentage of Population Living in Poverty' (2012) <http://en.wikipedia.org/wiki/List_of_countries_by_percentage_of_population_living_in_poverty> last accessed 31 March 2016.

54 The World Bank, 'Poverty and Disability' (26 January 2010) <http://web.worldbank.org/WBSITE/EXTERNAL/TOPICS/EXTSOCIALPROTECTION/EXTDISABILITY/0,,contentMDK:20193783~menuPK:419389~pagePK:148956~piPK:216618~theSitePK:282699,00.html> accessed 26 February 2012.

55 United Nations Enable, 'Convention and Optional Protocol Signatures and Ratifications' (2012) <www.un.org/disabilities/countries.asp? navid=12&pid=166> last accessed 31 March 2016.

56 art 2(6), The Constitution of Kenya (2010).

57 Ideally, this topic should be titled, 'Measures taken by the Government of Kenya towards Independent Living'. However, while these measures go towards facilitating independent living for people with disabilities, independent living is not identified by the government as being the aim towards which these measures are taken/the driver of these measures.

58 African Union of the Blind, Kenya Union of the Blind, and Centre for Disability Rights Education and Advocacy, 'State of Disabled Peoples Rights in Kenya' (2007) 9.

59 Established under s 32 of the Persons with Disabilities Act (2003) No. 14 (n 37).

60 Kenya UPR Stakeholders Coalition (n 47).

61 Ministry of Gender, Children and Social Development, 'Social Welfare/Persons with Disabilities Programme' (2012) <www.gender.go.ke/index.php/Gender-and-Social-Development-

from the payment of income tax.[62] The key strategy paper in the country currently is Vision 2030.[63]

3.5 Cash Transfers

The National Development Fund for People with Disabilities[64] was established under s 32 of the PDA[65] and operationalised in 2010. It has begun to disburse funds to persons with disabilities and to organisations and institutions that provide services to persons with disabilities. In 2009–2010 the Government allocated KES 200 million to the fund.[66] This fund provides only limited financial support to people with disabilities and their families on a means-tested basis.

The Government, through the Ministry of Gender, Children and Social Development, also began the Economic Empowerment Project in 2010. Through the project, the Government is disbursing funds on a continuous basis directly to groups of persons with disabilities for promoting their economic independence.[67]

Furthermore, the Ministry of Gender, Children and Social Development began a cash-transfer programme for persons with severe disabilities in every electoral constituency.[68] The programme started in April 2011, targeting ten households in every constituency.[69] The number of households targeted has since increased to seventy.[70]

Persons with disabilities are also exempted from the payment of income tax pursuant to s 12(3) of the PDA.[71] To this end, the National Council for Persons with

---

Divisions/social-welfare-persons-with-disabilities-programme.html> last accessed 31 March 2016.

62 Persons with Disabilities Act (n 37) s 12 (3).

63 Kenya Vision 2030, 'A Globally Competitive and Prosperous Kenya' (2011) <www.vision2030.go.ke/> last accessed 31 March 2016.

64 National Council for Persons with Disabilities, 'National Development Fund' (2012) <http://ncpwd.go.ke/national-development-fund-for-persons-with-disabilities/> last accessed 31 March 2016. The Fund currently supports the following funding categories:

1. Assistive devices and services – To improve mobility and access. Includes wheelchairs, crutches, surgical shoes, hearing aid, white cane and others.
2. Educational assistance – Scholarships for persons with disabilities who wish to pursue education but cannot do so because of financial difficulties.
3. Economic Empowerment & Revolving Fund – Help for groups of persons with disabilities to set up small businesses or revolving fund schemes.
4. Infrastructure & Equipment – Assistance or social care and education institutions that provide services to Persons with Disabilities.
5. Cash transfers – Support for households of persons with severe disabilities who are in extreme poverty.

65 Persons with Disabilities Act (2003) No. 14 (n 37).

66 Kenya UPR Stakeholders Coalition (n 47).

67 ibid.

68 Constituency populations for the 1997 elections ranged from as few as 3,635 people to as many as 301,558 people (with most constituency populations well above or below the population quota of 102,271). L Handley, 'Challenging the Norms and Standards of Election Administration: Boundary Delimitation' (International Fpundation for Electoral Systems 2007) 59.

69 Ministry of Gender, Children and Social Development (n 59).

70 Interview with P S Musakhi, Assistant Director for Gender and Social Development, Ministry of Gender, Children and Social Development (Nairobi, Kenya, 10 May 2012).

71 The exemption is upto KES 150,000 per month.

Disabilities facilitates the exemption of persons with disabilities registered with it from the payment of income tax.

3.6 Strategy Paper

Vision 2030 is Kenya's long-term development blueprint. Under its social pillar, it provides that key programmes for learners with special needs will be developed. It also aims at 'minimising vulnerabilities by upscaling training for people with disabilities and special needs.'[72] It also states that 'full implementation (including appropriate budgetary allocations) of the Disability Fund' will be undertaken as a flagship project alongside other strategies to reduce vulnerabilities.[73] Under its goals for 2012 is the aim '[e]mpower people with special needs'.[74]

3.7 Critique of the Measures Taken by the Government of Kenya Towards Providing Support

To start with, it is noteworthy that independent living as a concept is not used in any of the legislative and programmatic measures. Further, the Kenyan state-funded assistance enumerated above is limited and largely inadequate.[75] State-funded provision of assistive services and support is limited (in terms of scope, focusing on persons with physical disabilities, and geographically in that it tends to be concentrated in urban areas). The effect of this is that many people with disabilities living at home often have their human rights violated.[76] In this regard, the situation prevailing in Kenya is wanting. The fact that the primary caregiving role is situated in the family without support often means that the key caregivers cannot avail themselves of employment or pursue other socio-economic activities. Hence, not only is the person with disabilities unable to live as an equal citizen, neither can his or her family.[77]

The National Development Fund for people with disabilities is grounded in the PDA. However, the fact that the Act does not have adequate enforcement mechanisms severely hampers its impact on the ground. In addition, despite preparation by the Kenya National Council for Persons with Disabilities of a strategic plan to carry out the mandate of the PDA, a lack of resources has impeded its implementation.[78]

---

72 Kenya Vision 2030 (n 61).

73 ibid.

74 ibid. These are identified as the 25.7% who are lame and 18.4% who are mentally disabled.

75 Issues with regard to the Cash Transfer Programme for Persons with Severe Disabilities include how to widen the pool of the severely disabled, ie issues of assessment as well as how to sustainably fund the scheme in the long term.

76 For instance, often, their right to privacy and autonomy is infringed, as is their freedom of movement, among other key rights.

77 E Kamundia, 'Advanced Legal Research and Methods, Literature Review: Independent Living: Application of Article 19 of the UN Convention on the Rights of Persons with Disabilities to Kenya' (Essay National University of Ireland, Galway 2011).

78 Stakeholder Submission, Universal Periodic Review of Kenya, May 2010, submitted by the African Union of the Blind, Disability Rights Promotion International, Kenya Union of the Blind, Center for Disability Rights Education and Advocacy. Disability Rights Promotion International, 'UN Human Rights Council– Universal Periodic Review of Kenya' (2010). <http://drpi.research.yorku.ca/DRPIHeadlines/KenyaUPRSubmission> last accessed 31 March 2016.

With regard to Vision 2030, the government's focus as far as persons with disabilities are concerned is limited to education. It does not contain any measures with regard to improving accessibility, employment or awareness-raising to combat prejudices which is one of the key hindrances to inclusion and participation by persons with disabilities.

4. Kenya's State Report to the CRPD Committee

Kenya's state report[79] under Article 35 of the CRPD was due in 2010, but was completed in August 2011. It is yet to be addressed by the CRPD Committee. In reporting on the measures that it has taken towards implementing Article 19, Kenya's report states the following:

First, that the Government has enacted the PDA to prohibit discrimination on the grounds of disability.

Second, that it has enacted the Persons with Disabilities (Cost, Care, Support and Maintenance) Regulations 2009, which provides a legal framework for the development of community rehabilitation programs for persons with disabilities that provide training in vocational and trade skills, independent living skills and capacity-building of children and persons with disabilities and thereby enhance effective rehabilitation, independent living and inclusion within the community.

Third, that it supports and works with development partners and NGOs to provide rehabilitation services within government hospitals, and that equipment is imported duty free.

Fourth, that it is running training programmes in several schools[80] for occupational therapists, physiotherapists and orthopedic technicians who empower persons with disabilities to gain life skills that enable them to live independently.

Fifth, that it is undertaking programmes to enhance public acceptance of persons with disabilities thus enabling them to live among the community.

Sixth, that through the Department of Children Services, it has also established the Orphans and Vulnerable Children Cash Transfer Programme for children, including those with disabilities, thereby empowering the care givers and guardians socially and economically.[81]

The state report is very general, and does not provide data or evidence of any other

---

79 Kenya's Initial Report Submitted Under Article 35(1) of the United Nations Convention on the Rights of Persons with Disabilities – 31 August 2011. Committee on the Rights of Persons with Disabilities, 'Future Sessions, Consideration of Reports' (2012) <www.ohchr.org/EN/HRBodies/CRPD/Pages/futuresessions.aspx> last accessed 31 March 2016.

80 Being the Kenya Medical Training Colleges, Jomo Kenyatta University of Agriculture and Technology, the PCEA University and Moi University.

81 Other funds include one established under the Kenya Society for the Blind Act for persons with visual disability and the National Fund for the Disabled of Kenya which provides start up kits for promoting independence.

kind to support its assertions on a number of important issues. No data is provided on the numbers of persons with disabilities who have been provided with assistive devices at a subsidised rate.[82] No data is provided on the number of programmes, educational facilities and rehabilitation centres established to give persons with disabilities life skills and education, or on the number of government hospitals providing rehabilitation services and the number of people attended to there, or the number of Public Private Partnerships (PPP) initiatives that seek to provide additional services aimed at improving the lives of persons with disabilities. There is also no information on the content and/or form of the awareness-raising programmes that enhance public acceptance of persons with disabilities.

While the government has been offering rehabilitation services, demand for these services far outweighs the supply. The Kenya National Survey for Persons with Disabilities reveals that 75% of persons with disabilities were aware of medical rehabilitation services and 54% needed the services, but only 29% received the services.[83] The key lacuna in the State Report on Article 19 is that it does not address its core – self-determination, choice and autonomy – at all.[84] The state report identifies the high levels of poverty and lack of awareness on issues that affect persons with disabilities in Kenya as the key barriers hampering the efforts towards independent living.

5. Conclusion

To facilitate the right to independent living it is necessary to remove the barriers that hinder its realisation. In the context of Kenya, these barriers stem from a combination of various factors including stigma, inaccessibility of places, services and social structures and lack of support within the community.[85]

This section clusters the recommendations towards actualising independent living for people with disabilities in Kenya into three sets. The first set of recommendations touch on the law, the second address families while the third are with regard to the Ministry of Gender, Children and Social Development under which the mandate of disability in Kenya falls. It cannot be emphasised enough how critical it is for persons with disabilities and their organisations to be involved in these reform measures.

With regard to the law, it is necessary to establish an independent living policy to

---

82 The State Report asserts that the overall disability rate in Kenya is 3.5% which translates to 1.330,312 million persons with disabilities. This is likely to be a gross underestimate in light of the World Disability Report that estimates the prevalence of disability at 15%.

83 National Coordinating Agency for Population and Development and Kenya National Bureau of Statistics, 'Kenya National Survey for Persons with Disabilities – Main Report' (2008) <http://ncpd-ke.org/researches/KNSPWD%20Main%20Report.pdf> last accessed 31 March 2016.

84 The measure for success in implementing this right would be the actual lived experience of persons with disabilities. See Council of Europe Commissioner for Human Rights, 'The Right of People with Disabilities to Live Independently and be Included in the Community' (2012) (COMM (2012) 3, 13) <https://wcd.coe.int/ViewDoc.jsp?id=1917847#P188_14524> last accessed 31 March 2016.

85 Commissioner for Human Rights, 'The Right of People with Disabilities to Live Independently and be Included in the Community' (2012) (COMM (2012) 3, 13) <https://wcd.coe.int/ViewDoc.jsp?id=1917847#P188_14524> last accessed 31 March 2016.

implement Article 19 as part of a broader agenda of implementing socio-economic rights. This is tenable as Kenya has ratified most of the international instruments that provide for economic, social and cultural rights. The Constitution of Kenya also has extensive provisions on these rights. The fulfillment of economic, social and cultural rights would go a long way towards aiding the fulfillment of the right to live independently. Second, it is urgent that the existing law be implemented: Kenya has a legal framework which, if implemented, would go a long way towards actualising independent living for persons with disabilities in Kenya.[86] Third, it is important that the measures that are being taken by the government to support persons with disabilities be anchored in law. Fourth, there are instances that call for the amendment of the law. For instance, the Mental Health Act may need to be amended to lay emphasis on community-based care instead of institutionalisation in psychiatric hospitals.[87] The PDA may also need to be amended to include sanction mechanisms for failure to implement existing laws, as well as to strengthen the monitoring mechanisms.

With regard to families, it is extremely important to build their capacity in all respects, including through providing information to combat stigma, encouraging the formation of support groups among families, as well as providing financial support to families. This is especially critical in light of the fact that the majority of persons with disabilities in Kenya live with their families.

Several interventions are required with regard to the Ministry of Gender, Children and Social Development. First, it is important that the Ministry coordinates with other relevant ministries to ensure that accurate data is availed of on persons with disabilities in Kenya, including data on education, employment and institutionalization. Second, the Ministry should pilot state-funded independent living centres in several counties with the intention of replicating them all over the country in time. Third, the Ministry should liaise with other relevant ministries to reform community-based rehabilitation to ensure that it serves the purpose for which it is meant – social inclusion. Fourth, the Ministry, through the National Council for Persons with Disabilities, must step up its awareness-raising activities. It needs to find creative ways to involve vibrant community bodies, such as churches, mosques and temples, and target actors such as police, health care workers and judicial officers. It is also necessary for the Ministry to equip the Disability Mainstreaming Committees within each ministry to function effectively. Fifth, the Ministry should find ways to partner with Disable Peoples' Organisations (DPOs). This necessity includes building the capacity of DPOs to effect change. In conclusion, these recommendations have budgetary implications, involve multiple stakeholders, and necessitate co-ordination across government ministries. Nevertheless, these measures are necessary in order to ensure that persons with disabilities participate and are included in the community.

---

86 For instance, art 54 of the Constitution of Kenya provides for inclusive education as well as for 5% employment in public service.

87 D McKenzie and I Formanek, 'Kenya's mentally ill locked up and forgotten' (2011) <http://edition.cnn.com/2011/WORLD/africa/02/25/kenya.forgotten.health/index.html> last accessed 31 March 2016.

CHAPTER 21

CONTRADICTION IN TERMS? THE UK, SOCIO-ECONOMIC RIGHTS AND ARTICLE 19 CRPD

Tabitha Collingbourne

1. INTRODUCTION

In May 2009, the United Kingdom reported to the UN Committee on Economic, Social and Cultural Rights in Geneva. At that meeting, the UK delegation confirmed that '[t]he [International Covenant on Economic, Social and Cultural Rights] has not been and is not expected to be incorporated into domestic law, (…). The Government is not convinced that it can incorporate the rights contained in the ICESCR in a meaningful way within the British legal system.[1]

Three weeks later, the UK ratified the UN Convention on the Rights of Persons with Disabilities.[2] In doing so, it undertook to 'ensure and promote the full realization of all human rights' – civil, cultural, economic, political and social – for all disabled people in the UK.[3]

This chapter explores some effects of this contradiction in terms of implementation in England of the UN Convention on the Rights of Persons with Disabilities (CRPD), taking Article 19, the right to live independently, as a case study.

2. ECONOMIC, SOCIAL AND CULTURAL RIGHTS IN THE UK

The United Kingdom has no overarching written constitution. In line with its dualist legal system, the terms of international treaties only apply directly in domestic law where they have been specifically introduced by an Act of the UK Parliament. The only human rights treaty incorporated in that way so far is the European Convention on Human Rights, which predominantly protects civil and political rights. There is thus no domestic constitutional recognition of, or protection for, economic, social and cultural rights in the UK, and they receive very little attention. Successive UK governments have viewed socio-economic rights not as 'rights', but as non-

---

1 International Covenant on Economic, Social and Cultural Rights, Fifth Periodic Report from the United Kingdom, the Crown Dependencies, the British Overseas Territories July 2007, E/C.12/GBR/5, para 74.

2 8 June 2009.

3 art 4 (1), United Nation Convention on the Rights of Persons with Disabilities (CRPD) (2006) A/RES/61/106.

justiciable guiding 'principles and objectives' to be advanced by politicians through the specific legislation, policies and programmes of the welfare state.[4]

Over the past two decades, the 'constructive dialogue' between the UK and the UN Committee on Economic, Social and Cultural Rights has become increasingly fractious. In its Concluding Observations following their 2009 meeting, the Committee, 'regrets the statement made by the State party's delegation that economic, social and cultural rights are mere principles and values and that most of the rights contained in the Covenant are not justiciable.'[5]

The Committee urges the UK to give economic, social and cultural rights full domestic legal effect, to ensure that Covenant rights are justiciable, and to provide effective remedies for breach. It strongly reminds the UK of its legal obligation to fully realise the international treaties it ratifies.

However, there seems little likelihood that the UK will change its position in the foreseeable future. This chapter argues that the lack of domestic recognition of economic, social and cultural rights leaves a fundamental imbalance in UK human rights protection which goes to the heart of CRPD implementation.

3. 'Rights' and 'Needs'

The specific laws, policies and practices, such as those relating to health, housing or social security, on which UK governments rely for meeting their international economic, social and cultural rights obligations have their roots in the 1940s welfare state. The National Assistance Act 1948 still provides the legal foundation for social care provision. It empowers local authorities to make 'welfare arrangements for blind, deaf, dumb and crippled persons;'[6] and to provide residential accommodation for people who 'by reason of age, illness, disability or any other circumstances are in need of care and attention.'[7] Throughout the many social and political developments since the 1940s, the law has kept pace incrementally rather than through radical change. Socio-economic provision generally remains a 'target duty' for the State, not a 'right' for the individual; and 'welfare' decisions are consequently difficult for an individual to challenge.

Accordingly, socio-economic rights are understood not as 'rights', inherent in all human beings, but as 'needs', to be met, or not met, by democratically elected representatives making decisions in Parliament on the allocation of scarce resources. This perspective makes (at least) two assumptions: first, that socio-economic rights (as opposed to civil and political rights) are always expensive; secondly, that it is not appropriate for judges to determine socio-economic questions. Both of these assumptions are now widely discredited. The realisation of some civil and political

4 Dr V Rangarajan, Opening Statement to UK Examination, Geneva, 12/13 May 2009, para 10.

5 Committee on Economic, Social and Cultural Rights – Concluding Observations of the Committee on Economic, Social and Cultural Rights, E/C.12/GBR/CO/5, 22 May 2009 para 13.

6 National Assistance Act 1948 s 29.

7 ibid s 21.

rights costs more than the realisation of some socio-economic rights, and vice versa.[8] And there is a growing body of case law on economic, social and cultural rights from around the world which demonstrates a positive and useful role for the judges, and which does not threaten the politicians' control of the public purse.[9] But UK governments continue to insist that such issues are to be dealt with as welfare needs.

The fundamental rationale of the CRPD, as identified by its drafters, is by contrast precisely the paradigm shift from welfare to rights.[10] In its re-description of the world, disabled people are no longer excluded recipients of welfare, but active, valued and equal rights-holders. Economic, social and cultural rights play a key part in that transformation. Far from fulfilling a 'welfare' role in compensating disabled people for their exclusion, economic, social and cultural rights take on an 'enabling' function vital to their inclusion. They allow people to take charge of their own lives, to exercise autonomy and to participate in and contribute to society. The Convention's text inextricably melds socio-economic and civil and political rights together in order to ensure the full realisation of all human rights in the context of disability. Consequently, as Flóvenz suggests, implementation of the Convention may vary from one State Party to another depending on how each State implements economic and social rights in general: 'one might come to the conclusion that in those States in which economic and social rights have not been sufficiently implemented until now, there may arise some problems in implementing the Convention as a whole.'[11]

To see whether such problems may arise in the UK, the remainder of this chapter focuses on Article 19, the right to live independently and be included in the community. The indivisibility and interdependence of all human rights in the CRPD and in people's lives is exemplified in Article 19. To live independently, to take part in the community, to have the kinds of life choices and opportunities that others take for granted, is a necessary pre-requisite for exercise of all Convention rights. Realising such civil and political rights to autonomy, choice and participation for all disabled people, however, requires availability of housing options and personal support services, as well as access to transport, education, health care, an adequate standard of living and more – it requires the realisation of economic, social and cultural rights. How these rights are realised in the domestic setting will therefore be crucial to realisation here not only of Article 19, but of the Convention as a whole.

The following sections examine in turn the policy, law and practice relating to implementation in England of Article 19(b): the provision of 'a range of in-home, residential and other community support services, including personal assistance

---

8 S Fredman, *Human Rights Transformed: Positive Rights and Positive Duties* (Oxford University Press 2008).

9 M Langford (ed), *Social Rights Jurisprudence: Emerging Trends in International and Comparative Law* (Cambridge University Press 2008).

10 See Chair of the Ad Hoc Committee, Daily Summary, Third Session, January 9, 2004, morning session; O M Arnardóttir and G Quinn (eds), *The UN Convention on the Rights of Persons with Disabilities: European and Scandinavian Perspectives* (Martinus Nijhoff Publishers 2009).

11 B Flóvenz, 'The Implementation of the UN Convention and the Development of Economic and Social Rights as Human Rights,' in O M Arnardóttir and G Quinn (eds), *The UN Convention on the Rights of Persons with Disabilities: European and Scandinavian Perspectives* (Martinus Nijhoff Publishers 2009) 260.

necessary to support living and inclusion in the community, and to prevent isolation and segregation from the community.'[12]

4. Independent Living in England

4.1. Policy

Independent living arrived on the national policy agenda in England in 2005, when the New Labour government produced a report on 'Improving the Life Chances of Disabled People.' It set out the 'ambitious vision' that 'by 2025, disabled people in Britain should have full opportunities and choices to improve their quality of life and will be respected and included as equal members of society.'[13]

The report, written with strong input from disabled people, identified four areas as central to future strategy to bring this vision about, one of which was helping disabled people to achieve independent living. A government Office for Disability Issues (ODI) set up to help implement the report has worked hard to promote independent living and to support the introduction of individual budgets and services over which people themselves have some control. The New Labour government's 'personalisation' agenda aimed to 'put people first through a radical reform'[14] of those services, essentially shifting the role of the State from controller of services towards empowering people through 'co-production' to shape their own lives and the services they receive. And it recognised the need for a holistic approach. On its face, this policy fits well with the ethos of the CRPD, and augured well for realisation of Article 19.

However, there was one strange phenomenon: there was no mention of human rights in these policy developments. They were presented not as a 'rights' agenda, but as what the government called an 'enabling welfare state'.[15] Coming from a CRPD perspective, this absence of 'rights-talk' seemed extraordinary. The New Labour government helped to draft the CRPD,[16] and said it was proud to have ratified it. One might expect it to have trumpeted the fact that it was making such good progress towards implementing the rights set out under Article 19. If, on the other hand, one considers the UK's overall refusal to acknowledge socio-economic rights as 'rights', it becomes clear that the government was caught in a bind of its own making. It could hardly trumpet these developments as rights-based whilst at the same time insisting that service provision was a non-justiciable welfare need.

---

12 art 19(b), CRPD.

13 Prime Minister's Strategy Unit, 'Improving the Life Chances of Disabled People' (2005) <www.cabinetoffice.gov.uk/strategy/work_areas/disability.aspx> last accessed 31 March 2016.

14 Local Authority Circular (Department of Health), 'Putting People first: a shared vision and commitment to the transformation of adult social care' (2008) <http://webarchive.nationalarchives.gov.uk/20130107105354/http:/www.dh.gov.uk/prod_consum_dh/groups/dh_digitalassets/@dh/@en/documents/digitalasset/dh_081119.pdf> last accessed 31 March 2016.

15 Department of Health, 'Independence, Well-Being and Choice' (Department of Health 2005) Cm6499.

16 Where, with the EU, it argued against the inclusion of art 19(b) – see United Nations DESA –Daily Summary, 6th session, 1 August 2005, morning session, and Comments, proposals and amendments, 6th session, European Union. <www.un.org/disabilities/default.asp?id=1423> last accessed 31 March 2016.

Since 2010, New Labour's 'personalisation' agenda has been enthusiastically embraced by the new Coalition government. Its 'Vision for Adult Social Care' builds on and accelerates many aspects of New Labour's 'transformation,' with continuing emphasis on individual outcomes, and personal budgets rolled out to all who qualify by 2013. The shift from State to citizen, which was welcomed by disabled people as an exercise in 'co-production' under New Labour, becomes even more radical, re-interpreted through the strongly market-orientated ideology of the new government. Services will be delivered through a 'thriving social market', facilitated by the State. Disabled people will become individual consumers and employers, stimulating market competition by making choices about how and where they spend their personal budgets, and will be responsible for their own 'welfare' outcomes. New Labour's incipient plans for a National Care Service are replaced by policies of decentralisation and free competition.[17] There is no mention here of 'rights', and little acknowledgement of central strategic accountability. While policy strongly supports individual rights to autonomy and participation through concepts of 'personalisation,' choice and control, there is marked resistance to any acknowledgement of the economic, social and cultural rights fundamental to their exercise.

4.2. Law

There is general consensus that current legislation relating to social care in England is out-dated and has become 'exceptionally tortuous,' giving rise to many difficulties in its application.[18] In 2008, whilst acknowledging that 'there is a gap between national policy and people's real experiences,' the ODI did not feel that new legislation was necessary, hoping instead that its Independent Living Strategy would 'begin to fill the gap.'[19] Unlike its predecessor, the Coalition government does intend to legislate and, at the time of writing, has brought forward a draft Social Care Bill.[20] Those debating the Bill will have two recent and contrasting precedents on which to draw: a private member's Health and Social Care (Independent Living) Bill and a review of adult social care legislation conducted by the Law Commission.

The Independent Living Bill was drafted by the (then) Disability Rights Commission, informed, in line with CRPD Article 4(3), by wide consultation with organisations of disabled people, older people and carers, some of whom came together to campaign for its adoption.[21] The Bill 'seeks to enable people with disabilities to make decisions

---

17 Open Public Services, 'Open Public Services' (2012) <www.openpublicservices.cabinetoffice.gov.uk/> last accessed 31 March 2016; Localism; Communities and Local Government, 'A plain English guide to the Localism Act – Update' (2011) <www.communities.gov.uk/publications/localgovernment/localismplainenglishupdate> last accessed 31 March 2016.

18 Law Commission, 'Law Commission Adult Social Care Scoping Report 2008' in L Clements, *Community Care and the Law* (5th edn) (Legal Action Group 2011).

19 Office for Disability Issues, 'Independent Living Strategy' (2008) <http://odi.dwp.gov.uk/docs/wor/ind/ilr-executive-report.pdf> last accessed 31 March 2016. The Coalition Government's Disability Strategy, which looks to build on the 2008 strategy, is expected shortly at the time of writing (May 2012).

20 Department of Health, 'Draft Bill to modernise adult care and support in England included in Queen's Speech' (2012) <www.dh.gov.uk/health/2012/05/draftadultcarebill/> last accessed 31 March 2016. The Bill promises to 'put people in control of their care and give them greater choice,' but at the time of writing fails to address the issue of funding.

21 RADAR the Disability Network, ''Our Lives, Our Choices' campaign, RADAR Briefing on

about what care and assistance they receive, and about their living arrangements, by providing rights and entitlements to independent living.'[22]

It was introduced to Parliament three times between 2006 and 2009, where it was supported by the House of Lords but failed to complete the Parliamentary process to become law. The Bill takes respect for and promotion of disabled people's human rights as a primary objective,[23] and demands a range of emancipatory and inclusive outcomes. Statutory duties of service providers are matched by individuals' right to independent living, including rights to information, advice and assistance, to independent advocacy, and to holistic, self-directed assessment of their requirements. The language here is not about 'needs' and 'entitlements', but about 'requirements', 'assistance' and 'support.' Coordinated national and local frameworks are put in place, with built-in involvement of disabled people and other stakeholders at all levels, and inspected and enforced by independent regulators. Whilst there is no overt acknowledgement in the Bill that the services in question are economic, social and cultural rights, there is recognition that they should be provided 'to the maximum of available resources' in line with ICESCR Article 2(1) and CRPD Article 4(2). Although the Bill was drafted well before UK ratification of the CRPD, its terms are highly consistent with the Convention's requirements.

The Law Commission consulted on its review of adult social care legislation in 2010. Its aim was to create, as far as possible, 'a neutral legal framework that is not wedded to any particular policy and is capable of accommodating different policies and practices in the future, [whilst maintaining] the core entitlements and rights that are crucial to the existing community care legal framework.'[24]

The Consultation Paper lists a number of 'general concepts with a view to considering whether they are capable of forming the basis of statutory principles.'[25] Despite UK ratification of the CRPD, none of these concepts are rights-related.[26] Consultees responded accordingly: human rights are barely mentioned, and the concept of 'independent living' as a central principle is supported only by a minority. In their place, the Law Commission recommends 'wellbeing' as the legislation's core objective. Service providers have a duty to provide information, advice and assistance to all, and 'targeted' social services to those found eligible following assessment. The nature of those services reflects the status quo. Here too, focus should be on outcomes, and the individual and their carer should be 'consulted'. However, the outcomes chosen do not include choice, control or independent living, and consultation with the individual is hedged with provisos; there is no scope for self-assessment, and no ultimate requirement that the individual agrees with the arrangements.

---

the health and Social Care (Independent Living) Bill' (2009) <www.radar.org.uk/radarwebsite/tabid/167/default.aspx> last accessed 31 March 2016.

22 Parliament UK, 'Official summary of the Bill' (2009) <http://services.parliament.uk/bills/2009-10/healthandsocialcareindependentlivinghl.html> last accessed 31 March 2016.

23 Department of Health (n 20) s 1.

24 Law Commission (n 18) para 4.

25 Law Commission (n 18) para 11.

26 They are: that decision-makers must maximise the choice and control of service users; person-centred planning; that a person's needs should be viewed broadly; the need to remove or reduce future need; the concept of independent living; an assumption of home-based living; dignity in care; the need to safeguard adults at risk from abuse and neglect.

In its response to the consultation, the Coalition Government's position appears to lie somewhere between the Law Commission's proposals and the Independent Living Bill. It categorically states that it will not enact rights-based legislation, but is not content either with the Law Commission's cautious endorsement of the status quo. In line with the Coalition's 'localism' agenda, no strategic planning provisions are to be included in the statute. Instead, the focus is on individual autonomy and freedom to make choices, and regulation by market forces. However, the Government's response also incorporates – at individual though not at strategic level – elements of New Labour's (and disabled people's) discourse of co-production; understandings of the holistic nature of independent living; and recognition that service provision is about 'doing things with, not for, or to' disabled people. Again, there is no mention of the CRPD or of Article 19 in the government's response to the Law Commission – along with economic, social and cultural rights more generally, they remain invisible.

4.3. Practice

Coming to the 'practices' on which the UK relies for implementation of its international economic, social and cultural rights obligations, the 'personalisation' of public services – that shift of power from state towards individual which, as we have seen, has intensified under the new government – demands massive cultural, institutional and administrative change. The New Labour government invested in local government to try to bring about that change.[27] However, eligibility for services remained so tightly restricted that only those with substantial or critical needs would qualify,[28] leaving many without support and with an 'overwhelmingly poor'[29] quality of life; and leading Jane Campbell to identify levels of social care rationing as 'the major problem which blocks the transformation of social care from a welfare safety net to an empowering human rights, public support service.'[30]

Since then the Coalition government has responded to the global economic crisis by instigating deep public funding cuts in order to cut national borrowing.[31] Local authorities have shouldered real term reductions in funding of 28% over four years.[32] Although some new social care funding has been provided to counteract these cuts,[33] it will be insufficient to meet projected need,[34] and is not ring-fenced,[35] leaving local authorities free to cut their social care budgets in real terms in the face of overall

---

27 Local Authority Circular (n 14).

28 Immediately before the 2010 Spending Review, 72% of councils provided services only to those falling into the substantial or critical bands, with 3% meeting critical needs only.

29 Commission for Social Care Inspection, 'Report: Lost to the System? (Executive Summary)' (2008) para 32.

30 J Campbell, 'Social Care as an Equality and Human Rights Issue' *Independently Newsletter* (National Centre for Independent Living February 2008) 9.

31 Local Government Association, 'Briefing: The Spending Review 2010' (2010) <www.lga.gov.uk/lga/aio/14462985> last accessed 31 March 2016.

32 ibid. Tapering from £28.5bn in 2010–11 to £22.9bn in 2014–15; compared with cuts of 8.3% overall across all department budgets.

33 £1.5bn over four years, with a further £1bn to be transferred from the NHS to support joint working.

34 ibid. According to the Local Government Association, this additional funding will be insufficient to meet an estimated rise in the annual cost of adult social care by 2014–15 of around £6bn.

35 ibid. See also Dilnot Commission, 'Report: Fairer Care Funding' (2011) <www.dilnotcommission.dh.gov.uk/2011/07/04/commission-report/> last accessed 31 March 2016.

budgetary pressures; and some have done so,[36] reducing eligibility for services to those in critical need only.[37]

The combination of fast-changing 'transformative' policy agendas with severe and unpredicted funding restriction has left the administration of service provision under considerable strain.[38] Nevertheless, it is at this level that the vast majority of disabled people experience the decisions and interactions that affect their daily lives. And it is here also that some of the greatest barriers to the transition from welfare to rights are found. In this climate, whilst some emancipatory outcomes may still arise, for many individuals the experience of assessment remains oppressive rather than supportive, with risk of reversal rather than maintenance or improvement in any progress in the achievement of independent living. As the Joint Committee on Human Rights has identified, when such reductions in eligibility for services coincide with current restrictions in financial support, 'there seems to be a significant risk of retrogression of independent living and a breach of the UK's Article 19 obligations.'[39]

Where individuals seek to challenge Article 19(b) decisions, they must exhaust an internal complaints procedure before applying to the court for judicial review, or complaining to the Ombudsman. All of these processes focus not on the substance of the decision itself, but on decision-making procedure: they are not a 'right of appeal'. In the courts, common law precedent[40] has established that, beyond a 'core minimum' of provision, resources may be taken into account in decision-making, effectively reducing any incipient individual 'right' to services[41] to a discretionary power on the part of the provider. Introduction of the Human Rights Act in 2000 prompted some judges to interpret Strasbourg jurisprudence expansively in line with Article 19 requirements, particularly in relation to ECHR Article 8 rights to suitably adapted accommodation, dignity and participation.[42] However, such expansion was swiftly reversed, with imposition of a higher bar to engagement of Article 8 than that imposed in Strasbourg.[43] The work of the Ombudsmen provides potentially more promising developments. Whilst distancing themselves from court-based law enforcement, they seek to 'give force to' human rights standards

36 See *R (on the application of W) v Birmingham City Council; R (on the application of M, G and H) v Birmingham City Council* [2011] EWHC 1147 (Admin).

37 Department of Health, 'Fair Access to Care Services: Guidance on Eligibility Criteria for Adult Social Care' (2003) www.dh.gov.uk/en/Publicationsandstatistics/Publications/PublicationsPolicyAndGuidance/DH_4009653 last accessed 31 March 2016. The 'critical' band includes where life is at risk, or there is great risk of serious illness or harm; Department of Health, 'Prioritising Need in the context of Putting People First: A Whole System Approach to Eligibility for Social Care' (2010) <www.dh.gov.uk/en/Publicationsandstatistics/Publications/PublicationsPolicyAndGuidance/DH_113154> last accessed 31 March 2016.

38 See British Broadcasting Coperation, 'England social care 'underfunded and in crisis'' (2012) <www.bbc.co.uk/news/health-17987724> last accessed 31 March 2016.

39 Joint Committee on Human Rights, 'Implementation of the Rights of Disabled People to Independent Living' (Twenty-Third Report of Session 2010–2012) HL paper 257, HC1074, 50.

40 *R v Gloucestershire County Council ex p Barry* [1997] 2 All ER 1 (HL).

41 Chronically Sick and Disabled Persons Act 1970, s 2.

42 *R (on the application of Bernard and another) v Enfield* London Borough Council [2002] All ER (D) 383; *R (A, B, X & Y) v East Sussex County Council (No 2)* [2003] EWHC 167 (Admin).

43 *Anufrijeva v Southwark London Borough Council* [2004] QB 1124; J A King, 'United Kingdom: Asserting Social Rights in a Multi-layered System' in Malcolm Langford (ed), *Social Rights Jurisprudence: Emerging Trends in International and Comparative Law* (Cambridge University Press 2008) 288.

and principles, including (though not overtly) those underlying the progressive realisation of economic, social and cultural rights.[44] However, such promise is not without its challenges, including reliance on exhaustion of internal complaints procedures, resource constraints, lack of visibility and lack of statutory recognition of the Ombudsmen's constitutional role in the administrative justice system, or in the implementation of all human rights. Systems for redress thus offer at best a tortuous, exhausting and potentially frustrating means of challenging failure in the provision of the in-home, residential and other community support services required under CRPD Article 19(b).

Examination of implementation in England of the economic, social and cultural rights set out in Article 19(b) through policy, law and practice reveals endemic failure to acknowledge their basis in human rights law. In the absence of that legal and normative framework, policy efforts to implement Article 19 civil and political rights to autonomy, choice and control through 'personalisation' remain hostage to ideological re-interpretation and to economic restructuring of the socio-economic support systems required for their exercise, with no protection against regression. The opportunity to replace welfare-based statute with rights-based legislation in line with CRPD Article 4(1)(a) is side-stepped; tight eligibility criteria continue to leave many without support; and redress systems reflect rather than challenge dominant exclusionary understandings.

5. Conclusion

The UK maintains that it 'will not ratify a treaty unless the Government is satisfied that domestic law and practice enable it to comply.'[45] The UK has ratified the CRPD. The UK concurrently resists incorporation of economic, social and cultural rights into UK law. This chapter has argued that that contradiction in terms is simply not tenable, and that the resulting imbalance in domestic human rights protection impedes realisation of CRPD rights.

The CRPD demands a fundamental transformation in thinking from 'welfare' to 'rights'.[46] To enable the realisation in people's lives of that transformation, the Convention fully integrates civil, cultural, economic, political and social rights to the extent that they become equally important and truly indivisible. But the UK does not recognise or protect economic, social and cultural rights, seeing them not as 'rights', but as guiding 'principles and objectives.'[47] It already fails to comply.

The UK then argues that it implements these socio-economic 'principles and values' through the domestic policy, legislation and practice of its welfare state. On investigation, this chapter has found that, in England, such policy, legislation and practice relating to CRPD Article 19(b) still have their roots in the 1940s welfare

---

44 A Abraham, 'The Ombudsman and the Executive: the Road to Accountability' (2008) 61 Parliamentary Affairs (3) 535.

45 Ministry of Justice, 'UK National Report to UN Universal Periodic Review' (Geneva 2008).

46 United Nations, *From Exclusion to Equality: Realizing the Rights of Persons with Disabilities, Handbook for Parliamentarians* (2007) <www.un.org/disabilities/default.asp?id=150> 25/05/12.

47 Dr Vijay Rangarajan, 'Opening Statement to UK Examination' (12/13 May 2009) para 10.

state; that socio-economic rights are seen not as rights but as 'welfare needs' – an understanding likely to continue to be reflected in forthcoming legislation; and that even where policy does attempt to bring about a transformative shift in power from the State towards the individual, this is not acknowledged as rights-related, and is negated in practice by increasingly severe rationing and ineffective administrative redress systems.

In 2009, the UN Economic, Social and Cultural Rights Committee strongly reminded the UK of its legal obligation to fully realise the international treaties it ratifies, and to give economic, social and cultural rights full domestic legal effect, to ensure that Covenant rights are justiciable, and to provide effective remedies for breach. In the field of independent living in England, this chapter argues that the UK is not meeting those obligations. That failure impacts on implementation of CRPD Article 19: the right to live independently and be included in the community is meaningless without access to the range of housing options and personal support services required to realise it in practice. Furthermore, realisation in practice of Article 19 is a pre-requisite for the exercise of other Convention rights. Failure in its implementation calls into question the UK's undertaking on ratifying the CRPD to ensure and promote the full realisation of all human rights for all disabled people in its jurisdiction.[48]

As Flóvenz suggests, 'in those States in which economic and social rights have not been sufficiently implemented until now, there may,' indeed, 'arise some problems in implementing the Convention as a whole.'[49]

---

48 art 4(1), CRPD.

49 Flóvenz (n 11).

Chapter 22

SELF-DETERMINING OPTIONS: COMPARATIVE PERSPECTIVES IN INDEPENDENT LIVING LAW & POLICY

Andrew Power

1. Introduction

The adoption of the Convention on the Rights of Persons with Disabilities (CRPD)[1] by the United Nations (UN) General Assembly in 2006 marks the culmination of many years of work within the UN system to place disability rights on the international agenda. At the same time, the adoption of the CRPD is serving as an impetus for disability law and policy reform at domestic level.[2] In particular, the CRPD is directed towards enabling independence and full participation within the community for persons with disabilities. In this regard it signals a decisive break from historical practices, and indeed many earlier international documents on disability.[3] The thrust turns away from passive, paternalistic approaches that tended to privilege medical care and rehabilitation towards self-determination and independent living. Through its general principles and specific substantive obligations, the CRPD defines a framework which affirms that States Parties must 'recognize the equal right of all persons with disabilities to live in the community, with choices equal to others', and that they shall 'take effective and appropriate measures to facilitate full enjoyment by persons with disabilities of this right and their full inclusion and participation in the community.'[4]

---

1 UN Convention on the Rights of Persons with Disabilities (2006), G.A Res. 61/106, U.N Doc. A/61/611 (Dec 13, 2006), opened for signature 30 March 2007. An Optional Protocol providing for additional monitoring mechanisms was adopted at the same time. Optional Protocol to the Convention on the Rights of Persons with Disabilities, opened for signature 30 March 2007, (Optional Protocol).

2 See generally J E Lord and M A Stein, 'The Domestic Incorporation of Human Rights Law and the United Nations Convention on the Rights of Persons with Disabilities' (2008) 83 Washington University Law Review 449.

3 The first international instruments specifically addressing persons with disabilities included the adoption of the Declaration on the Rights of Mentally Retarded Persons followed by the Declaration on the Rights of Disabled Persons. While the adoption of these instruments certainly reflected an important development in terms of placing disability on the international agenda, these were non-binding and they did little to shape national law and policy and had no monitoring and implementation measures to facilitate national action. Moreover, they did not fully reflect – and in some cases diverged from – existing human rights principles as they tended to underscore passivity and dependence which underscored the ethos of welfare policy at the time.

4 UN Convention on the Rights of Persons with Disabilities (2006) A/RES/61/106, art 19.

At its core, these guiding principles are encapsulated by the philosophy of personalisation which focuses on a move away from passive, paternalistic provision of services *for* persons with disabilities, and an embrace of legal capacity and self-directed supports to promote and facilitate agency and self-determination.[5] The theoretical underpinnings behind personalisation and the model of self-directed supports emerged from a rejection of the assumption that persons with disabilities are unable to make life choices and determine what is best for them. In contrast, the independent living movement demands control and choice in everyday life as a human and civil right for people with disabilities,[6] and so embraces the full range of action to achieve those rights.[7]

Reinforcing these principles at the national level are a range of self-directed support mechanisms comprising individual funding packages that facilitate consumer control over choices about how disability support funds are spent. Funds are held by the person or their family, a facilitator or service provider, are portable between service providers or facilitators when the person chooses, and can generally be used to buy support from service providers or in an open market.[8]

In particular, the mechanism of self-directed supports through the use of individual funding is becoming a growing policy interest in Europe and North America and is emerging in various forms, demonstrating a continuum of approaches with varying levels of control and choice for the person.[9] Evaluations by both state[10] and independent third parties[11] have revealed that self-directed support can enhance choice, control and flexibility, when compared with conventional service provision. Sapey also suggests that Direct Payments, one form of individual funding, are an important means of challenging the 'culture of welfare' across social service departments.[12] For many, it is simply a pragmatic shift in the funding and management of support, with, in particular, the possibilities for independent living created by employing a personal assistant. For many disability organisations,

---

5 The United Nations High Commissioner for Human Rights emphasised this shift to a rights-oriented perspective on the adoption of the CRPD in December 2006. See United Nations High Commissioner for Human Rights, Statement by United Nations High Commissioner for Human Rights on Convention on Rights of Persons with Disabilities, delivered at the adoption of the convention in December 2006 (New York, December 6 2006) <www.ohchr.org/English/issues/disability/docs/statementhcdec06.doc> last accessed 31 March 2016 (noting that the CRPD dismisses the understanding of persons with disabilities as 'objects of charity, medical treatment and social protection' and instead reaffirms that persons with disabilities are 'subjects of rights, able to claim those rights as active members of society.').

6 A Ratzka, Independent Living: A Personal Definition (Independent Living Institute, 2003) <www.independentliving.org/def.html> last accessed 31 March 2016.

7 J Morris, *Independent Lives? Community Care and Disabled People* (Macmillan 1993).

8 S Riddell, C Pearson, D Jolly, C Barnes, M Priestley, and G Mercer, 'The Development of Direct Payments in the UK: Implications for social justice' (2005) 4(1) *Social Policy and Society* 75.

9 See A Power, *Active Citizenship and Disability: Towards the Personalisation of support* (Cambridge University Press, forthcoming). Department of Health, *Putting people first: a shared vision and commitment to the transformation of adult social care* (DOH 2007).

10 eg Individual Budgets Evaluation Network (IBSEN), *Evaluation of the Individual Budgets Pilot Programme* (Social Policy Research Unit, University of York 2008).

11 G Zarb and P Nadash, *Cashing in on Independence: Counting the costs and benefits of cash and services* (The British Council of Organisation of Disabled People (BCODP) 1994).

12 B Sapey 'Independent successes: implementing direct payments [review]' (2001) 31(3) British Journal of Social Work 506.

it has been heralded as much more than this: a key goal of the independent living movement and a 'potentially revolutionary' redistribution of power.[13]

Using examples from British Columbia (BC) in Canada, England, and Sweden, this chapter explores how these self-directed support models have been evolving and the extent to which they animate or otherwise the general principles of independent living put forth by the CRPD. After assessing how these different jurisdictions have implemented these options, the chapter subsequently explores the common challenges which each of these jurisdictions are facing in fully realising the expectations and obligations of rights enshrined in the Convention.

2. The Evolution of Personalisation at the Domestic Level

As noted, international human rights standards are designed to be implemented at the domestic level.[14] Ratifying states (as well as regional integration organisations such as the EU[15]) are expected to give legal effect to assumed treaty obligations and the CRPD sets forth general parameters for implementation at the domestic level.[16] In particular, given the CRPD's core focus on independent living, effective monitoring of a nation's commitment to the Convention's obligations hinges on the acknowledgement that social rights and supports are 'in the service' of a life in the community.

Many of the ratifying states have in various ways led the way in developing new initiatives for supporting people with disabilities towards this goal. In particular, BC, England and Sweden over the last 20 years have focused on demand-side reforms, which are particularly important in animating the principles of personalisation inherent in the Convention. One of the key demand-side reforms as identified has been the new individualised funding options, which seek to assist people to be in control of their *disability*-related support.[17] The comparative examples below explore how these pioneering models have evolved.

Firstly, signalling its commitment to these principles, Canada ratified the CRPD on March 11, 2010, on the eve of the Paralympic Games in Vancouver, imposing a fundamental shift from pastoral care towards integration of people with disabilities. Canada's ratification comes on the back of a strong history of human rights, evident from the Canadian Charter of Human Rights and Freedoms which was incorporated

---

13 E Hall 'Shopping for support: personalisation and the new spaces and relations of commodified care for people with learning disabilities' (2011) 12(6) *Social and Cultural Geography* 589; J Glasby and R Littlechild, *Social Work and Direct Payments* (Policy Press 2002).

14 T Buergenthal, D Shelton and D Stewart, *International Human Rights* (2nd edn, West Publishing Co. 2002).

15 The CRPD has been signed, and the decision taken to conclude it, by the European Community (EC) under the EC Treaty.

16 In order for a treaty to have domestic legal effect, an act of government is frequently required whereby the treaty norm is incorporated into its domestic law. Such legal systems are considered 'dualist' in nature, in contrast with monist systems where the State's legal system is considered to include international treaties without the need for separate, domestic-level action.

17 C Barnes and G Mercer (eds), *Disability Policy and Practice: Applying the Social Model* (The Disability Press 2004).

in 1985.[18] Alongside this there has been a steady commitment to deinstitutionalise persons with disabilities with BC, which closed all its institutions in 1996, and to refocus social policy on removing barriers to employment. In addition, the province has introduced the option of individual funding to enable people to have more choice in the supports they require to enable them to live independently.

Since 1990, self-managed support has slowly become a core part of the disability reform agenda in BC. A new programme called 'Choices for Support in Independent Living' (CSIL) was piloted in 1990 and became a permanent programme in 1993. It is funded by BC's Ministry of Health and provides direct funding to individuals (excluding children) with physical disabilities and individuals with both developmental and physical disabilities. The programme has two phases: Phase One is for individuals who are considered mentally capable of self-managing their support. Consumers receive funds directly and assume full responsibility for the hiring and training of personal attendants, and all payroll responsibilities of an employer. Phase Two is for those who are not considered mentally capable of managing their own support. In order to receive funding, consumers must form a support group including at least five members, and they must register as a non-profit society though the BC Society Act 1996[19] to receive funds on behalf of the individual. There are no restrictions as to who can be in the consumer support group, although family members are recommended.[20] In both phases, a case manager determines the amount of funding an individual is eligible for and the funds are administered by the Regional Health Authority. The funding is for a personal assistant only and cannot be used to purchase other goods or services such as equipment.

Since CSIL, the crown corporation for intellectual disability, Community Living British Columbia (CLBC), from its foundation in 2005 has introduced a choice of two individualised funding options: Direct Funding or Host Agency Funding. Direct Funding is paid directly to an individual or his/her agent (family member or representative) for the purchase of supports and services. Meanwhile, the Host Agency Funding is allocated to a support agency that administers the funds and works with the individual and family to arrange and manage the supports required. This option provides the benefits of individualised funding, but with less responsibility for the individual and family.

Some evaluations have shown that self-managed programmes have the potential to

---

18 The Charter includes a number of important fundamental rights relevant to self-determination. Chapter I (Fundamental Freedoms And Rights) includes '[e]very human being has a right to freedom' including 'freedom of expression,' 'a right to the safeguard of his dignity, honour and reputation,' and 'a right to respect for his private life.' Moreover, Chapter I.1 states every person has 'a right to full and equal recognition and exercise of his human rights and freedoms, without distinction, exclusion or preference based on (amongst other distinctions) a handicap or the use of any means to palliate a handicap.'

19 Refer to British Columbia Society Act 1996 <www.bclaws.ca/EPLibraries/bclaws_new/document/ID/freeside/00_96433_01> last accessed 31 March 2016.

20 Many who choose this self-managed support option in BC manages the budget through the Vela Microboard Association, a non-profit organisation which assists individuals with disabilities (excluding children) to develop 'microboards' to access government funding for support and to manage it on behalf of a particular individual. Refer to CSIL website: <www.health.gov.bc.ca/hcc/csil.html> last accessed 31 March 2016.

produce cost efficiencies[21] since individuals requiring support are generally better qualified to understand their own needs and to find ways of meeting them within available resources. In turn, some evidence suggests that their choices as consumers can help drive providers to be more responsive and to achieve innovations in support delivery.[22]

These models mirror what has been happening in England, where 'choice' is a central guiding principle in the design of support systems, as set out by the Independent Living Strategy.[23] The UK ratified the CRPD and the Optional Protocol in June 2009 (albeit with some general reservations) requiring the government to take action to remove barriers and give disabled people real freedom, dignity and equality.

The Independent Living Fund (ILF) was the first practical means through which individual funds could be allocated for the purchase of supports.[24] While it originally was envisaged to run for five years, there were a number of extension funds created to administer the payments of people beyond the original time frame. However, in December 2010, the Minister for Disabled People announced that the ILF was to be permanently closed to new applications.

Nonetheless, throughout the lifecourse of the ILF, there were a number of councils which began operating a number of 'work-around' indirect payment schemes in the early 1990s. Originally, direct payments (cash payments to individuals in lieu of services) were deemed illegal under the 1948 Social Security Act; however, these indirect payments enabled councils to give money to local Centres for Independent Living so they could support persons individually through the use of personal assistants. This developed organically in places where alliances had been developed between disabled people and helpful professionals and managers who began to question the model of institutional services, which did not fit with their philosophy of self-determination.

Meanwhile, an influential research report demonstrating the cost effectiveness of direct payments by Zarb and Nadash on behalf of The British Council of Organisations of Disabled People (BCODP) was published.[25] Having resisted individual funding for many years, due to fears over accountability and the previous legislation prohibiting it, this report led to the acceptance of direct payments as a future policy option.[26, 27]

---

21 J M Prince, S Manley and G G Whiteneck, 'Self-managed versus agency-provided personal assistance care for individuals with high level tetraplegia' (1995) 76 *Archives of Physical Medicine and Rehabilitation* 919.

22 K Spalding, J R Watkins and A P Williams, *Self-Managed Care Programs in Canada: A Report to Health Canada* (Health Canada June 2006).

23 HM Government Office for Disability Issues, *Independent Living Strategy* (HM Government 2008).

24 <www.dwp.gov.uk/ilf/about-ilf/> last accessed 31 March 2016.

25 G Zarb and P Nadash (n 11).

26 See also Department of Health, *Direct Payments Guidance: Community Care, Services for Carers and Children's Services (Direct Payments) Guidance England 2003* (Department of Health 2003).

27 For a more detailed account, please refer to: S Riddell, C Pearson, D Jolly, C Barnes, M Priestley, and G Mercer, 'The development of Direct Payments in the UK: Implications for social justice' (2005) 4 Social Policy and Society (1) 75.

The resulting Community Care (Direct Payments) Act 1996 enabled local authorities responsible for community care services to make payments to persons in respect of their securing the provision of such services and for connected purposes. 'Direct payments' are cash payments given to persons with disabilities in lieu of community care services they have been assessed as needing, and are intended to give them greater choice in their support. Direct payments confer responsibilities on recipients to employ people or commission services for themselves. Unlike other jurisdictions, which offer independent facilitation, such as some states in the US (eg Wisconsin, Michigan),[28] individuals or their representatives must take on all the responsibilities of an employer, such as payroll, meeting minimum wage and other legislative requirements. Some of these services can be contracted out and many councils have commissioned support organisations (eg Centres for Independent Living) to help service users handle these responsibilities.

Similar to Canada, a second option, 'personal budgets', evolved out of the need for a more suitable model for persons with intellectual disabilities. They were initially piloted by a charity called In Control,[29] who designed a Resource Allocation System (RAS) to create an individualised budget tool that operates within existing community care legislation and eligibility rates.[30] They are regarded as a broader allocation of funding to either pay for personal assistants or a wider array of supports. People can choose to receive them as a direct payment like above, or – while still choosing how their support needs are met and by whom – leave local councils with the responsibility to commission the services (or some combination of the two). People often choose to use them as an 'Individual Service Fund (ISF)' where a support provider ring-fences personal budgets for individual clients.[31] As a result, personal budgets provide a potentially good option for people who do not want to take on the responsibilities of a direct payment.

The process of expanding individual funding was bolstered by a major government piloting of personal budgets[32] and a subsequent commitment to this delivery model by the New Labour Prime Minister's Strategy Unit,[33] and various White Papers.[34] This

---

28 For a detailed discussion of self-directed support models in Wisconsin and Michigan, see Campaign for Real Choice Illinois, 'Understanding Self-Direction for People with Developmental Disabilities: A Choice for Change in Illinois' (2011) <http://realchoiceinillinois.org/documents/Self-Direction%20Research%20Paper_Final.pdf> last accessed 31 March 2016.

29 In Control, 'About Us' (2011) <www.in-control.org.uk/about-us.aspx> last accessed 31 March 2016.

30 In Control is working with subscribing authorities and central government to develop the best possible system to meet the government's goal of expanding personal budgets.

31 ISFs have the following common characteristics: the budget is held by the provider on behalf of the individual, the support plan is the key driving document behind the provider/the person's relationship, the individual is in control of how the money is spent. I deleted this as the reference is no longer available and the author does not have the dul citation

32 This involved the piloting of Individual Budgets which cover a multitude of funding streams, in addition to adult social care, including Supporting People, Disabled Facilities Grant, Independent Living Fund, Access to Work and community-equipment services. They can cover a wider array of supports in a person's life, bundled together in a single support package. The government has only piloted individual budgets, and has so far not called for their full implementation.

33 Prime Minister's Strategy Unit, *Report to Transform the Life Chances of Disabled People* (Office of the Deputy Prime Minister 2005).

34 Department of Health, *Our Health, Our Care, Our Say: Making It Happen* (Department of Health 2006); Department of Health, *Valuing People Now* (Department of Health 2007).

policy evolution has so far culminated with the Department of Health Concordat, Putting People First in 2008 calling on councils to significantly increase the number of people receiving individual funding.[35] The government currently envisages that all users of adult social care should have a personal budget from which to pay for their support services, apart from in emergencies, by Spring 2013.[36] It has been described as 'a massive cultural sledgehammer', by a Department of Health manager, redefining the entire context of social services.[37]

Finally, in Sweden, in pursuit of its fundamental goal of promoting independent living, the CRPD and Optional Protocol was ratified on 30 December 2008 and as a result has committed itself to ensuring that its policy goals remain faithful to the Convention's guiding principles. Sweden has implemented civil rights legislation for support and personal assistance called the 'Act on support and service for certain individuals with disabilities' (LSS) (1993). Through the creation of LSS, persons with disabilities are entitled to ten different kinds of social services[38] including personal assistance as a civil right. Independent living is unquestionably the philosophy behind the right to personal assistance in these reforms.[39] On the whole, this philosophy is mirrored in the national action plan, From Patient to Citizen, which fully embodies the vision of a society designed to allow disabled persons of all ages full participation in all aspects of life in the community.[40]

People with disabilities are entitled to access personal assistants (PAs) through the use of individual funding. The direct payment model of personal assistance was first instigated by User Cooperatives,[41] led by the Stockholm Cooperative for Independent Living (STIL) in 1987.[42] Following their pilot, STIL provided direct payments after reaching agreements with a number of municipalities in the Stockholm area. STIL's purpose was to show that personal assistance based on a direct payment system is cheaper and produces higher quality support than the residential homes provided by local authorities. Despite original opposition from the political left and the unions who, according to Berg, had a political interest in keeping the collective system of state-owned welfare, several new cooperatives in Stockholm and other parts of the country began adopting STIL's approach.[43]

---

35 This document is the Department of Health Concordat published with the Local Government Association (LGA), the Association of Directors of Adult Social Services (ADASS), the NHS and others.

36 M Routledge and J Lewis, *Personal Budgets: Taking Stock, Moving Forward* (Think Local, Act Personal Partnership 2011).

37 Interview with Department of Health manager (telephone interview, 15 July 2010).

38 SFS 1993:387, *Lag om stöd och service till vissa funktionshindrade*. Notisum (*Support and Service Act*) Section 9.

39 S Berg, *Personal Assistance in Sweden*. (Independent Living Institute 2003) <www.independentliving.org/docs6/berg20030520.html> last accessed 31 March 2016.

40 Prop. 1999/2000:79,, *From Patient to Citizen – The National Disability Action Plan* <www.regeringen.se/content/1/c4/14/78/e9da3800.pdf> last accessed 31 March 2016.

41 Cooperatives have a long and proud tradition in Sweden started by the labour movement, particularly economic cooperatives such as building societies, credit unions, funeral societies or food chains. However, they have a broader goal than economic activity; they have a general interest in human enhancement and the social integration of citizens. In short, they mean an organised cooperation of citizens – with a broad goal of improving the social economy.

42 From the outset, STIL was organised as a cooperative, and consequently was able to get political support and free technical assistance from the Swedish cooperative movement.

43 A Ratzka, 'Kort presentation av STIL' (1993) <www.independentliving.org/docs3/stil1993.html#14> last accessed 31 March 2016; S Berg, 'Personal Assistance Reforms in Sweden:

Following the successes of these direct payment initiatives, the Swedish government made a clear commitment to freedom of choice and integrity, and greater control over one's own life within their disability policy.[44] This was in contrast to the way in which social services were historically administered in Sweden; with an emphasis on 'care' and organised on communitarian ideals.[45]

Since these reforms, Sweden's choice of individual funding options is extensive; disability personal support can be organised through self-management, private agencies, and cooperatives, or provided through the municipality.[46] The municipality covers the first 20 hours of assistance and the state pays the hours granted which exceed 20 hours per week. The amount covering the agreed hours[47] is paid to the individual using personal assistance or to the administrator chosen by the individual.

Each of the three jurisdictions identified have made an important contribution to the global development of personalisation for people with disabilities. They are amongst the first nations to enable free choice in terms of personal assistance and use of social support funding, as part of a broader ongoing project to move away from welfare and congregated services to independent living and human rights.

Offering self-directed supports underpinned by individual funding is a radical shift in terms of how welfare and social policy is imagined. The employment of personal assistants, and specifically using direct payments for this purpose, is regarded by disability studies scholars as a key issue for those promoting 'independent living'[48] because, without it, disabled people who need help with everyday life activities, risk segregation and institutionalisation.[49] At the domestic scale, this model according to the UK Department of Health, 'is about *whole system change*, not about change at the margins.'[50] To enable this to happen, the reform of disability support requires a strategically planned, fundamental re-organisation of the old social care system.

While these policy options have been evolving throughout the decades preceding the CRPD, the philosophy underpinning these options nonetheless closely aligns with the idea of individual self-determination, a term used frequently within the context of the CRPD negotiations.[51] Indeed, the different jurisdictions discussed in

---

breaking the assumption of dependency?' in C Barnes and G Mercer (eds), *The Social Model of Disability: Europe and the Majority World* (The Disability Press 2005).

44 Prop. 1992/93:159, *Stöd och service till vissa funktionshindrade* Stockholm: Allmänna förlaget (*Support and service to persons with certain functional impairments*).

45 S Berg (n 46).

46 C Laragy, *Interview with Jämlikhet Assistans Gemenskap (Equality, Assistance, and Community)* (Unpublished manuscript, Sweden 2006).

47 The Swedish State sets out a standard hourly amount of the assistance benefit: €28 in 2010, of which 87% has to be used for salaries, bonuses for unsocial working hours, holiday pay, salary taxes, social fees and retirement insurance contributions. The remaining 13% is to cover the other costs due to the provision of personal assistance: administration, training of the assistant, costs of the assistant and costs associated with the work place.

48 J Morris (n 7).

49 M Oliver, *The Politics of Disablement* (Macmillan 1990); C Barnes, *Disabled People in Britain and Discrimination* (Hurst and Co., in association with British Council of Organisation of Disabled People 1991).

50 Department of Health, *Transforming Social Care* (Local Authority Circular 2008).

51 The term 'individual autonomy' was preferred, apparently because the concept of self-determination under international law carries with it a particular meaning – the idea of group

this chapter played leading roles in negotiating the UNCRPD and as identified, were in a position to ratify it. The theoretical underpinnings behind the self-determination philosophy encompasses the overall thrust of the CRPD, as articulated by the first enumerated general principle of Article 3; 'respect for inherent dignity, individual autonomy including the freedom to make one's own choices, and independence of persons.'[52] Clearly, the right to choice inherent in self-directed support, albeit not being a right to independent living per se, nonetheless makes a decisive step toward animating the general principles of independent living put forth by the CRPD. While the CRPD provides an impetus to States Parties of what ought to be done, the above examples serve to illustrate some of the potential ways reform at the domestic level can be done.

3. Challenges Ahead

Despite the successes identified above there exist a number of challenges, which to varying extents each of the comparative jurisdictions now face. Ultimately, with this new paradigm, persons with disabilities are being asked to take on greater responsibilities in managing their own support. The success of direct payments and personal budgets hinges on the ability and willingness of individuals and families to opt for this model, given the personal responsibilities involved. With support brokerage still in its infancy, particularly in many parts of England, there is still some reluctance by some groups of people with disabilities to use this model.[53] Analysis from an Economic and Social Research Council study has shown that support schemes (which help people to manage their direct payment) undoubtedly have a positive effect on numbers taking up direct payments.[54] Thus the lack of comprehensive support remains a barrier to its take-up. Consequently, self-directed support still remains a distant option for many persons with disabilities who continue to receive support and care from conventional group services.

Meanwhile, it is clear from commentators that within the paradigm of personalisation, safeguards will need to be in place to ensure that a sole focus on individualised support does not lead to a neglect of issues relevant to community connection, such as promoting good mental health, tackling isolation and fostering support networks.[55]

---

self-determination. The literature on the self-determination of peoples, springs principally from art 1 of both the International Covenant on Civil and Political Rights and the International Covenant on Economic, Social and Cultural Rights which provide that 'all peoples have the right to self-determination.' See generally A Cassesse, *Self-Determination of Peoples* (Cambridge University Press 1995); J Crawford (ed), *The Rights of Peoples* (Clarendon Press 1988); P Thornberry, 'Self-determination, minorities, human rights: A review of international instruments' (1989) 38 *International and Comparative Law Quarterly* 867.

52 Art 3(a) CRPD.

53 Individual Budgets Evaluation Network (IBSEN), *Evaluation of the Individual Budgets Pilot Programme* (Social Policy Research Unit, University of York 2008).

54 A Carmichael and L Brown, 'The future challenge for Direct Payments' (2002) 17 Disability and Society (1) 797.

55 P Beresford, J Fleming, M Glynn, C Bewley, S Croft, F Branfield and K Postle, *Supporting people: Towards a person-centred approach* (The Policy Press 2011); See also P Beresford, 'Are personal budgets really the way ahead for social care?' *The Guardian* (London, 17 January 2012).

At present, the social care systems operate in a context that itself creates tensions between individual choice and collective planning.

Safeguards are also required given the concerns about direct payments potentially driving down the cost of support and deregulating the employment rights for directly employed personal assistants.[56] In particular, there are concerns that a sole focus on direct payments without the necessary safeguard could potentially disempower the predominantly female support workforce and in the end destroy the quality of services provided.[57]

Given the significant shift in control of power and resources inherent in this model, full implementation is likely to take time, given the range of professionals involved. At times, traditions still act as a barrier. According to Stainton, structural conflicts of interest in relation to social workers' roles within the community care system will continue to be a source of resistance.[58] The governments in each jurisdiction are therefore attempting to build confidence and capacity in the service sector and provide a roadmap for the transformation of adult social support.[59] The implementation of this policy will be crucial to its future development.

More broadly, the effects of devolution and decentralisation on implementation of the CRPD poses a significant barrier to the full realisation of the right to independent living, given the extent of variations in the manner in which regional and local authorities implement national law and policy. In Sweden, for example, the sovereignty of municipalities still presents many barriers to the full implementation of LSS, and the continual battle with municip.lities not accepting the duties in the legislation is evidenced by continual enquiries proposing changes to the law.[60] Similarly, in England, recent restrictions in local authority eligibility criteria for social care support are evident and are posing a risk to the support persons with disabilities need to live independently.[61] Consequently, the devolution of such government decision-making has implications for the role played by the CRPD in policy development. There is often reluctance to invoke the role of the national governments in ensuring implementation of rights across local authorities. Each national focal point charged with coordinating and reporting on implementation of the CRPD must therefore ensure that it can assess the extent of regional disparities in the way the CRPD is being implemented.

Finally, while direct payments offer the potential to reposition people with disabilities as empowered citizens, ultimately the availability of good quality person-centred

---

56 See H Spandler, 'Friend or Foe? Towards a critical assessment of direct payments' (2004) 24 Critical Social Policy (2)187.

57 C Ungerson, 'Give them the money: Is cash a route to empowerment?' (1997) 31 Social Policy and Administration (1) 45.

58 T Stainton, 'Taking rights structurally: Disability Rights and Social Worker Responses to Direct Payments' (2002) 32 British Journal of Social Work 751.

59 For example, Department of Health *Putting People First* (Department of Health 2008).

60 See Official Government inquiries and committees (Regeringskansliet, 2012) <http://regeringen.se/sb/d/2461> last accessed 31 March 2016.

61 Joint Committee on Human Rights (JCHR), *Implementation of the Right of Disabled People to Independent Living* (Joint Committee on Human Rights, London 2012) <www.parliament.uk/business/committees/committees-a-z/joint-select/human-rights-committee/news/independent-living-report/> last accessed 31 March 2016.

supports remains central to supporting individuals. Clearly then, there is also the need for supply-side reforms which seek to make the support market more responsive, including options which enhance participation and community connection.

4. Conclusion

The CRPD defines, both through its general principles and specific substantive obligations, a framework within which to understand the concept of personalisation and operationalise it in both law and policy. While each jurisdiction examined in this study has been committed to the new paradigm of self-determination embedded in the Convention, it was clear from the comparative analysis that each country is still grappling with many challenges in implementing this vision. And yet, on the other hand, the self-directed support models identified in this chapter provide important examples for the future evolution of independent living policy. Together, it is possible to learn from both the 'success stories' which have emerged as well as the challenges which each country has faced.

Given the differences in approaches, this chapter provides a telling example of the complexities involved in implementing the right to independent living as crystallised in the CRPD. The achievements and challenges experienced in each of these States Parties serve to illustrate the practicalities of embedding the guiding principles of the CRPD at the domestic level and the role played by the Convention in policy development and decision-making at regional levels of government. While challenges remain, these examples nonetheless provide fully-fledged models of personalisation in practice to be built upon and to facilitate the further development of disability support strategies in other jurisdictions.

While these policy options have been evolving throughout the decades preceding the CRPD, they nonetheless represent the fruition of long-held policy debates over ways to enable independent living, which mirror those held in the negotiations of the CRPD. The philosophies which now underpin the Convention resonate with the different visions of self-determination found in the national policies. However, it must be cautioned that the delivery of personalisation focused solely and exclusively on individual funding arguably has the potential to dilute the broader vision of self-determination inherent in the Convention, and in some cases there is evidence to suggest that such a narrow focus could erode rather than reinvigorate much of the disability support environment.[62] Alongside the self-determining option of individual funding, this chapter is mindful that the implementation of the broader philosophy of personalisation should include access where required to independent planning and support co-ordination to enable full citizenship. Alongside these mechanisms, legislation also needs to permit supported decision-making and access to advocacy services to help people in institutions negotiate the challenges in moving into the community. Finally, it is important to emphasise that reform of disability support policy and implementation structures can only be truly effective where it occurs in

[62] E Hall, 'Shopping for support: personalisation and the new spaces and relations of commodified care for people with learning disabilities' (2011) 12(6) *Social and Cultural Geography* 589; See also: N Hanlon, M Rosenberg and R Clasby, 'Offloading social care responsibilities: recent experiences of local voluntary organisations in a remote urban centre in British Columbia, Canada' (2007) 15 Health and Social Care in the Community (4) 343.

conjunction with broader public sector reform, ie the 'mainstreaming' of disability issues across all levels of government. Cumulatively, these options for achieving a personalised support delivery system serve as the basis for further development and restructuring of disability law and policy at the domestic level. These examples thus serve to illustrate how welfare systems can be re-imagined to ensure the CRPD guiding principles are firmly embedded to enable persons with disabilities become more independent.

CHAPTER 23

THE UN CONVENTION ON THE RIGHTS OF PERSONS WITH DISABILITIES: EXPLORING THE SYNERGY BETWEEN ARTICLE 12 AND ARTICLE 19

Sinead O'Donnell and Charles O'Mahony

1. INTRODUCTION

The UN Convention on the Rights of Persons with Disabilities (CRPD) is driving a worldwide law reform programme as State Parties to the Convention seek to bring their law and policy in line with their commitments under international human rights law. This chapter considers the synergy between Article 12 on legal capacity and Article 19 on the right to live independently and be included in the community. The synergy between these two articles centres on the notion that in order to live independently in the community everyone's legal capacity to make decisions and have those decisions respected is recognised. Equally independent living allows for the facilitation of and the growth and exercise of legal capacity. The opportunity to acquire the necessary skills to live independently has historically been denied to persons with disabilities who have been perceived as lacking the legal capacity, a presumption that has resulted in segregation and institutionalisation. The chapter will go on to consider the interpretation by the UN Committee on the Rights of Persons with Disabilities of the meaning of Articles 12 and 19.

2. ARTICLE 12 OF THE CRPD

Article 12 (equal recognition before the law) is at the heart of the CRPD. One of main problems identified in necessitating a specific international human rights treaty on disability was the lack of visibility of persons with disabilities. Persons with disabilities tended to be treated in the past as objects to be managed as opposed to subjects with their own interests and desires and their own rights to pursue.[1] This out-dated view of disability was evident in highly restrictive laws on mental capacity. Being recognised as having full legal capacity is the key to making decisions for oneself. Having legal capacity restricted or completely denied allows third parties to engage in substitute decision-making in all areas including decisions about where and with whom a person can live. Until the arrival of the CRPD there have been three general approaches to

1 G Quinn and T Degener (eds) *Human Rights and Disability: The Current Use and Future Potential of United Nations Human Rights Instruments in the Context of Disability* (Geneva: Office of the United Nations Commissioner for Human Rights, 2002).

legal capacity. The first approach is referred to as the 'status approach', which means that once an individual is considered to be disabled then legal capacity should be removed. Under the status approach it was irrelevant whether the impairment is of a kind or degree that necessitated the stripping away of legal capacity. The decision to deprive legal capacity was not tailored to the circumstances of the person. The second approach is known as the outcome approach, and is rooted in the belief that in circumstances where a person makes a bad decision or a number of bad decisions that person should lose the right to continue to make decisions.[2] This approach to capacity is now out-dated, as there is recognition that 'we all have the right to make our own mistakes' and that it is unjust to set the decision-making bar higher for persons with disabilities.[3]

The third approach, the functional approach, involves a consideration of legal capacity on an issue-specific basis by assessing a persons' mental functioning. A person might not be considered able to make decisions about where they live but might be considered to have capacity to make other types of decisions. This approach rejects the status approach and outcome approach. The functional approach presumes that a person has capacity unless proven otherwise and involves the provision of supports in order for people to exercise decision-making. While the functional approach represented a significant improvement on the status and outcome approaches to legal capacity the CRPD now requires a shift away from all three approaches, which have looked at persons with disabilities in terms of deficits.

Article 12 requires State Parties to make a profound shift to the 'supported decision-making approach'.[4] In essence, it centres on the person and restores decision-making autonomy to them. The move to the supported decision-making model can be seen in Article 12(3), which requires States Parties to take appropriate measures to provide access to supports in order to exercise legal capacity. It is important to note that the discourse around Article 12 challenges the very legitimacy of the concept of mental incapacity. It is important to note also that the 'best interests' principle has emerged from law and policy focused on children, and it is an inappropriate concept in relation to adults.[5] Acting in the 'best interests' has been used in the past and continues to be used as justification for limiting the choice for persons with disabilities to live in the community.

The CRPD requires a move away from the 'best interests' principle. Article 3 of the CRPD sets out the principles underpinning the Convention, which include respect for inherent dignity; autonomy – including the freedom to make one's own choices – and independence; non-discrimination; full and effective participation and

---

2 G Quinn 'Personhood & Legal Capacity Perspectives on the Paradigm Shift of Article 12 CRPD' (HPOD Conference, Harvard Law School, 20 February, 2010). Available at: http://www.nuigalway.ie/cdlp/staff/gerard_quinn.html.

3 ibid.

4 For a discussion on this see M Bach and L Kerzner 'A New Paradigm for Protecting Autonomy and the Right to Legal Capacity' (Law Commission of Ontario, October 2010). To see the need to move to supported decision-making see 'Who Gets to Decide? Right to Legal Capacity for Persons with Intellectual and Psychosocial Disabilities' (Strasbourg: Council of Europe Commissioner for Human Rights, Issue Paper, 20 February 2012, CommDH/IssuePaper(2012)2).

5 For a discussion in the origin of the best-interests principle, see *The Best Interests of the Child: Towards a Synthesis of Children's Rights and Cultural Values* (Florence: UNICEF, 1996).

inclusion in society; respect for difference; and equality of opportunity. Nowhere does the CRPD refer to the 'best interests' of adults with disabilities, and in fact the suggestion that the 'best interests' be included in Article 12 was firmly rejected at the negotiations of the CRPD at the Ad Hoc Committee.[6] The paradigm shift in thinking required by the CRPD and in particular in Article 12 necessitates a move away from substitute decision-making by third parties based on what is adjudicated to be in a person's 'bests interests'. A central aspect of Article 12(4) is the focus on the 'will and preferences' of the person as the determining factor in decisions about their life. This new focus recognises that the 'best interests' approach brings with it a significant risk of paternalism and substitute decision-making. This is a hugely significant shift, which ought to have a significance in allowing the opportunity for persons with disabilities to realise their rights under Article 19 of the CRPD to live and be included in the community.

3. Article 19 of the CRPD

The inclusion of Article 19, much like Article 12, in the CRPD must be emphasised as being hugely significant. Article 19 enshrines in international human rights law the rights of persons with disabilities in the community for the first time. As discussed elsewhere in this edited collection, Article 19 of the CRPD sets out the right to live independently and to be included in the community, and as such is one of the key provisions that aim to restore autonomy, choice and independence for persons with disabilities.[7] Article 19 requires State Parties to the Convention to take action to facilitate them in fully enjoying inclusion and participation in the community. While there is no precise definition of independent living in Article 19, it is generally understood to reflect the principles of autonomy and choice and undoubtedly reflects the philosophical approach of the social model of disability. It is clear that the placement of persons with disabilities in institutions constitutes a 'pervasive violation' of Article 19 of the CRPD.[8] Article 19 sets out a non-exhaustive list of the effective and appropriate measures that State Parties to the Convention are required to take. For example, Article 19(a) requires State Parties to ensure a choice of residence: 'persons with disabilities have the opportunity to choose their place of residence and where and with whom they live on an equal basis with others and are not obliged to live in a particular living arrangement'.

It is self-evident that in order to live independently in the community a person needs to be recognised as having legal capacity and be able to make decisions. If a person is not legally recognised as being able to make decisions they will be unable to enter into the contractual arrangements necessary to live in the community and access the goods and services necessary to live in the community. The development of decision-making ability necessitates the building up of experience of living independently and being included in the community and in forming and maintaining relationships.

---

6 The only references to 'best interests' in the CRPD emerge in respect of children with disabilities (see arts 7 and 23).

7 L Clements and C Parker 'The UN Convention on the Rights of persons with Disabilities: A New Right to Independent Living?' (2008) 4 European Human Rights Law Review 508–523.

8 See 'The Right of People with Disabilities to Live Independently and be Included in the Community' (Strasbourg: Issue Paper, Council of Europe Commissioner for Human Rights, 13 March 2012, CommDH/IssuePaper(2012)3).

Persons with disabilities have been traditionally excluded from acquiring this experience on the basis of their status of being disabled and the supplementary presumption of incapacity.

4. CRPD Committee Statements on Article 12 and 19

To date the UN Committee on the Rights of Persons with Disabilities have made a number of statements on Articles 12 and 19 of the CRPD that have highlighted the important synergy between the articles. The Committee on the Rights of Persons with Disabilities in its General Comment on Article 12 expressly stated that the 'recognition of legal capacity is inextricably linked to the enjoyment of many other human rights provided for in the Convention' including Article 19.[9] The importance that the Committee attaches to this synergy was highlighted in a section in General Comment No. 1 dedicated to its relevance to Article 19.[10] The Committee noted that persons with disabilities needed opportunities to develop and express their 'will and preferences' by living in and being included in the community and by having 'control over their everyday lives, on an equal basis with others, as provided for in Article 19'.[11] The Committee expressly stated that the right to live in the community required providing support for persons with disabilities 'using a community-based approach'.[12]

The Committee specifically addressed the issue of segregation of persons with disabilities in institutional settings. Segregation was described as a 'pervasive and insidious problem that violates a number of the rights guaranteed under the Convention'.[13] The Committee noted that the problem of segregation was 'exacerbated by the widespread denial of legal capacity to persons with disabilities, which allows others to consent to their placement in institutional settings'.[14] The Committee singled out the directors of institutions for comment, noting that they often are given power to make decisions for persons resident in these settings. The Committee was explicit in stating that the CRPD requires deinstitutionalisation in conjunction with the restoration of legal capacity to all persons with disabilities. Deinstitutionalisation in conjunction with the restoration of legal capacity is essential if a person is able to then make decisions about where and with whom they live.[15]

5. Conclusion

As discussed above, Article 12 of the CRPD requires the removal of barriers that prevent persons with disabilities from exercising their legal capacity. The requirement in Article 12 that the State Parties provide the necessary supports to allow everyone make decisions has great potential for realising the rights to

---

9 Committee on the Rights of Persons with Disabilities, General Comment on Article 12 (CRPD/C/GC/1), paras 27.

10 ibid paras 40–42.

11 ibid para 40.

12 ibid para 41.

13 ibid para 42.

14 ibid.

15 ibid.

independent living and inclusion in the community. After all, Article 12 expressly states that persons with disabilities are entitled to enjoy legal capacity on an equal basis with others 'in all aspects of life'.

Article 19 of the CRPD defines the right to independent living as including '... the equal right of all persons with disabilities to live in the community, with choices equal to others'. Article 19 of the CRPD, for the first time in international human rights law, requires State Parties to the CRPD to ensure that persons with disabilities will have the opportunity to make choices about where and with whom they live. Importantly, that choice means that they will not be required to live in one particular type of living arrangement. Article 19 also involves having access to residential and community supports if necessary to support living and inclusion in community. Article 19 then has huge potential to propel the deinstitutionalisation movement throughout the world. Article 12(5) in that regard is important, in providing that States Parties to the Convention 'shall take all appropriate and effective measures to ensure the equal right of persons with disabilities to own or inherit property, to control their own financial affairs and to have equal access to bank loans, mortgages and other forms of financial credit, and shall ensure that persons with disabilities are not arbitrarily deprived of their property'. This provision will prove important in removing the barriers faced by persons with disabilities in accessing the financial services and credit that is required to live in the community.

In this chapter we have argued that the CRPD has great potential to remove barriers that prevent persons with disabilities from participating and living independently in the community on an equal basis with everyone else. The Committee on the Rights of Persons with disabilities have robustly asserted that recognition of persons with disabilities as persons before the law in Article 12 is essential in asserting, exercising the right to live independently and be included in the community. The denial of legal capacity means that the right contained in Article 19 is significantly compromised and, as such, State Parties to the Convention must ensure that law reform must ensure that restoration of legal capacity and the development of supported decision-making mechanisms is a priority.

PART 5: THE RIGHT TO INCLUSIVE EDUCATION

Chapter 24

THE RIGHT TO EDUCATION: ARTICLE 24 OF THE CRPD

Andrea Broderick and Shivaun Quinlivan

1. Introduction

The right to education has been described as 'a pre-requisite to the exercise of many other rights.'[1] This statement is fitting in the context of persons with disabilities. The right to education is intrinsically linked with empowerment and participation and inclusion of persons with disabilities in society on an equal basis with others. Article 24 of the United Nations Convention on the Rights of Persons with Disabilities (CRPD) contains the cornerstone principle of inclusive education. It has been stated that 'Article 24 arguably provides [a stronger] mandate for states to provide inclusive education than any previous human rights document.'[2]

The right to education has traditionally been described as falling within the category of rights known as economic, social and cultural rights. As such it is deemed to be subject to progressive realisation.[3] That being stated, the CRPD seeks to reframe the debate concerning the realisation of human rights. The Convention recognises, in its Preamble, the 'universality, indivisibility, interdependence and interrelatednesss of all human rights.'[4] Many of the rights in the CRPD may be termed so-called hybrid rights, imposing both immediate and progressive obligations on States Parties. Article 24 of the CRPD is one such right.

The objective of this chapter is to interpret and analyse the right to education contained in the CRPD from a legal perspective and to delineate the various obligations contained therein. In order to aid the interpretation of Article 24, the authors will have recourse to the rules of legal interpretation codified in the Vienna Convention on the Law of Treaties (VCLT), as well as referring to the observations and recommendations of the United Nations Committee on the Rights of Persons with Disabilities (CRPD Committee), among others. Throughout this chapter, we will also analyse the extent to which States Parties to the CRPD are living up to their commitments under Article 24 of the Convention.

---

1 C O'Mahony, Education Rights in Irish Law (Thomson Roundhall 2006) 18.

2 School of Oriental and African Studies, 'The Convention on the Rights of Persons with Disabilities: The Right to Education and the Obligations of States' (2011) 44, SOAS International Human Rights Clinic Project – Research Paper No. 06/2011, 23 <http://papers.ssrn.com/sol3/papers.cfm?abstract_id=1895726>.

3 For a more detailed analysis on the enforcement of socio economic rights and the duty to realise these rights progressively see Eide, Krause and Rosas (eds), Economic, Social and Cultural Rights: A Textbook (2nd Ed, Martinus Nijhoff Publishers, 2001).

4 United Nations Convention on the Rights of Persons with Disabilities (CRPD), Preamble (c).

To that end, this chapter is broken down into six sections. In Section 2 of this chapter we will provide a brief overview of the rules of legal interpretation contained in the VCLT, in order to demonstrate the methodology which will be applied in interpreting the right to education in Article 24 of the CRPD. In Section 3 we will reflect on the duty to realise progressively human rights, while also outlining the duties inherent in the obligation to realise progressively the right to education, as laid out by the various human rights treaty bodies. We will then go on, in Section 4 of this chapter, to interpret Article 24 of the CRPD and to consider the constituent elements of that article – those elements deemed to be realisable immediately and those elements subject to progressive implementation. In Section 5 of this chapter, we will highlight emerging trends in the realisation of the right to education for persons with disabilities. Finally, Section 6 will contain concluding remarks.

2. Methodology: The Vienna Convention on the Law of Treaties

In order to clarify the obligations imposed on States by international human rights treaties and to determine how best to implement such obligations, it is necessary to first interpret the duties imposed by human rights treaties. The VCLT contains the rules of legal interpretation that are widely accepted as being the most appropriate rules for interpreting the norms contained in international human rights treaties. Articles 31 and 32 of the VCLT essentially contain interpretative tools – literal (textual) interpretation, systematic (contextual) interpretation, teleological (functional) interpretation and historical interpretation. The literal approach to interpretation requires the reader to respect the primacy of the text. In that regard, words or phrases 'are to be given their normal, natural, and unstrained meaning.'[5] However, the ordinary meaning of CRPD provisions should not be determined in the abstract. Rather, it should be determined in the context of the treaty as a whole and in light of its object and purpose. This leads neatly onto the next two interpretive tools contained in the VCLT – the systematic (contextual) approach and the teleological (functional) approach to interpretation. The systematic approach mandates that one reads a human rights treaty as a whole and, furthermore, locates the interpretation of any phrases within their broader meaning. The Preamble and Annexes, as well as the General Principles and General Obligations of the CRPD (contained in Articles 3 and 4 of the Convention respectively) may provide interpretive context in that regard. Article 31(3) of the VCLT provides that, together with the context, any subsequent agreements between the parties or practices in the application of the treaty can be taken into account. Subsequent practice may be manifest in the general comments and concluding observations of the CRPD Committee. These general comments and concluding observations are deemed to be subsidiary, supplementary sources of interpretation and are not legally binding *per se*. The Committee has not yet adopted any general comments on the right to education so we will reflect on the Committee's concluding observations in this chapter as they may provide important interpretive context in determining the steps to be taken by States Parties in the realisation of Article 24.

---

5 Comment by Sir G *Fitzmaurice, International Law Commission Rapporteur on the Law of Treaties, cited by M Fitzmaurice, 'The Practical Working of the Law of Treaties' in M Evans (ed) International Law (2edn, Oxford University Press, 2006) 198.*

In addition to the foregoing interpretive tools, the object and purpose of a human rights treaty plays a major role, according to the teleological (functional) approach to interpretation. It essentially reflects an embodiment of the intention of States Parties to a Convention and it is a useful point of reference in the overall interpretive process. Finally, under Article 32 of the VCLT, a historical approach is allowed as a supplementary interpretation tool. That approach permits recourse to the *travaux prèparatoires* (or the record of negotiations), treaty drafts and other documents relating to the circumstances which preceded a treaty's enactment in order to clarify the intent of States Parties to the Convention.[6]

The interpretive tools outlined above will be relied on throughout this chapter to aid in the analysis of Article 24 of the CRPD. Before we actually analyse the obligations contained in Article 24 itself, we will consider the overall concept of the progressive realisation of human rights and its application to the right to education.

3. The Progressive Realisation of Human Rights: The Right to Education

Article 4(2) of the CRPD contains a clause on progressive realisation.[7] This concept is enshrined in numerous other international human rights treaties.[8] In essence, progressive realisation amounts to the recognition in international law that States require sufficient time to realise fully certain composite rights contained in a given treaty. The Office of the High Commissioner for Human Rights (OHCHR) has stated that progressive realisation is 'a practical device that acknowledge(s) the real world challenges' and helps to avoid overburdening states, employers and other duty-bearers.[9]

In light of the hierarchical, albeit somewhat artificial distinction,[10] which has been carved out between civil and political rights, on the one hand, and economic, social and cultural rights, on the other hand, several states have interpreted the notion of

---

6 The drafting history of a treaty should only be resorted to in order to confirm the meaning resulting from the application of Article 31, or to determine the meaning when the interpretation according to Article 31 'leaves the meaning ambiguous or obscure' or 'leads to a result which is manifestly absurd or unreasonable' [Vienna Convention on the Law of Treaties, art 32].

7 art 4(2) CRPD reads as follows: 'With regard to economic, social and cultural rights, each State Party undertakes to take measures to the maximum of its available resources and, where needed, within the framework of international cooperation, with a view to achieving progressively the full realization of these rights, without prejudice to those obligations contained in the present Convention that are immediately applicable according to international law.'

8 See, among others, art 2 of the International Covenant Economic and Social Rights (ICESCR) and art 4 of the Convention on the Rights of the Child (CRC).

9 OHCHR, 'From Vision to Action: The Road to Implementation of the Convention' (2007) 5.

10 The traditional dichotomy of human rights into civil and political rights, on the one hand and economic, social and cultural rights, on the other hand, has been increasingly eroded in academic discourse. On this point, see S Fredman, Human Rights Transformed: Positive Rights and Positive Duties (Oxford University Press 2008); See also M Sepúlveda Carmona, The Nature of the Obligations Under the International Covenant on Economic, Social and Cultural Rights (School of Human Rights Research Series Volume 18 Intersentia Antwerpen 2003) 127; See also I E Koch, 'From Invisibility to Indivisibility: The International Convention on the Rights of Persons with Disabilities' in O M Arnardóttir and G Quinn (eds) The UN Convention on the Rights of Persons with Disabilities: European and Scandanavian Perspectives (Martinus Nijhoff 2009).

progressive realisation to mean that the implementation of economic, social and cultural rights is not of immediate concern. As a result of this misconception, the UN Committee on Economic, Social and Cultural Rights (CESCR Committee) has explained that while the full realisation of such rights may be achieved progressively, 'steps towards that goal must be taken within a reasonably short time after the Covenant's entry into force for the Member States concerned. Such steps should be deliberate, concrete and targeted as clearly as possibly towards meeting the obligations recognised in the Covenant.'[11]

The CESCR Committee emphasises the fact that states have certain obligations which require immediate implementation, irrespective of the level of available resources.[12] This position is reaffirmed in Article 4(2) of the CRPD, which explicitly provides that the progressive realisation of economic, social and cultural rights is 'without prejudice to those obligations contained in the present Convention that are immediately applicable according to international law.'[13] The principal obligation, which is deemed to take effect immediately, is the guarantee of non-discrimination in the exercise of human rights.[14] The principle of non-retrogression is also deemed to be immediately applicable.[15] In other words, the existing level of human rights protection must be maintained, unless there are extenuating circumstances. In addition to this, there are certain obligations which are deemed to take effect immediately in order to meet the minimum essential levels of socio-economic rights provision. [16] These are termed the 'minimum core obligations'[17] of human rights. Coömans and Hallo de Wolf have stated that 'the core content of a right must be understood as meaning its essence i.e. that essential element without which a right loses its substantive significance as a human right.'[18] Coomans states that the 'essence of the right to education means that no one shall be denied a right to education.'[19] This

---

11 UN Committee on Economic Social and Cultural Rights (CESCR Committee), General Comment No. 3, 'The nature of States Parties' obligations' (1990) para 2 <http://www.unhchr.ch/tbs/doc.nsf/(symbol)/CESCR+General+comment+3.En>.

12 UNCESCR, General Comment No. 4 'The right to adequate housing' (1991) para 10; CESCR Committee, General Comment No. 11 'Plans of action for primary education' (1999) para 11 <http://www.unhcr.org/refworld/publisher,CESCR,GENERAL,,,10.html>.

13 art 4(2) CRPD.

14 See art 2(2) ICESCR.

15 In that regard, the United Nations Committee on the Rights of the Child (CRC Committee) has stated that it is not permissible to 'take any retrogressive steps that could hamper the enjoyment of economic, social and cultural rights,' Committee on the Rights of the Child (hereinafter CRC Committee), Day of General Discussion, 'Resources for the Rights of the Child: Obligations for States' (21 September 2007) para 13 <http://www2.ohchr.org/english/bodies/crc/discussion2012.htm>.

16 The United Nations Committee on the Rights of the Child (hereinafter CRC Committee) remarks, in its General Comment No. 3, that States Parties have 'a minimum core obligation to ensure the satisfaction of, at the very least, minimum essential levels of each of the rights [enunciated in the Covenant].'

17 It is noteworthy that the concept of minimum core obligations is controversial in certain quarters and has been effectively rejected by the South African Constitutional Court. In this regard, see S Fredman, Human Rights Transformed: Positive Rights and Positive Duties (Oxford University Press 2008) 84.

18 F Coomans and A Hallo de Wolf, 'Privitisation of Education and the Right to Education' in K De Feyter and F Gómez Isa (eds) Privatisation of Education and the Right to Education (Intersentia 2005) 232.

19 F Coomans, 'Clarifying the Core Element to the Right to Education,' SIM Special 18, 7 <http://www.uu.nl/faculty/leg/EN/organisation/schools/schooloflaw/organisation/departments/studieeninformatiecentrummensenrechten/publications/simspecials/18/Pages/default.aspx>

equates to an access right, namely the right to access on an equal basis with others the existing education system. In particular, access must be ensured in respect of the most basic forms of education. In that regard, Coomans notes that the core content of education must include free and compulsory primary education.[20] He asserts that 'primary education is so fundamental for the development of a person's abilities that it can be rightfully defined as a minimum claim.'[21] The CESCR Committee affirms that States Parties are 'obliged to prioritise the introduction of compulsory, free primary education.'[22] In other words, the obligation to provide primary education for all must be addressed as a matter of pressing concern, as it is 'an immediate duty of all State Parties.'[23]

Another obligation which is deemed to be immediately applicable is the duty to take steps to devote the maximum of available resources to achieving progressively the full realisation of human rights.[24] The obligation to take steps to the maximum of available resources was elaborated on in the case of *Autism Europe v France*,[25] which demonstrates the justiciability of the right to education and also serves as an example of a blatant failure by a State Party to realise progressively the right to education. In that case, the European Committee on Social Rights held that France had not made sufficient provision for the education of autistic children. The Committee found, inter alia, that the proportion of autistic children being educated in either general or specialist schools was disproportionately low in comparison to non-disabled children. The State Party had, in fact, passed relevant legislation in this area as far back as 1975.[26] However, it had failed to enforce the legislation in the interim. As a result, a high proportion of autistic children were deemed not to have received an appropriate education.[27] In view of this, the Committee ruled that the State Party was in breach of Article 15(1) and Article 17(1) of the Revised European Social Charter alone and in conjunction with Article E. These Articles relate to the right of persons with disabilities to education and the general right of children and young people to education and non-discrimination respectively. The Committee stated that when the achievement of a right is exceptionally complex and particularly expensive to resolve, State Parties must take measures to do so 'within a reasonable time with measurable progress and to an extent consistent with the maximum use of available resources.'[28]

In addition to delineating the immediate obligations imposed on States in the context of the realisation of socio-economic rights, it is also appropriate to refer to the 4As framework outlined by the CESCR Committee in its General Comment

---

20 ibid.

21 ibid.

22 CESCR Committee, General Comment No. 13, 'The right to education' (1999) para 51, <http://www2.ohchr.org/english/bodies/cescr/comments.htm>

23 ibid.

24 art 4 CRPD, art 2 ICESCR, art 4 CRC.

25 Autism Europe v France, Complaint No. 13/2002, Decision on the Merits, 7th November 2003 <http://www.coe.int/t/dghl/monitoring/socialcharter/complaints/CC13Merits_en.pdf>

26 The right to education of persons with disabilities in France was enshrined in two Acts: Act no. 75/534 of 30 June 1975, People with Disabilities (Policy) Act, and Act No. 75/535 of 30 June 1975 on social and medico-social institutions.

27 80-90% of autistic children did not receive an adequate education.

28 For further analysis of the duty to realise progressively the right to education see AEH v France, Complaint No. 81/2012, Decision on the Merits, 11 September 2013.

No. 13. In that general comment, the CESCR Committee expands on the various components of the progressive realisation of the right to education. The CESCR Committee states that education in all its forms and on all levels should be available, accessible, acceptable, and adaptable.[29] According to the Committee, the availability of education implies that States must create and maintain functional educational facilities, which include all the materials and resources needed for the education of the learners.[30] The second criterion outlined by the Committee is the accessibility of education – it must be accessible to all learners.[31] Accessible education has three overlapping dimensions. First, it must be provided on a non-discriminatory basis. Secondly, it must be physically accessible and within safe physical reach for all. Thirdly, it must be economically accessible or affordable to all, especially to vulnerable or marginalised groups.[32] The next criterion outlined by the Committee is the acceptability of education, which means that the form and substance of education, including curricula and teaching methods, have to be acceptable to students (eg relevant, culturally appropriate and of good quality).[33] Finally, education has to maintain adaptability. It must be flexible and must adapt to the needs of changing societies and communities and respond to the needs of students within their diverse social and cultural settings.[34] In other words, education must not be provided according to a 'one-size-fits-all' approach. Rather, it must change and adapt according to the needs of the learner.[35]

Each of the constituent elements outlined in this section with regard to the progressive realisation of human rights and, in particular, with regard to the right to education are equally applicable in the context of Article 24 of the CRPD. It is to that article that we now turn, in order to delineate the steps to be taken by States Parties to the CRPD in the realisation of the right to education for persons with disabilities.

4. The Right to Education in Article 24 of the CRPD

The right to education is a long established right at the level of international human rights law.[36] However, the touchstone of the right to education was not always the concept of inclusive education. Article 24 of the CRPD cements the right to inclusive education in international human rights law. Inclusive education can essentially be viewed as the means by which the right to education is operationalised for persons with disabilities and it is also a beneficial means of learning for non-disabled students. Inclusive education has been described as a 'process of addressing and responding to the diversity of needs of all learners by increasing participation in learning, cultures

---

[29] CESCR Committee, General Comment No. 13, 'The right to education' (1999) para 6, <http://www2.ohchr.org/english/bodies/cescr/comments.htm>

[30] ibid, para 6(a).

[31] ibid, para 6(b).

[32] ibid.

[33] ibid, para 6(c).

[34] ibid, para 6(d).

[35] The European Committee on Social Rights applied the principle of the 'four As' in the case of MDAC v Bulgaria, Complaint No. 41/2007, Decision on the Merits, June 3 2008.

[36] The right to education is contained, inter alia, in art 26 of the Universal Declaration of Human Rights and arts 13 and 14 International Covenant on Economic, Social and Cultural Rights. The right to education for disabled children is specifically mentioned in arts 23(3) and 23(4) of the Convention on the rights of the child.

and communities, and reducing exclusion within and from education.'[37] The goals of inclusive learning are, among others, equality of opportunities, the principle of non-discrimination, accessible structures and tailored, individual learning. The World Report on Disability recognises the benefits of inclusive education for persons with disabilities. It states as follows:

> The inclusion of children with disabilities in mainstream schools promotes universal primary completion, is cost-effective and contributes to the elimination of discrimination. Creating an inclusive learning environment will assist all children in learning and achieving their potential.[38]

In debating the initial drafts of the CRPD during the negotiation sessions of the Ad Hoc Committee, delegates were undecided as to whether segregated education should be explicitly prohibited under the Convention or whether it should in fact be permitted in certain circumstances. For example, the Canadian delegate argued that persons with disabilities should 'always [be] educated within the general education system.'[39] On the contrary, Japan stated that it could not accept any wording that obliged States to ensure inclusive education in all circumstances on account of the fact that it felt that 'the use of general or special schools should be decided according to the best interests of the child.'[40] In a similar vein, the Israeli delegate argued that 'the right to choose should also be considered, as there are many cases where parents, having considered all relevant considerations, opt for special schools.'[41] While the final text of the CRPD does not prohibit segregated education explicitly, it is very clear on a textual, systematic and teleological reading of the Convention that States are obliged to ensure that that education for persons with disabilities is inclusive.

Before the adoption of the CRPD, the Convention on the Rights of the Child (CRC) appeared to allude to many of the goals of inclusive learning, even though the CRC did not specifically mention a right to inclusive education. For example, Article 23(3) of the CRC recognises the special needs of disabled children and the entitlement to assistance designed to ensure that the disabled child has effective access to and receives, among other things, education and training in a manner conducive to the child's achieving the fullest possible social integration and individual development, including his or her cultural and spiritual development.[42] Furthermore, Article 28 of the CRC refers to the notion of accessibility in the context of secondary[43] and higher education.[44] Moreover, the aims of education addressed in Article 29 of

37 UNESCO, 'Overcoming Exclusion through Inclusive Approaches in Education: A Challenge and a Vision, Conceptual Paper' (UNESCO 2003) 7.

38 World Health Organization & World Bank, World Report on Disability 206 (2011).

39 Seventh Session of the Ad Hoc Committee (16/01/06 – 03/02/06), Daily summary of discussion at the seventh session 24th January 2006 <http://www.un.org/esa/socdev/enable/rights/ahc7sum24jan.htm>.

40 ibid.

41 ibid.

42 art 23(3) CRC.

43 art 28(b) of the CRC requires states to 'encourage the development of different forms of secondary education, including general and vocational education, make them available and accessible to every child, and take appropriate measures such as the introduction of free education and offering financial assistance in case of need.'

44 art 28(c) requires States Parties to 'make higher education accessible to all on the basis of capacity by every appropriate means,' and art 28(d) requires States Parties to 'make educational and vocational information and guidance available and accessible to all children.'

the CRC – including developing the child's potential, talents and abilities to their fullest potential and developing respect for human rights – also reflect the aims of inclusive education.

The CRPD goes much further than the CRC by specifically framing the right to education for children and adults with disabilities in terms of an inclusive educational framework. In order to interpret Article 24, we now turn to a textual, systematic and teleological analysis of the Convention. The object and purpose of the Convention is stated in Article 1 as being to promote, protect and ensure the full and equal enjoyment of all human rights and fundamental freedoms by all persons with disabilities, and to promote respect for their inherent dignity.[45] Furthermore, Article 1 of the Convention acknowledges the fact that the participation in society of persons with disabilities is hindered through interaction with various barriers.[46] The object and purpose of the Convention reflects the social model of disability which underlies the Convention as a whole, including Article 24. The social model identifies discriminatory systemic barriers (in the form of environmental, attitudinal and societal obstacles) as the main contributory factor in disabling people with impairments.[47] The object and purpose of the Convention also mirrors the 4 As framework above by requiring, in particular, that the criteria of adaptability and accessibility (including non-discrimination) are satisfied in the context of the right to education (as well as the other rights contained in the Convention).

The Preamble of the CRPD explicitly states that 'children with disabilities should have full enjoyment of all human rights and fundamental freedoms on an equal basis with other children.'[48] In addition, the Convention includes within its general principles '[r]espect for the evolving capacities of children with disabilities and respect for the right of children with disabilities to preserve their identities.'[49] By that token, the Convention recognises the inherent dignity of children with disabilities and the need to respect the diversity of disabled children, including in the implementation of Article 24. It also mirrors the principles of accessibility and adaptability.

Article 24 of the Convention itself specifically elaborates on the goals to be achieved by education in the context of persons with disabilities. In the first instance, Article 24 maintains that education should be directed towards 'the full development of human potential and sense of dignity and self-worth, and the strengthening of respect for human rights, fundamental freedoms and human diversity.'[50] The second goal to be achieved through inclusive education is furthering the 'development by persons with disabilities of their personality, talents and creativity, as well as their mental and physical abilities, to their fullest potential.'[51] The third goal of inclusive education under the Convention is to enable 'persons with disabilities to participate effectively

---

45 CRPD art 1.
46 ibid.
47 The social model of disability was originally labelled as such by Michael Oliver – see M Oliver, 'If I had a Hammer' in C Barnes and G Mercer (eds) Implementing the Social Model of Disability: Theory and Research (The Disability Press 2004) 18–31. For further information, see M Ashley Stein, 'Disability Human Rights' (2007) 95 California Law Review 75, 88.
48 ibid Preamble (r).
49 ibid art 3(h).
50 ibid art 24(1)(a).
51 ibid art 24(1)(b).

in a free society.'[52] This last goal of Article 24 is consistent with the overall object and purpose of the Convention, which seeks to remove barriers to the exercise of rights by persons with disabilities. Interestingly, during the negotiation process, delegates specifically drew attention to the fact that the various components of education – a sense of dignity and self worth, human potential, participating effectively in society, and the development of a child's mental and physical abilities – are 'often neglected in the education of persons with disabilities.'[53]

These goals of inclusive education are intended to be given effect through the implementation of the duties outlined in Article 24. As a hybrid right, Article 24 is subject to progressive realisation, with certain elements of the right to education being realisable immediately. In the sub-sections which follow, we will discern the obligations in Article 24 which can be described as taking effect immediately. These will be juxtaposed with the obligations of progressive achievement relating to the right to education under the CRPD. The concluding observations and recommendations of the CRPD Committee will be drawn on to clarify the steps to be taken by States in order to ensure that persons with disabilities are guaranteed the right to education on an equal basis with others.

4.1 Non-Discrimination and Non-Retrogression

In terms of the immediacy of obligations imposed on States, it is clear from the observations of the treaty bodies that the non-discrimination principle in Article 24 is not subject to the overall concept of progressive achievement. Thus, States Parties to the Convention will be required to ensure non-discrimination in the exercise of the right to education by persons with disabilities. Discrimination in education has been defined as including the treatment of any student in a way which separates him or her from the other students and negatively impacts his or her ability to participate in and receive education.[54] This includes depriving a person or a group from access to education,[55] limiting a person or group to an inferior education,[56] establishing or maintaining separate educational systems for certain groups,[57] or inflicting on any person or group conditions which are against their dignity.[58] States Parties to the CRPD will also be required to ensure non-retrogression in the realisation of Article 24. Thus, States will be required to ensure that already existing levels of educational provision for persons with disabilities are maintained, and that cutbacks due to economic crises do not impact negatively on the right to education.

4.2 Access to Education on an Equal Basis with Others

The right of access for persons with disabilities is specifically contained in Article

---

52 ibid art 24 (1)(c).

53 See the comments of the New Zealand delegate during the negotiations on art 24 CRPD, 3rd session of the Ad Hoc Committee, 28 May 2004, <www.un.org/disabilities/default.asp?id=150>, last accessed 31 March 2016.

54 UNESCO Convention against Discrimination in Education, Paris (1960) art 1.

55 ibid art 1(a).

56 ibid art 1(b).

57 ibid art 1(c). Article 2 of this Convention elaborates that separate educational systems are allowed if the separate systems offer equivalent access to education with teachers of the same qualifications, quality school premises and equipment, and equivalent courses.

58 ibid, art 1(d).

24(2)(b). That article requires States to ensure that persons with disabilities 'can access an inclusive, quality and free primary and secondary education on an equal basis with others in the communities in which they live.'[59] The paramaters of the immediate obligation to ensure non-discriminatory access under Article 24 were clarified by the Chair of the Ad-Hoc Committee, Mr Ronald Mc Callum, during the negotiation sessions. He stated that the CRPD obliges States not to deny access to free and compulsory education on the grounds of disability. Thus, if free and compulsory primary education is available, it should be made available to persons with disabilities without discrimination based on disability.[60] A similar observation was made by the Chair in respect of secondary and tertiary education.[61] The CRPD Committee has specifically recommended that States remove barriers that prevent people with disabilities from accessing the educational system without discrimination.[62] The Committee has also specifically drawn attention to the importance of ensuring access to higher education in its concluding observations. In that regard, the Committee notes that States should make greater efforts to enable students with disabilities to study at universities and other tertiary institutions.[63] This reinforces the duties on States Parties under Article 24(5) of the CRPD to 'ensure that persons with disabilities are able to access tertiary education, vocational training, adult education and lifelong learning without discrimination on an equal basis with others.'[64]

It is disconcerting to note that, given the priority accorded by the human rights treaty bodies to the issue over the years, there are still major anomalies in access to free and compulsory primary education for children with disabilities. For instance, the alternative reports considered by the CRPD Committee highlight the fact that, while the proportion of disabled children entering compulsory education in China is increasing (reaching 71.4% in 2010,[65] as a result of the implementation of education aid policies), 'there is still a clear gap compared with the national level of school-age children in compulsory education.'[66] Additionally, in Peru, 87.1% of school-age children with disabilities remain outside the education system.[67] This highlights the distinct lack of educational opportunities for persons with disabilities, when compared with their non-disabled counterparts.

In many of its concluding observations, the CRPD Committee expresses concern at the fact that children with disabilities are being placed in segregated education and not in inclusive educational settings.[68] In addition, the alternative reports submitted

---

59 CRPD, art 24(2)(b).

60 Quoting the words of Ronald Mc Callum, CRPD Ad Hoc Committee, Daily Summaries of the CRPD – Daily Summaries, Sixth Session, 3 August 2005 <http://www.un.org/esa/socdev/enable/rights/ahc6sum3aug.htm> last accessed 31 March 2016.

61 ibid.

62 ibid.

63 Concluding Observations, CRPD Committee, Costa Rica, U.N.Doc.CRPD/C/CRI/CO/1 (2014), para 48.

64 CRPD, art 24(5).

65 China Disabled People's Federation, 2010 Report on the Progress of the Well-Being of Disabled People in China.

66 Alternative Report of One Plus One Beijing (March 2012) <www.ecoi.net/file.../1930_1373293379_oneplusonebeijing-report-eng.p.>

67 See the Alternative Report On the Compliance with the Convention on the Rights of Persons with Disabilities submitted by the Peruvian National Confederation of People with Disabilities<www2.ohchr.org/SPdocs/CRPD/6thsession/CONFENADIP_Peru_en.doc>.

68 See, for instance, Concluding Observations, CRPD Committee, Austria, U.N. Doc. CRPD/C/

to the Committee also highlight gaps in educational provision for persons with disabilities. In the context of the Spanish examination, for instance, the alternative report submitted to the CRPD Committee criticises the legislative framework in that country, claiming that the relevant legislation,[69] although based on inclusive education and equal opportunities, allowed pupils with certain disabilities or high support needs to be referred to special education centres.[70] In order to ensure access to inclusive, quality education, it is vital that States Parties to the CRPD include in legislation a clear definition of what is meant by inclusive education. This has been recognised as a duty incumbent on States by the CRC Committee in its concluding observations.[71] Indeed, it is only by providing a clear legislative definition of what is actually meant by the term 'inclusive education' that States can then move forward to implement Article 24 of the CRPD. The CRPD Committee has also emphasised the fact that States should develop a comprehensive education policy for inclusive education.[72]A policy framework is not, however, sufficient to ensure fulfilment of the right to education. In that regard, the Committee makes it clear that States must conduct research into the effectiveness of their inclusion policies and the extent to which they are being implemented in practice.[73] To this end, States should set targets to increase the rates of participation and completion of education and training by students with disabilities.[74]

5. Reasonable Accommodations and Supports

Once access to education is ensured, educational systems must adapt to the individual needs of students. In that regard, and in order to achieve the full realisation of the right to education for persons with disabilities, the CRPD imposes a number of obligations on States, including the duty to provide reasonable accommodations and individualised supports. Article 2 of the CRPD defines reasonable accommodation as:

> 'Necessary and appropriate modification and adjustments not imposing a disproportionate or undue burden, where needed in a particular case, to ensure to persons with disabilities the enjoyment or exercise on an equal basis with others of all human rights and fundamental freedoms.'[75]

Article 24(2)(c) of the CRPD specifically sets out the duty to accommodate in educational settings. It provides that, in realising the right to education, 'States

AUT/CO/1 (2013), para 40; Concluding Observations, CRPD Committee, Spain, U.N.Doc. CRPD/C/ESP/CO/1 (2011), para 43; Concluding Observations, CRPD Committee, Costa Rica, U.N.Doc.CRPD/C/CRI/CO/1 (2014), para 45.

69 Organisation of Education Act (n 48, para 98).

70 Alternative Report of the Comité Espanol de Representantes de Personas Con Discapacidad (CERMI State Delegation) (2010), <www2.ohchr.org/SPdocs/CRPD/.../CERMI_Spain_5thSession_en.doc.>.

71 Concluding Observations, CRC Committee, Cyprus, U.N Doc. CRC/C/CYP/CO/3–4 (2012), paras 38, 39.

72 Concluding Observations, CRPD Committee, Argentina, U.N.Doc. CRPD/C/ARG/CO/1 (2012), para 38.

73 Concluding Observations, CRPD Committee, Australia, U.N.Doc. CRPD/C/AUS/CO/1 (2013), para 46.

74 ibid.

75 CRPD, art 2.

Parties shall ensure that reasonable accommodation of the individual's requirements is provided.'[76] The principle of reasonable accommodation is part of the armoury of tools provided for in the CRPD which gives practical effect to the non-discrimination norm. Reasonable accommodations are a central element of disability equality in the context of the right to education. The CRPD specifically defines discrimination on the basis of disability as including all forms of discrimination 'including denial of reasonable accommodation.'[77]

The CRPD Committee recognises that the duty to provide reasonable accommodation is immediately applicable and not subject to progressive realisation[78] (subject, of course, to the disproportionate burden defence). This is a challenging obligation for States. The first step to be taken by States Parties to the CRPD is to ensure that their laws reflect the fact that the failure to provide reasonable accommodation amounts to discrimination. Indeed, under the general obligations of the Convention, States are specifically required to align their laws with the principles contained within the Convention.[79] The provision of reasonable accommodations in the context of Article 24 will also require States to take active steps to ensure inclusive education for persons with disabilities. Reasonable accommodations, according to the CRPD Committee, will include such measures as assistive technology, accessible and adapted educational materials and curricula as well as accessible school environments.[80] The CRPD Committee reiterated the importance of the provision of reasonable accommodations to inclusive education in its concluding observations to Spain, in which it expressed its disconcertion:

> In view of reported cases of failure to provide reasonable accommodation, of continued segregation and exclusion, of financial arguments used as justification for discrimination and of the cases of children enrolled in special education against their parents' will.[81]

The Committee recommended that the State Party 'increase its efforts to provide reasonable accommodation in education by allocating sufficient financial and human resources to implement the right to inclusive education.'[82] In its examination of Hungary, the Committee also recommended that the State Party significantly increase its efforts to provide reasonable accommodation to children with disabilities and emphasised that the provision of such accommodations must be based on the student's individual requirements.[83]

In addition to the duty to provide individualised accommodations, Articles 24(d) and (e) set out the requirement to provide individualised supports to persons with

---

76 CRPD, art 24(2)(c)

77 CRPD, art 2.

78 Concluding Observations, CRPD Committee, Spain, Geneva 19–23 September 2011, UN Doc. CRPD/C/ESP/CO/1, para 44.

79 CRPD, art 4(1)(a).

80 Concluding Observations, CRPD Committee, Azerbaijan, U.N.Doc. CRPD/C/AZE/CO/1 (2014), para 41(a).

81 Concluding Observations, CRPD Committee, Spain, U.N.Doc.CRPD/C/ESP/CO/1 (2011), para 43.

82 ibid, para 44(a).

83 Concluding Observations, CRPD Committee, Hungary, U.N.Doc. CRPD/C/HUN/CO/1 (2012), para 41.

disabilities within the education system. Article 24(d) mandates that persons with disabilities receive support within the general education system in order to 'facilitate their effective education.'[84] Article 24(e), on the other hand, requires the provision of 'effective individualized support measures'[85] in 'environments that maximize academic and social development'[86] with a view towards full inclusion. The core issue in both of these sub-articles appears to be the necessity for the education itself to be effective for the disabled learner. Above all, it is not for the learner to adapt to a one-size-fits-all educational system. This is very much in line with the principles of adaptability and accessibility as set out in the 4As framework above and reinforces the notion that individuals should be in a position to actually draw benefit from the education provided.[87]

The provision of supports under Article 24 reflects the notion of progressive realisation in the context of the right to education, as the facilitation of effective education for persons with disabilities will not be realisable overnight. Indeed, the insertion of the phrase 'with the goal of full inclusion' in Article 24(e) evidences the intention of the drafters that the provision of fully inclusive education can be achieved in a gradual manner, where the resources of a given State are constrained. This is due to the fact that the implementation of adequate supports to ensure the effective education of people with disabilities may require significant resources and will be a difficult challenge for States Parties to the CRPD. There are currently gaps in the provision of effective education and sufficient supports for persons with disabilities within mainstream education systems. While approximately 80% of pupils with disabilities are educated in mainstream schools in Spain,[88] 11.55% of the population with disabilities have not completed primary education, compared to 2.15% of the population in general.[89] In addition, the Alternative Report of the Democratic Party of Hong Kong[90] highlights the fact that students with disabilities studying in mainstream settings do not receive the support they require.[91] The progressive realisation of the right to inclusive education requires much more than a mere legislative and policy framework on inclusion. It requires States to take concrete steps towards a budgetary framework to enable the provision of sufficient supports and full implementation and monitoring of laws and policies in the context of inclusive education. With regard to the progressive realisation of inclusive education, the CRC Committee has acknowledged in its General Comment No. 9 that 'the extent of inclusion within the general education system may vary.'[92] The Committee affirms the fact that the progressive realisation of inclusive education involves 'a continuum of services and programme options must be maintained

---

[84] CRPD, art 24(d).

[85] CRPD, art 24(e).

[86] ibid.

[87] This coincides with the jurisprudence of the European Court of Human Rights, in the Belgian Linguistics (No. 2) case Judgment of 23 July 1968, Series A, No. 6 para 4 that the applicants '[S]hould have the possibility of drawing profit from the education received.'

[88] Alternative Report of the Comité Espanol de Representantes de Personas Con Discapacidad (CERMI State Delegation) (2010) <www2.ohchr.org/SPdocs/CRPD/.../CERMI_Spain_5thSession_en.doc.>

[89] ibid.

[90] CRPD Committee, Seventh Session, Shadow Report of the Democratic Party of Hong Kong (September 2011).

[91] ibid.

[92] CRC Committee, General Comment No. 9 on the rights of children with disabilities (2007), UN Doc. CRC/C/GC/9, para 66.

in circumstances where fully inclusive education is not feasible to achieve in the immediate future.'[93] Nonetheless, the Committee reaffirms the fact that full inclusion 'should be the goal of educating children with disabilities.'[94]

Article 24(4) of the CRPD gives concrete examples of the types of measures that will be necessary in order to help ensure the realisation of the right to education for persons with disabilities. It provides that States Parties 'shall take appropriate measures to employ teachers, including teachers with disabilities, who are qualified in sign language and/or Braille, and to train professionals and staff who work at all levels of education.'[95] It further provides that 'such training shall incorporate disability awareness and the use of appropriate augmentative and alternative modes, means and formats of communication, educational techniques and materials to support persons with disabilities.'[96]Again, this will be a significant challenge for States, many of which have a lack of professionals trained in disability awareness working in mainstream schools.

In its concluding observations to Tunisia, for example, the CRPD Committee expressed its disquiet that many integrated schools are not equipped to receive children with disabilities, and that the training of teachers and administrators with regard to disabilities remains a concern.[97] In view of this, Committee has urged States to adopt a policy of training teachers in the inclusive education model, and to guarantee inclusive education by providing support for trained teachers, such as Braille, alternative means and modes of communication, easy reading texts and other auxiliary equipment and media.[98] In addition, the Committee has recommended that States should 'step up efforts to provide quality training for teachers, including teachers with disabilities, in the use of braille and sign language with a view to enhancing the education of all categories of children with disabilities, including deaf and hard-of-hearing girls and boys'[99] and that they should 'ensure that inclusive education is an integral part of core teacher training in universities.'[100]

6. Emerging Trends in Inclusive Education Provision

Progress is understandably slow in the implementation of such a complex right as the right to education for persons with disabilities and there is a long road ahead if States Parties to the CRPD are to succeed in the full implementation of Article 24. In spite of the laudable objectives of the CRPD to create inclusive educational structures, many persons with disabilities are still educated in segregated educational settings and those who are granted access to mainstream education are often not

---

93 ibid.
94 ibid.
95 CRPD, art 24(4)
96 ibid.
97 Concluding observations of the Committee on the Rights of Persons with Disabilities, Tunisia, CRPD/C/TUN/CO/1, para 31.
98 Concluding Observations of the Committee on the Rights of Persons with Disabilities, Costa Rica, U.N.Doc. CRPD/C/CRI/CO/1 (2014), para 46.
99 Concluding Observations of the Committee on the Rights of Persons with Disabilities, Azerbaijan, U.N.Doc. CRPD/C/AZE/CO/1 (2014), para 41(c).
100 ibid.

provided with sufficient supports to ensure that they can benefit from the right to education as laid down in the CRPD.

In some countries, such as Hungary, only a number of persons with disabilities are being educated in inclusive settings.[101] Moreover, the report submitted by the Tunisian Government to the CRPD Committee states that the country is in the process of implementing a phased integration policy for students with certain disabilities but it also refers to the planned construction and extension of alternative education centres.[102] The 'List of Issues' drafted by the Committee in respect of Tunisia includes a request for 'information about the progress achieved toward ensuring full scholastic inclusion of children with disabilities.'[103] It has been stated that 'this makes it very clear that the Committee expects full inclusion of persons with disabilities in the general education system to be the ultimate goal of States Parties.'[104] In its concluding observations to Tunisia, the Committee commended Tunisia for its drafting of the national programme of inclusive education for children with disabilities but also noted 'with deep concern'[105] the fact that, in practice, the inclusion strategy was not equally implemented in schools and, furthermore, that rules relating to the number of children in mainstream schools and to the management of inclusive classes are commonly breached.[106] The Committee therefore recommended that Tunisia should allocate sufficient financial and human resources to implement the national programme of inclusive education for children with disabilities and that it should also increase its efforts to enforce inclusive education for children with disabilities in all schools.[107]

Notwithstanding the challenges which have been highlighted above in respect of the implementation of Article 24 of the CRPD, an examination of the various state reports and shadow reports submitted to the CRPD Committee makes it clear that some progress has been made. In its Study on the challenges and good practices in the implementation of the UN Convention on the Rights of Persons with Disabilities, the European Foundation Centre contends that the Cypriot experience 'reveals positive ways of implementing Article 24 of the CRPD and can thus be considered as a good practice in this area.'[108] That study points to the fact that Cyprus has made considerable progress in integrating disabled children into a common learning environment.[109] This is primarily as a result of the 1999 Act of

---

101 National report on the basis of Article 35 (1) of the Convent ion on the Rights of Persons with Disabilities, Committee/C/HUN/1 (2010).

102 CRPD Committee, Report submitted by Tunisia, Implementation of the Convention on the Rights of Persons with Disabilities: Initial Report of State Parties Submitted Under Article 35 of the CRPD (July 2010), <http://tbinternet.ohchr.org/_layouts/treatybodyexternal/TBSearch.aspx?Lang=en&TreatyID=4&DocTypeID=29.>

103 Committee on the Rights of Persons with Disabilities, List of Issues to be Taken up in Consideration of the Initial Report of Tunisia (October 2010), para 20 <http://www.ohchr.org/en/hrbodies/crpd/pages/crpdindex.aspx>.

104 Supra n 3.

105 Concluding observations of the Committee on the Rights of Persons with Disabilities, Tunisia, UN Doc. CRPD/C/TUN/CO/1, para 30.

106 ibid

107 ibid para 31(d).

108 European Foundation Centre, Study on challenges and good practices in the implementation of the UN Convention on the Rights of Persons with Disabilities VC/2008/1214, 127.

109 ibid

Parliament on the Education and Training of Children with Special Needs,[110] which assigns responsibility to the State for safeguarding the right of disabled children to an inclusive education at all levels of the education system.[111] The aforementioned legislation is directed towards early identification of children with special educational needs. It also requires the implementation of a robust support system, whereby local district committees for special education and training must provide necessary measures in terms of curriculum adaptation, technical and staffing support, or other, for the effective education of the child in an ordinary school.[112] The law also requires evaluation of a child's progress at least once every year.[113] Sweden also provides a good example of a country that is making strides towards fully inclusive education for persons with disabilities. In its concluding observations, the CRPD Committee commended Sweden for its education system, in which only 1.5% of children are instructed outside inclusive, mainstream schools.[114]

7. Conclusion

The CRPD Committee has stated that '[t]he concept of inclusion is one of the key notions of the Convention and should be especially adhered to in the field of education.'[115] During the drafting of the CRPD, the concept of progressive realisation was deemed 'particularly contentious with regard to the right to education, for fear that it may be invoked by states, particularly developing states, as an "escape clause" from the obligations of the CRPD.'[116] This fear is a valid one, in light of the resource constraints encountered by States Parties. However, it is countered by Rieser's view that 'states must plan and develop their capacity in line with the [CRPD] from the moment of adoption.'[117] In the context of the right to education, this has been interpreted as examining current legislation, practices and procedures to ensure the continuing development of education systems so that all disabled children have access to education within an inclusive education system.[118] In the context of Article 24 of the CRPD, ensuring meaningful content to the right to education requires in the first instance the removal of legislative barriers to accessing education. It also requires the provision of reasonable accommodations. This will require States to amend their laws in line with the CRPD and to allocate sufficient resources – financial, human and other – to ensure the implementation of the right to education. The full realisation of Article 24 will require States to take active

---

110 Act of Parliament on the Education and Training of Children with Special Needs 113(1)/1999 <www.moec.gov.cy/eidiki/nomothesia/Number 113(1)_1999.pdf>.

111 Supra n 108.

112 ibid, Pt II, s3(1) of the Law 113(1)/1999 [Information taken from the European Foundation Centre, Study on challenges and good practices in the implementation of the UN Convention on the Rights of Persons with Disabilities VC/2008/1214.]

113 Information taken from the European Foundation Centre, Study on challenges and good practices in the implementation of the UN Convention on the Rights of Persons with Disabilities VC/2008/1214.

114 CRPD Committee, Concluding Observations, Sweden, UN Doc. CRPD/C/SWE/CO/1 (2014), para 4.

115 CRPD Committee Concluding observations, China, UN Doc. CRPD/C/CHN/CO/1 (2012), para 36.

116 Supra n 3, at 6.

117 R Rieser, Implementing Inclusive Education: A Commonwealth Guide to Implementing Article 24 of the UN Convention on the Rights of People with Disabilities.

118 ibid.

and concrete, targeted measures to provide individualised supports while working towards the goal of full inclusion.

The CESCR Committee has pointed to the fact that 'the right to education epitomises the indivisibility and interdependence of all human rights.'[119] In that regard, the Committee has stated that the right to education 'has been variously classified as an economic right, a social right and a cultural right. It is all of these. It is also, in many ways, a civil right and a political right, since it is central to the full and effective realisation of these rights as well.' The indivisibility and interdependence of all human rights is reflected explicitly in the CRPD[120] and can be seen in the hybrid nature of many of the rights contained in the Convention. Arguably a key indicator of the CRPD's effectiveness will be the extent to which States Parties realise such a fundamental right as the right to education. This point is neatly captured by the assertion that although the right to education in Article 24 'is a social right that must be realised progressively, elements of that right are immediately realisable and it is within this context that the right must be monitored.'[121]

---

[119] CESCR Committee, General Comment No. 11 on Plans of action for primary education (Twentieth Session, 1999), U.N Doc. E/C.12/1999/4 (1999), para 2. <http://www2.ohchr.org/english/bodies/cescr/comments.htm>.

[120] See, in particular, Preamble (c).

[121] A Mohitu, National Human Rights Commission of India in IHCHR, From Vision to Action: the Road to Implementation of the Convention (2007) 10.

Chapter 25

INCLUSIVE EDUCATION: MOVING BEYOND IDEOLOGY AND RESTRICTIVE THEORETICAL PERSPECTIVES

Joyce Mortimer

1. Introduction

There is an expansive international legal framework in place on the right to education.[1] However, the reality is that this right is denied in many parts of the world for children with disabilities. As there are between 120 and 150 million children with disabilities in the world, this human rights breach has far-reaching and devastating consequences.[2] The right to education for children with disabilities has been defined, re-defined and reformed continuously in international law, resulting, most recently, in the finely tuned Article 24 of the United Nations Convention on the Rights of Persons with Disabilities 2006 (CRPD) which is the most fundamental mandate for inclusive education to date. It is argued that inclusive education as prescribed by Article 24 is more than an ideological concept. What is required is a paradigm shift in thinking about student disability in order to ensure the right to an equal education on a non-discriminatory basis.

The CRPD promotes a holistic human rights understanding of disability which provides a departure point for the realisation of inclusive education. The Convention emphasises the view that 'disability' is a changing construct, with the environment causing the barriers to inclusion coupled with the individuals' impairments.[3] The preamble of the Convention states: 'Disability is an evolving concept, and that disability results from the interaction between persons with impairments and attitudinal and environmental barriers that hinders full and effective participation in society on an equal basis with others.'[4] Disability is described as neither a medical construct nor a social construct, but rather an interaction between a non-inclusive society and individual impairments.[5]

---

1 T Jonsson and R Wiman, 'Education, Poverty and Disability in Developing Countries. Poverty Reduction Sourcebook' (2011) paras 13–18.

2 ibid 11.

3 J Trani and J Dubois, 'Capability and Disability: An Approach for a better Understanding of Disability Issues' (Conference UN Convention on the Rights of Persons with Disabilities: A Call for Action on Poverty, Lack of Access and Discrimination, Addis Ababa, 19–22 May 2008).

4 Preamble, United Nations Convention on the Rights of Persons with Disabilities (CRPD) (2006).

5 A Silvers, 'On the possibility and desirability of constructing a neutral conception of disability' (2003) 24 Theoretical Medicine 471; S M Reindal, 'A social relational model of disability: A

This chapter will begin by examining the different meanings of disability and how societal values influence meanings and models. It will be shown how different models and understandings of disability ultimately influence educational provision at a given time. The orthodoxy of special needs education and the underlying understanding of disability will be considered and deconstructed. The international legal framework on the right to education will be laid out, both before and under the CRPD. It will be demonstrated that the holistic human rights model of disability upon which the CRPD is based can serve as a departure point for the realisation of an inclusive education system.

2. The Different Models of Disability

The parameters of normalcy or deviance are socially constructed. The view that disability is a matter of perspective is not new. It has long been argued that '"Difference" is only meaningful as a comparison.'[6] Disability categories and labels are based on the concepts of norm and normal.[7] What it means to be disabled and the models that inform these meanings differ from culture to culture and from time to time. Socially held values and opinions influence both meanings and models. Research shows that what is regarded as a disability in one society may not be percieved as such in another society.[8] If one considers stretching the parameters of normalcy to include people with disabilities, the onus then falls on the education system to adapt to include all people rather than on people to conform to the norm.

The different understandings of disability that have existed have had a direct influence on the type of educational provision at any given time. Disability policies have undergone numerous transformations, from a medical model to a civil rights or social model to the most recent human rights holistic model.[9] Those in favour of a social model of disability have criticised the medical model for focusing on medical defects or limitations and for seeing any difficulties as entirely due to personal impairments.[10] In contrast, the social model is based on the view that societal prejudice, bias and discriminatory attitudes create barriers that inhibit the inclusion of persons with disabilities in mainstream society.[11]

Regarding the medical model, Finkelstein states that the body of knowledge created by a traditional approach to disabled people

> 'crystallised into institutional menus of good practice expected from medical staff in rehabilitation centres, occupational therapists in social services,

---

theoretical framework for special needs education?' (2008) 23 European Journal of Special Needs Education (2) 135.

6 M Minow, 'The Supreme Court 1986 Term, Foreword: Justice engendered' (1987) 101 Harvard Law Review 13.

7 J Richardson, 'Common, delinquent, and special: On the formalization of common schooling in the American states' (1994) 31 American Educational Research Journal 695.

8 B Ingstad, S R Whyte (eds), *Disability and Culture* (University of California Press 1995).

9 D R Kelemen and L Vanhala, 'The shift to the rights model of disability in the EU and Canada' (2010) 20 Regional and Federal Studies (1) 5.

10 See M Oliver, *Understanding Disability: From Theory to Practice* (Macmillan 1996); M Priestley, *Disability Politics and Community Care* (Jessica Kingsley 1999).

11 M Oliver, *The Politics of Disablement* (Macmillan 1990).

> remedial teachers in special schools and so on. In all this activity the volume of understanding has increasingly rested on what, until recently, has been an unchallenged dogma; that the possession of an impairment leads to social vulnerability.'[12]

Shakespeare suggests that feelings of pity, tragedy and welfare in non-disabled people for those with disabilities may stem from an entrenched fear of their own impairments or mortality.[13]

The social model is based on the principle that 'differences are not intrinsic but socially constructed, which implies in turn that the criteria for comparison are not 'real' but humanly chosen.'[14] Oliver states

> '[i]n the broadest sense, the social model of disability is about nothing more complicated than a clear focus on the economic, environmental and cultural barriers encountered by people who are viewed by others as having some form of impairment – whether physical, sensory or intellectual.'[15]

The strength of the social model lies in its requirement to look at society as the problem and not the individual. This is also its inherent weakness. It is couched in negative terms. While it initially empowered people with disabilities, it has now become an assist in their continued segregation and oppression as it ignores the naturally occuring differences in people. A number of disabled people have voiced their criticisms of the social model for its neglect of impairment.[16] It is contended that a more affirmative model is needed, with the focus placed firmly on rights. The United Nations Convention on the Rights of Persons with Disabilities provides such an affirmative model – a holistic human rights model of disability.

---

[12] V Finkelstein, 'Emancipating Disabling Studies' (1998 unpublished papers). An edited version of this paper was published in T Shakespeare (ed), *The Disability Reader: Social Sciences Perspectives* (Cassell 1998).

[13] T Shakespeare, 'Cultural representation of disabled people: Dustbins for disavowal?' (2004) 9 Disability & Society (3) 283.

[14] Minow (n 6) 36.

[15] M Oliver, 'The social model in action: If I had a hammer,' in C Barnes and G Mercer (eds), *Implementing the Social Model of Disability: Theory and Research* (The Disability Press 2004) 21.

[16] See P Abberley, 'Work, utopia and impairment,' in L Barton (ed) *Disability and Society: Emerging Issues and Insights* (Longman 1996); L Crow, 'Renewing the social model of disability' (2008) Coalition 5; L Crow, 'Including all our lives: renewing the social model of disability,' in J Morris (ed) *Encounters with Strangers: Feminism and Disability* (Women's Press 1996); S French, 'Disability, impairment or something in between?' in J Swain, V Finkelstein, S French and M Oliver (eds), *Disabling Barriers – Enabling Environments* (Sage 1993); R G Thomson, 'Feminist theory, the body and the disabled figure,' in L J Davis (ed) *The Disability Studies Reader* (Routledge 1997); B Hughes and K Patterson, 'The social model of disability and the disappearing body: Towards a sociology of impairment,' (1997) 12 Disability & Society (3) 225.; L Keith (ed), *Mustn't Grumble: Writings by disabled women* (Women's Press 1994); J Morris, *Pride Against Prejudice: Transforming Attitudes to Disability* (Women's Press 1991); R Pinder, 'Sick-but-fit or fit-but-sick? Ambiguity and identity at the workplace,' in C Barnes and G Mercer (eds), *Exploring the Divide: Illness and Disability* (The Disability Press 1996); T Shakespeare and N Watson, 'Defending the social model' (1997) 12 Disability & Society (2) 293; S Wendell, *The Rejected Body: Feminist Philosophical Reflections on Disability* (Routledge 1996); S Wendell, 'Towards a feminist theory of disability,' in L Davis (ed), *The Disability Studies Reader* (Routledge 1997).

3. Institutionalisation, Segregation and Inclusion

The education system has been used throughout history as an instrument for maintaining society's status quo.[17] In the context of disability, there has always been a conflict between asserting sameness in order to be treated equally, and acknowledging difference in order to claim required accommodations to ensure equality. This has been entitled the 'dilemma of difference.'[18] Minow argues that this dilemma arises as a result of 'powerful unstated assumptions about whose point of view matters, and about what is given and what is mutable in the world.'[19]

Disabilities have been defined, re-defined and re-named continuously throughout history in accordance with socially held opinions. This, in turn, has had a direct effect on the type and standard of education provided to children with disabilities. The eugenic movement involved segregation and institutionalisation.[20] The medical model of disability was based on notions of welfare, paternalism and charity.[21] This model of disability influenced the creation of special education and 'pull-out' classes. The resulting educational provision came in the form of institutions (at worst) and segregated schooling (at best). This situation only served to perpetuate stereotypes and discriminatory assumptions and further isolate an already isolated group. Disability advocates, comprising a large representation of people with disabilities themselves, challenged the underlying assumptions and beliefs which gave rise to the medical model.[22] A paradigm shift in thinking was called for. The social model was welcomed as it represented a fundamentally new understanding of disability. Although it was recognised that the medical model did provide necessary benefits to people with disabilities, it did not protect rights. The social model is based on the principles of freedom, autonomy, dignity and ultimately civil rights. The social model asserts that people with disabilities are disabled by mainstream society and the way in which it excludes and restricts the participation of people with disabilities. The social model of disability forced a review of segregationist policies and a move towards inclusive education. Mainstream schools were criticised for excluding students with disabilities.

4. The Special Education Orthodoxy

It is argued that the special education orthodoxy is discriminatory and inadequate to protect the educational rights of persons with disabilities. Special education is a practice which has evolved over many centuries in response to a variety of societal factors. Special education is not an inherent aspect of schooling. It is based on concepts of standardisation, labelling and classification. Those opposing inclusive

---

17 F Coomans, 'Identifying violations of the right to education,' (1994) 20 Naam auteur/Artikel, SIM Special 141.

18 M Minow, 'Learning to live with The dilemma of difference: Bilingual and Special Education,' (1985) Law & Contemporary Problems 157.

19 Minow (n 6) 13.

20 See T M Cook, 'The American with Disabilities Act: The Move to Integration' (1991) 64 Temple Law Review 393.

21 B Blatt and F Kaplan, *Christmas in Purgatory: A Photographic Essay on Mental Retardation* (Human Policy Press 1974).

22 S French and J Swain, 'It's time to take up the offensive' (1997) 23 (34) Therapy Weekly 7.

education call for evidence of its effectiveness in advance of its implementation whilst ignoring the proven failures and shortcomings of the existing segregated system. Stereotypical, prejudicial beliefs inform the special education argument.[23] Segregated education mirrors the discriminatory stratifications existent in society. Inclusive education, on the other hand, is based on principles of equality, non-discrimination, autonomy and human rights.

The orthodoxy within special needs education is based on a medical model of disability. Classification systems form the basis of the system. In recent years, the orthodoxy of special needs education has been challenged by those proposing the social model of disability[24] (Oliver, Shakespeare and Watson, Swain et al). The Special education system is criticised for its categorisation of impairments and special needs into disabilities, through classification systems grounded in a medical understanding of disability. As Engel states '[t]he science of defectology pervades the culture that surrounds special education.'[25] In 1968, Lloyd Dunn wrote a provocative and often cited article in which he suggested that special education might fundamentally be doing more harm than good.[26] Dunn and Jane Mercer were especially concerned about the possibility that bias might underlie the schools' labelling and segregating disproportionate numbers of minority pupils.[27] Grant and Sleeter grouped handicap status with class, race, and gender in a critical analysis of ways in which social stratification occurs in schools.[28] Sleeter saw disability as a social construct that resulted from institutions' inability to accommodate diversity.[29] Barnes writes:

> 'The aims of education for all children and young people include the achievement of responsible personal autonomy and full participation in the communities in which they live. In practice, this usually means employment and a relatively autonomous lifestyle. The type of education that the overwhelming majority of young people with impairments receive does not provide them with the skills and opportunities to achieve either.'[30]

Those that favour separate systems of schooling generally believe that children with disabilities are either cannot receive education in mainstream settings or that it will cost too much. Historically, it was also believed that including children with disabilities in mainstream schools led to a drop in the overall quality of education being provided. The consequence was that mainstream schools began pushing out those children who did not measure up to performance goals, resulting in a reluctance

---

23 S J Peters, C Johnstone, P Ferguson, 'A disability rights in education model for evaluating inclusive education' (2005) 9 International Journal of Inclusive Education 2.

24 M Oliver, *'Disability and dependency: The role of education'* C Struiksma and F Meijer (eds), *Integration at Work* (Rotterdam, Pedagogical Institut 1989).

25 D M Engel, 'Law, culture and children with disabilties: Educational rights and the construction of difference' (1991) 1 Duke Law Journal 180.

26 L M Dunn, 'Special education for the mildly retarded: Is much of it justifiable?' (1968) 35 Exceptional Children 5.

27 J R Mercer, *Labelling the Mentally Retarded* (University of California Press 1973).

28 C Grant and C Sleeter, *After the School Bell Rings* (Falmer 1986).

29 C Sleeter, 'Learning Disabilities: The social construction of a special education category' (1986) 53 Exceptional Children 46.

30 C Barnes, *Disabled People in Britain and Discrimination: A Case for Anti-Discrimination Legislation* (C Hurst Publishers 1991).

to include students with disabilities and to expel students who were difficult to teach. In 1994, the United Nations Special Rapporteur, Bengt Lindqvist stated that '[a]ll children and young people of the world, with their individual strengths and weaknesses, with their hopes and expectations, have the right to education. It is not our education systems that have a right to certain types of children. Therefore, it is the school system of a country that must be adjusted to meet the needs of all children.'

5. Before the CRPD: The Right to Inclusive Education in International Law

The right to education is protected by a system of soft and hard law instruments. Most of these instruments do not explicitly protect the right to education of children with disabilities; however, education for all is a common theme throughout. According to Basser, the international legal framework 'supports inclusive education as the norm for all children, including children with disabilities' and if there is to be a segregated setting, 'it must be available on equal terms to that in the mainstream.'[31] In terms of the hard law instruments, before the CRPD the right to education was protected by the Convention on Economic, Social and Cultural Rights 1966 (CESCR) and the Convention on the Rights of the Child 1990 (CRC).

The Committee on Economic, Social and Cultural Rights has elaborated upon and expanded the protection of the right to education for children with disabilities through its General Comments. General Comment No.5 comments on the importance of inclusion in education.[32] The Committee outlines how people with disabilities are best educated in an integrated educational environment. General Comment No.13 states that the right to education has four intrinsic elements: availability, accessibility, acceptability and adaptability.[33] It states that the three principles of accessibility are non-discrimination, physical accessibility and economic accessibility.

Before the CRPD, the CRC was arguably the most significant legal instrument protecting the rights of persons with disabilities. Regarding the right to education, Article 23(3) states that it shall be ensured that the disabled child has 'effective access to and receives education, (…) in a manner conducive to the child's achieving the fullest possible social integration and individual development.'[34] The Committee on the Rights of the Child promotes the concept of inclusion of children with disabilities in mainstream education, stating '[i]nclusion of the child with disability in the groups of children of the class room can show the child that he or she has a recognized identity and belongs to the community of learners, peers, and citizens.'[35] The CRC states that inclusive education should be the goal of educating children with

---

31 L A Basser, 'Justice for all? The challenge of realizing the right to education for children with disabilities' (2004–5) 8 Journal of Gender, Race and Justice 538.

32 Committee on Economic, Social and Cultural Rights, General Comment No. 5 – (1994) Persons with Disabilities 09/12/1994, CESCR.

33 Committee on Economic, Social and Cultural Rights, General Comment No. 13 – (1999) The Right to Education 12/08/1999, E/C.12/1999/10, CESCR, paras 6–7.

34 art 23 (1990). UN General Assembly, Convention on the Rights of the Child, 20 November 1989, United Nations, Treaty Series, vol. 1577, 7.

35 Committee on the Rights of the Child, Forty-Third session (Geneva, 11–29 September 2006) CRC/C/GC/9, 27 February 2007 para 64.

disabilities. The Committee urges States Parties to provide the necessary supports and accommodations to help provide an appropriate education for children with disabilities in mainstream schools. The Committee also acknowledges the goal of inclusive education contained in the draft text of the international Convention on the Rights of Persons with Disabilities and encourages State Parties to develop plans of action for achieving this goal. The Committee states:

> [i]t is important to understand that inclusion should not be understood nor practiced as simply integrating children with disabilities into the regular system regardless of their challenges and needs. Close cooperation among special educators and regular educators is essential. Schools' curricula must be re-evaluated and developed to meet the needs of children with and without disabilities. Modification in training programmes for teachers and other personnel involved in the educational system must be achieved in order to fully implement the philosophy of inclusive education.[36]

There are a number of soft law instruments with also provide for the right to education for children with disabilities. The Standard Rules place an explicit expectation on Member States in relation to inclusive education. It states:

> [t]o accommodate educational provisions for persons with disabilities in the mainstream, States should:
> - Have a clearly stated policy, understood and accepted at the school level and by the wider community
> - Allow for curriculum flexibility, addition and adaption
> - Provide for quality materials, ongoing teacher training and support teachers.[37]

The focus on inclusion in the Standard Rules is clear. Rule 6.8 states:

> '[i]n situations where the general school system does not yet adequately meet the needs of all persons with disabilities, special education may be considered. It should be aimed at preparing students for education in the general school system. The quality of such education should reflect the same standards and ambitions as general education and should be closely linked to it. At a minimum, students with disabilities should be afforded the same portion of educational resources as students without disabilities. States should aim for the gradual integration of special education services into mainstream education.'[38]

The Salamanca Statement and Framework for Action opposes segregation as the main option for children with disabilities and promotes the realisation of inclusion. A definition for the inclusive school is given in paragraph 7 and was the first of its kind. It states:

> '[t]he fundamental principle of the inclusive school is that all children should

---

[36] ibid para 6.

[37] United Nations, Standard Rules on the Equalization of Opportunities for Persons with Disabilities G.A, A/RES/48/96 Rule 6.

[38] ibid Rule 6.8.

> learn together, wherever possible, regardless of any difficulties or differences they may have. Inclusive schools must recognize and respond to the diverse needs of their students, accommodating both different styles and rates of learning and ensuring quality education to all through appropriate curricula, organizational arrangements, teaching strategies, resource use and partnerships with their communities. There should be a continuum of support and services to match the continuum of special needs encountered in every school.'

Paragraph 26 explicitly calls for:

> 'the articulation of a clear and forceful policy on inclusion together with adequate financial provision – an effective public information effort to combat prejudice and create informed and positive attitudes – an extensive programme of orientation and staff training – and the provision of necessary support services. Changes in all the following aspects of schooling, as well as many others, are necessary to contribute to the success of inclusive schools: curriculum, buildings, school organization, pedagogy, assessment staffing, school ethos and extra curricular activities.'

The Dakar Framework for Action[39] explicitly recognises inclusive education as the main strategy for addressing the issues of marginalisation and exclusion in schooling.[40] The Dakar Final Report on Education For All states that 'Concern about inclusion has evolved from a struggle on behalf of children "having special needs" into one that challenges all exclusionary policies and practices in education, (…) Instead of focusing on preparing children to fit into existing schools, the new emphasis focuses on preparing schools so that they can deliberately reach out to all children.'[41]

6. The CRPD: A Holistic Human Rights Model of Disability and the Right to Inclusive Education

The draft article on education, Article 17, of the CRPD proved the most contentious of all the provisions. The draft stated that 'where the general education system does not adequately meet the needs of persons with disabilities, special and alternative forms of learning should be made available.'[42] The debate over the initial drafts was based on the continuing question of the appropriateness of inclusion over special provision for deaf children, blind children and deaf-blind children. The International Council for the Education of the Visually Impaired (ICEVI) – World Blind Union (WBU) – published a Position Paper on Inclusive Education affirming its support

---

39 United Nations Educational, Scientific and Cultural Organization, 'World Education Forum. The Dakar Framework for Action: Education for All – Meeting our Collective Commitments' (Paris, UNESCO 2000), (ED-2000/WS/27).

40 United Nations Educational, Scientific and Cultural Organization, 'Policy Guidelines on Inclusion in Education' (Paris, UNESCO 2009) (ED-2009/WS/31) 7.

41 United Nations Educational, Scientific and Cultural Organization, 'World Education Forum Final Report. Part II: Improving the Quality and Equity of Education for All – Meeting Special and Diverse Education Needs: Making Inclusive Education a Reality' (2000) 16.

42 United Nations Enable, 'Working Group, Draft Comprehensive and Integral Convention on the Protection of the Rights and Dignity of Persons with Disabilities' (2004) <www.un.org/esa/socdev/enable/rights/ahcwgreportax1.htm> last accessed 31 March 2016.

for Salamanca and the argument that education for deaf-blind persons 'may be more suitably provided in special schools or special classes and units in mainstream schools.'[43] It stated that it would continue to promote special schools, while also providing special support for blind children in inclusive settings. Commenting on a particular draft and the fact that segregation remained an option, the Centre for Studies of Inclusive Education (CSIE) argued that it upheld 'the segregation of disabled learners and learners with special educational needs into special schools as a legitimate human right.' The CSIE stated that it 'considers such a position to be a retrograde step in the field of education for persons with disabilities.'[44] Inclusion International stated that Article 17 would only be agreed upon by its organisation if based on the Salamanca principles of inclusive education.[45] The final draft contained no reference to separate or segregated education, placing a clear obligation on States to provide an inclusive education system.[46]

Article 24 of the CRPD provides the strongest mandate for the right to inclusive education for children with disabilities to date. It makes no explicit provision for segregated education. The Convention is based on the 'new' approach and attitude to disability, which began emerging in the decade before it.[47] It ensures people with disabilities are not seen as objects of charity, welfare or medical treatment but rather as human beings with rights.[48] The focus is on dignity and equal human rights.[49] The CRPD provides an understanding of student disability and impairment that accepts differences, abilities and inabilities. Upon acceptance of the continuum of human difference, a framework for inclusive education can be built. In the same way society changes its perceptions of all groups of people – on the basis of gender, age, religion, race etc – it is necessary to continue to question our perception of disability. As

---

43 The International Council for Education of People with Visual Impairment and The World Blind Union, 'Joint Position Paper on Inclusive Education of Children with Visual Impairment' (2003) www.icevi.org/publications/ICEVI-WBU_joint_policy_paper_on_inclusive_education.html 25 May 2012.

44 United Nations Enable, 'Contributions to the Third Session of the UN Ad Hoc Committee – Centre for Studies on Inclusive Education, Inclusive Education: Disabled Persons and Education in the New UN Disability Convention' (2004) <www.un.org/esa/socdev/enable/rights/contrib-scbrown.html> last accessed 31 March 2016.

45 United Nations Enable, 'Inclusion International's Position on the Draft Comprehensive and Integral International Convention on the Protection and Promotion of the Rights and Dignity of Persons with Disabilities' (2004) <www.un.org/esa/socdev/enable/rights/ahc3ii.htm> last accessed 31 March 2016.

46 F Ahmad, S Girijashanker and M Kemple, 'The Convention on the Rights of Persons with Disabilities: The Right to Education and the Obligations of States; SOAS International Human Rights Clinic Project' (2011) School of Oriental and African Studies, University of London, Research Paper No. 06/2011, 23.

47 R Kayess and P French, 'Out of darkness into light? Introducing the Convention on the Rights of Persons with Disabilities (2008) 10 Human Rights Law Review.

48 See H Szoke, 'From Welfare to Human Rights – the Rights of People with a Disability' (Conference Disability Advocacy and Information Service, City of Wodonga, 6 November 2008); United Nations Enable, Ad Hoc Committee on an International Convention, Fourth Session (23 August – 3 September 2004); International Disability Alliance, 'Submission: Towards a UN Disability Convention – Article 12 of the CRPD – The Right to Equal Recognition before the Law' (NSW Disability Discrimination Legal Centre 2009). T Hammarberg, 'Realising Children's Rights requires more than Rhetoric – Systematic and Concrete Actions are now Needed' (Council of Europe 2009).

49 United Nations Enable, 'Report of the Working Group looking at the Protection of the Rights of Persons with Disabilities' (2004) <www.un.org/esa/socdev/enable/rights/ahcwgreport.htm> last accessed 31 March 2016.

society continues to develop and modernise, so too must disability discourses. Swain and French recommend an 'affirmative model' of disability, which is, 'essentially a non-tragic view of disability and impairment which encompasses positive social identities, both individual and collective, for disabled people grounded in the benefits of life style and life experience of being impaired and disabled.'[50] This is in line with the holistic human rights model laid down in the CRPD. This advanced conceptual understanding of disability underpins the inclusive education movement.

There is an ever-increasing amount of research being conducted in support of inclusive education for children with disabilities.[51] The World Bank states that:

- there are personal, social and economic dividends to educating primary school aged children with special education needs in mainstream schools
- most special education needs can be successfully and less expensively accommodated in integrated schools than in segregated institutional settings,[52] and
- the vast majority of children with special education needs can be cost-effectively accommodated in regular primary schools.[53]

Additionally, according to the World Bank, 'programs that expand the access of excluded groups to education have led to important shifts in mind-set among community members and government leaders regarding the contributions that those groups can make to society.'[54]

In a report for UNICEF, Bengt Lindqvist, the United Nations Special Rapporteur on Human Rights, stated that '[s]chools are in need of reform, both structurally and also in terms of pedagogy and curriculum.'[55] An inclusive curriculum addresses every child's cognitive, emotional, social and creative development.[56] It is based on four pillars of inclusive education – learning to know, to do, to be and to live together.[57] Curricula need to be flexible enough to allow for differences in children's learning abilities and needs. Teachers should be afforded the space and opportunities to adapt and adjust education to diverse classrooms.[58] Pupil diversity needs to be responded to in a positive manner. All children need to be seen as capable of learning – to some degree. Multi-grade, multi-age and multi-ability classrooms are becoming a reality across the globe.[59] UNESCO views inclusion as, a 'dynamic approach of

50 J Swain and S French, 'Towards an affirmative model of disability' (2000) 15 Disability & Society (4)569.

51 For example, see the writings of Diane Ferguson and Susan Peters.

52 S J Peters, 'Inclusive Education: An EFA Strategy for All Children' (World Bank 2004).

53 R Metts, 'Disability, Issues, Trends and Recommendations for the World Bank' (World Bank 2000) Social Protection Discussion Paper No. 0007, xi.

54 Peters (n 56).

55 United Nations Educational, Scientific and Cultural Organization, 'Policy Guidelines on Inclusion in Education' (Paris, UNESCO 2009) (ED-2009/WS/31).

56 UNESCO 10 Questions on Inclusive Education.

57 J Delors and the International Commission on Education for the Twenty-first Century, 'Learning: The treasure within' (UNESCO 1996).

58 UIS 2004c. Investing in the Future: Financing the Expansion of Educational Opportunity in Latin America and the Caribbean, Montreal, QUE., UIS.

59 United Nations Educational, Scientific and Cultural Organization, 'Policy Guidelines on Inclusion in Education' (Paris, UNESCO 2009), (ED-2009/WS/31) 19.

responding positively to pupil diversity and of seeing individual differences not as problems, but as opportunities for enriching learning.'[60]

7. Conclusion

A paradigm shift in attitudes is vital to the practical realisation of the right to inclusive education for children with disabilities. The appropriateness of separate systems of education have been challenged from both a human rights perspective and also from the perspective of cost-effectiveness. A change in thinking can lead to a re-conceptualisation of 'disability' or 'special needs.' The challenge is to develop an understanding of impairments and disability, which provides a departure point for realising inclusive education in practice. It is argued that framing disability issues in terms of rights assists in 'the paradigm shift' and ensures the realisation of radical social change.[61] Disability must be seen as an issue facing all individuals, those with impairments and those without. Many non-disabled people have impairments, for example, poor sight or poor hearing. However, these people are disabled by barriers within the society that they live. The way in which society is structured and the values and beliefs upon which it is based must be questioned. The default reference point, ie the non-disabled person, must be deconstructed. Difference and diversity in people must be acknowledged and embraced. As Minow states, '[b]y taking difference into account, we can overcome our pretended indifference to difference, and people our worlds with those who can surprise and enrich one another.'[62]

Inclusive education opponents argue that it strives to enforce a type of 'normalisation' on children with disabilities. That is not what is proposed by the CRPD. Inclusive education ought to be based on the following general principles:

- Human diversity is inevitable and natural. It is futile to use a 'norm' as a comparator against which all people are to be assessed.
- Common human characteristics transverse the socially constructed delineations of gender, race, disability, class and sexual orientation.
- Diversity and varying educational competency is to be expected in any classroom. Learning is possible and even enhanced in an inclusive setting.
- Inclusive schooling fosters equality in encouraging a sense of community and co-operation. The fundamental tenet of inclusive education is the welfare of all students.

From a policy perspective, realising inclusive education in practice means adopting a holistic approach to school reform and therefore transforming the way exclusion is currently addressed.[63] Inclusive education involves changing and modifying educational content, approaches, structures and strategies with a common vision that it is the responsibility of the mainstream school to educate all children.[64] Inclusive

---

60 ibid 9.

61 D Kelemen and L Vanhala, 'The shift to the rights model of disability in the EU and Canada' (2010) 20 (1) Regional and Federal Studies.

62 Minow (n 6) 95.

63 United Nations Educational, Scientific and Cultural Organization, 'Policy Guidelines on Inclusion in Education' (Paris, UNESCO 2009), (ED-2009/WS/31) 4.

64 United Nations Educational, Scientific and Cultural Organization, 'Overcoming Exclusion

education, 'is a plan for educational development that is based on the concepts of human rights and peace and stresses respect for differences.'[65]

through Inclusive Approaches in Education. A Challenge and a Vision' (Paris, UNESCO 2003), (ED-2003/WS/63).

65 L Nai-Kwai Lo, 'The sustainable development of inclusive education' (2007) 40 Chinese Education and Society (4) 44.

CHAPTER 26

RECONCILING SAMENESS AND DIFFERENCE IN DISABILITY RIGHTS IDEOLOGY: THE CASE OF STUDENT IDENTITY

Bronagh Byrne

1. INTRODUCTION

Concepts of sameness and difference, equality and non-discrimination have long occupied a central position in international human rights law. Despite widespread guarantees of equality and non-discrimination in human rights treaties, the precise meaning and scope of these have been a source of contention and only a few human rights instruments have expressly provided for a definition of 'distinction' or 'non-discrimination'. As Judge Tanaka observed in the West Africa case, '[A]lthough the existence of this principle [of non-discrimination] is universally recognised..., its precise content is not very clear.'[1] The intricacies of 'equality' are equally compelling and associated debates are marked by significantly greater disaccord than any consensus. While 'equality' is not a new revelation, it could be argued that the tenacity and cumulative nature of inequalities more generally, have generated a reinvigorated examination of the concept.

The ways in which 'equality' is conceptualised and understood in international human rights law, and the extent to which it is underpinned by a formal or substantive approach, has important implications for assessing the 'degree of fit' between international law and lived experiences, not least with respect to the lived experiences of people with disabilities. Equality theories and traditional manifestations of 'formal equality' under international law have by and large, failed to fully consider or incorporate the logistics of disability, particularly in relation to the social construction of such. Nor have disabled people been included as subjects of liberal equality theorising and jurisprudence.[2] Instead, the 'problem' of equality in the disability context has been rooted in the perceived dilemma of 'difference,' not least in relation to other minority group statuses and inequalities. Attention to substantive equality, whilst undoubtedly much more relevant and far-reaching than formal equality, is arguably similarly problematic where it remains heavily contingent upon notions of 'support,' 'assistance' and 'reasonable accommodations' in restrictive forms. Achieving substantive equality for disabled people in a system where 'the game has already begun,' and where 'the rules and standards have already

[1] International Court of Justice South West Africa, Second Phase (1966) International Court of Justice 3(6) 302.

[2] A Silvers, '"Defective" agents: Equality, difference and the tyranny of the normal' (1994) The Journal of Social Philosophy's Twenty-Fifth Anniversary Issue. Reprinted in R Manning and R Trujillo (eds), *Social Justice in a Diverse Society* (Mayfield Publishing Company 1996).

been set,'[3] is somewhat contradictory since it implies a form of equality that requires disabled people to 'fit in' with an already constructed society and associated social systems; that is, a form of equality which fails to radically challenge the root of all inequalities. Rather, attention must be paid to practices of systemic discrimination which emanate from 'rules' of everyday practice(s), which are taken for granted and which can become subsumed by an unproblematised language of substantive equality. These 'routine regimes' of social action[4] are part of the deeper structures of domination and oppression with which this chapter is concerned.

The United Nations Convention on the Rights of Persons with Disabilities (CRPD) is grounded in the principles of, inter alia, equality and non-discrimination, and respect for diversity and difference. The language of the CRPD situates this premise firmly in the domain of substantive equality. This, combined with Article 24 of the CRPD (which provides for a right to education without discrimination and on the basis of equal opportunity), would appear to establish a strong rights base for young people with disabilities in education settings. Access to many CRPD rights are, however, contingent upon the acceptance of a 'disabled' identity; something which presents a particular dilemma for young people with disabilities in educational settings at a crucial point in their lifecourse. This chapter takes the latter dilemma as its starting point. It explores the extent to which the CRPD reflects and/or has the potential to engage with issues of identity in the educational context. To this end, the chapter draws on recent research which sought to explore barriers to education for young people with hearing and visual impairments and the 'crisis of belonging'[5] that emerged in the face of institutional claims to substantive equality and 'reasonable accommodations.'

2. Disability and Identity Ascription

People with disabilities have traditionally experienced particularly high levels of involuntary labelling and identity 'ascription.' In such instances, the social characteristics of disabled people and their implied possibilities are generally 'ascribed' to the individual by non-disabled others rather than being either selected or crafted by the individual through behaviours and attitudes. The possession by individuals of a particular characteristic(s) which allows them to be labelled 'disabled,' 'black,' 'gay' or 'straight' is deeply embedded. As Calhoun contends: '[w]e know of no people without names, no languages or cultures in which some manner of distinctions between self and other, we and they, are not made.'[6] Corker contends that such identity ascription becomes manifest as a form of legitimate control exercised by the dominant culture, which operates by attributing greater value to one side of the binary opposition (non-disabled people) over the other (disabled people).[7] The highly determinative role of social ascription and social structures

3 I Young, 'Social movements and the politics of difference' (1990) in R Manning and R Trujillo (eds), *Social Politics in a Diverse Society* (Mayfield Publishing Company 1996).
4 M Cassin, 'Routine Regimes: Systemic Discrimination, Inequality and Privilege' (Equality and Social Inclusion Conference, Belfast, February 2006).
5 Z Bauman, *Identity* (Cambridge Polity Press 2004).
6 C Calhoun (ed), *Social Theory and the Politics of Identity* (Blackwell 1994) 9.
7 M Corker, 'Disability discourse in a postmodern world' in T Shakespeare (ed), *The Disability Reader* (London: Continuum 1998) 18.

is particularly evident in the lives of young disabled people who are ascribed as 'dependent' and denied any consultative role or individual agency.[8] The way(s) in which 'disability' is defined and ascribed has powerful implications for students in determining access and entitlement to resources, services and opportunities through, inter alia, diagnosis and labelling, and acceptance or rejection of expressed need against set criteria.[9] In third-level education, for example, young people are required to actively disclose and identify as 'disabled' in order to gain access to appropriate 'support' and assistance.

The internalisation of ascribed identities can act as a form of 'self-discipline'[10] and lead to individuals, in this case young people with disabilities, emerging as the 'other.'[11] Thus, '[h]igh levels of ascribed identity and identification are very much part of the processes which create minority population subgroups as 'Other' and not part of 'We' or 'Us."[12] The categorical nature of identity ascription that assumes a single, fixed identity fails to recognise variations within as well as between categories. The assumption that all those who fall into the ascribed category 'disabled' are the same fails to recognise that disabled people, like non-disabled people, have different needs, backgrounds and characteristics, and that not all will wish to be labelled as such. Yet the term 'disabled' remains a powerful one, for both those who do and do not identify with it. As Shakespeare argues:

> 'There is a danger of ignoring the fact that disabled people are also men and women, straight and gay, and come from various ethnic groups. Just as white feminists were accused by black women of ignoring the specificities of black women's experience, and even of being racist, so disabled people risk ignoring difference.'[13]

3. Conceptualising Equality in Human Rights Law

The experiences of people with disabilities of complex institutional and systemic forms of discrimination have posed particular challenges to prevailing concepts of equality and non-discrimination. The dilemma associated with 'equality' more generally has been recognised by the Human Rights Commitee (HRC),[14] in its General Comment and in *Broeks v Netherlands*, which recognised that not all forms

---

8 K M Tisdall, 'A culture of participation?' in S Riddell and N Watson (eds), *Disability, Culture and Identity* (Pearson Education Ltd 2004); S Riddell, T Tinklin and A Wilson, *Disabled Students in Higher Education: Perspectives on widening access and changing policy* (Routledge 2005).

9 B Byrne and L Lundy, 'Protections for students with disabilities in international law?' in C Russo (ed), *The Legal Rights of Students with Disabilities* (Rowland and Littleman 2011) 5.

10 M Foucault, *A History of Sexuality: an introduction* (Penguin 1976).

11 Calhoun (n 7).

12 B Byrne and E McLaughlin, 'Disability and Equality: the case of Young adults and Third Level Education in Northern Ireland, Belfast' (Equality and Social Inclusion in Ireland Project 2005) 3.

13 T Shakespeare 'Disability, Identity, Difference', in C Barnes and G Mercer (eds) *Exploring the Divide: Illness and Disability* (Disability Press 1996) 109.

14 Human Rights Committee, General Comment No. 18 -... *supra* note 22, para 8; *Broeks v Netherlands Communication* No. 172/84, unreported, 9 April 1987, at para 13. This approach has been reinforced by the European Court of Human Rights in the *Belgian Linguistics* case (A/6) (1979–1980) 1 E.H.R.R 252.

of differential treatment are discriminatory.[15] The meaning of discrimination under the International Covenant on Civil and Political Rights (ICCPR) encompasses indirect as well as direct forms of discrimination, with the HRC noting in *Althammer v Austria* that: '[A] violation of article 26 can also result from the discriminatory effect of a rule of measure that is neutral at face value or without intent to discriminate...'[16] Elsewhere, the Committee on Economic, Social and Cultural Rights recognises both de jure and de facto discrimination against people with disabilities, and has gone so far as to define 'disability-based discrimination' as including any distinction, exclusion, restriction or preference, or 'denial of reasonable accommodation' based on disability which has the effect of nullifying or impairing the recognition, enjoyment or exercise of economic, social or cultural rights.[17] The Committee's most recent General Comment on non-discrimination expands on the HRC's previous observations considerably.[18] Of particular relevance is the recognition of the need for discrimination to 'be eliminated both formally and substantively;'[19] of the impact of systemic discrimination, and the impact of cumulative and intersectional discrimination.[20]

While the rights specified in the CRPD are largely specified in other human rights instruments, the Convention focuses on the actions that States must take to ensure that people with disabilities enjoy these rights on an equal basis with others. The CRPD makes extensive references to equality and non-discrimination throughout.[21] A definition of discrimination is set out in Article 2 while for the first time in a human rights instrument, Article 2 defines 'reasonable accommodation' as: 'Necessary and appropriate modification and adjustments not imposing a disproportionate or undue burden, where needed in a particular case, to ensure to persons with disabilities the enjoyment or exercise on an equal basis with others of all human rights and fundamental freedoms.'[22]

Article 5 of the CRPD sets these terms in their context. Article 5(3) obliges States Parties to take all appropriate steps to ensure that reasonable accommodation is provided in the pursuit of equality while Article 5(4) enunciates that: 'Specific measures which are necessary to accelerate or achieve de facto equality of persons with disabilities shall not be considered discrimination under the terms of the present Convention.'[23]

All provisions of the CRPD must be read in light of Article 3 (General Principles).

---

15 See also *Young v Australia* (No.941/2000 ICCPR) and *Pauger v Austria* (No. 415/1990 ICCPR) where distinctions in treatment was found to have no 'reasonable' or 'objective' aims.

16 *Althammer v Austria*, No,998/2001 ICCPR at para 10.3.

17 Committee on Economic, Social and Cultural Rights, General Comment No. 5 (1994) Persons with Disabilities at para 15.

18 Committee on Economic, Social and Cultural Rights, General Comment No. 20 (2009) Non-discrimination in Economic, Social and Cultural Rights, E/C.12/GC/20.

19 *Supra* n 17 at para 8.

20 *Supra* n 17 at paras 17 and 27.

21 See references contained in Preamble; art 2 (Definitions); art 3 (General principles); art 4 (General obligations); art 5 (Equality and non-discrimination); art 12 (Equal recognition before the law); art 24 (Education); art 25 (Health); art 27 (Work and employment); art 28 (Adequate standard of living and social protection); art 29 (Participation in political and public life) and art 30 (Participation in cultural life, recreation, leisure and sport).

22 art 2, CRPD (2006).

23 ibid art 5(4).

Whilst Article 3(b) explicitly sets out non-discrimination as a general principle alongside equality between men and women (3(g)), the remaining six principles constitute variants of the equality principle, encompassing the concepts of dignity and autonomy (3(a)), participation and inclusion (3(c)), respect for difference (3(d)), equality of opportunity (3(e)) and, in applying equality to disability, accessibility (3(f)). Paragraph 3(h) enunciates respect for the evolving capacities of children with disabilities. In the context of education, States Parties are required to provide 'reasonable accommodation' of an individual's requirements.[24]

The concept of reasonable accommodation has been identified as a crucial component of the CRPD. It has been coined as 'perhaps the most fundamental element of the Convention'[25] and conceptualised as reflective of the move away from assimilationist equality approaches towards one that recognises the ways in which people with disabilities have been disadvantaged by the immanent rules of a 'game' which has already begun, and of the remedies needed to ensure a more level 'playing field.'[26] However, the inclusion of reasonable accommodation, whilst a nod to the principle of substantive equality, arguably becomes something of a safety net for States Parties and educational institutions, allowing for discrimination to be justified in cases where an individual's needs are perceived to be 'unreasonable.' As shall be seen, it is also highly individualised since in order to identify what 'reasonable adjustment' is needed, a process of individual assessment and self-identification as 'disabled' is generally required; something which has parallels with an individual model of disability. The concept of reasonable accommodation in the CRPD must take account of and be reconciled against the lived experiences of people with disabilities. The substantive nature of reasonable accommodation and the CRPD's approach to equality more generally, assumes that such provisions are unproblematic in disabled people's lives and that 'reasonable accommodations' will always enhance an individual's enjoyment of their rights. What follows illustrates the potential pitfalls of substantive equality provisions in practice for young people with disabilities and the tensions that exist between the need to identify as 'disabled' in order to access forms of 'support' and the desire among young people to develop a student identity alongside their peers. These findings are based on a research project which explored the barriers to further and higher education for young people with visual and hearing impairments in Northern Ireland. Twenty young people were interviewed in total alongside thirty-one interviews with policymakers and representatives from further education colleges, universities and community and voluntary organisations.

4. The Case of 'Student Identity'

Most young people felt that their experience in third-level education was 'ok.' Some were genuinely impressed with the level of support provided, while others were critical of the pressures that had been borne on them by virtue of requiring support. The desire to assume a 'student identity' was understood by the young people who participated in the study to conflict with an ascribed 'disabled

---

24 ibid art 24(2)(c).

25 R Kayess and P French 'Out of the Darkness, Into the Light? Introducing the CRPD' (2008) 8(1) Human Rights Law Review 1–34, 27.

26 I M Young, 'Equality of Whom? Social Groups and Judgements of Injustice' (2001) The Journal of Political Philosophy (9)1, 1–18.

identity'. It is clear that the perceived marking of difference through the process of reasonable accommodation remains problematic. Most of the young people in the study associated this marking of 'difference' and the provision of reasonable accommodation with ideas of 'otherness.' Typical comments from young people included:

> 'I just want to be treated the same' (Rufus)
>
> 'It's difficult… you don't want to be treated any different. You don't want to be seen as something odd.' (Gareth)
>
> 'I think when you are treated [like] everyone else you are going to feel the same. When someone treats you different[ly] you are going to start thinking you are different… [that] there is an obvious difference between you and everyone else and you will notice the difference. The fact that I can't see really isn't any different.' (Cheryl)

These understandings of equality reflected an internalisation of what it is to be accepted and valued. The distinction between 'same' and differential treatment is also reflective of the ongoing dialectical relationship between impairment and disability, and which impinges upon understandings of equality. 'Disability' was here experienced as a shameful and corrosive social relation rather than a neutral social status, while differential treatment was interpreted as a source of devaluation or perceived failure to meet prescribed 'standards.' Cheryl for example, perceived differential treatment in the form of support as drawing unwanted attention to her visual impairment rather than to the presence of institutional barriers. Young people's understandings of disability and impairment are at odds with those asserted in the disability field where collective and positive identity as 'disabled' is viewed as an important political challenge.[27] This political challenge is one that has been taken up by the CRPD but, in the context of some young people at least, is not a challenge all wish to take up.

The assertion of a same-treatment ethos emerged as a form of resistance against individualised forms of support. It was clear that forms of support can become part of, and exacerbate, structures of domination and oppression. The emerging trend towards 'direct payment' to the individual, who then purchases the services or equipment required, is intended to foster a culture of independence and empowerment.[28] This suggestion is at odds with the perceptions of those young people in my study who were responsible for paying and organising their support and completing the necessary paperwork. Young people viewed this as burdensome, particularly given that this was not something that was bestowed on their peers. Attempts to enhance disabled people's autonomy through the direct payment of support can thus become a double-edged sword. For example:

> 'I was in the middle of doing my dissertation; I was under a load of pressure

---

27 See for example, C Barnes, G Mercer and T Shakespeare, *Exploring Disability: A Sociological Introduction* (Polity Press 1999); M Scott-Hill, 'Impairment, difference and "identity"' in J Swain, S French, C Barnes and C Thomas (eds), *Disabling Barriers – Enabling Environments* (2nd edn, Sage 2008).

28 R Kayess and P French (n 25).

> with uni. And [disability services] sent me emails and some of them I didn't like the tone of the emails…[for example]' if you don't fill this form in we won't be in a position to support you next year'. And it is like you are threatening me. Just stop it! Stop writing me these letters telling me if I don't do this or I don't do that then you are not going to do this... So I just ignored them in the end and they stopped emailing me and I was happy with that. It really did feel like, 'them and us'. So the next semester then I chose not to have any support. So here I am now, really in the same position as I was before struggling with the lectures.' (Gareth)

The practice of completing forms and liaising with Disability Services conflicted with Gareth's sense of self, and made him more aware of his disadvantaged position in the social order; something he had not previously considered to any great extent. It is through interaction with Disability Services that Gareth's feelings of difference come to the fore; 'Why do I suddenly feel different now that I have asked for support?' As such, support provision was generally perceived to be 'disabling' rather than 'enabling.' As a result, many of the young people in my study were keen to have both minimal and less visible support, while some chose to go without. Gareth's experience at university was hindered rather than enhanced by the support he received.

For young deaf people, the visibility of hearing aids and/or note takers was highlighted as frustrating and appeared to replace one 'problem' with another:

> 'Sometimes it is very hard to make friends because with note takers, it is very close to the front, and everybody sits away at the back so it is a bit hard at times.' (Anne)

Even though Anne was now able to understand her lectures better than previously, the act of sitting at the front of the class with her (elder) note taker, while everyone else sat at the back, became 'embarrassing.' Anne did not have many friends on her course and felt isolated. Thus, the act of receiving support becomes, on the one hand, a functional solution to an otherwise inaccessible situation, and on the other, a form of negative symbolic capital and social segregation.

While forms of support such as note takers have been successful in enabling pedagogic access for many young people with disabilities, focus remains on the young person's perceived 'inability' to readily participate and the need to get 'around' particular barriers, and does not always consider the negative implications that some forms of support may have for young people in practice. These experiences highlight how some forms of support offered by educational institutions can unwittingly become part of those deeper structures of domination and oppression, and of complex forms of discrimination by distinguishing between those students who are able to conform to naturalised pedagogies, and those who are not. What support mechanisms fail to sufficiently highlight is the ways in which the educational participation of young disabled people can be hindered by constructed norms and by practices that are taken for granted, rather than by the individual impairment. The reactive nature of disclosure policies place considerable pressure upon students to define and categorise themselves as inherently 'different' at a time when 'fitting in' is perceived by young people as crucial to positive experiences in the educational domain. Young people with disabilities are therefore less able to embrace an individualised 'choice identity'[29] than their non-disabled peers. Increases in disability support provision are widely perceived to be 'a good thing' or an indicator of institutional commitment towards 'inclusion' and substantive equality more generally. Yet individualised and needs-based assessment and support continue to be portrayed as a 'gift' or 'concession' rather than a fundamental human right. Forms of support as objectified by support services in further and higher education are in themselves 'carriers' and perpetrators of 'disablism.'[30] Supports which claim to facilitate 'inclusion' must be regarded with caution. Areas of provision which require the individual student to adjust have exacerbated 'deeper' and less-visible patterns of inequality. There were numerous instances in which the young people who participated in the study sought to improve their possession of symbolic capital, even if this meant rejecting support. It was clear that support provision was experienced as an instrument of communication, cognition and mode of distinction between the dominant and dominated.[31]

5. Conclusion

The ambiguity of equality in the context of disability is illustrative of the higher levels of social infrastructure and resources that are sometimes, but not always, necessary in order to achieve similar outcomes, and which require active identification as 'disabled' for their operationalisation. This ambiguity becomes particularly evident in educational settings where young people with disabilities may interpret 'inclusion' in ways that are more compatible with their identity development at a particular point in the lifecourse, and choose to adopt a 'passing strategy.' The articulation of a disabled identity and associated differential treatment therefore becomes confusing, not least when viewed in contradistinction to the (particularly social) benefits of a 'student identity'. This may lead to some forms of support, most notably those perceived as 'marking difference,' being experienced as disabling rather than enabling.

The need for substantive equality and its explication in the CRPD is not questioned. What is at issue, however, is the complexity of achieving genuine substantive equality in a way that accommodates the diverse lived experiences of people with disabilities and which facilitates inclusion as conceptualised by those 'seeking to be included.' While the CRPD clearly makes reference to 'individualised' forms of support, these continue, by and large, to be determined by what is on offer in particular settings. Moreover, in the context of reasonable accommodation, what is perceived as reasonable by an institution may be very different to what is considered reasonable for a young person receiving that support.

The practical realities of young disabled people's lives in education settings necessitates careful application of reasonable accommodation, and of substantive equality provisions more generally, to ensure that the enjoyment of rights is enhanced rather than impaired. More needs to be done to ensure that young people are actively involved in decisions about their educational experiences and that these processes are

---

29 U Beck, *Risk Society: Towards a New Modernity* (Sage 1992).

30 C Thomas, *Female Forms: Experiencing and Understanding Disability* (University Press 1999) 48.

31 P Bourdieu, *Outline of a Theory of Practice* (Cambridge University Press 1977).

sensitive to the realities of identity development. Rights should not, in their practical implementation, be contingent upon the forced acceptance of a medicalised disabled identity. In conclusion, the CRPD must be sensitive to the dilemma of difference and the potential dangers of identity ascription as the experience of young people with disabilities in this chapter demonstrates. Attention must be paid to those inequalities entrenched in practices that have been taken for granted. To do so will add richness to the development of the CRPD and the enjoyment of rights in practice.

Chapter 27

AFRICAN PERSPECTIVES ON ARTICLE 24 OF THE UNITED NATIONS CONVENTION ON THE RIGHTS OF PERSONS WITH DISABILITIES

Tsitsi Chataika

1. Introduction

Recent years have witnessed a considerable global improvement in the way in which persons with disabilities are viewed. Concerns for social justice, including recognition of equal rights and provision of equal opportunities driven by the success of the Civil Rights movement in the 1950s and 1960s, have increased awareness of the rights and abilities of individuals with physical, sensory and/or cognitive impairments. The result has been the enactment of numerous pieces of legislation related to various sectors, including education. However, in the absence of reasonable accommodations required by specific laws, the ability of affected individuals to fully participate in society remains limited. This chapter focuses on the African perspective of the educational rights of persons with disabilities, as provided for in Article 24 of the United Nations Convention on the Rights of Persons with Disabilities (CRPD), which calls for full rights to education in inclusive settings for persons with disabilities. Inclusive education is discussed from the African perspective, and the interplay between global and local interpretations of this concept is considered, using a post-colonial lens. The argument is that international human rights conventions are important, but should be understood from a local and cultural perspective. Meekosha and Soldatic[1] argue that the CRPD addresses the politics of human rights and disability, which has been central to the struggle for recognition of persons with disabilities. However, Northern discourses of disability rights have considerably influenced this international legal instrument. Their argument is that the daily experiences of many persons with disabilities in the global South (or the so-called 'developing' countries) lie outside the reach of human rights instruments. Therefore, disabled activists in the global South rightfully question the extent to which these instruments contribute to the struggle for justice for persons with disabilities in the global South. By implication, while Northern discourses promote an examination of disabled *bodies* in social dynamics, the politics of impairment in the global South must understand social dynamics in *bodies*. Accordingly, regional collaborations and local ownership of pragmatic solutions in achieving Article 24 of

1 H Meekosha and S Karen, 'Human Rights and the Global South: The Case of Disability' (2011) 32 Third World Quarterly 1383.

the CRPD may decrease accusations of cultural imperialism in Africa, and facilitate local innovation in inclusive education, which acts as a vehicle for socio-economic transformation.

2. Education as a Vehicle for Socio-economic Transformation

What do we mean by education? The question appears to be simple. However, there have been countless academic papers attempting to address this question from a philosophical, anthropological, sociological, or psychological perspective; and yet, there seems to be no definite answer.[2] Any definition of education reflects the ideological and ethical preconceptions of the definer of the meaning, rather than an absolute and unchanging reality. According to Peters, education can only be defined by its criteria, and she likens it to a *reform* because it would be 'a logical contradiction to say that a man [or woman] had been educated but that he [or she] had in no way changed for the better; or that in educating his [or her] son [or daughter], a man [or woman] was attempting nothing that was worthwhile.'[3]

The 1948 Universal Declaration of Human Rights (UDHR) is the starting point for any definition of education in which human rights are incorporated. The aims of education in the UDHR are outlined in Article 26 as follows:

> 1. Education shall be directed to the full development of the human personality and to the strengthening of respect for human rights and fundamental freedoms.
> 2. It shall promote understanding among all the nations, racial or religious groups, and shall further the activities of the United Nations for the maintenance of peace.

The above principles establish the requirements of an education to produce citizens who respect rights and freedoms within a global, rather than merely a national context. Education is defined as a right in itself, but the aforementioned article in the UDHR also implies that education is a means to an end, rather than an end in itself. Education is the process through which all citizens can become aware of their rights and responsibilities, so that peace and prosperity can be secured for all nations and peoples. In Article 3 of the UDHR, States are required to enact such legislation and to promote such educational programmes as may be calculated to secure the acceptance and observance of this policy.[4]

This means that education is a tool for the development of the human character and the strengthening of respect for human rights and basic freedom. The 1978 Warnock Report described the purpose of education as:

> 'First to enlarge a child's knowledge, experience and imaginative understanding and thus her/his awareness of moral values and capacity for enjoyment; and

---

2 T Chataika, 'Inclusion of Disabled Students in Higher Education in Zimbabwe: From Idealism to Reality – A Socio-ecosystem Perspective' (PhD thesis, University of Sheffield 2007).

3 R S Peters, *Ethics and Education* (Routledge and Kegan Paul 1966).

4 United Nations, Universal Declaration of Human Rights (UDHR) (United Nations 1948).

> secondly to enable her/him to enter the world after formal education is over as an active participant in society and a responsible contributor.'[5]

Therefore, in order to satisfy this purpose, education appears to be concerned with knowledge, imaginative understanding and creativity, moral values, capacity for enjoyment, involvement in society and, inter-dependence. Put simply, for education to be valuable, it should impart knowledge, promote imaginative understanding and creativity, instil positive moral values, provide room for enjoyment through various activities, involve and empower an individual and society at large, and finally promote inter-dependence amongst individuals at both micro and macro levels.[6] If education is such a powerful tool in human development, then no one has the right to deny it to anybody, including persons with disabilities. Regrettably, societal attitudes and perception of disability have relegated persons with disabilities to the periphery of any development initiative.

3. Global Situation of Persons with Disabilities

The first-ever world disability report estimated that there are now over one billion persons with disabilities, with 80 percent of them living in low-income countries.[7] These individuals are often limited by both physical and social barriers, which exclude them from society and prevent them from actively participating in the development of their nations. This is despite the obvious link between disability and poverty.[8] The key to unlocking the potential of person with disabilities rests in the provision of education and the respect for the rights of all individuals.[9] Inclusion in education is a process of effectively facilitating the learning and participation of all learners within the mainstream school systems, without segregation and prejudice. It is about shifting the focus from attempting to alter persons with disabilities to fit into society; to transforming society and the world by changing attitudes, removing barriers and providing the right support systems for them. Oliver, quoted by Chataika and her colleagues, argues that the social model of disability paves the way for social action by persons with disabilities to challenge barriers to participation, and promoting the realisation of their human rights.[10]

4. Education as a Human Right for Persons with Disabilities

Over the last sixty years, governments have adopted a number of general and thematic human rights Conventions and Declarations which are binding and create legal obligations on States to promote, protect and fulfil human rights. These

---

5 Warnock Committee, *Special Educational Needs: The Warnock Report* (D.E.S 1978).

6 T Chataika (n 2).

7 World Health Organization and World Bank, 'World Disability Report' (WHO 2011). <http://whqlibdoc.who.int/publications/2011/9789240685215_eng.pdf> last accessed 31 March 2016.

8 World Health Organization and World Bank (n 5).

9 T Chataika, 'Inclusion of Disabled Students in Higher Education in Zimbabwe' in J Lavia and M Moore (eds), *Cross-cultural Perspectives on Policy and Practice: Decolonizing Community Context* (Routledge 2010).

10 T Chataika, J A Mckenzie, E Swart & M Lyner-Cleophas 'Access to Education in Africa: Responding to the United Nations Convention on the Rights of Persons with Disabilities' (2012) 27 Disability & Society 385.

international human rights instruments reinforce the principle of universality of human rights including the right to education and development, which are clear in all United Nations human rights Conventions. The 1948 Universal Declaration of Human Rights asserted that everyone has a right to education, and yet persons with disabilities were, however, frequently denied this fundamental right. This is often based on the assumption that persons with disabilities do not count as full human beings, and so are somehow the exception in terms of universal rights.[11] Article 28 of the United Nations Convention on the Rights of the Child 1989 stated that primary education should be 'compulsory and available for free to all,[12] and Article 2 specifically mentions children with disabilities. The 1990 Jomtien World Declaration on Education for All attempted to address some of these challenges by stating that many different specific groups were vulnerable, with a particular mention on persons with disabilities. Although the term *inclusion* is not specifically mentioned, there are some statements which indicated the importance of ensuring that marginalised groups should have access to education in the mainstream system. The Millennium Development Goals (MDGs) were endorsed at the United Nations Millennium Development Summit in 2000; they were also reaffirmed by the World Bank. The second MDG specifically focus on achieving universal primary education.[13]

However, the above Conventions and Declarations have not been able to meaningfully address disability issues, thus leaving persons with disabilities unable to enjoy their full rights as enshrined in these instruments. As a result of pressure from disability activists, there were some initiatives specific to disability agreed upon by the international community, particularly in the past three decades. For example, 1981 was declared the International Year of Disabled Persons, which raised awareness and the profile of persons with disabilities. This was followed by the World Programme of Action Concerning Disabled Persons, which was a key instrument of action throughout the United Nations Decade of Disabled Persons (1982–1992). The Standard Rules on the Equalisation of Opportunities for Persons with Disabilities 1993 followed, which consisted of rules governing all aspects of persons with disabilities. Rule 6 focuses on education and agrees with what was stated in Jomtien, Thailand, that States should take the responsibility of educating persons with disabilities in integrated settings.

The principle of inclusive education was adopted at the 1994 Salamanca World Conference on Special Needs Education in Spain. The Dakar World Education Forum followed in 2000, to present the evaluation of the Decade of Education for All that the Jomtein Framework had begun. During this forum, governments pledged themselves to 'create safe, healthy, inclusive and equitably resourced educational environments conducive to excellence in learning with clearly defined levels of achievement for all.'[14] The above instruments restated the belief that all children and adults have the right to benefit from an education that will meet their basic learning needs.

---

11 S Stubbs, *Inclusive Education: Where there are Few Resources* (The Atlas Alliance 2008) United Nations (1989) Convention on the Rights of the Child.

12 United Nations, Convention on the Rights of the Child (United Nations 1989) www.unicef.org/crc last accessed 31 March 2016.

13 For more information on MGDs, refer to www.un.org/millenniumgoals/.

14 See art 8 of the Dakar Declaration.

Initiatives specific to Africa were also proclaimed. In 1999, the Organisation of African Unity (OAU), now African Union, adopted the African Decade of Persons with Disabilities (ADPD 1999-2009). The ADPD was an effort to raise awareness about disability issues on the continent, and to identify solutions tailored to the African experience. In 2010, the ADPD was extended to 2019, drawing on the lessons learnt from the previous dec ADPD, in order to plan for better access to services and participation of persons with disabilities in national development processes. In addition, Member States of the OAU adopted the African Charter on the Rights and Welfare of the Child, which affirmed the right of children with disabilities to protective services under conditions which would guarantee their dignity, encourage self-reliance, and enable active participation in the community. This Charter sought to ensure access to training, preparation for employment, and recreational opportunities designed to promote the fullest possible social integration of persons with disabilities.

The above policy environment, which paved the way for the CRPD and its tenets, was signed in March 2007 and came into force in May 2008.[15] This Convention re-affirms existing human rights, in the context of disability, and focuses strongly on the discrimination that persons with disabilities face on a daily basis. Countries that ratify this international instrument are obliged to implement its tenets, and ensure that persons with disabilities become part of the national development agenda. However, in most low-income countries, recognising the CRPD provisions presents a significant challenge, particularly implementing Article 24 that focuses on education in inclusive settings.

5. The African Perspective on Disability

Although African folklore has over the years been used to promote attitudes of tolerance and respect for individual differences, impairments are generally feared by society.[16] As Marfo points out, being disabled may be associated with supernatural phenomena such as the gods' anger at a parent for misconduct.[17] Some believe that an offended person sought the services of a traditional doctor to curse a family, causing someone to be born, or to become, disabled. Others believe that living a sinful life may be punished by being reincarnated as a person with a disability. River blindness, a parasitic eye disease and a leading infectious cause of blindness, may be attributed to spirits who live in the rivers.[18] Persons with intellectual impairments are often thought to be possessed by an evil spirit. Such beliefs are deep-seated in African traditional culture and religion and may be held to some degree even by more highly educated individuals. Health professionals, for instance, have been known to ignore patients who are disabled, giving preference to non-disabled ones.[19]

---

15 United Nations Enable, 'Convention on the Rights of Persons with Disabilities' (United Nations 2011) <www.un.org/disabilities/default.asp?id=150> last accessed 31 March 2016.

16 J Kisanji, 'The March Towards Inclusive Education in Non-Western Countries: Retracing the Steps' (1998) 2(1) International Journal of Inclusive Education 55.

17 K Marfo, 'Families in Non-Western Cultures: Africa as a Case Example' in J Paul and R J Simeonsson (eds), *Children with Special Needs: Family, Culture and Society* (2nd edn, Harcourt Brace Jovanovich 1993).

18 Marfo (n 14).

19 ibid.

Whether rejected as less worthy because of the impairment, or because they may be less able to pay for services, this clearly communicates disrespect and devaluation of the person who is disabled. There have been reported cases of disabled babies being killed, or be kept hidden from the public. Since a disabled child is seen as a curse, a bad omen, or an incomplete person unworthy of life, abandoning the child to the care of a hospital, orphanage, or special school is likely.

Contrary to the above, though, a study conducted in Zimbabwe among the Tonga people reported no indications of purposely hiding or neglecting children with disabilities.[20] Although the study reported that village elders narrated stories of how in the past, disabled children were hidden away or left to die in rural areas due to beliefs that such children would bring bad luck to the community, the villagers emphasised that this belief was no longer practiced in spite of the Tonga being one of the most deprived ethnic groups of people in Zimbabwe. In fact, the study indicated that parents did their best and displayed much love for their disabled children. Rather, when expecting a child, most Tonga people were more worried about whether or not the child would survive rather than would have a visible impairment. Bodily imperfections were seen as important only to the extent that they impaired normal functioning, and life was seen as superior to death. Impairment was seen as secondary, as illustrated in the proverb, 'kocilema kunywigwa maanzi' (it is better to be disabled than dead. Thus, it is better to have a disabled child than a dead one). With the high mortality of children among the Tonga, the sentiment among mothers was that they should be grateful to have a living child than to have him or her die. Similar findings have been documented among the Tswana.[21]

However, being a disabled person remains a major exclusionary factor of schooling in Africa.[22] A large-scale study reported a high degree of exclusion from any form of education for children with disabilities in Africa.[23] In addition, it was reported that about 77 million out-of-school children worldwide, approximately 25 million were excluded on the basis of disability.[24] The 2007 World Vision report also indicated that fewer than ten percent of disabled children of school-going age attended school in Africa; and most of those who attend school, do so in segregated settings.[25] Estimates by the Education for All (EFAs) Global Monitoring Report indicated that about 24 million primary school-aged children with disabilities are out of school. This is so because policies, laws and environments that currently exist do not embrace disability *per se*. Even in countries that have shown significant milestones in enacting

---

20 J Muderedzi and B Ingstad, 'Disability and Social Suffering in Zimbabwe, in A H Eide and B Ingstad (eds), *Disability and Poverty: A global Challenge* (Policy Press 2011).

21 J Muderedzi and B Ingstad (n 17).

22 World Vision, *Education's Missing Millions: Including Disabled Children in Education through EFA FTI Processes and National Sector Plans* (World Vision 2007).

23 Inclusion International, *Better Education for All: When We're Included Too* (Salamanca: INICO 2009).

24 UNICEF/UNESCO, Children Out of School: Measuring Exclusion from Primary Education (UNICEF/UNESCO 2006). http://www.osisa.org/sites/default/files/sup_files/girls_education.pdf> last accessed 31 March 2016.

25 World Vision, Missing Millions: Including Disabled Children in Education through EFA FTI Processes and National Sector Plans Main Report of Study Findings (World Vision 2007) < http://9bb63f6dda0f744fa444-9471a7fca5768cc513a2e3c4a260910b.r43.cf3.rackcdn.com/files/4613/8029/8799/Educations-Missing-Millions-Main-Report.pdf> last accessed 31 March 2016.

enabling legislation, like Uganda, persons with disabilities still lag behind in terms of accessing education, let alone in inclusive settings.[26]

6. Understanding Article 24 of the CRPD from an African Perspective

Article 24 of the CRPD is explicit about inclusive education as the preferred strategy for the education of persons with disabilities. In understanding Article 24, I adopt the social model of disability, which argues that it is the attitudinal, institutional and environmental barriers to participation that create disabling practices, and not a person with an impairment.[27] This understanding views discriminatory social practices as disabling, an effect that is caused by the way society is organised which exposes persons with disabilities to exclusion from the education system in Africa. The CRPD asserts that persons with disabilities should be guaranteed the right to inclusive education at all levels, without discrimination, and on the basis of equal opportunity.[28] This means that children with disabilities should have entitlement to free and compulsory primary education. In addition, persons with disabilities should have access to secondary and tertiary education, vocational training, adult education and lifelong learning. Central to this understanding should be the recognition of and commitment within the general education system to embrace different forms of communication which protect and promote the linguistic identity of the deaf community, for example.[29]

I am aware that countries from the global North were over-represented when the CRPD was developed. To say that the Global South was underrepresented, and therefore they should not consider ratifying the CRPD, is retrogressive. The CRPD was long overdue and its development had to be initiated somehow, as Conventions focusing on children and women seemed not to have advanced disability rights. Now that a Convention focusing on the rights of persons with disabilities has been enacted, it is critical that the CRPD should be understood from an African perspective, taking into account the socio-economic and cultural factors that characterise the continent. The obvious reason for not embracing inclusive education in Africa is that it is seen as a luxury by many countries, particularly those that claim to have many competing issues, such as the need to improve their economies. Most African countries may believe that inadequate funding and large classes are some of the barriers that make inclusive, diversity-friendly education unattainable, particularly for disabled children, who are seen as needing expensive equipment and individualised teaching.[30] Thus, inclusive education is usually regarded as a luxury in contexts where there are no funds for 'extras.' Thus, persons with disabilities are not usually seen as people who are capable of contributing to the national economy. Literally, it therefore means

---

26 M Wazakili, T Chataika, G Mji, A Kudakwashe Dube and M MacLachlan, 'Social Inclusion of People with Disabilities in Poverty Reduction Policies and Instruments: Initial impressions from Malawi and Uganda' in A Eide, and B Ingstad (eds), *Disability and poverty: A Global Challenge* (Policy Press 2011).

27 M Oliver, *Understanding Disability: From Theory to Practice* (Macmillan 1996).

28 United Nations (n 13).

29 ibid.

30 Save the Children UK, *Report of Making Schools Inclusive: How Change Can Happen – Save the Children's Experience* (Save the Children 2008).

that 'valuable resources' should not be wasted on 'unproductive people,' which is not the case. If given the opportunity and capacity, persons with disabilities can meaningfully contribute to the development agenda.[31]

Working towards inclusive education does not necessarily have to be expensive, although it requires strategic and focused investment of available resources. Inclusive education does not have to involve a host of specialist expertise, although teachers have to understand and respond to the needs of all children in their classes. Also, it does not have to involve extensive infrastructural changes, although modifications to the material set-up of schools can be valuable.[32] There are some examples of best practice of inclusive education in resource-poor countries.[33] What is important is to distribute any resources that are available as equitably as possible, avoiding situations where some people benefit from costly facilities, while others are totally deprived of education. Thus, 'inclusive education in a developing country implies the equal right of all children to the "educational package," however basic that package may be.'[34]

As Africa celebrated 'Africa Day' on 25 May 2012, 112 countries had ratified the CRPD worldwide, with just twenty-four out of fifty-four African countries having done so. This shows lack of political will to push the disability agenda forward among African countries. The flimsy excuse of lack of resources should not be used as a scapegoat to preventing the realisation of inclusive education. It has to start anyway, lest persons with disabilities continue to be marginalised, making it difficult for them to compete in the labour market because of lack of capacity, thus making it almost impossible for Africa to achieve the MDGs by 2015.

In post-colonial Africa, it is understandable that we are still dealing with a diverse range of human rights issues, and inclusive education is still a new concept. However, the 'ubuntu' (beingness) philosophy, which is emphasised in most African countries, should be the one guiding us towards realising the goals of Article 24 of the CRPD. 'Ubuntu' is a humanist philosophy focusing on people's allegiances and relations with each other.[35] The literal translation would be: 'I am what I am because of who we all are.' It entails being honest, accommodative, sharing, saving life at all cost, and respecting young and old; thus valuing human dignity.[36]

Despite Africa having embraced the 'ubuntu' philosophy, persons with disabilities have been marginalised for a very long time compared to other vulnerable groups; and so, it is almost a case of rights delayed being rights denied. In their study on inclusive education, Benjamin and colleagues[37] established that the process of

---

31 T Chataika, M Mulumba, G Mji and M MacLachlan, *African Policy on Disability and Development; Did what? Research project in brief: A-PODD in Uganda* (The Global Health Press 2011).

32 Save the Children UK (n 27).

33 S Miles, 'Engaging with Teachers' Knowledge: Promoting Inclusion in Zambian Schools' (2009) 24 Disability & Society 611.

34 Department For International Development, *Disability, Poverty and Development* (DFID 2001).

35 J S Mbiti, *African Religions and Philosophy* (Heinemann 1992).

36 T Chataika (n 2).

37 S Benjamin, M Nind, K Hall, J Collins and K Sheehy, 'Moments of Inclusion and Exclusion: Pupils Negotiating Classroom Contexts' (2003) 23 British Journal of Sociology of Education 547.

inclusion is a complex one, which requires moment-by-moment renegotiation between teachers and learners. Hence, the study concluded that:

> Inclusion is not a target to be hit, nor a goal to be reached; it isn't the final destination of a road of continuous linear improvement. Rather, inclusion is an ongoing process; marked out by struggle and negotiation, and worked out through interpersonal actions and relations in a wider social and political context.[38]

The point to emphasise here is that inclusion should better be understood as a process and not an event. Thus, supporting the inclusion process, especially politically, appears to be more helpful than critiquing a particular educational context as inclusive or not inclusive by making reference to the standards of high-income countries.[39] 'Ubuntu' is defined by qualities of the individual's participation in valued family and community activities, which should embrace all people, young and old, disabled or not. Inclusive education in Africa can therefore be built on the 'ubuntu' philosophy – a critical element that can promote inclusive practices and the advancement of the social model of disability. Therefore, the CRPD is relevant and timely, and Africa has to embrace it if she is to reduce her poverty levels; including any hopes of realising the MDGs. Substantial research evidence exists in mainstream education, but very little is available on the educational needs of persons with disabilities, and this has to be redressed if persons with disabilities are to enjoy their right to education within their own communities.[40]

The scenario described above does by no means suggest that inclusive education has been rejected by Africans. There are some countries in Africa that have embraced inclusive education as a concept. Chataika and her colleagues[41] established that the Ministry of Education in Botswana is now seeking to move towards an inclusive education system. The government has prioritised increasing access to education, with the first ten years of school being highly subsidised, although not compulsory. The impetus for inclusive education is based on the basic human rights and social justice philosophy of the education system of the country. There is also a concerted attempt to integrate special needs education courses into teacher training so that student teachers become aware of the varying needs of their potential learners.[42]

In Lesotho, an education policy was passed in the late 1980s, stating that all learners should have access to the curriculum and an integrated education system.[43] However, policy implementation still remains a challenge. Limited resources, such as insufficient teacher training, inadequate staff support and the lack of accountability and monitoring, have been some of the barriers to the effective implementation of inclusive education and training in Lesotho. Pockets of best practices for students

---

38 ibid 556.

39 ibid.

40 Chataika, McKenzie, Swart and Lyner-Cleophas (n 10).

41 ibid.

42 G Dart, 'Inclusive education in Botswana' in P Engelbrecht and L Green (eds), *Responding to the challenges of Inclusive Education in Southern Africa* (Van Schaik 2009).

43 C J Johnstone, 'Inclusive education in Lesotho' in P Engelbrecht and L Green (eds), *In Responding to the challenges of Inclusive Education in Southern Africa* (Van Schaik 2007).

with disabilities do exist, but are largely dependent on teachers who are willing to go the extra mile.[44]

In Zimbabwe, inclusive education involves the identification and minimisation or elimination of barriers to students' participation in tradition school settings. The School Psychological Services and Special Needs Education Department has the primary responsibility for supporting schools in their inclusive education practices, although there is no specific legislation on inclusive education. However, a number of government policy issues are consistent with the intent of inclusive education.[45] What is typical in most African countries, however, is that disabled children who receive education usually do so in segregated settings where their impairment determines the type and place of their educational experiences.[46] Whilst special schools or segregated settings are still the norm in the education of disabled children in Africa, minimal post-school employment levels and limited social inclusion have been reported.[47] Hence, in spite of the prevalence of segregated settings in Africa, the excessive cost of providing special schools has resulted in the continued exclusion of disabled children from the education system.

Important to note is that inclusive education projects have been introduced in many African countries. For instance, Leonard Cheshire International is assisting several African countries, which include Zimbabwe, to implement inclusive education in rural areas.[48] However, the main problem with such ventures, like what happens in most donor-driven programmes, is that the enthusiasm for continuation may just fade away after the support is withdrawn by the donor community, especially if the local government's input for sustainability is not forthcoming. This unfortunately compromises the realisation of Article 24 of the CRPD.

7. Conclusion

There is sufficient reason for despair about the progress of inclusive education in Africa. Although less than half of the countries in Africa have not yet ratified the CRPD, to suggest a wider applicability of all strategies is not helpful, given the diverse contexts in which inclusion has to be implemented in Africa. But more important, perhaps, than the specific inclusive strategies is the message that inclusion is not only desirable but also possible in spite of several challenges faced by various African countries, which include but are not limited to nominal resources and capacity, attitudinal barriers, and lack of political will. If persons with disabilities in Africa are to truly realise the rights enshrined in the CRPD, which include values of equality and non-discrimination (Article 5), awareness-raising (Article 7), social justice (Article 13), and access to information (Article 21), they inevitably have to be central to education for all in inclusive settings, which Article 24 is all about. Thus, inclusive education should not be another agenda to be debated or delayed. Rather, it should be seen as a process rather than an end in itself, taking into account

---

44 ibid.

45 M Mutepfa, E Mpofu and T Chataika, 'Inclusive Education Practices in Zimbabwe: Curriculum, Family and Policy Issues' (2007) 83 Childhood Education 342.

46 Chataika, Mckenzie, Swart & Lyner-Cleophas (n 10).

47 Inclusion International (n 20)

48 See Leonard Cheshire International Website.

the socio-economic and cultural dynamics of each African country. A commitment to inclusive education would ensure that every African child, irrespective of the challenges that he or she has, would experience the kind of education which Nelson Mandela so beautifully described in his autobiography, *Long Walk to Freedom*, as follows: 'Education is the great engine of personal development. It is through education that the daughter of a peasant can become a doctor, that the son of a mineworker can become the head of the mine and that a child of farm workers can become the president of a great nation.'[49]

[49] N Mandela, *Long Walk to Freedom: The Autobiography of Nelson Mandela – Volume 1 – 1918–1962* (Abacus 2002).

Chapter 28

THE EUROPEAN COURT OF HUMAN RIGHTS AND THE RIGHT TO INCLUSIVE EDUCATION

Joyce Mortimer

1. Introduction

The grounds of race and disability have historically been utilised as means to justify exclusionary educational policies and practices.[1] An analysis of the educational segregation experienced by both minority groups highlights unfounded assumptions of inferiority.[2] These assumptions fortify biases and prejudices, which perpetuate the cycle of discrimination and exclusion. The European Court of Human Rights (ECtHR) has yet to make a finding of disability discrimination in education. It has, however, updated its approach to discrimination generally and opposed the exclusion of children from mainstream education on the basis of race. The next big challenge is opposing segregated education on the ground of disability. It is argued here that the rationale used in the case of *DH & Others v the Czech Republic*[3] to reject racial discrimination can also be used to oppose disability discrimination.

It is acknowledged that there are differences in realising equality in education for both minority groups. While children discriminated against on the basis of race demand the same treatment, children discriminated against on the basis of disability demand different treatment in order to achieve real and effective equality.[4] Children with disabilities often require adaptations and accommodations in education. The United Nations Convention on the Rights of Persons with Disabilities (CRPD) provides for the right of reasonable accommodation. The provision of such is the means to achieving inclusive education for children with disabilities. 'It equips students with disabilities with the right to seek accommodation of their requirements on the basis of non-discrimination.'[5]

This chapter examines the jurisprudence emanating from the ECtHR on the issue of disability discrimination in education. It will be seen that challenges seeking

---

1 B A Ferri and D J Connor, 'Special Education and the subverting of Brown' (2004–2005) The Journal of Gender, Race & Justice 57.

2 ibid.

3 *D H and Others v the Czech Republic* App no 57325/00 (ECtHR, 7 February 2006).

4 See M Minow, 'The Supreme Court 1986 Term Foreword: Justice engendered' (1987–1988) 101 Harvard Law Review 10.

5 F Ahmad, S Girijashanker and M Kemple, 'The Convention on the Rights of Persons with Disabilities: The Right to Education and the Obligations of States; SOAS International Human Rights Clinic Project' (2011) School of Oriental and African Studies, University of London, Research Paper No. 06/2011, 5.

reasonable accommodations have not been successful to date, with the qualifier of disproportionate burden proving an easy escape clause for schools. The case of *D.H. & Others* is also examined, which, although dealing with racial discrimination, provides a basis for challenging discriminatory educational policies and practices on the grounds of disability.

2. The European Convention on Human Rights and the Right to Education

The right to education for children with disabilities is protected by Article 2 of Protocol 1 (securing the right to education), read in conjunction with Article 14 (prohibiting discrimination). Article 14 is limited in its narrow scope. It is not a general anti-discrimination provision in that it only applies to the explicit rights contained in the European Convention on Human Rights (ECHR) itself. This weakness was partly remedied by the adoption of Protocol 12 to the ECHR, Article 1 of which states: 'The enjoyment of any rights set forth by law shall be secured without discrimination on any ground such as sex, race, colour, language, religion, political or other opinion, national or social origin, association with a national minority, property, birth, or other status.' The Protocol does not alleviate the inherent shortcomings of Article 14 due to the fact that it only applies to Member States that ratify it. For Member States that do not raify it, the original Article 14 remains applicable. Another downfall of Article 14 stems from the fact that disability is not explicitly referred to as one of the protected grounds upon which discrimination is prohibited. It is generally accepted without argument that disability comes under the ground of 'other status.' However, like so many international legal norms, it is disappointing that disability discrimination is not expressly prohibited.

The potential of Article 14 in relation to the right to education has been even further eroded by the European Court of Human Right's reluctance to find violations of the Article.[6] The Court has adopted a stringent, narrow approach to discrimination, which pales in comparison to the more advanced conceptual thinking of the European Court of Justice. In a Bulgarian racial discrimination case in which the Court found no violation of Article 14, Judge Bonello vented frustration in a dissenting opinion, stating:

> 'Leafing through the annals of the Court, an uninformed observer would be justified to conclude that, for over fifty years democratic Europe has been exempted from any suspicion of racism, intolerance or xenophobia. The Europe projected by the Court's case-law is that of an exemplary haven of ethnic fraternity, in which peoples of the most diverse origin coalesce without distress, prejudice or recrimination. The present case energises that delusion, (…). Frequently and regularly the Court acknowledges that members of vulnerable minorities are deprived of life or subjected to appalling treatment in violation of Article 3; but not once has the Court found that this happens to be linked to their ethnicity. Kurds, coloureds, Muslims, Roma and others are

---

6 L Clements and J Read, *Disabled People and Human Rights: A Review of the 1998 Human Rights Act for Children and Adults with Disabilities in the UK* (The Policy Press 2003).

> again and again killed, tortured or maimed, but the Court is not persuaded that their race, colour, nationality or place of origin has anything to do with it.'[7]

The right to education provisions contained in international human rights instruments are broader in formulation than the educational provision set out in the ECHR.[8] Protocol 1 of Article 2 states that '[n]o person shall be denied the right to education. In the exercise of any functions which it assumes in relation to education and teaching, the State shall respect the right of parents to ensure such education and teaching in conformity with their own religious and philosophical convictions.' The restrictive and narrow wording used in this provision may be a result of the considerable debate and disagreement which ensued during its adoption.[9] The reluctance to fully adopt this provision is further highlighted by the significant number of States who have ratified the Protocol with reservations to Article 2.[10] Article 2 of Protocol 1 is couched in negative terminology, stating that 'no persons shall be denied the right to education.' Mountfield states that 'the right not to be denied an education contained in the ECHR is a limited and cautious right in comparison with some other instruments.'[11] The question then arises whether this 'peculiar formulation' of the right to education places a corresponding duty on State Parties.[12] The ECtHR held in the case of *Belgian Linguistics* that Article 2 of Protocol 1 did not actually require Member States to provide education to all children but merely required a right of access to educational institutions in existence at that time.[13] This level of protection appears inadequate at first glance. However, O'Mahony argues that as all State Parties had free primary education systems in existence when Article 2 of Protocol 1 was drafted, then 'a right of access' requires an equal right to free primary education.[14] Quinn and Alston argue that certain facts and circumstances seem 'to concede that Article 2 is capable of being interpreted robustly to give rise to substantive claims of State resources.'[15] In the *Valsamis*[16] case, the Court held that the obligation in the second sentence of the article implies 'some positive obligations on the part of the State.' It has also been held by the

7 *Anguelova v Ireland* App no 38361/97 (ECtHR 13 June 2002).

8 R J McManus, *Education and the Court* (Jordans 2004).

9 A H Robertson, 'The European Convention on Human Rights – Recent developments' (1951) 28 British Yearbook of International Law 359, 362; T Opsahl, 'The Convention and the right to respect for family life particularly regarding the unity of the family and the protection of the rights of parents and guardians in the education of children' in A H Robertson (ed), *Privacy and Human Rights* (Manchester University Press 1973).

10 For a summary of the reservations, see L Wildhaber, 'European System' 551.

11 H Mountfield, 'The implication of the Human Rights Act 1998 for the law of education' (2000) Education Law Journal 46.

12 P Gynther, *Beyond Systemic Discrimination – Educational Rights, Skills Acquisition and the Case of Roma* (Martinus Nijhoff Publishers 2007) 143.

13 Belgian Linguistics case (1979–80) 1 European Human Rights Law Reports 252.

14 See argument made by Dr C O'Mahony, 'National Mechanisms for Protecting the Right to Education,' (Irish Human Rights Commission/Law Society Annual Human Rights Conference 2009); C Ovey and J White, *European Convention on Human Rights* (4th edn, Oxford University Press 2006) 337.

15 P Alson and G Quinn, 'The Nature and Scope of States Parties' Obligations under the International Covenant on Economic, Social and Cultural Rights' (1987) 9 Human Rights Quarterly (2)156.

16 *Valsamis v Greece* App no. 21787/93 (ECtHR 18 December 1996), (1997) 24 European Human Rights Reports 294, para 27.

Court that the ECHR's provisions are to be interpreted in such a way as to ensure the instrument promotes the standards and values of a democratic society.[17]

It is argued by Van Dijk and Van Hoof:

> 'The exercise of the right to education, conceived as a right of equal access, presupposes the existence of a minimum of education provided by the state, since otherwise that right would be illusory. If a person is denied the opportunity of receiving minimal education, this involves far-reaching consequences for the development of the person and for the ability to enjoy the right and freedoms of the ECHR. A mere negative construction of the right to education in the first sentence of article 2 protocol 1 ECHR would conflict with the general purpose of the Convention, which is the effective protection of human dignity and human rights. It is in the light of this general purpose that article must be interpreted.'[18]

As primary and secondary education are compulsory in most European education systems, '[i]t may be accepted, therefore, that States tacitly consider themselves obliged to ensure that public schools, which guarantee a minimum of education, are available.'[19] Wildhaber argues that it must be held, therefore, that Article 2 entails for States a positive obligation to guarantee this minimum of education.[20] Frowein and Peukert state that 'the state is in a position to guarantee an appropriate system of education for the whole population. Article 2 must be understood to mean that this is a duty of the state which flows from the right of every child to education.'[21]

3. Discrimination, Reasonable Accommodation and the Right to Inclusive Education

O'Mahony highlights that Article 2 of Protocol 1 is phrased in terms of inclusivity in that it states that 'no person shall be denied the right to education.' This choice of wording, ie 'no person', implies that the provision covers all children, including those with disabilities. The case law of the ECtHR on the right to education for children with disabilities has been, to date, very disappointing. The Court has been reluctant to find violations of the non-discrimination provision in conjunction with the right to education.[22] In *Belgian Linguitisc*, case the Court stated that the ECHR did

---

17 *Kjeldsen, Busk Madsen and Pedersen v Denmark* (ECtHR 7 December 1976), Series A, No. 23; (1979–80) 1 European Human Rights Reports 711, para 54; *Valsamis v Greece* App no 21787/93 (ECtHR 18 December 1996) (1997) 24 European Human Rights Reports 314, para 25. See also C Ovey and R White, *European Convention on Human Rights* (3rd edn, Oxford University Press 2002) 321.

18 P Van Dijk and F van Hoof, *Theory and Practice of the European Convention on Human Rights* (3rd edn, Kluwer Law International 1998)/Utrecht: Stichting Studie – en Informatiecentrum Mensenrechten (SIM) (Utrecht University).

19 K D Beiter, *The Protection of Right to Education by International Law – International Studies in Human Rights* (Martinus Nijhoff Publishers 2005) 161.

20 L Wildhaber, 'Right to education and parental rights', in R MacDonald, F Matscher and H Petzold (eds), *The European System for the Protection of Human Rights* (Dordrecht 1993) 531.

21 J A Frowein and W Peukert, 'EMRK – Kommentar (2nd edn, 1996) 829.

22 See *P and L.D. v the United Kingdom, Simpson v the United Kingdom and McIntyre v the United Kingdom.*

not place an obligation on States 'to establish at their own expense, or to subsidise, education of any particular type or at any particular level.'[23] A resource-focused theme surfaces throughout the Strasbourg case law on this area, and clearly this is not amenable to litigating on the rights of claimants with special education needs. In the cases of *P&LD*[24] and *McIntyre*,[25] the Court left a questionable amount of discretion to States regarding the expenditure of resources and too low a threshold in relation to the qualifier 'disproportionate burden'. In *Graeme v United Kingdom,*[26] the European Commission ('Commission') stated that 'there must be a wide measure of discretion left to the appropriate authorities as to how to make the best possible use of the resources available to them in the interests of disabled children generally.'[27]

In *P & L.D. v the United Kingdom*,[28] the applicants argued that there was a breach of Article 2 of Protocol 1 to the ECHR, which in their view guarantees the provision of a reasonable range of practical choices within the state-education system for parents in respect of their children's schooling. The applicants held deep philosophical convictions about the type of schooling best suited to their daughter's needs and believed that segregated education was inappropriate and harmful in the long term to her due to its overall fundamental direction. The applicants wholly rejected the assumptions made about Lydia's learning potential. The applicants recognised that while Lydia requires an education with a low teacher/pupil ratio, this could be provided in a specialist unit in a mainstream school. The applicants also claimed a violation of Article 14 of the ECHR, read in conjunction with Article 2 of Protocol 1, as Lydia's education has offered her less intellectual and social opportunity than that which a child without disabilities could expect within the United Kingdom state-education system. The applicants argued that the continued segregation of children with disabilities cannot be objectively or reasonably justified in light of contemporary knowledge.

The Commission acknowledged the duty placed on the State by virtue of the second sentence of Article 2 of Protocol 1, requiring the State in exercising any educational function to ensure that the education and teaching of a child is as far as possible in conformity with the parents' religious and philosophical convictions. The Commission went on to draw attention to the United Kingdom Government's reservation to this provision, accepting the second sentence only so far as it is compatible with the provision of efficient instruction and training and the avoidance of unreasonable public expenditure. This reservation is in line with the aforementioned Education Act 1981. The Commission stated that it was aware of the growing body of opinion in favour of inclusive education for all children, including children with disabilities. The Commission, unfortunately, failed to commit to an inclusive educational policy, stating that there must be a wide measure of discretion left to the appropriate authorities as to how to make the best possible use of available resources in the interests of disabled children generally. The Commission opined that the second sentence of Article 2 of Protocol 1 could not be interpreted as requiring

---

23 Belgium (Belgian Linguistic Case (No2)), (ECtHR 23 July 1968) Series A, No. 6; (1979–80) 1 European Human Rights Reports 252, 32.

24 *P & LD v United Kingdom* App no 14135/88 (ECtHR October 2 1989).

25 *McIntyre v United Kingdom* App no 29046/95 (ECtHR October 21 1998).

26 *Graeme v United Kingdom* App no 13887/88 (ECtHR February 5 1990).

27 ibid.

28 *P & LD v United Kingdom* App no. 14135/88 (ECtHR October 2 1989).

the placement of a child with severe developmental delay in a general school rather than in an available place in a special school. The Commission stated that the compromise made by the Local Education Authority whereby Lydia would receive her education two days a week in the mainstream school and three days in the special school was acceptable and respected Lydia's right to have as effective an education as possible. The Commission concluded that there was therefore no violation of Article 2 of Protocol 1. Regarding the applicant's complaint of discrimination in breach of Article 14 of the ECHR read in conjunction with Article 2 of Protocol 1, the Commission noted that while the legislation encourages the integration of children with disabilities in mainstream schools, it also provides that their special needs be met, if necessary in specialised institutions. The Commission concluded that it found no element of discrimination in such a policy.

Similarly, the issue of 'disproportionate burden' and the expenditure of resources was at the heart of the decision in *McIntyre v the United Kingdom*.[29] The applicant, by her mother and next friend, brought a judicial review action against the LEA's refusal to install a lift in the applicant's school. This action was dismissed by the High Court in 1995. The applicant applied to the Court of Appeal for leave to appeal against the previous decision. This application was also dismissed. The Court stated that there was no legal obligation on the LEA to provide a lift. The applicant complained that she was discriminated against by virtue of her disability, contrary to Article 14 of the ECHR, in that she was denied full enjoyment of her right to education according to Article 2 of Protocol 1 of the ECHR. She argued that she was not afforded the same access to all classes attended by her able-bodied peers and therefore she did not have access to the national curriculum. The Government responded that the right to education includes the right of access to existing state-educational institutions, and a right to an effective education, but that neither of these rights were absolute. They argued that the applicant had access to existing state institutions and had an effective education, even though she did not have access to each and every room in the school. They considered that Article 2 of Protocol 1 and Article 14 did not secure a right to the most effective possible education. The Government argued that a balance must be struck between the needs of disabled pupils, the wishes of parents, the interests of other pupils, and the availability of public funds. They contended that this balance was struck in the case of the applicant. The Government further argued that the words 'or other status' in Article 14 of the Convention did not cover discrimination on grounds of disability.[30]

The Commission recalled that the right to education under Article 2 of Protocol 1, 'by its very nature calls for regulation by the State, regulation which may vary in time and place according to the needs and resources of the community and of individuals,' as long as the substance of the right to education is preserved.[31] The Commission also noted that 'that there must be a wide measure of discretion left to

---

[29] *McIntyre v United Kingdom* App no 29046/95 (ECtHR October 21 1998).

[30] Regarding the latter complaint, the Commission did not determine whether the words 'or other status' in art 14 covered disability, as it concluded that the application was inadmissible in any event for reasons laid out below. This was unfortunate as it is a fundamental weakness of art 14 that disability is not expressly covered. It is necessary that the Commission (now the Court) consistently acknowledge 'disability' as a protected category covered by way of the words 'or other status.'

[31] See Belgian Linguistic (ECtHR 23 July 1968), Series A, no 6, 30–32, paras 3–5.

the appropriate authorities as to how to make the best use possible of the resources available to them in the interests of disabled children generally.'[32] Regarding Article 14 of the ECHR, the Commission noted that a difference of treatment is discriminatory if it 'has no objective and reasonable justification,' that is, if it does not pursue a 'legitimate aim' or if there is not a 'reasonable relationship' of proportionality between the means employed and the aim sought to be realized.[33]

The Commission opined that the fact that the applicant's statement of needs included the need for full access to the national curriculum did not entail the specific need for a lift to be installed as long as the applicant still received an adequate education. The Commission concluded that the LEA had provided the applicant with a number of accommodations (ie re-arranging the location of her fixed classroom), and therefore the refusal to install a lift did not deny the applicant 'the right to education.'

Regarding the complaint of discrimination under Article 14 of the ECHR, the Commission noted that the applicant was treated differently from her able-bodied peers in that they could attend classes on the first floor whereas she could not, on the grounds of her disability. The Commission examined the LEA's policy and found that the legitimate aim was to provide educational facilities in a manner consistent with a practical and efficient use of resources and public funds. The Commission noted that the LEA had carefully considered the applicant's request for a lift and found the cost to be comparatively large when balanced with the other demands of the area's schools. The Commission concluded that, in light of all the other measures taken by the LEA to assist the applicant, the refusal to provide a lift could not be said to be disproportionate to the legitimate aim of the LEA. The application was therefore declared inadmissible. In response to this decision, Kilkelly explains that in determining whether measures adopted in a particular case are compatible with the ECHR will depend on the principle of proportionality.[34]

In both these cases, the applicants sought accommodations in their education. Both schools evaded such requests by relying on the qualifier of disproportionate burden. The principle of disproportionate burden is a proportionality test, as stated by Kilkelly (above). The proportionality test requires states to 'balance the rights of, and burden and benefits to, all persons affected by the proposed accommodation or adjustment.'[35] During the drafting of the CRPD, concerns were raised regarding the inclusion of the qualifier of disproportionate burden. The International Disability Caucus proposed deleting the qualifier, as it had apprehensions regarding the adjudication by States on what was essentially an escape clause.[36] Such a qualifier allows States to rely on insufficient resources when asked to provide reasonable accommodations. As stated by Ahmad, Girijashanker and Kemple, 'if the threshold at which the obligation ceases or it is set too low or if the obligation is easily

---

32 See App no. 14688/89 (ECtHR 4 December 1989) D.R 64, 194; App no 28915/95 (ECtHR 17 December 1997), unpublished.

33 See *Marckx v Belgium* (ECTHR 13 June 1979), Series A, no 31, 16, para 33.

34 U Kilkelly, *The Child and the European Convention on Human Rights* (Ashgate 1999) 67.

35 United Nations Enable, 'Seventh Session of the Ad Hoc Committee (16/01/06 – 03/02/06), Daily summary of the discussion at the seventh session 16th January 2006' (2006) <www.un.org.esa.socdev/enable/rights/ahc7sum16jan.htm> last accessed 31 March 2016.

36 United Nations Enable, 'Seventh Session of the Ad Hoc Committee (16/01/06 – 3/02/06), Daily summary of discussion at the seventh session 31st January 2006' (2006) <http://www.un.org/esa/socdev/enable/rights/ahc7sum31jan.htm> last accessed 31 March 2016.

evaded, reasonable accommodation may result in little or only marginal changes to an exclusionary norm.'[37]

4. The ECtHR: First Finding of Discrimination in Education

The recent case of *DH v Czech Republic*[38] (which was subsequently upheld in *Sampanis and Others v Greece*),[39] marks a change in direction for the ECtHR. The Court held that the exclusion of Roma children from mainstream education was a violation of Article 14 (non-discrimination) in conjunction with Article 2 of Protocol 1 (right to education).

This case highlights the tension between the promise of law and the strength of politics. A stated by Claud Cahn, '[t]o date, no efforts by civil society, international monitoring bodies, the European Union, or even good-willed corners of the Czech government itself have been powerful enough to persuade the Czech government to undertake anything other than cosmetic changes to the school system.'[40] Governments cannot be relied upon to protect the human rights of all people at all times and therefore '(...) a corrective is sometimes needed since "normal" politics can predictably fail to deliver for certain groups who lack political clout or impact – or worse still, they may be deliberately targeted or ignored.'[41] This problem was visible in the case of *D.H.*, where the Court failed to come to a decision on the very acceptability of segregated education for children with disabilities. In the Chamber judgment, the Court stated that the question of whether segregated education should exist for children with intellectual disabilities was solely a matter of 'expediency' and did not disclose issues of high principle or rights. Numerous human rights laws enshrine the right to education for children with disabilities, including most recently Article 24 of the CRPD which provides the right to inclusive education.

Nevertheless, this landmark decision by the Grand Chamber of the European Court

---

37 Supra n 5.

38 Case of *D.H. and Others v the Czech Republic* App no 57325/00 (ECtHR 7 February 2006).

39 Case of *Sampanis and Others v Greece* App no 32526/05 (ECtHR 5 June 2008). This case involved an action by 11 applicants of Roma origin living in Greece. The applicants argued that their children had been subjected, without any objective or reasonable justification, to treatment that was less favourable that that given to non-Roma children in a comparable situation and that this situation constituted discrimination contrary to the Convention. The applicants' children were not provided with an education during the 2004–2005 school year and were subsequently placed in segregated classes, a measure which the applicants claimed was related to their Roma origin. The Court considered that the evidence adduced by the applicants and other evidence in the case file could be regarded as sufficiently reliable to create a strong presumption of discrimination, and that it was therefore for the Government to show that this difference in treatment was the result of objective factors, unrelated to the ethnic origin of the persons concerned. The Court concluded that, in spite of the authorities' willingness to educate Roma children, the conditions of school enrolment for those children and their placement in special preparatory classes – in an annex to the main school building – ultimately resulted in discrimination against them. Accordingly, there had been a violation of art 14 of the Convention taken together with art 2 of Protocol 1 in respect of each of the applicants.

40 C Cahn, 'On not tackling systemic racial discrimination at the European Court of Human Rights' (European Roma Rights Centre).

41 G Quinn, 'The European Social Charter and EU anti-discrimination law in the field of disability: Two gravitational fields with one common purpose' in G de Burca and B DeWitts (eds), *Social Rights in Europe* (World Bank 2005).

of Human Rights in *DH v Czech Republic* is to be greatly welcomed. The case arose out of the disproportionately high rates of Roma children who were assigned places in segregated schools for children with intellectual disabilities in the Czech Republic. It was alleged that this practice discriminated indirectly against Roma children who had normal, or even above normal, levels of intelligence. The complaint was brought by the European Roma Rights Centre on behalf of eighteen Romani children who were receiving their education in 'special schools' or 'remedial special schools' in Ostrava. The lawsuit was originally brought before the domestic tribunals in 1999 and dismissed. In 2000, the applicants filed their complaint at the European Court of Human Rights. The judgment of the Chamber is worth noting as it gives an insight into the Court's repeated inability to make findings of discrimination. The Court held that 'the Government have (sic) nevertheless succeeded in establishing that the system of special schools in the Czech Republic was not introduced solely to cater for Roma children, (….)' and '[t]he Court observes that the rules governing children's placement in special schools do not refer to the pupils' ethnic origin.'[42] The Court went on to conclude that although 'the general situation in the Czech Republic concerning the education of Roma children is by no means perfect, the Court cannot in the circumstances find that the measures taken against the applicants were discriminatory.' This ruling was at odds with recent decisions of the European Committee of Social Rights.[43]

'The Chamber judgement seemed to indicate a future of constricted, formalistic Court interpretations of discrimination, an approach which would nullify possibilities for remedy in all but the most egregious cases. Careful governments and others were evidently given license to discriminate at will, provided they did so politely.'[44] On 13 November 2007, the Grand Chamber made a ground-breaking judgment, reversing the Chamber decision. For the very first time, the European Court of Human Rights found a violation of Article 14 in relation to racial discrimination in education. Numerous aspects of the Court's judgment are worth noting:

The Court clarified its view on whether the European Convention on Human Rights protects against indirect discrimination. The Court adopted the EU's more advanced thinking, accepting that the Convention's ban on discrimination includes indirect discrimination, which

> shall be taken to occur where an apparently neutral provision, criterion or practice would put persons of racial or ethnic origin at a particular disadvantage compared with other persons, unless that provision, criterion or practice is objectively justified by a legitimate aim and the means of achieving that aim are appropriate and necessary.

The Court also adopted the EU law approach to the question of the burden of proof, which now is to be reversed once a prima facie case of 'indirect discrimination'

---

42 Case of *D.H. and Others v the Czech Republic* App no 57325/00 (ECtHR 7 February 2006) paras 48, 49.

43 *International Association Autism Europe v France*, Complaint No. 13/2002; *Mental Disability Advocacy Center v Bulgaria*, No. 41/2007.

44 C Cahn, '*D.H. and Others v Czech Republic*: Establishing Council of Europe System Anti-Discrimination Law in Economic and Social Rights Area' (2007) <www.upr-info.org/IMG/pdf/COHRE_CZE_add1.pdf> last accessed 31 March 2016.

has been made. The Court acknowledged the role of statistics as a method of proving racial discrimination, particularly in the event of an allegation of indirect discrimination: 'As to whether statistics can constitute evidence, the Court has in the past stated that statistics could not in themselves disclose a practice which could be classified as discriminatory, (…).' However, in more recent cases on the question of discrimination, in which the applicants alleged a difference in the effect of a general measure or *de facto* situation, (…) the Court focused extensively on statistics produce by the parties to establish a difference in treatment between two groups (men and women) in similar situations. Thus,

> '[W]here an applicant is able to show, on the basis of undisputed official statistics, the existence of a prima facie indication that a specific rule – although formulated in a neutral manner – in fact affects a clearly higher percentage of women than men, it is for the respondent Government to show that this is the result of objective factors unrelated to any discrimination on grounds of sex. If the onus of demonstrating that a difference in impact for men and women is not in practice discriminatory does not shift to the respondent Government, it will be in practice extremely difficult for applicants to prove indirect discrimination.'[45]

> '(...) the Court considers that when it comes to assessing the impact of a measure or practice on an individual or group, statistics which appear on critical examination to be reliable and significant will be sufficient to constitute the prima facie evidence the applicant is required to produce. This does not, however, mean that indirect discrimination cannot be proved without statistical evidence.'[46]

5. Implications of the DH Judgment for Future Disability Discrimination Cases

The decision of the Grand Chamber will have significant implications as it reforms the principle of discrimination under the European Convention on Human Rights. The Court firmly equivocates that racial segregation in education is prohibited in all Council of Europe Member States. The Court stated that the effect of the mis-placement of Roma children compounded their difficulties and compromised their subsequent personal development instead of tackling their real problems or helping them to integrate into ordinary schools and develop the skills that would facilitate life among the majority population. The Court failed to acknowledge the same consequences for children with disabilities placed in segregated educational settings. Worryingly, the Court also stated: '[T]he (policy or legislative) choice between a single school (system) for everyone, highly specialised structures and unified structure with specialised sections is not an easy one. It entails a difficult balancing exercise between the competing interests. As to the setting and planning of the curriculum, this mainly involves questions of expediency on which it it not

[45] Case of *D.H. and Others v the Czech Republic* App no 57325/00 (ECtHR, 7 February 2006) para 181.

[46] ibid para 188.

for the Court to rule.'[47] The Court should have had regard to the growing consensus, within the Council of Europe Member States rejecting segregated education for children with disabilities.[48] However, no reference was made in the judgment to the increasing body of caselaw of the European Committee on Social Rights on the need for integrated education for children with disabilities.[49] Neither was there reference to the Council of Europe's own 2006 Action Plan on disability which expresses the need to ensure mainstream education for children with disabilities. It must be remembered that the ECtHR has held that the ECHR is a living document, to be interpreted in light of modern and changing values and legal standards.[50] The Court has stated that the ECHR is intended to protect rights in a practical and effective manner[51] and not so that they remain illusory and theoretical.[52] Interpreting the ECHR in this way increases the scope of its provisions.

Ultimately, the effective realisation of the right to education for children with disabilities depends largely on the political will of governments. The implementation of human rights norms is ultimately vested with sovereign states and unfortunately the normative strength of law is all too often matched by political weakness. The European Court of Human Rights has the power to drive positive social change in its position as the sole court protecting and promoting human rights within the Council of Europe.

6. Conclusion

The ruling in favour of Roma children permits future challenges to discriminatory education policies. The Court has shown the ECHR is powerful enough to prohibit racial discrimination in education. Tackling the issue of segregated education for children with disabilities will be the next big challenge. There is a need for a paradigm shift in thinking, unreservedly adopting the holistic human rights model of disability proposed by the CRPD. Protecting the right to reasonable accommodation is the means to ensure the right to inclusive education is achieved in practice. The European Court of Human Rights has broadened its approach to discrimination in the provision of education and has opposed segregated education on racial grounds. While this is a reason to celebrate, there is a lot yet to be done. It must be acknowledged that while segregated education is still permitted for any minority group, full inclusion can never be realised. Segregated schooling has traditionally mirrored the stratification that occurs in society at large. Misconceptions, prejudices and biases result in separate educational provision for all minority groups. Discrimination on grounds of race, disability, gender, class and ethnicity is rife in education systems. Opposing segregation on one, or some of these grounds will not suffice. For as long as there is

---

47 Ibid.

48 In a collective complaint against Ireland (*World Organisation against Torture v Ireland* Complaint No 18/2003), the European Social Rights Committee stated that both the Charter and the ECHR are living instruments to be interpreted in light of contemporary knowledge and social conditions. The Committee also held that it was entirely appropriate to rely on international treaties.

49 See specifically *Mental Disability Advocacy Center v Bulgaria*, No. 41/2007, and *Autisme-Europe v France*, No. 13/2002.

50 *Tyler v United Kingdom* (1979) 2 European Human Rights Reports 1.

51 *Airey v Ireland* (1981) 2 European Human Rights Reports 301.

52 U Kilkelly, *Children's Rights in Ireland – Law, Policy and Practice* (Totell 2008) 39.

a separate system of schooling, society will use it to discriminate, be it on grounds of race or disability. Therefore, while *DH* is a welcome development in the area of discrimination law, it does not tackle the fundamental issue of the acceptability of segregated education.

> 'If history is any lesson, as long as there remains a dual system of general education and special education, one will be used by the other to uphold the status quo: exclusion, (...). In this way, race is a special education issue, just as disability is a racial issue. Perhaps a more intersectional approach to disability and civil rights law could begin to address inequality and exclusion in all of its forms and thus transform education into a space of inclusion and justice for all.'[53]

[53] B A Ferri and D J Connor, 'Special Education and the subverting of Brown' (2004–2005) The Journal of Gender, Race & Justice 57.

PART 6: EMPLOYMENT AND PERSONS WITH DISABILITIES

Chapter 29

REASONABLE ACCOMMODATION IN THE CONVENTION ON THE RIGHTS OF PERSONS WITH DISABILITIES AND NON-DISCRIMINATION IN EMPLOYMENT: RISING TO THE CHALLENGES?

Anna Lawson

1. Introduction

Reasonable accommodation duties are expressly articulated, for the first time in a binding UN human rights treaty,[1] in the Convention on the Rights of Persons with Disabilities (CRPD).[2] By defining 'discrimination on the basis of disability' as 'including a denial of reasonable accommodation',[3] the CRPD situates these duties unequivocally within the ambit of its cross-cutting non-discrimination requirement. Thus, the obligation imposed on States Parties by Article 5(2) to 'prohibit all discrimination on the basis of disability' carries with it a requirement to impose reasonable accommodation duties on public bodies, employers, educators, transport providers, places of detention and other social actors who control access to any of the substantive rights protected by the CRPD. In addition, explicit reference is made to reasonable accommodation duties in a number of the articles dealing with substantive rights, including Article 27, which is entitled 'work and employment.'

Article 27(1) affirms that disabled people have the right to work 'on an equal basis with others', and the opportunity to 'gain a living' through 'work freely chosen or accepted in a labour market, (...) that is open, inclusive and accessible.'[4] In order to realise this right, the Article specifies that States will take appropriate steps, including legislative ones, to prohibit discrimination against disabled people in relation to all aspects of employment (including recruitment, job retention, promotion, working conditions, pay and grievance procedures) and ensure that they have access, on an

1 They had, however, been previously recognised as integral elements of the non-discriminatory realisation of human rights in other UN documents – see, in particular, the ground-breaking General Comment No. 5 of the Committee on Economic, Social and Cultural Rights (Eleventh Session, 1994), UN Doc E/1995/22, 19.

2 United Nations Convention on the Rights of Persons with Disabilities (2006) UN Doc A/Res/61/106 (CRPD).

3 art 2 CRPD.

4 art 27(1) CRPD.

equal basis with others, to employment-related benefits and opportunities (including those relating to trade union activities and technical and vocational training).[5] These obligations to prohibit disability discrimination necessarily include an obligation to impose reasonable accommodation duties because, as already explained, failure to provide such accommodation constitutes discrimination for purposes of the CRPD. However, Article 27(1)(i) makes this explicit by insisting that States Parties will '[e]nsure that reasonable accommodation is provided to persons with disabilities in the workplace.' These non-discrimination obligations are thus no more than are required by the cross-cutting demand of Article 5(2) that disability discrimination should be prohibited. However, the restatement of these obligations in Article 27(1) enables context-specific detail to be included – a practice which has been identified as one of the many innovative features of the CRPD and which, it is to be hoped, will facilitate domestic implementation.[6]

The focus of this chapter is the reasonable accommodation duty and its operation in the employment field. It is impossible to embark on a detailed discussion of this topic without at least a brief mention of the employment situation of disabled people. The global picture has recently been presented in the World Report on Disability.[7] According to this, despite some national variation (which is likely to be due in part to inconsistency in data gathering and definitions of disability[8]) disabled people of working age have 'significantly lower employment rates and much higher unemployment rates' than non-disabled people – the likelihood of a disabled person having a job being less than one-third of the chances of a non-disabled person having one in South Africa, just over one-third in Japan, but four-fifths in Switzerland and just over nine-tenths in Malawi.[9] The World Report refers to research carried out in twenty-seven countries by the Organisation for Economic Co-operation and Development (OECD),[10] according to which the average employment rate for working age disabled people was 44%, compared with an average of 75% for non-disabled people. These averages disguise important differences between the employment situation of different disabled people. Factors such as gender and impairment type are also important: disabled women and people who have, or are regarded as having psycho-social or intellectual disabilities are particularly at risk of employment exclusion and disadvantage.[11] For those disabled people who do have work, the World Report suggests that they are disproportionately likely to work in the informal unregulated market, to have part-time or fixed-term posts and to have low pay.[12]

The implementation of effective reasonable accommodation duties might be expected to improve the employment prospects of disabled people. Accommodations made

---

5 art 27(1)(a)–(d), CRPD.

6 F Megret, 'The Disabilities Convention: Human Rights of Persons with Disabilities or Disability Rights' (2008) 30 Human Rights Quarterly 494, 504.

7 World Health Organisation and World Bank, 'World Report on Disability' (World Bank, 2011).

8 ibid, ch 2.

9 ibid, tables 8.1 and 8.2.

10 OECD, 'Sickness, Disability and Work: Breaking the Barriers. A Synthesis of Findings across OECD Countries' (2010) (OECD).

11 See n 7 at 237 (referring to '*Ready, Willing, and Disabled: survey of UK employers*' (Scope, 2003); and G Thornicroft, '*Shunned: Discrimination against People with Mental Illness*' (Oxford University Press 2006)).

12 See n 7 at 39 and ch 8.

during the application process will be essential for removing disabling barriers which might otherwise disadvantage disabled applicants; and accommodations provided during the course of employment will be essential for ensuring that disabled employees have equal opportunities to perform their jobs to the full extent of their ability and are not disadvantaged by disabling physical, informational or procedural barriers. It should be acknowledged at the outset, however, that the effectiveness of such duties will depend not only on how they are crafted and put into practice, but also on what other measures and policies are put in place alongside them. Of obvious relevance are measures designed to improve the accessibility of workplaces and transport systems; to ensure equal access to education and training; and to establish supported employment and affirmative action schemes to boost the numbers of disabled people in work.

This chapter will examine some, but by no means all,[13] of the challenges which may arise in the process of formulating strong reasonable accommodation duties and putting them into practice. Its focus will be employment but much of the discussion will be of relevance to reasonable accommodation duties in other spheres of life. It will draw on literature and experience from a range of countries including the US (where the duty first emerged) and the EU (the Member States of which have recently been required by EU law[14] to transpose a reasonable accommodation duty into their national laws).

To facilitate analysis, the challenges discussed here will be divided into three broad categories – 'conceptual,' 'ideological' and 'implementation.' As will be seen, however, these categories are not entirely discrete and there is some overlap between them.

Attention will first be turned, in Section 2 below, to a number of what are termed 'conceptual challenges.' These are challenges associated with developing a clear understanding of the concept of 'reasonable accommodation' and the distinctive role which it has to play in modern human rights law – a challenge which consists largely of disentangling reasonable accommodation from other distinct but related concepts with which it regularly becomes entwined. In Section 3, focus will shift to some of the 'ideological' challenges which reasonable accommodation duties have encountered. These take the form of alleged tensions between reasonable

---

13 Some important challenges will be omitted here. These include issues concerning whether the reasonable accommodation duty should be available to people who are not themselves disabled but are regarded as disabled or associated with somebody who is disabled (examined in E F Emens, 'Disabling Attitudes: US Disability Law and the ADA Amendments Act' (2012) 60 *American Journal of Comparative Law* 205; and challenges connected with putting reasonable accommodation to work in contexts where it is less familiar, such as in places of detention (on which see A Lawson, 'Disability Equality, Reasonable Accommodation and the Avoidance of Ill-Treatment in Places of Detention: The Role of Supranational Monitoring and Inspection Bodies' *International Journal of Human Rights (forthcoming); and, on this and other relatively new areas for reasonable accommodation,* J Lord and R Brown, 'The Role of Reasonable Accommodation in Securing Substantive Equality for Persons with Disabilities: The UN Convention on the Rights of Persons With Disabilities' in M H Rioux, L Basser and M Jones (eds), *Critical Perspectives on Human Rights and Disability Law* (Martinus Nijhoff Publishers/Brill Academic 2011) 273.

14 Council Directive 2000/78/EC of 2 December 2000 establishing a general framework for equal treatment in employment and occupation [2000] OJ L 303/16.

accommodation and rights to property or freedom of contract. In Section 4, a number of what are termed 'implementation challenges' will be discussed.

2. Conceptual Challenges

2.1. Defining Reasonable Accommodation

Article 2 of the CRPD defines reasonable accommodation as 'necessary and appropriate modification and adjustments not imposing a disproportionate or undue burden, where needed in a particular case, to ensure to persons with disabilities the enjoyment or exercise on an equal basis with others of all human rights and fundamental freedoms.'

It thus consists of 'modification' or 'adjustments' which, first, are 'necessary and appropriate' to ensure that 'in a particular case' a disabled person is able to exercise or enjoy human rights (including those relating to employment) on an equal basis with others; and which, second, do not impose a 'disproportionate or undue burden' on the duty-bearer. In order to identify which modifications or adjustments are required in a particular case, two issues must therefore be addressed – each of which merit further consideration.

First, the modifications or adjustments must be 'necessary' or 'appropriate' to remove the relevant disadvantage for the particular disabled person in question. Ascertaining what such adjustments might be will demand some dialogue between that person and the duty-bearer. Impairments vary enormously in nature and severity and so too do the characters, experiences and preferences of people with similar impairments. This variety inevitably results in differences in the appropriateness or necessity of various adjustments that might be made by the duty-bearer. The individual-orientated nature of reasonable accommodation thus requires duty-bearers to resist making assumptions as to what might be most appropriate for a particular disabled individual and demands that instead they engage in a dialogue with such a person about how the relevant disadvantages might most effectively be tackled.[15] This is well illustrated by the English case of *Project Management Institute v Latif*.[16]

Ms Latif, who was registered blind and training to be an accountant, argued that PMI (*Project Management Institute)* had discriminated against her by failing to provide her with reasonable accommodation in connection with a professional exam. PMI had rejected her request to take the exam on a computer equipped with her screen-reading software and insisted that instead, and in line with its standard procedure for blind candidates, she would be provided with a reader and additional time. The Employment Appeal Tribunal found that PMI had indeed failed to discharge its duty to make reasonable adjustments for Ms Latif. The judge observed that the case represented 'a good example' of a situation in which 'a failure to carry out a proper assessment, (…) may well result in a respondent failing to make adjustments

[15] This is termed the 'procedural' component of reasonable accommodation duties by S J Schwab and S L Willborn, 'Reasonable Accommodation of Workplace Disabilities' (2003) 44 William and Mary Law Review 1197.

[16] *Project Management Institute v Latif* [2007] Industrial Relations Law Reports 579.

which he ought reasonably to make'[17] and that a duty-bearer 'cannot rely on that omission as a shield to justify a failure to make a reasonable adjustment which a proper assessment would have identified.'[18]

The second issue of relevance in any assessment of what modifications or adjustments a reasonable accommodation duty might demand is that of the potential burden of a proposed step on the particular duty-bearer. A 'burden', for these purposes, would not be confined to financial cost and might, for instance, include factors such as disruptiveness to working arrangements or deterioration in the quality or nature of core services. It is important to remember, however, that many adjustments will carry net benefits rather than burdens for duty-bearers[19] – in addition to the benefit of securing the employment of the particular disabled individual, benefits might flow from modifications (such as a ramp or accessible intranet system) that improve accessibility and ease of use for disabled and also non-disabled customers and co-workers.[20] Further, the introduction of a modification for a particular individual (such as flexitime) might usefully trigger consideration of whether it might benefit the entire workforce and be implemented as a general measure instead of by way of an exceptional concession made for the particular disabled employee in question.[21]

Reasonable accommodation requires assessments of the level of any potential burden to be conducted in a manner that is sensitive to the circumstances of the particular duty-bearer. Thus, a financial cost that represents a small fraction of the annual budget of a large, wealthy organisation might nevertheless represent so large a sum as to threaten the financial health of a small and poorly resourced organisation. Clearly, an adjustment that might represent an undue burden for the latter might well not do so for the former. However, if one modification would impose too heavy a burden on a particular employer, consideration should be given to whether the disadvantage in question might effectively be tackled by other measures – a process which will require on-going dialogue between the employer, the disabled employee and potentially also others with expertise in relevant types of equipment or facility.

2.2 Disentangling Reasonable Accommodation from Affirmative Action

Affirmative action, often termed 'positive action' in European contexts,[22] generally refers to measures which an organisation may choose to adopt, but which it is not required to adopt, in an effort to reduce the obstacles confronting disadvantaged groups. An example is an employer's policy of requiring lower qualifications of applicants who are disabled, female or from a particular ethnic minority group than it requires of non-disabled applicants. In many jurisdictions, affirmative action schemes are at risk of being challenged by people falling outside the selected group on the ground that the scheme treats them less favourably because they do not have the

---

17 ibid para 35.

18 ibid.

19 R Kayess and P French, 'Out of Darkness into Light' (2008)1 Human Rights Law Review 27.

20 See, for insightful analysis of this point, E F Emens, 'Integrating Accommodation' (2008)156 University of Pennsylvania Law Review 839.

21 ibid.

22 See eg O de Schutter, 'Positive Action' in D Schiek, L Waddington and M Bell (eds), *Cases, Materials and Text on National, Supranational and International Non-Discrimination Law* (Hart Publishing 2007).

required race, sex or other characteristic to become part of that group and thereby entitled to the benefits conferred by the scheme. Nevertheless, such schemes are an important means by which to tackle the engrained societal disadvantage which may be experienced by certain disadvantaged groups. Their importance is recognised in various UN human rights treaties, including the CRPD. According to Article 5(4) of the CRPD, '[s]pecific measures which are necessary to accelerate or achieve de facto equality of persons with disabilities shall not be considered discrimination under the terms of the present Convention.'

This makes it clear that affirmative action schemes in favour of disabled people should not be open to the challenge that they discriminate against non-disabled people. Such schemes are thus permitted, but not required. The establishment of such a scheme does not amount to discrimination against non-disabled people and neither does the failure to provide one amount to discrimination against disabled people. Unlike other international human rights treaties, the CRPD places no time limit (related to de facto equality being achieved) on the legitimacy of affirmative or positive action schemes for disabled people.

There is an unfortunate tendency, even amongst eminent scholars and practitioners, to refer to reasonable accommodation duties as a form of affirmative or positive action measure.[23] Indeed, the 2009 General Comment on non-discrimination of the Committee on Economic, Social and Cultural Rights[24] was not unambiguous on this point. Although this Comment helpfully states that failures to provide reasonable accommodation constituted discrimination and should therefore be included in non-discrimination prohibitions,[25] it also makes the following rather confusing observations about 'specific,' 'special' or affirmative action measures:

In order to eliminate substantive discrimination (sic[26]), States Parties may be, and in some cases are, under an obligation to adopt special measures to attenuate or suppress conditions that perpetuate discrimination. Such measures are legitimate to the extent that they represent reasonable, objective and proportional means to redress de facto discrimination (sic) and are discontinued when substantive equality has been sustainably achieved. Such positive measures may exceptionally, however, need to be of a permanent nature, such as interpretation services for linguistic minorities and reasonable accommodation of persons with sensory impairments in accessing health-care facilities.[27]

---

23 See eg for UK examples, K Monaghan, *Blackstone's Guide to the Disability Discrimination Legislation* (Oxford University Press) 96. See also B Doyle, 'Enabling Legislation or Dissembling Law? The Disability Discrimination Act 1995' (1997) 60 Modern Law Review 64, 74 where reasonable adjustments are described as a form of 'legally mandated positive action'; elsewhere, however, Doyle insists that: 'reasonable accommodation must be seen as an integral part of the non-discrimination standard' and that it 'should not be regarded as a species of affirmative action, thereby attracting heightened scrutiny, judicial suspicion and narrow application'– B Doyle, *Disability, Discrimination and Equal Opportunities: A Comparative Study of the Employment Rights of Disabled Persons* (Mansell Publishing 1995), 245.

24 Committee on Economic, Social and Cultural Rights, General Comment No. 20 – Non-Discrimination an Economic, Social and Cultural Rights (2009) UN Doc E/C.12/GC/20.

25 ibid, para 28.

26 It is respectfully suggested that by 'discrimination' here (and where it appears in the next sentence in the text, also marked with '(sic)'), the Committee meant 'inequality' or 'disadvantage.' Such a reading would be more consistent with the relevant treaty provisions.

27 (n 24) para 9.

This tendency to regard reasonable accommodation as a form of legally mandated affirmative action is presumably linked to the fact that such duties concern the taking of positive measures in order to place disabled people on an equal footing with their non-disabled peers. Although understandable, it is unfortunate because it risks generating misunderstanding and confusion about the nature of the reasonable accommodation duty. It risks creating the impression that reasonable accommodation duties, like affirmative action measures, are optional and not compulsory. Further, because affirmative action measures tend to confer benefits on the basis of group membership and nothing more, this tendency creates a risk that the highly individualised nature of the reasonable accommodation duty will be overlooked. More fundamentally, regarding reasonable accommodation as a form of affirmative action risks removing it from the non-discrimination domain and obscuring the fact that the function of reasonable accommodation is to ensure basic equality for a particular disabled person by removing a disadvantage to which they would otherwise have been subjected by the standard procedures, structures or operation of the duty-bearer. For all these reasons, the concepts of reasonable accommodation and affirmative action must be disentangled.[28]

2.3 Disentangling Reasonable Accommodation from Accessibility

Accessibility is a general principle of the CRPD and also an obligation, which is set out in a number of articles.[29] Thus, Article 4, which sets out the CRPD's 'general obligations', includes duties to promote the development of universally designed goods, services, equipment and facilities.[30] Article 21 sets out a range of duties relating to accessible information and communication, including the use of alternative formats and sign language. The most significant provision on accessibility, however, is Article 9 – which is itself entitled 'Accessibility.' This Article lays down accessibility obligations relating to physical infrastructure, information and signage as well as to information and communication technologies and transport.

Accessibility differs from reasonable accommodation in that it is not a duty owed to a specific individual to make an appropriate adjustment necessary to remove a particular disadvantage or obstacle. Instead, it is a duty on States Parties to plan for the removal of barriers affecting disabled people as a group and to invest resources, in accordance with the principle of progressive realisation,[31] in the fulfilment of these plans. This difference between accessibility and reasonable accommodation

---

28 See, for a more detailed discussion, A Lawson, *Disability and Equality Law in Britain: The Role of Reasonable Adjustment* (Hart Publishing 2008) 223; see also L Waddington and A Hendriks, 'The Expanding Concept of Employment and Discrimination in Europe: From Direct and Indirect Discrimination to Reasonable Accommodation Discrimination' (2008) 8 International Journal of Comparative Labour Law and Industrial Relations 403; and L Waddington and M Bell, 'Exploring the Boundaries of Positive Action under EU Law: A Search for Conceptual Clarity' (2011) 48 Common Market Law Review 1508.

29 For a thorough analysis of the concept of accessibility as used in the CRPD, see J Lord, 'Accessibility and Human Rights Fusion in the CRPD: Assessing the Scope and Content of the Accessibility Principle and Duty under the CRPD', paper delivered at the Committee on the Rights of Persons with Disabilities Day of General Discussion, 7 October 2010, available at: <www.ohchr.org/EN/HRBodies/CRPD/Pages/DGD7102010.aspx> last accessed 31 March 2016.

30 art 4(1)(f), CRPD.

31 art 4(2), CRPD.

has implications for the way in which duty-bearers should involve disabled people in decisions about how to implement both duties.[32] In order to discharge a reasonable accommodation duty (as explained above) the dialogue required is between the duty-bearer and the specific disabled person in question. This ensures that the resulting modifications will address the disadvantage, as it is experienced by that person, in a way that is appropriate for them – even if this involves taking measures which many people with the same impairment would find unhelpful. The implementation of accessibility duties, however, requires dialogue between the duty-bearer and disabled people's organisations about types of measure which would provide access to disabled people (or people with particular impairment types) more generally.[33]

Unlike reasonable accommodation, accessibility is not positioned within the CRPD's conception of discrimination. Thus, the requirement in Article 5(2) to prohibit disability discrimination does not carry with it a duty to ensure accessibility. Nevertheless, some countries have chosen to introduce into their equality laws mechanisms by which individuals can sue organisations for failing to make adequate progress in ensuring accessibility. Examples of this sort of action include the UK's anticipatory reasonable adjustment duty[34] and Norway's duty to provide universal design.[35] Although these countries have chosen to introduce failures to implement accessibility into the realms of their non-discrimination law, this is not required by the CRPD.

For these reasons, it is important to maintain clarity about the distinction between reasonable accommodation and accessibility duties. However, the two duties have a close and mutually reinforcing relationship.[36] This is because the more accessible an environment or organisation is, the less likely it is that aspects of its structure or functioning will place a disabled person at a disadvantage which calls for reasonable accommodation. The most obvious illustration of this point is a disadvantage caused to people with mobility impairments by an inaccessible physical structure or building, and their consequent need for reasonable accommodation – a need which would not have arisen had the structure or building been accessible. Similarly, the disadvantage caused to a person with intellectual disabilities by inaccessible information would call for reasonable accommodation (perhaps in the form of a verbal explanation) whereas, had the information been accessible to that person (eg because it was available in easy read format) there would have been no disadvantage and therefore no requirement for reasonable accommodation. Thus, providing accessibility can remove the need for many reasonable accommodations. In addition, as mentioned above, the provision of some reasonable accommodations may result in making a

---

32 I am grateful to Prof T Degener for her clear articulation of this point at a meeting of the Disability Rights in Employment and Accessible Markets project, Leeds, February 2012.

33 art 4(3) of the CRPD demands that disabled people and their organisations should be consulted and actively involved in the design and implementation of all policies affecting them.

34 Equality Act 2010 – replacing but, in this respect not changing, the Disability Discrimination Act 1995; see generally, A Lawson, *Disability and Equality Law in Britain: The Role of Reasonable Adjustment* (Hart Publishing 2008); and A Lawson, Disability and Employment in the Equality Act 2010: Opportunities Seized, Lost and Generated' (2011) 40 Industrial Law Journal 359.

35 Law on Discrimination and Accessibility 2009 (Norway).

36 See further A Lawson 'Reasonable Accommodation and Accessibility Obligations: Towards a More Unified European Approach?' (2011) 11 European Anti-Discrimination Law Review 11.

building or information system accessible to other disabled people as well as to the individual in whose favour the accommodation was made.

3. Ideological Challenges

Reasonable accommodation duties have sometimes been challenged on ideological grounds – generally because they are considered to threaten the property rights of duty-bearers or to undermine freedom of contract. The most dramatic illustration of such opposition is perhaps to be found in the struggle to introduce such duties in Ireland.

In the case of *Re Article 26 and the Employment Equality Bill*,[37] the Irish Supreme Court was asked to assess the constitutionality of the Employment Equality Bill 1996 – a Bill which sought to introduce anti-discrimination protection on the basis of nine grounds, one of which was disability. The Bill would have required employers to 'do all that was reasonable to accommodate' the needs of a disabled employee or applicant, subject to the limit of 'undue hardship.'[38]

The court accepted that the Bill's reasonable accommodation provisions were designed to further the 'totally laudable aim'[39] of promoting 'equality in the workplace between the disabled and their more fortunate fellow citizens.'[40] In its view the cost of furthering that aim – unlike costs arising from the production process (such as those relating to health and safety or environmental pollution) – should not fall on employers but be borne instead by society as a whole. The Bill, however, imposed the entire cost on employers and this, according to the court, was 'so contrary to reason and fairness' as to amount to an 'unjust attack' on the constitutional rights of employers to enjoy their property and their freedom to make a living.[41]

The Employment Equality Bill was therefore ruled to be repugnant to the Constitution. It was allowed to become law only after the reasonable accommodation provisions had been modified so as to restrict their scope to accommodations which imposed no more than a 'nominal' cost on employers.[42] European Union law has since resulted in the lifting of the nominal cost restriction in relation to employment[43] but

---

37 *Re Article 26 and the Employment Equality Bill* [1997] 2 IR 321; see generally, G Quinn and S Quinlivan, 'Disability Discrimination: The Need to Amend the Employment Equality Act 1998 in Light of the EU Framework Directive on Employment' in C Costello and E Barry (eds), *Equality in Diversity: The New Equality Directives* (Irish Centre for European Law, 2003).

38 Employment Equality Bill (Ireland) cll 16(3) and 35(4).

39 *Re Article 26 and the Employment Equality Bill* [1997] 2 IR 321.

40 ibid 366.

41 Under arts 40(3) and 43 of the Irish Constitution. The language quoted in the text was accepted as representing the correct approach in this case; see [1997] 2 IR 321 at 334 (C J Hamilton, quoting *Tuohy v Courtney* [1994] 3 IR 1 47).

42 Employment Equality Act 1998 (Ireland) s 16(3)(c). For discussion of the meaning of this phrase see G Quinn and S Quinlivan, 'Disability Discrimination: The Need to Amend the Employment Equality Act 1998 in Light of the EU Framework Directive on Employment' in C Costello and E Barry (eds), *Equality in Diversity: The New Equality Directives* (Irish Centre for European Law, 2003), 230.

43 The Equality Act 2004 (Ireland) amends s 16(3) of the Employment Equality Act 1998 (Ireland) by replacing the reference to 'nominal' with a reference to 'disproportionate burden.'

it remains in operation in the context of goods and services.[44] Clearly, such a limit on the reasonable accommodation duty would be inconsistent with the CRPD and it is to be hoped that ratification of the CRPD will at last result in the loosening of these chains on the Irish reasonable accommodation duty. There is, however, the troubling possibility that resistance to an unfettered reasonable accommodation duty may impede progress toward Irish ratification of the CRPD.

The concern about reasonable accommodation which emerges from the approach of the Irish Supreme Court thus relates to the potential imposition of heavy burdens on employers which will put their businesses at risk and constrain the exercise of their property rights. Similar concerns have been expressed in US academic literature, particularly in the years immediately following the enactment of the Americans with Disabilities Act 1990,[45] which imposed a reasonable accommodation duty on employers in the private as well as the public sector. Notable amongst these reasonable accommodation critics is Richard Epstein,[46] according to whom the imposition of such duties 'necessarily impedes the operation and efficiency of firms'[47] by forcing them to bear the costs of an inefficient social policy. Some commentators have called simply for the abandonment of a system which both requires reasonable accommodations to be made and prohibits reductions in wages for the recipients.[48] Others have gone further and argued for the repeal of all disability discrimination law in the field of employment.[49] Epstein has gone still further and called for the abandonment of all regulatory intervention designed to counter discrimination.[50] The part of this budget that would have been devoted to disability should instead, he suggests, be devoted to 'programs that deal with rehabilitation, training, and counselling and direct assistance' or to 'grants to certain firms to allow them to offer employment to particular classes of disabled workers.'[51]

It is remarkable that a duty, which is explicitly limited by concepts of 'reasonableness', 'undue hardship' or 'disproportionate burden' should have been met with such alarm. The strength of such concepts is generally a task entrusted to the courts and there is little evidence to suggest that courts are likely to impose overly heavy obligations on employers. Much has been written about the tight control over access to reasonable accommodations exercised by the US judiciary, through restrictive interpretations of the definition of disability[52] – the tightness of this control being loosened in 2008

---

44 Equal Status Act 2000 (Ireland).

45 Pub L No 101-336, 104 Stat 327 (1990) – 42 USC s 12101.

46 See eg R Epstein, *Forbidden Grounds: The Case Against Employment Discrimination Laws* (Harvard University Press, 1992). For criticism see eg M A Stein, 'The Law and Economics of Disability Accommodations' (2003) 53 Duke Law Journal 79.

47 ibid 484.

48 See eg C L Weaver, 'Incentives versus Controls in Federal Disability Policy' in C L Weaver (ed), *Disability and Work: Incentives, Rights and Opportunities* (University Press of America, 1991) 5.

49 See eg C J Willis, 'Title I of the Americans with Disabilities Act: Disabling the Disabled' (1995) 25 Cumberland Law Review 715.

50 See n 46.

51 ibid 484.

52 See eg R L Burgdorf, '"Substantially Limited" Protection from Disability Discrimination: The Special Treatment Model and Misconstructions of the Definition of Disability' (1997) 42 Villanova Law Review 409; W Wilkinson, 'Judicially Crafted Barriers to Bringing Suit Under the Americans with Disabilities Act' (1997) 38 South Texas Law Review 907; M Diller, 'Judicial Backlash, the ADA & the Civil Rights Model' (2000) 21 Berkeley Journal of Employment

by statutory intervention in the form of the Americans with Disabilities Amendment Act.[53] This experience does more to fuel the concerns of proponents of disability equality than its critics. Indeed, any discussion of concerns about the burdens that reasonable accommodation duties might place on employers would not be complete without reference to the converse concerns that the duties will not require employers to do enough.

Within the disability movement, the controlling role of the concept of 'reasonableness' has been condemned for its conservative tendencies.[54] Proponents of disability equality have drawn attention to the relatively limited nature of the concept of reasonable adjustment or accommodation.[55] This concept, it is argued, is premised on the acceptance of a non-disabled norm from which some departures will be required in order to accommodate the needs of people with impairments. Because such departures will be required only if they are deemed to be 'reasonable', they will necessarily be modest and limited. A departure from normal practice will not be deemed reasonable, and therefore not required, if it would inflict an undue level of hardship on the duty-bearer. The notion of 'reasonableness' thus represents a compromise. It anticipates and legitimises failures to achieve the ideal. These concerns will be revisited in Section 4 below. Here, however, it should be stressed that reasonable accommodation duties cannot be expected to perform all the work of removing disabling barriers. Their strength lies in their sensitivity to the circumstances of particular individuals. Accessibility obligations are more suited to carry out the heavy work of systematically dismantling disabling barriers.

Ideological resistance to reasonable accommodation does not seem to be a thing of the past. The Hungarian Supreme Court has recently ruled that a bank was under no obligation to make its ATM services accessible to the claimants, who were blind customers, because they were aware of the inaccessible machines when they had entered their contract for services with the bank.[56] Freedom of contract therefore outweighed any obligations to remove disadvantages that disabled customers might experience. This case has been referred to the UN Committee on the Rights of Persons with Disabilities. It provides a perfect scenario for the analysis of conflicts

---

& Labor 19; and C R Feldblum, 'Definition of Disability under Federal Anti-Discrimination Law: What Happened? Why? And what can we do about it?' (2000) 21 Berkeley Journal of Employment and Labour Law 91.

53 Pub L No 110-325, 122 Stat 3553 (2008) – 42 USC 12101 ff; see generally E F Emens, 'Disabling Attitudes: US Disability Law and the ADA Amendments Act' (2012) 60 American Journal of Comparative Law 205.

54 See eg S Prideaux, *Good Practice for Providing Reasonable Access to the Physical Built Environment for Disabled People* (Disability Press 2006) 38.

55 See in particular M T McCluskey, 'Note, Rethinking Equality and Difference: Disability Discrimination in Public Transportation' (1988) 97 Yale Law Journal 863, 871; M C Weber, 'Beyond the Americans with Disabilities Act: A National Employment Policy for Persons with Disabilities' (1998) 46 Buffalo Law Review (1998) 123, 148, and accompanying text; L Waddington and M Diller, 'Tensions and Coherence in Disability Policy: The Uneasy Relationship Between Social Welfare and Civil Rights Models of Disability in American, European and International Employment Law' in M L Breslin and S Yee (eds), *Disability Rights Law and Policy: International and National Perspectives* (Transnational Publishers Inc, 2002), 275; and C O'Cinneide, 'A New Generation of Equality Legislation? Positive Duties and Disability Rights' in A Lawson and C Gooding (eds), *Disability Rights in Europe: From Theory to Practice* (Hart Publishing 2005) 223.

56 Judgement Pfv. IV21.144/2008/7.

between equality, on the one hand, and property or freedom of contract, on the other. Although not an employment situation, it will have obvious significance for the employment field.

4. Implementation Challenges

4.1 Clear Articulation of the Duty

As mentioned above, experiences of transposing the reasonable accommodation requirement of the Employment Equality Directive 2000[57] into the domestic law of EU Member States provides useful indications of the types of challenge which may arise in connection with the implementation by States Parties of the CRPD's reasonable accommodation duties. By way of context, it is worth noting that the Employment Equality Directive requires Member States to prohibit discrimination on grounds of disability (as well as age, sexual orientation and religion and belief) in employment and occupation. A variety of forms of conduct must be prohibited, including direct discrimination, indirect discrimination, harassment and victimisation. In relation to disability only there is a requirement to impose reasonable accommodation duties on employers.[58]

According to a 2009 report of the EU Network of Legal Experts in the Non-Discrimination Field (the Legal Network study),[59] two disability-related aspects of this Directive have proved particularly problematic for Member States to transpose into their domestic law. These were, first, the definition of disability[60] and, second, the formulation of reasonable accommodation duties. The fact that transposing the reasonable accommodation duty into domestic law has not been straightforward was perhaps to be expected, given that the Directive 'brought the concept of reasonable accommodation to the attention of many European legislators, and indeed "forced" the notion onto these legislators.'[61] Problematic cases, in which domestic law appears to be in breach of the Directive's requirements, fall into two broad categories – the first of which will be considered here, and the second in the next section.

The first type of problematic transposition consists of national laws which fail to include a clear and unambiguous reasonable accommodation duty applying to the full range of employment and occupation covered by the Directive. The Legal Network study gives Italy, Slovenia and Poland as examples of countries falling

57 Council Directive 2000/78/EC of 2 December 2000 establishing a general framework for equal treatment in employment and occupation, [2000] OJ L 303/16.

58 ibid, art 5.

59 L Waddington and A Lawson, *Disability and non-discrimination law in the European Union: Analysis of disability discrimination law within and beyond the employment field* (Network of Legal Experts in the Non-Discrimination Field, 2009). <www.ec.europa.eu/social/BlobServlet?docId=6154&langId=en> last accessed 31 March 2016.

60 There is no guidance on this in the Directive itself, but some was subsequently provided in the judgment of the Court of Justice of the EU in Case C-13/05, *Chacón Navas v Eurest Colectividades SA* [2006] ECR 1-6467.

61 See n 59 at s 2.3.3.

into this category.[62] In Italy's case, this resulted in a referral by the Commission to the Court of Justice of the EU (CJEU) in April 2011.[63]

The absence of an explicit articulation of the reasonable accommodation duty, covering the required range of policy domains, would obviously also be a problem for CRPD implementation. It would, in particular, appear to fall foul of the Article 5(3) requirement that '[i]n order to promote equality and eliminate discrimination, States Parties shall take all appropriate steps to ensure that reasonable accommodation is provided.'

4.2 Extending the Duty to All Disabled People

The second category of problematic reasonable accommodation transpositions identified in the Legal Network study consists of laws which restrict entitlement to reasonable accommodation to a subset of disabled people. According to another study, carried out by the EU Agency for Fundamental Rights (FRA),[64] this approach is adopted in France, Germany, Hungary and Spain.[65] The legislative restriction of entitlement to reasonable accommodation in Germany to those people classified as 'severely disabled' (which therefore denied reasonable accommodation claims to people regarded as having more minor impairments) resulted in the initiation of infringement proceedings by the Commission. These were dropped in October 2010, however, on the basis of Germany's plans to revise this approach.

This tendency to restrict reasonable accommodation duties to people who are regarded as having more severe impairments is perhaps linked to a tendency to think of reasonable accommodation as a form of social welfare handout – access to which must be rigorously guarded. Such a tendency, as mentioned above, has been identified as an explanation of restrictive judicial interpretations of disability in the US. In the words of Matthew Diller:

> '[t]he failure of many judges to fully embrace the concept of equality reflected in the ADA has led courts to construe the statute in ways that make no sense as a matter of civil rights policy, (…). [I]n the absence of a grounding in principles of equality, the ADA can only be read as a means of dispensing subsidies to a targeted group of people. Seen from this vantage point, the case law has a certain coherence, although not the coherence intended by the framers of the law.'[66]

Such an approach is plainly inconsistent with the CRPD, which requires reasonable accommodation to be available to all disabled people.

---

62 ibid.

63 European Commission, '*Employment Equality: European Commission refers Italy to the EU's Court of Justice*' Press Release, IP/11/408, 6 April 2011.

64 European Union Agency for Fundamental Rights, *The Legal Protection of Persons with Mental Health Problems Under Non-Discrimination Law: A Comparative Study of the Definition of Disability and of the Duty to Provide Reasonable Accommodation in European Union Member States* (Publications Office of the EU, 2011).

65 ibid, s 2.2.1; see also UN Committee on the Rights of Persons with Disabilities, Concluding Observations: Spain, Sixth Session 19–23 September 2011, para 19.

66 ibid at 47.

Even where reasonable accommodation duties are not explicitly restricted to a subset of disabled people, there are risks that certain groups of disabled people may find it more difficult to harness such duties to remove the disadvantages they experience in the workplace and beyond. Employers are likely, for instance, to be more familiar with, and therefore more willing to make, the types of adjustment that might be appropriate to remove a disadvantage experienced by employees with physical or sensory impairments than those which might be experienced by employees with psychosocial or intellectual disabilities.[67] The provision of adjustments (such as flexible or part-time working hours or access to a quiet room) may, however, have a significant impact on whether a person with psychosocial disabilities is able to remain in employment, particularly at times of crisis.[68] Similarly, the prospects of employees with intellectual disabilities are likely to be considerably enhanced by the provision of adjustments (such as the provision of clear information or instructions in easy read format, the opportunity to perform repeat tasks, and access to additional training). It is therefore important that States Parties rise to the challenge of ensuring that reasonable accommodation duties operate effectively in favour of all, and not just some, disabled people.

4.3 Extending Awareness of the Duty

There is some evidence that, in the EU, difficulties have arisen in connection with putting the reasonable accommodation duties into practice so that they can be used to remove the disadvantages which affect disabled applicants and employees.[69] Many of these difficulties appear to be linked to lack of awareness or understanding of the existence and nature of the reasonable accommodation obligation amongst employers, disabled people, trade unions, and even lawyers and judges. The need to provide additional guidance and information on this issue was included in the Committee on the Rights of Persons with Disabilities' concluding observations on Spain[70] and also features amongst the plans set out in the European Disability Strategy 2010-2020.[71] Forms of guidance that have proved helpful in some countries (eg the UK[72]) are codes of practice, authorised by parliament and to which judges must have regard when deciding relevant cases, containing detailed explanations and practical examples. The European Disability Forum has drawn attention to the crucial role played by disabled people's organisations in raising awareness about reasonable accommodation and other equality entitlements, and also to the fact that,

---

67 This point emerged clearly from the empirical evidence presented in European Union Agency for Fundamental Rights, *Choice and Control: The Right to Independent Living* (Publications Office of the EU, 2012).

68 See generally A Lawson, 'People with Psychosocial Impairments or Conditions, Reasonable Accommodation and the Convention on the Rights of Persons with Disabilities' (2008) 26 *Law in Context* 62.

69 See generally European Disability Forum, *Ten Years On: Practical Impact of the Employment Directive on persons with disabilities in Employment* (EDF, 2010).

70 See n 65 at paras 19–20.

71 European Commission, *Initial plan to implement the European Disability Strategy 2010–2020, List of Actions 2010–2015*, SEC (2010) 1324 final, ss 1.3 and 1.4.

72 See eg the Equality Act 2010 (UK) Codes of Practice, available at: <www.equalityhumanrights.com/legal-and-policy/equality-act/equality-act-codes-of-practice/> last accessed 31 March 2016.; for discussion of earlier versions of these codes, see N O'Brien, 'The GB Disability Rights Commission and Strategic Law Enforcement: Transcending the Common Law Mind' in A Lawson and C Gooding (eds), *Disability Rights in Europe: From Theory to Practice* (Hart Publishing 2005) 249.

owing to austerity measures, many such organisations have experienced funding cuts with the result that they are now struggling to survive.[73]

4.4 Providing State Support

In addition to enhancing awareness, the effectiveness of reasonable accommodation duties could be enhanced by the provision of State support in the form of facilitative policies.[74] Such policies might include funding schemes (eg the Access to Work scheme in the UK[75]) whereby the costs of employment-related reasonable accommodations are substantially paid by the State and not subject to an upper limit. The development of schemes to provide expertise and advice as to technical devices and other forms of assistance that might be helpful to disabled employees might also increase the likelihood of accommodations being as effective as possible.

In addition, general employment structures that facilitate flexibility are likely to have a positive impact on the implementation of reasonable accommodation duties. Examples include policies which facilitate the taking of disability leave (eg to train with a new guide dog, to deal with a mental health crisis or to acquire new skills at the onset of an impairment); and policies which facilitate flexible hours or working from home. Maria Liisberg, drawing on her comparative analysis of Denmark and Sweden, has argued that the concept of reasonable accommodation is likely to be interpreted and applied more expansively in countries which include strong protection for disabled people against dismissals.[76] She concludes that the lack of protection against dismissal in Denmark, integral to its 'flexicurity' model of employment, is a significant contributing factor to the startling disparity in the employment rates of disabled people in the two countries – 26% in Denmark and 50% in Sweden. Liisberg therefore calls for the flexicurity model, operating in Denmark and promoted by the EU, to be modified so as to include explicit protection against dismissal on grounds of impairment-related reduced work capacity along the lines of the Swedish approach. This would prohibit employers from dismissing disabled people on grounds of reduced work capacity unless, after having been provided with appropriate training and adjustments, the disabled employee could not perform work of value to the employer. Such an approach would also contribute

---

73 See n 69 at 3.

74 See eg KMU Forschung Austria, 'Providing Reasonable Accommodation for Persons with Disabilities in the Workplace in the EU – Good Practices and Financing Schemes' (2008) www.ec.europa.eu/social/BlobServlet?docId=1961&langId=en last accessed 31 March 2016.; see also European Disability Forum, Ten Years On, above n 69.

75 Details of which are available at: <www.direct.gov.uk/en/DisabledPeople/Employmentsupport/WorkSchemesAndProgrammes/DG_4000347> last accessed 31 March 2016. For analysis of this scheme, and the way in which it contrasts with the US equivalent, see A Lawson, *Disability and Equality Law in Britain: The Role of Reasonable Adjustment in Britain* (Hart Publishing 2008), especially chapter 6; see also Department of Work and Pensions, *Disability Employment Support: Fulfilling Potential* (Stationery Office, 2012). See also n 69 for descriptions of schemes which are similar (but apparently more limited) than that of the UK which operate in Lithuania, Sweden and Finland.

76 M Ventegodt Liisberg, *Disability and Employment: A Contemporary Disability Human Rights Analysis applied to Danish, Swedish and EU Law* (Intersentia, 2011); see also M Ventegodt Liisberg, 'Flexicurity and Disability in a Contemporary Human Rights Perspective' in G Quinn, L Waddington and E Flynn (eds), *European Yearbook of Disability Law* (Intersentia, forthcoming).

to the creation of an environment in which reasonable accommodation duties, with all their disadvantage-removing potential, are more likely to flourish.

5. Conclusion

It is still less than a quarter of a century since reasonable accommodation duties caught the world's attention when they appeared in the Americans with Disabilities Act 1990.[77] Now, by virtue of the CRPD, they are internationally acknowledged to be an integral element of prohibitions of disability discrimination. Their rise to prominence has been swift. However, despite their promise, they will not perform the task asked of them unless certain challenges are met. In this chapter, an attempt has been made to outline some of these challenges and, where appropriate, to offer suggestions as to how they might be tackled.

As Lord and Brown have observed, 'the CRPD animates both theoretical as well as practical discussions about rendering all rights meaningful for some 650 million persons with disabilities worldwide.'[78] The issues discussed above, under the heading of 'conceptual challenges' raise theoretical questions. The issues discussed under the heading of 'implementation challenges' raise practical questions. However, the two cannot be cleanly divided because, without clarity at the conceptual level, practical implementation is doomed to failure.

The issues discussed under the heading of 'ideological challenges' demonstrate that there is still important work to be done in winning the hearts and minds of judges, scholars and no doubt others – and persuading them that equality for disabled people necessarily involves reasonable accommodation and that it should not automatically be subordinated to concerns, often misplaced, about maximising profit and retaining freedom of contract. The implementation of effective reasonable accommodation duties raises profound questions about balancing apparently competing rights and values. The emergence of the CRPD will undoubtedly intensify the need for these questions to be answered and the balances to be struck – both at international and at national levels. It is to be hoped that reasonable accommodation, and proponents of disability equality, are ready and able to rise to the challenges.

---

77 See n 45.

78 J Lord and R Brown, 'The Role of Reasonable Accommodation in Securing Substantive Equality for Persons with Disabilities: The UN Convention on the Rights of Persons With Disabilities' in M H Rioux, L Basser and M Jones (eds), *Critical Perspectives on Human Rights and Disability Law* (Martinus Nijhoff Publishers / Brill Academic, 2011) 273.

Chapter 30

THE CRPD AND THE GENERAL OCCUPATIONAL REQUIREMENT IN EMPLOYMENT

Olivia Smith

1. Introduction

The emergence of the CRPD reflects the 'universal consensus' that now exists on the need to protect persons with disabilities from discrimination and to realise their enjoyment and the protection of the full range of human rights.[1] It embraces a wide range of substantive rights that stretch across the civil and political versus social, economic and cultural divide,[2] and obliges State Parties to move beyond reliance on anti-discrimination law as the summit of a rights-based approach to disability issues. Of course, this extension of anti-discrimination law to the disability ground has been a welcome and developing worldwide phenomenon from the late 1990s onwards.[3] Its significance as one of the first legal paradigms that viewed people with disabilities as rights-holders (as opposed to subjects of social welfare or rehabilitation programmes) cannot be overlooked, nor can its recognition of the role which the structural environment and negative attitudes play in the exclusion of people with disabilities.[4] However, anti-discrimination law's well-recited limitations lie in its ability to bring about the structural alterations necessary to support people with disabilities towards the realisation of their opportunities. By contrast, the CRPD contains an array of altogether more ambitious policies and standards that are designed to tackle the interlocking processes of exclusion, disadvantage and invisibility which diminish the life chances of people with disabilities. At the same time, the CRPD breathes new life into the principles of non-discrimination and equality, which remain at its interpretive core.

This chapter's concern is with the sustenance that the Convention could provide to anti-discrimination law's 'general occupational requirement' (herafter the GOR) provision.The GOR principle is a reasonably familiar staple of employment discrimination law, particularly sex discrimination law, although it has been

---

1 See *Glor v Switzerland* App No 13444/04 (ECtHR, April 2009), where the European Court of Human Rights noted, citing the Convention, that 'there is a European and universal consensus on the necessity to protect persons suffering from a disability from discrimination.'

2 Although art 5(2) of the CRPD makes reference to the traditional formula of 'progressive achievement of the full realization' of economic, social and cultural rights.

3 See T Degener, 'Disability Discrimination Law: A Global Comparative Perspective' in C Gooding and A Lawson (eds), *Disability Rights in Europe: From Theory to Practice* (Hart Publishing 2005) 87.

4 As reflected in the duty to make reasonable accommodation and the prohibition on direct discrimination respectively.

somewhat neglected in the disability context. There is little consensus on the GOR as extended to disability – it has been adopted by some national employment law discrimination frameworks and omitted in others. It is permitted by the provisions of the EU's Framework Employment Directive[5] and completely unreferenced within the employment provisions of the CRPD. The implications of its application, or otherwise, to the disability ground has also tended to be glossed over in the literature. This circumspection regarding the disability-based GOR can be traced to the predominance of a particular interpretive strain that makes it (for many) intuitively unsustainable – this is, the actual requirement of a disability for the purposes of an employment position. Thus disability as a GOR appears at odds with the lingering welfarist construct that has long equated disability with reduced functioning, productivity and non-participation. However, the CRPD disrupts significantly this understanding of disability and it creates some space for a more positive construct of the GOR provision in the disability context.

In this chapter I consider the potential of a disability GOR to contribute towards States Parties' obligation under Article 27 of CRPD to safeguard and promote the realisation of the right to work. While the text to Article 27 makes no reference to the GOR, I suggest that provisions therein, as interpreted through the lens of the Article 3 principles, provide scope for a positively constructed disability-based GOR. Moreover, given the EU's involvement in driving the development of the Convention's standards,[6] its refusal to exclude a disability GOR reinforces support for the arguments developed. I also suggest that the adoption by States Parties of a GOR in employment could contribute to their obligation under Article 8 to raise awareness of the contribution and potential of people with disabilities to counter stereotypes and to promote positive images of disability.

2. Background to the GOR

The GOR principle, which situates the protected ground or characteristic as legitimately relevant to the performance of a particular occupation, has garnered most attention in the sex discrimination context.[7] Its genesis can be traced back to the long-standing rule that direct sex discrimination is incapable of justification and also to the symmetrical nature of sex discrimination law.

The principle of equal treatment, upon which the prohibition on direct discrimination is predicated, is based on a process that sees the protected characteristic as irrelevant to determinations of job qualifications, competence and performance. Its purpose is to expunge any sex-based determinations (or on the basis of the other protected characteristics) from decision-making processes that govern access to life's opportunities and is the foundation of the classic formal model of equality's concern with historical and socially constructed forms of (sex) discrimination. The reduction of this idea to legal doctrine is through direct discrimination's

---

5 Council Directive 2000/78/EC of November 27, 2000 establishing a general framework for equal treatment in employment and occupation [2000] OJ L202/16.

6 See G De Burca, 'The EU in the negotiations of the UN Disability Convention' (2010) 35 European Law Review 174.

7 For discussion, see D Schiek, L Waddington and M Bell, *Cases, Materials and Text on National, Supranational and International Non-Discrimination Law* (Hart Publishing 2007) 275.

prohibition of 'less favourable treatment' on the protected grounds.[8] This formula has always been constructed as symmetrical: both men and women are equally protected against unlawful sex-based determinations, an approach that confirms the narrow anti-differentiation basis of sex discrimination law and lessons its concern with the unpacking the wider processes of disadvantage.[9] In addition, statutory discrimination law has consistently refused to countenance any justifications for proven direct discrimination. Once the process or treatment has been accepted as having been 'on the grounds of' sex, race, etc, an employer cannot avoid liability by arguing that economics, customer or co-worker preference,[10] or a benign motive[11] was the reason for the decision, or that it had no intention to discriminate.[12] While the justification of direct discrimination has received renewed focus of late,[13] the continued refusal to countenance justifications for direct discrimination places a spotlight on its exceptions, of which the GOR is one.

The basis of the GOR exemption can be seen in its departure from the direct discrimination matrix and its shift away from the irrelevancy of the protected characteristic. In short, it situates the protected characteristic as required for the performance of the particular occupational activity in question. Thus, as applicable to the gender ground, being a woman or a man can be a genuine and determining occupational requirement, which means it will not be unlawful discrimination to exclude members of the other sex from the position in question. However, given that the GOR is a derogation from the principle of equal treatment, its operation is policed by proof of a legitimate objective and a proportionate requirement.[14] GOR case law illustrates the types of circumstances in which GORs have been raised – ranging from public security,[15] to privacy,[16] to role modelling and counselling/welfare,[17] and authenticity.[18]

---

8 A typical formulation is Article 2(2)(a) of the Framework Employment Equality Directive.

9 See Nicola Lacey, 'From individual to group? A feminist analysis of the limits of anti-discrimination legislation' in Nicola Lacey, *Unspeakable Subjects: Feminist Essays in Legal and Social Theory* (Hart Publishing 1998) 25.

10 See US decision in *Wilson v Southwest Airlines* 517 F Supp. 292 (ND Rex, 1981).

11 Though note the early decision of *Peake v Automotive Products Ltd* [1978] QB 233, eventually modified by the Court of Appeal in *Ministry for Defence v Jeremiah* [1980] QB 87 and *James v Eastleigh Borough Council* [1990] 2 AC 751.

12 See *R v Birmingham City Council ex parte EOC* [1989] AC 1155 and *R (On the application of E) v Governing Body of JFS* [2009] UKSC 15; [2010] 2 AC 728.

13 In *R (On the application of E) v Governing Body of JFS* [2009] UKSC 15; [2010] 2 AC 728, para 69, Baroness Hale noted a developing view that 'discrimination law should modify its rigid adherence to formal symmetry and recognize a greater range of justified departures than it does at present' but concluded that such an allowance, if it were to be made, ought to be made by Parliament.

14 See art 2(6) of the Amended Equal Treatment Directive 2002/73/EC OJ L269/15.

15 *Johnston v Chief Constable of the RUC* [1986] ECR 1651.

16 See US decision of *Fesel v Masonic Home of Delaware Inc* 447 F Supp. 1346 (1978); K Manley, 'The BFOQ Defense: Title VII's concession to gender Discrimination' (2009) 16 Duke Journal of Gender Law and Policy 169.

17 *City of Philadelphia v Pennsylvania Human Relations Commission* 300 A 2.d 97; *Lambert London Borough Council v Commission for Racial Equality* [1990] ICR 768.

18 This reason is often raised as legitimating sex-based distinctions in acting roles, though note the criticism of M A Case, 'Disaggregating gender from sex and sexual orientation: The effeminate man in the law and feminist jurisprudence' (1995) 105 Yale Law Journal 1.

3. Employment and CRPD

Article 4 of the CRPD sets out the general obligations of State Parties to adopt 'strategies ... in pursuance of the general obligation to ensure the full realisation of all human rights' for people with disabilities. These include, inter alia, refraining from practices inconsistent with the Convention; mainstreaming disability perspectives into all policies and programs; and introducing legislative, administrative and other measures to secure relevant rights for disabled people.

Articles 24 to 28 and Article 30 of the CRPD fall under the canon of economic, social and cultural rights, with Article 27 of the Convention focused on employment. As noted above, the EU played a central role in driving the CRPD negotiations and, given its existing competence in the area of employment discrimination law, these standards have been described as 'largely reflect[ing] those already established by EU law.'[19] However, the CRPD goes significantly further than anti-discrimination law orthodoxy by requiring State Parties to positively develop substantive and positive responses that facilitate people with disabilities right to work 'on a free and equal basis with others [which] includes the right to the opportunity to gain a living by work freely chosen' in an open, inclusive and accessible labour market. The substantive advance with the CRPD's adoption is two-fold: first, the Convention's more rounded approach to employment is supported by its inclusion alongside the range of substantive rights which impact on the realisability of employment rights, including, inter alia, health and education rights, accessibility, and independent living.[20] Second, non-discrimination is framed as central to the supports States Parties are obliged to develop in order to 'safeguard and promote the realisation of the right to work' by taking appropriate steps, including through legislation, to, inter alia, 'prohibit discrimination on the basis of disability with regard to all matters concerning all forms of employment, including conditions of recruitment, hiring and employment, continuance of employment, career advancement and safe and healthy working conditions.' [21]

The promotion of employment opportunities, including assistance in finding, obtaining and maintaining employment is referenced, as is the promotion of the employment of persons with disabilities in both the public sector and the private sector, which includes the development of appropriate policies, including positive action, incentives and other measures.[22] In addition, Article 3 has eight paragraphs that provide the interpretive lens through which its substantive provisions must be applied and include references to anti-discrimination and equality and intersecting values and principles, including respect for difference, dignity, diversity and autonomy.[23] Clearly, then, States are mandated to go beyond non-discrimination whilst simultaneously placing its core ethic at the heart of its Convention obligations. The discussion below considers how a positive construction of the GOR could form

---

19 A Lawson, 'Disability and employment in the Equality Act 2010: Opportunities seized, lost and generated' (2011) 40 Industrial Law Journal 359, 360.

20 This is neatly summed up in the description in art 1 of the CRPD's general purpose to 'promote, protect and ensure the full and equal enjoyment of all human rights and fundamental freedoms by all persons with disabilities, and to promote respect for their inherent dignity.'

21 art 27(1)(a), CRPD (2006).

22 arts 27(1)(g)–(h), CRPD (2006).

23 art 3(a)–(h), CRPD (2006).

part of the legislative program of State Parties in pursuit of their obligations under Article 27 and what this would entail.

4. Towards A Disability-Based GOR

The essence of the GOR is its construction of the protected characteristic as an occupational requirement necessary for the performance of a particular job position.

Prior to considering the GOR as a possible positive construct of employment discrimination law, it is worth noting that the one domain in which a de facto type of disability GOR already operates is in the context of sheltered and supported employment. The Convention makes no such distinction between mainstream employment and sheltered employment but, as Lawson points out, the 'blanket consignment of people with certain impairments to certain forms of occupation may amount to a violation of their right to an opportunity to gain a living through work that is freely chosen.'[24] Moreover, the CRPD charges States Parties to mainstream a disability perspective into all policies and programs, and the requirement to enhance access to mainstream employment settings that are 'open and inclusive'[25] to people with disabilities mandates a consideration of the GOR in open employment settings.

The GOR has proven to be controversial when applied to the gender ground.[26] Some of the problems that beset gender GOR claims can be traced to the symmetrical nature of sex discrimination, difficulties that may be possibly side-stepped in the disability context. I will first deal with a couple of issues that ensue in respect of the disability ground prior to focusing on a positive construction of the disability GOR as refracted through a Convention lens. One is the question of the asymmetrical nature of disability discrimination protection because where this is accepted, it actually could, somewhat paradoxically, raise the necessity of a disability-based GOR. Briefly put, anti-discrimination precepts construct the law's protection against identity-based discrimination as operating in both directions, that is, for example, in the sex discrimination context, in favour of both women and men. The extension of this type of reciprocal protection to the disability ground does seem suspect: otherwise the legislative scheme would be read as protecting non-disabled people from less favourable treatment on the grounds of disability.[27] This assumption of asymmetry coupled with the permissibility of treating people with disabilities more

---

24 A Lawson, 'The United Nations Convention on the Rights of Persons with Disabilities: New era or false dawn' (2007) 34 Syracuse Journal of International Law and Commerce 563, 605, relying on Office of the High Commission for Human Rights, Committee on Economic, Social and Cultural Rights, General Comment No. 5 – Persons with Disabilities 12/09/1994, UN Doc E.1995/22, CESCR para 19.

25 art 27(1), CRPD (2006).

26 The problem lies in the reinforcement of gender stereotypes regarding women's suitability for particular types of employment which can arise both where the GOR works against or in favour of women.

27 However, note the decision of *McCall v Area Development Management Ltd* DEC-S2007-058, para 24, handed down under Ireland's Equal Status Acts 2000–2011, in which the Equality Tribunal rejected an argument that the direct disability-discrimination principle was asymmetrical in operation, instead holding that the statutory language did 'not support the view that the discriminatory grounds operate only in one direction.'

favourably than non-disabled persons,[28] combine to suggest that on one reading, the GOR in favour of disability is perhaps unnecessary. This reasoning, which is predicated on a link between the symmetrical nature of discrimination protection and the construction of the GOR as an exception to thereto, distracts, however, from the possible positive value that could be constructed within a Convention framed disability GOR that is developed here. Before moving to that point, it is worth stressing the risks over the reach of the GOR in the disability context, particularly where an asymmetrical construct of direct discrimination is not accepted. It is not too much of a leap to suggest that the reality of reduced opportunity for meaningful employment among certain groups of people with disabilities reflects a position that in many respects constructs 'not having a disability' as a (less than genuine) but common occupational requirement. Consequently, commentators have noted the need to 'successfully police the invocation of this defence in the disability context (as) a segregationist ethic could too easily masquerade as a genuine and determining occupational requirement.'[29]

However, I would suggest that given how the Convention provides 'breadth and context'[30] to the EU's anti-discrimination framework the better construction to States Parties discrimination law's protection would be to conceive the direct discrimination principle as being asymmetrical. This would mean that the GOR would not need to be interpreted as a strict derogation from the (symmetrical) principle of equal treatment. Such an approach lends itself to a more benign interpretation of the GOR in the disability context, that is, one that supports its operation in one direction – in favour of the disability ground. This would stipulate that the presence of 'disability' (what this might mean is interrogated below) can be an actual requirement for an occupation in a particular context.[31] This construct of the principle is further reinforced by the broad account of discrimination adopted in the Convention, which discards the categories of direct and indirect discrimination in favour of a prohibition on any 'distinction, exclusion or restriction of rights on the basis of disability,' and which avoids the wrangling over the symmetry or otherwise that besets the comparator model of anti-discrimination law.[32] Consequently, I argue that the GOR in this positive, enabling sense, ought not to be excluded from the disability ground, and to do so would be to construct an impermissible restriction of rights on the basis of disability.

---

[28] Which is said to be implicit in the reasonable accommodation duty: note the view of Baroness Hale that '(...)to the extent that the duty to make reasonable adjustments requires it, the employer is not only permitted but obliged to treat a disabled person more favourably than others,' *Archibald v Fife Council* [2004] 4 All E.R 303, 322.

[29] EU Network of Independent Experts on Disability Discrimination, 'Baseline Study: Disability Discrimination in the EU Member States' (November 2004) 20.

[30] A Lawson (n 19) 360.

[31] Disability as a GOR is not excluded from the UK's Equality Act 2010, the Framework Employment Directive. Cf. The Netherlands, where the government's view is that 'no scenario is imaginable in which 'disability' would constitute a genuine occupational requirement.' M Gitzen, 'Report on Measures to Combat discrimination: Country Report Netherlands' (European Commission 2005).

[32] See text (n 26).

5. Actualising a Disability GOR

The above discussion implicated the Convention in deconstructing the barriers to a positive disability GOR that derive from the dominance of the formal model of equality. Next, I go on to consider how the CRPD could construct the GOR in a way as to build a bridge between the substantive right to work and the disability non-discrimination right in such as way as to increase the representation of people with disabilities and the visibility of disability within employment structures, which can help foster more inclusive attitudes.[33]

A positive disability-based GOR could be a valuable means of furthering the Convention's employment provisions, particularly where read through Article 3 and Article 8, the latter of which obligates States Parties to raise awareness of the contribution and potential of people with disabilities and to counter stereotypes and to promote positive images of disability. In this way, the GOR could be one of many 'appropriate measures' of promoting the 'realisation of the right to work' given its construction of a positive nexus between work and disability. As suggested below, the GOR can assist in deconstructing the stereotypical assumption that disability and work are mutually exclusive. More tenuously it could be suggested that the CRPD can be said to indirectly support this construction by virtue of the relationship between the GOR and positive action,[34] given that States Parties are obliged to 'promote the employment of persons with disabilities in the private sector, (…) which may include affirmative action programmes, incentives and other measures.'[35]

Like much of discrimination law, the GOR leans on the meaning of disability with respect to its operation. What exactly a 'characteristic related to the disability ground'[36] opens up, is a range of possible interpretations, including the construction of disability within discrimination law, which, given that the EU has ratified the CRPD, must now be read in light of the how the Convention itself constructs the meaning of the term. The debate over settling a Convention definition of disability has been well documented,[37] with the resulting compromise situating an account of disability that recognises its 'evolving' nature within Article 1 and not in the definition section. The CRPD references persons with disabilities as including 'those who have long-term physical, mental, intellectual or sensory impairments which in interaction with various barriers may hinder their full and effective participation in society on an equal basis with others.'[38] The Preamble reinforces the social dimension to disability and how it 'results from the interaction between persons with impairments and attitudinal and environmental barriers that hinders their full and effective participation in society on an equal basis with others.'[39] As a result,

---

33 This invisibility can 'foster social attitudes of fear and condescension.' M Weber, 'Beyond the Americans with Disabilities Act: A national employment policy for people with disabilities' (1998) Buffalo Law Review 123, 130.

34 Pressures of space prevent further discussion on the relationship between the GOR and positive action; but, briefly put, similarities exist in respect of how both positive action and a positive GOR aim to increase the representation of people with disabilities in employment. There remain, however, considerable doctrinal differences between the two.

35 art 27(1)(h), CRPD (2006).

36 art 2(2)(a) of the Framework Employment Equality Directive.

37 See A Lawson n 24 pp 593–595.

38 art 1, CRPD (2006).

39 Preamble (e), CRPD (2006).

some form of impairment must be present in order for the GOR to be applicable, but it could also be argued, in keeping with a vision of disability for the purposes of positive action,[40] that it ought to include some experience with the socially constructed experience of disablement that arises from the interplay between inhospitable environments and negative attitudes.

It follows then to consider what roles can be constructed as positive and enhancing disability-based GORs in line with the Convention directive to 'promote recognition of the skills, merits and abilities of persons with disabilities.'[41] The first type of occupational position suggested borrows from an example of the GOR applied to the sexual-orientation ground in UK discrimination law. It has been suggested that a valid GOR could arise where 'an organisation advising on and promoting gay rights may be able to show that it is essential to the credibility of its chief executive who will be the public fact of the organisation that s/he should be gay.'[42] Similar reasoning could be adopted in respect of a disability rights organisation, although a couple of practical issues emerge here. First, as noted above, as compared with the types of sexual orientations, there is a vast array and range of impairments, which correspond to differing experiences of disablement. This raises questions as to whether an organisation could insist on employing a person with a certain type of disability or, indeed, in reflection of the social model, a particular experience of disability. This raises many difficult issues on the politics of the visibility/invisibility of disability. However, the statutory construct could provide some guidance on this issue. The GOR principle explicitly requires a link between the occupational requirement (or context in which the job is performed) and the characteristic 'related' to the protected ground.[43] Thus the provision is ultimately governed by the nature of the job occupation at issue, including the context in which it is performed, and that these requirements will ultimately determine the nature of the characteristic that is related to the protected ground. For instance, it could be determined that part of the public role of the chief executive of a disability rights/representative organisation is to draw attention both to the socially constructed nature of disability and the positive contributions which people with disabilities can make; therefore it may argue that it wishes to hire an individual with an impairment that is visible in order to best impart its political message to the general public and other important constituents.[44] Similarly, a mental health charity may form the view that the public face of its organisation should have personal experience of mental health issues so as to better connect its message to the public and to help attack stigma and stereotypes around the employability of persons with mental health experiences. Again, it would

---

40 The claim that there ought to be a distinction between the definition of disability for the purposes of non-discrimination and positive action arises in those jurisdictions which include a broad definition of disability that is not predicated on measuring severity of the impairment in terms of its substantial functional limitations. This is so that positive action measures can be better targeted towards advancing the inclusion of the more acutely excluded and so avoid the 'creamy top' indictment directed towards non-tailored positive action programmes.

41 art 8(1)(a)(iii) CRPD.

42 Acas, *Sexual Orientation and the Workplace: Putting the Employment Equality (Sexual Orientation) Regulations 2003 into practice for Employers and their Staff*, para 1.6.

43 art 2(2)(a) of the Framework Employment Equality Directive (n 5).

44 Of course if would still be necessary to determine the 'legitimacy' and 'proportionality' of this objective. Certainly the Convention's standards help to bolster the legitimacy argument on the basis that people with disabilities are to be actively involved in decision-making processes – Preamble (o), CRPD.

be expected that any disability GOR claimed in this context would be specifically tailored to the disability at issue. Therefore, an individual with diabetes ought not to be able to litigate should the organisation try to insist on a disability-specific GOR because the characteristic – the specific disability of experience of living through mental illness – is related to the particular occupational activities.

Further, disability GORs can be raised in the context of counselling and professional support roles. In the United States, the courts have legitimated the use of the GOR exception to allow supervisors of juvenile detainees to be the same sex as the detainees based on 'common sense' evidence that vulnerable persons were more likely to confide in and open up to a person of their own sex.[45] The now repealed Race Relations Act 1976 in England and Wales also contained a broadly similar type of GOR applicable to the race ground.[46] Given the frequently unhappy experiences that people with disabilities report with the medicalisation of disability,[47] it could be suggested that a positive welfare-enhancing approach could be to provide access to professional persons who have accumulated experience in navigating the life path with disability. Thus, it could be argued that in such instances a disability GOR could be adopted in respect of counselling or support positions, for example, where persons provide support for individuals following the onset of disability as a result of illness or accident. Thus, the context in which the job activities are carried out and the nature of the work could require that a sense of understanding, empathy and practical connection to the experiences of the service user, may make a particular experience of disability a genuine and determining requirement of the job. Peer-leader positions are also useful examples of positions that require disability as a GOR. Such positions can be usefully harnassed towards consciousness-raising around disability, and one of the best examples is the Moving On with Learning Programme which operates in England.[48] These job positions involve people with intellectual disabilities providing training and seminars regarding the treatment of people with intellectual and other impairments to the many professions that have had powerful influences over the quality of life of people with disabilities, including doctors, nurses, social workers and lawyers. In the context of the entertainment industry the application of the GOR has been queried in some instances,[49] and has generally not been mandated in favour of people disabilities so as to create employment opportunities for actors with disabilities.[50] Thus, many productions with characters with disabilities have not been played by actors with disabilities. However, many actors and performers with disabilities consider the portrayal of disabled characters in films and other media as equivalent to 'blacking-up' in the

---

45 See *City of Philadelphia v Pennsylvania Human Relations Commission* 300 A.2d (1973).

46 This provision permitted a race-based GOR in the following terms: 'the holder of the job provides persons of that racial group with personal services promoting their welfare and those services can most effectively be provided by a person of that racial group.' Discussed in *Lambeth London Borough Council v Commission for Racial Equality* [1990] ECR 768.

47 M Oliver, *Understanding Disability: From Theory to Practice* (Palgrave 1996).

48 'Moving on with Life and Learning' (2011) www.mowll.net/default.html last accessed 31 March 2016.

49 For discussion of the tension between the First Amendment's protection for artistic freedom and employment discrimination law, see R K Robinson, 'Casting and caste-ing: Reconciling artistic freedom and antidiscrimination norms' (2007) 95 California Law Review 1.

50 The opposite side of the coin, of course, is that one of the barriers to work in the acting profession cited by performers with disabilities is 'only being considered for disabled roles.' See O Raynor and K Hayward, *The Employment of Performers with Disabilities in the Entertainment Industry* (Screen Actors Guild, 2005) <www.iampwd.org/resources> last accessed 31 March 2016.

context of race or ethnicity acting. Of course, this is a separate point to the tenor of the productions and how disability is constructed and represented within the arts and wider entertainment industry, more generally.[51]

6. Conclusion

The CRPD addresses, in a holistic way, the human rights obligations of States Parties to people with disabilities. In the employment context, this will require States Parties to develop a range of provisions and programmes that can help to actualise the right to work in an open and inclusive labour market. This chapter has suggested ways by which a reinvigorated disability GOR could form part of a State's employment policy for people with disabilities. Where adopted it legitimises disability as a positive and necessary requirement for the purposes of certain forms of employment and, in so doing, contributes to the integration of people with disabilities into work settings in a way that recognises the value of their specific experiences and their worth. However, it is important not to overstate its transformative potential. Its operation in this manner will still be dependent on employers recognising the value of and need for a disability GOR in relevant circumstances. Hence, it is dependent on a robust commitment to the Article 8 obligation of promoting awareness – for example, training programmes on disability and the rights of persons with disabilities.

---

51 ibid 9. This report shows how characters with disabilities are often portrayed in stereotypical ways (as suffering, special victims, or courageous or deserving of sympathy – with rare characterisations of persons with disabilities as more rounded characters participating – in typical activities which reinforces stereotypical views. One recent exception is the role of Walter Jr played by the actor R J Mitte in the television series *Breaking Bad.*

CHAPTER 31

GENETIC DISCRIMINATION IN EMPLOYMENT: THE RELEVANCE OF THE UNITED NATIONS CONVENTION ON THE RIGHTS OF PERSONS WITH DISABILITIES

Aisling de Paor

1. INTRODUCTION

Ground-breaking genetic discoveries and technological advances have opened up a new era in genetic exploration, and technological advances have enabled geneticists to successfully chart the genetic basis of a wide range of diseases, and detect potential future disabilities. However, genetic tests and the information they are able to reveal provide a classic example of 'technology's double edged sword'.[1] Questions arise as to whether an appropriate framework and safeguards exist to protect the interests of individuals (specifically to protect the privacy of sensitive genetic information, and to prevent the discriminatory use of genetic information) and also to encourage further advances in the scientific field.

Against the backdrop of rapidly advancing genetic science, this chapter will focus on the misuse of genetic information in the employment context, highlighting the implications of using genetic information, from the perspective of both the employer and the employee. This chapter will look at the regulatory framework at EU level and whether this framework sufficiently protects sensitive genetic information. Specifically this chapter will focus on the United Nations Convention on the Rights of Persons with Disabilities (CRPD) and its application to the issue of genetic discrimination. In particular, it will look at the relevance and implications of the conclusion of the CRPD by the EU, and whether this adds weight to the argument that an EU-level response to genetic discrimination is preferable, and perhaps indeed necessary. It will also explore the impact of the EU Charter of Fundamental Rights as a possible tool to enhance EU-level regulation of this area.

2. THE NEW GENETIC AGE

The rapid surge in genetic research and technological discoveries, provoked in large

1 D Suzuki, 'Inventing The Future: Reflections On Science, Technology And Nature '(Stoddart 1990) 55.

part by the success of the Human Genome Project,[2] anticipates a future in which information about a vast amount of disease genes can be more easily accessible. These unprecedented scientific advances have led to an increase in the practice of genetic testing for medical and non-medical purposes.

The advent of this new genetic age also offers the possibility of personalised medicine, which potentially promises to introduce a health care revolution – it has the potential to transform health care with earlier diagnosis, more effective prevention and treatment of disease, and avoidance of drug side effects. Some tests may confirm a diagnosis and direct a physician toward appropriate treatments, while other tests highlight individuals at high risk for conditions that may be preventable. In particular, a family history of a condition or disease may be confirmed by undergoing a genetic test. Genetic testing offers opportunities for individuals to be more informed of their genetic status and health, so that they can effectively manage their health care and treatment plans.

Whole genome sequencing is quickly evolving as science is advancing, with scientists competing to sequence the human genome at an ever-decreasing cost.[3] In addition, scientific advances are facilitating the development of pharmacogenetics, which has the potential to revolutionise not only individual treatment and health care, but also the pharmaceutical industry.[4] There has also been an increase in the use and availability of direct-to-consumer (DTC) genetic testing, which are genetic tests that are accessible directly to the consumer and bypass the requirement for a medical professional in the process of discovering one's genetic make-up.[5]

Further advances in genetic science are revealing the potential to detect certain behavioural traits, such as the existence of the risk-taking gene, and more recent research indicates that predisposition towards determination and success is determined by one's genes (in conjunction with environmental and other external factors). These rapid advances in gene discovery and technological advances result in genetic information becoming widely available and accessible to individuals and

---

2 The Human Genome Project was a 13-year endeavour to sequence the human genome. The Human Genome Project began in 1990, and in 2003 it was announced that they had successfully mapped the human genome, two years ahead of schedule. For further details about the Human Genome Project and its success, see www.genome.gov/10001772 and www.genome.gov/ last accessed 31 March 2016.

3 It was recently reported that the human genome can now be sequenced for $1,000, and no doubt this will further decrease in price. See J Markoff, 'Cost of Gene Sequencing Falls, Raising Hopes for Medical Advances' *The New York Times* (New York, 7 March 2012) <www.nytimes.com/2012/03/08/technology/cost-of-gene-sequencing-falls-raising-hopes-for-medical-advances.html?> last accessed 31 March 2016.

4 Pharmacogenetics is the area of genetic research that analyses how drug therapies may impact differently depending on individual people's specific genetic code. See T Lemmens, 'Selective Justice, Genetic Discrimination, and Insurance: Should we Single Out our Genes in Our Laws?' (2000) 45 McGill Law Journal 347, 351. See generally, W E Evans and M V Relling, 'Moving towards individualized medicine with Pharmacogenomics' (2004) 429 Nature 464–468. See also H R Abbing, 'Pharmacogenetic data: Mapping the subject's rights' (2006)13 Good Clinical Practice Journal 28–30.

5 The increase in interest and availability of DTC genetic testing is partly the result of the emergence of several companies, such as: 23andMe <www.23andme.com/ > last accessed 31 March 2016, offering tests using genome-wide technology direct to consumers over the internet. One of the significant challenges of direct-to-consumer testing is that it shifts the control of genetic testing from the clinical context and medical professionals to consumers.

third parties. This deluge of genetic information infiltrating society raises a variety of ethical, social and legal issues that, in the absence of appropriate regulation, can not only threaten advancing science, but can also result in the discriminatory use of genetic information, and violation of one's genetic privacy. Ultimately, there is a risk of the creation of a potential genetic underclass and the segregation of certain vulnerable individuals. In light of the potential for abuse, it is necessary to explore the implications of third-party use of genetic information.

3. Genetic Testing in Employment: A Battlefield of Competing Rights

3.1. What is Genetic Discrimination?

In consideration of technology's 'double-edged sword,' it is necessary to explore the undesirable and unintentional consequences of advancing science, and in particular, the implications of third-party use and misuse of genetic information. One of the main concerns arising is the discriminatory use of genetic information, particularly by employers, leading to genetic discrimination.[6] Discrimination involves differentiating between individuals on the basis of certain characteristics, such as age, race or sex, and using those distinctions as the basis for differential treatment. The increasing incidence of genetic testing and the resulting rise in the availability of genetic information have essentially unveiled a new dimension or layer of difference, that of genetic makeup.[7] The concept of genetic discrimination has been discussed extensively in academic literature.[8] Genetic discrimination has been described as 'discrimination against an individual or against members of that individual's family solely because of real or perceived differences from the "normal" genome in the genetic constitution of that individual.'[9] Rothstein has used the term to describe the differential treatment based on genetic status.[10] It can also be construed as discrimination on the basis of genetic information or genetic features.[11] From a

6 There is also a myriad of undesirable ethical issues that may arise, for example, the right not the know, the psychological consequences of knowing one's genetic make-up and the potential obligation to inform family members of genetic test results. For further discussion of the ethical issues see A Mainsbridge, 'Employers and Genetic Information: A New Frontier in Discrimination' (2002) 2 Macquarie Law Journal 61, 67.

7 ibid.

8 The concept of genetic discrimination has also been translated in the motion picture *Gattaca*.

9 M R Natowicz et al, 'Genetic Discrimination and the Law' (1992) 50 American Journal of Human Genetics 465. The authors 'distinguish genetic discrimination from discrimination based on disability caused by altered genes', and thereby clarify the point that genetic discrimination is not based on any notion of the present function of the individual; rather the discriminating party relies on that individual's genotype to assess risk of future dysfunction. See also Billings et al, 'Discrimination as a Consequence of Genetic Testing' (1992) 50 American Journal of Human Genetics 476. Billings et al describes genetic discrimination as 'discrimination directed against an individual or family based on an apparent or perceived genetic variation from the "normal" human genotype.' For further discussion, see M A Rothstein and M A Anderlik, 'What is Genetic Discrimination, and when and how can it be prevented?' (2001) 3(5) Genetics in Medicine 354.

10 M A Rothstein, 'Genetic Discrimination in Employment: Ethics, Policy and Comparative Law', in Swiss Institute of Comparative Law (ed), *Human Genetic Analysis and the Protection of Personality and Privacy* (Schulthess Polygraphisher Verlag 1994) 129, See also M A Rothstein, 'Discrimination based on Genetic Information'(1993) 33 Jurimetrics Journal 13.

11 The European Union Charter of Fundamental Rights refers specifically to the concept of 'genetic

disability perspective, genetic testing can predict a propensity to or probability of future disability. Genetic discrimination can therefore be described as discrimination on the basis of perceived disability, or on the basis of potential future disability.[12] Accordingly, if genetic information is too widely available, it exposes putative persons with disabilities (which, with the ageing process, includes most of us) to overt and covert discrimination, (therefore potentially violating the CRPD). We are all therefore potential victims of genetic discrimination, as no one has perfect genes, and everyone carries genes that predispose to a variety of common conditions and illnesses (for example, cancer, coeliac disease, colour-blindness, anaemia, cystic fibrosis, diabetes, and eyesight problems).

3.2 Genetic Discrimination in Employment

Interested third parties (including employers) may use the results of genetic tests (as well as genetic information elicited from family history) to discriminate based on perceptions of health risks and possible future disabilities. Although genetic testing by employers is not yet taking place on a widespread basis, rapidly advancing genetic technology indicates that testing will undoubtedly become cheaper,[13] more sophisticated and therefore more accessible to employers and other third parties. Indeed it has been acknowledged that advances in genetics have led some to anticipate that widespread genetic discrimination is inevitable.[14]

Genetic testing in the workplace generally incorporates the practices of genetic screening and genetic monitoring. Genetic screening may be used as a test to determine the genetic predisposition of an employee (or potential employee).[15] Genetic monitoring focuses on the workplace as a potential risk for genetic conditions, and may be viewed as a means to improve the workplace environment, and therefore protect employees.[16] Such testing is often carried out to monitor workplace exposure to hazardous substances, which may indicate increased likelihood of future illness or disability.[17] This section will explore the practice of genetic testing in the workplace and the consequences for the employee and society. It will also look at the employer's potential right to know and the limits

---

features' in art 21.1. Charter of Fundamental Rights of the European Union, proclaimed by the Commission, 7 December 2000. O.J (C 364) 1.

12 See generally, P S Miller, 'Genetic Testing and the Future of Disability Insurance: Thinking about Discrimination in the Genetic Age' (2007) Journal of Law, Medicine and Ethics 47. See also G Wolbring, 'A Disability Rights Approach to Genetic Discrimination', in J Sandor (ed), *Society and Genetic Information: Codes and Laws in the Genetic Era* (Central European University Press 2004) 161.

13 Markoff (n 3).

14 J Chorpening, 'Genetic Disability: A Modest Proposal to Modify the ADA to Protect Against some forms of Genetic Discrimination' (2004) 82 North Carolina Law Review 1441, 1443. See also P T Kim, 'Genetic Discrimination, Genetic Privacy: Rethinking Employee Protections for a Brave New Workplace' (2002) 96 Northwestern University Law Review 1497, 1498.

15 M B Kaufman, 'Genetic Discrimination in the Workplace: An Overview of Existing Protections' (1999) 30 Loyola University Chicago Law Journal 393, 397.

16 K D Weaver, 'Genetic Screening and the Right not to Know' (1997)13 Issues in Law and Medicine 243, 246.

17 The purpose of genetic monitoring is to help employers determine if the employees are being affected by any toxins that they come into contact with through various daily tasks. See Kaufman (n 15) at 389–399.

that must be placed on this right, striving towards a balance in the recognition of these competing rights.

3.3 Employers' Interest in Genetic Information

All employers have an economic interest in the health and welfare of their employees. They want to capitalise employees' fitness and productivity and minimise employee absenteeism and turnover.[18] It is generally accepted that when employees are in ill health, they are less productive,[19] may require sick leave, are more likely to suffer injury and illness on the job, and their illnesses may negatively impact upon the morale of co-workers and other third parties.[20] These factors collectively result in increased costs for the employer.

Therefore, when hiring, training or promoting employees, employers have strong financial incentives to select the healthiest and most productive individual. Genetic information may assist employers to manage the productivity of the workforce. Indeed, to many employers, obtaining genetic information about employees and potential employees may be viewed as rational commercial practice.[21] Hiring or promoting an under-qualified and under-productive worker is inevitably costly to the employer.[22] Employers may seek to take advantage of advancing genetic technology by requiring the use of genetic testing as a prerequisite to employment, or by requesting existing genetic test results and details of family medical history.

Employers may argue that they have a valid interest in obtaining as much information as possible about a prospective employee in order to ensure selection of the best possible candidate for the position.[23] As well as revealing details of an individual's potential future health, advancing genetic science (together with environmental and other factors) can reveal potentially valuable behavioural profiles – for example, the prevalence of the 'risk-taking' gene,[24] which, some employers may view as desirable in a potential employee, while others may see this as indicative of a high-

---

18 M A Rothstein et al, 'Protecting Genetic Privacy by Permitting Employer Access Only to Job-Related Employee Medical Information: Analysis of a Unique Minnesota Law' (1998) 24 American Journal of Law and Medicine 399, 401.

19 The final financial effect of hiring genetically susceptible workers is that their productivity suffers as a result of a disease or condition that might develop. See K A Jensen, 'Genetic Privacy in Washington State: Policy Considerations and a Model Genetic Privacy Act' (1997) 21 Seattle University Law Review 357, 369.

20 B Knoppers and M A Rothstein, 'Legal Aspects of Genetics, Work and Insurance in North America and Europe' (1996) 3 European Journal of Health Law 143,144.

21 S Carr, 'Invisible Actors: Genetic Testing and Genetic Discrimination in the Workplace' (2008) 30 University of Arkansas at Little Rock Law Review 2.

22 In addition, employers who facilitate health insurance for employees have increased economic incentives to be concerned about the productivity of workers and costs such as health benefits and insurance. This is particularly relevant in the United States, where employers generally facilitate health insurance for employees.

23 Mainsbridge (n 6) at 66.

24 R Alleyne, 'Why risk taking runs in the family – scientists find gene that makes you gamble' *The Telegraph* 6 May 2009. <www.telegraph.co.uk/news/newstopics/howaboutthat/5279222/Why-risk-taking-runs-in-the-family-scientists-find-gene-that-makes-you-gamble.html > last accessed 31 March 2016. See also S Shane, 'Explaining Innate Risk-Takers', *Bloomberg Business Week*, 12 February 2010 www.businessweek.com/smallbiz/content/feb2010/sb20100211_567240.ht last accessed 31 March 2016.; citing S Shane, *Born Entrepreneurs, Born Leaders – How your Genes Affect your Work Life* (Oxford University Press 2010); See also M J Kreek et al,

risk candidate who may financially jeopardize a company. Advancing science may also reveal which candidates are more inclined to succeed, which would likely be of interest to employers.[25] As genetics becomes more closely associated with behavioural traits, employers have additional incentives to take advantage of new technologies to find an individual who fits the profile of their organisation.

3.3.1. Use of genetic information for health and safety purposes

An employer's desire to obtain genetic information about employees may also be motivated by occupational health and safety factors.[26] Genetic information may potentially determine whether or not an employee has a genetic predisposition that may pose a safety risk to the employee, co-workers or the public or that may result in a susceptibility to workplace hazards. Genetic monitoring can therefore be used to screen employees and potential employees, who, because of their genetic status, may be more likely to develop illnesses, if exposed to certain workplace or occupational elements, including chemicals.[27] Individuals with the sickle cell trait, for example, may be at increased risk for sickle cell anaemia if exposed to carbon monoxide or cyanide.

Use of genetic technology is therefore often advocated as a means of reducing occupational illness, both for the benefit of the employer and the employee.[28] Employers could potentially use genetic information to ensure that prospective or current employees are not placed in environments that might cause harm.[29] By

---

'Genetic Influences on impulsivity, risk-taking, stress, responsibility and vulnerability to drug abuse and addiction' (2005) 8 Nature Neuroscience 1450.

[25] C Hsu, 'New Findings Suggest that Winners are Born, not Bred', *Medical Daily* 16 May 2012 <www.medicaldaily.com/news/20120516/9908/success-genes-dna-characteristics-failure-twins.htm> last accessed 31 March 2016.

[26] Employers have obligations under European health and safety law: Directive 89/391/EEC on Safety and Health at Work (there are also certain common law duties to provide a safe place of work, see *Wilson and Clyde Coal Co Ltd v English* [1937] 3 All ER 628 establishing the modern day duty of care owed to the employee, including, inter alia, the duty to provide a safe place of work).

[27] Genetic monitoring involves periodic testing of employees to monitor any changes in employees' genetic material that occurred during the course of employment. For further discussion, see Kaufman (n 15).

[28] Employees arguably have an increased interest in obtaining information about their genetic composition in hazardous workplaces in order to monitor their health closely and make an informed decision about remaining at their job. Periodic genetic screening of employees working under hazardous conditions or being exposed to dangerous toxins with the aim of detecting problematic genetic changes, or pre-employment testing for heightened susceptibility, may induce the employer to introduce adequate workplace modifications or preventative measures, or to offer (potential) employees a different function that does not entail a heightened risk to disease. J H Gerards and H L Janssen, 'Regulation of Genetic and Other Health Information in a Comparative Perspective' (2006) 13 European Journal of Health Law 339, 363. See also Carr (n 21) at 2.

[29] Employers have an interest in maintaining a healthy and productive workforce to guard against being held negligent. Some may advocate genetic screening on the grounds that all individuals have a right not to be harmed, and employers therefore have a duty to provide a safe workplace. Employers have obligations under European health and safety law: Directive 89/391/EEC on Safety and Health at Work (there are also certain common law duties to provide a safe place of work, see *Wilson and Clyde Coal Co Ltd v English* [1937] 3 All ER 628 establishing the modern day duty of care owed to the employee, including, inter alia, the duty to provide a safe place of work).

controlling occupational illness, genetic testing may reduce employment costs (including costs incurred from lowered productivity, absenteeism, as well as liability for occupational disease).[30]

Although employers may argue that use of genetic monitoring in hazardous workplaces is legitimate, caution is needed to ensure that employees' rights are maintained, having particular regard to privacy and confidentiality, and preventing the discriminatory use of such monitoring, particularly in accordance with EU Data Protection legislation.[31] In addition, the limited accuracy and scientific validity, as well as the effectiveness of genetic testing must be taken into account. It is important that any potential genetic testing is used fairly by employers, with legitimate objectives, and not as a cloak to shield the segregation and potential weeding out of 'high-risk' employees.[32] This is where the line blurs and the balance between the respective rights of employers and employees becomes more difficult to achieve.[33]

Overall, it is arguable that the use of genetic technologies in hazardous workplaces can give employees relevant health information, contribute towards scientific research in understanding occupational diseases, and potentially facilitate an employer in discharging their safety obligations. Accordingly, there are some arguments in favour of controlled and limited use of genetic testing in the workplace, in limited circumstances, with a view to achieving a balance between the rights of employers and employees. In achieving the appropriate balance between employers and employees, and having explored the limited right to know of employers, it is important to highlight the implications of misusing genetic information, and the potential consequences for employees and society.

---

30 For a more in-depth view of this argument, see R A Bohrer, 'A Rawlsian Approach to Solving the Problem of Genetic Discrimination in Toxic Workplaces' (2002)39 San Diego Law Review 747. The author argues that with appropriate limits and safeguards, it is appropriate to exclude individuals from some employment opportunities if they are known to have genetic factors that predispose them to diseases. See also M Baram, 'Genetic Testing for Susceptibility to Disease from Exposure to Toxic Chemicals: Implications for Public and Worker Health Policies' (2000–2001) 41 Jurimetrics 165.

31 Directive 95/46/EC of the European Parliament and of the Council of 24 October 1995 on the protection of individuals with regard to the processing of personal data and on the free movement of such data.

32 For example, in the United States, genetic monitoring for sickle cell anaemia became prevalent in the 1970s. It has been discovered that some carriers of the sickle cell gene might be hyper-susceptible to certain workplace toxic chemicals such as benzine, lead, cadmium, carbon monoxide and cyanide. Accordingly, employers relied on the submission that in hazardous workplaces they should be allowed to engage in genetic monitoring of employees. Some job applicants were denied employment, while others were terminated from their jobs because they were found to be carriers of the sickle cell gene. A public health initiative escalated into a method of stereotyping and discriminating against African-Americans who are more susceptible to sickle cell anaemia than other races. See Kaufmann (n 15) at 402–403; See also M A Pagnatarro, 'Genetic Discrimination and the Workplace: Employee's Right to Privacy v Employer's Need to Know' (2001) 39 American Business Law Journal 139, 147.

33 It has been suggested that any regulation of genetic information in the employment context should contain a clear exception for requesting or requiring genetic information in the case of genetic monitoring of employees in hazardous workplaces. See Carr (n 21) at 11. In providing for this exception, it has also been acknowledged that employee rights be upheld. Accordingly, the exception should contain protections for workers, including a requirement that employees provide voluntary, written and informed consent. It has also been pointed out that if employers engage in genetic monitoring, they also need to take precautions to protect employee confidentiality.

3.4. Undesirable Implications: A Potential Genetic Underclass?

Employers arguably have no right to require that an individual take a genetic test (or use the results of genetic tests previously taken) when that individual does not have an illness that would impact upon his or her current capacity to do a job. Making an employment decision on the basis of the probability of an individual developing a certain illness or disability, as opposed to based on his or her actual ability to carry out the work, may amount to unfair discrimination.[34] Discrimination based on genetic factors can be as unjust as that based on race or gender, and such discrimination based upon actual or perceived genetic traits creates unnecessary barriers to an individual's right to equal opportunity. The right to be treated equally and according to one's abilities in all the diverse aspects of human endeavour is a core social value.[35] Genetic discrimination therefore violates basic tenets of individual justice and is potentially detrimental to core societal values.

In addition, misuse of sensitive genetic information can result in the violation of an employee's privacy, with implications not only for that employee but also for his or her family.[36] Genetic information contains personal, sensitive information about an individual, and has been described as an individual's 'future diary' as it effectively 'informs our younger selves about our aging selves.'[37] Genetic information reveals sensitive, personal information about ourselves, our ancestors, and other blood relatives such as sisters and brothers.[38] Unauthorised access to and disclosure of genetic information to employers may breach an individual's (as well as family

---

[34] In the European Union there is strong legislation in favour of equality in the workplace – Directive 2000/78/EC of 27 November 2000 –establishing a general framework for equal treatment in employment and occupation, [2000] OJ L 303/16. Article 2 of this Directive defines four types of discrimination including direct discrimination, which occurs 'where one person is treated less favourably than another is, has been or would be treated in a comparable situation on any of the grounds referred to in Article 1 [including disability].'

[35] L O Gostin, 'Genetic Discrimination: The Use of Genetically Based Diagnostic and Prognostic Tests by Employers and Insurers' (1991) 17 American Journal of Law and Medicine 109, 112. See European Convention on Human Rights, the EU Charter of Fundamental Rights and the European Social Charter, in which there is a strong focus on core social values and fundamental human rights principles. [2001] C 364/01; Council of Europe, 'European Social Charter (Revised)' 3 May 1996 ETS 163.

[36] In the European Union, there is a strong emphasis on the protection of an individual's and the family's privacy and data protection: art 8 European Convention on Human Rights (1950); art 8 EU Charter of Fundamental Rights [2001] C 364/01; art 16 Treaty on the Functioning of the European Union [2008] C/115/47. In addition, the EU Data Protection Directive is an important component of EU privacy and human rights law. The Directive was designed to protect the privacy and protection of all personal data collected for or about citizens of the EU, particularly as it relates to processing, using or exchanging such data. Directive 95/46/EC of the European Parliament and of the Council of 24 October 1995 on the protection of individuals with regard to the processing of personal data and on the free movement of such data (1995) OJ L281/31.

[37] G J Annas, 'Genetic Privacy: There Ought to be a Law' (1999) 4 Texas Review of Law and Policy 9, 11. He does however clarify that 'it is coded and probabilistic: we are not necessarily going to get every disease that we are genetically predisposed to develop.' Annas borrowed this analogy from William Safire's description of diaries, which 'inform our aging selves about our younger selves'. W Safire, 'Sleazy Senate Inquiry', *The New York Times* (New York 25th October 1993) 19.

[38] Linked to this, genetic information has implications for spouses and potential spouses in terms of reproduction and reproductive choices, thereby raising further privacy and confidentiality concerns.

members') fundamental right to privacy,[39] and may violate the public interest in privacy protection.[40]

On further examination of the potential effects of misusing genetic information, it has been observed that genetic discrimination may perpetuate further discrimination against already marginalised and historically victimised groups in society, such as racial and ethnic minorities and amongst the sexes.[41] Genetic conditions are sometimes more prevalent in certain racial and ethnic groups, or in specific local communities.[42] For example, the sickle-cell trait generally affects Africans and African-Americans at a higher rate than other races,[43] and the two genetic mutations associated with breast cancer (BRCA1 and BRCA2[44]) are more common among Ashkenazi Jews.[45] When the faction affected is one which has previously been stigmatised in society, there is a risk of further exacerbating negative attitudes and focusing on the significance of the connection.[46] This can result in increased discrimination, social exclusion and marginalisation, both in the employment context and in the wider society.[47]

The misuse of genetic information has potentially undesirable implications, not only for the individual, but also for the scientific community. Considering the possibility of putting their current or future employment at risk, as well as the fear of discrimination and the fear of privacy violations, individuals may be reluctant to undergo genetic testing and take advantage of advancing genetic technology that could enhance their

---

39 In one of the few United States cases on the issue of genetic testing in employment, the Ninth Circuit stated: 'one can think of few subject areas more personal and more likely to implicate privacy interests than that of one's health or genetic make-up.' *Norman Bloodsaw v Lawrence Berkeley Laboratory* 135 F.3d 1260, 1269 (9th Cir. 1998) (citing *Dee v City of New York*, 15 F.3d 264, 267 (2d. Cir. 1994).

40 For further discussion on the topic of genetic privacy see M Taylor, *Genetic Data and the Law: A Critical Perspective on Privacy Protection* (Cambridge University Press 2012).

41 L Gostin, 'Genetic Discrimination: The Use of Genetically Based Diagnostic and Prognostic Tests by Employers and Insurers' (1991) 17 American Journal of Law and Medicine 109,111, states that the 'fact that genetic diseases are sometimes closely associated with discrete ethnic or racial groups such as African Americans, Ashkenazi Jews or Armenians compounds the potential for invidious discrimination.' See generally I V Motoc, 'The International Law of Genetic Discrimination: The Power of Never Again' in T Murphy (ed), *New Technologies and Human Rights* (Oxford University Press 2009).

42 Mainsbridge (n 6) at 71. There has recently been discussion and controversy in relation to screening for sickle cell anaemia in the NCAA – for further discussion see, L B Jordan et al, 'Screening U.S. College Athletes for their Sickle Cell Disease Carrier Status' (2011) 41 American Journal of Preventative Medicine 406.

43 Substantial controversy has already arisen over sickle-cell screening: in the 1970s in the United States, massive sickle-cell screening, which was introduced as a health care program, led to discrimination against African-Americans. See generally Lemmens (n 4) at 372–373.

44 For further information on BRCA1 and BRCA2 see link to the National Cancer Institute at the National Institutes of Health: <www.cancer.gov/cancertopics/factsheet/Risk/BRCA> last accessed 31 March 2016.

45 See S V Hodgson et al, 'Risk Factors for Detecting Germline BRCA1 and BRCA2 Founder Mutations in Ashkenazi Jewish Women with Breast or Ovarian Cancer' (1999) 36 Journal of Medical Genetics 369.

46 J L Dolgin, 'Personhood, Discrimination and the New Genetics' (2000–2001) 66 Brook Law Review 755, 786–87. For a more general discussion of the racial and ethnic disparities in health care and health status, see E Singer et al, 'Racial and Ethnic Variations in Knowledge and Attitudes about Genetic Testing' (2004) 8 Genetic Testing 1.

47 This risk of perpetuating further discrimination against already marginalized groups may also be contrary to the CRPD [2006], A/RES/61/106.

health and wellbeing.[48] In addition to individual health implications, this reluctance to engage in genetic testing may also have the effect of stifling genetic science and advancing technology. Scientists may experience difficulty in collecting research data as people become unwilling to submit to genetic tests.[49] This may have further implications for public health, as potentially beneficial genetic discoveries and technological innovations become hampered.

3.4.1. Societal Implications of Genetic Discrimination

In addition to the impact which misuse of genetic information has on an individual and on science, there are also wider societal implications that merit consideration in this debate. Individuals who are denied employment on the basis of genetic test results may be left without a job and in some situations, without access to health care (for example, which is often the case in the US.[50])[51]

Consequently, genetic technology can create employment barriers by effectively categorising individuals according to potential future health risk. Employer deference to such classifications could lead to a genetic underclass of 'unemployable' and in some cases 'uninsurable' individuals and deny health care (and other benefits) to certain employees and their families, thereby intensifying this underclass. This 'underclass' may be denied employment, yet never actually develop the illness for which they have a higher than normal genetic risk of acquiring. Society may be denied the contribution of these individuals, who are in a position to make a productive addition to the community, and who are being denied this opportunity, despite their current ability. This may result in the further exclusion and isolation of vulnerable persons such as persons with disabilities, and the elderly, and create further barriers to their integration into the community.[52]

Access to fruitful employment may also affect access to other social and economic goods and services, such as ownership of a property,[53] leisure activities, and in certain cases, health insurance. It may impact upon fulfilling civic engagement,

---

48 M R Santiago, 'Chapter 99: Preventing Employment Discrimination Based on One's Genetic Characteristics' (1999) 30 McGeorge Law Review 703, 705.

49 P S Miller, 'Genetic Discrimination in the Workplace' (1998) 26 Journal of Law, Medicine and Ethics 189, 190.

50 There is currently no universal health care provided by the government in the US; therefore, most health insurance is provided for by private health insurers. In addition, the majority of individuals in the US obtain insurance cover through their employers. Access to health care is therefore a serious problem, particularly for the un-employed or the under-employed. The provision of insurance is therefore closely linked to employment in the US. In comparison, most European countries have some form of universal access to health care.

51 By excluding qualified individuals from employment, education, government service or insurance, the marketplace is robbed of skills, energy and imagination. Such exclusion promotes physical and economic dependency, draining rather than enriching social institutions. See L O Gostin, 'Genetic Discrimination: The Use of Genetically Based Diagnostic and Prognostic Tests by Employers and Insurers' (1991) 17 American Journal of Law and Medicine 109, 112, 113.

52 Creating barriers to employment is contrary to the CRPD, which specifically promotes equality in employment – art 5, CRPD [2006] A/Res/61/106. The Convention also promotes the right to dignity and integrity of the person (art 17, UNCRP and focuses on the inclusion of persons with disabilities (in education, political life, health and society) – see art 3, UNCRP. See also art 24, art 25 and art 29, UNCRP.

53 In certain jurisdictions (for example, in Ireland and the United Kingdom) access to insurance

including access to political life and active involvement in the community. Access to employment may also potentially affect an individual's social life and interaction with peers, which has a meaningful impact on inclusion and active participation in society.[54] If uncontrolled, this may ultimately lead to growing unemployment, poverty and other issues, resulting in a myriad of social and economic problems.

3.5. Accuracy and Predictive Value of Genetic Testing

On evaluating the implications of misusing genetic information, and the concept of genetic discrimination in the workplace, it is important to refer to the accuracy of genetic testing and the popular perception of such testing.[55] There is a common misperception that genetic tests can fully and accurately predict whether a person will develop a genetic condition. In this regard, it is relevant to point out that the majority of genetic tests still lack accuracy, and the probability that an individual will develop a particular condition is usually dependent upon the interaction of a complex range of elements, including environmental factors. Employers may misinterpret and misuse genetic test results to weed out those whom they perceive to be high risk and undesirable (based on a misunderstanding that having a genetic trait is the same as having the actual disease or condition).[56] In overestimating the predictive value and accuracy of genetic testing, genetic-based discrimination may take place because of employer ignorance in affording validity to genetic information that is not sufficiently precise for that purpose.[57] In most cases, genetic testing is not diagnostic, but predicts only risk or susceptibility. The information gleaned from genetic testing will not determine whether a person will actually develop a condition, but only that they have a higher than normal likelihood to do so than others.[58] In the employment context, it is simply 'bad science' for an employer to use the existence of a particular gene or genetic marker to make employment decisions, because those genes cannot predict how effectively an individual will succeed in the workplace.[59] However, in looking forward, considering the rate at which genetic science is advancing, it is anticipated that genetic tests will become more accurate, and scientists' understanding of disease will become more refined.

---

may also affect access to property ownership (for example, the necessity to have life insurance prior to obtaining a mortgage).

54 This may impact more heavily on the elderly, the disabled and other vulnerable (and perhaps already marginalised) groups in society.

55 Most genetic conditions are multifactorial, whereby manifestation of the condition is a result of a complex interaction between genes and environment (for example, heart disease). It is only in the case of monogenetic genetic conditions that the onset and severity of the condition can be more accurately predicted (for example, Huntington's disease).

56 E M Holmes, 'Solving the Insurance/ Genetic Fair/ Unfair Discrimination Dilemma in Light of the Human Genome Project' (1996–1997) (85) 3 Kentucky Law Journal 503, 529. See also D K Casey, 'What Can the New Gene Tests Tell Us?' (1997) 36 (3) Judges Journal of the American Bar Association 14.

57 Holmes, ibid 515.

58 C MacDonald and B Williams-Jones, 'Ethics and Genetics: Susceptibility Testing in the Workplace' (2002) 35 Journal of Business Ethics 235, 237. See also E Draper, 'The Screening of America: The Social and Legal Framework of Employers' Use of Genetic Information' (1999) 20 Berkeley Journal of Employment and Labor Law 286, 290–291.

59 P S Miller, 'Is there a pink slip in my genes? Genetic discrimination in the workplace' (1999–2000) 3(2) Journal of Health Care Law and Policy 225.

3.6. Striking a Balance

Employment-based genetic testing is a technology both 'full of promise and fraught with ethical peril.'[60] Although genetic technology may potentially improve the health and wellbeing of individuals, the use of genetic testing in employment can potentially exacerbate existing stigma and classification of individuals, and provokes concern regarding employee privacy, justice and protection of fundamental rights. In the employment context, discrimination on the basis of genetic information can be compared to discrimination on the basis of other immutable characteristics such as race and gender. Based on the same argument that it is unlawful to refuse to hire someone on the grounds of race or gender,[61] it should be unlawful to refuse to hire an individual on the basis of genetic information (without reference to an individual's current ability to do the job).[62] An otherwise qualified and experienced individual should not be restricted from obtaining or securing a job based upon having a genetic marker or a genetic predisposition for a disease, disorder or disability.

In addressing this area, it is important to consider the competing rights between employer and employee, and assess where the appropriate balance should be struck. An employer's 'right to know' (for example, potential use of genetic monitoring in hazardous workplaces, albeit under strict conditions) must be acknowledged, and necessary controls need to be placed on this right. In acknowledging an employee's rights, it is important to ensure protection against unfair discrimination in hiring, promotion and employee benefits, and to maintain employee privacy. In achieving this balance, it requires that the harms and benefits of genetic testing be considered (for the individual, the scientific community and society as a whole), together with the values placed on fundamental human rights, and society's interest in reaping the benefits of advancing genetic science. This balance may be reached by ensuring that the area is appropriately regulated, taking account of the fundamental rights of employees, and the limited right of employers to know.

4. The Regulation of Genetic Discrimination

In light of the potential for misuse of genetic information, it is necessary to address the issue of regulation as a tool to address genetic discrimination and achieve balance between the competing interests.[63] In Europe there is effectively a patchwork of

---

60 MacDonald and Williams-Jones, ibid 238.

61 Discrimination on the basis of gender and race is prohibited in Europe pursuant to Directive 2000/43/EC of 29 June 2000 implementing the principle of equal treatment between persons irrespective of racial or ethnic origin, and Directive 2000/78/EC establishing a general framework for equal treatment in employment and occupation, [2000] OJ L303/16.

62 (n 59) 264.

63 Such questions of regulation also provoke consideration of the concept of 'genetic exceptionalism' – whether genetic information is worthy of special protection. See generally T H Murray 'Genetic Exceptionalism and 'Future Diaries: Is Genetic Information Different from Other Medical Information?' in M A Rothstein (ed),*Genetic Secrets: Protecting Privacy and Confidentiality in the Genetic* (Yale University Press 1997). See also G J Annas, 'Genetic Privacy: There Ought to be a Law' (1999) 4 Texas Review of Law and Policy 9, 11. An alternative approach would be to consider legislation that regulates all health information, both genetic and non-genetic. For further discussion see M A Rothstein, 'Genetic Exceptionalism and Legislative Pragmatism' (2007) Journal of Law, Medicine and Ethics 59; C S Diver and

protections throughout the individual Member States.[64] At EU-level, the foundation for equality in the workplace is the Employment Equality Directive.[65] The question arises as to whether the Employment Equality Directive could potentially be applied to genetic discrimination regarding a potential future disability or a perceived disability. The Employment Equality Directive offers limited protection against genetic discrimination in the employment context, and it is unlikely that the scope of the legislation would stretch to cover this area.[66] This is particularly evident in light of the restrictive and conservative approach taken by the European Court of Justice in interpreting the disability ground under the Employment Equality Directive.[67] There is accordingly no concrete EU-level position addressing genetic discrimination. In consideration of the limited EU-level protections, it is therefore necessary to highlight the possibility of considering a new regulatory regime at EU-level, specifically targeting genetic discrimination.[68] On looking at the possibility of a new scheme of regulation, it is important to look at the impact of the CRPD, its conclusion by the EU and how this might contribute towards and facilitate EU-level regulation in this area. It is also relevant to highlight the EU Charter of Fundamental Rights, its elevated status pursuant to the Lisbon Treaty, and its potential to enhance EU-level regulation of genetic discrimination.

5. The UN Convention on the Rights of Persons with Disabilities: An Introduction

This section will explore the CRPD, its conclusion by the EU, and its potential impact on the area of genetic discrimination. In particular, this section will examine the content and intention of the relevant CRPD provisions, as well as the relevance of the paradigm shift towards the social model of disability. It is the first international human rights treaty of the twenty-first century and has been described as providing a 'moral compass for change.'[69] The adoption of the CRPD has been hailed as 'the

---

J M Cohen, 'Genophobia: What is Wrong with Genetic Discrimination?' (2000–2001) 149 University of Pennsylvania Law Review 1439.

64 S Soini, 'Genetic testing legislation in Western Europe – a fluctuating regulatory target' (2012) 3 Journal of Community Genetics 143; O Varga and S Soini, 'Definitions of Genetic Testing in European Legal Documents' (2012) 3 Journal of Community Genetics 125. Genetic information is regulated to varying degrees by the different Member States and two general approaches can be observed: prohibitive legislation (for example, the Medical Examinations Act 1997 in the Netherlands which seeks to regulate the use of medical examinations and to restrict the scope of health inquiries in the context of employment) and voluntary moratoria (for example, the voluntary agreement between the Association of British Insurers and the Department of Health in the United Kingdom upon not requiring collection or disclosure of genetic information up to a certain amount of insurance).

65 Directive 2000/78/EC of 27 November 2000 establishing a general framework for equal treatment in employment and occupation, [2000] OJ L 303/16.

66 A de Paor, 'US and EU Perspectives on Genetic Discrimination in Employment and Insurance: Striking a Balance in a Battlefield of Competing Rights' in L Waddington et al (eds) 4 *European Yearbook of Disability Law* (Intersentia 2013) 99, 116

67 ibid. C-15/05, *Chacon Navas v Eurest Colectividades* [2006] ECR 1-6467. The *Chacon Navas* case has been criticized and is regrettable particularly in light of the restrictive view taken on the definition of disability. The European Court of Justice took the old-fashioned medical model approach to disability.

68 See n 102 for details in relation to the legal basis for action at EU level.

69 G Quinn, 'The United Nations Convention on the Rights of Persons with Disabilities: Toward

dawn of a new era'[70] and it intends to provide for and facilitate the fundamental human rights and equal treatment of persons with disabilities. In addressing all facets of life, the CRPD 'melds civil and political rights with economic, social and cultural rights.'[71] The principles and rights provided for in the CRPD are not ground-breaking in themselves, but are novel in the application to the disability field,[72] and therefore the objective of the CRPD is to ensure that all existing human rights are equally applicable for persons with disabilities.[73]

From the perspective of disability law, genetic testing can predict a low or a high propensity to or probability of future disability. As noted above, genetic discrimination can therefore be described as discrimination on the basis of perceived disability, or on the basis of potential future disability.[74] Accordingly, if genetic information is too widely available, it exposes putative persons with disabilities to obvious, as well as subtle discrimination, therefore potentially violating the CRPD.

5.1. The CRPD and Genetic Discrimination

The CRPD is an innovative human rights treaty with the objective of facilitating human rights for all persons with disabilities. The CRPD's overall intention and objectives, as well as its substantive provisions can be interpreted as applying to the concept of genetic discrimination and to putative persons with disabilities. Accordingly, the CRPD can potentially be a useful tool in the regulation of genetic information and can potentially act as a trigger for EU-level regulation of the area.

As a State Party to an international human rights treaty, the EU has an obligation to respect, protect and fulfill rights. Article 1 of the CRPD confirms the social construction of disability whereby limitations arise from a person's interaction with environmental barriers, rather than as the consequence of an individual impairment.[75] Article 1, paragraph 2 of the CRPD states: 'Persons with disabilities include those who have long-term physical, mental, intellectual or sensory impairments which in interaction with various barriers may hinder their full and effective participation in society on an equal basis with others.'[76] It has been asserted that 'this is not necessarily a definition, but more accurately, a bare minimum, and therefore, any

---

a New International Politics of Disability' (2009–2010) 15(1) Texas Journal on Civil Liberties and Civil Rights 33.

70 General Secretary Kofi Annan, in a message delivered by Deputy Secretary-General at the Press Release, General Assembly, General Assembly adopts Groundbreaking Convention, Optional Protocol on Rights of Persons with Disabilities: Delegations, Civil Society Hail First Human Rights Treaty of the Twenty-First Century, U.N Doc. GA/ 10554 (13th December 2006) <www.un.org/News/Press/docs/2006/ga10554.doc.htm> last accessed 31 March 2016.

71 M A Stein and J Lord, 'Future Prospects for the United Nations Convention on the Rights of Persons with Disabilities', in O M Arnardóttir and G Quinn (eds), *United Nations Convention on the Rights of Persons with Disabilities*, 24.

72 Quinn (n 69) at 42,

73 Ambassador McKay, UN Enable, Statements made on the Adoption of the Convention on the Rights of Persons with Disabilities (2007) <www.un.org/esa/socdev/enable/convstatementgov.htm> last accessed 31 March 2016.

74 See generally, Miller (n 12) at 47. See also G Wolbring, 'A Disability Rights Approach to Genetic Discrimination', in J Sandor (ed), *Society and Genetic Information: Codes and Laws in the Genetic Era* (Central European University Press 2004) 161.

75 Stein and Lord (n 71) at 25.

76 CRPD art 1.

interpretation of the CRPD should include not only persons with disabilities, but also persons who have genetic differences, and those to whom disabilities are imputed.'[77]

The principles of equality and non-discrimination are key underlying concepts which pervade the Convention. The CRPD actually obliges the EU to uphold higher standards of non-discrimination regarding persons with disabilities. The content of the CRPD, as well as its objective, could potentially have a significant impact on the overall framework of human rights in the EU.[78] In line with the concept of the 'moral compass' for change, as explained by Quinn,[79] the values in this compass are contained in Article 3, which emphasises the fundamental importance and guiding force of these principles. In Article 3, the values or principles that animate the CRPD are dignity, individual autonomy, non-discrimination, full and active participation and inclusion, respect for difference, equality of opportunity, accessibility, equality between men and women, and respect for the evolving capacities of children with disabilities.[80] These principles are in accordance with the paradigm shift and the overall ethos of the CRPD. In applying the principles enshrined in Article 3 to the debate surrounding genetic discrimination, it can be further hypothesised that discrimination on the basis of genetic information can result in a violation of the above principles, resulting particularly in isolation from the community and from society, denial of equal opportunities and ultimately, denial of the fundamental rights of dignity and integrity.

Article 2 reinforces upon this theme to define discrimination on the basis of disability as:

> 'any distinction, exclusion or restriction on the basis of disability which has the purpose or effect of impairing or nullifying the recognition, enjoyment or exercise, on an equal basis with others, of all human rights and fundamental freedoms in the political, economic, social, cultural, civil or any other field. It includes all forms of discrimination, including denial of reasonable accommodation.'[81]

Disability-based discrimination as set out in the CRPD therefore 'includes all forms of discrimination; direct, indirect, structural, multiple or other, as well as discrimination by association and discrimination based on assumed or future disability.'[82] Consequently, discrimination on the basis of genetic features or genetic information could very well come within the ambit of this definition, and any potential EU legislation in the field of genetic discrimination could be regarded as implementation of the Convention. In addition, Article 5 provides specifically for the principles of equality and non-discrimination and requires, inter alia, the

---

77 D Ferri, 'Legislating at EU level: Challenges and Possibilities', at 'Genetic Discrimination – Transatlantic Perspectives on the Case for a European Level Legal Response' (19 November 2011, Galway, Ireland).

78 D Ferri, 'The Conclusion of the UN Convention on the Rights of Persons with Disabilities by EC/EU: Some Reflections from a 'Constitutional' Perspective' 4 Universita di Catania Online Working Paper 3/2010.

79 G Quinn (n 69).

80 CRPD art 3.

81 CRPD art 2 [2006] A/Res/61/106.

82 European Foundation Centre, Study on challenges and good practices in the implementation of the CRPD VC/ 2008/ 1214 Final Report, 54.

prohibition of discrimination on the basis of disability and the guarantee to persons with disabilities equal and effective legal protection against discrimination on all grounds.[83] Article 5, read in conjunction with the overall intention of the CRPD, could arguably be interpreted as applying to discrimination on the basis of genetic information.

In continuing the theme of non-discrimination, Article 27 specifically focuses on work and employment, recognising the right of persons with disabilities to work on an equal basis with others, and prohibiting discrimination on the basis of disability.[84] Article 27 (a) 'prohibits discrimination on the basis of disability with regard to all matters concerning all forms of employment, including conditions of recruitment, hiring and employment, continuance of employment, career advancement…' An expansive interpretation of Article 27 would encompass genetic discrimination in employment, and would prohibit discrimination on the grounds of genetic features during all the stages of employment listed in Article 27 (a), including during the recruitment stage and throughout employment, for example in relation to promotional opportunities.

In conjunction with the overall objectives and rationale of the CRPD, particularly the principles of equality and non-discrimination[85] which permeate the CRPD, Article 27 could therefore be interpreted to cover discrimination in employment on the basis of genetic differences. Such an interpretation is also in line with underlying principles of inclusion and active participation in society, for which the CRPD provides. By creating barriers to employment, by misusing genetic information, this may result in the unjustified exclusion of certain vulnerable individuals, with undesirable social consequences. Unfettered access to fruitful employment is essential for an individual's participation in and contribution to the community. Such access to employment is also necessary in ensuring an individual's rights to dignity and integrity, which the CRPD also promotes. It has been observed that the scope and coverage of the Convention is unprecedented.[86] An expansive interpretation of Article 27 to include discrimination on the basis of genetic features would therefore seem appropriate, justified and in line with the overall objectives of the CRPD.[87]

Article 22 in relation to respect for privacy also merits discussion in the debate

---

83 CRPD art 27

84 art 5.

85 For example, art 5.

86 A Kanter, 'The Promise and Challenge of the United Nations Convention on the Rights of Persons with Disabilities' (2006–2007) 34 Syracuse Journal of International Law and Commerce 287, 289.

87 In delving deeper into the intention and scope of art 27, it is interesting to look at art 27(1)(a) and (b) which provides that, inter alia, that States Parties shall provide for 'safe and healthy conditions.' This may potentially be interpreted in favour of employer use of genetic information as a means of ensuring a safe and healthy working environment, in detecting potential occupational disease/disability. This could also be in line with an employer's obligations under EU health and safety legislation, as well as general common law principles that dictate the duty to provide a safe place of work. Employers have obligations under European health and safety law: Directive 89/391/EEC on Safety and Health at Work (there are also certain common law duties to provide a safe place of work, see *Wilson and Clyde Coal Co Ltd v English* [1937] 3 All ER 628, establishing the modern day duty of care owed to the employee, including, inter alia, the duty to provide a safe place of work).

surrounding protection of genetic information.[88] Genetic information reveals a myriad of particularly sensitive and unique details about an individual and that individual's family, relating to health status and future health risks, including potential future disabilities. Access to and disclosure of such information to third parties without consent interferes with the privacy of an individual and that individual's family.[89]

It is therefore clear that the overall rationale and tenor of the CRPD, as well as the objectives of the substantive provisions are applicable to the issue of genetic discrimination and the need to ensure the protection of genetic information. It is also submitted that the emphasis on the social model of disability, as advocated by the CRPD is particularly relevant and applicable to the debate on genetic discrimination.

5.2 Genetic Discrimination and the Social Model of Disability

One of the most revolutionary and welcomed aspects of the CRPD is the paradigm shift away from the medical model of disability towards the social model of disability. The social model, as accepted and promoted by the CRPD, views persons with disabilities as rights holders and valued members of our societies who are often more disabled by the physical and attitudinal barriers societies erect to exclude and stigmatise them. The medical model of disability proposes that individuals with disabilities are defined by their disability and by the perception that they are ill and require a cure. Attitudinal barriers often exacerbate the ethos of the medical model of disability.[90] In reaffirming the CRPD's emphasis on the social model of disability, Ferri notes that the Preamble states that 'disability is an evolving concept and that disability results from the interaction between persons with impairments and attitudinal and environmental barriers that hinder their full and effective participation in society on an equal basis with others.'[91]

In the context of genetic discrimination, employers may take the view that an individual with a genetic predisposition to a certain condition has a disability, and may therefore be perceived by the employer as unable to do a particular job. Indeed it has been observed that attitudes, rather than resource constraints, often create

---

88 CRPD art 22.

89 Another article of the CRPD that is relevant in this debate is art 25 on health. Article 25 provides that persons with disabilities are entitled to the highest standard of health without discrimination on the basis of disability. It is observed that the fear of genetic discrimination (and breach of privacy) by employers, insurance companies or other interested third parties may result in some individuals being reluctant to engage in genetic testing that may benefit their health, and therefore may act as a barrier to access to health care and advances in genetic technology. In order to eliminate this fear, and instill confidence in individuals, appropriate protections are necessary, allowing access to health care and medical advances for all persons.

90 M Priestley, 'Constructions and Creations: Idealism, Materialism and Disability Theory' (1998) 13 Disability and Society 75; M Oliver, *Understanding Disability: From Theory to Practice* (Macmillan Press Ltd 1996); V Finkelstein, '"We" are not disabled, "you" are,' in S Gregory and G Hartley (eds), *Constructing Deafness* (Continuum 1990); C Barnes, 'The Social Model of Disability: A Sociological Phenomenon Ignored by Sociologists?' in T Shakespeare (ed) *Disability Reader: Social Science Perspectives* (Continuum 1998).

91 D Ferri, 'The Conclusion of the UN Convention on the Rights of Persons with Disabilities by the EC/EU' in G Quinn and L Waddington (eds), 2 *European Yearbook of Disability Law* (Intersentia 2010) 52.

the strongest barriers to employment.[92] Not only is this negative attitude towards genetic conditions and positive genetic test results reflective of the medical model, but it is also in disregard of an individual's current ability to do a job, resulting in discrimination and violation of the principles and values espoused in the CRPD, as explained above. In line with the paradigm shift to acceptance of the social model, and, in particular, the rejection of attitudinal barriers to disability, it is submitted that a forward-thinking and creative approach be taken to the issue of genetic discrimination. This submission is also in accordance with the overall rationale and underlying theme of the CRPD, as well as the emphasis on equality and non-discrimination.

5.3 The Conclusion of the CRPD by the EU: The Implications

The European Union concluded the UN Convention on the Rights of Persons with Disabilities in December 2010, and it came into force on 22 January 2011.[93] This historic action signifies the first time that the European Union has concluded an international human rights treaty.[94] It is significant development and a positive step forward in the protection of human rights by the EU. It has been observed therefore that the 'CRPD will take on a completely new legal status with EC law, and will have to be respected in its totality, and not as a mere add on to be referred to in passing in Community instruments.'[95] However, although this welcomed development is a positive promotion of human rights and recognition of disability rights, it provokes challenging questions regarding the obligations and responsibilities of the EU and its Member States.[96] In particular, questions arise as regards the particular obligations of the EU and the legislative competence of the EU. In the context of regulating genetic discrimination, it is interesting to examine the EU's potential obligations and responsibilities.

5.4 EU Obligations Under the CRPD

The CRPD is an example of a 'mixed agreement', referring to the concept that part of an international agreement comes under the scope of the powers and responsibilities of the EU, and part of an agreement comes under the ambit of the powers and responsibilities of the Member States. Addressing discrimination on the grounds of disability is an area of shared competence between the EU and the Member States.[97] It has been asserted that it is unlikely that there is a legal obligation

---

92 Statement by L Arbour, UN High Commissioner for Human Rights, General Assembly Ad Hoc Committee, Seventh Session (27 January 2006).

93 Council Decision of 26 November 2009 concerning the conclusion, by the European Community of the CRPD (2010/48/EC), [2010] OJ L.

94 The EU's competence to negotiate and sign the CRPD derived from art 19 (art 13), addressing (disability) discrimination, and art 95, addressing the internal market.

95 L Waddington, 'A New Era in Human Rights Protection in the European Community: The Implications the United Nations Convention on the Rights of Persons with Disabilities for the European Community' 4 Maastricht Faculty of Law Working Paper (2007). See also G de Burca, 'The EU in the negotiation of the UN Disability Convention' (2010) 35 European Law Review 2; Fordham Law Legal Studies Research Paper No. 1525611. < http://ssrn.com/abstract=1525611 > last accessed 31 March 2016.

96 L Waddington, 'The European Union and the United Nations Convention on the Rights of Persons with Disabilities: A Story of Exclusive and Shared Competences' (2011) 18 Maastricht Journal 4.

97 D Ferri (n 77). See also Case C-239/03 *Etang de Berre* at (25): 'In accordance with case-law,

on the EU under the CRPD to take proactive steps (for example, adopting a new directive addressing discrimination on the ground of disability). It follows that any EU action that is taken needs to comply with the CRPD, but there does not seem to be any legal obligation under international law to take action in the fields of shared competence. Waddington however, expresses the view that 'it can nevertheless be desirable for the EU to act in such areas of shared competence.'[98]

Therefore, as regards discharging its obligations under the CRPD, the EU could take a minimal type of approach, by ensuring that the EU does not breach the provisions of the CRPD when acting in areas of shared competence.[99] Alternatively, and perhaps preferably, the EU could take a wider approach,[100] particularly considering that this is the first instance of the EU concluding an international human rights treaty. Pursuant to the CRPD, the EU is under an obligation not only to respect human rights but also to protect them.[101] This submission is also in line with the overall tenor of the CRPD and has regard to the fundamental principles of equality, dignity, integrity and inclusion, which animate the CRPD. In the context of genetic discrimination, EU legislative action in this area could be viewed as interpretation of the CRPD, in line with the EU's obligations. Before looking at the EU's obligations in this area, it is necessary to highlight the value of the EU Charter of Fundamental Rights in this context.

6. EU Charter of Fundamental Rights

An interesting addition to this debate is the EU Charter of Fundamental Rights,[102] which is an important factor in further ascertaining the legal framework applicable to genetic discrimination in Europe, and in generally setting a high standard as regards fundamental human rights. Pursuant to Article 21.1, genetic discrimination has been singled out as a priority area of reform. Article 21.1 specifically prohibits discrimination on the grounds of genetic features.[103] The Lisbon Treaty changed the status of the EU Charter of Fundamental Rights. Pursuant to Article 6(1) Treaty on

mixed agreements concluded by the Community, its Member States and non-member countries have the same status in the Community legal order as purely Community agreements in so far as the provisions fall within the scope of Community competence.'

98 L Waddington, ibid 448.

99 ibid.

100 One of the arguments in favour of EU action in areas of shared competence is to prevent diverging national CRPD implementation approaches in the field of non-discrimination. Individual national implementation measures are likely to create diverse standards and differing levels of protection in the EU, which may negatively impact on the internal market. In addition, concerted action by the EU is arguably the most efficient method of implementing the CRPD effectively. A uniform response by the EU will negate the need for individual action from each Member State. See L Waddington, ibid 448.

101 Some commentators advocate in favour of an expansive approach by the EU. The dynamic of the Convention, the requirement to set up structures to promote, protect and monitor the implementation of the Convention, and the desirability, from the point of view of EU law and EU cohesion, to find coordinated responses to the obligations imposed by the Convention on the EU and Member States in combination, all argue in favour of a far more active approach to implementation of the Convention by the EU.

102 Charter of Fundamental Rights of the European Union, proclaimed by the Commission, 7 December 2000. O.J (C 364) 1.

103 art 21.1 European Union Charter of Fundamental Rights states: 'Any discrimination based on any ground such as sex, race, colour, ethnic or social origin, genetic features, language,

European Union (TEU),[104] the Charter now has the same legal value as the Treaties, and the EU is now obliged to comply with the Charter in all its activities, as are the Member States when they are implementing EU law.[105] Although in-depth discussion of the impact of the EU Charter of Fundamental Rights is outside the scope of this chapter, it can be hypothesised that, on initial consideration, the added strength of the EU Charter of Fundamental Rights may increase the obligations on the EU to ensure the protection of genetic features. It is also relevant to acknowledge the value of the EU Charter of Fundamental Rights, and how the specific provisions of the Charter (prohibiting genetic discrimination on the basis of genetic features[106]) might enhance the interpretation of the CRPD and the interpretation of the EU Treaty. The Charter may therefore operate to trigger potential EU regulation of this area.

7. What Next: An EU Level Response?

In light of the reality of potential widespread abuse of genetic information, and having considered the impact and potential of the CRPD, together with the added value of the EU Charter of Fundamental Rights, it is necessary to highlight the merits of a new genetic information non-discrimination directive.[107] This may be a unique opportunity to take a proactive and forward-thinking approach towards

---

religion or belief, political or any other *opinion,* membership of a national minority, property, birth, disability, age or sexual orientation shall be prohibited.'

104 art 6(1) TEU states: 'The Union recognises the rights, freedoms and principles set out in the Charter of Fundamental Rights of the European Union of 7 December 2000, as adapted at Strasbourg, on 12 December 2007, which shall have the same legal value as the Treaties. The provisions of the Charter shall not extend in any way the competences of the Union as defined in the Treaties.' It must be pointed out that although the Charter has been given additional status, it does not afford an independent basis for legislative action.

105 L Waddington at 433. In addition, in 2010 the Commission published a communication stating that the EU Charter of Fundamental Rights must be taken into account when the EU is legislating (Communication from the Commission: Strategy for the effective implementation of the Charter of Fundamental Rights by the European Union COM (2010) 573 final). The Charter is a point of reference for new legislation (an assessment of compatibility of legislation with the Charter must be carried out before passing legislation at EU level).

106 art 21.1 EU Charter of Fundamental Rights. Charter of Fundamental Rights of the European Union, 7 December 2000, Official Journal of the European Communities, 18 December 2000 [2000]C 364/01.

107 In the context of regulating genetic information at European Union level, it is necessary to refer to the legal basis for action. It is submitted that the most viable legal basis for the introduction of non-discrimination legislation in the area of genetic information can be found in art 19, Treaty on the Functioning of the European Union (TFEU) (formerly art 13, TFEU). [2008] C/115/47. On the basis of this article, the Council of Ministers of the EU may take action against discrimination on any of the grounds mentioned in art 19 by means of directives. Although art 19 TFEU itself does not mention 'genetic information' or 'health' as a prohibited ground, it could be a suitable legal base for a piece of legislation on genetic discrimination, through an extensive interpretation of the ground of disability (future disability and imputed disability), and in accordance with art 21 of the EU Charter of Fundamental Rights. In addition, art 16 TFEU establishes a clear basis for the Council and the Parliament to regulate the processing of personal data in the EU. It is therefore submitted that a dual approach to this issue be considered: a non-discrimination approach and a privacy approach. Another approach is to consider the possibility of amending existing directives; however, although politically and legally this would be an easier option, a new directive specifically targeting genetic information would arguably be preferable, considering the sensitive nature of the subject matter and the unique concerns to which it gives rise.

regulating human rights for EU citizens in the twenty-first century.[108] A concerted, uniform approach by the EU would contribute towards guaranteeing fundamental rights and principles, ensuring the effective operation of the internal market and ensuring against any potential obstacles to the realisation of these rights. Such an approach is welcomed, not only from a legal perspective, but also from a political and social perspective; it may succeed in facilitating the further advancement of genetic science and eliminate any fears of genetic discrimination that may prevent individuals from undergoing genetic testing for the benefit of their health. Any EU legislation in the field of genetic discrimination could be regarded as proactive implementation of the Convention and adherence to the principles set out in the EU Charter of Fundamental Rights. In this context, the EU could look to the US as a model framework on taking a progressive approach at federal level, and acting in anticipation of advancing technology and the protection of human rights.[109]

8. Conclusion

Addressing the issue of genetic discrimination in employment provokes a societal conflict between the rights of individuals and the rights of employers and other institutions, as well as scientific interests, leading to an inevitable conflict of rights. As employers become more aware of the potential and the benefits of genetic information (as a useful tool to select and maintain whom they perceive to be the most genetically desirable and productive employees), and if the area is left insufficiently regulated, there is a real possibility that discrimination and breach of privacy will become more widespread, and that employers will take advantage by abusing sensitive genetic information. Further, as genetic information proliferates, and as more and more people may be considered genetically flawed, this may potentially signal the creation of a genetic underclass, and the relegation of what are perceived to be 'genetically undesirable' individuals. This may lead to the practice of genetic cleansing, not just in employment but also in other facets of life, such as education, political life and society in general. Such a regulatory vacuum may accelerate this genetic underclass, and could operate to inhibit the inclusion of persons with disabilities (and older persons) into employment and into society, with potentially disastrous social and economic consequences. Indeed, it has been observed that 'genetic discrimination foreseeably will be the civil-rights issue of the twenty-first century.'[110]

The introduction of the CRPD, and in particular the conclusion of the CRPD by the EU, represents a landmark in human rights law and in facilitating the rights for persons with disabilities. A holistic interpretation of the CRPD would encompass the protection of discrimination on the basis of genetic characteristics, and on the basis

108 This forward-thinking approach was taken in the US with the introduction of GINA and adoption of a pre-emptive legislative model.

109 The US is a pioneer in this field: The Genetic Information Nondiscrimination Act (GINA) was introduced in 2008: Genetic Information Nondiscrimination Act of 2008, Pub. L No. 110–233, 122 Stat. 881 (2008). GINA targets genetic discrimination by employers and health insurers. The legislation is novel, as it is the first pre-emptive anti-discrimination statute in American history, meaning that it attempts to eliminate a new brand of discrimination before it becomes widespread. This is different than predecessor civil rights statutes, which typically look for a documented history of discrimination as the basis to prohibit similar conduct in the future.

110 Holmes (n 56) 507.

of putative disabilities. Such an interpretation is also in accordance with the overall objectives and intention of the CRPD. The CRPD therefore has the potential to guide and trigger the regulation of genetic discrimination in the field of employment and other areas. In addition, the strengthened value of the EU Charter of Fundamental Rights further verifies the need to seriously consider EU-level regulation to address the issue of discrimination on the basis of 'genetic features.' Indeed, there is now arguably a responsibility on the European Institutions to seriously reflect on the case for some form of legislative or other response to the issue of genetic discrimination. Although we are stepping into uncharted territory, such a combined interpretation of the CRPD, the EU Charter of Fundamental Rights and the overall constitutional framework of the EU is to be welcomed in adopting a proactive and forward-thinking approach to this issue. As we witness the dawn of this new genetic age, such rapidly advancing genetic technology offers enormous potential benefits for humankind. However, as interest in genetic science escalates, so too does the potential for abuse and violation of fundamental human rights, thereby signalling the importance of appropriate regulation and consideration of the balance of rights.

Chapter 32

DISABILITY, EU LAW AND THE CRPD: A NEW DAWN?

Claire Bruton and Shivaun Quinlivan

1. Introduction

This chapter will examine the definition of disability in anti-discrimination employment law in Europe. It reviews some of the approaches to defining disability both within the European Union and by the European Union. The underlying theme of this chapter is to assess what, if any, impact the European Union's ratification of the United Nations Convention on the Rights of Persons with Disabilities (CRPD) will have on those definitions.

The CRPD is a significant development for persons with disabilities, described by some commentators as 'ground[-] breaking.'[1] It is ground-breaking for a number of reasons, but most significantly for ensuring that it embodies the social model of disability.[2] The main focus of this chapter is to assess whether the various definitions of disability perpetuate the medical/individual model of disability or support the social model of disability, and to determine the most appropriate approach to the definition within the EU.

2. Medial Model v Social Model

In order to place the concept of 'disability' within context, it is important to examine the two primary models of disability. According to the medical/individual model of disability the problems disabled persons face in their daily life are mainly caused by their impairment, either physical or mental, and these impairments inhibit the ability of such individuals to participate in the workforce. The response has been to focus on the 'problem' caused by the particular impairment or condition. Additionally the medical model approach is based on the belief that any reduction in the individual's quality of life is a result of the condition intrinsic to the individual. The entire focus

---

1 L Waddington, 'A New Era in Human Rights Protection in the European Community: The Implications of the United Nation's Convention on the Rights of Persons with Disabilities for the European Community,' Maastricht Faculty of Law, Working Paper No. 2007 4, 1–22.

2 See generally, C Barnes, 'Theories of Disability and the Origins of the Oppression of Disabled People in Western Society' in L Barton (ed), *Disability and Society: Emerging Issues and Insights* (Longman, 1996); M Oliver, 'A Sociology of Disability or a Disablist Sociology?' in L Barton (ed), *Disability and Society: Emerging Issues and Insights* (Longman, 1996); T Shakespeare and J Watson, 'The social model of disability: An outdated ideology?' (2001) 2 Research in Social Science and Disability 9–28.

is on addressing the functionality of the individual to allow them to live a more 'normal' life; in other words all the failings are with the individual.[3]

By contrast, the second model of disability – the social model – focuses on how society and societal constraints and barriers seek to limit or inhibit full participation by, and inclusion of, persons with disabilities in society.[4] Consequently it is society that disables people through designing everything to meet the needs of a perceived norm, ie those without disabilities. The social model recognizes that there is a significant amount that society can do to reduce and remove disabling barriers. This is the responsibility of society and not the individual. The purpose of anti-discrimination legislation invoking this model is to govern societal actions and prohibit objectionable behaviours. Anti-discrimination legislation ascribes equality rights to people with disabilities, thus endorsing the social model of disability as it sites the problem of disability outside the individual.

The social model of disability underpins the entire CRPD.[5] In adopting this approach, the legal landscape has changed within the EU, the social model adopts a rights-based approach to inclusion. This is what many have described as the 'paradigm shift.' We have moved from the charity-based to the rights-based approach to disability policy. The theoretical battle has been won the social model has triumphed. But, as Degener highlighted, the social model does not 'give any guidance as to how to legally define disability alternatively.'[6] However, it can be said that in adopting the social model of disability, a solid base is provided from which an expansive definition of disability can be built.

3. Legal Definitions of Disability: Some Problems

What is apparent is that the attempts to provide a legal definition of disability have been the subject of much debate. This debate has failed to culminate with an internationally accepted definition of disability, a failing not remedied by the CRPD.[7] In fact there are often several different definitions of disability within any particular jurisdiction dependant on the purpose of the legislation.[8] Legislation whose purpose is to distribute a social benefit may adopt a narrow definition of disability, or may

---

3 S Quinlivan, 'The United Nations Convention on the Rights of Persons with Disabilities: An Introduction' (2012) 13 (1) S. ERA Forum 71 http://www.springerlink.com/content/74541066131743p/

4 C Barnes, 'A Working Social Model? Disability Work and Disability Politics in the 21st Century' (2000) 20 Critical Social Policy 441. See also Waddington, 'Case note Chacón Navas' (2007) 44 CMLR 487 at 491.

5 See Ambassador MacKay's comments, http://www.un.org/disabilities/default.asp?id=160

6 T Degener, 'Definition of Disability' *EU Network of Experts on Disability Discrimination,* August 2004, 5–6.

7 See for example: B M Altman, 'Disability Definitions, Models, Classification Schemes and Applications' in G L Albrecht, K D Seelman and M Burg, *Handbook of Disability Studies* (Thousand Oaks: Sage Publications 2001), 97–122; T Degener, 'Definition of Disability' *EU Network of Experts on Disability Discrimination,* August 2004; L Waddington and A M Lawson, 'Disability and Non-Discrimination Law in the EU: An Analysis of Disability Law in employment and beyond' (Luxembourg, EU Commission, 2009).

8 In Ireland for example there are a multitude of definitions; see, for example: Disability Act 2005, Education for Persons with Special Educational Needs Act 2004, Employment Equality Acts 1998–2011 all of which adopt different definitions/approaches to disability.

adopt a needs-based approach. For the purposes of this chapter it is contended that no such limiting factors are necessary in the context of anti-discrimination legislation, the purpose of which is to prohibit objectionable behaviour: discrimination.

It is undoubtedly the case that disability is hard to define as it encompasses a variety of conditions: physical, mental and sensory. Further disabilities span a range, including mild, moderate, severe and profound. Moreover, disabilities may be temporary in nature or may be controlled by medication. This leads to demarcation disputes (eg 'when does a visual limitation constitute an impairment?')[9] and questions as to the appropriate filter for disabilities. In addition, definitions of disability change according to developments in medical science. New disabilities emerge with new medical developments and discoveries. Genetic dispositions to certain diseases are recent examples.[10]

There is a further issue to consider. The CRPD adopts the social model of disability; therefore, there is no place for the medical model or individual model of disability. However, anti-discrimination law by its nature is individualistic; it provides in the main individual remedies or solutions to specific events or situations. The protection is not a group protection, but an individual protection for members of a group, ie a woman may claim gender discrimination but this does not necessarily translate into a right for all women. One potential solution suggested by a number of commentators is that we do not need to define disability – rather we need to prohibit disability-based discrimination, thus ensuring that the focus is on non-discrimination and not on the individual. To a large extent this is the approach adopted by the Framework Employment Directive[11] (FED), and it is contended that the resulting case law is in the main disappointing.

It may be a gross generalisation but there appear to be three distinct approaches to defining disability: the non-definitional approach, such as that adopted by the FED; the restrictive approach, which attempts to restrict the application of discrimination laws to the 'deserving' disabled by including limiting factors such as the necessity for the disability to be substantial, long-term and to severely impact on the individual (this is the approach adopted by the American's with Disabilities Act[12] and the United Kingdom's Equality Act 2010);[13]; finally there is the purposive approach,

---

9 T Degener, 'Definition of Disability' *EU Network of Experts on Disability Discrimination,* August 2004, 4.

10 In Australia the definition of disability has recently been expanded to expressly include a genetic predisposition to a particular disability; see the Disability Discrimination Act 1992, as amended by the Disability Discrimination and Other Human Rights Legislation Amendment Act 2009.

11 Council Directive 2000/78/EC.

12 s 4 of the Americans with Disabilities (Amendment Act) 2008 defines disability, inter alia, as 'long term physical, mental, intellectual or sensory' impairments.

13 s 5(1) of the Equality Act 2010 provides that a person has a disability if they have 'a physical or mental impairment and the impairment has a substantial and long-term adverse effect on the person's ability to carry out normal day-to-day activities.' For a discussion on the difficulties with the definition of disability in the ADA and the DDA see, generally, R Burgdorf, 'Substantially Limited Protection from Disability Discrimination: The Special Treatment Model and Misconstructions of the Definition of Disability' (1997) Villanova Law Review 409; C Anderson, '"Deserving Disabilities": Why the Definition of Disability Under the Americans with Disabilities Act Should Be Revised to Eliminate the Substantial Limitation Requirement' 65 Missouri Law Review (2000) 83; T Degener, 'Definition of Disability' *EU Network of*

which may be based on impairment but contains no threshold of severity, or time limitations on the applicant. This approach will be discussed below.[14]

4. Non-Definitional Approach

The FED prohibits discrimination on 'grounds of disability'[15] but does not provide any definition of disability or provide any guidance on who is protected from such discrimination. This absence of a definition of the protected ground is common in EC anti-discrimination legislation: for example the Equal Treatment Directive[16] (now subsumed into the Recast Gender Directive)[17] prohibits discrimination on grounds of sex but no further detail is provided. Many Member States do not provide any legislative definition of disability[18] and therefore guidance will have to be sought from the relevant courts or tribunal as to the elucidation of the precise parameters of the definition.

In *Chácon Navas v Eurest Colectividades SA*[19] the CJEU was asked to consider the parameters of the definition of disability for the purposes of the FED given that there was no express definition contained in the Directive.[20] The applicant in this case challenged her dismissal as discriminatory as she had been on leave of absence and temporarily unfit for work for eight months. The Spanish Court asked the CJEU for its view on the relationship between sickness and disability and whether sickness was subsumed into disability for the purposes of the FED.

The Advocate General argued for a restrained interpretation of 'disability' due to the economic consequences that might flow from claims by disabled persons.[21] He saw it as desirable that a uniform interpretation of the concept of disability be developed in the European Community.[22] Interestingly, he expressly acknowledged the existence of the social model of disability, whereby account is taken of social perception of a disability, together with changes in the biomedical understanding of disability, and that it 'cannot be excluded in this context that certain physical or mental shortcomings are in the nature of "disability" in one social context, but not in another.'[23] However, he adopted a medical definition of disability and stated that

---

Experts on Disability Discrimination, August 2004; A Hendriks, 'Different Definition – Same Problems – One Way Out?' DREDF – From Principles to Practice – http://www.dredf.org/international/Hendricks.html; C Woodhams, 'Defining Disability in Theory and Practice: A Critique of the British Disability Discrimination Act 1995,' (2003) 32 (2) Journal of Social Policy.

14 Such as the approach in the Irish Employment Equality Acts 1998–2011.

15 art 1 of the Framework Employment Directive.

16 Council Directive 76/207/EEC.

17 Recast Directive 2006/54/EC.

18 J Gerards 'Discrimination Grounds' in D Schiek, L Waddington and M Bell, *Cases, Materials and Texts on National, Supranational and International Non-Discrimination Law* (Oxford, Hart Publishing 2007) 128.

19 (C-13/05), [2006] E.C.R I-06467, [2006] IRLR 706.

20 See also D L Hoskins, 'A High Bar for EU Disability Rights' [2007] 36(2) ILJ 228 and L Waddington, 'Case note Chacón Navas' (2007) 44 CMLR 487.

21 (C-13/05) [2006] E.C.R I-06467, [2006] IRLR 706 at 711 (paras 47–51).

22 ibid para 64.

23 ibid para 58.

it would apply to persons 'with serious functional limitations (disabilities) due to physical, psychological or mental afflictions.'[24]

The Grand Chamber of the CJEU in its judgment followed the decision of the Advocate General in July 2006.[25] The Court took the view that the concept of disability must be understood to refer to a limitation which results in particular from physical, mental or psychological impairments, and which hinders the participation of the person concerned in professional life,[26] and that by using the concept of disability in Article 1 of the Directive – which provides the aim of the Directive is to combat certain types of discrimination (including disability) as regards employment and occupation – the legislature deliberately chose a term which differs from sickness. Therefore the court stated that the two concepts could not be treated the same.[27] While in certain cases the two may overlap, not every sickness may qualify as a disability in the meaning of the FED. The CJEU examined the provisions of the FED concerning the obligation to provide reasonable accommodation, and stated:

> The importance which the Community legislature attaches to measures for adapting the workplace to the disability demonstrates that it envisaged situations in which participation in professional life is hindered over a long period of time. In order for the limitation to fall within the concept of 'disability', it must therefore be probable that it will last for a long time.[28]

The definition of disability propounded by the CJEU is certainly in line with definitions in other jurisdictions,[29] instruments[30] and that developed by the CJEU[31] which require the disability to be long-term in nature in order to be worthy of inclusion in a protected characteristic.

Finally, the CJEU held that the Directive could not be extended to cover 'sickness' as an additional ground of discrimination as the grounds listed in the Directive were exhaustive.[32] In fact earlier in its judgment, the CJEU stated that it could see nothing in the FED allowing for workers to be come within its ambit of protection 'as soon as they develop any type of sickness,' and therefore distinguished itself from the finding of the Advocate General that persons with sicknesses of the nature of a long-term limitation should be regarded as disabled.[33]

The judgment of the CJEU and opinion of the Advocate General are open to criticism on a number of grounds. The primary difficulty with the reasoning adopted by the CJEU is the ramifications of the decision to determine that disability for the purposes

---

24 ibid para 76.
25 (C-13/05), [2006] E.C.R I-06467, [2006] IRLR 706.
26 ibid, 715, para 43.
27 ibid, para 44.
28 ibid, para 45.
29 s 5(1) of the Equality Act 2010 provides that a person has a disability if they have 'a physical or mental impairment and the impairment has a substantial and long-term adverse effect on the person's ability to carry out normal day-to-day activities.'
30 art 1 of the United Nations Convention on the Rights of Individuals with Disabilities defines disability as 'long term physical, mental, intellectual or sensory' impairments.
31 *Chácon Navas v Eurest Colectividades SA* C-13/05 [2006] IRLR 706.
32 ibid 716, para 56.
33 ibid 75, para 47.

of the FED encompasses only narrow medically based disability of a long-term nature.[34] While it was acknowledged by the CJEU that the applicant's sickness was one which resulted in her being unfit for work for eight months and required an operation, neither the CJEU or the Advocate General gave any consideration as to whether this relatively serious (though unspecified) condition was sufficient to amount to a disability. It has been argued that by labelling the applicant as sick, this excluded her from also being labelled as disabled.[35] It is also apparent from the decision of the CJEU that it felt it necessary to devise a definition of disability that would only include those deserving of being cloaked with the protection of the Directive in that they have a disability that will last for a lengthy period of time. Further the CJEU provided no consideration of the now recognised social model of disability and instead apparently unthinkingly adopted the classic medical model of disability. By adopting a purely medical model of disability without any reference to the social constructs of the reality of disability, it is arguable that the definition of disability developed by the CJEU is not capable of extending to discrimination on the basis of a past disability or imputed disability.[36]

The failure to define disability within the FED ensured that the ultimate arbiter as to what could amount to a disability would be the CJEU. As is evident from the decision in *Chácon Navas v Eurest Colectividades SA*[37] the courts cannot always be relied on to provide a positive and expansive definition of disability. That said, the second decision of the CJEU pertaining to disability – *Coleman* – took an admirably progressive and expansive approach to the protection.[38]

5. Purposive Approach

The approach adopted by Irish legislators has been defined as the purposive approach for this chapter. The rationale for this term is that the definition of disability employed by the Employment Equality Acts 1998–2011 does not act as a gatekeeper to the protections contained within the legislation. The purpose of these Acts is to prohibit discrimination, thus the focus of the Acts is primarily on whether or not discrimination has occurred, not whether or not a person comes within the terms of a particular definition. There is the necessity to come within the definition of disability but in the main this is not a difficult threshold to meet.

The definition within the Employment Equality Acts 1998–2011 has been criticised as being an example of the medical model or individual model of disability. The authors disagree with that analysis. The World Health Organisation defines disability thus:

---

[34] Waddington and Lawson argue that the adopting of an exclusive medical model of disability is questionable in light of the recognition by the EU Parliament and the EU Commission in a number of documents and communications of the social model of disability. See L Waddington and A M Lawson, 'Disability and Non-Discrimination Law in the EU: An Analysis of Disability Law in employment and beyond' (Luxembourg, EU Commission, 2009) 16.

[35] D L Hoskins, 'A High Bar for EU Disability Rights' (2007) 36(2) ILJ 228, 232–233.

[36] See also D L Hoskins, 'A High Bar for EU Disability Rights' (2007) 36(2) ILJ 228, 233.

[37] (C-13/05) [2006] E.C.R I-06467, [2006] IRLR 706.

[38] (C-203/06) [2008] ECR I-05603, [2008] IRLR 722.

> Disabilities is an umbrella term, covering impairments, activity limitations and participations restrictions. An impairment is a problem in the body function or structure; an activity limitation is a difficulty encountered by an individual in executing a task or action; while a participation restrictions is a problem experienced by an individual in involvement in life situations. Thus disability is a complex phenomenon, reflecting an interaction between features of a person's body and features of the society in which he or she lives.[39]

Consequently, the WHO, which provides the closest thing we have to an international definition of disability, defines disability as the interaction between an impairment and society, which give rise to a disability. Thus it is: Impairment + Discrimination = Disability. Degener therefore contends:

> 'A discrimination law has to separate these two things by saying which treatment is regarded prohibited discrimination against whom. Disability discrimination laws thus need to define discrimination as well as disability and it makes no sense to define disability as the outcome of discrimination.'[40]

Accordingly, disability discrimination is almost always a negative or prejudicial act based on an actual or presumed impairment. An example is a factory manager firing a person with epilepsy on the false assumption that his or her impairment means he or she cannot perform the functions of the job.[41] Impairments may be visible or invisible, real or imputed, but the common denominator is the response to such impairment . Consequently, it seems logical that any definition of disability in discrimination laws should refer to impairment and that reference does not in itself perpetuate the individual or medical model of disability.[42]

Assuming that a reference to impairment does not in itself offend the social model of disability, there are still concerns to be addressed. Ideally a definition based on impairment should not be drafted too narrowly. The terminology adopted should be neutral,[43] and there should be no threshold of severity to overcome, or arguably a threshold of duration.[44] Finally, the ideal definition of disability should recognize that disability discrimination could happen to those with a history of disability, those who are imputed a disability, those who may have a future disability, or those associated with a person with a disability. To achieve all this in one definition seems like a herculean feat of drafting magic. But it is contended here that the definition

---

39 World Health Organisation, http://www.who.int/topics/disabilities/en/.

40 T Degener, 'Definition of Disability' *EU Network of Experts on Disability Discrimination*, (August 2004) 6.

41 See *McCrory Scaffolding (NI) Limited v A Worker* EED055 (Labour Court).

42 See T Degener, 'Definition of Disability' *EU Network of Experts on Disability Discrimination*, August 2004.

43 For example, the Irish Disability Act 2005 defines disability as: 'disability' in relation to a person, means a substantial restriction in the capacity of the person to carry on a profession, business or occupation in the State or to participate in social or cultural life in the State by reason of an enduring physical, sensory, mental health or intellectual impairment.' This definition focuses on the individuals inability or their restrictions in carrying on a profession, business or occupation. The focus of the definition is therefore quite negative and not neutral.

44 That stated, even the CRPD has included a threshold of duration, therefore it would appear that it is now universally accepted that only disabilities that will persist for a long-time will be covered.

of disability utilized in the Employment Equality Acts 1998–2008 meets these requirements.

The Employment Equality Acts 1998–2008 prohibit discrimination against individuals who come within the definition of 'disability'[45] contained in those Acts.[46] The definition does not list conditions but sets out general statements that will include most, if not all, impairments; for example, paragraph (a) provides: the total or partial absence of a person's bodily or mental functions, including the absence of a part of a person's body.

As is evident from this there are no thresholds to overcome; similarly, the definition does not exclude any conditions from the ambit of the definition of disability.[47] The Equality Tribunal and Labour Court have interpreted the definition of disability in an extremely broad and all-encompassing manner. Accordingly, claimants in Ireland have not faced the difficulties which their counterparts in the UK and US have whereby the issue of whether the condition was within the definition of disability is often the deciding preliminary issue prior to any examination of the merits of the substantive cases alleging discrimination on grounds of disability.[48]

An example of the pragmatic approach taken by the Equality Tribunal is well-illustrated by the decision of the Tribunal in *A Government Employee v A Government Department*[49] where it was held that hypertension was a disability within the meaning of the Acts, even when it was treated and being well-managed.

To date, conditions which are minor and temporary in nature have been found to be within the protected ground.[50] The primary reason relied in these decisions is the

---

45 'disability' means—

(a) the total or partial absence of a person's bodily or mental functions, including the absence of a part of a person's body,
(b) the presence in the body of organisms causing, or likely to cause, chronic disease or illness,
(c) the malfunction, malformation or disfigurement of a part of a person's body,
(d) a condition or malfunction which results in a person learning differently from a person without the condition or malfunction, or
(e) a condition, illness or disease which affects a person's thought processes, perception of reality, emotions or judgement or which results in disturbed behaviour,

and shall be taken to include a disability which exists at present, or which previously existed but no longer exists, or which may exist in the future or which is imputed to a person.

46 s 2(1) of the Employment Equality Acts 1998–2011. This definition is based on the definition of disability contained in the Australian Disability Discrimination Act 1992. For more detail on the Australian definition see G Quinn, M McDonagh and C Kimber, *Disability Discrimination Law in the United States, Australia and Canada* (Oak Tree Press, 1993) 124–128.

47 Disability Discrimination (Meaning of Disability) Regulations 1996. On disability discrimination in the United Kingdom see, generally, B Doyle, *Disability Discrimination Law and Practice* (6th ed, Jordans, 2008) and S Keen and R Outlon, *Disability Discrimination in Employment* (OUP 2009). This was amended by the Equality Act 2010 so now no exclusions of any conditions exist.

48 G Quinn and S Quinlivan, 'Disability Discrimination: the need to amend the Employment Equality Act 1998 in light of the EU Framework Directive on Employment' in C Costello and E Barry (eds), *Equality in Diversity: The New Equality Directives* (ICEL 2003) 218.

49 DEC-E2010-055

50 For example, see *Customer Perception Limited v Leydon* [2004] 15 ELR 101 (injuries sustained from road traffic which resulted in reduced movement in back, neck and shoulder) and

express reference within the definition to disabilities which 'previously existed but no longer exists' in section 2 of the Acts. In *Customer Perception Limited v Leydon*[51] the complainant was involved in a road traffic accident that resulted in reduced movement in her shoulder, back and neck. The Labour Court held that the injury at issue came within the meaning of paragraph (c) of the definition of disability:

> 'taking the ordinary and natural meaning of the term malfunction…the condition from which the complainant suffered in consequences of her accident amounted to a malfunction of parts of her body. It thus constituted a disability within the meaning of the Act. Moreover, in providing that the term comprehends a disability which existed but no longer exists, it is clear that a temporary malfunction comes within the statutory definition.'

Moreover, in *Fernandez v Cable & Wireless*[52] the complainant suffered complications from her treatment with an intravenous injection used to deal with her kidney infection and was hospitalised for one week. Upon her return to work she requested time off to attend hospital for a check up whereupon she was informed if she did so she could be open to disciplinary action. The Equality Officer had no difficulty in finding that the illness, although temporary in nature, suffered by the complainant amounted to a disability. This decision stands in marked contrast to the finding of the CJEU in *Chácon Navas*,[53] discussed above, which eschewed the approach of allowing an illness or sickness to be subsumed into the definition of disability in the FED.

The definition of disability extends to situations where the disability exists, existed in the past, may exist in the future or is imputed to the person concerned, thus fully reflecting the social model of disability as it reflects and takes cognizance of the discrimination against the individual as opposed to the disability itself. The Equality Tribunal in *HSE Employee v HSE*[54] addressed the issue of an imputed disability. In this case the complainant's appointment to staff nurse was deferred by approximately nine months on the receipt of an Occupational Health Report which found the complainant to be morbidly obese. The Equality Tribunal found that the HSE had imputed a disability to the complainant without carrying out a risk assessment and without communicating directly with the complainant about the situation, and had discriminated against the employee based on this imputed disability. The Equality Officer made no finding on whether obesity of itself is a disability, as the complainant had not made any such claim. Rather the Equality Officer found, as argued by the complainant, that a disability had been imputed to the complainant by the HSE on the basis of her serious weight problem.[55]

Not only does the definition of disability include disabilities actually faced by

Fernandez v Cable & Wireless DEC-E2002-052 (illnesses as a result of reaction to intravenous injection which required hospitalisation).

51 [2004] 15 ELR 101. See also more recently *An Granian Hotel v Langford* EDA1211 (Labour Court, 2012).

52 DEC-E-2002-052.

53 [2006] IRLR 706.

54 DEC-E2006-013 (Equality Tribunal). See also *HSE East Coast Area v A Worker* EDA 0711 and *Ms X v An Electronic Company* DEC-2006-042.

55 No test has yet been established to determine when a disability is imputed to an employee. The test utilised in Australia provides useful guidance – see particularly *Gordon v Commonwealth of Australia* [2008] FCA 603.

claimants at the time of the alleged discrimination, it also includes past disabilities (such as mental health difficulties), disabilities which may arise in the future (for example, a genetic predisposition to a particular disability), and disabilities which are imputed to an individual (for example, an intellectual disability to a claimant who is in a wheelchair). The Employment Equality Acts 1998–2011 also prohibits discrimination on the basis of a person's association with a person with a disability.[56]

In a recent decision, the Labour Court provided useful guidance on the issue of whether work-related depression could amount to a disability, but in doing so expressed the opinion that there has to be a certain minimum level of symptoms manifest in the condition suffered by the individual concerned to be sufficient to be considered a disability.[57] The Labour Court noted that while the definition in the Acts did not refer to a minimum level of extent to which the symptoms were to be present, the Labour Court held that a de minimis rule must be applied such that 'effects or symptoms, which are present to an insignificant extent, would have to be disregarded.' Significantly the Court expressed the view, on an obiter basis,[58] that mere unhappiness, ordinary stress or disappointment would not amount to a disability. In a similar vein, a more recent decision has determined that work-related stress of itself does not constitute a disability for the purposes of the Acts.[59] The decision of the Labour Court establishes for the first time that there must be a minimum level of symptoms of a particular condition present for the condition to amount to a disability and receive the ascribed protection provided by the Acts. Should a claimant only have symptoms of a condition which are of an insignificant or lower extent, it appears that they would not meet the threshold established by the decision.[60]

Further, recent case law from Ireland suggests that more employers are raising preliminary arguments as to whether particular conditions amount to disabilities, most particularly where the conditions are manifested in a very minor way and there is an absence of medical evidence. Thus, an element of demarcation about when does a limitation become an impairment has crept into Irish case law. The worrying element about this trend has been the willingness of the Equality Tribunal to utilize dicta from the Court of Justice in *Chácon Navas* to import a threshold of requiring the condition to last for a long time into Irish case law.[61] In addition, the reliance of the Equality Tribunal on the CJEU decision in *Chácon Navas*[62] is worrying (and it is submitted incorrect) given the wide definition of disability in this jurisdiction without reference to any temporal limits. It is also arguably in breach of Article 8 and Recital 28 of the FED which clearly provide that the Directive cannot be used by Member States to reduce or regress the level of protection provided in their law.[63]

56 Section 6(1)(b) of the Employment Equality Acts 1998–2011. See also the decision of the CJEU in *Coleman v Attridge Law* [2008] IRLR 722.

57 *A Government Department v A Worker* EDA094, Labour Court, 2009.

58 The Labour Court expressly stated that it was not reaching a concluded view on the issue as it was not required to do so in the matter before it.

59 *Mr A v A Charitable Organisation* DEC-E2011-049.

60 See also *O'Rourke v JJ Red Holdings Limited t/a Dublin City Hotel* DEC-2010-045.

61 *Colgan v Boots Ireland Ltd* DEC-E2010-008. See also *O'Rourke v JJ Red Holdings Limited t/a Dublin City Hotel* DEC-2010-045.

62 [2006] IRLR 706.

63 Council Directive establishing a general framework for equal treatment in employment and education Directive 2000/78/EC. See also *Catholic University School v Dooley* [2010] IEHC

The importance of the decision in *Chácon Navas* becomes evident when it impacts on a detailed legislative definition of disability and serves to restrict that definition. This adds weight to the arguments that this decision should be revisited, and the CRPD may provide the legal basis to do just that.

6. CRPD

Article 1 of the CRPD is described as 'the purpose' of the Convention, and part of that purpose contains what has been described as the definition – or non-definition – of disability.[64] The Convention is often described as not including a definition of disability; however, there are elements within the Convention that provide significant guidance on who is covered for the purposes of the Convention. There was significant concern during the drafting of the CRPD regarding the inclusion of a precise definition of disability as advocated by NGOs, not least from the EU Commission and government delegations.[65] As a compromise, the approach which has been described as providing 'a soft threshold definition in the form of guidance which is open-ended and inclusive' was adopted within the CRPD.[66] The first element of that definition or meaning is contained in the Preamble at paragraph (e) which is the part of the CRPD on purposes (rather than the second article, which is concerned with definitions). The meaning of disability contained in the preamble provides as follows:

> Disability is an evolving concept and that disability results from the interaction between persons with impairments and attitudinal and environmental barriers that hinders their full and effective participation in society on an equal basis with others.

The above statement must be read with the provision in Article 1 which provides:

> Persons with disabilities include those who have long-term physical, mental, intellectual or sensory impairments which in interaction with various barriers may hinder their full and effective participation in society on an equal basis with others.

This definition clearly endorses the social model of disability. The focus is on the barriers and obstacles that hinder or prevent full, equal and effective participation in society, ie on the failings of society and not the perceived failings of the individual.

---

496 where, in the context of the Part-Time Workers Directive (Directive 97/81/EC) and the Fixed-Term Workers Directive (99/70/EC), Ms Justice Dunne of the Irish High Court accepted the argument made by the employees that 'the Directive rights are a floor not a ceiling. In other words, the Directive provides the minimum rights that may be provided and the State legislature can expand on that.' For an excellent overview of the non-regression clause in EU law see S Peers, 'Non-Regression Clause: The Fig Leaf has Fallen' [2010] 39(4) Industrial Law Journal 436.

64 For a discussion for the rationale for not including a definition of disability see S Trömel, 'A Personal Perspective on the drafting history of the United Nations Convention on the Rights of Persons with Disabilities' *European Year Book of Disability Law* Vol 1, 115–137, 121–122.

65 G de Burca, 'The European Union in the negotiation of the UN Disability Convention' (2010) 35(2) European Law Review 174, 186 and 191.

66 ibid 191.

That said this definition also includes a potential limiting factor with the inclusion of the phrase 'long-term.' However this definition does not require a disability to be long-term so much as provide that 'persons with disabilities' include those who have long-term impairments. The focus of the definition is on the disabling effects of the interaction between an impairment and attitudinal and societal barriers – a very different focus to that adopted in *Chácon Navas*. It is clear that the European Union's definition of disability as encompassed by the decision of *Chácon Navas* is not in compliance with the CRPD.

The CRPD is the first human rights convention ratified by the European Union in its own right.[67] Thus the CRPD will have a new 'legal status within EC law, and will have to be respected in its totality, and not as a mere add on to be referred to in passing in Community instruments.'[68] While the exact impact of EU ratification is as yet unclear, it is the case that in areas of EU competence, international treaties, once ratified by the EU, are binding on Member States and European institutions alike.[69] Further, it is the case that directives are subordinate to international treaties, and human rights treaties, like all other international agreements, once ratified by the EU, form an integral part of the EU legal order. The role of the CJEU is to uphold the law of the EU[70] and to ensure that the EU executive and legislative bodies comply with that law which now includes the CRPD.

In 2011 a reference for a preliminary ruling was referred to the CJEU: *Jette Ring v Dansk Almennyttig Boligselskab DAB*.[71] The reference requests the CJEU to

---

67 See Council Decision 2010/48/EC.

68 L Waddington, 'A new era in human rights protection in the European Community: the implications of the United Nation's Convention on the Rights of Persons with Disabilities for the European Community' Maastricht Faculty of Law, Working Paper No. 2007-4, 1–22.

69 art 300(7) TEC, and see also art 216(2) Treaty of Lisbon.

70 art 19 TFEU.

71 Case C-335/11: the question referred:

1.(a) Is any person who, because of physical, mental or psychological injuries, cannot or can only to a limited extent carry out his work in a period that satisfies the requirement as to duration specified in para 45 of the judgment of the Court of Justice in Case C-13/05 Navas covered by the concept of disability within the meaning of the directive?

(b) Can a condition caused by a medically diagnosed incurable illness be covered by the concept of disability within the meaning of the directive?

(c) Can a condition caused by a medically diagnosed temporary illness be covered by the concept of disability within the meaning of the directive?

2. Should a permanent reduction in functional capacity which does not entail a need for special aids or the like but means only that the person concerned is not capable of working full-time be regarded as a disability in the sense in which that term is used in Council Directive 2000/78/EC?

3. Is a reduction in working hours among the measures covered by art 5 of Directive 2000/78/EC?

4. Does Council Directive 2000/78/EC preclude the application of a provision of national law under which an employer is entitled to dismiss an employee with a shortened notice period where the employee has received his salary during periods of illness for a total of 120 days during a period of 12 consecutive months, in the case of an employee who must be regarded as disabled within the meaning of the directive, where

(a) the absence was caused by the disability, or

(b) the absence was due to the fact that the employer did not implement the measures appropriate in the specific situation to enable a person with a disability to perform his work?

consider the parameters of the definition of disability along very similar lines to those initially referred in *Chácon Navas*. For example, amongst the questions raised is whether a 'condition caused by a medically diagnosed temporary illness be covered by the concept of disability within the meaning of the directive?'[72] While there are some nuanced differences between the issues referred to in *Chácon Navas* and those currently before the CJEU as a result of *Jette Ring*, the issues are in the main the same. The issue then is what would allow the CJEU to re-consider or revisit its decision in *Chácon Navas*, and it is contended that the EU-adoption of the CRPD will require a different approach. A new decision is warranted as there is a new source of law – the CRPD – and the CRPD is steeped in the social model of disability. Thus the CJEU must now read the FED in light of the CRPD, which in turn should lead to a reassessment of *Chácon Navas*.

7. Conclusion

From the foregoing, it is axiomatic that the Irish definition of disability, straddling a combination of impairments and discrimination, is the most comprehensive and legally sophisticated definition discussed in this chapter. The CRPD provides an opportunity for a re-assessment of the definition so disappointingly and restrictively adopted in EU law and the FED in the CJEU decision in *Chácon Navas*.[73] Given the opportunity provided by the ratification of the CRPD by the EU, and the brave expansive approach adopted by the CJEU in *Coleman*,[74] it is likely that illnesses will be covered by the term 'disability' within the FED, and the view expressed by the CJEU on sickness not being covered by the Directive in *Chácon Navas* will need be to be approached in light of these considerations. However, the threshold of long-term disability may not be disturbed given the inclusion of this in the CRPD.

---

72 Para 1 (c), Case C-335/11.

73 (C-13/05) [2006] E.C.R I-06467, [2006] IRLR 706.

74 (C-203/06) [2008] ECR I-05603, [2008] IRLR 722.

Chapter 33

DISABILITY QUOTA SYSTEMS IN PUBLIC SERVICE EMPLOYMENT, POSITIVE DISCRIMINATION AND ARTICLE 27 OF THE CRPD

Charlotte May-Simera and Elizabeth Kamundia

1. Introduction

Inclusion is a key concept intrinsic to any efforts towards creating a just and equal society. It is particularly important for persons with disabilities, who are often excluded from society as result of their impairment and societal attitudes that equate difference with inferiority.[1] As a result of developments in all areas of human rights over the previous century, law has developed responding to the call from civil rights movements, consolidating the concepts of equality and non-discrimination on the grounds of gender, religion, ethnicity, and most recently sexuality and disability. Inclusion has come to be seen as a goal worth pursuing, carrying with it many benefits for society. One attempt to foster inclusion by the Irish government focuses on the employment of persons with disabilities, through the introduction of a quota system to regulate the numbers of persons with disabilities employed by the State. By improving their employment in the public sector the State sets a standard of behaviour it wishes to see replicated elsewhere in society whilst responding to the demands for improved conditions and greater awareness for the disadvantaged and excluded. The decision to take measures to influence the employment of persons with disabilities was also a result of the realization of the great potential and gains to be had by including persons with disabilities in all spheres of life. Not least also the economic value of this task force and hidden source of human capital heightened government interest, subsequently fuelling the impetus to legally enforce the employment of persons with disabilities.

This chapter will commence by introducing the quotas system as it operates in Ireland and will discuss the Irish Disability Act 2005, Part 5, which covers public service employment, throughout. Internationally, the UN Convention on the Rights of Persons with Disabilities (CRPD) came into force in 2006 and is the leading framework for disability policy. Ireland has yet to ratify the Convention; however, this international treaty is a valuable tool to inform legislation. This chapter will attempt to gauge whether or not the use of quotas systems as provided for by Part 5 of the 2005 Disability Act is in line with the novice approach to disability rights embodied by the Convention.

---

1 R Kayess and P French, 'Out of Darkness into Light? Introducing the Convention on the Rights of Persons with Disabilities (2008) 8 Human Rights Law Review 1.

Next, this chapter will address the policy measures taking place elsewhere within the European Union in a similar effort to address the employment of persons with disabilities. While the European Union does not have the competence to enforce a quota system on its Member States, since the European Employment Directive (2000/78/EC) and its new focus on disability, many Member States have since introduced or revised such systems. A comparative view is relevant because the experience of disability is universal as are the challenges that ensue. Further, through describing structures, practices and attitudes and how they differ between societies, strengths and weaknesses, commonalities and uniqueness can be detected more easily. Through comparative studies, we can learn how understandings are constructed through reflections and considerations on characteristics, cultures, politics and economies of numerous countries.[2] Finally, by comparing and differentiating we arrive at a clearer internal reflection of the merits and demerits of the quota system in Ireland and the added value of the CRPD.

2. Quota Systems – A Brief Introduction

The employment rate of persons without disabilities compared to persons with disabilities is significantly high. According to the 2006 Irish census, only 35% of persons with disabilities who were of working age (aged between 20 to 64) were in formal employment.[3] Employers are hesitant to employ persons with disabilities for various reasons, including their fear of additional costs towards supporting their employment as a result of their obligations to provide reasonable accommodation[4] and the assumption that persons with disabilities are not as productive as their able-bodied counterparts.[5]

On a general note, a quota system is used to regulate the labour force to employ a specific number of certain groups of people, in our case persons with disabilities. Quotas can either be established on a voluntary basis or as a legal requirement.[6] A disability employment quota is the most common approach taken to regulate and ensure the employment of persons with disabilities. When the quota system is established as a legal requirement, there are consequences for non-compliance with it. Further, the quota system can only be effective in an appropriate work environment.[7] In this sense, a work environment may mean the built environment, information accessibility, awareness of disability and/or a willingness to take all

---

2 C May-Simera, *Comparative Analysis of Adoption policies in England and Germany* (MA Dissertation, London Metropolitan University, 2010).

3 National Disability Authority, 'Frequently Asked Questions on recording the disability status of staff in the Public Service – Part 5 Disability Act 2005' (National Disability Authority, 2011) <www.nda.ie/website/nda/cntmgmtnew.nsf/0/A3FA97F7EF093251802573D900393654/$File/FAQ_Dis_Status.html> last accessed 31 March 2016.

4 Definition of reasonable accommodation: 'the necessary and appropriate modification and adjustments not imposing a disproportionate or undue burden, where needed in a particular case, to ensure to persons with disabilities the enjoyment or exercise on an equal basis with others of all human rights and fundamental freedoms', art 2 CRPD (2006).

5 D Mont, 'Disability Employment Policy' (2004) GLADNET Collection. Paper 431. <http://digitalcommons.ilr.cornell.edu/gladnetcollect/431> accessed on 7 January 2012.

6 GLADNET (n 5).

7 GLADNET (n 5).

the costs for the purpose of reasonable accommodation.[8] Since 2005, with the introduction of the Disability Act 2005 the quota has become a legal requirement in Ireland. For the first time the Act imposed a target of 3% employment of persons with disabilities in all public sector bodies. This approach, we argue, constitutes one of the affirmative action measures suggested in the CRPD under Article 27 on work and employment.

3. The CRPD

The Convention specifies States' obligations to ensure the 'legal right of persons with disabilities to earn a living through work that they voluntarily choose or accept, and to prohibit discrimination based on disability in all forms of employment.'[9] In 2007, on the International Day of Persons with Disabilities, the UN High Commissioner for Human Rights in a press release concisely and definitively declared that, unambiguously, the Convention guarantees the right to work. Additionally, the High Commissioner asserted that States shall safeguard this right to work by actively promoting the employment of persons with disabilities (public and private sector) by adopting appropriate strategies, 'which may include affirmative action programmes.'[10] Indeed, Article 27(1) of the UN CRPD reads 'States Parties recognize the right of persons with disabilities to work, on an equal basis with others; this includes the right to the opportunity to gain a living by work freely chosen or accepted in a labour market and work environment that is open, inclusive and accessible to persons with disabilities.'[11] Further, this Article provides that States should protect and promote the recognition of the right to work by employing persons with disabilities in the public sector[12] as well as encouraging the employment of persons with disabilities in the private sector,[13] and urges States to do so 'through appropriate policies and measures, which may include affirmative action programmes, incentives and other measures.'[14]

While Article 27 does not specifically mention quotas systems as a means to achieve the realization of the right to work, arguably it implies this, however, by the use of the wording 'affirmative action measures.' In fact, the Secretariat for the Convention on the Rights of Persons with Disabilities understands that 'affirmative-action measures' include employment quotas that aim to create equal opportunities by tackling structural disadvantages faced by certain groups. The Secretariat goes on to explain: 'unlike reasonable accommodation, such measures are not intended to meet the needs of individuals. Affirmative-action measures are temporary and are

8 NDA (n 3).

9 UN Enable, 'Handbook for Parliamentarians on the Convention on the Rights of Persons with Disabilities-Work and Employment' www.un.org/disabilities/default.asp?id=241 last accessed 31 March 2016.

10 UN Enable, 'Report of the United Nations High Commissioner for Human Rights on progress in the implementation of the recommendations contained in the study on the human rights of persons with disabilities' (A/HRC/4/75, para 45, 17 January 2007) <http://www.un.org/disabilities/default.asp?id=135> last accessed 31 March 2016.

11 art 27, CRPD (2006) G A Res 61/106.

12 art 27.1(g), CRPD (2006) G A Res 61/106.

13 art 27.1(h), CRPD (2006) G A Res 61/106.

14 art 27.1(h), CRPD (2006) G A Res 61/106.

intended to last only until the structural disadvantages have been overcome, either through compensation or by creating a more equitable system.'[15]

Waddington identifies quotas systems as a form of positive action that is used to promote employment of certain groups of people. In light of the current Convention then, this approach can be interpreted as an accepted means to accelerate the de facto equality of persons with disabilities in employment situations.[16] This assumption that quota systems, in general, are in line with the CRPD is further supported when we look to Article 5.4 of the Convention, which proposes that principles of equality and non-discrimination are to be achieved via 'specific measures which are necessary to accelerate or achieve the de facto equality of persons with disabilities;' further, these 'shall not be considered discrimination under the terms of the present Convention.'[17] After all, Marianna Schulze identifies that 'employment for persons with disabilities is essentially a non-discrimination and an accessibility issue.'[18] In fact, in her discussion of Article 27, Schulze explains that positive discrimination via the use of quotas systems was amongst the two main themes of debate during the drafting stages of the CRPD, the other being the implications of the wording of 'alternative' employment.[19]

As we have established, the right to work on an equal basis with others is provided under Article 27 of the CRPD. States are particularly recognized as having enhanced role in realizing this right. Having regard to the fact that the employment of persons with disabilities is hampered by negative stereotypes and attitudes informed by notions that disability equates to inability, evidenced in low employment rates, the Convention addresses this in Article 8. Article 8 requires State Parties to raise awareness throughout society regarding persons with disabilities to promote awareness of their capabilities and contributions, to combat stereotypes and prejudices against them as well as to foster respect for their rights and dignity. Towards this end, State Parties are required to initiate public awareness campaigns designed to promote recognition of the skills, merits and abilities of persons with disabilities, and of their contribution to the workplace and the labour market. Awareness-raising could be undertaken through conducting public enquires or studies,[20] for instance to find out the employment rates for persons with disabilities in public and private spheres (indeed, this is provided for in Part 5 of the Irish Disability Act 2005).[21] In their capacity as employers, States have an important role to play in promoting positive attitudes towards people with disabilities, and therefore,

15 UN Enable, 'Handbook for Parliamentarians on the Convention on the Rights of Persons with Disabilities-Work and Employment' www.un.org/disabilities/default.asp?id=241 last accessed 31 March 2016.

16 L Waddington, 'Reassessing the employment of people with disabilities in Europe: From Quotas to anti-discrimination laws' (1997) 18 Comp. Lab. L.J 62, 73.

17 art 5.4, CRPD (2006) G A Res 61/106.

18 M Schulze, 'A Handbook on the Human Rights of Persons with Disabilities: Understanding the UN Convention On The Rights Of Persons With Disabilities' (Handicap International 2010).

19 ibid.

20 United Nations, 'From Exclusion to Equality: Realizing the Rights of Persons with Disabilities: Handbook for Parliamentarians on the Convention on the Rights of Persons with Disabilities and its Optional Protocol' (2007) <http://www.un.org/disabilities/default.asp?id=212> last accessed 31 March 2016.

21 art 31 of the Convention promotes statistics and data collection on the situation of persons with disabilities.

under Article 8, should serve as a model towards this end. Awareness-raising would also ensure that individuals, private entities and government entities know about the rights of persons with disabilities and the corresponding responsibilities. For instance, it would popularize the 3% employment quota in the Irish public service (discussed below), increasing the chances of compliance.

4. General Description of the Disability Act 2005 (Part 5)

The Disability Act 2005 is the latest, most comprehensive disability statute in Ireland. It addresses the employment of persons with disabilities in the public service and establishes that the National Disability Authority as the commissioning body of the provisions laid out by it. This means that it is the main enforcer and supervisor of the 3% quota in public service employment. On a general level, the National Disability Authority (NDA) is an independent statutory agency that provides expert advice on disability policy and practice to the Minister for Justice and Equality in Ireland.[22, 23]

The Act, in its preliminary and general provision, also defines disability and other key terms. Accordingly, 'disability in relation to a person means a substantial restriction in capacity of the person to carry on a profession, business or occupation in the State or to participate in social or cultural life in the State by reason of an enduring physical, sensory, mental health or intellectual impairment.'[24] In comparison, the CRPD does not define disability for various reasons, generally stating that it is an evolving concept arising from the interaction between persons with impairments and their environment. In the Irish context applied to employment, to fall under the definition, the impairment must be, as described by the NDA, a long-term condition which continues or is expected to continue for 12 months or more. Most importantly, the disability must significantly restrict the capacity of the person to work and participate in the day-to-day life of the social and cultural engagement of the society.

Of particular interest here is Part 5 of the Disability Act 2005 which deals with public service employment and sets new obligations on public bodies. Public bodies are responsible to ensure that not less than 3% of persons employed by them are persons with disabilities unless there is a good reason for not this not being taking place.[25] Moreover, similar to Articles 8 and 27 of the CRPD, public bodies shall take all reasonable measures to promote and support the employment of persons with disabilities.[26] The reasonable measures provided for by the Disability Act 2005 include delivery of disability training for staff, having support and retention policies for those who have acquired a disability in their work, flexible working hours, adjustment of work schedules and duties, stress-management policies, confidential employee assistance programmes and provision of specialist equipment.[27]

---

22 National Disability Authority, 'What we do' (National Disability Authority, 2011) <www.nda.ie/website/nda/cntmgmtnew.nsf/0/D2E2BF6F07A969B880256C790064011E?OpenDocument> last accessed 31 March 2016.

23 The NDA was established in 2000 under the auspices of the Department of Justice, Equality and Law Reform by the National Disability Authority Act, 1999.

24 Disability Act 2005, s 2(1).

25 ibid s 47(4).

26 ibid s 47(1)(a).

27 National Disability Authority, '2008 Report on Compliance with Part 5 of the Disability Act 2005

If a public body does not fulfil its obligations under Part 5 and fails to do so consecutively for two years, the NDA will contact the said body and inform the relevant Minister and can recommend that 'specific action be taken to achieve compliance, and can recommend that individual public bodies undertake specific steps to improve recruitment, training and promotion of staff with disabilities.'[28] Indeed, some of the changes requested in employment policy, which can follow from non-compliance by a public body, are quite significant.[29]

Data-collection is central to the effective monitoring of the quota system and the NDA reports that this improves from year to year. The data assessing whether the 3% target is met is sent to monitoring committees (the transfer of data is handled in accordance with Data Protection legislation).[30] The monitoring committee of each department will then prepare a comprehensive report on that body and share this with its Minister and the NDA. The overall aim is to distil information from the data, which will help inform the NDA on the recommendations they provide on how to best recruit and support persons with disabilities. This is also sought by way of bench-marking best practice examples and sharing experiences. In cases where the target is met, the Act allows Ministers to set new and higher targets beyond the statutory minimum.[31] On a general note, it can be said that the NDA reports are a valuable source of information and of good quality.

---

on Employment of People with Disabilities in the Public Service' <www.nda.ie/cntmgmtnew.nsf/0/584C604587AEE6BE8025768D00574AFE?OpenDocument > last accessed 31 March 2016.

28 National Disability Authority, 'Frequently asked Questions on recording the disability status of staff in the Public Service: Part 5 Disability Act 2005,' (National Disability Authority, 2011) <http://www.nda.ie/website/nda/cntmgmtnew.nsf/0/A3FA97F7EF093251802573D900393654/$File/FAQ_Dis_Status.html > last accessed 31 March 2016.

29 According to s 47(3)d, the Minister may specify:
   i. the numbers or percentages of persons with disabilities to be employed by the public body concerned;
   ii. the holding of recruitment competitions confined to persons with disabilities in relation to specific posts or employments;
   iii. measures for the filling, by suitably qualified persons with disabilities, of specified categories of vacancies for such period as he or she considers appropriate; and
   iv. that the public body concerned shall offer a specified number of work experience placements of specified duration to persons with disabilities each year.

30 'Information on an individual's disability status comes under the heading of "sensitive personal information" in the Data Protection Acts 1988 and 2003. There is a particular onus on public bodies to ensure this information is stored safely and securely; that only nominated officials have access to it; and that the information is only used for stated purposes of which the individual concerned has been made aware. Management and protection of this data would normally be a function for the Human Resources or Personnel Unit.' National Disability Authority, 'Frequently asked Questions on the statistical monitoring of Public Service Staff: Part 5 Disability Act 2005,' (National Disability Authority 2011) <http://www.nda.ie/website/nda/cntmgmtnew.nsf/0/A3FA97F7EF093251802573D900393654/$File/FAQs_on_stat_monitoring.html > last accessed 31 March 2016.

31 National Disability Authority, 'Frequently asked Questions on recording the disability status of staff in the Public Service: Part 5 Disability Act 2005,' (National Disability Authority, 2011) <http://www.nda.ie/website/nda/cntmgmtnew.nsf/0/A3FA97F7EF093251802573D900393654/$File/FAQ_Dis_Status.html > last accessed 31 March 2016.

5. Comparative European Perspectives

Employment policy has often played a peripheral role in the European project, largely focusing on the rights of workers in relation to mobility between EU Member States.[32] Employment regulation has usually been contested as national labour markets are embedded in diverse political and social economic systems or varieties of capitalism, this makes harmonization of social protection and job-creation strategies impossible.[33]

By the time of the Treaty on the European Union (Maastricht Treaty) there was a broader coalition of Member States in favour of European regulation of employment and other social issues to provide safeguards against a feared regulatory race to the bottom as the single market deepened. In the final agreement adopted as the Social Protocol only health and safety, work conditions and equal pay fell under EU competence with the system of Qualified Majority Voting in place to adopt any legislation in this area. Only under the Treaty of Amsterdam (1997) did this extend to worker information and consultation and the integration of persons excluded from the labour market.

The Employment Equality Directive of 2000 resulted from the Treaty changes made at Amsterdam. Directive 2000/78/EC prohibits discrimination on grounds of religion and belief, age, disability and sexual orientation now under the Treaty Establishing the European Union (EC Treaty, now TFEU).[34] Articles 136 and 137 of Part XI of the EC Treaty address social policy in relation to working conditions, protection of workers and, as noted above, the integration of persons excluded from the labour market. The European Commission notified in a Communication, that the impact of this Directive would be great and that it would oblige Member States to change existing rules. Similarly, it would have 'huge implications for employers – public and private – and their employment practices towards people with disabilities.'[35] This Directive created new rights and responsibilities on behalf of employers and employees, in relation to this. The idea was that a renewed commitment to the concept of 'reasonable accommodation' in the workplace would be central to addressing the issue of the right to employment of persons with disabilities (The EU does not have competence to make provisions for a quota system). At this point it is important to note that in December 2009, the EU as a regional body ratified the Convention. The full effects that this will have on EU policy in relation to disability are yet to be determined.

Referring to the use of the quota system in EU Member States, Waddington points out that 'the quota system has emerged as the main legislative tool in Europe to promote the employment of disabled people.'[36] In a report from 2002, the European

---

32 K Jacobsson, 'Soft regulation and the subtle transformation of states: the case of EU employment policy' (2004) 14 Journal of European Social Policy 4, 355–370.

33 ibid.

34 EC Treaty Title XI c I arts 137–39.

35 European Commission, 'Communication on Equal Opportunities for people with disabilities: A European Action Plan' (EC COM 2003650 final), 16 <www.eur-lex.europa.eu/LexUriServ/LexUriServ.do?uri=COM:2003:0650:FIN:EN:PDF > last accessed 31 March 2016.

36 L Waddington, 'Reassessing the employment of people with disabilities in Europe: From Quotas to anti-discrimination laws' (1997) 18 Comp. Lab. L.J 62, 64.

Commission identifies that in about 'half of the EU states a quota-levy scheme is applied. Within the EU the developments of quota schemes vary considerably.'[37] This report particularly highlights the dismal enforcement of the quotas, similarly identifying that penalties (where the quota is not achieved) do not seem to deter employers from underperforming. The Commission claims that the system only truly seems to be running in France and Germany (which is why they are discussed below in more detail). However, 'this does not mean necessarily that employment targets are generally met, but that levies are collected to provide funds for additional measures.'[38] Interestingly, Scandinavian countries refrain from any quota-like provisions due to their belief in disability-neutral legislation as a basis for equal treatment, rather than singling out specific categories of people and thus labelling, stigmatizing and defining them as different from others.

A solid quota system is a fundamental part of German employment law.[39] The 'Social Rights Book IX' codifies Germany's social rights, and was amended in 2001 to include participation rights of persons with disabilities. Part 2 (71) establishes that both public and private bodies with twenty employees or more must ensure that a disability quota of at least 5% is met. The Act specifies that particular regard must be given to women with disabilities and also calculates the quotas differently according to the number of job positions that are filled across the year. Failure to comply with the quota obligation means that a penalty called 'Ausgleichsabgabe' (Compensation charge) must be paid to a regional integration office ('Integrationsamt'). The penalty is calculated referring to the difference between the legal requirement of 5% and reported percentage (for example, if the figure is below 2%, a monthly fine of €260 must be paid; if it is between 3% and 5% the sum is €105).[40] Doyle notes that 'the proceeds of this penalty are ploughed back into positive disabled employment policies pursued by the state.'[41] The definition of disability is established on the basis of an assessment and official registration system, through which disability is measured in percentages. According to the percentage of disability, relevant benefits can be claimed. To be counted as an employee with a disability the percentage is set at 50%.[42]

France has employed a quota scheme for the private sector since 1987 (companies with twenty employees or more are subject to a 6% quota).[43] In 2005, 'Association Nationale de Gestion du Fonds pour l'Insertion Professionnelle des Personnes Handicapées' (AGEFIPH), an organisation established in 1987 following the

---

37 European Commission, Directorate-General for Employment and Social Affairs Unit E.4, 'Active Labour Market Programmes for People with Disabilities: Facts and Figures on Use and Impact' (European Commission, 2004).

38 ibid 23.

39 Gesetz zur Sicherung der Eingliederung Schwerbehinderter in Arbeit, Beruf und Gesellschaft (Schwerbehindertengesetz – SchwbG).

40 Sozialgesetzbuch, Neuntes Buch, 'Rehabilitation und Teilhabe behinderter Menschen' (2001) SGB IX Teil 2, §77.

41 B Doyle, *Disability Discrimination and Equal Opportunities: A Comparative Study of the Employment Rights of Disabled Persons* (Mansell, 1995).

42 Sozialgesetzbuch, Neuntes Buch, 'Rehabilitation und Teilhabe behinderter Menschen' (2001) SGB IX Teil 2, §72.

43 Ministre des Solidarités et de la Cohésion sociale, 'La loi du 11 février 2005′ (Ministre des Solidarités et de la Cohésion sociale, 2009) < www.solidarite.gouv.fr/espaces,770/handicap,775/> last accessed 31 March 2016.

Employment of Disabled Workers Act that promotes the employment of persons with disabilities and manages the contributions made by non-compliant businesses, became the monitoring body of the quota scheme.[44] In their research the NDA explain that 'from 2006 public and state functions have also had to declare how many people with disabilities they employ and the severity of each disability.'[45] Failure to comply on behalf of public and state employers results in the obligation to pay into a fund that addresses professionals' integration in public service, 'le Fonds pour l'Insertion Professionnelle dans la Fonction Publique' (private sector penalties are diverted to a different fund). The calculation of the penalty is a high multiple of the hourly rate per job not filled by a person with a disability that would make up the quota. In cases where non-compliance exceeds three years the amount multiplies.

Germany and France impose heavy sanctions, compared to the weak enforcement mechanisms applied in Ireland. However, despite these heavy fines, the NDA find in their review of the French situation that 'evidence suggests that many employers prefer to pay the contribution rather than consider employing a person with a disability.'[46] This consequence then raises questions on the merits and demerits of the quota system generally.

6. Evaluating Quota Systems

The quota system remains one of the most widely used elements of employment policy for people with disabilities.[47] Generally, much of its success results from the fact that employer penalties or compensatory payments are directly used to finance employment promotion programmes (not applied in Ireland). This has the effect of stimulating the employment of people with disabilities, either directly (through the quota) or indirectly (through funded employment programmes).[48]

Despite the popularity of the quota scheme and their legal provisioning, their full potential is still far from being realised, according to many disability scholars. Gundersen complains that 'quota positions are often filled through internal rather than external recruitment,' and that employers' fulfilment of quota obligations is most likely to benefit those who are closest to the labour market in the first place, rather than bringing about real change towards the participation of persons with

---

44 L'Association Nationale pour la Gestion du Fonds pour l'Insertion Professionnelle des Personnes Handicapees, 'Qui sommes nous?' (2011) <www.agefiph.fr/#agefiph> last accessed 31 March 2016.

45 National Disability Authority, 'Statutory Targets on Employment of People with Disabilities in the Public Sector'(National Disability Authority 2011) <www.nda.ie/cntmgmtnew.nsf/0/84AA79B029E870AE8025729D0046CAED/%24File/people_with_disabilities_in_public_sector_04.htm > last accessed 31 March 2016.

46 ibid.

47 Organization for Economic and Cooperation and Development, 'Transforming disability into ability: Policies to promote work and income security for disabled people (OECD Publishing, 2003) 104 available at <www.oecdbookshop.org/oecd/display.asp?K=5LMQCR2K51D0&DS=Transforming-Disability-into-Ability> last accessed 31 March 2016.

48 National Disability Authority, 'Statutory Targets on Employment of People with Disabilities in the Public Sector' (National Disability Authority, 2011) <www.nda.ie/cntmgmtnew.nsf/0/84AA79B029E870AE8025729D0046CAED/$File/people_with_disabilities_in_public_sector_04.htm> last accessed 31 March 2016.

disabilities in society.[49] Here, it is important to consider that persons with disabilities often do not even qualify for certain positions due to insufficient training or levels of education as a result of inaccessible education systems.

Quite comprehensively, Brennan and Conroy have criticized the very nature of the quota system in that they start from the presumption that persons with disabilities are unable to enter or maintain employment in the open labour market.[50] Further, they complain, that the quota system as applied in Ireland does not report on actual work status, indicating what type of positions they occupy. They question the use of such a system is if persons with disabilities are only employed in low-level jobs or simply to fulfil the purpose of the achieving the quota. Moreover, unlike the German system for example, the Irish system does not target women with disabilities specifically.[51] Finally, they argue that experiences in quota countries show that employees who become disabled and are thus eligible for counting towards the quota are more likely to be kept in a job, while quota schemes give little incentive to employ a disabled job applicant.[52] Also, many have argued that quota policies tend to emphasize difference and incapacity rather than ability which partly explains why some quota countries have introduced new anti-discriminatory policy elements as well.[53]

To conclude the list of criticisms, some disability academics claim that 'there is a lack of clear consensus or convergence in this area, and recent years have seen European countries moving both towards and away from disability quota systems.'[54] Moreover, writing for the Academic Network of European Disability Experts, Greve claims that there also exists 'some tension between the maintenance of quota systems and the shift towards rights-based employment policies.'[55] While there are concerns that the rights-based implications of quotas systems set apart people with disabilities, we argue that by maintaining the label, positive discrimination as provided for in Article 5.4 of the CRPD justifies the means to achieve de facto equality temporarily. Similarly, the UN Secretariat for the Convention also interprets that affirmative action measures are temporary and should be employed until more equitable systems are established.

7. Conclusion

This chapter has addressed the employment of persons with disabilities particularly in the public sector, and how this is promoted using quota systems that set a target

---

49 T Gundersen, 'Quota system in European Countries for People with Disabilities' (Translation) Rapport nr. 8/08 (2002).

50 A Brennan, P Conroy and Ralaheen Ltd, 'The Three Percent Target for the Employment of People with Disabilities in the Public Service' (NDA 2010) <www.nda.ie/cntmgmtnew.nsf/0/E7AF211E4C77D7408025706600506DFE?OpenDocument> last accessed 31 March 2016.

51 OECD (n 47).

52 OECD (n 47) 105.

53 OECD (n 47) 106.

54 B Greve, 'The labour market situation of disabled people in European countries and implementation of employment policies: a summary of evidence from country reports and research studies' (Academic Network of European Disability Experts 2009) <www.disability-europe.net/content/aned/media/ANED%20Task%206%20final%20report%20-%20final%20version%2017-04-09.pdf> last accessed 31 March 2016.

55 ibid.

percentage rate of positions to be filled by person with disabilities. From the brief overview provided above it becomes evident that the quota systems are regulated differently between EU Member States. These differences begin at the definition of who is to be included in the quota count in the first place. Some States require an official registration of the disability in a registration system to be eligible for counting towards the quota. Some even add a definition set by a percentage of disability (Germany). Further, to establish the disability and be registered requires a medical assessment. While the more rigorous assessment-requirement can be seen as discriminatory in itself, the NDA identifies that this can be a positive measure in that it reduces the possibility of ambiguity 'with regard to whether specific impairments qualify the person to be counted in connection with employment quotas.'[56] Ireland does not apply financial sanctions for non-compliance as, for example, France or Germany do, and does not involve the medical profession to the same extent.

The regulation of the employment of persons with disabilities in public sector employment in Ireland is pursued to ensure inclusion, which is increasingly felt to be a socially desirable behaviour the world over, not least since the coming into force of the CRPD. However, for a mechanism of this kind to work, several measures need to be in place. First, the establishment of disability should be unambiguous, as is the case with the German system. The Disability Act 2005 is silent on how a public body is to calculate the number of people with disabilities for the purposes of making returns. In most countries in which the quota system is in place, only registered disabled people who fulfil the eligibility criteria count towards the quota.[57] This is not the case in Ireland, in light of the fact that it is at the employees' discretion to choose whether or not to disclose their disability, and a number of factors can lead to a person with a disability choosing not to. As a result, a true reflection of the number of employees with a disability employed is not being portrayed.[58] Second, there is a need to establish a more uniform measurement system. Currently, the monitoring of the Irish quota is conducted by civil and public service employers who appear to rely on a variety of measurement systems and depend on voluntary disclosure by employees. Not surprisingly, low results, hovering above or below the 3% percent target, have been the pattern of counts in recent years.[59] Third, it may be useful to explore the introduction of a quota to private firms which meet a particular threshold of employees, such as is the case in France and Germany. This would be in line with Article 27.1(h), which specifically addresses the private sector.

A final recommendation would be that a greater focus is placed on the recruitment process[60] and on encouraging people with disabilities to participate in competitions for positions in the public service, through the advertising of accommodations

---

56 National Disability Authority, 'Statutory Targets on Employment of People with Disabilities in the Public Sector' (National Disability Authority, 2011) <www.nda.ie/cntmgmtnew.nsf/0/84AA79B029E870AE8025729D0046CAED/%24File/people_with_disabilities_in_public_sector_08.htm> last accessed 31 March 2016.

57 OECD (n 47).

58 Department of Community, Equality, and Gaeltacht Affairs.

59 A Brennan, P Conroy and Ralaheen Ltd, 'The Three Percent Target for the Employment of People with Disabilities in the Public Service' (NDA 2010) available at <www.nda.ie/cntmgmtnew.nsf/0/E7AF211E4C77D7408025706600506DFE?OpenDocument> last accessed 31 March 2016.

60 Under s 47, the Minister may make an order to set alternative compliance targets, including targets for recruitment or measures such as special recruitment competition.

available to facilitate participation.[61] The Disability Act 2005 should make it clear that the quota is not an end in itself but a means which should lead to better supports for people with disabilities. Ireland is yet to ratify the UN CRPD; however, with the approach taken towards employment in Part 5 of the Disability Act 2005 we argue that Ireland demonstrates great willingness and is prepared to live up to the requirements of the Convention.

61 Review of the operation of the Disability Act 2005 <www.justice.ie/en/JELR/Review%20of%20the%20Operation%20of%20the%20Disability%20Act%202005.pdf/Files/Review%20of%20the%20Operation%20of%20the%20Disability%20Act%202005.pdf> last accessed 31 March 2016.

PART 7: COMPARATIVE AND REGIONAL PERSPECTIVES

Chapter 34

HUMAN RIGHTS AND DISABILITY: REINTERPRETING DISABILITY WITHIN THE OAS IN LIGHT OF THE CRPD

Francisco J Bariffi

1. Disability within the OAS

The Organization of the American States (OAS) is a regional organisation which came into being in 1948 with the signing in Bogotá, Colombia, of the Charter of the OAS, which entered into force in December 1951. The OAS brings together all 35 independent states of the Americas and constitutes the main political, juridical, and social governmental forum in the Hemisphere. In addition, it has granted permanent observer status to 67 states, as well as to the European Union (EU).

Within the structure of the OAS, disability is regarded as a priority issue. As the OAS expresses, 'integrating persons with disabilities fully into the societies of the countries of the Americas has become an important priority for the OAS.'[1] In the field of the rights of persons with disabilities, the Department of Social Development and Employment (DSDE) is responsible for promoting the two main normative instruments of the Inter-American System on the subject: The Inter-American Convention for the Elimination of All Forms of Discrimination against Persons with Disabilities, and the Program of Action for the Decade of the Americas for the Rights and Dignity of Persons with Disabilities (PAD).

Accordingly, the OAS's action in the field of disability rights is focused basically in monitoring compliance of Member States to the Inter-American Convention, including the provision of adequate technical support to the Committee in charge of monitoring the Convention and to promote and monitor the compliance of Member States with the Program of Action, including evaluation and monitoring of the compliance reports submitted by the States.

2. The Inter-American Convention on Disability

The Inter-American Convention for the Elimination of All Forms of Discrimination against Persons with Disabilities (IACD) was adopted on 7 June 1999 by the OAS General Assembly in Resolution AG/RES. 1608 (XXIX-O/99), during its

---

1 Organization of American States, 'Persons with Disabilities' (2011) <www.sedi.oas.org/ddse/english/index-4.asp> last accessed 31 March 2016.

twenty-ninth ordinary session in Guatemala. Therefore, the IACD became the first instrument in international human rights law to set forth binding obligations to the States Parties.

The IACD entered into force on 14 September 2001 and has been ratified for nineteen Member States of the OAS. The treaty is a quite small instrument with only fourteen articles, among which only a few have real substantive content. The IACD can be regarded as a 'non-discrimination' type. Pursuant to Article 2 the 'objectives of this Convention are to prevent and eliminate all forms of discrimination against persons with disabilities and to promote their full integration into society.'[2]

Article 1 is devoted to defining what 'disability' means on the one hand, and on the other hand what 'discrimination against persons with disabilities' means. Paragraph 1 states that the term disability 'means a physical, mental, or sensory impairment, whether permanent or temporary, that limits the capacity to perform one or more essential activities of daily life, and which can be caused or aggravated by the economic and social environment.'[3]

At first glance, this definition seems to acknowledge the human rights perspective and the underlying principles of the social model of disability. The two elements of the social model, ie the impairment on the one hand and the social barriers on the other hand, can be identified. Yet the wording is perhaps not the most adequate and can give room for misconception.

A positive element of the IACD's definition of disability is perhaps the reference to 'permanent or temporary' impairment, which in most domestic jurisdictions, as well as in the UN Convention on the Rights of Persons with Disabilities (CRPD), is restricted to long-term situations. Likewise, the last sentence of Article 1(1) expresses that disability 'can be caused or aggravated by the economic and social environment.' This may provide a good basis to address the close relationship between disability and poverty, which in most of the Americas region is a major concern.

On the negative side, the IACD's definition of disability dangerously approaches the medical model of disability when it refers to an individual's impairments with the limitation of the capacity to carry out daily life activities. It is true that the definition that follows makes clear that the limitation is caused or aggravated by the economic and social environment. However, the first part of the sentence still remains confusing and gives room for interpreting the definition from a medical model perspective. In addition, and unlike CRPD, this definition does not include an equality standard.

Paragraph 2(a) states that term discrimination against persons with disabilities 'means any distinction, exclusion, or restriction based on a disability, record of disability, condition resulting from a previous disability, or perception of disability, whether present or past, which has the effect or objective of impairing or nullifying

2 art 2, Inter-American Convention for the Elimination of All Forms of Discrimination against Persons with Disabilities AG/RES 1608 (XXIX-O/99).

3 art 1(1), Inter-American Convention for the Elimination of All Forms of Discrimination against Persons with Disabilities AG/RES 1608 (XXIX-O/99).

the recognition, enjoyment, or exercise by a person with a disability of his or her human rights and fundamental freedoms.'

The definition adopts the classical triangular discriminatory structure in which there is an action or omission (including public or private behaviour and also restrictive legislation), followed by a disability-based ground (including past, present, future or perceived disabilities), and ending with a rights violation outcome (including impairing or nullifying the recognition, enjoyment, or exercise of human rights). Accordingly, this legal definition of discrimination against persons with disabilities clearly adopts a human-rights based approach, and has an overarching aspect which covers both direct and indirect discrimination. Paragraph 2(b) states that:

> '[A] distinction or preference adopted by a state party to promote the social integration or personal development of persons with disabilities does not constitute discrimination provided that the distinction or preference does not in itself limit the right of persons with disabilities to equality and that individuals with disabilities are not forced to accept such distinction or preference and continues asserting that "if, under a state's internal law, a person can be declared legally incompetent, when necessary and appropriate for his or her well-being, such declaration does not constitute discrimination"'

The first part of paragraph 2(b) deals with affirmative action measures which most of the Member States include in their legislation and which should not be considered as discrimination provided that the distinction or preference does not in itself limit the right of persons with disabilities to equality, and that individuals with disabilities are not forced to accept such distinction or preference. The last sentence of paragraph 2(b) deals with another common practice in most Member States ie the deprivation of legal capacity through a declaration of incompetence or incapacity which, in light of the IACD, should not be considered as discrimination. This statement brings up some conflicting implications in relation to the CRPD and will be addressed in detail in below.

As regards the obligations set forth by the IACD in relation to implementation of this definition of discrimination against persons with disabilities, Article 3 states that States Parties shall:

> '[A]dopt the legislative, social, educational, labor-related, or any other measures needed to eliminate discrimination against persons with disabilities and to promote their full integration into society, including, but not limited to: a. Measures to eliminate discrimination gradually and to promote integration by government authorities and/or private entities in providing or making available goods, services, facilities, programs, and activities such as employment, transportation, communications, housing, recreation, education, sports, law enforcement and administration of justice, and political and administrative activities; b. Measures to ensure that new buildings, vehicles, and facilities constructed or manufactured within their respective territories facilitate transportation, communications, and access by persons with disabilities; c. Measures to eliminate, to the extent possible, architectural, transportation, and communication obstacles to facilitate access and use by persons with

disabilities; and d. Measures to ensure that persons responsible for applying this Convention and domestic law in this area are trained to do so.'[4]

3. The Inter-American Committee on Disability

Article 6(1) of the IACD expresses that 'to follow up on the commitments undertaken in this Convention, a Committee for the Elimination of All Forms of Discrimination against Persons with Disabilities, composed of one representative appointed by each state party, shall be established.'[5] The Committee, known as CEDDIS, is the legitimate forum to review the progress of the IACD's implementation and to exchange experiences among States Parties. According to the rules of procedure the Committee is composed of one representative from each of the States Parties to the IACD. The members serve in their personal capacity, perform their functions autonomously, and must be technically well-versed and experienced in the various issues addressed in the IACD, among others, expertise on human, disability issues and public policy.[6]

In order to monitor the IACD, States Parties must submit a report to the Secretary General of the Organization for transmission to the Committee so that it may be examined and reviewed. The reports shall include information on measures adopted by the Member States pursuant to the IACD and on any progress made by the States Parties in eliminating all forms of discrimination against persons with disabilities. The reports shall also indicate any circumstances or difficulties affecting the degree of fulfilment of the obligations arising from the IACD.

Reports prepared by the Committee on the basis of its review of progress made in implementing the IACD, of the discussion by States Parties of their experiences, and of the consideration and analysis of reports presented by States Parties shall reflect the deliberations and include, inter alia, information on any measures adopted by the States Parties pursuant to the IACD. Such information shall reflect any progress States Parties have made in eliminating all forms of discrimination against persons with disabilities, and on any circumstances or difficulties they have encountered in the implementation of the IACD. Reports shall also include the Committee's conclusions, observations, and general suggestions for the progressive fulfilment of the IACD. Considering that the Committee held its first meeting in March 2007, so far there has been only one States Report examination[7] with the corresponding recommendations and observations of the Committee issued.[8]

---

4 ibid.

5 ibid.

6 According to art 2, Committee for the Elimination of All Forms of Discrimination against People with Disabilities, 'Rules of Procedure of the Committee for the elimination of all forms of discrimination against persons with disabilities' (5 March 2007) OEA/Ser.L/XXIV.2.1, CEDDIS/doc.4/07.

7 Copies of the state reports available at: Organizations of American States, 'CIDDAS Compliance Reports' (2014) <www.sedi.oas.org/ddse/english/index-4_reports.asp> last accessed 31 March 2016.

8 Copies of the Committee's observations available at: Organization of American States, 'Official Documents' (2010) <http://www.sedi.oas.org/ddse/documentos/Discapacidad/informe%20del%20CEDDIS.doc> 1 September 2014 (OEA/Ser.L/XXIV.2.3, CEDDIS/doc.63/10 rev. 2, 10 May 2010).

4. Disability within the OAS Human Rights System

The human rights system within the OAS, known as Inter-American Human Rights System, relies basically on two specific organs ie the Inter-American Commission on Human Rights (IACHR) and the Inter-American Court of Human Rights (IACtHR). The IACHR is a principal organ within the structure of the OAS which, pursuant to Article 106 of the OAS Charter, has the function of promoting 'the observance and protection of human rights and to serve as a consultative organ of the Organization in these matters.'[9] The work of the IACHR rests on three main pillars: a) the individual petition system; b) monitoring of the human rights situation in the Member States, and c) the attention devoted to priority thematic areas.

In relation to the individual petitions framework the IACHR has different procedures depending on the status ratification of the different human rights treaties within the scope of the OAS. The IACHR has the general competence to hear individual complaints in relation to all the Member States of the OAS regarding violations of the rights included in the Inter-American Declaration of Rights of Duties of Men of 1948.[10] This competence derives from the OAS Charter so any Member State may be examined by the Commission. Additionally, the IACHR has the specific competence to hear individual complaints in relation to those Member States which are part of the American Convention on Human Rights of 1969 (ACHR).[11] This competence derives from the ACHR so any Member State to the treaty may be examined by the Commission.

The ACHR has no explicit reference to disability yet it could be included as an implicit ground for non-discrimination under Article 1(1). In turn, the San Salvador Additional Protocol to the ACHR in the Area of Economic, Social and Cultural Rights has several references to disability in relation to the right to work (Article 6.2), the right to social security (Article 9.1); the right to education (Article 13.3.e); and a whole specific provision on the right to protection of the handicapped (Article 18).[12]

The IACtHR is a judicial organ composed of seven judges created by the ACHR with competence to hear cases of violations of the rights enshrined on the IACD, but only in relation to those Member States which have explicitly accepted the competence of the IACtHR whether generally or in relation to a specific case.[13]

---

9 The Commission is not a political body and is composed of seven members who shall be persons of high moral character and recognized competence in the field of human rights.

10 Inter-American Commission on Human Rights (IACHR), American Declaration of the Rights and Duties of Man, 2 May 1948, available at: http://www.refworld.org/docid/3ae6b3710.html last accessed 31 March 2016.

11 Organization of American States (OAS), American Convention on Human Rights, 'Pact of San Jose', Costa Rica, 22 November 1969, available at: http://www.refworld.org/docid/3ae6b36510.html last accessed 31 March 2016.

12 Organization of American States (OAS), Additional Protocol to the American Convention on Human Rights in the Area of Economic, Social and Cultural Rights ('Protocol of San Salvador'), 16 November 1999, A-52, available at: http://www.refworld.org/docid/3ae6b3b90.html last accessed 31 March 2016.

13 art 62(3) of the Organization of American States, American Convention on Human Rights, 'Pact of San Jose' (Costa Rica, 22 November 1969) <http://www.oas.org/dil/treaties_B-32_American_Convention_on_Human_Rights.htm> last accessed 31 March 2016. The jurisdiction of the Court shall comprise all cases concerning the interpretation and application of the provisions of this Convention that are submitted to it, provided that the States Parties to the

Both Member States and individuals can file complaints before the Court against other Member States. However, individuals are not entitled to bring a case directly to the IACtHR but must go through the Commission.

There are only three cases that have specifically addressed disability issues within the Inter-American Human Rights System. In *Victor Rosario Congo v Ecuador* the IACHR concluded that Ecuador was responsible for the violations of the ACHR in relation to the applicant – Mr Congo – who had a mental disability and who was placed in a detention center where he died, according to the fact-findings, as a result of physical abuse and lack of medical treatment.[14] The interesting approach of this case is that the Commission considered it 'pertinent to apply special standards to the determination of whether the provisions of the Convention have been complied with in cases involving persons suffering from mental illnesses'. More specifically the Commission asserted that 'in this case the person whose physical, mental and moral integrity was allegedly violated, suffered from a mental disability. Therefore, the Commission considers that in the present case the guarantees established in Article 5 of the American Convention must be interpreted in light of the Principles for the Protection of Persons with Mental Illness and for the Improvement of Mental Health Care'.[15]

In *Ximenes-Lopes v Brazil*, the IACtHR found Brazil responsible for the violation of the ACHR in relation to the applicant, Mr Ximenes-Lopes, who had a mental disability and who was placed in a mental institution where he died, according to the factfindings, as a result of physical abuse and lack of medical treatment.[16] The case was resolved a couple of months before the UN Convention on Disability was adopted so there is no reference to it in the reasoning of the IACtHR, nor is there a real acknowledgment of the social model of disability perspective. The IACtHR restricted its analysis to determine whether the Brazilian State had violated the rights to life and integrity, but left aside the question whether forced institutionalization was compatible with the OAS human rights framework. However the IACtHR did acknowledge that this case was 'special' in the sense that involved the human rights violations of a person with a 'mental disability' and accordingly emphasized 'the special attention the States must give to the persons with mental disabilities for they are particularly vulnerable.'[17] More specifically the IACtHR asserted that 'any person who is in a vulnerable condition is entitled to special protection, which must be provided by the States if they are to comply with their general duties to respect and guarantee human rights' and reaffirmed that 'not only should the States refrain from violating such rights, but also adopt positive measures, to be determined according to the specific needs of protection of the legal person, either because of his personal condition or the specific situation he is in, such as his disabilities.'[18]

In *Furlan v Argentina*, the IACtHR for a time used the CRPD in order to interpret

---

case recognize or have recognized such jurisdiction, whether by special declaration pursuant to the preceding paragraphs, or by a special agreement.

14 Inter-American Commission on Human Rights, 'REPORT 63/99, CASE 11.427 VICTOR ROSARIO CONGO ECUADOR '(April 13, 1999).

15 ibid 54.

16 *Ximenes-Lopes v Brazil* (IACtHR 4 July 2006) C 149.

17 ibid para 101.

18 ibid para 103.

the rights of a person with disability within the OAS system. According to fact-findings, Sebastian Furlan, a 14-year-old child, entered into a facility property of the Argentinian Army and was severely injured. He was certified as being 70% disabled. His father filed suit for civil liability against the Government, and the Lower Court found the State responsible and awarded compensation. However, the enforcement of the judgment was irregular due to the application of an internal law which converted the compensation in consolidated bonds issued for sixteen-year terms.[19]

While Furlan was not a strategic case in the sense of directly addressing challenges derived from the implementation of the social model of disability (the case was basically about adequate state compensation towards to victim), it allowed the IACtHR to elaborate several relevant considerations in relation to the right to access to justice. And perhaps the most interesting approach of this ruling is the cross-reference of both child and disability perspectives.[20]

First, the IACtHR acknowledges that both the IACD and the CRPD take into account the 'social model of disability' 'which implies that disability is not only defined by the presence of a physical, mental, intellectual or sensory impairment, but is interrelated with the barriers or limitations that exist socially for persons to exercise their rights effectively'.[21] Second, the IACtHR reaffirms previous doctrine in relation to the special protection principle asserting that '...any person who is in a vulnerable situation is entitled to special protection, based on the special duties that the State must comply with to satisfy the general obligation to respect and ensure human rights. The IACtHR calls to mind that it is not sufficient for States to refrain from violating rights, and that it is imperative to adopt affirmative measures to be determined according to the particular protection needs of the subject of rights, whether on account of his personal situation or his specific circumstances, such as disability...'[22] Third, the IACtHR acknowledges the fact that persons with disabilities are often subjected to discrimination, and accordingly '...States must adopt the appropriate legislative, social, educational, employment or other measures necessary to prevent all discrimination associated with mental disabilities, and to promote the full integration of such persons into society. Appropriate access to justice plays a fundamental role to address these types of discrimination...'[23] Finally the IACtHR recognizes that the CRPD contains rules on the importance of effective access to justice for persons with disabilities 'on an equal basis with others, including through the provision of procedural and age-appropriate accommodations'. Therefore, the

---

19 *Furlan and Family v Argentina* (IACtHR 31 August 2012) C 246.

20 '...the Court notes that in the instant case, the alleged violations of the rights enshrined in the American Convention are in relation to the fact that Sebastián Furlan was a child at the time of the accident and that, consequently, this accident resulted in his becoming an adult with disabilities. Taking these two facts into account, the Court considers that the alleged violations must be analyzed in light of: i) the international body of law on the protection of children, and ii) the international standards on the protection and guarantee of the rights of persons with disabilities. These two legal frameworks should be considered as cross-references in the analysis of the instant case...', ibid, para 124.

21 In fact, the Court goes on asserting that '...The types of limitations or barriers commonly encountered by people with functional diversity in society are, among others, physical or architectural types of barriers, communication, attitudinal or socioeconomic barriers...', ibid, para 133.

22 ibid, para 134.

23 ibid para 135.

IACtHR '...considers that when vulnerable persons are involved, as in the case of a person with disabilities, it is imperative to take the pertinent actions, such as ordering the authorities to give priority to addressing and settling such cases, in order to avoid delays in their processing so as to ensure a prompt decision and execution thereof...'[24]

5. CRPD within OAS Member States

Among the thirty-five Member States of the OAS, nineteen have ratified the IACD. Twenty-seven Member States of the OAS have ratified the CRPD. All nineteen Member States to the IACD have also ratified the CRPD.[25] Eight members of the OAS have ratified the CRPD but not the IACD.[26] Cuba is a Member State to the CRPD but not to the IACD, yet it should be pointed out that Cuba was excluded from participation in the OAS under a decision adopted by the Eighth Meeting of Consultation on 31 January 1962.

The panorama within the OAS shows two clear trends. On the one hand, all members of the IACD are also members of the CRPD, and on the other hand, a growing number of Member States of the OAS are ratifying the CRPD without an apparent need to ratify the regional treaty. Consequently, the need to analyse the relationship and possible overlaps between these two international instruments becomes crucial. For this reason, a brief analysis of the applicable rules of international law on treaties status and relationships will be carried out.

Unlike most domestic legal systems, international law does not have a unified or centralized legislative body. Consequently, international law is considered as a fragmented legal system at both institutional and substantive levels.[27] The phenomenon of the fragmentation of international law has been intensively addressed by the UN International Law Commission (ILC) from 2002–2006 ending with the adoption of a series of conclusions[28] and an analytical study entitled: The 'Fragmentation of International Law: Difficulties arising from the Diversification and Expansion of International Law.'[29]

According to the ILC, in 'applying international law it is often necessary to determine the precise relationship between two or more rules and principles that are both valid and applicable in respect of a situation. For that purpose the relevant relationships fall into two general types:

Relationships of interpretation. This is the case where one norm assists in the

---

24 ibid para 196.

25 Argentina, Bolivia, Brazil, Chile, Colombia, Costa Rica, Dominican Republic, Ecuador, El Salvador, Guatemala, Haiti, Honduras, Mexico, Nicaragua, Panama, Paraguay, Peru, Uruguay and Venezuela.

26 Belize, Canada, Jamaica, St. Vincent & Grenadines, Cuba, Dominica, Grenada and Barbados.

27 M Koskenniemi and P Leino, 'Fragmentation of International Law? Postmodern Anxieties' (2002) 15 Leiden Journal of International Law 553.

28 Study Group on the Fragmentation of International Law, 'Difficulties arising from the Diversification and Expansion of International Law' (A/CN.4/L.682, 13 April 2006) <www.untreaty.un.org/ilc/texts/instruments/english/draft%20articles/1_9_2006.pdf> last accessed 31 March 2016.

29 ibid.

interpretation of another. A norm may assist in the interpretation of another norm, for example as an application, clarification, updating or modification of the latter. In such situation, both norms are applied in conjunction.

Relationships of conflict. This is the case where two norms that are both valid and applicable point to incompatible decisions so that a choice must be made between them. The basic rules concerning the resolution of normative conflicts are to be found in the Vienna Convention on the Law of Treaties (VCLT).[30]

At first glance, the interaction between the IACD and the CRPD reveals a potential for both interpretation and conflict relationships. As regards interpretation relationships, most provisions of the IACD are likely to be interpreted and complemented in the light of the CRPD; some other provisions of the IACD will provide a good basis for broadening the interpretation of the UN CRPD. As regards the conflicting aspect, the IACD enshrines at least one provision which is clearly incompatible with the CRPD, discussed below. In this respect, and as ILC points out, international law provides some tools to address these relationships, yet these tools are rather vague if they are not considered in relation to a specific situation.

It is generally accepted that all treaties have equal status, and accordingly there is no formal hierarchy between them.[31] However, there are some substantive rules which can be issued in international law to deal with the content of the treaty and not with the status of the treaty itself. These rules can be summarized in the *jus cogens* rule,[32] the *lex specialis derogare lege generali* rule,[33] and the *lex posterior derogat priori* rule.[34]

The analysis to the present case is in some way less problematic, as there is no apparent relationship between a general rule of international law and a specific rule of a so-called 'self-contained regime,' nor does there seem to be a manifest conflict between a general and a *jus cogens* norm.

It is less clear, however, if the CRPD should be considered as a *lex specialis* in relation to the IACD or vice versa. Both treaties can be considered as part of international human rights law, and both treaties address the rights of persons with disabilities from a non-discrimination perspective. The regional character of the IACD does not seem relevant as an element of special law. The ILC's analytic study on fragmentation deals with differentiation between types of special law but only in relation to rules derived from two different self-contained regimes.[35] In the present case the *lex specialis* rule does not seem to provide clarity on the conflicting relationship between the IACD and the CRPD, yet it may be used to deal with

---

30 ibid 2.

31 Perhaps the only exception to this rule is art 103 of the UN Charter which reads as follows: 'In the event of a conflict between the obligations of the Members of the United Nations under the present Charter and their obligations under any other international agreement, their obligations under the present Charter shall prevail.' United Nations, Charter of the United Nations, 24 October 1945, 1 UNTS XVI, available at: http://www.refworld.org/docid/3ae6b3930.html last accessed 31 March 2016.

32 Study Group on the Fragmentation of International Law (n 28) 324–409.

33 ibid 46–222.

34 ibid 223–323.

35 ibid 55.

differences in interpretation. For example, IACD's definition of 'disability' could be used to interpret the CRPD's definition of 'persons with disabilities' as to cover both long or temporary impairments, which the wording of the latter restricts solely to 'long-term impairments.'

The *lex posterior derogat priori* rule seems to be much more helpful to the present case. According to Article 30 of the VCLT, when all the parties to a treaty are also parties to an earlier treaty on the same subject, and the earlier treaty is not suspended or terminated, then it applies only to the extent its provisions are compatible with those of the later treaty. This is an expression of the principle according to which 'later law supersedes earlier law.'[36] When there is a manifest conflict of two provisions like Articles 1(2)(b) of the IACD and Article 12(2) of the CRPD, the *lex posterior* rule clearly points towards the prevalence of the earliest law, ie the CRPD. As regards interpretation relationships, the *lex posteriori* rule should be used in a more flexible way, especially considering the human rights character of the provisions at stake. The CRPD's provisions should not be considered as constantly derogating the IACD's provisions, as long as the latter reflect a more protective or far-reaching scope than the former.

The conclusions referred to above can provide some clarity on the substantive aspect of fragmentation, yet they cannot solve further conflicts arising from the institutional fragmentation of international law. Both the IACD and the CRPD have fragmented monitoring mechanisms which can bring an additional element of conflict to the equation.

Within the OAS system the IACD can only be directly applied by the IACHR but with some restrictions and in a subsidiary way by the IACtHR. Additionally, the CEDDIS has no competence to deal with individual complaints, and can only monitor compliance with the IACD through the analysis of state reports.[37] In turn, the CRPD cannot be directly applied by any OAS bodies and can only be used as an interpretative tool in deciding on violations of any Inter-American human rights treaties.[38]

6. The Need to Reinterpret Disability Law within the OAS in the Light of the CRPD

The previous analysis within this article reveals the need to reinterpret disability law within the OAS, especially the IACD, in light of the CRPD. A good step forward was given by the IACtHR when addressing the *Furlan* case. It relied on several provisions of the CRPD in order to analyze the alleged violations of the rights enshrined on ACHR. Explicitly the IACtHR stated '...in the instant case, the alleged violations of the rights enshrined in the American Convention are in relation to the fact that

[36] Study Group on the Fragmentation of International Law (n 28).

[37] This has not prevented the Committee from issuing an important general observation on the relationship between CEDDIS and CRPD, which will be addressed in Part 6.

[38] As seen above, in the recent case *Furlan and Family v Argentina* the IACtHR considered that the alleged violations must be analyzed in light of (....) '...ii) the international standards on the protection and guarantee of the rights of persons with disabilities...', namely, the CRPD (n 19).

Sebastian Furlan was a child at the time of the accident and that, consequently, this accident resulted in his becoming an adult with disabilities. Taking these two facts into account, the IACtHR considers that the alleged violations must be analyzed in light of: i) the international body of law on the protection of children, and ii) the international standards on the protection and guarantee of the rights of persons with disabilities. These two legal frameworks should be considered as cross-references in the analysis of the instant case…'

Accordingly the Court uses as guidelines for interpreting the human rights of Sebastian Furlan the following CRPD provisions: Article 1(2) on the concept of person with disability,[39] Article 3 on general principles,[40] Article 7 on children with disabilities,[41] Article 13 on access to justice,[42] Article 25 on the right to health,[43] Article 26 on habilitation and rehabilitation,[44] and Article 28 on the right to adequate standard of living and social protection.[45] Another important step towards an integrated interpretation of disability rights within the OAS system was given on 28 April 2011, when CEDDIS issued an important 'General Observation' in relation to the need to interpret Article I.2(b) in line of the IACD in the context of Article 12 of the CRPD.[46]

On October 2010, CEDDIS considered the regulatory and conceptual discrepancy between the IACD and the CRPD with respect to the institution of legal incompetence and protection rules as a mechanism for the exercise of the legal capacity of persons with disabilities. In this respect, and given that the process of reforming the IACD could be complex and cumbersome the CEDDIS suggested that they, as a Committee, adopt an interpretation criterion that could be disseminated on a larger scale. The observation begins by acknowledging that:

> 'most Civil Codes, especially in Latin America, still retain in their legal provisions institutions such as declaration of insanity and protection as a way to afford legal representation to persons with disabilities, particularly persons with hearing or mental disabilities, and that said institutions need to be revised in light of the provisions of Article 12 of the United Nations Convention on the Rights of Persons with Disabilities, as mandated in Article 4.1(a) and (b) of said Convention.'[47]

The Committee declares that the criterion established in Article I.2(b) of the IACD, in as much as it establishes that 'If, under a state's internal law, a person can be declared legally incompetent, when necessary and appropriate for his or her well-being, such

---

39 *Furlan and Familiy v Argentina* (n 23) para 132.
40 ibid para 131.
41 ibid paras 136 and 229.
42 ibid paras 137, 196, 229 and 241.
43 ibid para 282.
44 ibid para 288.
45 ibid para 254.
46 General Observation of the Committee for the Elimination of All Forms of Discrimination against Persons with Disabilities on the need to interpret art I.2(b) in fine of the Inter-American Convention on the Elimination of All Forms of Discrimination against Persons with Disabilities in the context of art 12 of the United Nations Convention on the Rights of Persons with Disabilities, OEA/ Ser.L/XXIV.3.1, CEDDIS/doc.12(I-E/11) rev.1, 28 April 2011.
47 ibid 3.

declaration does not constitute discrimination,'[48] seriously contradicts the provisions of Articles 2 and 12 of the CRPD, and accordingly, 'that the aforementioned criterion must be reinterpreted in light of the latter document currently in force.'[49]

The Committee shows its concern in relation to the existing substituted decision-making mechanisms in the region and that 'what the CRPD demands is that support be based on trust, provided with respect, and never against the will of the person with disabilities. The Committee states that:

> '[P]ersons with disabilities do very often need support, but not replacement. The support envisioned by the Convention as "appropriate" focuses on abilities (more than on disabilities) and on elimination of obstacles in the environment so as to facilitate access and pro-active inclusion in social life (the physical and cultural environment, justice system, housing and transportation, social and health services, educational and labor opportunities, cultural, professional, and political life, sports, and recreation).'[50]

Moreover the Committee asserts that:

> '[U]nlike substitutive protection systems, in which people are trapped and objectified as wards, support guided by the new human rights approach is geared toward increasing personal freedoms in people's lives, broadening the spheres in which they can decide for themselves, and enhancing recognition of the value of their contribution to the society they form part of as citizens and "as part of human diversity and humanity" (Articles 3(d), 8.1(c), and 8.2(a) iii of the Convention.'[51]

The Committee observes that the CRPD does not include a definition of disability like the IACD, but it does, however, include a definition of 'person with disability' in Article 1. In the view of the Committee:

> '(...) [T]he strategy used in the Convention is to make explicit mention of certain groups in the definition, to highlight their greater vulnerability to discrimination and the more pressing need to design strategies for strengthening these groups' ability to exercise and claim their rights. A review of domestic legislations and of the actual practices of states shows that it is precisely these groups to whom legal capacity is denied (...).'[52]

To conclude, the Committee states that 'Article I.2(b) of the OAS Inter-American Convention on the Elimination of All Forms of Discrimination against Persons With Disabilities needs to be reinterpreted in light of the new paradigm set forth in the aforementioned Article 12'.[53]

---

48 ibid 3–4.
49 ibid 5.
50 ibid 6.
51 ibid.
52 ibid 7.
53 ibid.

Chapter 35

THE CONVENTION ON THE RIGHTS OF PERSONS WITH DISABILITIES AND THE EUROPEAN UNION

David Hosking

1. Introduction

The United Nations Convention on the Rights of Persons with Disabilities (CRPD)[1] is the first international treaty that the European Union (hereafter EU or Union)[2] has signed and ratified. The CRPD touches on policy areas exclusive to the EU and many more which are shared between the EU and its Member States. After outlining where the CRPD fits in the EU legal order, its potential impact on three policy areas will be considered – personal equal treatment policy, transport policy and the European Social Fund. With one notable exception, EU law and policy in the three areas substantially incorporate the principles and objectives of the CRPD. While it is too early to say exactly how the CRPD will affect developments in EU disability law, it will be a highly persuasive authority supporting the EU taking a more vigorous approach to implementing its disability strategy, and actually bringing to completion or making substantial progress towards achieving many of its long-term policy objectives.

2. EU Adherence to the CRPD

The EU signed the CRPD, but not the Optional Protocol, on 30 March 2007 and ratified it on 23 December 2010; it came into effect for the EU on 22 January 2011.[3] In the EU legal order, the CRPD is second in priority to the EU treaties. It takes priority over all secondary EU legislation, the interpretation of which must, as much as possible, be in conformity with the obligations assumed under the CRPD. Where

---

1 United Nations Convention on the Rights of Persons with Disabilities (CRPD) (2006) A/Res/61/106 (13 December 2006).

2 The EU is the successor organisation to the European Community which negotiated and ratified the CRPD.

3 Council Decision of 26 November 2009 concerning the conclusion, by the European Community, of the United Nations Convention on the Rights of Persons with Disabilities (2010/48/EC) [2010] OJ L 23/35. Annex II sets out the declaration of Community competences as required by art 44(1) of the CRPD (2006), and notes that as the scope and exercise of Community competence evolves, the declaration will be amended. See G de Burca, 'The European Union in the Negotiation of the UN Disability Convention' (2010) 35 European Law Review 174.

EU legislation is ambiguous or open to more than one interpretation, the institutions of the EU should adopt the interpretation most consistent with the CRPD.[4]

In its declaration of competences, required of regional integration organisations, the EU set out its areas of exclusive and shared competence. The EU shares competence with the Member States in matters of discrimination, free movement of goods, persons, services and capital, agriculture, transportation, taxation, internal market, equal pay for men and women, trans-European networks and statistics.[5] In these areas, the declaration states that the EU assumes competence only if it has exercised its option to legislate or if existing common rules apply. Because of the shared competence, the role of the EU in the implementation of the CRPD in these areas becomes indeterminate and subject to legal and policy options. But where the EU does act, its legislation takes precedence over domestic legislation. A key unresolved issue is whether the EU is only required to act to implement a provision of the CRPD if it has decided to act upon a matter within its competence, or whether if a matter is or could be within its competence it must act to implement the CRPD.[6]

The practical consequences of the EU's adherence to the CRPD are hard to assess at this time. Its provisions are sufficiently indeterminate that there is much room for interpretation about the scope of the rights and what is required to implement them. It will not be until the European Court of Justice (ECJ) decides cases engaging provisions of the CRPD that its extent and impact on EU law will be known. Apart from its impact on EU law, in the development of policy and design of programmes EU officials will have an eye to what they think the CRPD requires. An appeal to CRPD commitments will have an important, though hard to define, impact on EU policy. The indeterminate nature of the rights protected by the CRPD also allows for a variety of interest groups to argue that the EU has or has not lived up to its commitments, that the rights in question are already adequately protected or that proposed measures will not adequately advance those rights or meet the EU's commitments.

3. Personal Equal Treatment Policy

Article 19 of the Treaty on the Functioning of the European Union TFEU authorises the Council of the EU to 'take appropriate action to combat discrimination based on [...] disability'.[7] Article 5 of the CRPD requires contracting parties to prohibit discrimination based on disability, ensure there is 'effective legal protection' from discrimination and take 'all appropriate steps to ensure that reasonable accommodation is provided.'[8]

---

4 See European Foundation Centre, 'Study on challenges and good practices in the implementation of the UN Convention on the Rights of Persons with Disabilities' (Brussels 2010) 28.

5 Council Decision (n 3) Annex II, para 2.

6 G Quinn and E Flynn, 'The Past and Future of EU Non-Discrimination Law and Policy on the Ground of Disability' (2012) 60 American Journal of Comparative Law 23, 27.

7 Consolidated Version of the Treaty on the Functioning of the European Union [2008] OJ C115/47.

8 Article 5 CRPD.

In 2000, the EU adopted the Employment Equality Directive (hereafter EED)[9] which prohibits discrimination based on disability in relation to all aspects of employment, vocational guidance and training, and membership of and participation in worker, employer and professional organisations in the public and private sectors.

Although the Commission proposed a Goods and Service Equality Directive (hereafter the proposed GSED) that would prohibit discrimination in the provision of goods and services in 2008, the EU has not been able to reach an agreement on a legislative text. The current draft would prohibit discrimination in both the public and private sectors in the areas of social protection, social assistance, social housing, health care, education and access to and supply of goods and other services, including housing, which are available to the public.[10] The EU has clearly failed to live up to the expectations that were raised when it signed the CRPD by its failure to adopt this anti-discrimination legislation.

In the CRPD, persons with disabilities 'include those who have long-term physical, mental, intellectual or sensory impairments which in interaction with various barriers may hinder their full and effective participation in society on an equal basis with others.'[11] Who else might be included as a person with disabilities for the purposes of implementing the CRPD is left to the contracting parties. Although there is no definition of disability in the EED, the ECJ has held that, as used in that Directive, disability 'must be understood as referring to a limitation which results in particular from physical, mental or psychological impairments and which hinders the participation of the person concerned in professional life' and which will 'probab[ly] [...] last for a long time.'[12] (The proposed GSED incorporates the CRPD definition of persons with disabilities.) Since the CRPD does not positively require an expansive interpretation of disability, it will be necessary to resort to arguments based on the CRPD's description of disability and its general principles to try to introduce a much broader conception of disability into EU law.

The definition of discrimination in the CRPD includes the 'denial of reasonable accommodation,' which is defined as 'necessary and appropriate modification and adjustments not imposing a disproportionate or undue burden, where needed in a particular case.'[13] Article 5 of the CRPD requires the contracting parties to take 'all appropriate steps to ensure that reasonable accommodation is provided.' Article 5 of the EED requires employers to provide reasonable accommodation by taking

---

9 Council Directive 2000/78/EC of 27 November 2000 establishing a general framework for equal treatment in employment and occupation [2000] OJ L303/16, which also prohibits discrimination based on religion or belief, age or sexual orientation.

10 Council, 'Proposal for a Council Directive on implementing the principle of equal treatment between persons irrespective of religion or belief, disability, age or sexual orientation – Consolidated text' (22 May 2014) 9876/14. There is the possibility that the proposed GSED will be withdrawn and replaced with an entirely new proposal: See L Waddington, 'Future prospects for EU equality law: lessons to be learnt from the proposed Equal Treatment Directive' (2011) 36 European Law Review 163.

11 art 1 CRPD.

12 Case C-13/05 *Chacón Navas v Eurest Colectividades SA* [2006] ECR I-6467, paras 43 and 45. In 2013, the Court modified this definition in light of the CRPD by the addition of the nine italicized words: '(...) a limitation which results in particular from physical, mental or psychological impairments which *in interaction with various barriers may* hinder the *full and effective* participation (...)': Joined Cases C 335/11 and C 337/11 *HK Danmark.*

13 art 2 CRPD.

'appropriate measures, where needed in a particular case, to enable a person with a disability to have access to, participate in, or advance in employment [...] unless such measures would impose a disproportionate burden on the employer.' (The Directive makes no mention of any duty on unions to cooperate with employer efforts to provide an accommodation.) In contrast to the EED, the proposed GSED includes the denial of reasonable accommodation in its definition of discrimination. Both reasonable accommodation and the duty to provide it are, however, described in similar language in both the EED and the proposed GSED.

The EED and proposed GSED differ in how they deal with the factors to be considered in assessing claims that an accommodation would impose a disproportionate burden. In the EED those factors, set out in the introductory recitals which have only an interpretative role in EU law, are 'the financial and other costs entailed, the scale and financial resources of the organisation or undertaking and the possibility of obtaining public funding or any other assistance.'[14]

In contrast, the proposed GSED sets out the factors in a substantive provision. These include 'the size and resources of the organisation or enterprise,' 'the estimated cost,' 'the estimated benefit for persons with disabilities' taking into account the impact of not providing the accommodation and the frequency of use of the goods or services, 'the life span of infrastructures and objects which are used to provide a service,' 'the historical, cultural, artistic or architectural value of the (...) property' and 'whether the measure in question is impracticable or unsafe.'[15]

Although the descriptions of the duty to provide reasonable accommodation in the existing and proposed Directives accord well with that found in the CRPD, there is a clear danger that the judicial and administrative interpretation of a 'disproportionate or undue burden' will give much too much weight to the interests of employers and service providers as opposed to the needs of the particular disabled person. The general principles set out in the CRPD may be used to argue for the broadest interpretation of the duty to accommodate and the narrowest interpretation of its limiting parameters of disproportionate or undue burden.

The CRPD may be the catalyst to resolving the impasse in achieving agreement on a Directive to prohibit discrimination in the provision of goods and services. It may also prompt the ECJ to take a more expansive approach to the meaning of disability in EU law and to adopt a generous interpretation of the duty to provide reasonable accommodation.

4. Transportation

The EU shares competence in the transportation sector with the Member States. Under the TFEU, the EU may establish rules for international transport into and within the EU, set operating conditions for non-resident carriers, take measures to improve safety, and make 'any other appropriate provisions' consistent with

---

14 Employment Equality Directive, recital 21.

15 Proposed Goods and Service Equality Directive, art 4b(1).

implementing the EU's transport policy.[16] EU transport policy is directly affected by the overarching prohibition against discrimination in Article 5 of the CRPD and the requirement to promote accessibility of transportation systems in Article 9.

EU Regulations prohibiting discrimination based on disability cover air, rail, coach, inland waterways and marine passenger services. The first such Regulation was the Disabled Air Passenger Rights Regulation.[17] This Regulation applies to persons whose mobility when using transportation is reduced due to any disability or their age and 'whose situation needs appropriate attention and the adaptation to his or her particular needs of the service made available to all passengers.'[18] It prohibits airlines from refusing to accept reservations from, or to carry, a disabled person except if the refusal is based on safety requirements or if it is 'physically impossible' to embark the person or load accompanying mobility equipment. In these cases, the airline has to 'make reasonable efforts to propose an acceptable alternative.'[19] A person who is refused carriage must be immediately told the reasons for the refusal.[20] Provisions are also made for providing scheduling and safety information in alternative formats. The 'managing body of the airport' is responsible for ensuring that assistance is provided without charge in the airport terminal and immediately adjacent service areas if the traveller provides 48 hours' notice or, if no notification is made, for making 'all reasonable efforts to provide' the required assistance.[21] Airlines are responsible for providing assistance on their planes.[22] Both the managing body and the airline are responsible for ensuring that their staff receive suitable training.[23]

Unlike the Disabled Air Passenger Rights Regulation, the rights of disabled people to assistance when travelling by rail, coach, bus, inland waterways and sea are mainstreamed into Regulations covering the rights of all passengers.[24] These Regulations cover information to be provided by the transport provider, ticketing, insurance obligations, obligations in cases of delay, special provisions for disabled persons, the definition and monitoring of service quality standards, security and complaint procedures. The specific provisions related to disabled people are modelled on those found in the Disabled Air Passenger Rights Regulation.

---

16 Treaty on the Functioning of the European Union, art 91(1). See generally the transport policy provisions in TFEU arts 90–100.

17 Council Regulation (EC) 1107/2006 concerning the rights of disabled persons and persons with reduced mobility when travelling by air [2006] OJ L 204/1 arts 3, 4(a) and 4(b).

18 ibid art 2(a).

19 ibid art 3 and 4(1).

20 ibid art 4(3) and (4).

21 ibid art 7. The types of assistance which must be provided are set out in Annex I of the Regulation and include assistance getting to the check-in counters, checking in, getting to the departure area, boarding the aircraft and being seated by means of lifts and associated equipment, disembarking, collecting baggage and exiting the airport: provisions are made for persons assisting the disabled traveller and service animals.

22 ibid art 10. The types of assistance which must be provided are set out in Annex II of the Regulation.

23 ibid art 11.

24 Council Regulation (EC) No 1371/2007 of 23 October 2007 on rail passengers' rights and obligations [2007] OJ L 315/14; Council Regulation (EU) No 1177/2010 of 24 November 2010 concerning the rights of passengers when travelling by sea and inland waterway and amending Regulation (EC) No 2006/2004 [2010] OJ L 334/1; Council Regulation (EU) No 181/2011 of 16 February 2011 concerning the rights of passengers in bus and coach transport and amending Regulation (EC) No 2006/2004 [2011] OJ L 55/1.

The passenger rights Regulations are examples of legislation to ensure equal treatment (non-discrimination) with reasonable accommodation. However, the scope of the duty to accommodate is limited by the degree to which current modes of transport are physically inaccessible to many disabled people. Article 9 of the CRPD requires the contracting parties to 'take appropriate action to ensure [...] access, on an equal basis with others, to [...] transportation,' including taking 'appropriate measures' to develop and enforce minimum accessibility standards.

An example of an EU measure setting minimum standards for accessibility is the Directive setting out a common standard for passenger vehicles carrying more than eight people.[25] The Directive sets out detailed technical specifications for the manufacture of these vehicles and has special provisions dealing with accessibility for disabled passengers. Any vehicle which meets these standards may be granted a 'type-approval' certificate which means that it can be sold and used everywhere in the EU. The effect of this Directive will be that manufacturers who tool up to meet the specifications will make all their vehicles meet them and, by default, as older vehicles are pulled from the road the only new ones available will meet these standards. It is doubtful that the CRPD requires that inaccessible buses be replaced with accessible ones before their regular replacement schedule. Since buses may be serviceable for up to 20 years, this is a long-term process. However, the CRPD's provisions remain important in many ways: at a political level, appeals to the commitments made through the CRPD will affect transportation planning at both national and local levels; when new equipment is ordered, their specifications should meet CRPD requirements; and, when transportation infrastructure, such as stations, terminals or bus stops are constructed or undergo significant renovation, they too should be made fully accessible. The CRPD will also provide political support for developing similar technical standards for other modes of transportation which have not yet attracted EU attention.

EU transport policy includes a variety of measures to ensure disabled people have equal access to transportation. The passenger rights legislation and the type approval procedures deal with barriers due to discrimination and barriers due to inaccessible transport infrastructure. Article 9 of the CRPD commits the contracting parties to take 'appropriate measures' to ensure equal access to the physical environment, including transportation, as well as information and services and facilities. Unlike the immediacy of the commitment to prohibit discrimination set out in Article 5, the parties need only take steps to progressively achieve a fully accessible society. Transportation policy is an example of how a legal right to non-discrimination intersects with a programmatic right to accessibility. Apart from relatively minor modifications to infrastructure or adjustments to the policies and practices of transportation services and prohibiting adverse treatment due to bias and stereotyping, it is unlikely that significant improvements in access to transport services can be achieved through individual discrimination complaints. The CRPD will provide a legal and political basis for the wide variety of other hard and soft law initiatives which will be required to make the transportation system truly accessible.

---

[25] Council Directive 2001/85/EC of 20 November 2001 relating to special provisions for vehicles used for the carriage of passengers comprising more than eight seats in addition to the driver's seat, and amending Directives 70/156/EEC and 97/27/EC [2001] OJ L 42/1.

5. European Social Fund – Employment

The European Social Fund (ESF)[26] is the largest of the EU's financial instruments to implement employment and social policies, with an annual budget in the order of €10 billion and some 8.5 million people a year benefiting from ESF programmes.[27] The ESF provides co-financing along with the Member States for vocational training, counselling and other supports to increase the employability of people who are unemployed, under-employed and first entering or returning to the labour market. Projects supported by the ESF must contribute to increasing the participation rate of economically inactive people, combating social exclusion— especially for disadvantaged groups such as disabled people— and promoting equality and non-discrimination.

Under Article 27 of the CRPD, which deals with work and employment, the contracting parties recognise the right for disabled people to work, on an equal basis with others, in a labour market and work environment that is 'open, inclusive and accessible.'[28] The Article adds a number of employment-related details to the general principles of non-discrimination and inclusion. Contracting parties must take 'appropriate steps' to safeguard and promote these rights, which include prohibiting discrimination, providing effective access to work-readiness, job-search and rehabilitation programmes, employing disabled persons in the public sector and promoting self-employment and employment in the private sector.

The general Regulation governing the Structural Funds, which includes the ESF, specifies that the Commission and Member States must take appropriate steps to prevent any discrimination based on sex, racial or ethnic origin, religion or belief, disability, age or sexual orientation during the various stages of implementation of the Funds and, in particular, in the access to them. In particular, accessibility for disabled persons shall be one of the criteria to be observed in defining operations co-financed by the Funds and to be taken into account during the various stages of implementation.[29]

The EU's involvement in the management of the ESF is proportionate to its contribution. Its ability to monitor and require changes to particular projects is constrained because of the role and function of the Member States in the programme. The EU, however, can set all the criteria that need to be met to apply for and receive funding. When developing the programme's parameters, the EU must ensure its rules, at a minimum, comply with and, preferably, promote the objectives of the CRPD. At the EU level it is arguable that the Regulations contain the essential obligations imposed by the CRPD for inclusion, non-discrimination, and consultation with disabled people even if there is much room for improvement in the application of

---

[26] Council Regulation (EU) No 1304/2013 of 17 December 2013 on the European Social Fund and repealing Council Regulation (EC) No 1081/2006 [2013] OJ L 347/470.

[27] European Commission, 'Progress: The EU programme for employment and social solidarity 2007–2013' (OOPEC 2007) 8. The 2014 – 2020 ESF budget will be at least €70 billion.

[28] art 27 CRPD.

[29] Council Regulation (EC) No 1083/2006 of 11 July 2006 laying down general provisions on the European Regional Development Fund, the European Social Fund and the Cohesion Fund and repealing Regulation (EC) No 1260/1999 [2006] OJ L 210/25, art 16 (currently Council Regulation (EU) No 1303/2013 of 17 December 2013).

the provisions supporting social inclusion at the Member States' overall planning and the individual project stages.

The most likely influence of the CRPD on ESF policy will be as a persuasive authority for more and better inclusion of disabled people in the various projects it funds. Projects which cannot show how they are, or will become, physically accessible, and how their employment practices implement the duty to provide accommodation, should not receive funding. Disability interest groups will have to scrutinize the individual projects funded by the ESF in order to know how much disabled people are actually included and what form their participation takes. With that data, the ESF can be measured against the standards of inclusion mandated by the CRPD. Adjustments to the programme's project selection criteria, improved assessment of project applications and EU-mandated data-collection procedures may be required to ensure the CRPD rights are respected throughout the administration of the ESF.

6. Conclusion

The CRPD affects most of the policy areas within the competences conferred on the EU. EU disability policy already reflects the CRPD's guiding principles. Its practical impact will depend on how broadly or narrowly the CRPD's provisions are read by the ECJ and EU policy drivers.

The failure to adopt legislation to prohibit discrimination in the provision of goods and services is the most glaring gap in implementing the EU's immediate commitments under the CRPD. To avoid the embarrassment of the CRPD's Committee on the Rights of Persons with Disabilities commenting adversely on this failure, the Council will be under strong political pressure to adopt something similar to the Commission's 2008 proposal. However, the devil will be in the details and it will be important for disability interest groups to appeal to the CRPD in arguing for a sufficiently robust Directive to make a real change in the lives of disabled people.

Champions of disability policy within EU institutions will find ample support for more vigorous implementation of EU disability policy initiatives as set out in the EU's most recent iteration of its disability strategy.[30] Organisations which represent disabled people will be expected to continually hold the EU accountable for implementing the commitments it undertook when it ratified the CRPD.

---

[30] European Commission, 'European Disability Strategy 2010–2020: A Renewed Commitment to a Barrier-Free Europe' COM (2010) 636 final.

CHAPTER 36

HUMAN RIGHTS AND PERSONS WITH DISABILITIES IN NIGERIA: BEYOND POLICY FORMULATION

Omolara Funmilola Akinpelu

1. INTRODUCTION

This chapter examines issues relating to human rights and persons with disabilities in Nigeria. It also discusses the need to go beyond formulating human rights policies and stresses the need to implement such policies. Human rights refer to the basic rights to which all humans are entitled, often held to include the right to life and liberty, freedom of thought and expression, and equality before the law.[1] Human rights cover those individual entitlements and freedoms that pertain to a person's humanity, whether they are civil and political or economic, social and cultural. The Fundamental Human Rights as provided in the Nigerian Constitution[2] are in harmony with the Universal Declaration of Human Rights adopted by the General Assembly of the United Nations in 1948[3] and 1966,[4] respectively. Griffo notes that 'societies' low regard for the abilities of persons with disabilities has resulted in discrimination and stigma attached to disability, which pose great barriers in their participation in economic, cultural, political and social life.[5]

In order to include persons with disabilities in the wider society, there has been a dramatic shift over the past two decades in the recognition of their fundamental human rights. This shift to a human rights perspective has been authoritatively endorsed at the level of the United Nations. This is reflected in several developments, for instance, the General Assembly declared the year 1981 as the 'International Year of the Disabled' under the slogan 'Full Participation and Equality.' In 1982, the General Assembly adopted the World Programme of Action concerning Disabled Persons which set the guidelines for a world strategy to promote 'equality' and 'full participation' by persons with disabilities in social life and development. As a follow-up to the World Programme of Action, the General Assembly, in 1993, adopted a resolution entitled 'Standard Rules on the Equalization of Opportunities for People with Disabilities.' The Standard Rules explicitly take the International Bill on Human Rights (which comprises the Universal Declaration on Human Rights and the two international Covenants on Economic, Social and Cultural Rights and

---

1 The Charter of the United Nations (2012).
2 Nigerian Constitution (1999).
3 General Assembly of the United Nations (1948).
4 General Assembly of the United Nations (1966).
5 Griffo et al 'Human rights, UN convention, and the International Classification of Functioning, Disability and Health: collecting data on persons with disabilities?' (Am J Phys Med Rehabil: 13(1), 2012).

Civil and Political Rights) as their political and moral foundation.[6] These formal statements con3stitute an important reference guide in identifying the relevant obligations of States Parties under the existing human rights instruments. These international policy documents aim at ensuring that 'girls, boys, men and women with disabilities, as members of their societies, may exercise the same rights and obligations as others, and require states to remove obstacles to equal participation.'[7] Also in 1993, the Vienna Declaration of Human Rights reaffirmed that 'all human rights and fundamental freedoms are universal, and thus unreservedly include persons with disabilities,' and placed the active participation of persons with disabilities in all aspects of civil society explicitly in a human rights context.

Nigeria is a signatory to most of these universal declarations of human rights policy documents. For instance, Nigeria became a signatory state to the United Nation Convention on the Rights of Persons with Disabilities (CRPD)[8] on March 30, 2007. The fundamental question is has Nigeria implemented these human rights policies?

2. Country Situation Report

Lang and Upah[9] in 2008 presented a SWOT analysis (Strengths, Weaknesses, Opportunities and Threats) in a final report on Nigeria on disability issues. In terms of strengths they identified the following: two Bills had been introduced into the National Assembly to secure rights; disability advisors had been appointed in nine of Nigeria's thirty-six states; rehabilitative centres had been established in six administrative regions (although it had not been possible to ascertain how effective they had been); limited attempts had been made to engage with DPOs in policy dialogue; and the Ministry of Health had been provided some funding for Leprosy and TB medical rehabilitation service. In terms of weaknesses they pointed to the perception by government officials and Nigerian society at large of disability issues in terms of charity and not in terms of human rights; the failure of the Nigerian Government to enact any disability legislation by that date; the lack of any robust statistics on disability; the lack of political will on the behalf of policy-makers to raise the political profile of disability issues; the fact that government-funded services had virtually no long-term sustainable impact of service provision; and that there was no main government ministry that actively promotes disability issues. Available opportunities were shown to include: the 1999 Nigerian Constitution was currently under review, which was seen as potentially providing an opportunity for disability rights to become enshrined; the CAN CBR conference was to be held in Nigeria in 2010, which was seen as an opportunity to provide an impetus for the Nigerian Government to take disability issue more seriously; civil society institutions, including DPOs were keen to establish effective partnerships with relevant government ministries to advance disability issues. The threats identified were that the 'charity ethos' was so deeply entrenched in mainstream Nigerian culture that disability issues would continue to be primarily perceived as an issue of

---

6 General Assembly of the United Nations (1993) para 13.

7 General Assembly of the United Nations (1993) para 15.

8 United Nation Convention on the Rights of Persons with Disabilities (CRPD) (2006).

9 Lang & Upah 'DFID Scoping Study in Nigeria' (Department for International Development, UK, April 2008).

charity, not rights, and that the current inefficient administrative infrastructure would frustrate the implementation of effective disability policy and service provision.

3. Disability and Human Rights

The Fundamental Human Rights are contained in Chapter IV of the Nigerian Constitution (1999). They are as follows:

i) right to life
ii) right to dignity of the human person
iii) right to personal liberty
iv) right to fair hearing
v) right to private life
vi) right to freedom of thought, conscience and religion
vii) right to freedom of expression and the press
viii) right to freedom of movement and
ix) right to freedom from discrimination.

The United Nations had described persons with disabilities as the world's largest minority with the World Health Organization estimating that there are 1 billion persons with disabilities in the world.[10] While living conditions vary, people with disabilities are united in one common experience: being exposed to various forms of discrimination and social exclusion. This negative attitude, low expectations and prejudice leads to exclusion and marginalization of persons with disabilities. A dramatic shift in perspective has been taking place over the past two decades, especially in developed nations. Persons with disabilities have started to be viewed as holders of rights.

These formal standards constitute an important reference guide in identifying the relevant obligations of States Parties under the existing human rights instruments. They aim at ensuring that 'girls, boys, and women with disabilities, as members of their societies, may exercise the same equal rights and obligations as others,' and require States Parties to remove obstacles to equal participation.[11] Also in 1993, the Vienna Declaration of Human Rights reaffirmed that 'all human rights and fundamental freedoms are universal, and thus unreservedly include persons with disabilities,' and place the active participation of persons with disabilities in all aspects of civil society explicitly in a human rights context.[12] The disability rights movement continues to grow and the awareness to adopt new laws prohibiting discrimination on the basis of disability is on the increase. For instance, the Beijing Declaration on the Rights of People with Disabilities came into existence in 2000. The Americans with Disabilities Acts (ADA 1990) is another major landmark in the history of the disability rights movement. The most recent is the CRPD,[13] which was adopted and entered into force in May 2008. The Nigerian Government

10 'World Report on Disability' (Geneva: World Health Organization and the World Bank, 2011), p. 44.
11 General Assembly of the United Nations (1993) para 15.
12 General Assembly of the United Nations (1993) para 13.
13 UN Convention on the Rights of Persons with Disabilities (2006)

also formulated the 'Nigerians with Disability Decree' in 1993.[14] The purpose of this decree is to provide clear and comprehensive legal protection and security for Nigerians with disabilities. The Nigerians with Disability Decree 1993 defines a 'disabled person' as:

> A person who has received preliminary or permanent certificate of disability to have condition which is expected to continue permanently or for a considerable length of time which can reasonably be expected to limit the person's functional ability substantially, but not limited to seeing, hearing, thinking, ambulating, climbing, descending, lifting, grasping, rising, and any related function or any limitation due to weakness or significantly decreased endurance so that he cannot perform his everyday routine, living and working without significantly increased hardship and vulnerability to everyday obstacles and hazards.[15]

It is also on record that the Nigerian Government signed the protocol of the CRPD on March 3, 2009. A further development on the issue of human rights of persons with disabilities was the Nigerian Senate passing the Discrimination Against Persons with Disabilities Bill 2009. The Bill is referred to as House Bill 219.[16] The question now is: to what extent are persons with disabilities in Nigeria able to enjoy their fundamental human rights? That is, is it a mirage or reality in terms of the implementation of these rights as they relate to persons with disabilities in Nigeria? People with disabilities are faced with many challenges. They are denied access to basic social services and the protection of their human rights. Lang notes that 'disability discrimination encompasses rights to appropriate health, education, employment, and social services.'[17] The following analysis is therefore subdivided into education, health care and social services, telecommunications, employment and accessibility issues.

3.1 Education

Education is a right and not a privilege for every member of any given society. The Nigerian National Policy of Education[18] states that the guiding principles of Education in Nigeria is to equip every citizen with such knowledge, skills and attitudes to enable him or her to derive maximum benefits from his or her membership in society, lead a good life and contribute to the development and welfare of the community. Section 5 of the Nigerians with Disability Decree 1993 also elaborates on the rights to education of persons with disabilities. It is stated in this section that 'Disabled persons shall be provided in all public educational institutions free education at all levels.' This provision is in line with the Individuals with Disabilities Act (IDEA)[19] in the United States of America. This Act states that free, appropriate public primary and secondary education are to be made available to all eligible children with disabilities in an environment that is least restrictive to their individual

---

14 Nigerians with Disability Decree (1993).

15 ibid.

16 Bill 209 (2009).

17 Lang "Disability Policy Audit in Namibia, Swaziland, Malawi and Mozambique: Final Report", (Southern African Federation of the Disabled, Zimbabwe, 2008).

18 Nigerian National Policy of Education (1998, 1981).

19 Individuals with Disabilities (2011-IDEA).

needs. Article 24 of the CRPD[20] is devoted to the right to education of persons with disabilities. In Nigeria education is supposed to be free and available at all levels to students with disabilities, but in most cases there is no legislation to enforce this educational provision. The Country Report on Nigeria on Human Rights Practices by the US Department of State[21] notes that:

> 'There are no laws that prohibit discrimination against persons with physical and mental disabilities in employment, education, access to health care, or the provision of other state services. There are no laws requiring physical accessibility for persons with disabilities. Children and women with disabilities face social stigma, exploitation, and discrimination, and were often regarded as a source of shame by their families. Children with disabilities who could not contribute to family income were seen as a liability, and in some cases were severely neglected. Significant numbers of indigent persons with disabilities begged on the streets. Literacy rates among various categories of persons with disabilities were significantly lower than among the general population for both men and women.'[22]

Garuba[23] alludes to the fact that the education of people with special needs has received wide attention at policy level, but that this has attention has not yet reached the level of implementation. The following problems have been identified with the education of persons with disabilities in Nigeria: inadequate plans for the identification of children with disabilities; lack of adequate guidance services for parents to understand the nature and the extent of special education facilities available for their children; the predominant location of most schools that can serve children with disabilities in urban areas; and begging, which is fast assuming the status of an occupation among children and adults with disabilities, not being conducive to school attendance.

The National Blueprint on Education of the Handicapped[24] states that progress has been made so far in the delivery of special education in Nigeria, although it is minimal in terms of anticipated impact, largely due to inadequate funds. It is therefore not surprising that the literacy rates of people with disabilities in Nigeria are significantly lower than among the general population, for both men and women. [25]

3.2 Health Care and Social Services

There are no provisions for subsidized social services in Nigeria. It is stated in Section 4 of the Nigerians with Disability Decree 1993 that 'Disabled persons shall be provided in all public health institutions free medical and health services including general medical needs.'[26] Persons with disabilities face many challenges

---

20 art 24, CRPD.

21 'Country Report on Nigeria on Human Rights Practices' (U.S Department of State, Bureau of Democracy, Human Rights, and Labor 2011).

22 ibid.

23 Garuba 'Inclusive Education in the 21st Century: Challenges and Opportunities for Nigeria' (Asia Pacific Disability Rehabilitation Journal: 14(2), 2003).

24 The National Blueprint on Education of the Handicapped (Nigeria, 1989).

25 Leonard Cheshire Disability (2012).

26 Nigerians with Disability Decree (1993, s 4).

in accessing health care and social services. They pay for their own medical bills and buy their own drugs; for example, parents procure hearing aids, where required, for deaf children. Many people with disabilities pay for rehabilitation services.[27] Accessibility to rehabilitation services is currently poor in many developing countries (Nigeria inclusive).[28] In the aspect of social services, persons with disabilities are being denied their rights because there are no provisions for them to enjoy social amenities.

3.3 Telecommunications

Telecommunications are vital in the life of any individual in any given society because they provide information and entertainment. Deaf individuals are being denied and deprived of this right in Nigeria because there is no provision for interpreting services and captioning, even on the Nigerian Television Authority (NTA). Individuals with visual impairment also do not have access to vital information because most of the materials (books, magazines and newspaper) which are sources of this information are not in Braille or other alternate formats, such as large print. One can then conclude that the telecommunications rights under Section 5 of the Nigerian Disability Decree 1993 is still a mirage.

The marginalization and social exclusion of persons with disabilities was summarized by the charity, Leonard Cheshire Disability:

> 'The abuses that disability communities face are such that they are contrary to [the] spirit of the Nigerian Constitution, the African Charter on Human and People[']s Rights, the Continental Plan of Action for the African Decade of Persons with Disability, and the CRPD. They are often … treated as second-class citizens, shunned and segregated by physical barriers and social stereotypes. This discrimination occurs in a range of arena, including the workplace, schools, health centres, recreational facilities, and many societal contexts. As a fall-out of social discrimination, economic marginalization, and a broad range of other human rights violations, people with disability face difficult challenges in living a normal life. To add salt to their injuries, they are ignored and sometimes excluded from development policies and programs. While some governments and societies have adopted a social inclusion and rights-based approach to disability issues, Nigeria relies on charity models of assistance and a narrow medical model focuses on finding medical "solution" to limitations caused by a disability and ignores the need to address the vast array of limitations created and imposed by discrimination, exclusion, ignorance, and lack of access.'[29]

3.4 Employment

There are many qualified persons with disabilities who are unemployed in Nigeria. There are no accurate statistics to support this but it could be estimated that only

---

27 Amusat 'Disability Care in Nigeria: The need for professional advocacy' (AJPARS: 1(1), 2009).

28 M Mji, et al 'Realizing the rights of disabled people in Africa: An introduction to the special issue' (*Disability and Rehabilitation:* 31, 2009).

29 Leonard Cheshire Disability (2007) 5 https://www.ucl.ac.uk/lc-ccr/downloads/scopingstudies/dfid_nigeriareport last accessed 10 October 2016.

two out of every thirty qualified people with disabilities are employed. Employers' attitudes create the largest barrier to employment opportunities; they often have stereotypical assumptions that underestimate the capacities and abilities of persons with disabilities. Employers often refuse to hire individuals with disabilities because of their unjustified fears that such workers cannot perform the job satisfactorily. For instance, employers use communication barriers as the reason for limiting job opportunities for deaf applicants and employees. Mba[30]notes that most prejudiced employers claim that: disabled people constitute employment hazards and are usually not covered by the company's policy; disabled workers rarely work as hard as their able-bodied counterparts; employing disabled individuals could ruin the company because other workers could protest or abandon their jobs because they loathe the sight of a crippled or blind persons working alongside them; the workers' trade union might not extend membership to disabled workers; and the attitude of most disabled is anti-social and antagonistic.[31]

It is stated under Section 6 of the Nigerians with Disability Decree 1993[32] that the Vocational Rehabilitation and Employment right that 'all employers of labour shall reserve for the disabled' should extend to not less than 10% of work force. The question is what is the percentage of persons with disabilities employed in federal government ministries in Nigeria?

3.5 Accessibility Issues

Article 9 of the CRPD[33] refers to accessibility as a right to enable persons with disabilities to live independently and participate fully in all aspects of life. That is, persons with disabilities must have access, on equal basis with others, to the physical environment, to transportation, to information and communications, buildings, roads and other indoor and outdoor facilities, including schools, housing, medical facilities and workplaces. Accessibility issues are covered in Sections 6–12 of the Nigerians with Disability Decree 1993, but it is obvious that these provisions are yet to become reality. For instance, physically challenged individuals regularly encounter architectural barriers because most buildings in Nigeria are not designed to meet their needs. This situation would violate the Architectural Barrier Act 1968 (ABA)[34] of the United States, and Article 9 of the CRPD on accessibility, both of which require that buildings and facilities be designed, constructed, or altered to ensure standards for physical accessibility, such as pathways, that will enable the physically challenged and wheelchair-users to move freely and easily.

The final report submitted by Lang and Upah[35] on disability issues in Nigeria describes some of the barriers to social inclusion of people with disabilities in

---

30 Mba 'Fundamentals of Special Education and Vocational Rehabilitation' (Ibadan: Codat Publication, 1995).

31 ibid.

32 Nigerians with Disability Decree 1993.

33 Art 9 UN Convention on the Rights of Persons with Disabilities (2006).

34 Architectural Barrier Act 1968 (US). this is as piece of legislation from the United States – I have added a reference to this

35 Lang & Upah 'DFID Scoping Study in Nigeria' (Department for International Development, UK, April 2008)..

Nigeria. These barriers are summed up into three categories: environmental, institutional and attitudinal (see Table 1).

Table 1: Barriers to the Social Inclusion of Disabled People in Nigeria[36]

Environmental	Institutional	Attitudinal
• Inaccessible public buildings • Inaccessible transport system • Lack of access to computers and internet • Poor lighting • Lack of accessible information	• Lack of disability legislation • Lack of robust and reliable disability statistics • No social protection • Inadequate provision of medical and rehabilitation services • Lack of access to micro-finance and banking services • Inaccessibility of mainstream public services (especially education)	• The cause of impairment often attributed to a 'curse' • Disability issues are predominantly perceived in terms of charity/welfare, not in terms of human rights • Lack of understanding of disability issues by the general public

6. Recommendations

There are many factors acting against the social inclusion of persons with disabilities in Nigeria which Lang and Upah[37] identified to include environmental, institutional and attitudinal. It can be concluded that the main factor is institutional because if laws and regulations regarding disability issues are in place and enforced, environmental and attitudinal factors would be taken care of. They further note that 'two separate disability bills have been introduced into the National Assembly, but both failed to be enacted.'[38] There are individuals with disabilities and allies that are disgruntled with the state of affairs regarding disability issues in Nigeria. Some of the major disability right movement organizations are: Joint National Association of Persons with Disabilities (JONAPWD); Association for Comprehensive Empowerment of Nigerians with Disabilities (ASCEND) and Affirmation of the Rights of Persons with Disabilities (ARPWD).

It is good, of course, to formulate policies, enact laws, and establish statutes but the most important issue is implementing them. Grugel and Piper state that 'there is no real evidence that ratification of international charters always lead to dramatic

36 R Lang and L Upah, 'Scoping Study: Disability Issues in Nigeria' (DFID 2009) <www.ucl.ac.uk/lc-ccr/projects> last accessed 31 March 2016.

37 ibid 20.

38 ibid 21.

changes in the state behavior'.[39] This is the situation in Nigeria regarding the CRPD. Nigeria is one of the signatories to the Convention and passed the Bill in 2009 and passed a piece of disability legislation in 2014, after much delays. The delay in enacting the legislation has been a barrier to people with disabilities in enjoying basic human rights. It is thus imperative for the Nigerian Government to move beyond policy formulation because implementation is crucial.

In moving forward, the Nigerian Government should consider empowering persons with disabilities by involving these individuals in the affairs that are related to them. Most of the disability organisations are directed by people without disabilities; it is time that the Nigerian Government and public heed the clarion of the slogan 'Nothing About Us Without Us.' People with disabilities should be given a chance to be their own voices. The government should align priorities by providing adequate funds to assist disability organisations to carry out their activities. All disability organisations should forget their differences and work together to focus on the same theme for the progress of people with disabilities. For instance, Affirmation of the Rights of Persons with Disabilities (ARPWD)[40] has proposed the following: central organisations of persons with disabilities should be strengthened to drive the affirmation of the rights of persons with disabilities; focal stakeholder groups and organisations with active interest in disability issues should coalesce to pursue the affirmation of persons with disabilities' rights; mechanisms should be put in place to support the passage of the Disability Bill and the development of relevant laws and policies that facilitate the rights of persons with disabilities; and key areas for change identified by the coalition should be understood by persons with disabilities, policy makers and the wider public. It is therefore recommended that other disability organisations should support these actions in order to achieve common goals.

There is also a need to promote the understanding of the rights-based concept of disability. Presently, the medical and charity models are entrenched in the attitude of parents, families, government and the general public towards people with disabilities. Parents see disabilities as diseases and are commonly engaged in what is called the 'shopping principle,' referring to the search for medical and/or spiritual cures at the expense of seeking as early as possible services from which children could benefit . Government, especially the offices of the First Lady, dole out equipment, wheelchairs, clothes, and food items to people with disabilities. Disability should be seen as a social construct, recognizing the need to provide accessible services and environment for people with disabilities. Most schools are not accessible for people with physical disabilities; transportation is not accessible; there is lack of adequate interpreters for people who are deaf; information for the blind is limited due to the lack of printed materials in Braille or in alternate formats; children with cognitive disabilities are still referred to as 'mentally retarded' and are seen as incapable of amounting to much in life. Those with psychiatric disability are seen as insane people who should be confined in institutions in remote areas. People with HIV/AIDS are still stigmatized and are likely to be ostracised from their families, jobs, and the community.

---

39 Grugel and Piper 'Do Rights Promote Development?'(Global Social Policy, 2009 9(1), 79-98)

40 http://coalitions4change.org/index.php?option=com_content&task=blogcategory&id=21&Itemid=59

There are no accurate figures for the number of people with disabilities in Nigeria, but it is estimated that there are about 19 million with disabilities out of a total population of 150 million. It is crucial that accurate, valid numbers are available to assist the Government when planning for service provision. This information will also be helpful for both national and international bodies that are interested in disability issues in Nigeria. It is also important to introduce disability studies into the curriculum of higher institutions. The present emphasis is on special education but it is highly recommended that students acquire knowledge in disability rights movements, independent living philosophy, models of disability, and disability critical theory. This will motivate students to be engaged in disability issues and know how other nations of the world are embracing the social model of disability; most importantly, it will change disability from a charity/welfare perspective to a human rights-based view. Another issue that can come from introducing disability studies in Nigerian higher institutions of learning is research. There is a need for research on disability issues in Nigeria because this will go a long way in promoting scholarly activities in this field and will broaden the scope of knowledge in this field.

In moving forward, the Nigerian Government must create a new ministry that will be dedicated to handling disability issues. Currently, disability issues are under the supervision of Ministry of Women's Affairs and Social Development; this will not suffice. For the newly created Ministry to function efficiently the staff employed should have relevant background and experience in social work, rehabilitation, counselling, and disability studies. It is recommended that qualified individuals with disabilities are part of the team to enhance the quality of service delivery. The intention of this is that Nigeria should ensure that she embraces the slogan 'Nothing About Us Without Us' by involving people with disabilities in the affairs that are related to them. They should be encouraged to be their own voices as much as possible.

Lastly, the Nigerian Government should incorporate national coordinating committees that will be responsible for monitoring disability issues. These committees will ensure that ministries, organizations, and even individuals committed to disability are accountable for and in a position to produce measurable deliverables.

7. Conclusion

There is need for the Nigerian Government to ensure the implementation of fundamental human rights policies of persons with disabilities in Nigeria. Boutros-Ghali, former Secretary General of the United Nations, states that: 'disability issues have gone beyond the category of humanitarian concern. They are now recognized in the dimension of human rights and development. Disability has moved from charity to integrated social development planning. Definitions have changed, disability has improved'.[41]

The time has come in Nigeria for individuals with disabilities to assert themselves in advocating for their fundamental human rights. There is also the need for parents, professionals, para-professionals, and other interest groups to join forces with

[41] Boutros-Ghali 'An Agenda for Development' (United Nations, 1995).

persons with disabilities to form a disability rights movement. It is not enough to formulate policies or promulgate law; implementing them will go a long way in helping persons with disabilities to have a sense of belonging in their own country.

Chapter 37

OF RIGHTS AND WRONGS: THE NATIONAL DISABILITY STRATEGY IN PORTUGAL

Paula Campos Pinto

1. Introduction

On 30 March 2007 Portugal was among the States that signed the Convention on the Rights of Persons with Disabilities (CRPD) on the first day it opened for signature at the headquarters of the United Nations in New York. In the statement read at the ceremony, the then State Secretary for Rehabilitation reaffirmed the 'commitment in the promotion of universal respect and observance of the human rights, fundamental freedoms and equality of all human beings', firmly founded upon the belief that 'human rights are the rights of persons with disabilities!'[1]

By then, the Government had already put in place the First Action Plan for the Inclusion of Persons with Disabilities (PAIPDI) and had adopted a National Accessibility Plan. The two documents were presented at this occasion as key political instruments in the elimination of disability-based discrimination and the removal of obstacles to the full participation of these citizens in the labour market, community life and the knowledge-based society.

Like a number of other countries in Europe and beyond, Portugal has plunged into a deep economic recession. In the disability field, the First Action Plan has given place to a National Disability Strategy (ENDEF) enacted in 2010 to cover the period 2011–2013. What have these changes done to the legal and policy landscape around disability in the country? What has been the impact, if any, of the Convention? How far has Portugal moved in the protection of disability rights over the last five years?

Addressing these questions is important to understand the significance of international human rights law in moulding domestic legal frameworks and societal practices. Portugal, in this regard, is a particularly interesting case study, since it is facing a harsh economic and financial crisis in which priorities of fiscal restraint compete with human rights goals. Assessing how the Government is tackling its international human rights commitments, in such an adverse context, may thus illuminate the complex interplay of law, policy and politics in contemporary societies.

---

1 Statement of the Secretary of State for Rehabilitation, Idália Moniz, at the signature of the CRPD (United Nations, New York, 27 March 2007) <http://search.un.org/search?q=persons+disabilities+Portugal&spell=1&output=xml_no_dtd&client=UN_Website_en&num=10&lr=lang_en&proxystylesheet=UN_Website_en&sort=date%3AD%3AL%3Ad1&oe=UTF-8&ie=UTF-8&ud=1&exclude_apps=1&site=un_org> assessed 25 May 2012.

This chapter sets out to examine these issues by monitoring the implementation of the National Disability Strategy in Portugal and assessing this policy document against the formal rights commitments of the Portuguese State, as these are laid out in the CRPD. Then it moves on to a rights assessment in practice. Drawing from data collected through individual monitoring interviews recently conducted throughout the country, it discusses the gap between rights in theory and on the ground. The chapter concludes with reflections on the impact of the current economic crisis on disability rights progress in Portugal.

2. The National Disability Strategy: An Overview

The ENDEF was adopted in December 2010 by the Resolução do Conselho de Ministros 97/2010. In contrast with the previous Action Plan – a sixty-page, mostly theoretical paper – the new Strategy is a concise document, of roughly twelve pages, organized around fives axes: (1) disability and multi-discrimination; (2) justice and exercise of rights; (3) autonomy and quality of life; (4) accessibility and design for all; and (5) administrative modernization and information systems. For each of these axes the Strategy lists measures, indicators, the responsible entities for the implementation of each measure, and the deadlines for setting them in place. All this information is presented in tables, which further provides for a synthesized view of the Strategy's content.

This format is clearly different from the one followed in the previous Action Plan, analysed elsewhere,[2] which discussed at length the 'new' rights-based and bio-psychosocial approach to disability before going into the description of the measures advanced by the Plan. The ENDEF, on the contrary, goes straight to the point. After a brief introduction that alludes to the ratification of the Convention to highlight the commitment of the Portuguese State to 'promoting, protecting and ensuring a life with dignity for persons with disabilities', the need to proceed with policies that 'fight discrimination and improve the quality of life of persons with disabilities and their families' is recognised. Viewed as a policy benefiting 'the Portuguese society as a whole', the Strategy is introduced as an inter-departmental framework which relies on, and calls upon, the contribution of a variety of areas of government as well as civil society organizations and the disability movement. The obligation of mainstreaming disability in societal life and at all levels and areas of government, stated in Article 4(c) of the CRPD, is thus clearly embraced in this document.

The five axes in which the Strategy is organised represent another leap forward in bringing into life the rights-based approach enacted by the Convention. The axes chosen – Multi-Discrimination, Justice and Access to Rights, Autonomy and Quality of Life, Accessibility and Administrative Organization – suggest a more holistic rights-based approach to disability than the discussion around discrete issues such as employment or education, labour market integration or culture, leisure and sports, of the earlier Action Plan. More in accordance with current human rights theory (eg the Vienna Declaration) the new headings imply a vision of rights as indivisible

---

2 P Pinto, 'Between the lines: A critical discourse analysis of disability policy in Portugal' [2011] Disability Studies Quarterly 31 (3) <http://www.dsq-sds.org/article/view/1678/1592> assessed 30 April 2012.

and interdependent and therefore requiring integrated and interrelated measures that mobilize a variety of areas to tackle the factors which cause the disadvantages facing persons with disabilities.

The first axel – disability and discrimination – provides a clear illustration of this. In addressing this section, the ENDEF recognizes that beyond the discrimination that persons with disabilities in general face, 'there are [...] certain groups such as women, children, immigrants and unemployed [...] who accumulate social disadvantages' and therefore need to be the target of 'additional measures'. This statement is important as it is the first time that a national policy document addresses persons with disabilities, not as a monolithic group, but in their heterogeneity. Traditionally, in the policy discourse, people with disabilities have been talked about as a monolithic group – a collective of people with the same characteristics and needs. Such a view amounts to a form of discrimination, as it denies the subjectivity of each person and ignores the power of broader social and economic structures that constrain the lives of men and women with disabilities. The ENDEF breaks away from this conventional approach and while doing so embodies the spirit of the CRPD which also clearly recognises 'the diversity of persons with disabilities'.[3]

Such a perspective enables the emergence of new policy goals. For example, tackling the discrimination that arises at the intersection of disability and gender, an issue completely ignored in the preceding Action Plan, has now become a new focus area for disability policy in Portugal, as the Convention also requires.[4]

In a similar trend, the axel Autonomy and Quality of Life brings together measures that address disability-prevention through early intervention programmes, support to families, education, vocational training and employment, as well as measures to promote the social integration of persons with disabilities. The fact that all these areas are discussed under the same heading provides for a more comprehensive perspective on the issues affecting the quality of life of persons with disabilities and their families.

The three remaining axels – Justice, Accessibility and Administrative Organisation – deal with a matter that is transversal and which to a great extent is a precondition to the exercise of rights. The matter is access, whether it translates into access to justice (through recognition of legal capacity and equal rights in the legal system), access to the physical environment, or access to information systems, particularly in the public sector. Here again the Strategy is attuned with the text of the CRPD which calls attention to the 'importance of accessibility to the physical, social, economic and cultural environment, to health and education and to information and communication, in enabling persons with disabilities to fully enjoy all human rights and fundamental freedoms'[5].

In short, an overall perspective of the structure of the ENDEF suggests a more progressive outlook of this document than could be found in its predecessor, the Disability Action Plan. It becomes interesting, then, to assess whether this new

---

3 Convention on the Rights of Persons with Disabilities 2006 (CRPD 2006) Preamble (i).
4 art 6 CRPD.
5 Preamble (v) CRPD.

package translates in fact in more progressive content and, more importantly, if it does, how much of it has already been transposed to reality.

3. The Devil is in the Details? Assessing the ENDEF from Within

Altogether, the new Strategy proposes 133 measures to be implemented over three years, from 2011. Of these, only 15% were to be realized by the end of 2011; 11% were planned to be completed by 2012, and the great majority, or 74%, were to be achieved by 2013. While this timeline immediately indicates that a large number of policy goals is being pushed forward in time, it seems more relevant to examine how innovative are the measures being advanced.

The outcome is disappointing. Of the twenty measures proposed for 2011, only seven are entirely 'new' – the majority is just the re-statement, re-enactment or the extension of actions previously undertaken. Moreover, in many instances the measures proposed appear clearly insufficient to promote the broad change that the Strategy envisions.

For example, to tackle issues of multi-discrimination, the government primarily offers awareness-raising training programmes, targeted to a variety of audiences: the staff at the Ministry of Culture, professionals of the tourism industry, advisors of the Justice Department, journalists and civil servants at local, regional and national levels. To raise awareness about disability among these professionals is certainly an important goal but this is also a purpose which has been inscribed in the mission of the National Disability Institute (INR) for a long time, and yet has so far met with little success. Two main reasons explain this failure: one is the reduced number of training opportunities provided, which is partly related to a lack of public demand; the other is the limited range of attendees, which tend to come from within, rather than from outside, the disability sector. There are reasons to believe that this panorama did not radically change in 2011: disability-awareness tends to be a neglected area of training for civil servants and the business sector, and therefore it is not uncommon for training offered by the INR to be cancelled at the last minute for lack of registrations. This too is a reflection of the marginalized position of people with disabilities within Portuguese society. Until such training becomes a requirement for workers in public offices and those in the business sector who are in close contact with the public, the situation will probably remain unchanged. Unfortunately, the Strategy does not go that far and in this sense the continuing efforts to mainstream disability and raise awareness among a variety of professionals will likely continue to reach limited effectiveness.

Similarly, the measures proposed under the heading Autonomy and Quality of Life are mostly a prolongation of programmes and services already in place for persons with disabilities, whether in education, rehabilitation, vocational training or employment. The few truly innovative proposals – including setting in place a much-needed project of personal assistance (PA) services – were all scheduled to take place in 2013. PA schemes, which have been described as fundamental pillars for independent living,[6] are currently non-existent in Portugal, which greatly contributes

---

6 A Ratza, Keynote address at the conference on personal assistance in Strasbourg, France <www.

to perpetuate the disadvantageous and dependent status of persons with disabilities within their families and in society at large[7].

It is in the area of administrative modernisation that more originality can be found in the measures proposed in the Strategy. This is perhaps not surprising given that this area primarily concerns state reform and is focused on simplifying administrative processes and improving access to public information to citizens in general. Mainstreaming disability in these ongoing reforms seems therefore an obvious goal. Some of the initiatives proposed include making better use of information technologies to improve access to public services and information for persons with disabilities or waiving requirements of periodic presentation of the medical certification of incapacity in order to access certain benefits. They are certainly welcome as they are likely to have a positive impact in the lives of many disabled people.

In contrast, the measures proposed under the heading Accessibility are disappointing. Of the twenty-fix measures listed, seventeen (or over 65%) were to be concluded only in 2013, and this despite their urgency. In fact, it seems too long to have to wait yet another couple of years before having information about the schedule of the Lisbon subway trains available in accessible formats, or before making pathways in the subway stations of the capital city accessible to people with visual impairments, or before ensuring accessibility to all health facilities in the NHS, or even before ensuring physical accessibility to the entire building in which the INR, the government body for disability issues, is currently located.

Equally disappointing is how the Strategy deals with gender inequalities. Despite recognizing that women with disabilities may face multiple discrimination the ENDEF does little to redress their disadvantage. In fact, the one action proposed to tackle this issue is 'to produce a brochure about the rights of women with disabilities in accessible formats'.[8]

Finally, the Strategy mentions a couple of actions directly responding to the monitoring requirements of the CRPD. Both were scheduled for 2011. Results, however, have been mixed: while the first national report on the implementation of the Convention has been written and publicly discussed (although not yet submitted) the independent mechanism to promote and monitor implementation of the CRPD, also scheduled to 2011, is yet to be created.

In short, despite important advances in the overall framework proposed, denoting a clearer orientation to a rights-based approach to disability, the changes introduced by the ENDEF appear to be more in form than in substance. Hence, Portugal continues to be lagging in disability policy development. Moreover, there is already some delay in the implementation of measures that would impact significantly on the exercise

---

independentliving.org/docs2/enilpakeytoil.html> assessed 12 February 2012.

7 P Pinto, 'Family, disability and social policy in Portugal: Where are we at, and where do we want to go?' (2011) Sociologia On Line, nº2 <http://revista.aps.pt/?cad=REV4dc1582d76418&tipo=TAR4b223cfff053b&art=ART4dc4205994c60> assessed 26 May 2012.

8 Resolução do Conselho de Ministros 97/2010, ENDEF, 18.

of human rights of persons with disabilities. It thus becomes important to monitor how disabled people are accessing their rights.

4. From Policy to Practice: Human Rights on the Ground

To understand the barriers faced by persons with disability in Portugal to realize their human rights, policy analysis need to be complemented with the collection and analysis of personal stories. This section is based on thirty-two in-depth interviews conducted on a purposeful sample of adults with a variety of impairments living in three regions of Portugal. Interviews were conducted during the summer of 2011 as part of the pilot project, DRPI-Portugal. This research used the methodologies and tools developed in the context of Disability Rights Promotion International, an international project that has been working since 2002 to create a system to monitor disability rights around the world. Two initial questions were asked: 'What has brought you more satisfaction in life over the last five years?' and 'What have been your major obstacles or barriers?' Typically, respondents listed two or three situations that interviewers then probed to explore their human rights implications. This free format enabled interviewees to identify the issues more relevant to them in terms of human rights experiences. Individual stories were then analysed and coded to identify their implications in terms of human rights principles.

The group interviewed was balanced and diverse with the three independent variables considered relevant to this investigation – sex, age group and type of disability. It included individuals of both sexes, with ages that ranged between eighteen and seventy, with higher incidence of the age group twenty-six to forty, which is also the widest. All types of impairment were represented with a higher prevalence of persons with mobility impairments. In most cases (twenty-eight), respondents reported a lived experience of disability that was relatively long (five years or more). Nevertheless, in terms of employment and education, the sample represents a relatively privileged group. In this sense, the experiences of discrimination and violation of human rights that this study has identified may acquire even greater significance.

The stories gathered through this study concerned all domains of life. However, most reports related to the domains of social participation (found in all interviews), economic security and support services (found in twenty-fix interviews or 78%) and work (found in nineteen interviews or 59%). These three domains thus represent the most significant areas for the exercise of human rights of the group interviewed. Moreover, the large majority of the stories gathered reported instances of denial and violation of rights principles with negative consequences for the well-being and quality of life of persons with disabilities.

The most frequent forms of violation of rights principles experienced by participants were disrespect for difference (reported by thirty-one participants), exclusion (reported by thirty participants) and discrimination and unequal treatment (reported by twenty-seven respondents). The persistence of negative perceptions about disability is one of the most significant factors limiting opportunities for inclusion and social participation of persons with disabilities. As one interviewed put it,

> '[t]here must not be a person with disability in this world that has not been

labelled in a way or another: look the lame, the poor blind, the poor thing (Male, aged fifty-three years).'

Demeaning images of persons with disabilities emerged in social interaction as well as in the workplace, creating serious obstacles for persons with disabilities to obtain a job or progress in their careers.

Another form of violation of the principle of respect for difference was found in the failure of existing support services to properly address the needs of persons with disabilities. For lack of personal assistance schemes in Portugal, disabled persons have to turn to homecare services to get some assistance with daily activity tasks, including self-care tasks. However, as they are currently offered, these services operate on the assumption that persons with disabilities do not live productive lives, do not work or study, and are not involved in any activities outside the house. The gap between the actual support needs of persons with disabilities to live independent lives and what the services provide configures an instance of lack of respect for difference, as the following report clearly illustrates:

> 'My personal hygiene tasks take some time and the homecare service starts at 8am only – exceptionally in my case, because usually it begins at 9 am, they opened an exception for me – but still, I only get to work at 11am and often at 11:30am, which causes me a lot of problems. In the evening, I do not use the service to get to bed because they often end up the service and I'm still at work. Sometimes they end up at 6pm, they put people in bed at 6, 7, 8pm (Man, age–unknown.)'

When their needs are not properly addressed persons with disabilities are prevented from participating in society on equal grounds with other citizens. Yet their lack of participation is viewed as the natural consequence of their impairments, which allows the stereotyped images of dependency, often associated with disability, to be perpetuated. On the contrary, respect for difference, which the CRPD advances as a guiding principle for disability policy and action, would require the design and implementation of suitable supports, thus ensuring a true equality of opportunities.

To participate as equal in social, economic and cultural life many people with disabilities need more accessible environments. In Portugal, the law defines accessibility standards for all public-use buildings, public spaces and housing, and stipulates a time limit for existing buildings to adapt to these new norms[9]. The law, however, is not sufficiently enforced and therefore lack of accessibility remains a huge obstacle in the daily lives of persons with disabilities. One interviewee commented:

> 'The health care centre was recently built, and I don't have access to family planning services. I don't have access to, I can't do some examinations. The Taxes Office is the same – it has not easy access, it does from one side but not from the other. (Female, aged twenty-eight)'

For those with sensory impairments, communication barriers constitute the biggest

---

9 Decreto-Lei 163/2006 de 8 de Agosto.

obstacle to social participation: lack of information available in Braille and other accessible formats, lack of sign-language interpretation services or close-captioning services. Despite improvements over the last years, this is an area that greatly contributes to the isolation and social exclusion of this group, as one deaf respondent reported:

> 'For example, the TV: what are they saying? I never know what they are saying. I can only see. On RTP [the public channel] they have subtitles but sometimes they write "temporary error" and there are words missing. The news rarely [has] subtitles, and when they do, it does not follow what is being said, it's not at the same time. (Male, age unknown)'

Reports such as these contrast with the promises of the ENDEF. Moreover, while there were fewer women in the sample than men, females' reports of denial and violation of human rights outnumbered those of the males in this study. This result suggests that intersections of gender and disability are creating in the Portuguese society added disadvantages for women with disabilities. A renewed attention to these intersections, beyond what is outlined in the Strategy, appears quite pertinent.

5. Conclusion

This chapter set out to explore the impact of the CRPD on disability policy and action in Portugal. As discussed earlier, in its outline, the new Disability Strategy, enacted after the Convention was signed and ratified, embodies some of the general principles contained in the treaty. However, it promises more than it actually delivers. Indeed, most of the measures proposed are a simple continuation of activities and programmes already on the ground. Moreover, where innovation exists, the deadline suggested for policy implementation tends to be the longest possible – that is, the end of the validity period of the ENDEF itself or 2013.

This raises questions about the effectiveness of the Strategy in promoting rights progress on the ground, as qualitative data from a monitoring study recently conducted in Portugal also revealed. Portuguese citizens with disabilities continue to face serious obstacles to exercise their human rights: lack of accessibility, lack of adequate personal assistance services and the persistence of demeaning images about disability, in particular, create significant barriers to social participation and a life with dignity. While attitudes can hardly be changed by decree, improving access to public places, services and goods, and ensuring appropriate assistance that enables persons to take part as active members in their communities would do a great deal to shift current negative perceptions about disabled people in the Portuguese society. Yet the Strategy is behind schedule in tackling these issues.

One of the reasons for such delay might be that improvements in these areas require public investment, just at a time when the Portuguese State is under heavy international pressure to reduce its debt. After the bail-out received in 2011 from the EU and IMF, Portugal has had to agree to a severe austerity plan and set in place a number of measures to reduce spending, including in the social policy arena.

This creates an inescapable paradox for disability policy in Portugal: despite the formal commitment to a progressive human rights agenda, the State is operating under a neoliberal agenda that prioritizes fiscal restraint. What has been missing from the debate is the voice of persons with disabilities themselves, challenging the status quo and claiming their rights. Crashed by the economic crisis many disability organizations are struggling to survive and this has had an impact on their ability to advocate disability rights.[10] At the same time, however, new alliances are being forged, notably around the preparation of the Portuguese alternative report, as we are witnessing an increased interest of the academia and broader human rights organizations in disability issues and disability rights. This is unprecedented in the country. And so, in spite of the very difficult context, there is now a renewed opportunity to build a wide coalition that can help shape, influence and change disability policy in Portugal in the years to come.

[10] F Fontes, 'Pessoas com deficiência em Portugal: Da caridade à cidadania social' (2009) Revista Crítica de Ciências Sociais 86, 73; P C Pinto, 'At the crossroads: Human rights and the politics of disability and gender in Portugal' (2011) ALTER: European Review of Disability Research 5(2) 116.

CHAPTER 38

ARTICLE 33 OF THE CRPD: ITS POTENTIAL FOR REALISING THE HUMAN RIGHTS OF PERSONS WITH DISABILITIES

Meredith Raley

One of the largest and most enduring problems facing international human rights law has been the gap between the standards set by various international human rights instruments, and the laws enacted by States that have ratified these documents and pledged to abide by their standards. Too often, these States fail to enact policies that would fully realise the rights enshrined in the treaties they have signed. This failure to implement human rights treaties has many causes, and there is no one solution, but it is one of the most urgent problems in international human rights law.

The drafters of the Convention on the Rights of Persons with Disabilities (CRPD or 'the Convention') took steps to address this problem in the Convention. Article 33 takes an innovative approach to the implementation gap by, for the first time, requiring States Parties to the CRPD to take concrete administrative and organisational steps towards implementing the Convention. This sets the CRPD apart from past treaties, which have set out a series of obligations, but remained silent on how a States Party should ensure that its obligations were realised.

One of the most important developments leading up to the drafting of the CRPD and the creation of Article 33 was the rise both in numbers and influence of National Human Rights Institutions (NHRIs). These national bodies monitor and promote international human rights standards within their States, and without them innovations in international law such as Article 33 would be nearly impossible. Understanding the role, function and history of NHRIs is a crucial part of understanding the importance and potential of Article 33.

International law has always relied on domestic legal systems.[1] Without a centralised authority to oversee and enforce international law, treaties can only be given force by States themselves.[2] For these reasons, national implementation of international law is crucial. Despite this, there has traditionally been very little regulation of the method by which States implement treaties that they are a party to.[3] While States may not use their domestic law as an excuse for failing to meet their international obligations, States have traditionally been otherwise free to implement treaties in any way they see fit.[4] This has been as true of human rights treaties as any other kind,

---

1 A Cassese, *International Law in a Divided World* (Clarendon Press 1986) 14.
2 ibid 13–14.
3 ibid 15.
4 ibid 15–16.

until the drafting of the CRPD. Like past UN human rights treaties, the Convention prescribes a set of obligations that States Parties must adhere to, and like past treaties, the Convention has a traditional accountability mechanism in a treaty body that States Parties must report to.[5] The innovation in the CRPD is found in Article 33, which for the first time requires States to take clearly defined administrative and procedural action in the process of implementing the Convention.[6]

Article 33 of the CRPD requires States to put in place a national structure tasked with implementing and monitoring the Convention. The article is unprecedented in the history of human rights treaties.[7] It was drafted and written into the treaty in the hope that the CRPD would avoid the problems of slow and patchy implementation that have plagued other human rights treaties.[8] The article has three parts, and reads as follows:

> 1. States Parties, in accordance with their system of organization, shall designate one or more focal points within government for matters relating to the implementation of the present Convention, and shall give due consideration to the establishment or designation of a co-ordination mechanism within government to facilitate related action in different sectors and at different levels.
>
> 2. States Parties shall, in accordance with their legal and administrative systems, maintain, strengthen, designate or establish within the State Party, a framework, including one or more independent mechanisms, as appropriate, to promote, protect and monitor implementation of the present Convention. When designating or establishing such a mechanism, States Parties shall take into account the principles relating to the status and functioning of national institutions for protection and promotion of human rights.
>
> 3. Civil society, in particular persons with disabilities and their representative organizations, shall be involved and participate fully in the monitoring process.[9]

The article divides the responsibly for implementation and monitoring into distinct sections, with Article 33(1) dealing with a governmental framework for implementation, while Article 33(2) describes an independent framework to promote,

---

5 Canadian Human Rights Commission, *Survey of National Human Rights Institutions on Article 33.2 of the UN Convention on the Rights of Persons with Disabilities* (Prepared for the International Coordinating Committee of National Institutions for the Protection and Promotion of Human Rights, 2011) 3.

6 Canadian Human Rights Commission, *Survey of National Human Rights Institutions on Article 33.2 of the UN Convention on the Rights of Persons with Disabilities* (Prepared for the International Coordinating Committee of National Institutions for the Protection and Promotion of Human Rights, 2011).

7 Human Rights Council – Thematic Study by the Office of the United Nations High Commissioner for Human Rights on the Structure and Role of National Mechanisms for the Implementation and Monitoring of The Convention on the Rights of Persons with Disabilities (22 December 2009) UN Doc. A/HRC/13/29, para 15.

8 MDAC, *Written submission by the Mental Disability Advocacy Center to the UN Committee on the Rights of Persons with Disabilities With respect to Article 33 of the UN Convention on the Rights of Persons with Disabilities* (2011) 3.

9 art 33, Convention on the Rights of Persons with Disabilities (CRPD) (2006).

protect and monitor national progress on ensuring the rights provided by the CRPD. The purpose of this framework is to address the gap between what rights a treaty grants in theory, and how those rights are realised by a State Party in practice. For most human rights treaties, there exists a wide gap between theory and practice, where a treaty has not been fully implemented.[10] This implementation gap has several causes, including a lack of co-ordination and cooperation among various governmental bodies when implementing human rights treaties, a lack of effective monitoring, and a lack of awareness of international human rights standards among those who should be most affected by these treaties.[11]

Article 33(1) sets out a framework that State governments must establish to guide the process of translating the rights enshrined in the Convention into domestic law. To ensure that responsibility for this process of implementation is clear and that action within the government is properly coordinated, governments must establish one or more focal points to oversee the process.[12] While the text in the Convention does not provide much guidance on where or how focal points should be established, the OHCHR has suggested that governments should designate at least one focal point at every level of government that will be involved in the implementation process, and that the highest focal should be found at the Ministry level, and close to the heart of government, in recognition of the fact that implementation of the CRPD will require work at the highest levels of government.[13] The OHCHR also stresses that the focal point's goal must be developing some kind of coherent national strategy for implementation, and guiding the rest of government towards that goal, rather than the focal point being directly responsible for delivering services.[14]

Article 33(1) also gives States the option to set up a co-ordination mechanism, as well as a focal point, to co-ordinate action at various levels and sectors of government. The OHCHR suggests that a co-ordination mechanism is appropriate whenever a State has chosen to create or appoint more than one focal point, to ensure that there is no duplication or contradiction of effort in the implementation process.[15]

While the first part of Article 33 deals with the responsibilities of government in implementing the CRPD, the second part, Article 33(2), mandates the creation or appointment of a framework, which must at minimum contain an independent mechanism, which will promote, protect, and monitor the rights laid out in the Convention. The idea that this framework will operate independently of the State government is central to Article 33(2), as is the idea that this independent mechanism must follow the principles laid out for the functioning of national institutions for the protection and promotion of human rights, which is an implicit reference to the Paris Principles.[16] Except for the requirement that the framework contain one Paris Principles-compliant body, States have considerable leeway in setting up their Article

---

[10] MDAC, 'Building the Architecture for Change: Guidelines on Article 33 of the UN Convention on the Rights of Persons with Disabilities' (2011) 13.

[11] ibid.

[12] Human Rights Council, para 17.

[13] ibid para 25.

[14] ibid para 29.

[15] ibid para 36.

[16] ibid para 18.

33(2) framework. Some may choose to have only the single NHRI, while others may choose to include several bodies, not all of which need to be independent.[17]

To fully understand Article 33(2), it is important to understand more about NHRIs. The term National Human Rights Institution (NHRI) covers a wide variety of national bodies around the world. While these bodies vary in their makeup and duties, they have in common the fact that they are all independent bodies within the national structure of a State, with a mandate to promote and protect human rights.[18] The idea of establishing institutions to ensure the implementation of international human rights treaties dates back to 1946, when the Economic and Social Council of the United Nations invited its Member States to consider setting up 'human rights committees' to work with both the States and the Commission on Human Rights.[19] One year later, the first NHRI was created in France, the French National Advisory Commission for Human Rights.[20]

The creation and operation of NHRIs is governed by a set of guidelines known as 'the Paris Principles.'[21] The full title of the document is 'Principles Relating to the Status of National Institutions, Competence and Responsibilities.'[22] The Paris Principles were written at the first International Workshop on Institutions for the Promotion and Protection of Human Rights, held in Paris in October 1991. The guidelines were written by the currently existing NHRIs themselves, and later adopted by the UN General Assembly in 1993.[23] The Principles require a NHRI to have a broad, stable mandate,[24] to be independent of the State's government,[25] and to be adequately funded.[26] The Paris Principles also lay out the areas for which a NHRI should be responsible, including but not limited to submitting opinions and proposals to the government, working on the ratification, promotion, and implementation of human rights treaties,[27] co-operating with the UN, and educating the public on human rights.[28] To meet all of its responsibilities, a NHRI must, among other things, be free to consider all questions and obtain all information that falls within its mandate, address the public, consult with other bodies, and develop relationships with NGOs.[29] A NHRI may also be authorised to hear individual complaints, but

---

17 ibid para 38.

18 R Carver, 'A new answer to an old question: National human rights institutions and the domestication of international law' (2010) 10 Human Rights Law Review 1, 4.

19 Gauthier de Beco, 'National Human Rights Institutions in Europe' (CRIDHO Working Paper 01.2007) <http://cridho.uclouvain.be/documents/Working.Papers/CRIDHO.WP.2007-1.pdf> last accessed 31 March 2016.

20 ibid.

21 United Nations General Assembly 'National institutions for the promotion and protection of human rights' (4 March 1994) U.N Doc A/Res/48/134, 7.

22 ibid.

23 Gauthier de Beco, 'National Human Rights Institutions in Europe' (CRIDHO Working Paper 01.2007) <http://cridho.uclouvain.be/documents/Working.Papers/CRIDHO.WP.2007-1.pdf> last accessed 31 March 2016.

24 United Nations General Assembly 'National institutions for the promotion and protection of human rights' (4 March 1994) U.N Doc A/Res/48/134, 7.

25 ibid.

26 ibid.

27 ibid.

28 ibid.

29 ibid.

this is not a requirement for an institution to be considered in compliance with the Paris Principles.[30]

A broad, clear mandate was important so that both the NHRI itself and the public are aware of the exact powers and responsibilities of the institution.[31] The principles require that a NHRI be established either in the Constitution or by legislative mandate, and discourage establishment by executive decree, because an institution so established is vulnerable to being abolished if it offends the Executive.[32]

Within the guidelines of the Paris Principles there is still considerable room for States to manoeuvre and create NHRIs that are best suited to their particular State. For instance, within the EU there are three different broad types of NHRI – Commissions, Ombudsmen, and Institutes. All three types can be and have been fully accredited under the Paris Principles by the UN.[33] Commissions are multi-member institutions that operate by consensus. They tend to have broad mandates and wide-ranging responsibilities, covering investigation of human rights abuses, public education, and review of legislation.[34] Ombudsman NHRIs are typically single-member institutions, which focus largely on hearing complaints of human rights abuses. Although the single-member model makes it more difficult to meet the standards of pluralism required by the Paris Principles, these institutions can be accredited.[35] The final type of NHRI is the Institute. Institutes focus on research, education and advising, and typically do not have the power to investigate abuses or handle individual complaints. They are multi-member bodies and generally have a broad mandate.[36]

NHRIs are accredited at the international level by both the UN and regional bodies. At the UN, accreditation is handled by the International Coordinating Committee (ICC),[37] which reviews the NHRIs compliance with the Paris Principles. The ICC is composed of sixteen NHRIs, four from each of the four regions within the ICC. The Chair and Vice-Chair are chosen from these sixteen members.[38] The ICC is part of the National Human Rights Institutions Forum, a co-ordinating body for NHRI worldwide, that works closely with both the OHCHR and the UN Commission on Human Rights.[39] There are three levels of accreditation awarded to NHRI by the ICC. A NHRI that is designated a Level A NHRI is considered fully in compliance with the Paris Principles, and is a voting member of the ICC. A Level B accreditation

---

30 United Nations General Assembly 'National institutions for the promotion and protection of human rights' (4 March 1994) U.N Doc A/Res/48/134, 7.

31 B Burdekin, assisted by J Naum, *National Human Rights Institutions in the Asia-Pacific Region* (Martinus Nijhoff Publishers 2007).

32 ibid.

33 European Agency for Fundamental Rights, *National Human Rights Institutions in the EU Member States* (2010).

34 ibid.

35 ibid.

36 ibid.

37 Office of the High Commissioner for Human Rights, 'International Coordinating Committee for Institutions for the Protection and Promotion on Human Rights' (2012) <http://nhri.ohchr.org/> last accessed 31 March 2016.

38 R Murray, *The Role of NHRIs at the International and Regional level* (Hart Publishing 2007).

39 Office of the High Commissioner for Human Rights, 'International Coordinating Committee for Institutions for the Protection and Promotion on Human Rights' (2012) <http://nhri.ohchr.org/> last accessed 31 March 2016.

designates a NHRI that is not in full compliance, and is a non-voting member of the ICC. Level C accreditation is given when a NHRI is not in compliance with the Paris Principles, and these institutions have no status within the ICC.[40] Currently (as of August 2011), there are a total of ninety-six NHRIs registered with the ICC. Of these, seventy have full Level A accreditation, sixteen have Level B accreditation, and ten have Level C accreditation.[41] This shows a marked increase in the number of NHRIs in the world, as in 2009 only eighty-nine NHRIs were registered with the ICC.[42]

In addition to the UN-based National Human Rights Institutions Forum, there are a number of regional bodies of NHRIs. There is the Network of African National Human Rights Institutions (NANHRI), which coordinates and supports NHRIs in Africa, as well as encourages their creation in States where they do not currently exist.[43] The membership of NANHRI includes many NHRIs that are not accredited by the ICC,[44] as the Network has its own accreditation committee, though the standard of accreditation is still the Paris Principles. There do not appear to be varying levels of membership based on compliance with the principles, as in the ICC and some other regional bodies.[45]

The Asia Pacific Forum of National Human Rights Institutions (APF) is the regional body of the Asia Pacific region, and works to coordinate NHRIs within that region.[46] The APF has three levels of membership. Full members are NHRI that are considered to be in full compliance with the Paris Principles.[47] Each full member is represented on the Forum Council, the decision-making body of the APF. There are currently fifteen full members, and the list of full members[48] corresponds exactly to those States in the Asia Pacific region who hold Level A status on the ICC.[49] Candidate Members are NHRIs who do not fully comply with the Paris Principles, but could

40 Office of the High Commissioner for Human Rights, 'Association International Coordinating Committee for Institutions for the Protection and Promotion on Human Rights: Statute' (1993) <http://nhri.ohchr.org/EN/AboutUs/Documents/ICC%20Statute%20as%20amended%20at%20ICC%2025.pdf> last accessed 31 March 2016.

41 Office of the High Commissioner for Human Rights, 'Chart of the Status of National Institutions Accredited by the International Coordinating Committee of National Institutions for the Protection and Promotion of Human Rights: Accreditation Status as of August 2011' (2011) <www.ohchr.org/Documents/Countries/NHRI/Chart_Status_NIs.pdf> last accessed 31 March 2016.

42 Office of the High Commissioner for Human Rights, 'Chart of the Status of National Institutions Accredited by the International Coordinating Committee of National Institutions for the Protection and Promotion of Human Rights: Accreditation Status as of June 2009' (2009) (Copy available from the author).

43 Network of African National Human Rights Institutions, 'Network of African National Human Rights Institutions' (2009) <http://www.nanhri.org/> last accessed 31 March 2016.

44 ibid.

45 ibid.

46 Asia Pacific Forum, 'Asia Pacific Forum' (2011) <www.asiapacificforum.net/about> last accessed 31 March 2016.

47 ibid.

48 ibid.

49 Office of the High Commissioner for Human Rights, 'International Coordinating Committee for Institutions for the Protection and Promotion on Human Rights' (2012) <http://nhri.ohchr.org/> last accessed 31 March 2016.

do so within a reasonable period of time.[50] Associate Members are members who do not comply with the Paris Principles, and are unlikely to do so within a reasonable period of time. To qualify as an Associate Member, a NHRI must still have a broad mandate on human rights, and only one organisation will be admitted from each Member State.[51] Associate and Candidate members can participate in APF activities, but cannot participate in decision-making.[52] There are no current Candidate members of the APF, and the two current Associate members are NHRI who currently have B status at the ICC.[53]

In the Americas, NHRIs are organized in the Network of National Institutions for the Promotion and Protection of Human Rights on the American Continent.[54] Rather than accredit NHRIs itself, the Network will only accept members who have been accredited by the ICC.[55] Currently, the Network has fifteen members,[56] which are the same fifteen NHRIs accredited with Level A status by the ICC.[57]

The European regional body is the European Group of NHRIs. It is made up of thirty-four NHRIs, which seems to include not only Level A status European NHRIs, but also those granted Level B or C status by the ICC.[58]

The CRPD is not the first human rights treaty to assign a role to NHRIs. Instead, the first treaty to mention NHRIs as a monitoring body is the Optional Protocol to the Convention Against Torture (OPCAT).[59] The primary aim of OPCAT is to prevent torture, and so one of the requirements of the treaty is that States appoint or establish a National Preventive Mechanism (NPM). While nothing in the treaty requires that this mechanism be a NHRI, in practice this is generally the body assigned the role of NPM.[60]

Finally, Article 33(3) requires civil society, in particular people with disabilities and their representative organisations, to be involved in the implementation process at every stage. This is in line with one of the main principles of the CRPD, the full participation of people with disabilities in society, which recurs throughout the

---

50 Asia Pacific Forum, 'Asia Pacific Forum' (2011) <www.asiapacificforum.net/about> last accessed 31 March 2016.

51 ibid.

52 ibid.

53 Office of the High Commissioner for Human Rights, 'International Coordinating Committee for Institutions for the Protection and Promotion on Human Rights' (2012) <http://nhri.ohchr.org/> last accessed 31 March 2016.

54 Network of National Institutions for the Promotion and Protection of Human Rights on the American Continent, 'Network of National Institutions for the Promotion and Protection of Human Rights on the American Continent' (2009) <http://www.rindhca.org.ve> last accessed 31 March 2016.

55 ibid.

56 ibid.

57 Office of the High Commissioner for Human Rights, 'International Coordinating Committee for Institutions for the Protection and Promotion on Human Rights' (2012) <http://nhri.ohchr.org/> last accessed 31 March 2016.

58 Irish Human Rights Commission, 'European Group of NHRIs' (2012) <www.ihrc.ie/international/euronhrigroups.html> last accessed 31 March 2016.

59 R Carver, 'A new answer to an old question: National human rights institutions and the domestication of international law' (2010) 10 Human Rights Law Review 1, 25.

60 ibid.

Convention.[61] The participation of people with disabilities in all levels of society is recognised as a general principles of the Convention in Article 3, and as a general obligation in Article 4(3).[62] It should be noted that full participation is a much stronger idea, and requires a much stronger role than mere consultation, and that this article makes ensuring full and meaningful participation of people with disabilities a responsibility of the State Party.[63]

The goal of Article 33 is to combat the problem of States failing to implement human rights treaties, and improve the implementation of the CRPD. Article 33 is not a perfect solution. It will do little in the case of States that are indifferent or hostile to human rights treaties, as it contains no mechanism of enforcement. In the case of States which fail to implement treaties through a lack of co-ordination, or a failure to properly assign responsibility for following up on ratification, however, the framework laid out in the Article has the potential to be extremely effective. By obligating the State to set up some kind of governmental framework to lead the process of implementation, and providing some guidance as to how that framework should look, the Convention can focus State's efforts and minimize organisational and administrative problems.

The Convention also helps to solidify the role of NHRIs in international human rights law, not only because Article 33(2) requires an independent monitoring mechanism, but because of its implicit reference to the Paris Principles, which despite not being explicitly stated, has been widely accepted by States and international organisations. This means that while monitoring progress on treaty implementation has been a function of NHRIs at least since the drafting of the Paris Principles, for the first time this role has been set down as an obligation that States must fulfil.

Article 33(2) does more than confirm the important role of NHRIs. It also creates a framework that can solve another common problem that prevents implementation: the lack of oversight to ensure that States Parties continue to take action on a treaty, rather than continually delaying implementation. This framework, which must include a Paris Principles compliant body and must, under Article 33(3), ensure the participation of civil society, can work to keep the issue of implementation in the minds of stakeholders at all levels of society, and so push governments to take action to fulfil their obligations under the Convention. With all of the tools provided by Article 33, it is to be hoped that the CRPD will not fall victim to the problems that plague so many human rights treaties, and that the rights it sets out will be realised more quickly and fully than would otherwise have been the case.

---

61 Human Rights Council (n 7).

62 MDAC (n 10).

63 ibid.

INDEX